THE

FEDERALIST.

A COMMENTARY

ON THE

CONSTITUTION OF THE UNITED STATES.

A Collection of Essays,

EDITED BY

JOHN C. HAMILTON,

AUTHOR OF *THE HISTORY OF THE REPUBLIC OF THE UNITED STATES.*

Since 1947
**REGNERY
PUBLISHING, INC.**
An Eagle Publishing Company • Washington, DC

Library of Congress Cataloging-in-Publication Data

Published in the United States by
Regnery Publishing, Inc.
An Eagle Publishing Company
One Massachusetts Avenue, NW
Washington, DC 20001

Distributed to the trade by
National Book Network
4720-A Boston Way
Lanham, MD 20706

Printed on acid-free paper.
Manufactured in the United States of America

10 9 8 7 6 5 4 3 2 1

Books are available in quantity for promotional or premium use. Write to Director of Special Sales, Regnery Publishing, Inc., One Massachusetts Avenue, NW, Washington, DC 20001, for information on discounts and terms or call (202) 216-0600.

HAMILTON

CONSERVATIVE LEADERSHIP SERIES

EAGLE PUBLISHING, INC.

REGNERY PUBLISHING, INC.

EAGLE BOOK CLUBS, INC.

CONSERVATIVE BOOK CLUB

The Conservative Leadership Series is a joint project of Regnery Publishing, Inc., and Eagle Book Clubs, Inc., divisions of Eagle Publishing, Inc., to make the classics of conservative thought available in hardcover collectors' editions.

CONTENTS.

CONTENTS.

N.B.—In frequent instances quotations are italicized to point attention
where there are no italics in the original.

THIS EDITION.

The text of this volume is taken from the 1864 edition of *The Federalist* edited by John Church Hamilton, Alexander Hamilton's fourth son and fifth child. It includes a lengthy Historical Notice by the editor, along with a number of documents important for understanding the context and development of the Constitution and *The Federalist*. These additional materials provide a useful corrective to the many histories of America's founding era that ignore or downplay the long, heated controversy that raged over the proper nature and extent of federal power from the Declaration of Independence in 1776 until well after the Constitution's ratification by the states.

This volume also provides a truly Hamiltonian interpretation of the founding era and *The Federalist*. Its editor, John Church Hamilton, was a strong partisan of his father. Before editing *The Federalist* John Church had written a massive, eight-volume biography of Alexander Hamilton and an extremely nationalist *History of the Republic of the United States*, as well as editing his father's collected works.

Here Alexander Hamilton's influence on the Constitution is boldly set forth. It is traced through the elder Hamilton's repeated calls for a convention to put together a stronger central government, through his report from the ill-starred Annapolis Convention intended to revise certain aspects of the Articles of Confederation, and through his primary role in writing and publishing *The Federalist*. The reader will find documents and speeches, most of them from Alexander Hamilton's own hand, setting forth the argument for a stronger union and denying the feasibility of half-measures, such as economic and taxation agreements among the states. To these are added the Constitution that *The Federalist* was written to justify, the Articles of Confederation, against which so much of *The Federalist's* brilliant fire was aimed, and Hamilton's own plan for a federal union.

Four separate calls for a national convention, with delegates appointed from Hamilton's state of New York, are included, as well as a letter from Hamilton to New York's Governor George Clinton, who became a strong opponent of the new Constitution.

This edition also includes, at the end of the Historical Notice, six essays written by Hamilton under the pen name "The Continentalist." These writings, published between in 1781 and 1782, serve as a spirited precursor to *The Federalist*. They show Hamilton's concern that the weak central government prescribed in the Articles of Confederation could endanger America's international prestige. They also propose a national convention to draft a plan for an independent federal government capable of directly taxing and legislating for the people.

After *The Federalist* there are three short essays written by William Duer, a one-time member of the New York legislature who had submitted essays for possible inclusion in *The Federalist*, but which were not included. Published under the pen name "Philo Publius," or "friend of Publius"—Publius being the pen name under which Hamilton, James Madison, and John Jay wrote *The Federalist* papers—these short essays provide an interesting footnote to *The Federalist*. They add color and support to Publius's writings on the need to tame officeholders' self-interest, and speak of the problems of Athenian democracy and the necessity of union for an effective navy.

Also in this edition is Alexander Hamilton's plan of government, presented to and rejected by the Constitutional Convention. Hamilton's plan outlined a significantly stronger and more centralized federal government than appears in the Constitution. This plan called for a president and Senate elected indirectly by the people and a House of Representatives elected

directly by them, but in no case through the agency or authority of the states. Districts were to be drawn by the federal
Congress on the basis of population alone, leaving the federal
government independent of state attachments.

In many ways Hamilton's plan of government is central to the
Historical Notice written by his son. This notice, written during
the Civil War by a strong partisan of the Union cause, presents
an extremely nationalist, Hamiltonian reading of the Constitution. In it, John Church Hamilton insists that the Declaration of
Independence created one people and one nation, the survival
and growth of which was properly the object of all Americans
and American states. Asserting that a nation can have only one,
unquestioned sovereign if it is to survive, he blames insurrections in the United States, including the Civil War, on the insuf-
ficiently national character of the Union. He then calls for
reforms along the lines of his father's rejected outline, which he
terms "Hamilton's Plan of a True National Government."

Clearly John Church Hamilton's views owed much to his
father. Alexander Hamilton was perhaps the most nationalist of
the framers. His rejected plan of government sought to undermine the ability of the separate states to govern themselves and
their people so that the national government might become the
object of loyalty that people then reserved for their home states.
Ironically, this most nationalist interpretation of the Constitution in no way contemplates the current subordination of states
to the central government.

John Church Hamilton's concern, like his father's, was to
solidify the union through direct taxation and representation by
the central government. He did not seek a system in which the
federal government could usurp state, local, and private responsibility for social regulation, economic well-being, justice, and
public peace, let alone one in which the central government
could reduce the states to mere creatures of administrative convenience. Both Hamiltons shared the almost universal American
concern for limited government, decentralized administration,
and the separation of powers. And these concerns, as shown by

The Federalist, required strong state and local governments and strict separation of powers at the national level. Those today who share the framers' concern for well-ordered liberty will find much in this volume to bolster their arguments.

AUTHORSHIP OF *THE FEDERALIST*.

Because *The Federalist* was originally published under the combined pen name Publius, for decades doubts persisted about who wrote which essay. In every case of doubt, John Church ascribes authorship to his father.

But established scholarly opinion now divides authorship of *The Federalist* essays as follows: 1, 6–9, 11–13, 15–17, 21–36, 59–61, and 65–85 are by Hamilton; 10, 14, 18–20, 37–58, 62, and 63 are by Madison; and 2–5 and 64 are by Jay, who was too sick to write more during the course of the ratification debates.

Madison's essays on "faction" and the separation of powers are perhaps the most quoted in *The Federalist*, while Hamilton was responsible for the crucial essays dealing with judicial review, the need for a unitary executive, and the need for energy in government to protect liberty and union.

Hamilton conceived *The Federalist*, chose those who would assist him in the project, and saw the whole effort through to its conclusion. As such, Hamilton was the guiding hand behind the crucial polemical document that won passage for the Constitution of the United States, and this edition does him his full justice.

THE

FEDERALIST.

A COMMENTARY

ON THE

CONSTITUTION OF THE UNITED STATES.

𝔄 Collection of Essays,

BY

ALEXANDER HAMILTON,

JAY AND MADISON.

ALSO

The Continentalist and Other Papers,

BY

HAMILTON.

EDITED BY

JOHN C. HAMILTON,

AUTHOR OF *THE HISTORY OF THE REPUBLIC OF THE UNITED STATES.*

PHILADELPHIA:

J. B. LIPPINCOTT & CO.

1864.

HISTORICAL NOTICE.

SOME time since, the intention was announced of publishing an edition of the Federalist, which would "state all the evidence known to exist, to designate the respective contributions of its authors."*

The great Rebellion which, while imperilling, has developed the power of our Government, and by its suppression will establish the Unity of the American Empire, has been a sufficient cause of delay; independent of those personal interests which have irresistibly drawn the mind from the study to the camp and to the battle-fields. This task is now performed.

As Alexander Hamilton is known to have been chiefly instrumental in the series of measures which finally resulted in the establishment of the Constitution of the United States—was its principal expounder—and as he had a large share in the practical exposition of its powers, under the Presidency of Washington and of his successor, I have permitted myself to believe, that a preliminary exhibition of his progressive opinions and acts—onward toward the goal of his great desires and hopes—the organization of a firm National Government, resting directly on the shoulders of the American people; acting directly upon them as individuals; and pervading the entire limits of their country, might not be without interest or instruction. And, in no other mode could this be more effectually done than by including in this volume—precedent to the Federalist—certain papers from his pen, which have hitherto had a very limited publicity, together with some elucidatory observations.

In a retrospect of the rise of the British Provinces in North America, from their Colonial condition to that of an Independent

---

* History of the Republic of the United States of America as traced in the writings of Alexander Hamilton and of his contemporaries. iii. 371. 1859.

power among the Nations of the World; what that condition
was, has at different periods been much discussed. At first, it
was treated as a question of the rights and duties of these
Colonies in reference to the parent Government; later, it has
been more often investigated as a question, of the relation of
the Colonies to their Sovereigns, and to each other, in regard
to the relations which have existed and now truly exist,
between the particular States within the Union and the whole
United States; or between the People of each of those States
and the whole People of the United States, ordaining and establishing a Constitution for the United States of America. The
Declaration of Independence disposed of the first of these questions, the latter has a living interest. In the second of his early
productions,* Hamilton touches this great question. Totally
denying the claim of parliamentary supremacy over the British
Colonies, except as conceded by them, he remarks, "In order
to form one State, that is, a number of individual societies, or
bodies politic united under one common head, there must
indeed be some connecting, pervading principle. This is found
in the person and prerogative of the King. He it is that con-
joins all these individual societies into one great body politic."
"He is King of America, by virtue of the compact between us
and the Kings of Great Britain." Their claim to allegiance was
founded upon the title derived from the Crown to the lands in
America, and on the King's being "the supreme protector of the
Empire," and having bestowed that protection. As fellow subjects of one common Sovereign, the Colonists had the common
rights of British subjects, those rights which are the natural
rights of every human being, except as limited by statutes.
These common rights extended over the whole territory of
Great Britain in North America. The colonists of each Colony
had the rights of traffic with, of migration to; of residence in,
and of inheritance by descent of real estate situate in, every
other Colony. To secure which common rights the local legislation of all the Colonies was required to be in accordance with
the laws of England.

Thus, the British colonists of North America, were, in chief
respects, "one people,"† and as such, the delegates chosen to the

* Hamilton's Works, ii. 55, February 5, 1775. "The Farmer Refuted"—
written in his eighteenth year.

† Story's Commentaries, i. § 163, 165. 2 Dallas Reports, 470. Opinion of
Chief Justice Jay.

first "American Continental Congress," were chosen, and declare themselves chosen by "the good people of the several Colonies" there represented. The powers exerted by it were exerted for their common protection; and the Union of the Colonies was symbolized to the world by that of "The Great Union Flag," in which they still recognized their common allegiance to the crown.*

Notwithstanding this still recognized allegiance, Congress representing the power of the United people, became, in place of the King, their "supreme Protector;" and ere long, on this protection being withdrawn from its subjects by the Crown, that allegiance was likewise withdrawn, and was transferred to the whole people of the United Colonies represented in that Congress. Thus, the Declaration of Independence by the Continental Congress, as the act of "one people," about "to assume among the powers of the earth," a "separate and equal station"—AS A NATION—and "in the name and by the authority of the *good people* of these colonies," declares, "that these United Colonies are, and of right, ought to be free and independent States;" and, as such, "have full power to levy war, conclude peace, contract alliances, establish commerce, and to do all other acts and things which independent States may of right do."

This manifestly was the joint act of all the people of the United colonies of North America, not a single colony being named. It was a Declaration of the Independence of the United colonies—of Great Britain—not of an independence of each colony of the other colonies—it was a declaration of the sovereignty of the people of the United States conjointly, not of the sovereignty of any one colony, for the colonial condition then ceased; not of the sovereignty of any one State, for no State Government, with a view to permanence, had then been formed. Hamilton accurately pronounced, before the present Constitu-

* A flag combining the Crosses of St. George and St. Andrew united (the distinctive Emblem of the United Kingdom of Great Britain) with a Field composed of thirteen stripes alternate red and white, the combination of the Flags previously used in the camp, on the cruisers and the floating batteries of the Colonies, was adopted for this purpose, ("the declaration of their union under a common sovereign") and called the "Great Union Flag."—*The National Flag of the United States*," p. 80–85, by Captain, since Major General Schuyler Hamilton. The change from this flag to that of the flag of the United States was ordered by a Resolution of Congress June 14, 1777, thus providing a substitute for the crosses of St. George and St. Andrews, that—"the Union be thirteen stars, white in a Blue Field—representing a *new constellation*."

tion was established, such to be the true political condition. "The
UNION and INDEPENDENCE of these States are blended and
incorporated in one and the same act"*—the Declaration of
Independence. "The sovereignty and independence of the peo-
ple," he declared, "began by a *federal* act. The Declaration of
Independence was the fundamental Constitution of every
State." "Congress had complete sovereignty." "Its constitutional
powers are not controllable by any State."†

In prosecution of the great purpose of the Declaration of
Independence—the establishment of a nation of free men—
Congress proceeded in the exertion of many of the sovereign
powers necessary to that purpose—powers of action and of prohibition. They had exerted and continued to exert the powers of
levying war on land and on sea, pledging the whole property of
the inhabitants of the twelve Colonies for the redemption of
their joint debt; and they had prohibited exportations to the
British dominions, with certain exceptions; the receipt and negotiation of British government bills by, or supplies of money to,
British officers; and of necessaries to the British army and navy
in Massachusetts, or transports in their service,‡ acting directly
upon the people of the United States for many purposes, and
through the agency of the States when organized, for other
purposes.

It is not to be supposed that a people keenly jealous of their
liberties would long be content with the large discretionary
powers Congress was exercising; and, in midsummer of seventeen hundred and seventy-five, Benjamin Franklin submitted to
Congress a sketch of "Articles of Confederation," in the name of
"The United Colonies of North America." These articles
declared their purpose to be "common defence—the securities of
their liberties and properties—the safety of their persons and
families—and their mutual and general welfare." They were to
"be proposed to the several provincial Conventions or Assemblies," for their approval and ratification; and "the Union
thereby established," was to continue firm until a reconciliation
with Great Britain; but, "on failure thereof," the Confederation
was "to be perpetual." Conferring upon Congress the power of
making "such General Ordinances as though necessary to the
general welfare, particular assemblies cannot be competent
to"—they declared, "that each Colony shall enjoy and retain as

---

* Hamilton's Works, ii. 358.   † Hist. Rep. iii. 16.
‡ Journal of Congress, June 2, 1775.

much as it may think fit of its own *present* laws, customs, rights, privileges, and peculiar jurisdictions within its own limits; and may amend its own Constitution, as shall seem best to its own assembly or convention."* Viewed as a merely temporary project, this scheme was in accordance with the existing condition of affairs; but regarded in its future, as a plan "to be perpetual," it wanted the comprehensiveness and reach which that future must demand. It was not acted upon.

The next step in our political organization was, a recommendation to the Colonies to form themselves into Governments—first temporarily, then permanently. The terms of this recommendation are very significant—to "adopt such Government as shall best conduce to the happiness and safety of their constituents, in particular, and to America in *general*."

The People of the several Colonies, now emerged from their colonial condition, proceeded under this recommendation, though at long intervals, to the formation of State Constitutions. In all these constitutions are seen a recognition of the then existing Congress by provisions for its continuance, and a reservation, as States, of the powers and rights incident and necessary to the guardianship of their particular interests.

A month later,† a Declaration of Independence having been ordered to be prepared, a draft of the form of a confederation between the Colonies was the next day directed to be made. Articles of confederation were soon after proposed, in the name of "The United States of America," the second of which declared, that the Colonies "unite themselves so as NEVER to be divided by any act whatever," and enter into a firm league of friendship with each other for "their common defence, the security of their liberties and their mutual and general welfare."‡ This draft having undergone frequent modifications—after discussions chiefly affecting the representative power of each State—the measure of its contributions, and their separate or joint interest in the public lands, the "Articles of Confederation" became operative, by the final ratification of them on the first of March, 1781, by the State of Maryland.

A comparison of the Articles ratified with those which preceded them, evince a growing jealousy as to the deposit, extent, and exercise of the general powers, necessary to "the mutual and general welfare." While in the earlier draft the reservation

* Secret Journals of Congress, i. 283, July 21, 1775.
† June 10, 1776.   ‡ Secret Journal, July 12, 1776.

was simply "of the sole and exclusive regulation and government of" the "internal police in all matters which shall not
interfere with the Articles of the Confederation"—as a provision secondary to the general league—in the later and in the
ratified Articles, the *primary* declaration is, that "each State
retains its sovereignty, freedom, and independence, and every
power, jurisdiction, and right which is not by this confederation
expressly delegated to the United States in Congress assembled." Even, for a "Council of State" to be appointed by
Congress, and to act during its sitting and in its recess—"with
power to direct military operations by sea or land"—was substituted a "Committee of Congress" to sit only during its
recess; and it was provided, that no person be allowed to serve
in the office of President "of Congress more than one year in
any term of three years."

Instead of a National Government of undefined powers, it
had dwindled down to a league of States with limitations inconsistent with the great purposes and ends of a general government; and more in the spirit of a penal statute. It had become
a mere league of States, disproportionate in territorial dimensions, in wealth, in population—each having an equal vote in
their general Council, and of these equal votes, nine requisite
to the exercise of many of the most important powers conferred—several of those powers of questionable authority
because of the intercipient reservations of powers in the States,
and without any common exponent; and it fixed a measure of
contribution unequal, impracticable, and therefore never carried
into effect—with a process of requisitions, not of impositions—
without legislative departments, without a Judiciary, without an
Executive—without any direct relation to, or civil power over
the People as individuals, whose general welfare was committed to it, and with a debated question as to whom allegiance
was due. "The Union," in the words of Hamilton, originally had
"complete sovereignty." "The Confederation was an abridgement of this original sovereignty."* Although not binding upon
any of the States until its ratification by the whole, the influence on the public mind of this very imperfect contrivance was
prominent in the proceedings of Congress and of the States—
delaying, and imperilling, during several years of the revolu-
tionary contest, the independence and sovereignty it professed
to assure.

* Hamilton's Works, i. 358.

The Congress issued pledges for money it had no means to pay, called for soldiers it had no means to support, entered into treaties it could not fulfil; while States endangered and did injustice to their associate States, by disproportionate, inadequate, contributions of men and money;* by the assumption of powers inconsistent with a community of rights; and by the refusal of powers essential to the preservation of those rights.†

In Virginia it was proposed to abolish all private commerce and to establish commercial companies including a State, or parts of a State in districts. Their commercial operations were to be represented by stock; the price of every article to be fixed by the companies; and the power to be conferred upon them "of taking private goods into their custody;"—called a plan "for *appreciating* the currency and reducing the price of necessaries." An embargo of provisions followed. And the day after Jefferson's election as Governor—the second of June, 1779—fearful of the breaking up of the Confederacy, and to secure a strong foreign protector; a resolution unanimously passed her legislature, by which, "the treaties of Alliance and Commerce between France and the Congress of the United States were ratified, confirmed, and declared binding; so far as in the power of this Commonwealth." A special favor from France was granted to her.

The sufferings in Virginia were a type of the general condition of this country. "The enemy," Washington wrote in November seventy-nine, "are in great hopes of terminating the war in their favor in another campaign, as they expect confidently the entire ruin of our money and a failure of provisions for the supply of our army." In the following month, he again wrote, "I

---

* The inefficiency of Virginia, the then most populous State of the Confederacy, is thus exposed by its Governor Patrick Henry:—"Public spirit seems to have taken its flight from Virginia. It is too much the case; for the quota of our troops is not half made up, and no chance seems to remain for completing it. Great bounties are offered. But I fear the only effect will be to expose our State to contempt, for, I believe no soldiers will enlist, especially in the Infantry. Can you credit it? No effort was made for supporting or restoring public credit. I pressed it warmly on some, but in vain. This is the reason you get no soldiers. *Let not Congress rely on Virginia for soldiers.* I tell you my opinion—they will not be got here, until a different spirit prevails."—*Memoir of R. H. Lee*, i. 195. 1778.

Washington soon after wrote, "At present they are but a handful, compared to the quota they should furnish, and unless something is done, this handful will dwindle to nothing."—*Hist. Repub.* i. 559.

find our prospects are infinitely worse than they have been at any period of the war, and unless some expedient can be instantly adopted, a dissolution of the army for the want of subsistence is unavoidable. *** We have never experienced a like extremity at any period of the war." Well might be feared "the entire ruin of the money." The bills in circulation amounted to the enormous sum of *one hundred and sixty millions* of dollars—and the total product of the taxes since the beginning of the war was only *three millions*.

It was in the midst of this chaotic confusion, this vast distress, so discouraging to the people, and so encouraging to the enemy—five years of indecisive war having nearly elapsed—that Hamilton (Washington's "principal and most confidential aid,") familiar with all his embarrassments and intimate with all the wants of the army and of the country, at the age of twenty-two, soon after the army entered winter quarters at Morristown, is seen to have projected an enlarged plan for the restoration of the public credit, proposing an indispensable change in the whole administration of the public affairs. After an argued exposition of this plan, he wrote, "Congress have too long neglected to organize a good scheme of administration and to throw public business into proper EXECUTIVE DEPARTMENTS. For commerce, I prefer a Board, but for most other things single men. We want a Minister of War, a Minister of Foreign Affairs, a Minister of Finance, and a Minister of Marine. There is always more decision, more dispatch, more secrecy, more responsibility, where single men, than where bodies are concerned. By a plan of this kind we should blend the advantages of a Monarchy and a Republic in a happy and beneficial Union."*

The adoption of this plan was not immediate, but the almost desperate situation of affairs† prompted and induced Congress, though reluctantly, to vest certain executive powers in a committee of its own body. The immediate motive to this measure was an occurrence which was of great immediate benefit, but was afterwards productive of most deleterious consequences.

---

* History of Republic, i. 577. 1779.

† Ibid. ii. 11, February 25, 1780. "Re-inforcements are expected—General Hagan is within a few miles. The Virginia troops are somewhere! *Assistance from that sister State has been expected these eighteen months*." Colonel Laurens to General Lincoln—who, for want of this aid, was compelled to surrender Charleston.

The American people, instead of the glory of achieving their final victory by their own unassisted valor, were obliged to ask foreign aid. Foreign arms now came; and subsequently abusing its gratitude, foreign influence, for a time, poisoned the councils of this yet infant nation. "It appears to me," Hamilton wrote by the order and in the name of Washington, "of the greatest importance, and even of absolute necessity that a *small* committee should be immediately appointed to reside near Head Quarters, vested with all the powers Congress have, so far as respects the purpose of a full co-operation with the French fleet and army on the *continent*. Their authority should be plenipotentiary; to draw out men and supplies of every kind and to give their sanction to any operations which the commander in chief may not think himself at liberty to undertake without it, as well *beyond* as *within* the limits of these States. This committee can act with dispatch and energy. The conjuncture is one of the most critical and important we have seen. All our prudence and exertions are required to give it a favorable issue. Hesitancy and delay would, in all probability, ruin our affairs."*

A committee was appointed, but its powers were far short of those suggested in this letter. Critical as was the state of the public affairs, no adequate remedy had been provided. The Emissions of credit bills were almost valueless. This accumulation of promises† fell to the ground; and Congress at last adopted the measures proposed by Hamilton the preceding year,—by a pledge to reimburse the subscribers to a Bank, and by the sending a commissioner to Europe to negotiate a Loan. The continental paper money had been a substitute for Revenue. This failing, the fate of the Revolution was cast on the voluntary action of twelve States ungoverned by a common government, untied by any other tie than their common necessities. This was the natural and necessary consequence of the impotence which had prevailed. The repeated recommendations of Congress without power to enforce them, were as repeated proclamations of weakness. The influence of a lavish treasury, ceasing with the cessation of the emissions of bills of credit, Congress almost without weight; and the patriotism of many was seen to sink in an equal ratio with the scale of the paper depreciation. The actual power being in the States, this portion of society turned towards them, and gave to their real an arti-

* History of Republic, ii. 17, April 28, 1780.   † Ibid. 77.

ficial, baneful preponderance—"Congress," to use the words of
a member,* "gradually surrendering or throwing upon the several States the exercise of powers they should have retained,
and to their utmost have exercised themselves, until at length
they have scarce a power left, but such as concerns foreign
transactions." The repeated recommendations to the States
were not the only public admissions of weakness. All the measures to impart a temporary force to the action of Congress
were equally acknowledgments of its want of power. The dic-
tatorial authority conferred upon Washington was the most
objectionable form national necessities could assume. Thus,
every motive of experience, of justice, of honor, of reputation,
of interest, of safety—demanded a Government of the People
of the United States, a general will and a general united power
to direct, express and enforce that will—in Hamilton's words,
"*a solid* COERCIVE UNION."

The great industrial interests of New England early felt and
early suggested a concert of action; and by successive conventions prepared the way for this great measure of political sal-
vation. A Convention held at Providence in 'seventy-six was followed by another at Springfield of the four New England
States and of New York, in 'seventy-seven. A third convention
met at New Haven in 'seventy-eight, where New Jersey and
Pennsylvania are stated also to have been present; and a fourth
at Hartford in 'seventy-nine. The earlier conventions had in
view limited but important, though, in part, impracticable,
objects. The last convention shewed a great advance in public
opinion. Massachusetts, at that time, the first of the States in
active power and large intelligence, instructed her delegates,
not only to consult as to measures to prevent a further depreciation of the money medium, but "to agree on a mode of internal trade and commerce in consistency with the general welfare;" and invited a larger meeting of Commissioners. This fifth
Convention was held at Philadelphia on the twenty-ninth of
January, 'eighty, at which were present the New England
States, New Jersey, Pennsylvania, Delaware, Maryland. New
York was unavoidably absent, her legislature not having met
to appoint commissioners; and Virginia was not represented.
The objection to her conferring on Congress a power of taxa-
tion—that such taxes would fall upon the owners of lands was

* John Matthews, of South Carolina.

soon after urged. Resolved to ascertain definitely her views, the President of this convention was directed to request the Governor of that State, "to give the earliest notice of her determination" as to meeting the other States in Convention. Waiting her concurrence, it adjourned first until February, and then to April; when a call was made for a meeting in August. At this Sixth convention the only States represented were Massachusetts, Connecticut and New Hampshire.

Wise resolutions as to finance were there passed; and the great, much to be desired result, an invigoration of the power of the general Government, was approached. "They conceived it," they declared, "to be essential to our final safety, that the Union of these States be fixed in a more solid and permanent manner,—that the power of Congress be more clearly ascertained and defined,—and that the important national concerns of the United States be under the superintendency and direction of one Supreme head—that the proper estimates of our public wants be seasonably made; and the necessary resources drawn forth and expended." With this purpose, the States were recommended "to invest their Delegates in Congress with powers competent for the Government and direction of all those common and national affairs, which do not, nor can come within the jurisdiction of the particular States;" urging "a permanent system—establishing proper Boards, officers, and regulations for the direction of the several Departments necessary to be executed under Congress."—To carry this proposal into effect, a new confederation was to be acceded to by the States.

Insufficient as these suggestions were, Hamilton grasped at them as a promise of greater good. The powers proposed to be conferred would indeed be only revocable grants, at the mercy of any State; and as the public mind then was, the probability that the States would concur in conferring them was small. But these proceedings proved, that the necessity of a change was widely felt; and he resolved to endeavor by his counsels to rescue the great cause of American liberty from its present, its menacing, and menaced dangers.

An inaccurate statement of the proceedings of this Convention reached him by the twenty eighth of August; and on the third of September, seventeen hundred and eighty, in conformity with a previous promise, he communicated to a member of Congress, the grave thoughts with which his mind long had laboured. The enquiry during his non-age, written in his company pay-book,

"Would it not be advisable to let all taxes, even those imposed by the States, be collected by persons of Congressional appointment"?* indicates the early direction of his views; and he subsequently wrote, "it has *ever* been my opinion that Congress ought to have complete sovereignty in all but the mere municipal law of each State." This opinion is expatiated upon in this communication, very important in itself and most important in all its consequences,† generally admitted to be the first proposal made in this country of a Convention to frame a National Government.

"The fundamental defect," Hamilton observed, "is a want of power in Congress. It is hardly worth while to show in what this consists as it seems to be universally acknowledged; or to point out, how it has happened, as the only question is, how to remedy it. It may however be said, that it has originated from three causes—an excess of the spirit of liberty, which has made the particular States show a jealousy of all power not in their own hands; and this jealousy has led them to exercise a right of judging in the last resort, of the measures recommended by Congress, and of acting according to their own opinions of their propriety or necessity,—a diffidence in Congress of their own powers, by which they have been timid and indecisive in their resolutions, constantly making concessions to the States, till they have scarcely left themselves the shadow of power:—a want of sufficient means at their disposal to answer the public exigencies, and of vigor to draw forth those means, which have occasioned them to depend on the States individually to fulfil their engagements with the army, the consequence of which has been to ruin their influence and credit with the army, to establish its dependance on each State separately, rather than *on them*—that is than on the whole collectively. It may be pleaded that Congress had never any definitive powers granted them; and of course could exercise none—could do nothing more than recommend. The manner in which Congress was appointed would warrant, and the public good required, that they should have considered themselves; as vested with full power to *preserve the Republic* from harm.

"They have done many of the highest acts of sovereignty, which were always cheerfully submitted to—the declaration of independence,—the declaration of war,—the levying an army,—creating a navy,—emitting money,—making alliances with For-

---

* Hist. Repub. i. pp. 4, 7.

† Ibid. ii. 86. Hamilton to James Duane, Sept. 3, 1780.

eign powers—appointing a Dictator, etc. All these were implications of a complete sovereignty, were never disputed and ought to have been a standard for the conduct of administration. Undefined powers are discretionary powers, limited only by the object for which they were given;—in the present case, the independence and freedom of America. The Confederation made no difference; for as it has not been generally adopted, it had no operation.

"But, from what I recollect of it, Congress have even descended from the authority which the spirit of that act gives them, while the particular States have no farther attended to it, than as it suited their pretensions and convenience. It would take too much time to enter into particular instances, each of which separately might appear inconsiderable, but united are of serious import. I only mean to remark, not to censure.

"But, the Confederation itself is defective and requires to be altered. It is neither fit for war, nor peace. The idea of an uncontrollable sovereignty in each State, over its internal police, will defeat the other powers given to Congress, and make our Union feeble and precarious. There are instances without number, where acts necessary for the general good, and which rise out of the powers given to Congress must interfere with the internal police of the States; and there are as many instances in which the particular States by arrangements of internal police can effectually, though indirectly, counteract the arrangements of Congress. You have already had examples of this, for which I refer you to your own memory.

"The Confederation," he proceeds, "gives the States individually too much influence in the affairs of the army. They should have nothing to do with it. The entire formation and disposal of our military forces ought to belong to Congress. It is an essential cement of the Union; and it ought to be the policy of Congress to destroy all ideas of State attachments in the army and make it look up to them. The Confederation too, gives the powers of the purse too entirely to the State legislatures. It should provide perpetual funds in the disposal of Congress by a land-tax, poll tax, or the like. All Imposts upon commerce ought to be laid by Congress and appropriated to their own use. For without certain revenues, a Government can have no power. That power which holds the purse strings absolutely must rule. This seems to be a medium which without making Congress altogether independent will tend to give reality to its authority. Another defect in our system is want of method and energy in the administration. This has partly resulted from the other defect, but, in a great degree, from prejudice and the want of a proper Executive. Congress have kept the power too much in their own hands, and have meddled too much with details of every sort. Congress is properly a deliberative corps; and it forgets itself when it attempts to play the Executive." Passing on from particular errors, he advanced to a fuller statement. "The Confederation, in my opinion, should give Congress complete sovereignty; except as to that part of internal police which relates to the rights of property and life among individuals, and to raising money by internal taxes. It is necessary, that every thing belonging to this should be regulated by the State legislatures. Congress should have complete sovereignty in all that relates to war, peace, trade, and finance, and to the management of foreign affairs; the right of declaring war, of raising armies, officering, paying them, directing their motions in every respect; of equipping fleets, and doing the same with them; of building fortifications, arsenals, magazines &c. &c.; of making peace on such conditions as they think proper; of regulating Trade, determining with what countries it shall be carried on, granting indulgences, laying prohibitions on all the articles of export or import: imposing duties, granting bounties, and premiums for raising, exporting or importing; and applying to their own use the product of these duties, only giving credit to the State on whom they are raised in the general account of revenues and expense; instituting Admiralty Courts, &c.; of coining money, establishing Banks, on such terms and with such privileges as they think proper; appropriating funds, and doing whatever else relates to the operations of finance, transacting every thing with foreign nations; making alliances, offensive and defensive, treaties of commerce &c. &c."

"The Confederation should provide certain perpetual revenues, productive and easy of collection; a land tax—poll tax—or the like, which, together with the duties on trade, and the unlocated lands, would give Congress a substantial existence; and a stable foundation for their schemes of finance." The next step recommended by him, was, a repetition of that of the previous year—the appointment of Five "great officers of State." Another step was, the recruiting of the Army for the war, or at least for three years—and eventually a draft—and the placing the officers on half pay. "The providing supplies," he added, "is the pivot of every thing else;" and four ways to be united are mentioned—"a foreign loan—heavy pecuniary taxes—a tax in kind—and a Bank founded on public and private credit."

Having stated the want in Congress of powers, competent to the public exigencies, he observed as to the remedy; "This may happen in two ways: one by resuming and exercising the discretionary powers, I suppose to have been originally vested in them for the safety of the States, and resting their conduct on the candor of their countrymen and the necessity of the conjuncture;—the other by calling immediately a CONVENTION of all the States with full authority to conclude finally upon a general confederation; stating to them beforehand explicitly the evils arising from a want of power in Congress and the impossibility of supporting the contest on its present footing; that the Delegates may come possessed of proper sentiments, as well as proper authority to give efficacy to the meeting." ... "The reasons for which I require them to be vested with plenipotentiary authority are, that the business may suffer no delay in the execution, and may in reality come into effect. A CONVENTION may agree upon a Confederation, the States individually never will. We must have one at all events, and a vigorous one; if we mean to succeed in the contest and be happy hereafter. I am persuaded a solid confederation, a permanent army, a reasonable prospect of subsisting it would give us treble consideration in Europe and produce a peace this winter. If a CONVENTION is called, the minds of all the States and the people ought to be prepared to receive its determinations by *sensible and popular writings* which should conform to the views of Congress." ... "The measure of a convention would revive the hopes of the People, and give a new direction to their passions, which may be improved in carrying points of substantial utility."

Six days after the date of this remarkable letter, New York, in the person of General Schuyler, who was in intimate communion with Hamilton, in answer to a message from its Governor, avowed its strong convictions.* "Our embarrassments in the prosecution of the war," Governor Clinton then declared, "are chiefly to be attributed to a defect of power in those who ought to exercise a Supreme jurisdiction; for while Congress only rec-

---

* Hist. Repub. ii. 110, 111, 112.

ommend, and the different States deliberate upon the propriety of the recommendation, we cannot expect a union of force or council." "We perceive," Schuyler answered in behalf of the Senate, "the defects in the present system and the necessity of a supreme and coercive power *in the government of these States*; and are persuaded, that unless Congress are authorized to direct uncontrollably the operations of war, and enabled to enforce a compliance with their requisitions, the common force can never be properly united."

This idea of *enforcing* States seemed at these critical times to be the only remedy in view; and in fact, in such a confederation, force was the only possible sanction for the laws. Beside contemplating the appointment of a DICTATOR, with a Vice Dictator in each State, to be recommended by a *seventh* convention about to meet at Hartford, New York, by a unanimous vote, instructed her delegates to it, "to propose and agree, that Congress, during the present war or until a perpetual Confederation shall be completed, should be explicitly authorized and empowered to exercise every power which they may deem necessary for the effectual prosecution of the war;" and that, whenever it shall appear to them that any State is deficient in its contributions, they should "direct the Commander in Chief without delay to march the army, or such part of it as may be requisite in such State; and, by military force, *compel* it to furnish its deficiency."

Rash as this proposal was,* it was only a proposal to carry into effect upon a more extended scale a recent precedent in Pennsylvania; where, a few months before, martial law was proclaimed, to enable the State officers to procure supplies for the army—; Nor was this substitution of the arbitrary violence of military law for the regular and mild processes of civil government, only approved in the Middle States. In the following month, a leading delegate to Congress from Virginia, among his first essays† in that body, proposed as an expedient, that the requisite supplies for the army "be impressed with vigor and impartiality, and paid for in certificates *not* transferable; and to be redeemable at some period subsequent to the war, at specie value, and bearing an intermediate interest." The advantages promised were—an anticipation "of the future revenues of peace,"—"the *compelling* the

---

* Hist. Rep. ii. 112, 1780.

† By James Madison—Madison Papers, i. 56. October 1780.

people to *lend* the public their commodities; and that it would be a *permanent* resource by which the war might be supported as long as the earth would yield its increase." It was to be a *system of impress*—of forced loans—which, merely as an occasional resort, Hamilton had recently condemned as "violent, unequal, oppressive and odious."

Such are the dangers of an unbalanced government. It threatened, as Hamilton afterwards deprecated, that "anarchy would shoot into monarchy." Defeat and disaster following, only called forth the powers of Hamilton's mind, in repeated calls by him for increased governmental energies, but all were to be the energies of an adequately constituted government. "But, above all things," he wrote, "let us have without delay a vigorous *government*, and a well constituted army for the war."* "We must have an administration distinct from Congress, and in the bands of single men, under their orders."† "I am sorry to find," referring to his recent letter of September, "we do not seem to agree in the proper remedies to our disorders, at least in the practicability of applying those which are proper. Convinced, as I am, of the absolute insufficiency of our present system to our safety, if I do not despair of the Republic, it is more the effect of constitution than of judgment."‡ The disasters which pressed at this time, were occurring at the South, whence General Greene wrote to him; "There is nothing but murders and devastations in every quarter. Government here is much more popular than to the northward; and there is no such thing as national character or national sentiment. The inhabitants are numerous, but they would be rather formidable abroad than at home. *There is a great spirit of enterprize among the black people*, and those that come out as volunteers are *not a little formidable* to the enemy."§ On the twelfth of December previous, a circular from the Convention, which had met at Hartford, addressed to the several States, was presented to Congress. This Convention proposed, "that the several States should make the necessary provisions by law, to enable Congress to levy and collect such taxes, and duties within them respectively, as Congress should call for;" and that the delegates thereto should be authorized to pledge the faith of their respective States that they will pass the requisite laws for that purpose. The States were called upon

* Hist. Rep. ii. 124—Hamilton to Duane.
† Ibid. 134, to Isaac Sears, Oct. 12, 1780.   ‡ Ibid. 135, to Duane.
§ Hist. Rep. ii. 164, Greene to Hamilton, January 10, 1781.

to sink their full quotas of the continental bills; and were to call "for a return of the number of persons, blacks as well as whites, in each State," as the basis of a rule of contribution.* This circular boldly urged the necessity of these grants. "Our present embarrassments, we imagine to arise in a great measure from a defect in the present government of the United States. All government supposes the power of coercion. This power, however, in the general government of the Continent never did exist; or which has produced equally disagreeable consequences, never has been exercised. By the expulsion of the enemy we may be emancipated from the tyranny of Great Britain. We shall however, be without a solid hope of peace and freedom, unless we are properly cemented among ourselves; and, although we feel the calamities of war, yet we have not sufficient inducements to wish a period to them, until our distresses, if other means cannot effect it, have, as it were, forced us into a Union." In pursuance of its suggestion, a Continental Judicature was ere long appointed by Congress, "for the trial and determination of all causes, in relation to offences committed against the United States in the civil departments thereof."†

These departments were soon after constituted. On the tenth of January, seventeen hundred and eighty one, Hamilton's proposal of "an Administration by single men" was brought before Congress;‡ and subsequently a Secretary of Foreign affairs—a Superintendent of Finance—a Secretary of Marine—and a Secretary of War were appointed, with defined powers. Hamilton was in contemplation as head of the finance, but Robert Morris was wisely elected.§

This measure gave much alarm, yet in despite of factious jealousies and opposition, Congress recommended to the States, "as indispensably necessary to vest Congress with a power to levy for the use of the United States," a duty on imports, and on condemned prizes and prize goods. Wiser and more honest counsels had now begun to prevail; and this body, being without power to provide any means for their redemption, declared that their bills of credit, should *not* be a *tender*, in any other manner, than at their current value compared with gold and silver;‖ and recom-

---

* Hist. Rep. ii. 198. † Ibid. ii. 199.

‡ Duane, to whom Hamilton had proposed this measure, was of this Committee. Ibid. ii. 200.

§ Ibid. 201. ‖ February 3, 1781.

mended the States, where laws making paper bills a tender still existed, to repeal those laws.* But the dominant jealousy yet prevailed; and a proposal to vest Congress with the exclusive right of laying duties on all imports, and that these duties should be uniform, was rejected. Hamilton, nevertheless, with unfailing purpose, soon after renewed his financial suggestions, and again urged a Convention. "'Tis, in a National bank, alone," he wrote, "that we can find the ingredients to constitute a wholesome, solid, and beneficial paper credit." "Congress must," he added, "demand an instant, positive, and perpetual investiture of an Impost on trade, a land tax, and a poll tax *to be collected by their own agents.* This Act to become *a part* of the Confederation. It has ever been my opinion, that Congress ought to have complete sovereignty in all, but the mere municipal law of each State; and I wish to see a CONVENTION OF ALL THE STATES, with full power to alter and amend, finally and irrevocably, the present futile and senseless Confederation."† Ere the end of the following month, a bank was chartered by Congress.‡

Hamilton's plan of a national bank was, it is seen, but a part of that larger system of measures on which his mind was fixed. His proposed Convention of all the States to establish a Constitution of Government, met with little countenance in Congress. The Articles of Confederation were to them a new, and an untried experiment. Not alive to the dangers of unbalanced power, they were content to seek relief to the public necessities, in solicitations to the States, to vest them with new powers, With this view, a grand committee, as it was called, of the States; after frequent deliberations, presented a report to Congress late in July 1781, nearly three months subsequent to Hamilton's letter to Morris. After enumerating the instances in which the Confederation needed execution, it recommended a grant by the States of certain specified powers;—a grant of powers, from their very nature, certain to be refused. Of these proposed powers, one was "to prescribe rules for *impressing property* into the service of the United States during the present war;" another was, "to *distrain the property* of a *State* delinquent in its assigned proportion of men or money;" with

* A short time before, Virginia enacted a law rendering her paper a *legal tender.* Edmund Pendleton to Madison, Dec. 4, 1780.

† Hist. Rep. ii. 224. Hamilton to Robert Morris, April 80, 1781.

‡ Ibid. 227, May 26, 1781.

which were others of obvious utility—to appoint collectors of, and direct the mode of accounting for taxes imposed, to admit into the Union any part or more of the dismembered States, to stipulate in treaties with foreign nations for the establishment of consular powers without reference to the States individually; to vary the rules of suffrage in Congress; adding the paralysing limitation "to require a concurrence of *two thirds* of the States" in the exercise of the most urgent powers—those, "of emitting bills of credit, or of borrowing money; the regulating the value of coin; determining the total number of land and sea forces, and allotting to each State its quota of men or money; fixing the number and force of vessels of war, and appointing a commander in chief of the army and navy."

The proposition to the States to impart to Congress the power of distraint upon them in case of delinquency—and the proposed limitations on several general and necessary powers, are among the most remarkable incidents in the political history of this country; yet New York had urged the grant of this power of distraint, and it had been vindicated by a delegate from Virginia, on the ground, that, "as the confederation now stands, and according to the nature even of alliances much less intimate, there is an *implied right of coercion* against the delinquent party, and the exercise of it by Congress," "whenever a palpable necessity occurs, will probably be acquiesced in."*

---

* Madison to Jefferson, April 16, 1781—Madison papers, i. 87. Jefferson sustained this right subsequently on the ground that it was not necessary to give Congress that power expressly, *"they have it by the law of nature."* Jefferson's writings, ii. 203. The proposed report is in these words; "It is understood and hereby declared in case *one* or *more* of the Confederated States shall *refuse* or *neglect* to abide by the determinations of Congress, and to observe all the Articles of Confederation, as required by the 18th Article, the said United States in Congress assembled are fully authorized to employ the force of the United States, as well by sea as by land, *to compel* such State or States to fulfil their federal engagements; and particularly to *make distraint* on any of the effects, vessels, and merchandizes of such State or States, or *of any of the citizens thereof,* wherever found; and to prohibit and prevent their trade and intercourse as well with any other of the United States and the citizens thereof as with any foreign State, and as well by land as by sea; until full compensation or compliance be obtained with respect to all requisitions made by the United States in Congress assembled, in pursuance of the Articles of Confederation." This new article was "to be binding on all the States not actually in possession of the enemy, as soon as the same shall be acceded to and ratified by each of the said States." Report to Congress for consideration—Madison Papers, i. 89.

What the probability of this acquiescence was, may be judged from the past history of this country; for this tremendous power, the analogy to which is seen in the worst feature of the ancient confederacies, proving fatal to them; contemplated the delinquency of, and distraint not merely of one, but of "*one* or more States." Well might Hamilton pronounce it a proposition to ENACT a civil war! That, in war, Government should rise with plume and mighty arms to the exertion of all the energies which war demands, is at times, the great necessity, the very condition of its existence; but that these energies should be so exerted as to cause the least unnecessary sacrifice of public and private rights, and interests; and that in peace, Government by its manly prudence, avoiding war, should by its policy render peace truly a blessing, these Hamilton felt, were objects worthy all a Statesman's care. Looking also, upon the States as essential parts of a compound Federal system, he never forgat, that they were "artificial beings"—existing and to exist for certain limited purposes; but regarding first and most the all involving general interests, before his clear view ever was present the grand perspective of the people of the United States, as ONE NATION. And thus, it was, the steady aim of his whole life, that this Unity should be perpetuated, not merely by parchment forms and artificial ties, but by the lasting ties of a great brotherhood of mutual affections and interests under paternal counsels, able not only to direct but to protect. To him nothing was more distasteful than an irregular and unnecessary exercise of power. Order working by its proper means to secure and enlarge the sphere of order, was all his favorite thought—Moderation in the selection and use of means, his favorite practice. To effect a permanent system of order, was with him as yet, only a hope; but to aid in securing the present means, by which that hope might become a certainty, was a duty. He felt it to be such. Hitherto he had confined himself to private instances. Now he came forward, and opened his embassy of great truths to all the people. Having temporarily retired from active service in the army; while Congress were engaged in preparing the recommendations to the States, previously mentioned, he wrote a series of essays, "to confirm an opinion already pretty generally received, that it was necessary to augment the powers of the Confederation;" and to fix the public judgment definitely on the points which ought to compose that augmentation. These Essays—the precursors of the Federalist,—he entitled, as a term most expressive of their purpose—"THE CONTINENTALIST," the first of which was published on the twelfth of July seventeen hundred and eighty one. They open in a tone of kind persuasion, well adapted to conciliate and to enlighten the prevailing doubts, and fears, and prejudices. Then, stating the object of his remarks—to shew "a want of power in Congress," they proceed. "History is full of examples, where in contests for liberty, a jealousy of power has either defeated the attempts to recover or preserve it in the first instance, or has afterwards subverted it by clogging the government with too great precautions for its felicity, or by leaving too wide a door for sedition and popular licentiousness. In a government framed for durable liberty, not less regard must be paid to giving the Magistrate a proper degree of authority to make and execute the laws with vigor, than to guard against encroachments upon the rights of the community. As too much power leads to despotism, too little leads to anarchy; and both eventually to the ruin of the people.... If the Federal government is too weak at first, it will continually grow weaker. The ambition and local interests of the respective members, will be constantly undermining and usurping upon its prerogatives, till it comes to a dissolution; if a partial combination of some of the more powerful ones does not bring it to a more *speedy* and *violent end.*"

Having, in the succeeding numbers, strongly marked the distinctive dangers proper to a single State and to a Confederacy; and, from a comparison of the different situations of the United States with those of the European Confederacies, drawn the conclusion, that, "if the FEDERAL GOVERNMENT SHOULD LOSE ITS AUTHORITY," CIVIL wars "WOULD CERTAINLY FOLLOW," he points to the probability of the larger States, in a short time become "prosperous, rich, and powerful, being inspired with ambition and nourishing ideas of separation and independence." "Though, it will ever be their true interest to preserve the Union, their vanity and self importance will be very likely to overpower that motive; and make them seek to place themselves at the head of particular confederacies, independent of the general one. A schism once introduced, competitions of boundary and rivalships of commerce will easily afford pretexts for war." The prostrate condition of this country; not from a deficiency of resources, but from a want of governmental power to employ them, is the next, and a most fertile and instructive topic; teaching the conclusion; that "we ought, without delay, to enlarge the powers of

Congress. Every plan, of which this is not the foundation, will be illusory. The separate exertions of the States will never suffice. Nothing but a well proportioned exertion of the resources of the whole under the direction of a Common Council, with power sufficient to give efficacy to their resolutions, can preserve us from being a conquered people now, or can make us a happy people hereafter." From these general views, he proceeds to a specification "of the points which ought to compose the contemplated augmentation of these powers." Primarily is stated, "the power of regulating trade," preceding a specification of the sources of revenue to be granted, "in *perpetuity*," to Congress; together with the power "of disposal of all unlocated lands for the benefit of the United States and the appointment of all land as well as naval officers of every rank." Having argued the necessity of permanent revenues as the basis of loans, and the policy of *funding* the debt, he dwells at some length on the necessity "of authorizing the Federal Government to regulate the trade of these States."

In the frame of the Articles of Confederation, nothing is more remarkable than the absence of an express power of regulating the external commerce of this country—a power which had been conceded to the British parliament by the Congress of 1775, "for the purpose of securing the commercial advantages of the whole empire to the mother country, and the *commercial benefits of its respective members*." In vain, did New Jersey, when consulting of the Confederation, avow her opinion; that "the sole and exclusive power of regulating the trade of the United States with foreign nations ought to be clearly vested in the Congress; and that the revenues therefrom ought to be appropriated to such public and general purposes as to Congress shall seem proper, and for the common benefit of the States; thereby deriving "a great security to the Union from the establishment of a common and mutual interest." Her proposal was rejected by *two thirds* of the voting States. And the Articles of the Confederation provided, that "the free inhabitants of each of the States shall be entitled to all the privileges and immunities of free citizens in the several States," and "shall enjoy therein all the privileges of trade and commerce, subject to the same duties, impositions, and restrictions as the inhabitants thereof respectively." They provided, that "no State, without the consent of the United States in Congress, shall enter into any conference, agreement, alliance, or treaty with any King, Prince, or State."

They provided, that, "no two or more States shall enter into any
treaty, confederation, or alliance whatever between them, without the consent of the United States in Congress." They gave to
Congress the power of, "entering into treaties and alliances,"
declaring that "no State shall lay any imposts or duties which
may interfere with stipulations in such treaties;"—but they also
provided, that, "no treaty of commerce shall be made whereby
the legislative power of the respective States shall be restrained
from imposing such imposts and duties on foreigners as their
own people are subjected to, or from prohibiting the exportation
or importation of any species of goods or commodities whatever." They provided, "for regulating the trade with the Indians;" but, by their previous limitations, they withheld the necessary plenary power "to regulate commerce with foreign
nations and among the several States."

The wise proposition of New Jersey—closed up among the
secret proceedings of Congress—was made in 1778. Two years
later, Hamilton is seen urging the conferring upon Congress this
great power, with all those incidents which look to the protection and encouragement of domestic industry. The following
year, New Jersey, again, in the person of a distinguished delegate,* proposed to vest Congress with a right "of superintending the commercial regulations of every State," and "with the
exclusive right of laying uniform duties on all imported articles."
A proposal, to vest in it the power of appropriating these duties
permanently, was rejected.

To impress on the public mind the necessity of imparting this
important power to Congress in all its extent was the next and
the most labored argument of "the Continentalist." The source
of the general prejudice against its being granted is there
stated; and next, those comprehensive and economical views,
which have since, in the main, governed the policy of this country, are developed with decisive force. But Hamilton's views did
not stop here. It was a part of his plan, that Congress should
have the power "of appointing all officers of the Customs,"
thereby, in fact, combined with the power of appointment of all
land (as well as naval officers) of every rank, to constitute a
Government of self-sustaining properties. That this defect of a
power to regulate their commerce should have continued until
the Confederation ceased to exist, among a people, which, in

* Dr. Witherspoon.

three quarters of a century, has risen to be the second, and soon must be the first commercial nation of the world; is only another instance of the obstinacy of local systems, often seen, not merely in confederacies but in single kingdoms, of which each member or province had differing rates of duties, and differing modes of collection.

The latest of the Essays of the "Continentalist" was published on the fourth of July 1782. It closes with this fine peroration. "There is something noble and magnificent in the perspective of a Great Federal Republic, closely linked in the pursuit of a common interest, tranquil and prosperous at home—respectable abroad; but there is something proportionately diminutive and contemptible in the prospect of a number of petty States, with the appearance only of Union, jarring, jealous, and perverse, without any determined action, fluctuating and unhappy at home, weak and insignificant by their dissensions in the eyes of other nations. Happy America, if those to whom thou hast entrusted the guardianship of thy infancy, know how to provide for thy future repose, but miserable and undone, if their negligence or ignorance permits the spirit of discord to erect her banner on the ruins of thy tranquility!!"

The true, the only remedy was a total change of system. To commence it by means of a Convention, Hamilton is seen to have been the foremost to have proposed; and only seventeen days elapsed after the publication of this essay, when he effected a purpose, to be classed among the most memorable acts of his short but variously and widely useful life. In the autumn of 'eighty, Hamilton, when recommending the appointment by Congress of a Superintendent of Finance, had also intimated the importance of appointing in each State a "Continental Superintendent." This appointment was conferred upon him; and a few months after on the thirteenth of July 'eighty two he attended the legislature of New York, then in session at Poughkeepsie, to consult with it on the financial measures deemed necessary. This body had, late in the preceding year, declared; "their readiness to comply with any measures to render the Union of these United States more intimate." This emphatic declaration had been preceded by an Act granting to Congress a revenue from the customs; by the authorization of a census; by the levy of a tax chiefly for continental use; and, by a declaration, in order to secure exclusive privileges to the recently established bank of North America, that no bank should be established within the State of New York. It was now convened in extra session, at the express instance of a Committee of Congress, to provide "for a vigorous prosecution of the war." Three days after Hamilton's arrival, on the motion of General Schuyler, the Senate, of which he was still the leader, resolved itself into a Committee, "to take into consideration the state of the Nation." The next day, the most important resolutions then proposed in this country, excepting those declaring its Independence, were reported. They were unanimously concurred in, the following day—Sunday the twenty first of July 1782—and were approved by the Governor, who was requested to transmit them to Congress, and to the Executive of each of the States. These Resolutions were from the pen of Hamilton, embodying much that had appeared in the "Continentalist." After a series of resolutions stating the importance and necessity of the measure, the closing Resolution, declared, "that it is essential to the common welfare that there should be as soon as possible a conference of the whole" of the States on the subject, and that it would be advisable for this purpose to propose to Congress "to recommend, and to each State to adopt the measure of assembling a GENERAL CONVENTION of the STATES, specially authorized to revise and amend the CONFEDERATION, reserving a right to the respective LEGISLATURES to ratify the same." Thus a legislative sanction was given to the great conception, he had, nearly two years before, first suggested. By almost all historical writers, under the enthralment which the slave power seemed to have imposed upon the mind of this country, the precedence in this great movement has been ascribed to Virginia. But, acting upon the examples* given in the previous New England Conventions, to which New York had been a frequent party, this precedence unquestionably belongs to New York.† This procedure, Hamilton announced to the Superintendent of Finance. I think this "a very eligible step, though I doubt of the concurrence of the other States, but I am *certain without it* they never will be brought to co-operate in any reasonable or effective plan. Urge reforms or exertions; and the answer constantly is, what avails

* History of Repub. ii. 108.

† Kent's Commentaries, i. 228, note. Adverting to this statement, "there is no doubt, that Colonel Hamilton ... was the distinguished individual, who by his wisdom suggested, and by his influence promoted, that *earliest authoritative* measure taken for a general Convention of the States."

it for one State to make them without the consent of the others? It is in vain to expose the futility of this reasoning. It is founded on all those passions which have the strongest influence on the human mind." The day after the passage of these resolutions, General Schuyler retired from the canvass to make room for Hamilton. He was elected a delegate to Congress. Ere long, he replied to his friend Colonel Laurens, announcing his election, "Peace made, my dear friend, a new scene opens. The object then will be to make our Independence a blessing. To do this we must secure our UNION on *solid* foundations, an herculean task; and to effect which mountains of prejudice must be levelled. Come to Congress. We know each other's sentiments. Our views are the same. We have fought side by side to make America free, let us, hand in hand, struggle to make her happy." To expedite this great plan of a national re-organization, a meeting of public creditors was held at Albany, at which a State delegation to a general convention was appointed.

Hamilton's doubts "of the concurrence of the other States," in this great measure, were too well founded. Instead of a spirit of union, a spirit of jealous discord prevailed. The question of territorial rights had delayed the ratification of the Articles of Confederation and was attended with circumstances most unpropitious. The charters of some of the Colonies extended their bounds to the South sea; and these Colonies, now States, claimed that, on the Declaration of Independence, the property and jurisdiction of the crown lands passed from the crown to these Colonies. A jealousy of these claims early prompted a proposition, that "to render the Union and Confederacy firm and perpetual; it was essential that the limits of each respective territorial jurisdiction should be ascertained by the Articles of Confederation." This proposition was rejected. A second, asserting to the United States the sole and exclusive power of ascertaining this boundary, was also rejected. This proposition being repeated the next year, met with the same fate. It was founded on the opinion, that, as "from the crown, of Great Britain, the sovereignty of its territory passed to the people, the unappropriated lands, which belonged to the crown, passed, not to the people of the Colony or State within whose limits they were situated, but to the whole "people of the United States."*

---

* Opinion of Jay, Chief Justice. 3 Dallas Rep. 419.

Under this conviction, a bounty in the public lands—as an inducement to enlistments—was offered by Congress, in the second year of the war. Averse to this measure, Maryland suggested the substitution of a money bounty. Two years later, Virginia passed a law, opening offices for the sale of her lands. Congress urged her to "forbear." New Jersey, Delaware, Maryland, each asserted its common right in these lands. In her true solicitude for the preservation and peace of the Union, New York, though with a strong conviction of her territorial rights, ceded them to the United States "to enure to their use and benefit."—Virginia did not willingly yield any part of her wide domain, but adopted a remonstrance to Congress, asserting "her exclusive rights of sovereignty and jurisdiction within her own territory;" until, affrighted by the invasion of her State, and the occupation by Arnold of her undefended Capital, at that very moment,* she also passed a vote of cession. This cession was clogged with conditions, which Congress pronounced "incompatible with the honor, interest and peace of the Union."

To ascertain what territory belonged to the United States, and to establish a plan for the disposal of it, in order to a discharge of the national debts, was soon after proposed in Congress. But, Virginia, now freed from the presence of an enemy by the victory at Yorktown, resumed her pretensions; protested against the proposed action of Congress; refused to give evidence of her title; and looked to a civil war in support of her claims.† In Congress the advocates of a national policy, again reported a recommendation to the States, of the cessions of the late crown lands—as "an important fund for the discharge of the National debt." On the final vote, this report was lost by a geographical division—the States North of the Potomac being unanimous in favor of it, and the four Southern States, with the exception of two members‡ opposing it. Powerless as Virginia

* January 2, 1781.

† Hist. Repub. ii. 327. Madison writes—"We are very anxious to bring the matter to an issue, that the State may know what course their *honor* and *security* require them to take."—Nov. 1, 1780. Again, "Considering the extensive interests and claims which Virginia has and the *enemies* and *calumnies* which these very claims form against her, she is perhaps under the strongest obligation of any State in the Union to *preserve* her *military contingent on a respectable footing*; and unhappily, her line is, perhaps of all, in the most *disgraceful* condition." April 1782. Madison Papers, vol. i. pp. 99, 101, 117.

‡ Colonel Bland, of Virginia, and Izard, of South Carolina.

was in money, in arms, in discipline, Congress had declared, in an address to the several States, while the integrity of the Union was thus being menaced, "We possess no funds which do not originate with you. We can command no levies which are not raised under your own acts."

The same spirit was shewn by Virginia in reference to a matter of much greater interest to the whole people of the United States—the right of navigating the Mississippi. During the pending negotiations with Spain, Virginia instructed her delegates in Congress "to use their utmost endeavors to obtain an express stipulation in favor of the United American States for the free navigation of the Mississippi *to the sea*, with a free port and other privileges at its mouth."* With the same affright under which she had tremblingly thrown up her claim to the late "crown lands," she authorized our negotiator "to recede from his former instructions; and, if Spain unalterably insisted on it, to content himself with a grant of its navigation to the *thirty-first degree* of *North latitude*." Thus, was the Unity of this great Empire in the enjoyment of this great national right, trifled with by the then most populous of the States. Jay disregarded the timid instruction, and Hamilton, as Chairman of a Committee of Congress subsequently reported, "that the free navigation of the Mississippi is a clear and essential right of the United States, and that the same ought to be considered and supported as such."† These were questions of the future, but the urgency of the present necessities was most grievously shown. Congress was compelled to pass a resolution, suspending the payment of the interest on the loan office certificates. The wide spread public and private distress resulting, and the impending pressing dangers, from the want of an efficacious government, at last drew forth from Hamilton this melancholy sentence— "The more I see, the more I find reason for those who love this country to weep over its blindness."

It was in the midst of an almost hopeless national bankruptcy, that he took his seat in Congress.‡ In the proceedings of that body he had a large share; and, it will be remarked, the Articles of Confederation having then been ratified by all the States; that, while he interpreted their provisions so as to give to them their full scope, he guardedly and strictly observed their limitations. A compliance by all of the

* Nov. 5, 1779.   † Sept. 16, 1788.   ‡ Nov. 25, 1782.

States with the past requisitions for money was the first
urgency—to provide for the immediate demands of the public
service—to secure additional aids, and to fulfil the public obligations. The cry for justice by the public creditors was a loud,
and indignant, and remonstrating wailing. Among these creditors were the suffering army about to be disbanded. Hamilton
deeply felt their wrongs; and, soon after he had taken his seat
in Congress, moved a resolution, directing the Superintendent
of Finance to represent to the States, the indispensable necessity of their complying with the last requisition, "assuring them,
that they were determined to make the fullest justice to the
public creditors an invariable object of their counsels and exertions." His resolution embraced the appointment of a deputation to Rhode Island to urge a grant of the impost—"as a measure essential to the safety, and reputation of these States." In
vindication of her refusal, that State communicated, through her
Governor, her reasons to Congress. These reasons involved in
their principles and in their policy the existence of the Confederacy; and Hamilton forthwith came forward, as the cham-
pion of the UNION against the contumacy of a STATE. He prepared a Report, the first, on the journals of Congress, which
discussed at length, the relations of the States, to the Confederation; and explained and vindicated its powers. Having primarily combated the objection of the unequal bearing of the
Impost on the Commercial States, he met that founded on its
alleged invasion of "the Constitution of the State." He asserted,
that a State had "a discretionary power of appointing officers,
not expressly known to its Constitution;" including "that of
authorizing the federal government to make the appointments,
in cases where the general welfare may require it;" and also,
that such a discretionary power existed in the Confederation.
"No federal constitution," he averred, "can exist, without powers, that in their exercise, affect the internal police of the component members. All that is required is, that the Federal government confine its appointments to such as it is empowered
to make, by the original act of Union, or by the subsequent
consent of the parties. Unless there should be express words
of exclusion in the constitution of a State, there can be no reason to doubt, that it is within the compass of legislative discretion, to communicate that authority." The propriety of so
doing was next urged. The inadequacy of the revenue to be
raised within the States rendering loans necessary; "the next

resource," he remarked, "is to borrow." We must not only stipulate a proper compensation for what "is lent," but we must
give security for the performance." "We must pledge an ascertained fund, simple and productive in its nature, general in its
principle, and at the disposal of a *single will*." "This will not
be the case, unless *the collection* as well as *the appropriation*,
is under the control of the United States."—They "have a common interest in a uniform and equally energetic collection; and
not only policy but justice to all the parties of the Union, designate the utility of lodging the power of making it where the
interest is common." *** "By the Confederation, Congress have
an absolute discretion in determining the quantum of revenue
requisite for the national expenditure. When this is done, nothing remains for the States, separately, but the mode of raising.
No State can dispute the obligation to pay the sum demanded,
without a breach of the Confederation; and when the money
comes into the treasury, the appropriation is the exclusive
province of the Federal Government." The strong motive for
the compliance with the requisition, that of funding the debt;
and that, thereby, "the national credit would revive and stand
hereafter on a secure basis," having been stated; Hamilton
closed this paper with these observations—"There is a happy
mean between too much confidence and excessive jealousy, in
which the health and prosperity of a State consist. Either
extreme is a dangerous vice. The first is a temptation to men
in power to arrogate more than they have a right to; the latter enervates Government, prevents system in the administration; defeats the most salutary measures; breeds confusion in
the State, disgusts and discontents among the people; and may
eventually prove as fatal to liberty as the opposite temper." To
this Report was appended, the first public pledge to establish
a SINKING FUND.

An estimate now made by him showed that the probable
receipts from the Impost would be insufficient. Before the
assent of the States to an increase could be obtained, it was
necessary to remove their discontents as to the late requisitions. With this view; and with the much higher view, of keeping the public faith, he moved the appointment of a Committee
to report the further provision necessary "for discharging the
interest on the loan office certificates, and other liquidated
debts; to revise the existing requisitions, and to report, whether
they should be continued or altered." One great cause of these

discontents was the absence of a practical rule for the apportionment of the public burthens: and while the demands for revenue were being considered, feeling the obligation of an effort
to act upon the existing provision of the Confederation—a valuation of the land within the States,—Hamilton offered a resolution "in order to enable Congress to form an *eventual* plan
towards carrying it into execution." In obedience also to his
sense of the importance of unswerving fidelity to the public
engagements, he sought to make provision for the Continental
bills, of which the people of New England were large holders.
In this he failed, the Southern States being much opposed to
their redemption. But there were other interests that could not
be wantonly disregarded. The main army presented a memorial
to Congress, setting forth its claims. In strict justice, these
claims had no precedence over those of other public creditors;
and Hamilton reported a declaration by Congress, that the
troops of the United States, "*in common with all their creditors*, have an undoubted right to expect security for their
claims;" and that Congress will make every effort in its power
to obtain from the respective States, substantial funds, adequate to the object of funding the whole debt of the United
States; and will enter upon an immediate and full consideration
of the nature of such funds, and the most likely mode of obtaining them."—To fulfil this pledge, he presented a resolution,
"that it is the opinion of Congress, that complete justice cannot be done to the creditors of the United States, nor the
restoration of public credit be effected, or the future exigencies
of the war be provided for, but by the establishment of *permanent* and *adequate funds*, to operate generally throughout
the United States, to be collected by Congress."*

This great advance towards an effective general Government
acting upon individuals, Virginia had recently barred. In the
previous month of October, she passed a resolution; not merely
in opposition to the grant to Congress of the power of levying
an impost, but formally and utterly hostile to the grant of any
power to Congress of raising a national revenue. Its terms are,
"Whereas the permitting *any power*, *other* than the general
Assembly of this Commonwealth, to *levy duties or taxes* upon
the citizens of *this State within the same*, *is injurious to its
sovereignty*; may prove destructive of the rights and liberty of

---

* Hist. Rep. ii. 360.

the people; and, so far as Congress might exercise the same, is contravening the spirit of the Confederation in the eighth article thereof;"* therefore the act previously passed granting it was repealed. Unpropitious as this procedure of Virginia was, Hamilton adhered to his purpose; and, declared by a resolution of Congress, "notwithstanding the discouraging obstacles they have hitherto encountered, they conceive it a duty to themselves and their constituents, to persevere in their intentions to renew and extend their endeavors to procure the establishment of revenues equal to the purpose of *funding all the debts* of the United States." Immediately after this renewed pledge, the mode of valuing the public lands—the rule of contribution—was considered. The plan approved by Congress he deemed very objectionable. It was acceded to by others from a persuasion that "some plan was expected by the States, and that none better could be fallen upon." Hamilton did not concur. His reasons detailed in a letter to the Governor of New York, have great weight. "A leading rule," he wrote at the close of this letter, "which I have laid down for the direction of my conduct is this; that, while I would have a just deference for the expectations of the States, I would never consent to amuse them by attempts which must either fail in the execution or be productive of evil. I would rather incur the negative inconveniences of delay, than the positive mischiefs of injurious expedients. *** There should, in my opinion, be a character of wisdom and efficiency in all the measures of the federal council—the opposite of a spirit of temporizing expedients. Every part of a business which is of so important and universal concern should be transacted on uniform principles, and under the direction of that body which has a common interest.... I regard the present moment, probably the dawn of peace, as peculiarly critical; and the measures which it should produce, as of great importance to the future welfare of these States."

Having urged that the proposed plan should be deferred; he offered a pledge, that an accurate valuation of the land should be made by Commissioners, *appointed by Congress and acting under their authority*. Though this pledge was supported by a majority of members, it was lost by a vote of States; and the plan he opposed was then rejected; and was never adopted.

The consideration of the Financial policy was long interrupted

* Henning's Statutes, xi. 171.

by a discussion of the claims of, and the provision made for the army; the necessity of adequate and permanent funds, having been declared by Congress. This subject was at last deliberately resumed; and on the motion of Madison, a proposition was made re-asserting the principle—the necessity of permanent and adequate funds; but omitting the provision in Hamilton's previous resolution, that these *funds should be collected by Congress.* This fatal concession to State prejudices was followed by another. It was the limitation of the grant of these funds to a period of *twenty five* years, defeating the intended purpose—the making them a basis for loans.* In vain, did Hamilton attempt by a modification of his plan, which gave to Congress the *nomination* of the officers of collection, but left the approval and *appointment* of them to the States, to secure his primary objects. His proposal was defeated; and a report was adopted, inviting the States to confer on Congress the power of levying, for the use of the United States, specific duties on certain enumerated articles, and an ad valorem duty on others—the duties to be continued for *twenty five years;*—the Collectors to be appointed by the States, removable by and amenable to Congress; with power, in case a State omitted to appoint, to make the appointment. Hamilton persisted in withholding his vote from this plan as being violative of his principles; but expressed "the hope, that New York would consent to it," upon special and general considerations. A similar plane of thought and system of principles are manifest in the several other plans submitted by him to Congress; among which is his report of a continental peace Establishment, land and naval. These plans, though not adopted by this negative Congress, were important, not only for the principles set forth as to the construction of the powers of the Confederacy, but as preliminary to the measures of a later period. Nor was his influence then unfelt as to the foreign policy of this country. The terms of a treaty of peace with Great Britain long and much agitated its counsels, these agitations chiefly proceeding from the subservience of Virginia to the views of France; from the questions which arose as to the national boundaries; and from the firmness of the negotiators of this treaty, shewn in the insisting upon the common rights of

---

* This limitation was in consequence of the opposition of Massachusetts, New Hampshire, Connecticut, and Virginia—(Madison, Lee, and Mercer, voting for it, Colonel Bland against it.) A similar limitation, much urged by Madison in 1790, was then decisively rejected, and Hamilton's view prevailed.

the people of the United States to the American fisheries. As to all these matters Hamilton's policy is seen to have been comprehensive and steadfast; nor were his efforts less strenuous to give a fair construction to the terms of this treaty, when concluded; and to persuade honest and moderate counsels in the execution of those of its provisions, as to which unhappy opinions had prevailed,* and existed.

Having prepared the instrument of ratification of this treaty, Hamilton wrote to Jay—its chief and most able negotiator, "We have now concluded the great work of independence, but much remains to be done to reap the fruits of it. Our prospects are not flattering. Every day proves the inefficacy of the present Confederation. Yet the common danger being removed, we are receding instead of advancing in a disposition to amend its defects. The road to popularity in each State is, to inspire jealousies of the power of Congress; though nothing can be more apparent, than that they have no power; and, that for the want of it the resources of the country during the war could not be drawn out; and we at this moment experience all the mischief of a bankrupt and ruined credit. It is to be hoped, that when prejudice and folly have run themselves out of breath; we may return to reason and correct our errors."

Discouraging as this view is, Hamilton resolved, before retiring from Congress to make another effort to retrieve by a great public act, the public affairs. The proposal made by New York to the other States to unite in a General convention to amend the Confederation, framed by himself, had met with no response. He well knew, that it was not easy to relieve the atrophy of a nation. Nevertheless, though disappointed in his exertions to recover it to health, full of apprehensions as to the continuance of the Union, he felt that it was a high duty to the people of this young country, while yet united in a general Confederacy, again, to appeal to them in their own behalf, through their several States, to save that Union. With this paramount

* On the 17th December 1781 Virginia passed resolutions, directing the Commissioners at Paris; "neither to agree to any restitution of property confiscated by the State; nor to submit that the laws made *by any independent* State of the Union be *subjected* to the *adjudication of any power* or *powers on Earth.*" Congress resolved "that this stipulation could not be retracted, without a violation of the national faith; and that the honor and interest of these United States require that it *should be substantially complied with.*" Hist. Rep. ii. 531, 532.

object in view, he framed a series of Resolutions, setting forth
in much detail the defects of the Articles of the Confederation,
enumerating briefly the injurious consequences of these defects;
declaring the necessity of "a Government, capable, both in peace
and war, of making every member of the Union, contribute in
just proportion to the common necessities; and of combining and
directing the forces and wills of the several parts to a general
end;" and recommending to the States, "to appoint a CONVEN-
TION to meet on a fixed day; with full powers to revise the Confederation; and to adopt and propose such alterations, as to
them shall appear necessary to be finally approved or rejected
by the States respectively."

On the draft of these resolutions Hamilton recorded the fact,
that they "were intended to be submitted to Congress, but
abandoned for want of support." Full of an equal apprehension
as to the continuance of the Union, Washington, on the eighth of
June on the disbanding of the army, addressed a circular letter
to the Governors of all the States. In this parting appeal, he
urged, "as essential not only to the well being, but to the existence of the United States as an independent power, an *indissoluble union* of the States under one common head;" "a sacred
regard to justice; the adoption of a proper peace establishment,"
and "the prevalence of that pacific and friendly disposition
among the people of the United States, which will induce them
to forget their local prejudices and policies, to make those
mutual concessions, which are requisite to the general prosperity; and, in some instances, to sacrifice their individual advantages to the interest of the community."

Referring to these paternal counsels, Hamilton thus
addressed his late commander in chief.

"In a letter which I wrote to you several months ago, I intimated that it might be in your power to contribute to the
establishment of our federal UNION upon a more solid basis. I
have never since explained myself. At the time, I was in hopes
Congress might have been induced to take decisive ground; to
inform their constituents of the imperfections of the present
system, and of the impossibility of conducting the public affairs
with honor to themselves and advantage to the community;
with powers so disproportioned to their responsibility; and having done this in a full and forcible manner, to adjourn, the
moment the definitive treaty was ratified. In retiring at the
same juncture, I wished you, in a solemn manner, to declare to

the people, your intended retreat from public concerns; your opinion of the present Government, and of the absolute necessity of a change. Before I left Congress, I despaired of the first; and your circular letter to the States had anticipated the last. I trust it will not be without effect; though I am persuaded it would have had more, combined with what I have mentioned. At all events, without compliment, sir, it will do you honor with the sensible and well meaning; and ultimately it is to be hoped, with the people at large; when the present epidemic frenzy has subsided."*

That frenzy did not soon subside; and the interval between the ratification of the Provisional treaty of Peace with Great Britain; and the operative influence of the present Constitution, exhibits an unvarying scene of national degradation and unrelieved distress. The compromising spirit which had induced the concessions by Congress in the financial policy of seventeen hundred and eighty three failed wholly of its purpose. Surrendering all that could commend these concessions to the confidence of true national views, they retained too much to satisfy the distrusts of opposite opinions. This twilight soon passed into utter darkness. Not more than six months had elapsed since the conclusion of the Definitive treaty of peace cheered the public heart; and now, at the time that Congress, insulted by a contemptible party of mutinous soldiers, clamoring for their pay, abandoned, under their menaces, the seat of Government, the rejection by Virginia of the recent financial plan, reprobating the principles enunciated by Hamilton in his reply to Rhode Island, was announced.† Blind as was this jealousy; under an impression that she had contributed disproportionately to the general treasury; a few months later, Virginia passed a resolution, in precise conformity with the previously expressed views of Madison; "declaring that Congress ought to *enforce* the payment of the balances due from any of the States by *distress*" on the property of the defaulting States or of their citizens.‡ Virginia had offensively rejected the recent financial plan, chiefly on the ground of the assertion of the safe and necessarily implied power of the Confederation to impose and levy duties on imports; and she now urged the exertion of a power— founded solely on a dangerous implication of that power, as inci-

* Hamilton's Works, i. 402.
† Joseph Jones to Madison, June 14, 1783.—Madison Papers.
‡ Journal of House of Delegates of Virginia, 11, 12. May 1784.

dental to a league. This resolution—addressed to a Congress whose army numbered only eighty men—fell lifeless before the Councils of the Country, now called upon to consult the great interests which peace had just opened to its view. A general power in Congress to regulate commerce, as previously stated, was not embraced in the Articles of Confederation; and though proposed to be after granted was not conferred; and the measures resorted to by the separate States only proved their utter incapacity of self protection. Fully aware of this weakness, and sore at her defeats; England, by a proclamation issued in 1783, the first act of her commercial policy towards her recent subjects; closed her West Indies to all American vessels; and prohibited in her own vessels the introduction there of fish and other articles. Virginia, smarting under recent disgraces, resolved to rush into a peaceful war of commercial restrictions—long the after favorite policy of her leaders. At the next session of her Legislature, in early winter, she recommended Congress to prohibit all intercourse with England, until the restrictions upon the commerce of the United States were removed. Congress, now composed of inferior men, recommended to the States to invest them with powers of commercial retaliation, for a limited term. These powers, though again asked, were never imparted to the Confederation. The lessons of a short experience told upon Virginia, as they did upon the other States. Ere two years had elapsed; she proposed to authorize Congress to regulate the foreign and internal trade of the States, and to collect the revenue therefrom, but for a limited term, *two thirds* of the States concurring; superadding other limitations. She, at the same time refused authority to collect an Impost. A year more intervened, when Virginia passed a countervailing law; and an Act giving preference of duties to her own citizens. Nor in these effete measures was she alone. Instead of one general, uniform, commercial policy to pervade the whole Union, are beheld, similar inchoations of strenuous weakness—the conflicting laws of conflicting States, each bidding for preferences by rival tariffs; each seeking to compel, by countervails and prohibitions, the advantages which those preferences did not obtain. The results of these commercial rivalries taught the needed lesson. Pennsylvania, while enacting a restrictive law, pointed to the true remedy—a grant to Congress of one of the powers, which Hamilton had so earnestly urged should be engrafted on the Confederation. She

declared, that "the privilege in the degree retained by the
States individually, of controlling and regulating their own
trade was no longer compatible with the general interest and
welfare of the United States." Connecticut, tired of vain experiments, under the same conviction, at last passed an Act "vesting Congress with power to regulate the commerce of the
United States;" and Massachusetts wearied of the narrow counsels which had too long prevailed there, also asserted, through
her Governor,* the duty of vesting in Congress the power of
regulating the trade of the whole country. Nor did this enlightened person stop here. "It is of great importance," he proclaimed, "and the happiness of the United States depends upon
it, that Congress should be vested with ALL the powers necessary to preserve the Union, to manage the general concerns of
it, and promote its common interest." With this intent, he proposed a CONVENTION, whose agreement, when confirmed by the
States, would comprehend these powers. The approving legislature, declaring that the powers of Congress were "not fully
adequate to the great purposes they were originally designed
to effect," urged Congress to recommend, "a Convention from
all the States, to revise the Confederation; and report to
Congress, how far it may be necessary in their opinion, to alter
or enlarge the same, in order to secure and *perpetuate* the primary objects of the Union." This resolution was *not* submitted
to Congress by her delegates; under an impression that the proposed powers ought only to be "temporary, until approved by
experience;" and, that, if a Convention was necessary, its members, should be limited in their authority, and confined to the
revision of such parts of the Confederation, as are supposed
defective; and not be intrusted with a general revision of the
articles, and a right to report a "plan of federal government
essentially different from the Republican form, now administered." In consequence, a resolution passed, declaring that no
further proceedings be had for revising the Confederation. A
sterner will was at this time curbing New York.

An enlargement of the powers of Congress to countervail
Great Britain was there proposed,—not granted; but a discriminating duty against British vessels was imposed by her legislature. The next year, Congress were vested by this body with the
retaliatory commercial powers it had asked; but were expressly

---

* Message of Governor Bowdoin. May 31, 1785. Hist. Rep. iii. 135.

forbidden collecting any revenue *within* the State *without its sanction*. The declaring her bills of credit a *legal tender* followed, a vicious example—forthwith copied by North Carolina and Georgia, and enforced in Rhode Island, by penal laws. Amid this wide distemperature, an abdication of the Union by New England became a current topic; and disaffection was exasperated into violence among large bodies of their people, by the honest vigor of Massachusetts, and of New Hampshire, maintaining the obligations of their public faith. This threatened collapse was prevented there. But in the two chief planting States, where the tone of the public pulse was weaker, and the necessary vigor of government was suspended; all was tending to an early dismemberment. Kentucke broke from unresisting Virginia. North Carolina was dissevered, and a fragment of her domain was forming into an independent State; while the vast Western region of the United States,—the present seat of mighty opulence and patriotic power, seemed sliding off from the feeble hold of a dissolving league. In the midst of this huge discord, the basis of a concentrated vigorous government might have been laid in the region extending from the St. Croix to Maryland; but below, on the Atlantic coast, physical obstacles are seen in many an aspect. Virginia, though looming with pride at her vast interior space, early felt the impossibility of a total isolation; and in the second year of Independence, sought a compact with Maryland to arrange the jurisdiction of their confluent waters, and common Estuary. In the first year of peace; she again appointed a commission of conference, which was renewed the following year, when her Commissioners met at Mount Vernon with those of Maryland. There they agreed upon an Act, regulating the commercial intercourse through the Potomac and Chesapeake, and defining the jurisdiction of each State. But, at the moment of framing this compact, these commissioners deemed it necessary to extend its provisions, so as to authorize the establishment of a naval force to protect their intervenient waters, and the formation of a mutual tariff. This compact, by the Articles of Confederation, required the previous consent of Congress. To obviate this difficulty, these deputies recommended to their respective States, the appointment of other Commissioners with enlarged powers, to whose proceedings the permission of Congress was to be solicited. In the first month of the ensuing year,* Virginia passed resolutions for an

---

* January 13, 1786.

uniformity of duties between the two States; and that Commissioners be chosen to meet annually, if required, to regulate their mutual commercial interests. A few days after,* she directed the projected arrangement to be communicated to all the other States, inviting a general meeting of deputies for the precise purpose of considering, "how far a uniform system of taxation in their commercial intercourse and regulations might be necessary to their common interest and permanent harmony; and to report to the several States, such an act relative to this great object, as when unanimously ratified by them; will enable the United States in Congress assembled, effectually to provide for the same."† A circular letter, transmitting this resolution, named Annapolis, as the place of meeting in the following September. This procedure merely contemplated a *commercial* arrangement, far short of the previous proposals—first of New York, then of Massachusetts.

It is the province of the highest order of minds, to see in the embryo of events, the fruits that are being born, and that may ripen to a rich maturity. By the intelligent interests of the navigating States, Hamilton felt almost assured, that every obstacle to the organization of an efficacious Government, would yield to wise persuasions; but so far the planting States, slow to learn and obstinate in their prejudices, had given no promise of enlightened convictions. This proposition was their first great advance; and he seized with delight the opportunity of earnest necessities that would not long be baffled. The first thing was to accomplish the co-operation of New York. While the commercial strifes of the several States were going on, the grant to Congress of the long sought power of raising a revenue from imports was still deferred,—partly owing to the fallacious schemes of 1784 and 1785; but chiefly to the non compliance of the two Central States,—Pennsylvania and New York.

Hemmed in by these great States, jealous of their commercial superiority, and disappointed in her efforts to induce a liberal general policy, New Jersey now took a decisive step. She passed a resolution, reciting, as a reason for it, the delinquency of other States, refusing a compliance with the requisition of Congress for her quota; "until all the States in the Union had complied with the revenue system of seventeen hundred and eighty

---

* Hist. Repub. iii. 160.

† Moved by John Tyler, father of a late President of the U.S.

three; or until, States having peculiar commercial advantages, should forbear a system of partial legislation." Yielding to wise influences she rescinded this resolution; but declared, that the requisition had no binding force. There was reason to expect that Pennsylvania would perform her federal duty, and would enlarge the federal powers; but that New York would depart from her then selfish and obnoxious policy, there was little ground of hope. The improvident importations made on the return of peace had poured into her coffers a large revenue, increased by the navigation acts of other States; rendering her the entrepôt of the region east of the Delaware. Under these circumstances, it was not difficult to inculcate a persuasion, "that the commercial advantage of the State depended upon retaining the power to collect her own revenues."* Thus cupidity, and ambition, and pride were all united in blinding her to exterior dangers; in giving her an undue sense of her own importance; and in rendering her, for the time, a jealous advocate of State sovereignty! This was seen in all her recent persistent legislation. An act passed, in accordance with the first recommendation of Congress, in seventeen hundred and eighty one, of the grant of power to raise an impost, giving them the fullest authority to levy, and collect it *by their own* officers, was repealed; and, although the grant was renewed, the duties were to be collected *by the officers*, and *under the authority of the State*. The second recommendation of Congress, in seventeen hundred and eighty three, was rejected by the two successive legislatures of seventeen hundred and eighty four, and eighty five; and in eighty six, though a power of raising a revenue by an impost was granted, "the sole power of levying and collecting the duties" was reserved to the State. Thus denied all virility, Congress could only implore. Hamilton felt that it was now time to bring to a definite issue, the pregnant question in her policy, of granting or refusing the means of maintaining the Union; if refused by her, of her entering into a concert in a general arrangement embracing leading national objects.†

* Curtis—History of the Constitution, i. 344. In opposition to the adoption of the present Constitution was a busy organization called "The Republican Club," the most active person of which in his correspondence with the opponents of it in other States, was the Collector of *the New York Customs*. George Mason agreed to act as chairman of the "Republican Society" in Virginia.—*Life of John Lamb.*

† "Hamilton," Colonel Troup relates, "had no idea that the legislature could be prevailed on to adopt the system as recommended by Congress;

Massachusetts, checked for a time in her forward action, was now again in motion. Her Governor, after descanting upon the importance of conferring the requisite powers upon Congress, placed before her legislature the grave enquiry—"Shall the Union cease to exist?"; and, as soon as he received the Circular of Virginia, recommended an appointment of Commissioners to the contemplated Commercial Convention, which was made. New Jersey, Pennsylvania, and Delaware united with Virginia in the mission to Annapolis, where Benson, the Attorney General, and Hamilton, two of the representatives appointed by the legislature of New York, arrived on the seventh of September. After some delay, awaiting the deputies from other States who did not appear, this assemblage of only twelve persons, appointed a committee to prepare a report, which being accepted, the Convention adjourned.

The draft of this report was by Hamilton, though not formally one of the Committee.* In this draft, as originally framed, Hamilton exhibited at large, the condition of the country, and the necessity of an efficient national Government. But, from the opinions he met there, and from the lukewarmness manifested by the non-attendance of the delegates of most of the States, it was thought, that his statements were too full, and explicit; and he reduced the report to the form in which it was issued† on the fourteenth of September seventeen hundred and eighty six. It was addressed to the five States there represented; and copies of it were transmitted to Congress and to the executives of the other States. The terms of this Address are seen to have been very carefully guarded, so as to be in strict accordance with the thirteenth of the articles of the Confederation, which required

neither had he any partiality for a commercial convention, otherwise than as a stepping stone to a general convention, to form a General Constitution. In *pursuance of his plan*, Mr. Duer, the late Colonel Malcolm and myself, were sent to the State legislature, as part of the city delegation, and we were to make every possible effort to accomplish Hamilton's objects. * * * We went all our strength in the appointment of commissioners to attend the commercial convention, in which we were successful—Hamilton was appointed one of them. Thus it was, that he was the principal instrument to turn the State to a course of policy that saved our country from incalculable mischiefs, if not from ruin."

* Memoir published by Judge Benson.

† Edmund Randolph, Governor of Virginia, objected to the Report as first framed; Madison then observed to Hamilton, "You had better yield to this man, otherwise all Virginia will be against you."

that, "any alteration of them should be *agreed to in Congress,* and confirmed by the *legislature of every State;*" while the latitude with which the object of the proposed Convention is expressed—"to devise such further provisions as shall appear to them necessary to render the Constitution of the federal government *adequate to the exigencies* of the Union," indicates clearly Hamilton's determined purpose to endeavor to establish a well organized NATIONAL GOVERNMENT. The contemplated general Convention was asked to meet at Philadelphia on the second Monday of the coming May.

This interval was momentous. The insurrection in New England, suppressed by a local force, raised without waiting the sanction of Congress, which the Articles of Confederation required, proved the want of the peace establishment which Hamilton in vain, had planned and urged; and New York, in stolid stubbornness, was defying every appeal to her better reason, to her great interests, and to her highest duty. The other States had at length granted to Congress, power to levy and collect an impost. These grants, the last act of New York in relation to it, rendered nugatory. In this great emergency, Congress requested her Governor to convene an extra session of her legislature. Clinton refused on the ground, that his power to convene it was limited, to "*extraordinary occasions.*" Congress, then sitting at New York, declared that the act of New York was not a compliance with the general plan—that "the present critical and embarrassed state of the finances was such as to require that the system of impost should be carried into immediate effect;" that they consider this as "an occasion sufficiently important and extraordinary" for the convening of the legislature, and earnestly recommended that it should be immediately called. Clinton was deaf to this most earnest appeal. The friends of the Union in New York were roused with indignation. They resolved to endeavour to redeem their State from such misguiding. General Schuyler had again been elected to its Senate. Hamilton, though opposed by the men whose cupidity he had exposed in 'eighty four, and who were among the chief adherents of Clinton, was chosen by the City of New York, one of its members of Assembly. His services in this body have left a marked impress on the legislative code of this State; but these were secondary to the influence he was enabled to exert upon the counsels of the Confederacy. The question before it, which rose in magnitude above all others, was—that of the grant to Congress of the power to raise an Impost. In behalf of this grant, Hamilton made an effort of argument and of eloquence not below the momentous topic— the union and general welfare of a free people. Around him were standing the few disheartened members of an anxious Congress; and most of the most distinguished men of the State. His effort, though thwarted, was not in vain, for he then and there established an influence, which, perhaps, it may not be erroneously stated, established the Federal constitution. What force of mind he displayed is seen in the fact, that not one of the numerous opposition ventured a reply. The resolution for the grant was defeated by a *silent* vote—as was said—"the Impost was *strangled by a band of mutes.*" This vote was given on the fifteenth of February 1787 while Congress were still hesitating their approval of the proposed General Convention. Though outvoted in this measure, Hamilton felt that in all this exertion of his powers, his gracious temper had rightly touched the temper of the Assembly; and, the day after this vote, a notice was given of an intended motion for an instruction to Congress to recommend the call of a general Convention. This proposed instruction was expressive of the great purpose in Hamilton's thoughts;—that "of revising the Articles of Confederation and perpetual Union, by such alterations and amendments, as *a majority* of the representatives shall judge proper and necessary to render them *adequate* to the preservation and *government* of the Union." Had this instruction as thus framed passed, the present civil conflict would not have taken place, and the question of the duration of this Government would not continue to agitate thoughtful minds. Though injuriously modified in its terms by the State party in the House, this Instruction passed; and through the influence of Schuyler, at an urgent moment, was adopted by the Senate, by a majority of *one* vote. The next day, Hamilton's Report from Annapolis was called up in Congress. By some it was supposed their sanction of the Convention might stimulate; by others it was alleged, that it would impede the action of the States. Some looked with jealousy at a body so formed, others doubted its "legality." Amid this perplexity—at this critical moment—the instruction of New York was presented to them and determined their action. Its precise instruction failed, though supported by Massachusetts and Virginia. A new resolution, offered by a member of the former state, being amended, passed.

Referring to the provision for their alteration, in the Articles of the Confederation, and to "the instructions of several States; and *particularly* the *State of New York;*" and declaring it to be "the most probable means of establishing in these States a *firm national* Government," it sanctioned the contemplated Convention, for the purpose "of revising" the Confederation, and reporting to Congress and to the several States "such alterations and provisions therein, as shall, when agreed to by Congress, and confirmed by the States, render the Federal Constitution, adequate to the exigencies of government and the preservation of the Union." One great barrier, Hamilton had now removed. Congress had surrendered its exclusive right to innovate upon the Articles of the Confederation. His great purpose was attained—the calling of a Convention to be composed of men of the highest intellect, and the longest and largest experience in this country,—by Congress, thus giving its sanction to this new body when convened—and trusting to the indeterminate commissions of its members, to organize a government fully capable of promoting and perpetuating the welfare of a great nation. Nor was this all. The existing Government was, by this act, made auxiliary to its own modification, or even subversion, by the substitution of another government, without violating the constitutional provisions of the Confederation; and, still looking to every contingency, the ligaments of the imperfect league were preserved; until, perhaps, the coming of some more favorable moment for its reconstruction. This may be pronounced a masterly achievement.

Having thus successfully exerted the influence of this act of reluctant New York upon the reluctant Congress; Hamilton was eager to derive the benefit of the influence of this recommendation of Congress upon that State; and five days after, he presented a resolution to the assembly of New York, conforming to that recommendation, for the appointment of five commissioners to meet in the General Convention. The proposed number was reduced to three; and a proviso was urged, that the alterations and provisions of the Confederation "should be not repugnant to, or inconsistent with the *Constitution of this State.*"* This proviso was lost by the vote of the presiding officer of the Senate. Hamilton's resolution was passed; and on the eighth of March, Hamilton, Lansing and Yates were appointed the three commissioners. As the rule of the Confederation of voting by

---

* Proposed by Chief Justice Yates.

States, probably would be adopted; and as his colleagues differed from him in their views, Hamilton proposed, near the end of the session, to add two delegates. This motion prevailed in the assembly, but was defeated in the Senate. Happily for his fame, this result did not prevent his assuming, finally, a responsibility from which he did not shrink, and which proved of large benefit to the American people. Virginia, New Jersey, Pennsylvania, Delaware, and North Carolina appointed their Commissioners, not waiting the sanction of Congress. This sanction being given, each of the other States, Rhode Island excepted, also chose a deputation.

Amid a great diversity of opinions, and of interests, the Federal Convention met at Philadelphia on the fourteenth of May seventeen hundred and eighty seven, when, a majority of States not being represented, it adjourned to the twenty-fifth of that month. It is an evidence of the uncertain anticipations of the result of its consultations, that Washington long hesitated becoming a member of it; and that Connecticut deferred the choice of her delegation to it until May; and New Hampshire until the following June. Nine States having appeared on the day to which it had adjourned, they gave to its proceedings all the weight and influence of Washington's great character and popularity, by electing him to preside. To secure to its deliberations the utmost freedom from external pressure, these deliberations were ordered to be secret.

Four days later, on the twenty ninth of May, a series of propositions for a National government were submitted for consideration to a committee of the whole body* by Edmund Randolph, of Virginia, and having been discussed and amended, were reported to the House on the thirteenth of June. They were called "the VIRGINIA Plan." Two days after, a number of resolves, framed by several of the representatives of States, especially sedulous for a large retention of power in the States, were presented. They were called "The JERSEY Plan." These being referred to a Committee of the whole House, the Virginia resolutions were recommitted.

The broad question, whether "a national government ought to be established, consisting of a Supreme legislative, executive

* A plan of Government was submitted by Charles Pinckney, *not that on the Journal*, but that stated in "No. 2687 of Select Tracts of New York Historical Society." It does not appear to have gained any special attention.

and judiciary," or the Articles of Confederation with enlarged powers, was now before the Convention. The VIRGINIA plan, as essentially modified, proposed a National Legislature to consist of two branches—the first "to be elected by the people of the several States for the term of three years"—the second, "by the individual legislatures;"—and it was resolved, that this legislature so organized, "ought to be empowered to enjoy the legislative rights vested in Congress by the Confederation;" and, moreover, "to legislate on all cases to which the separate States are incompetent, or in which the harmony of the United States may be interrupted by the exercise of individual legislation; and to negative all laws passed by the several States contravening in the opinion of the national legislature the articles of union, or any treaties subsisting under the authority of the Union." It was declared, that the right of suffrage in the first branch ought to be "in proportion to the whole number of white and other free citizens and inhabitants of every age, sex, and condition, including those bound to servitude for a term of years, and three fifths of all other *persons* not comprehended in the foregoing description, except Indians, not paying taxes in each State;" and, that the right of suffrage in the second branch ought to be according to the same rule;—that a National Executive be instituted to consist of one person, to be chosen by the National legislature, for the term of seven years, with power to carry into execution the National laws; to appoint to offices in cases not otherwise provided for; to be ineligible a second time; to be removable on impeachment and conviction of malpractice or neglect of duty; and to receive a fixed stipend from the national treasury, with a veto on any legislative act, unless afterwards passed by two thirds of each branch of the legislature;—and that a National Judiciary be established; to consist of one Supreme tribunal, appointed by the second branch of the legislature, to hold office during good behaviour, with fixed compensations, unalterable as to the incumbents— with power to the National legislature to appoint inferior tribunals. The judicial jurisdiction was to extend to all cases respecting "the collection of the National revenue, impeachments of any National officers; and questions which involve the National peace and harmony." The several departments being thus organized and their powers expressed; a provision was added, for "the admission of States lawfully arising without the limits of the United States." A provision was also made, for the continuance of Congress and its authorities until a given day after the reform of the Articles of Union shall be adopted, and for the completion of all their engagements. Likewise, a resolution, that a *republican constitution* and its existing laws, ought to be guaranteed to each State by the United States— another resolution, that provision ought to be made for the amendment of the Articles of Union—and that the legislative, executive and judiciary powers ought to be bound by oath to support the Articles of Union;—and a final resolution, that the amendments "offered by the Convention, ought, after the approbation of Congress, to be submitted to an assembly or assemblies of representatives, recommended by the several legislatures, to be expressly chosen by *the people*, to consider and decide thereon."

"The JERSEY plan;" in direct contrast with that originating with Virginia, proposed; "that the Articles of Confederation be so revised, corrected and enlarged, as to render the federal constitution adequate to the exigencies of government and the preservation of the Union." In addition to the existing powers, were proposed those of levying certain revenue duties and of regulating commerce—retaining the system of requisitions— numbers being substituted as the measure of contribution;— retaining a single legislative body with the command of the purse and of the sword, deriving its authority from the States; and with equality of suffrage by the States; but giving no negative upon the States. It contemplated a plural Executive, with authority to execute the federal acts, to appoint federal officers, and to direct all military operations; removable for misconduct, on application by a majority of the *executives of the several States*; and without a negative on the acts of this single legislative body. It proposed also, a federal judiciary to consist of a Supreme tribunal; to be appointed by the Executive, and to hold during good behaviour; authorized to hear appeals in several specified cases, and to try impeachments of federal officers, without any other original jurisdiction, and without providing for inferior tribunals. It was likewise resolved; "that the legislative, executive, and judiciary powers within the respective States, ought to be bound by oath to support the Articles of Union;" and that Acts of Congress, "lawfully made, and all treaties made and ratified under the authority of the United States, shall be the supreme law of the respective States, as far as those acts and treaties shall relate to the said States or to their citizens;" and that the State judiciaries shall be bound thereby. To this impotent system, was superadded an express power to the federal executive "to call forth the powers of the Confederated States to enforce and compel" by States or individual bodies, an obedience to the acts of the Confederacy or an observance of its treaties. It also provided for the admission of new States, and for the hearing and decision of territorial disputes.

It is seen, that this plan proposed merely a modification of the Articles of Confederation; and in most respects a modification embracing the several propositions made to Congress, from time to time, prior to the call of the Convention. It was in accordance with the policy of its advocates, to place themselves on the ground of a strict observance of the terms of their Commissions from their several States. The resolutions of Virginia, even much as they had been amended, presented features little less objectionable. With the undefined powers given to the national legislature, it was also empowered "to negative all laws passed by the several States, contravening, in the *opinion* of the national legislature, the articles of Union, or any treaties subsisting under its authority;" superadding the election of the Executive by the general legislature, and the choice of the Judiciary by the second branch of this legislature. A Government so constituted could not have been established; or if established, could not have maintained itself, without constant collisions with the States, early fatal to its existence, or without resulting in an intolerable tyranny. The two plans before the Convention were hopelessly irreconcilable. A dissolution of the Convention, and a dissolution of the frail union were impending—almost instant.

Hamilton, though by the uniting controlling voice of his two colleagues from New York, without a vote, resolved to present a plan—himself free from any weak reserves—in the approach to which might be framed a Government, resting entirely on the free voice and power of the American people. Aware of the existing heresy, that "a *party* to a *compact* has a right to revoke that *compact*"—the very heresy upon which the existing rebellion places its vindication, asserting that the Constitution of the United States is a mere compact of several sovereign States;—he fully saw "the necessity of laying the foundations of the National Government deeper than in the mere sanction of delegated authority." "The fabric of the American Empire," are his words, "ought to rest on the solid basis of the CONSENT OF THE PEOPLE."

"The streams of national power ought to flow immediately from that pure original fountain of all legitimate authority." This elementary, leading principle of his policy was avowed by him, on the *first* day of the deliberations of the Convention. The initial proposition of Virginia in the formation of a new Government was; "that the right of suffrage in the National legislature, ought to be proportioned to the quotas of contribution, *or* to the number of free inhabitants, as the one or the other may seem best in different cases." Hamilton met the open question at once by a resolution, "that the rights of suffrage in the National legislature ought to be proportioned to the number of FREE INHABITANTS."*

This principle having been adopted, as to the first branch of the legislature, was, with his concurring vote, extended to the second branch;† and, upon a motion for the choice of the Executive by electors to be chosen by the people in districts, as the vote of New York was divided;‡ (its other representatives strictly adhering to the theory of a State corporate vote); and as this was the mode of election provided for in his plan of a Constitution, it cannot be doubted, that Hamilton voted for it. Thus, did he propose to stamp upon the new system its primary essential character in his view, that of an Institution founded in the free voice of the whole people of the United States; and deriving all the departments of government from them;—confronting at the same time—at the very outset,—in the foreground,—the theory of the separate, controlling sovereignty of the mere, "artificial beings"—the States; and restoring to all the "free inhabitants of the United States"—"as one people," in Union, the united sovereignty and united independence they had asserted to themselves in the Declaration of Independence, when assuming, "among the powers of the earth, a separate and equal station." Thus, did he carry into effect his own pregnant, explicit, never to be forgotten attestation, that "the sovereignty and independence of the People began by a federal act"—that, "the declaration of Independence was the fundamental Constitution of every State"—"that the Union and Independence of these States are blended and incorporated in one and the same act." The Convention had unanimously pledged themselves to establish a *republican* Government. The only question, therefore, which remained,

* Journal of the Federal Convention, p. 83. The resolution moved by Hamilton, seconded by Spaight, May 30, 1787.

† Ibid. 112. *Moved* by Wilson, *seconded* by Hamilton. June 11, 1787.

‡ Ibid. 92.

was, what form that republican government ought to take? The first resolution of the States right, or "New Jersey Plan"—is seen to have been, "that the Articles of the Confederation ought to be so revised, *enlarged* and corrected, as to render the *federal constitution adequate to the exigencies of government*, and the preservation of *the Union*." To declare a purpose beyond this; and to open the whole subject of the best form of Government to be framed, this resolution was postponed; and it was now resolved;—"that the Articles of the Confederation ought to be revised and *amended*, so as to render the *government of the United States* adequate to the exigencies, the preservation, and *the prosperity* of the Union."

At this moment of most critical, deepest, emergent interest, Hamilton took the floor. After stating* the importance of the occasion, he urged the obligation of adopting "a solid *plan* without regard to temporary *opinions*"—that "if an ineffectual plan were again proposed, it will beget despair; and no Government will grow out of the CONSENT of the people—; that there seemed to be but three lines of conduct—; a league offensive, a treaty of commerce, and an apportionment of the public debts—; an amendment of the existing Confederation, by adding such powers as the public mind deems nearest being matured to grant—; or, *the forming a* NEW government to *pervade the whole*" country, "with *decisive* powers," in short, "with complete sovereignty." The last, he stated, seemed to be the prevailing sentiment, and he therefore fully examined its practicability. He next exposed at much length "the *objections*" to the existing Confederation, concluding, that it could not be amended, unless the most important powers were given to Congress, constituted as they were, shewing that this would be liable to all the objections against any form of general government, with the addition of "the want of *checks*." On this point his speech took a large scope; setting forth "the principles of Civil obedience," and the absence of their operation in such a plan; and stating in succession, the causes of opposition to it which would exist, and would be active, as the necessary consequences of such a scheme; sustaining his positions by a full exhibition from history, of the fate of ancient and modern Confederacies. The result, he declared, would be, "dismemberment," promoted by "foreign influence;" followed by "standing armies," and "domestic factions;" ending in "monarchy in the Southern

---

* Hist. Rep. iii. 275. June 18, 1787.

States"—; the jeopardy of "federal rights," especially, the "fisheries," and the loss of their great natural "advantages"—that,
"foreign nations" would not respect our rights, nor grant us
reciprocity; and would reduce us to a passive commerce,—that
the fisheries, the navigation of the lakes—of the Mississippi; and
the protection and power of a fleet—would all be hazarded or lost.
That to prevent all these evils, and to secure permanently the
national happiness; the General Government, must not only have
a strong soul, but *strong organs* "by which that soul is to operate." What that Government ought to be was the great question.
Here he gave his "sentiments of the best form of Government—
not as a thing attainable by us, but as a model which we ought to
approach as near as possible." That the "British Constitution was
the best form"—was the conclusion of the inquiries of the wisest
philosophic investigators of the nature and characteristics of government,—of Aristotle, of Cicero, Montesquieu, and Neckar. The
advantages of this form of Government were next fully pourtrayed; the difficulties of establishing a republican government
with adequate *checks* were shewn, and its defects exposed. The
results of this wide survey were, that it was "impossible to secure
the Union by any modification of federal government"—that, "a
league offensive and defensive was full of certain evils, and
greater dangers;" and that the organization of "a General Government was very difficult, if not impracticable," and liable to
various "objections."—"What," he asked, "is to be done? Balance
inconveniences and dangers, and choose that which seems to have
the fewest objections." He then "read his plan of a Constitution,
as illustrative of his views, not as a project, but so prepared that
it might have gone into immediate effect if it had been adopted."*

Some of the objections to such a plan were then adverted to
and met—the apprehended increase of expense, by the fact,
that the expences "of the State Governments will be proportionably diminished"—that "the interference of officers would
not be so great, because the objects of the General Government
and the particular ones would not be the same"—that the
finances would be the care of the former—the administration of
private justice that of the States;—and that energy would not
be wanting in essential points because the administration of private justice will be carried home to men's doors by the partic-

* Hist. Rep. iii. 301. Statement by Madison, that this plan "was a full plan
as long as the present Constitution; and so prepared, that it might have
gone into immediate effect, if it had been adopted."

ular governments, and that the revenues might be collected from imposts, excises, &c., and, if necessary to go further, the general government may make use of the particular governments. The objection as to the non-attendance of members—a frequent and most serious embarrassment in Congress—is answered, by stating, that the Government must be so constituted as to offer strong motives to exercise its powers—in short, "to interest all the *passions* of individuals and to turn them into that channel."

Having stated, without reserves, his theoretical opinions of the different kinds of Government; Hamilton declared, "that the republican theory ought to be adhered to in this country, as long as there was any chance to its success—that the idea of a perfect equality of political rights among the citizens, exclusive of all permanent or hereditary distinctions, was of a nature to engage the good wishes of every good man, whatever might be his theoretic doubts; that it merited his best efforts to give success to it in practice;—that, hitherto, from an incompetent structure of the government, it had not had a fair trial; and that the endeavor ought then to be to secure to it a better chance of success, by a government more capable of energy and order."*

The plan of Government read by him commences with a preamble, brief, simple, comprehensive, fully expressive of its purpose. "The People of the United States of America, do *ordain* and *establish* this Constitution for the government of themselves and their posterity." It consists of *ten* articles, each divided into sections.

The *first* of these declared that the legislative power should be vested in an assembly and senate, subject to a negative; the executive power, with specified qualifications, in a president of the United States; and the supreme judicial authority, with certain exceptions, in a supreme court, to consist of not less than six, nor more than twelve, judges.

The assembly of representatives were (by the *second article*) to be chosen by the free male citizens and inhabitants of the several states in the union, all of whom, of the age of twenty one years and upwards, were to be entitled to an equal vote. The first assembly was to consist of one hundred members, which

* Hist. Rep. iii. 283.

were apportioned among the states—the most populous state, Virginia, having sixteen, and the least populous, Delaware, having two representatives. The whole number was never to be less than one hundred, nor more than a given number, which was not fixed, to be apportioned among the states by a decennial census of the whole number of free persons, except Indians not taxed, and three-fifths of all other *persons*: the term of service was to be determined by the legislature, but was not to exceed three years, and to commence and end the same day. It was to choose its own officers, to judge and decide on the qualifications and elections of its members, and to have the exclusive power of impeachment; but the concurrence of two-thirds was necessary to impeach a senator.

Revenue bills and appropriations for the support of fleets and armies, and for the salaries of the officers of government, were to originate in this body, but might be altered or amended by the senate. The acceptance of office under the United States, vacated a seat in it. Thus, in the constituency of this branch of the government, (all the citizens and inhabitants of the union,) the principle of UNIVERSAL SUFFRAGE was recognised, and the democratic interests were fully represented. Its power over the purse, the sword, and over impeachments, gave it the means to resist usurpation, and rendered it an efficient counterpoise to the more durable members of the government, and the natural guardian of the rights and liberties of the people.

The *third article* related to the second branch of the legislature. The senate were also representatives of the people, but under the modifications that the senators were to be chosen by electors elected in districts of the states for that purpose, and only by persons who had an estate in land for life, or for an unexpired term of not less than fourteen years. The first senate was to be apportioned among the states as the convention should decide. For the purpose of future elections, the states which had more than one senator, were to be divided by the act of the general legislature into convenient districts to which the senators were to be apportioned; a state having one senator, to be a district. In case of death, resignation, or the removal of a senator from office, his place was to be supplied by a new election in the district from which he came; and upon each election there were to be not less than six nor more than twelve electors chosen in a district. The senate was never to consist of less than forty members, nor was any state to have

a less number than that originally allotted to it; but the number might be increased in proportion to the whole number of
representatives in the ratio of forty to one hundred; the
increase to be apportioned among the states according to the
respective numbers of their representatives. The senators were
to hold during good behaviour, removable only by conviction on
impeachment for some crime or misdemeanor, and might vote
by proxy, but no senator present was to hold more than two
proxies. To the senate, thus representing the numbers and
property of the country, composing a not numerous body, and
removed from immediate popular influences and passions, were
confided the sole power of declaring war, and a control over
the patronage of the government, by requiring its consent to
executive appointments, which consent was also necessary to
the ratification of treaties.

By the *fourth article*, the president was to be elected by electors chosen by electors chosen by the people in election districts. The first electors of each state were to be equal in number to the whole number of senators and representatives of
such state in the national legislature. They were to be chosen
by its citizens having an estate of inheritance, or for three lives
in land, or a clear personal estate of the value of a thousand
Spanish dollars of the then standard. These *first* electors of
each state, meeting together, were to vote for a president by
ballot, not being one of their own number. Then they were to
nominate openly two persons as *second* electors; and out of the
nominees having the four highest numbers, were to choose by
ballot, by plurality of votes, two who were to be the second
electors of each state. These second electors, neither of whom
could be voted for as president, were to meet on an appointed
day, and in the presence of the chief-justice, or of a senior
judge of the supreme court of the United States, were to open
the lists of the persons voted for by the *first* electors. The person having a majority of the whole number, was to be president. If there was not a majority, then the *second* electors were
to vote for one of the three persons having the highest number of the votes of the first electors; and the person having a
number of votes equal to a majority of the whole number of
the second electors chosen, was to be the president. But if no
such second choice should be made, then the person having the
highest number of votes of the first electors, was to be president. By this complicated process, it was hoped to obtain a cor-

rected expression of the public wishes in the choice of the chief magistrate, who was still the representative of the people.

The president was to take on oath, "faithfully to execute his office, and to the utmost of his judgment and power to protect the rights of the people, and preserve the constitution inviolate." He was to hold his office during good behaviour, removable only by conviction upon impeachment of some crime or misdemeanor. He was to have power to convene and to prorogue the legislature; to have a negative on the acts and resolutions of the assembly and senate; to take care that the laws be faithfully executed; to be commander-in-chief of the army, navy, and militia; and to have the direction of war when commenced, but not to take the actual command in the field without the consent of the senate and assembly; to have the absolute appointment of the chief officers of the four great executive departments, and the nomination, and, with the advice of the senate, the appointment of all other officers, except such as were differently provided for by the constitution, reserving to the legislatures the power of appointing by name, in their laws, persons to execute special trusts, and leaving to ministerial officers the appointment of their deputies. He might fill vacancies temporarily in the recess of the senate, and could pardon all offences, except treason, which required the assent of the senate and assembly. He might be impeached by two-thirds of the legislature, two-thirds of each house concurring. If convicted, to be removed from office, and then tried and punished in the ordinary course of law. His impeachment was to operate as a suspension, until determined. His compensation was to be fixed, and not to be increased or diminished during his term of service. If he departed the United States, his office was abdicated.

The president of the senate was to be vice-president; to exercise all the powers of the president in case of his death, resignation, impeachment, removal from office, or absence from the United States, until another was chosen.

The chief-justice, and other judges of the supreme court, were (by the fifth article) to hold during good behaviour, removable by impeachment and conviction. They were to have original jurisdiction in all causes in which the United States shall be a party; in all controversies between the United States and a particular state, or between two or more states, except questions of territory; in all cases affecting foreign ministers, consuls, and agents: and an appellate jurisdiction, both as to law and fact, in

5

all cases concerning the citizens of foreign nations; in all questions between the citizens of different states, and in all others in which the fundamental rights of the constitution were involved, subject to specified exceptions, and to the regulations of the legislature. The judges of all courts which might be constituted by the legislature, were also to hold during good behaviour, removable by impeachment, and were to have competent salaries, to be paid at stated times, and not to be diminished during their continuance in office; but the legislatures might abolish the courts themselves.

All crimes, except on impeachment, were to be tried by a jury of twelve men, in the state where committed; and all civil causes arising under the constitution, before triable by jury in the states, were also to be tried by jury, unless two-thirds of the national legislature should, in special cases, concur in a different provision.

When offices were of such duration as good behaviour, it was felt to be highly important to provide an efficacious and independent tribunal of impeachment; and as not only the rights of the nation, but of the states, were to be guarded, to have reference in its constitution to the general and particular governments.

With this view, a court of impeachment was to be instituted, by which the president, vice-president, the senators, governors, and presidents of the states, the principal officers of the great executive departments, ambassadors and other like public ministers, judges of the supreme court, generals and admirals of the navy, were to be tried. This court was to consist of the judges of the supreme court, and of the chief-justice, or first or senior judge, of the supreme court of law of each state, of whom twelve were to compose a court, and a majority might convict. All other persons, when impeached, were to be tried by a court to consist of the judges of the supreme court and six senators, drawn by lot, a majority of whom might convict. Provisions were made for conducting these impeachments. Such was to have been the permanent structure of this government.

The danger of collisions between the states, arising out of conflicting claims of territory, had been presented to Hamilton, in the progress of the controversy between New-York and Vermont. Other claims were unsettled. He proposed (*in a sixth article*) that a court should be formed, when territorial controversies should arise, of persons to be nominated by the controverting states, not their own citizens, double the number of the judges of the supreme court, one-half of whom, elected by the senate, should, with the judges of that court, decide the appeal.

In the resolutions prepared by Hamilton in seventeen hundred and eighty-three, it is seen that the leading defect of the confederation proposed to be corrected by him was, its "confining the federal government within too narrow limits; withholding from it that *efficacious authority* and influence in all matters of general concern, which are indispensable to the harmony and welfare of the whole; embarrassing general provisions by unnecessary details and inconvenient exceptions, incompatible with their nature, tending only to create jealousies and disputes respecting the proper bounds of the authority of the United States, and that of the particular states, and a mutual interference of the one with the other."

It was a settled maxim in his mind, "that a *government* ought to *contain within itself* every power requisite to the full accomplishment of the objects committed to its care, and to the complete execution of the trusts for which it is responsible; free from every other control but a regard for the public good, and to the sense of the people."

Another maxim was, "that every power ought to be commensurate with its object; that there ought to be no limitation of a power destined to affect a purpose which is of itself incapable of limitation." Applying these enlarged and obvious principles, and having sought to guard, in the structure of the government, against an abuse of its powers, he declared, in the *seventh article* of this constitution, that "the legislature of the United States shall have power to pass all laws which they shall judge necessary to the common defence and general welfare of the union."

As a check upon this power, every act, bill, or resolution, was to have the assent of the president, which, if not given within ten days after such act being presented to him, was to become a law, of which the enacting style was to be, that it was "enacted by the people of the United States of America;" thus recognising in every exercise of legislative power the sovereignty and unity of the American people. This general power was followed by the declaration of a few general restrictions in the nature of a bill of rights, either suggested by the experience of this country, or having reference to the nature of the government.

The danger of legislative tyranny, and of retrospective laws, not only to the domestic peace, but to the foreign relations of the country, had been too immediately before him not to have commanded his attention. To provide an efficient check to such pernicious proceedings, he framed a clause declaring "that no bill of attainder or ex post facto law shall be passed;" and adopting the language of the articles of the confederation, and thus adding guards to the republican system, he provided that no title of nobility should be granted by the United States, or either of them, and that no person holding any office or trust under the United States should, without permission of the *legislature*, accept any present, emolument, office, or title, from a foreign prince or state. "The prohibition of titles of nobility," he said, "may truly be denominated the corner-stone of republican government; for, so long as titles of nobility are excluded, there can never be serious danger that the government will be any other than that of the people."

To preclude the recurrence of such an attempt as he had recently defeated in the assembly of New-York, and carrying out the principle which is seen in his system of public instruction, he embodied in the constitution the proviso, so important to the interests of religion, to freedom of opinion, and to the peace of society, "nor shall any religious sect, or denomination, or religious test for any office or place, be ever established by law."

In forming a government founded upon a full recognition of the sovereignty of the people, it is seen that he had apportioned the representation to the number of free persons, except Indians not taxed, and three fifths of all other persons; thus following this great principle to its appropriate result. So in apportioning the direct contributions of the states to the public treasury, there being no common measure of a nation's wealth, he took the same basis, which, in the peculiar condition of this country, promised a nearer approach to equality than any other. "Taxes on lands, houses, and other real estate, and capitation taxes, were to be proportioned in each state to the whole number of free persons, except Indians not taxed, and three-fifths of all other persons."

As the command over the purse of the nation was intended by him to be a real check upon the action of the government, and with this view the originating revenue bills had been given to the popular branch, he provided "that the two houses might by joint ballot appoint a treasurer of the United States," thus securing the custody of the revenues of the nation to the department it had intrusted with raising and appropriating them.

A government performing its great office of providing for the common defence and safety, and for the general welfare, by its own comprehensive organs, acting upon individuals, the only proper objects of government, would perhaps have possessed a sufficiently central power to have maintained its due ascendency. But as the state governments were to continue, in order to prevent a collision, it was declared that the laws of the United States, and treaties made under the articles of the confederation, and to be made under the constitution, were to be the supreme law of the land, and to be so construed by the several courts of the several states. The legislature was to convene once in each year, which, unless otherwise provided for by law, should be on the first Monday in December; to receive a reasonable compensation fixed by law, no succeeding assembly to increase its own compensation.

The preceding injunction, that the laws and treaties of the United States "shall be the supreme law of the land," obligatory on all the courts, guarded against conflicts with the legislation of the states, and in theory secured the necessary supremacy to the judiciary power of the general government; but that power might be rendered nugatory by a defective execution of those laws. The position of New York at that moment indicated the danger to be apprehended from the executive trust of the states being independent of the government of the union.

To provide against both these evils, he declared (*in the eighth article*) that the governor or president of each state shall be appointed by the authority of the United States, shall have a negative on all laws about to be passed in the state of which he shall be governor or president, subject to such regulations as the legislature of the United States shall prescribe, but in all other respects, except as to the appointment of the officers of the militia, to have the same powers the constitution of the states then did or should allow. Each governor or president of a state was to hold his office until a successor was actually appointed, which could not be during the recess of the senate, "unless he died, resigned, or was removed on impeachment."

The officers of the militia might be appointed under the authority of the United States, unless its legislature authorized their appointment by the governors or presidents of the states; and, to avoid any obstruction from that source, the governors and presidents of the states at the time of the ratification of the constitution, were to continue in office in the same manner, and with the same powers, as if they had been appointed by the president and senate of the United States.

"If it be possible," Hamilton observed, "to construct a federal government capable of regulating the common concerns, and preserving the general tranquillity, it must carry its agency to the persons of its citizens. It must stand in need of no intermediate legislations, but must itself be empowered to employ the arm of the ordinary magistrate to execute its own resolutions. The majesty of the national authority must be manifested through the medium of the courts of justice. The government of the union, like that of each state, must be able to address itself immediately to the hopes and fears of individuals, and to attract to its support those passions which have the strongest influence upon the human heart. It must, in short, possess all the means, and have a right to resort to all the methods, of executing the powers with which it is intrusted, that are possessed and exercised by the governments of particular states."

Under this important provision as to the appointments of these governors and presidents, the administration of the general government, pervading the states, would have executed itself, while their legislatures would have retained the control of that part of internal police which relates "to the rights of property and life among individuals, the administration of justice, the supervision of agriculture, and of such things as are proper for local legislation." The advantages would thus have been attained of the reproductiveness of the civil power, and of its diffusive force throughout the whole extent of the republic, and the state legislatures would have acted as sentinels to warn against the first approach of usurpation.

The *ninth* article provided that the president must then be "a citizen of one of the states, or hereafter be born a citizen of the United States;" that senators and representatives must be citizens and inhabitants of the state in which they were chosen.

Prompted by the recent proceeding in New-York, he also provided that no person eligible as president, or to the legislature, shall be disqualified but by the conviction of some offence for which the law shall have *previously* ordained the punishment of disqualification; but that the legislature might provide by law that persons holding offices under the United States, or either of them, shall not be eligible to the assembly, and "shall be, during their continuance in office, suspended from sitting in the senate." The citizens of each state were to be entitled to all the immunities of citizens of other states, and full faith and credit was to be given to the public acts, records, and judicial proceedings of each; fugitives from justice were to be delivered up;—provisions taken from the articles of confederation. No new state was to be formed without the concurrent consent of the United States, and of the states concerned; but new states might be admitted by the general legislature into the union. The United States were "declared bound to guarantee a republican form of government to each state, and to protect it as well against domestic violence as against foreign invasion;" a provision drawn from the propositions of Randolph, but essentially enlarged—supplying, as Hamilton observed, "a capital imperfection" in the articles of the confederation.

All treaties, contracts, and engagements under those articles, were to have equal validity under the constitution; no state could enter into a treaty or alliance with another, or with a foreign power, without the consent of the United States. The members of the legislature of the United States and of each state, and all officers, executive and judicial, were to take an oath or affirmation to support the constitution of the United States.

Though a change of government would not have dissolved existing treaties not inconsistent with its principles, yet Hamilton's knowledge of the distinctions of international law would teach him the importance of a full and explicit declaration on this important subject, as a guard of the interests and of the faith of the nation. In the absolute prohibition of treaties by the states with foreign powers, the restrictive clause of the confederation was extended, and the requisition of an oath to support the constitution was a useful additional bond. Amendments to it were to be proposed by two-thirds of both houses, to be ratified by the legislatures or conventions in two-thirds of the states.

Finally, to secure the immediate operation of the new system, and to give it the solemn sanction of the people, it was provided (*in the tenth article*) that the constitution should be submitted to conventions of the People of each state, by their deputies, chosen under the direction of their respective legislatures; that each convention ratifying the constitution should appoint the first representatives and senators from such state, the representatives so appointed to continue in office only one year.

When the constitution shall have been duly ratified, congress were to give notice of a day and place of meeting of the senators and representatives from the several states; a majority of whom, when assembled, it was provided, shall, by plurality of voices in joint ballot, elect a president of the United States, "and the constitution, thus organized, shall be carried into effect."

From this abstract it will be seen, though Hamilton would have made use of the state governments for certain purposes, thus completely refuting the allegation that he contemplated their abrogation, yet it was his desire to have established a simple government pervading the whole union and uniting its inhabitants as *one people.* As it was necessary that "each department should have a will of its own," this government was so constituted that the members of each had no agency in the appointment of the others, and, with the exception of the judiciary, each was "drawn from the same fountain of authority, the people, and through channels having no communication whatever with one another." "In the constitution of the judiciary in particular," Hamilton remarked, "it might be inexpedient to insist rigorously on the principle; because peculiar qualifications being essential in the members, the primary consideration ought to be to select that mode of choice which best secures these qualifications, and because the permanent tenure by which the appointments are held in that department must soon destroy all sense of dependence on the authority conferring them."

"It is equally evident," he observed, "that the members of each department should be as little dependent as possible on those of the others, for the emoluments annexed to their offices:" hence is seen the provision that the compensation of the executive and the judiciary should be fixed by law; that of the judges not to be diminished during their term, and to guard against executive influence, that of the president to be neither increased nor diminished. "In framing a government which is to be administered by men over men, the great difficulty," he said, "lies in this—you must first enable the government to control the governed, and, in the next place, oblige it to control itself. A dependence on the people is, no doubt, a primary control on the government; but experience has taught mankind the necessity of auxiliary precautions." Of these, the chief was "in the distribution of the supreme powers of the state." "But it is not possible," he observed, "to give to each department an equal power of self-defence. In republican governments, the legislative authority necessarily predominates. The remedy for this inconvenience is, to divide the legislature into different branches; and to render them by different modes of election, and different principles of action, as little connected with each other as the nature of their common functions and their common dependence on the society will admit." With these views, in the structure of this government, while by the frequent choice of the popular branch elected by universal suffrage, the democratic influence was to be constantly renewed and invigorated, in the duration of the senate and executive chosen by constituents with property qualifications, he hoped to secure efficient and enduring checks on the impetuosity and instability of the many. The power of the people was to be kept up by a constitutional augmentation of the number of these representatives; and thus the barrier against executive usurpation, if attempted, was steadily strengthened; and "as the weakness of the executive," he remarked, "may require that it should be fortified," he gave him an "absolute negative on the legislature, as the natural defence with which the executive magistrate should be armed."

Having provided these precautions, by the deposit of the national trusts with representatives of different interests freely chosen by the people, and holding by a responsible and defeasible tenure, governed by the great maxims previously stated, he empowered the legislature "to pass all laws necessary to the common defence and safety, and to the general welfare of the union."

The speech of Hamilton accompanying the presentation of this plan, was soon followed by a decisive procedure. This was a resolution, which passed the next day, by the votes of seven States, rejecting the Jersey plan, and for the reconsideration of the amended resolutions from Virginia.

After the interval of one day,* Dr. Johnson of Connecticut

* June 21. Secret Debates, p. 147.

was the first to take the floor; and in the course of his remarks made a suggestion, which being subsequently adopted, gave a leading character to the Constitution.

"It appears to me," he observed, "that the JERSEY plan has for its principal object, the preservation of the State Governments. So far it is a departure from the plan of Virginia, which although it concentres in a distinct national government, it is not totally independent of that of the States. A gentleman from New York, with boldness, and decision, proposed a system totally different from both; and though he has been praised by every body, he has been supported by none. How can the State governments be secured on the Virginia plan? I could have wished that the supporters of the Jersey system could have satisfied themselves with the principles of the Virginia plan; and that the individuality of the States could be supported. It is agreed on all hands, that a portion of government is to be left to the States. How can this be done? It *can be done by joining the States in their legislative capacity with the right of appointing the second branch of the legislature to represent the States individually.*"

The discussions which followed this important suggestion, naturally related to the principle of representation. The Convention having decided, that the first branch of the national legislature should be chosen by the people, whence the Senate was to be derived was the great question? The advocates of a purely National government again urged its election, directly, or indirectly through the medium of electors by the *people*; those of a Federal government by the legislatures of the States. In support of the first system, Madison and Hamilton were conspicuous. The former urged the necessity of protecting the landed interest. "Landholders," he remarked, "ought to have a share in the government to support these valuable interests, and to balance and check the other. They ought to be so constituted, as to protect the majority of the opulent against the minority. The Senate ought to be this body; and to answer the purpose ought to have permanency and stability. Various have been the propositions; but my opinion is *the longer they continue in office* the better will" this "view be answered."* Roger Sherman replied, that, "a bad Government was the worse for being long, that frequent elections give security and permanency." Hamilton answered—"This question has already been considered in several points of view. We are now forming a *republican* govern-

* Secret Debates, p. 169.

ment. Real liberty is neither found in despotism, nor in the extremes of democracy, but in moderate governments. Those who mean *to form a solid republican government* ought to proceed to the confines of another government. As long as offices are open to all men; and no constitutional rank is established, it is pure republicanism. *But if we incline too much to democracy we shall soon shoot into a monarchy.* The difference of property is already great among us. Commerce and Industry will still increase the disparity. Your Government must meet this state of things; or combinations, in process of time, will undermine your system."*

At the close of this debate, the question was more broadly discussed, of the representation of the people, or of the States, resulting in an equal division of the votes by States—five to five—except the State of Maryland, whose vote was divided.†

It was now obvious, that some accommodation must be made, or that the Convention must break up. To meet the emergency, a committee of compromise, consisting of one member from each State, was appointed; whose report declared, that the first branch of the legislature should represent the people, and that, in the second "each State shall have an equal vote," which passed in the affirmative. The decisive manifestations that followed, of a purpose to depart from a purely federal to a compound government, determined the course of Hamilton's colleagues from New York. They *both* abandoned the Convention.‡ The advocates of a national Government had reluctantly yielded, in part. The friends of a Federal system sought to secure to it other advantages. Amid great alarms, successive propositions were discussed, until late in July, when a committee of detail was appointed who reported the outline of a Constitution on the sixth of August. This outline was discussed, not in Committee, but in the house, until the eighth of September; when many of its articles having been approved, it was referred to a Committee appointed by ballot, to *"revise its style and to arrange its articles."* Of this Committee Hamilton was second to Johnson of Connecticut,§ who, it is seen, at a moment of great discordance, first proposed the great compromise of a representation of the people in one branch of the legislature and of the States in the other. This distinguished man

---

* Secret Debates, p. 170.   † July 2, 1787. Journal of the Convention.
‡ July 10, 1787.
§ The other members were James Madison, Gouverneur Morris, Rufus King.

remarked, "If the Constitution did not succeed on trial, Hamilton was less responsible for the result than any other member, for he fully and frankly pointed out to the Convention what he apprehended were the infirmities to which it was liable. And, if it answered the fond expectations of the public, the community would be more indebted to Hamilton than to any other member; for, after its essential outlines were agreed to, he labored most indefatigably to heal those infirmities; and to guard against the evils to which they might expose it."* Owing to the mutilation of the Journal of the Convention at late stages of its proceedings, it is not possible to state some of the important modifications which, it is ascertained from other sources, were proposed. Two very important changes, however, demand notice. The twenty-second article of the plan reported by "the Committee of Detail," on the sixth of August, declared, that the Constitution "shall be laid before the United States in Congress assembled, *for their approbation*; and it is the opinion of this Convention, that it should be afterwards submitted to a Convention chosen in each State, under the recommendation of its legislature, in order to receive the ratification of such Convention." This article, had it been adopted, would probably have proved fatal; for from the temper the Congress had shown, its "approbation" was not to have been expected. Hamilton's plan of a Constitution anticipated this dangerous contingency. It provided, in its tenth article, that "the Constitution *shall* be submitted to the consideration of Conventions in the several States, the members whereof *shall* be chosen by *the people* of such States respectively, under the direction of their respective legislatures," the ratification of each convention being final, with power to each convention, to appoint the first representatives and senators from such State; who, when the Constitution was duly ratified, "shall by joint ballot, by plurality of votes, elect a President of the United States; and the Constitution thus organized shall be carried into effect." By this provision, the establishment of the Constitution would have been ensured. Its ratification, by the Conventions of several of the

---

* The distinguished person Guizot remarks,—"Hamilton must be classed among the men who have best known the vital principles and fundamental conditions of a government; not of a government such as this, but of a government worthy of its mission and of its name. There is not in the Constitution of the United States an element of order, of force, of duration, which he has not *powerfully contributed to introduce into it* and *to cause* to predominate.

States, was certain; and a Government incipiently organized by them would inevitably have drawn to it the concurrence of the other States, instead of leaving its fate to the very dubious contingencies which existed. But, what would be the practical operation of so new a system, what the state of public opinion in respect to it might permanently be, or what new circumstances might arise to indicate the necessity of a change, were open questions. The nineteenth article of the plan reported by the Committee looked wholly to the action of the States in the provision for these possibilities, and placed a change in the system entirely in their power. It declared, that, "on the application of the legislatures of two thirds of the States in the Union, for an amendment of this Constitution, the legislature of the United States shall call a convention for that purpose." Hamilton, in consistency with all his views, regarded the national legislature—representing the whole people of the United States in one body politic—as the safest judges, whether any and what alterations should be made in the national charter. Under this conviction, and with this intent, his plan confided the proposal of alterations and amendments solely to that body, two thirds concurring,—such alterations or amendments to be ratified by the legislatures of, or by conventions chosen by the people in two thirds of the States composing the Union. The Constitution as adopted, confided the power of proposing amendments to two thirds of Congress, *or* to a Convention applied for by two thirds of the States, which when ratified by the legislatures of, or by conventions in three fourths of the States were to be valid as part of the Constitution. Thus the initiation of changes in the system was confided either to the national legislature, or to the States, while the facility of a change was diminished by requiring the final ratification of a larger number of the States. How far this substitute was wise may be deemed problematical. The Report of the Committee of revision was made on the twelfth of September, which having been corrected still further in style; amended, and engrossed, was on the seventeenth of September, signed by Washington—"President and Deputy from Virginia;" and attested by the Secretary, which attestations were followed by the signatures of all the members present, with three exceptions.* The single name of

* The exceptions were Gerry of Massachusetts—Mason and Randolph of Virginia. The importance of the services of Madison and of Marshall in the convention of their State which adopted the Constitution and the great influence of Washington's approval may be the more estimated by the fact that

"Alexander Hamilton," as representing New York, speaks his position in this body.* This plan of a Constitution was submitted to the President of Congress, in a letter, which stated it to be, "the result of a spirit of amity and of that mutual deference and concession which the peculiarity of our political situation rendered indispensable. That it will meet the full and entire approbation of every State is not perhaps to be expected; but each will doubtless consider, that had her interests alone been considered, the consequences might have been particularly disagreeable or injurious to others:—that it is liable to as few exceptions as could reasonably have been expected, we hope and believe; that it may promote the lasting welfare of that country so dear to us all, and secure her freedom and happiness, is our most ardent wish."

Uniting heartily and sincerely as Washington did in recommending the adoption of the Constitution; it is evident, that he accepted it with reserves. He had previously stated, "Persuaded I am, that the primary cause of all our disorders lies in the different State Governments, and in the tenacity of that power which pervades their whole system."—But, after the Constitution had been submitted to the people, he wrote, "there are some things in the new form, I will readily acknowledge, which never did, and I am persuaded never will, obtain my cordial approbation; but I do now most firmly believe, that, in the aggregate, it is the best Constitution that can be obtained at this epoch; and, that this, or a dissolution of the Union, awaits our choice; and is the only alternative before us."† Jay, was also the advocate of a strong government: "Might we not have," he wrote, to Washington, "a governor-general limited in his pre-

in that State evidence exists that the adoption of the Constitution was regarded as a measure of temporary expedience. April 5, 1790. R. B. Lee, the grandfather of the commander in chief of the present rebel army wrote a letter recently found in the dwelling of General Stuart—also of Virginia. "The Southern States are *too weak* at *present* to *stand by themselves*; and a General Government will certainly be advantageous to us, as it produces no other effect than protection from hostilities and uniform commercial regulations. And when we shall attain our natural degree of population, I *flatter myself that we shall have the power to do ourselves justice*, with *dissolving the bond which binds us together*. It is better to put up with these little inconveniences than to run the hazard of greater calamities."

* The signatures of the members were set opposite their respective States; The name of each of the States is in the *handwriting* of Hamilton.

† Washington's Writings, ix. 297.

rogatives and duration? Might not Congress be divided into an upper and lower house—the former appointed for life, the latter annually; and let the governor-general, (to preserve the balance), with the advice of a Council, formed for that *only* purpose, of the great judicial officers, have a negative on their acts?*** What powers should be granted to the government so constituted is a question which deserves much thought. I think *the more the better*, the States retaining only so much as may be necessary for domestic purposes; and all their principal officers, civil and military, being commissioned, and removable by the national government."

"I am not sure," he wrote to Washington as soon as the plan of the Constitution reached him, "I am not sure, that the new government will be found to rest on principles sufficiently stable to produce a uniform adherence to what justice, dignity, and liberal policy may require."—But, while the Constitution was before the People, admitting its imperfections, he addressed them, urging its adoption.—"Is it probable," he asked, "a better plan can be obtained? If attainable, is it likely to be in season? What would be your situation, if, after rejecting this, all the efforts to obtain a better should prove fruitless?" Madison avowed, "I hold it for a *fundamental* point, that an *individual* independence of the States is utterly irreconcilable with an aggregate sovereignty. I think at the same time, that a consolidation of the States into a single republic is not less unattainable, than it would be inexpedient. Let it be tried, whether any middle ground cannot be taken which will support a due supremacy of the national authority, and leave in force the local authorities, so far as they can be subordinately useful." With this view, he proposed, that the general government should "have a negative *in all cases whatsoever* on the legislative acts of the States as the King of Great Britain had. This I conceive to be essential, and the least positive abridgment of the State sovereignties." "The right of *coercion* should be expressly declared." It is not surprising, therefore, that he voted in the Convention, for a President to hold office during good behaviour.* General Washington, and Madison, Hamilton stated, "entirely concurred in his views regarding the plan which he submitted to the Convention, as not exceeding in stability and strength what the exigencies of the country required." He

* Journal of Convention, p. 185.

added, "that his final opinion was against an Executive during good behaviour on account of the increased danger to the public tranquillity incident to the election of a magistrate of this degree of permanency."* Though entertaining doubts similar to, but probably stronger than those, of these other distinguished men; Hamilton remarked, "the truth is, the plan in all its parts, was a plan of accommodation;" and he declared,—"I am persuaded, it is the best which our political situation, habits and opinions will admit, and superior to any the revolution has produced. Though it may not be perfect in every part, it is, upon the whole, a good one; is the best the present situation and circumstances of the country will permit." Still the ominous future was before him, and he recorded in private, his hopes, his fears, and his expectation. "If the government be adopted," this solemn minute states, "it is probable, General Washington will be President of the United States. This will ensure a wise choice of men to administer the government, and a good administration. A good administration will conciliate the confidence, and affection of the people; and, *perhaps*, enable the Government to acquire *more consistency* than the proposed Constitution seems to promise for so great a country. It may then triumph altogether over the State governments; and reduce them to an entire subordination, dividing the larger States into smaller districts. The *organs* of the general government may also acquire additional *strength*. If this should not be the case, in the course of a few years, it is probable that the contests about the boundaries of power between the particular governments and the general Government; and the *momentum* of the larger States in such contests will produce a dissolution of the Union. This, after all, seems to be the most likely result. But, it is almost arrogance in so complicated a subject, depending so entirely on the incalculable fluctuations of the human passions, to attempt even a conjecture about the event."

Were these doubts of these eminent persons without foundation? Let the history of this young country give the answer. Ere the first decade of the existence of the present Constitution had expired, the doctrine of NULLIFICATION was avowed and approved by the legislatures of two of the planting States—that a State had a right to decide as to the measure of its obedience to "the supreme law of the land;" and at its will to annul that

---

* Hist. Rep. iii. 345—*note*.

law. This incipient Rebellion was avoided by the elevation of the party, originally hostile to the Constitution, to the supreme power of this nation, and by the election to the Presidency of the person who was—the author, the advocate, the abettor of this treasonable doctrine. Ere the second decade of its existence had elapsed, another incipient Rebellion was prevented, within six months after he had established the liberty of the Press, by the self sacrifice of Hamilton's life in behalf of the Union. "If they break this Union," were among his latest words, "they will break my heart." This rebellion was menaced by two of the Commercial States. Ere a third decade had elapsed, another Rebellion, also by Commercial States denying to the national government the command of their militia, was avoided by the timely conclusion of a peace, terminating a war begun in the interests of a foreign despot—a peace the result of an event over which this, country had no control—the dethronement of that despot. After an interval of murmuring discontents—of nullification become an act—of menaced hostilities; in the fifth decade of the Constitution, another incipient Rebellion was prevented by the firmness of a successful soldier wielding by his popularity a power dangerously strong—denouncing NULLIFICATION, and proclaiming and maintaining the supreme power of the national government. The seventh decade had only closed, when, aided by the imbecility of the Chief Magistrate of the Union, denying to it the right of coercion—of self defence; and rejecting the wise monitions of a great patriotic soldier, while a conspiracy was being plotted under his eyes in the Senate house, the existing Rebellion began, unparalleled in might and in extent. A million of lives well sacrificed and millions of treasure expended tell the sublime patriotism of the loyal American people—assuring their triumph.

But when suppressed will this Rebellion leave no unremoved evil? Do the results of other Rebellions teach no lessons and promise no compensations? Is the history of our progenitors an empty page? The insurrections against William the Conqueror resulted in the establishment in England of the feudal system and of the master power of the great military barons. After two centuries of the vassalage of her people another Rebellion took place, when these barons rose in arms; and in the presence of hostile encampments at Runnemede, extorted from the King the great deed of MAGNA CHARTA, granting or securing most "important liberties and privileges to every order of men

6

in the kingdom—to the clergy, to the barons, and to the people."*

Before half a century had elapsed, another Rebellion resulted in the establishment of the House of Commons, one of the most useful and, in process of time, one of the most powerful members of the National Constitution.† Centuries of discord ensued, until the great Rebellion terminated in a Convention which settled the crown on a new dynasty,‡ annexing "a declaration of rights," which circumscribed and defined the powers of the royal prerogative, and established over the British people a limited government; the ecclesiastical independence of England having been in the mean time secured, the Protestant religion established, and every British subject clothed with an absolute security against arbitrary imprisonment by the act of *Habeas Corpus*.

Another and the last important Rebellion gave birth to us as a nation of freemen.

All these rebellions were waged by subjects in their own cause of liberty. The existing Rebellion is waged by rebel States in the cause of Slavery!—alone in the history of man— a rebellion against a righteous unoffending Government to secure and perpetuate the lash and the fetters of human bondage. And here again will be seen ere long the compensating result—the universal emancipation of an unfortunate race continued in chains by the heathen barbarism that made captives in war the property of the captors. But in the full broad aspect of our Constitutional System, with the great good thus gained is there not to be seen a great remaining evil? All the incipient rebellions and the existing Rebellion have been within three quarters of a century of this nation's life. Such a life, so soon, so often, so much imperilled, ought no longer to be at hazard. All these menaced and this existing Rebellion are seen to have been begun by an array of STATE governments against a General Government dependent, by its very structure, upon the acts of States, of minor bodies politic too weak to protect themselves and entitled to its guarantee, too strong to be effectually controlled and to render that guarantee a thing of value. As the Federal Constitution now is, "a republican form of government" cannot be permanently secured to the people as a nation, nor to any part of the people as States. Where is the

---

* Hume's History of England, i. 106.   † Ibid. i. 265.   ‡ Ibid. ii. 648.

remedy? It is found in the precedent of Hamilton's plan of a Constitution, providing that the President and the Senate of the United States be indirectly, and the Representatives be directly chosen by the people, divided into districts by Congress from time to time according to their numbers—by rendering the NATIONAL GOVERNMENT self existent and self sustaining as are the governments of the several States. An eventual "dissolution of the Union" Hamilton apprehended as the probable result of the imperfect structure of our system. If prevented, it will be either by the usurping power of the sword, or by the consenting reason of the whole American people, restored to all the rights and powers and sovereignty which their own Declaration of Independence asserted to them. Let those who read the comments on the present Constitution by Hamilton's hand, when commending it to the favour of the public, perceive how strong though veiled were his apprehensions, apprehensions in which Jay and Washington concurred. "The men," he earnestly wrote to Hamilton, then temporarily absent from the Convention— "The men who oppose a *strong* and *energetic* government are, in my opinion, narrow minded politicians, or are under the influence of *local* views. I am sorry you went away. I wish you were back."

The Constitution is a reform of the Confederation. In the words* of the friend of Cromwell, the immortal penman,— "Reform the Reformation."—Establish the Constitution on its proper basis—not as a Federal, but as a National Government— and this done—"Go on hand in hand, O nation, never to be disunited, be the praise and heroic song of all posterity; merit this, but seek only virtue, not to extend your limits, but to settle the pure worship of God in his Church and justice in the State: then shall the hardest difficulties smooth out themselves before ye; envy shall sink to hell, craft and malice be confounded, whether it be HOMEBRED MISCHIEF or OUTLANDISH CUNNING; yea, other nations will then covet to serve ye, for lordship and victory are but the pages of justice and virtue. Commit securely to true wisdom the vanquishing and uncasing of craft and subtlety, which are but her two runagates; join your invincible might to do worthy and godlike deeds; and then he that seeks to break YOUR UNION, a cleaving curse be his inheritance to all generations."

* Of Reformation in England. The Prose Works of John Milton, i. 26.

PART SECOND.

THE great question now was, would this plan of government be adopted by the people. After stating the influences "in favor of its success, and against its success;" Hamilton observed—"It is difficult to form any judgment whether the plan will be adopted or rejected. It must be essentially matter of conjecture. The present appearances and all other circumstances considered, the probability seems to be on the side of its adoption. But the causes operating against its adoption are powerful, and there will be nothing astonishing in the contrary." To secure its adoption was not the chief care of the able men, who, surrendering their doubts and preferences, had united in framing it. No where, except in Rhode Island, were the obstacles so great, or was the opposition so stubborn as in the State of New York. The abandonment of the Convention by Yates and Lansing, was in itself an act certain to alarm the great body of its people. This alarm would be the greater, because of the grounds on which they publicly declared they had retired;— the refusal of their "assent to measures," they conceived "destructive to the political happiness of the citizens of the United States;" their "conviction of the impracticability of establishing a general government pervading every part of the United States and extending essential benefits to all;" and the duty, under their instructions, to preserve "the individual States, in their uncontrolled constitutional rights." Its "government," Hamilton wrote, had already discovered strong marks of disapprobation; and its adherents "were constantly employed in disseminating opinions unfavorable to its reception." Ere long these opinions were promulgated in several series of hostile essays.*

---

* Washington wrote—Nov. 30, 1787—"I have hardly seen one" publication, "that is not addressed to the passions of the people, and obviously calculated to alarm their fears."—*Writings of Washington*, ix. 283.

Private influences were not easy to be met, but an appeal to the public reason Hamilton welcomed. It was through the Press he had acquired his earliest title to distinction,* as by its after defence he secured to it for ever, its proper liberty.† Indeed, he has been seen in his first suggestions of a new system of government to have contemplated such an appeal. "If a convention is called," he wrote to Duane in seventeen hundred and eighty, "the minds of all the States, and the people, ought to be prepared to receive its determinations by sensible and popular writings." This expedient he had resorted to in the numbers of "The Continentalist;" and he now resolved to write a Vindication of the Constitution. This purpose gave birth to the Essays—entitled "The Federalist"—over the signature of "Publius," which Hamilton had used in 'seventy eight, exposing the grave misconduct of a member of Congress. To give to the country the united benefit of the talent and influence of two persons, both of whom at that time concurred in his opinions, he proposed to Jay, then Secretary of Foreign Affairs, and to Madison, to take part with him; and also to William Duer; recently a useful member of the New York legislature.‡ The efforts of Madison in the general Convention had shewn his ability; and Jay, though excluded therefrom by the antagonists of a truly National government, enjoyed a wide and well founded confidence.§ The first number of this Work was written by Hamilton in the cabin of a sloop, as he was descending

---

* Hamilton's Works, i. 1–140.   † Hist. Rep. vii. 736.

‡ "The undertaking," Madison states, "was proposed by Alexander Hamilton to James Madison with a request to join him and Mr. Jay in carrying it into effect. William Duer was also included in the original plan; and wrote two or more papers, which, though intelligent and sprightly, were not continued, nor did they make a part of the printed collection."—*Unpublished paper, in the State Department, by Madison, entitled "The Federalist."*

§ When Hamilton proposed to add two delegates to the number chosen to represent New York in the Convention, he observed, "I think it proper to apprise the house of the gentlemen on some of whom I wish their choice to fall, and with a view to which I bring forward the present motion. Their abilities and experience in the general affairs of the country cannot but be useful on such an occasion. I mean Mr. Chancellor Livingston, Mr. Duane, Mr. Benson, and Mr. Jay; the particular situation of the latter, may require an observation. His being a servant of Congress might seem an objection to the appointment; but surely this objection, if it had any weight, would apply with equal force to a member of that body. In the case of Mr. Lansing, the two houses appear to have thought there was no force in it, and I am persuaded there can be no reason to apply a different rule to Mr. Jay. His knowledge, abilities, tried integrity and abundant experience in the affairs of the country, foreign and

the Hudson. On the nineteenth of October, he transmitted it to
Washington. "The Constitution proposed," he wrote, "has in this
State warm friends and warm enemies. The first impressions
every where are in its favor, but the artillery of its opponents
makes some impression. The event cannot yet be foreseen. The
inclosed is the first number of a series of papers to be written in
its defence."

This number was published in the "Independent Journal,"
issued in the city of New York, on the twenty seventh of October, 1787, and was announced as "The Federalist, addressed to
the People of the State of New York." After the publication of
the seventh number, it was advertised, "in order, that the whole
subject of the papers may be, as soon as possible, laid before the
public, it is proposed to publish them four times a week."* And
it will be remarked in their dates, that, with the exception of the
interval between the fourth of April† and the seventeenth of
June, during which period, in part owing to the pendency of the
election of the delegates to the State Convention of New York,
and in part of Hamilton's professional engagements, the publication by numbers was suspended, these Essays usually appeared
at an interval of three days, two numbers being generally published at a time. Originally intended to be comprised within
twenty or at most twenty five‡ numbers, they were extended to
a series of eighty five Essays.

domestic, will not permit us to allow any weight to any objection which would
imply a want of confidence in a character that has every title to the fullest confidence."—*Hist. Rep.* iii. 242.

* Madison states, "the haste with which many of the papers were penned in
order to get through the subject whilst the Constitution was before the public,
and to comply with the arrangement, by which the printer was to keep his
paper open for four numbers every week, was such, that the performance must
have borne a very different aspect without the aid of historical and other notes
which had been used in the Convention, and without the familiarity with the
whole subject produced by the discussions there. It frequently happened, that,
whilst the printer was putting into types parts of a number, the following parts
were under the pen and to be furnished in time for the press."—*Paper by
Madison in the State Department, entitled "The Federalist."*

† Hamilton to Madison—April 3, 1788.—"I send you the Federalist from the
beginning to the conclusion of the Commentary on the executive branches. If
our suspicions of the author be right, he must be too much engaged to make a
rapid progress in what remains. The *Court of Chancery*, and a *Circuit Court*
are now sitting."

‡ Archibald McLean, one of the proprietors of the "Independent Journal,"

Having caused the earlier numbers, as they appeared, to be published in several gazettes, on the first of January, 1788, an edition of The Federalist, together with "Philo Publius," was announced for publication. And, on the twenty second of March, in order that these Essays might reach other States, where the question of the adoption of the Constitution was pending, a duodecimo volume, containing the first thirty six numbers, was issued with a preface, dated the seventeenth of March, and a syllabus or table of contents from the pen of Hamilton. The title page to this edition is in these words. "The Federalist: A Collection of Essays, written in favor of the NEW CONSTITUTION, AS AGREED UPON BY THE FEDERAL CONVENTION, September 17, 1787, IN TWO VOLUMES, Volume i. NEW YORK. Printed & sold by J and A M^cLEAN No 41 Hanover Square 1788."

The Preface states,—

"It is supposed that a collection of the papers which have made their appearance in the Gazettes of this City, under the Title of the Federalist, may not be without effect in assisting the public judgment on the momentous question of the Constitution for the United States, now under the consideration of the people of America. A desire to throw full light upon so interesting a subject has led, in a great measure unavoidably, to a more copious discussion than was at first intended. And the undertaking not being yet completed, it is judged advisable to divide the collection into two Volumes, of which the ensuing Numbers constitute the first. The second Volume will follow as speedily as the Editor can get it ready for publication.

"The particular circumstances under which these papers have

wrote to Colonel Robert Troup, "When I engaged to do the work it was to consist of *twenty* numbers, or at the utmost *twenty-five*, which I agreed to print for thirty pounds—five hundred copies. I made my calculations accordingly, and issued out proposals, each subscriber to pay six shillings."—Madison wrote to Edmund Randolph from New York—December 2, 1787, "The enclosed paper contains two numbers of the Federalist. This paper was begun about three weeks ago. It proposes to go through the subject. I have not been able to collect all the numbers, since my return from Philadelphia, or I would have sent them to you. I have been the less anxious, as I understand the printer means to make a *pamphlet* of them, when I can give them to you in a more convenient form. You will probably discover marks of different pens. I am not at liberty to give you any other key, than, that *I am in myself* for *a few* numbers; and that one, besides myself, was a member of the Convention."—*Madison Papers*, ii. 655.

been written, have rendered it impracticable to avoid violations
of method and repetitions of ideas which cannot but displease a
critical reader. The latter defect has even been intentionally
indulged, in order the better to impress particular arguments
which were most material to the general scope of the reasoning.

"Respect for public opinion, not anxiety for the literary character of the performance, dictates this remark. The great wish
is, that it may promote the cause of truth, and lead to a right
judgment of the true interests of the community."

The residue of the Essays was completed early in May, and
on the twenty eighth of that month was published in a second
volume, also with a table of Contents. The publication of them
in the Gazettes was resumed on the seventeenth of June, and
was concluded on the fifteenth of August. Two days before,
Hamilton wrote to Washington, "I have delivered to Mr. Madison, to be forwarded to you, a set of the papers under the signature of Publius, neatly enough bound to be honored with a
place in your library. I presume you have understood that the
writers of these papers are chiefly, Mr. Madison and myself,
with some aid from Mr. Jay." On the 28th of August, Washington acknowledged them, observing—"When the transient circumstances and fugitive performances which attended this crisis shall have disappeared, that work will merit the notice of
posterity, because in it are candidly discussed the principles of
Freedom and the topics of government, which will always be
interesting to mankind, so long as they shall be connected in
civil society."

No other edition was published in the United States until the
year eighteen hundred and two, three or more translations—the
first in seventeen hundred and ninety two—having, in the mean-
time, appeared in Paris, during the exciting discussions which
then occupied the minds of the people of France. Talleyrand
appreciating it, said to the Duc D'Aranda, envoy at the French
Court from Spain—"Vous avez lu Le Fédéraliste?"—"Non,"
replied D'Aranda.—"Lisez donc—lisez,"—was the significant
answer. Guizot, another distinguished statesman of France,
observed, "In the application of elementary principles of government to practical administration, it was the greatest work
known to him." I am not aware of any edition of this work having been published in Great Britain, though it was noticed in
two leading Reviews. One of these remarks, in an article on a
proposed amendment of the Constitution of the United States.*

---

* Edinburgh Review, No. 24.

The Federalist, "written principally by the late General Hamilton—a work little known in Europe—but which exhibits an extent and precision of information, a profundity of research, and an acuteness of understanding which would have done honor to the most illustrious statesmen of ancient or modern times." Another,† of a later period, observes, "The Federalist, which may be called seriously, reverently, the Bible of Republicanism. It is a work altogether, which for comprehensiveness of design, strength, clearness, and simplicity has no parallel. We do not even except or overlook those of Montesquieu and Aristotle among the writings of men."

The estimate of it in American minds could not be less. Chancellor Kent states—"I know not, indeed, of any work on the principles of free government that is to be compared in instruction and in intrinsic value, to this small and unpretending volume of the Federalist: not even if we resort to Aristotle, Cicero, Machiavel, Montesquieu, Milton, Locke, or Burke. It is equally admirable in the depth of its wisdom, the comprehensiveness of its views, the sagacity of its reflections, and the fearlessness, patriotism, candor, simplicity, and elegance with which its truths are uttered and recommended." The late Judge Story, of the Supreme Court of the United States, has made it "the basis of his Commentary on the Constitution;" and the author of a recent History of the Constitution remarks—"As soon as the Constitution was promulgated, Hamilton came forward and placed himself in the foremost rank of its advocates; making himself, for all future time, one of the chief of its authoritative expounders. He was very ably assisted in the Federalist by Madison and Jay; but it was from *him* that the Federalist derived the weight and the power which commanded the careful attention of the country, and carried conviction to the great body of intelligent men in all parts of the Union. The extraordinary forecast with which its luminous discussions anticipated the operation of the new institutions, and its profound elucidation of their principles, gave birth to American constitutional law, which was thus placed at once above the field of arbitrary construction, and in the domain of legal truth. They made it a science; and so long as the Constitution shall exist, they will continue to be resorted to as the most impor-

† Blackwood's Magazine, January, 1825.

tant source of co-temporaneous interpretation which the annals
of this country afford.*

On the thirteenth of January, eighteen hundred and two, proposals for the publication of the second American edition of this
work, were advertised in the city of New York by George F.
Hopkins. These proposals stated, that *the whole* would be
"*revised and corrected;*" and mentioned that Hamilton was the
principal writer of it, adding that "two other gentlemen of distinguished talents occasionally contributed some essays, which
will be marked in the publication"—Madison and Jay. This edition was in two octavo volumes. Instead of the title page to the
first, and at that time the only, American edition, the title page
to this edition is—"THE FEDERALIST, ON THE NEW CON-
STITUTION. BY PUBLIUS. Written in 1788; to which is
added, Pacificus on the Proclamation of Neutrality."—"*Revised
and Corrected.*" The preface to this revised edition states, that,
"in presenting to the public a new edition of this work, the
object has been to render it correct, as well as neat. Some verbal alterations will accordingly be found, though they have been
made with caution; and in such instances only as are supposed to
have escaped the writers in the hurry of composition, or to have
arisen from the manner of the first publication." Though
announced in January, owing probably to the time which could
be spared in making and revising these alterations, it was not
published until the following December. In neither of these two
editions is any designation given of the authors of the respective
numbers. "It was at first intended," the preface to this revised
edition states, "to mark the numbers distinctly which were written by each; but considerations have since occurred which would
perhaps render this measure improper."

A public disclosure of the authorship of the several numbers
having been made after Hamilton's decease, three volumes, entitled "The Works of Hamilton," were published in eighteen hundred and ten. Two of these volumes embrace "The Federalist,"
in which there is a designation of the respective authors.† Other
editions followed, until the year eighteen hundred and eighteen,
when the work was published in one octavo volume, of which
the title page states—"the numbers written by Madison" are
"corrected by himself." It included the "Letters of Pacificus" by

* History of the Constitution, by George Ticknor Curtis, i. 417, 419.
† By Williams & Whiting, New York.

Hamilton, and the reply entitled, "The Letters of Helvidius," by Madison. This is known as Gideon's Edition;* the name of the publisher. In its preface it states, that the numbers of Madison, as previously published, "*contained many inaccuracies.*" Frequent other editions have been since published. It is from the text of that of Hopkins published in eighteen hundred and two, *revised and corrected,* by John Wells, an eminent barrister of New York, and *supervised* by *Hamilton,* as to the numbers claimed by him; and from the text of that of eighteen hundred and ten, *corrected* by Madison as to the numbers claimed by him, that the present edition has been printed. Having in view a republication of The Federalist, to complete an edition of Hamilton's "Works," which I had then been engaged in preparing for the Press, an enquiry was made by me on the sixth of February, eighteen hundred and forty seven, of Mr. Hopkins— the publisher of the second edition of this work—for information respecting it. Mr. Hopkins made a verbal statement to me, which on the same day I reduced to writing on the fly leaf of the first volume of this edition. "Mr. Hopkins informed me to-day that this edition was in the first instance corrected by John Wells, who compared it with the original edition, published by McLean in 1788; and that it was subsequently revised by my father, at whose casual suggestion Pacificus was printed with it. New York, February 6, 1847."† At this interview, I requested him to address me a note on the subject, which I received two days after.

"NEW YORK, Feb. 8, 1847.

"DEAR SIR:

"In reply to your inquiries concerning the edition of the Federalist, that I published in 1802 (being the first octavo edition of

* Jacob Gideon.

† Hist. of Rep. 1859, vol. iv. 433. The editor is indebted to Thomas L. Wells, Esqr., son of John Wells, for this note, dated February 16, 1864. "In reply to your letter respecting the early editions of the *Federalist,* I can only say that I was told by Mr. Hopkins, now deceased, that an edition of the *Federalist* had been published under the care and revision of my father, the late John Wells, but I do not remember to have heard my father say any thing on the subject. I have always understood that an edition of that work was put to press under his examination, and suppose Mr. Hopkins, who was a printer, referred to the edition published by him in New York. There were a number of letters, notes, and communications in the handwriting of your father, addressed to my father, which he told me were in the handwriting of Gen. Hamilton, and which, I very much regret, were destroyed by fire."

the work), your father's attention was called to the subject through the urgent solicitude of two respectable professional gentlemen, both of whom have long since departed this life. Your father, it appeared, did not regard the work with much partiality; but, nevertheless, consented to its republication on condition that it should undergo a careful revision by one of the gentlemen above alluded to. Accordingly the work (two coarse duodecimo volumes, abounding with errors) was obtained with some difficulty, and placed in his hands for correction. Having performed his duty, he put the volumes into the hands of your father, who examined the numerous corrections, most of which he sanctioned, and the work was then put to press. Here, I deem it proper to remark, that the most scrupulous delicacy was observed in relation to any alterations in the numbers written by Mr. Madison; so much so, indeed, that the alteration of one word (a favorite one with Mr. M.) having escaped notice, that part of the work was required to be re-printed and the original word restored.

"It was proposed, that the name of the writer should be prefixed to each number; but this, as I was told, met with your father's decided disapprobation. But, after the publication appeared, the Hon. Egbert Benson gave me in writing, a key to the respective numbers, which I understood he had previously received from your father; and which I kept for many years. This key was subsequently made use of in an edition published by Williams and Whiting of this city, in three volumes, to which was appended the official Reports made by him to Congress, while Secretary of the Treasury.

"The letters of Pacificus were added at your father's suggestion; and corrected with his own hand. He remarked to me, at the time; that 'some of his friends had pronounced them to be his best performance.'

"With sincere respect I am your ob serv^t.

"G. F. HOPKINS.*

"JOHN C. HAMILTON, Esq."

---

* On the 28th March, 1817, a publication was made in "The New York Evening Post"—a paper then of large and leading influence, by the editor, William Colman, a gentleman of eminent literary ability, in reference to the subject of the authorship of the respective numbers of the Federalist. He mentions, as his motive, the "duty" he felt he owed "to the revered memory of the great and good man who honored him" during seven years with his "friendship." This editorial article states, "In the year 1802, Mr. Hopkins, printer of

In this edition, the syllabus which was printed in the first edition—that of eighty-eight—as the table of "Contents," is also printed as the table of "Contents" to it; and in addition, the subject of each number, copied from the table of "Contents," is prefixed to the proper number which treats of it precisely as was done in the first edition of the work. No dates of the time of publication of these essays are given in either of these editions. These will be seen at the head of each essay, with a designation of the author of it. The dates of the first thirty of these numbers, I have taken from a file of the "Independent Journal," in which they were first published. Not having had access to the residue of this file, of which I have found no complete copy in this city, I have taken the dates of the residue of the essays, with one exception, from another gazette—"The New York Packet." A comparison of the numbers of the edition of eighty-eight, which are in Roman characters, with the numbers, as printed in the two gazettes (those in the Independent Journal being also Roman numerals, and those in the Packet being in Arabic figures), shews a material variance in the numbering.

Before this edition passed from Hamilton's hands to distant points, a new enumeration of these Essays was made. The numbers, as printed in the two gazettes, were prefixed to those in the first volume, until the number of which the head is *"Concerning the Militia."* This number was not published until after the number, *thirty-four* (XXXIV); and was printed in the gazettes, as number thirty-five (XXXV), at the end of a series of essays immediately preceding it, of which the subject is totally different—*taxation.* In the first edition—that of 1788—it is transferred, and is placed next after number *twenty-eight* (XXVIII), being "concerning the Militia," following in its appropriate place the essays which relate to the military force. The number printed *thirty-four* (XXXIV) in the newspaper is consequently designated in this edition, as number *thirty-five* (XXXV), being a continuation of the subject of *"taxation."* Another variance is to be seen as printed in the "original text."

this city, intending to publish a new edition of *The Federalist*, took this opportunity to apply to Gen. Hamilton, and solicit him to correct and revise the numbers; and, so far succeeded, as *to obtain his consent to assist in the revisal, provided a gentleman of competent literary talents would undertake to make the first verbal corrections,* for the original idea was to be strictly adhered to. He *then examined the whole with his own eye,* previous to its being committed to the press, and saw that it was free from literary blemishes."

The closing paragraph in the original number, thirty-five (XXXV), when transferred and placed in its proper order as number twenty-nine (XXIX), is omitted; and a *new* paragraph beginning with a few words in this original closing paragraph of thirty-five (XXXV); but otherwise of entirely different and more fitting purport, is added to the number *thirty-four*, as numbered in the newspaper; but which is enumerated, when collected in the volume, as *thirty-six* (XXXVI). This number completes the Essays "concerning taxation," closing this first volume; the *new additional* paragraph forming an appropriate termination of it. This change, obviously, is the work of the admitted author of both these Essays—Hamilton—before this volume passed finally through his hands from the press to the public. Another variance is to be noted. In the first volume of this first edition, the number printed in the "Independent Journal," as number (XXXI) is published, as divided into *two* numbers, designated (XXXII) and (XXXIII); a new sentence being introduced at the beginning of number XXXIII, to mark more distinctly the reply to an objection, in respect to taxation, ingrafted on certain specified "clauses" of the Constitution. The effect of this division is, to render each subsequent number in this volume, and in the second volume, including number (LXXVII), one number higher in the enumeration than the numbers of the essays, as printed in the gazettes. Another consequence of this change is seen. The number (LXXVII) in the second volume concludes the view of "the constitution of the President;" and was printed in "the Packet," on the fourth of April and called 76—and when the publication in this gazette was resumed in June, with the number LXXVIII printed from the second volume*—this essay is

---

* It has been previously mentioned that the second volume of the first edition was published on the 28th of May, 1788. On the 19th of that month Hamilton wrote to Madison, "I executed your commands respecting the first volume of the Federalist. I sent forty of the common copies and twelve of the finer ones to Governor Randolph. The printer announces the second volume in a day or two, when an equal number of the two kinds shall also be forwarded." To preserve the incognito, he adds, "he informs, that the 'Judicial Department'—'Trial by Jury'—'Bill of Rights,' &c., is discussed in some additional papers, *which have not yet appeared in the gazettes*." On the 8th of June Hamilton again wrote to Madison, "The number of the volumes of the Federalist which you desired have been forwarded, as well the second as the first, to Governor Randolph. It was impossible to correct a certain error."— *Hamilton's Works*, vol. i. 454, 455.

also printed in "the Packet" by the same number 78; and I find no number seventy seven in its series. The enumeration with the syllabus in the first edition of this work, published by McLean in 1788, was retained in the second edition published by Hopkins in 1802, and is that, I believe, used in all the subsequent copies, including that sanctioned by Madison, with *one* exception. It ought manifestly to be retained to prevent much confusion in the frequent references to the numbers of these essays *above* the *twenty eighth*, heretofore made in the published adjudications of the Courts, and by the writers on subjects pertaining to the Constitution. The enumeration of the essays, as printed in the "original text," from which the departure in the volumes is seen to have had a sufficient motive, can only embarrass for general use; a remark which also applies to a reprint "from the original text, for which no sufficient motive will be seen to exist."*

The attribution which is seen to have been made to Hamilton, both in Europe and in America, of the principal and characterizing share in the production of "the Federalist," may have proceeded, either from a conviction of the superior merit of the Essays of which he was the undisputed author; or from a political affinity or bias towards his political opinions; or from the unlimited confidence of Washington which he enjoyed, and his large participation in his administration; or because of his ascription to himself, long unquestioned, of the authorship of much the larger portion of this work. How far this ascription is well founded, it is my purpose to examine, hoping to explain and to correct the errors into which "the fallibility of memory" has led.

The total number of these essays by Hamilton's enumeration, approved by Madison, is seen to be eighty-five. Of this enumeration, an abbreviated copy by Hamilton from his original minute, both in Hamilton's autograph, ascribes to himself the sole authorship of sixty three numbers, and the joint authorship with Madison of *three* numbers, leaving to the latter the sole authorship of *fourteen* numbers; and to Jay, of *five* numbers.

In November eighteen hundred and seven, three years after

---

* The alterations in Numbers 29 & 36 have been referred to. So in Number 83, also by Hamilton, there is an omission in his revised edition of superfluous matter.

Hamilton's decease, a publication was made,* which gave a list being a copy of the memorandum made by him. This list was not disputed until the year eighteen hundred and fifteen; when, in a sketch of the life of Jay,† the number *sixty four* was ascribed to him. In the same work, in a biographical notice of Hamilton, a copy of the list published in eighteen hundred and seven was republished. Early in the year following this notice, the accuracy of this list was denied; and a list was published,‡ being a copy of a memorandum "in Madison's handwriting," in which Madison appropriated to himself, *thirty* numbers; to Jay, *four* numbers, and to Hamilton, the residue—*fifty one* numbers. Three other lists were subsequently published, each of which gives a designation *by* Madison of the authors of the respective numbers. In one of these lists, Madison ascribes *twenty nine* numbers to himself—*five* to Jay, and *fifty two* to Hamilton. In the other two, the same total number is apportioned to each writer with those in the two first of the Madison lists. The variance, where it exists in these two lists, is seen in the designation of the respective writers.

Two statements are also traced to Jefferson's knowledge. One of these ascribes *thirty* numbers to Madison, *five* to Jay, and *fifty* to Hamilton. The other ascribes *fourteen* to Madison solely; *three* to Madison and Hamilton jointly, *five* to Jay, and *sixty three* to Hamilton.

A more minute comparison of these several statements will not be without interest. As to the paper left with Benson by Hamilton, two days previous to his decease, it is stated that, he called at the office of Judge Benson, where he found his nephew Robert Benson, who relates, "I was then a student in the office and well known to the General, and enquired for the Judge. I replied that he had left the city with Mr. King. The General in his usual manner then went to the book case and took down a book which he opened and soon replaced, and left the office. Some time after the General's death, a memorandum in his own handwriting was found in a volume of Pliny's letters, I think,

---

* The Port Folio, Nov. 14, 1807.   † Delaplaine's Repository.

‡ National Intelligencer, March 20, 1817, "Corrector," and May 3, 1817, "Corrector." In the former of these, it is stated by the writer, that he had "been *for several years* in possession of the information upon which this statement is predicated;" and he adds, "if it be doubted or denied, I will venture to appeal to the papers of General Hamilton for the confirmation of my assertion."—Dated March 10, 1817.

which, I believe, was the book he took down, and which memorandum was afterwards wafered by the Judge in the inside of
the cover of the first volume of the Federalist, and where it
remained for several years. He subsequently removed it, and, as
I understood, gave it to some public library." It was accompanied with a certificate that it was in the handwriting of Hamilton. This list and this certificate remained in "The New York
Society Library" until the year eighteen hundred and eighteen,
but has been purloined. This paper was, as stated, a designation
of the names of the respective authors of each number of the
Federalist when written by one person, and of the authors of
certain numbers when written conjointly, of which designation a
copy was taken and preserved by Benson. "The marks of the
wafers still remain in the volume, and above them in Judge Benson's handwriting is, what is presumed, and I believe to be, a
copy of the General's memorandum above referred to, and is as
follows—

"Nos. 2, 3, 4, 5, 54, by J.
"Nos. 10, 14, 37 to 48 inclusive, M.
"Nos. 18, 19, 20, M. and H. jointly.
"All the others by H."*

Some time after Hamilton's decease, it appears from a publication in 1807, that a copy of the Federalist was deposited in the
New York Society Library, in which were designated in his own
handwriting the parts of it written by himself, as well as those
contributed by Madison and Jay.

This minute is—

"Nos. 2, 3, 4, 5, 54, Mr. Jay.
"Nos. 10, 14, 37 to 48 inclusive, Mr. Madison.
"Nos. 18, 19, 20, by Mr. Hamilton and Mr. Madison jointly.
—All the rest by Mr. Hamilton."

A copy of this list was published previously to this copy of the
Federalist being purloined from this Library. This designation
was copied by me in the Federalist in my childhood, at the
request of my father.†

---

* *Copy* of a statement in my possession made for me by Egbert Benson,
Esq., a nephew of Judge Benson.

† In a letter addressed to me by Philip Church, a nephew, and previously
an Aide de Camp of General Hamilton, he states: "Some time in the years, I
believe, of 1802, or 1803, I am inclined to believe in the latter year, I handed
out of our Library, to your father, the two volumes of the Federalist; and
asked him to designate the authors of the different numbers. He promised to

7

Of the four several statements of Madison, one was published, as previously mentioned, in the National Intelligencer of the twentieth of March eighteen hundred and seventeen; and stated to be from "indubitable authority." It was copied from "a pencilled memorandum in the handwriting of Madison."* This memorandum appropriates to Madison the Nos. 10, 14, 18, 19, 20, 37, 38, 39, 40, 41, 42, 43, 44, 45, 46, 47, 48, 49, 50, 51, 52, 53, 54, 55, 56, 57, 58, 62, 63, and 64—Nos. 2, 3, 4, and 5, to Jay,—and the residue to Hamilton. Thus, Madison by this list, ascribes to himself *thirty* numbers; to Jay *four* numbers; to Hamilton *fifty one* numbers.

Another designation by Madison exists, in his handwriting, in a copy of the Federalist which belonged to Richard Rush deceased, a member of Madison's Cabinet.† The attribution in this designation, by Madison, to *himself* is, 10, 14, 18, 19, 20, 37, 38, 39, 40, 41, 42, 43, 44, 45, 46, 47, 48, 49, 50, 51, 52, 53, 54, 55, 56, 57, 58, 62, 63,—to Jay; 2, 3, 4, 5, 64,—to Hamilton; 1, 6, 7, 8, 9, 11, 12, 13, 15, 16, 17, 21, 22, 23, 24, 25, 26, 27, 28, 29, 30, 31, 32, 33, 34, 35, 36, 59, 60, 61, 65, 66, 67, 68, 69, 70, 71, 72, 73, 74, 75, 76, 77, 78, 79, 80, 81, 82, 83, 84, 85. Thus, it is seen, that in this list, Madison ascribes to *himself twenty nine numbers*, to Jay *five*, and to Hamilton *fifty one* numbers.

On the fifteenth of December, 1817, "The City of Washington Gazette" published another designation, "furnished by Madison himself." This designation is very detailed—stating the number— the topic and the name of the writer. In it, Madison ascribes to *himself*, Nos. 10, 14, 17, 18, 19, 21, 37, 38, 39, 40, 41, 42, 43, 44, 45, 46, 47, 48, 49, 50, 51, 52, 53, 54, 55, 56, 57, 58, 62 and 63—; to Jay— 2, 3, 4, 5, 64—to Hamilton 1, 6, 7, 8, 9, 11, 12, 13, 15, 16, 20, 22, 23,

---

do so, saying he would employ you as his amanuensis. The edition is printed by J. and A. McClean, New York. The following is an exact copy of the memorandum on the blank page of one volume.

"Nos. 2, 3, 4, 5, 54, John Jay.

 10, 14, 37 to 48 inclusive—James Madison.

 18, 19, 20, Hamilton and Madison.

"All the rest by Alexander Hamilton.

JOHN C. HAMILTON."

"Angelica, July 25, 1834."

* National Intelligencer, April 18, 1817.

† This memorandum in the handwriting of Mr. Rush is on a fly leaf of the second volume of the Federalist which was shewn by Mr. Rush at Paris to an American gentleman now residing in this vicinity; and is now in Philadelphia, in the possession of one of his sons.

24, 25, 26, 27, 28, 29, 30, 31, 32, 33, 34, 35, 36, 59, 60, 61, 65, 66, 67, 68, 69, 70, 71, 72, 73, 74, 75, 76, 77, 78, 79, 80, 81, 82, 83, 84, 85, to Hamilton. Thus, in this list he ascribes *thirty* numbers to himself, *five* to Jay, and *fifty* to Hamilton. In the following year, 1818, another, the fourth list, by Madison, was published, in an edition in which the numbers whereof he claimed to be the author were "corrected by himself," and the names of the respective writers were furnished by him. In this specification, Madison assigns to *himself* Nos. 10, 14, 18, 19, 20, 37, 38, 39, 40, 41, 42, 43, 44, 45, 46, 47, 48, 49, 50, 51, 52, 53, 54, 55, 56, 57, 58, 62 and 63—to Jay, Nos. 2, 3, 4, 5, 64—to Hamilton, numbers 1, 6, 7, 8, 9, 11, 12, 13, 15, 16, 17, 21, 22, 23, 24, 25, 26, 27, 28, 29, 30, 31, 32, 33, 34, 35, 36, 37, 59, 60, 61, 65, 66, 67, 68, 69, 70, 71, 72, 73, 74, 75, 76, 77, 78, 79, 80, 81, 82, 83, 84 and 85.

To number XVIII this note is seen, by Madison. "The subject of this and the two following numbers happened to be taken up by both Mr. H. and Mr. M. What had been prepared by Mr. H., who had entered more briefly into the subject, was left with Mr. M. on its appearing that the latter was engaged in it, with larger materials, and with a view to a more precise delineation, and from the pen of the latter the several papers went to press."*

Of the two statements traced to Jefferson's knowledge, the first is to be seen in his handwriting in a copy of the earliest edition of the Federalist, now in the Library of Congress. In this minute, Nos. 10, 14, 17, 18, 19, 21, 37, 38, 39, 40, 41, 42, 43, 44, 45, 46, 47, 48, 49, 50, 51, 52, 53, 54, 55, 56, 57, 58, 62 and 63, are attributed to Madison,—2, 3, 4, 5, 64 to Jay, and 1, 6, 7, 8, 9, 11, 12, 13, 15, 16, 20, 22, 23, 24, 25, 26, 27, 28, 29, 30, 31, 32, 33, 34, 35, 36, 59, 60, 61, 65, 66, 67, 68, 69, 70, 71, 72, 73, 74, 75, 76, 77, 78, 79, 80, 81, 82, 83, 84 and 85 to Hamilton. This statement agrees precisely with that furnished by Madison "in the City of Washington Gazette." The other statement is in a copy of the Federalist, formerly belonging to Gideon Granger, a member of Jefferson's Cabinet. This minute is in the handwriting of Granger, who states, that, "it was made *upon information derived from Jefferson.*"† In this minute Nos. 2, 3, 4, 5, 54, are

---

* It is added at foot, "Note by Madison written on the margin of the leaf commencing with the present number, in the copy of the Federalist loaned by him to the publisher."

† For this information the Editor is indebted to Lieutenant-Governor Francis Granger of Canandaigua, in a letter to him of the 7th July, 1855.

"The memorandum in the first volume 'of the Federalist,' is in these

attributed to Jay. Nos. 10, 14, 37, 38, 39, 40, 41, 42, 43, 44, 45, 46, 47, 48, to Madison. Nos. 18, 19, 20, to Madison and Hamilton jointly—and all the rest to Hamilton.

An unpublished paper prepared by Madison—entitled "The Federalist," now in the Department of State at Washington, gives these remarks.

"The particular papers assigned to each of the writers have been differently presented to the public. The statement from a memorandum left by Mr. Hamilton with Mr. Benson just before his death, is very erroneous, owing doubtless to the hurry in which the memorandum was made out. Besides the considerable number of papers written by J. M., and in the lump classed with those written by himself, he ascribes to himself No. 14 written by Mr. Jay, and to Mr. Jay No.　　written not by himself but by J. M. (See Life of Mr. Jay by Delaplaine.) The paper No. 49 also, in which Mr. Jefferson is painted in such strong colours, was not likely to be even approved by Mr. H., and the paper No. 54 on the subject of the negroes as comprised in the ratio of representation, was most likely to be within the share executed by the Southern member of the club.*** A true distribution of the numbers of the Federalist among the three writers is contained in the Edition of that work by Jacob Gideon. It was furnished to him by me, with a perfect knowledge of its accuracy, as it relates to myself, and a full confidence in its equal accuracy as it relates to the two others."

It will be observed, that in this comment prepared by Madison, notwithstanding the variation of his several statements had been publicly and pointedly criticised, there is no attempt to reconcile them nor to explain the inaccuracy. That this criticism came to Madison's knowledge may be inferred from the fact, that a part of the exposition and vindication published in the National Intelligencer *immediately under his eye*, is placed precisely on the same ground with that taken by Madison in his comment as to Number 49.*

words. 'The authors of the following work were as follows: Nos. 2, 3, 4, 5, 54, Mr. Jay. 10, 14, 37, 38, 39, 40, 41, 42, 43, 44, 45, 46, 47, 48, Mr. Madison. Nos. 18, 19, 20, Madison and Hamilton jointly. All the rest were from the pen of Alexander Hamilton.' This entry is in the handwriting of my father, who informed me, that it was made upon information derived from Mr. Jefferson; and, according to my recollection, *from a memorandum furnished by him.*"

* The quotation from No. 49 goes far to prove that Mr. Madison wrote it. Mr. Jefferson is there referred to in terms of distinguished approbation.

As to the variations in the several statements of Madison, it will be noticed, that in the enumeration by him in the volume possessed by Rush, and likewise in that in the "National Intelligencer" also made by him, number seventeen (XVII) is *not* claimed by him, but is *conceded* to Hamilton; while in "The City of Washington Gazette," made not long after that made to Rush, and published the same year with that in the "National Intelligencer," this same number seventeen (XVII) *is claimed* by Madison; and is also ascribed to him in one of Jefferson's lists, and is *not* claimed in the list furnished by Madison to Gideon for publication, but is *conceded* to Hamilton in that list, and is also ascribed to Hamilton in the other Jefferson list. In the three designations made by Madison of numbers XVIII and XIX; in that for Rush;* in that in "The Intelligencer;" in that in "The City of Washington Gazette," and that in one of the Jefferson lists, the *sole* title to the numbers eighteen (XVIII) and nineteen (XIX) is claimed by Madison, but in the list furnished by him to Gideon, there is a memorandam by Madison shewing a joint contribution to these numbers by Hamilton,† as is seen in the other Jefferson list. As to number twenty (XX); though the *sole* title to it *is claimed* by Madison in his list, made for Rush, and also in his list in "The National Intelligencer," it is *not* claimed, but is *conceded* by him to Hamilton in "The City of Washington Gazette;" and in Gideon's edition the memorandum by Madison also shews a joint contribution to this Number by

None but a zealous friend would have expressed such an unqualified eulogium on him; and it is well known, that Mr. Madison has always manifested the most unbounded regard to that gentleman."

* In the statement by Richard Rush, he says, "Number XVIII according to the printed designation appears to be by Mr. Hamilton and Mr. Madison. But the pen is *drawn* over the word 'Mr. Hamilton and,' leaving the printed designation to read simply 'By Mr. Madison,' the manuscript initials 'J.M.' occupying the usual place to the right of the number. Precisely the same remark applies to numbers XIX and XX, of which, therefore, we have Mr. Madison's authority for saying that he was himself the *sole* author, equally as to number XVIII."

† "The subject of this and the two following numbers happened to be taken up by both Mr. H. and Mr. M. What had been prepared by Mr. H., who had entered more briefly into the subject, was left with Mr. M., on its appearing that the latter was engaged in it, with larger materials and with a view to a more precise delineation; and from the pen of the latter the several papers went to the press."—*Note by Madison* written in the margin of the leaf commencing with the present number in the copy of the Federalist loaned by him to the publisher.

Hamilton, while in *both* the Jefferson lists this number is solely ascribed to Hamilton.

Number twenty one (XXI) is *conceded* to Hamilton by Madison in the list made by him for Rush, and in the list by him in "The National Intelligencer," and also in his list in Gideon's edition; but in the list in "The City of Washington Gazette" it *is claimed* by Madison. In one of the Jefferson lists it is ascribed to Madison, and to Hamilton in the other. As to numbers, forty eight (XLVIII) to fifty eight (LVIII), both inclusive, the sole authorship to these essays is claimed by Hamilton in his designation, and by Madison in all his lists, with the exception of fifty *four*. As to this number, the designation made by Madison in Rush's Copy—the edition of 1810—has this feature. This number in the printed designation of this copy is ascribed to Hamilton. There the memorandum of Rush states, "the pen" of Madison "is drawn across Mr. Hamilton's name," and the manuscript initials "J.M." substituted, "showing Mr. Madison to have been the writer." "The single number LIV shows the name 'Jay' in manuscript, near those initials, over which the pen has been again drawn leaving the manuscript initials 'J.M.' as before."

As to numbers sixty two and sixty three (LXII and LXIII) the sole title to each of them is claimed by Hamilton in his list, and by Madison in all his lists; and is ascribed to Hamilton in one of Jefferson's lists and to Madison in the other. Number sixty-four—LXIV—in the three lists, that of Rush, that in "The City of Washington Gazette" and in the Gideon edition is *assigned* by Madison to Jay, but in the memorandum by Madison published in "The National Intelligencer," it is *claimed* by Madison to *himself*. In one of the Jefferson lists it is ascribed to Hamilton, in the other to Jay.

In the inquiry which it is now proposed to enter upon in order to throw some light on the subject of the authorship of certain numbers of the Federalist, or of separate parts of them it is deemed proper to indicate the spirit in which it is the aim of the editor to pursue it. Hamilton's principal agency in the suggestion, preparation and superintendence of this work has never been a matter of controversy, nor that Jay and Madison were efficient co-operators with him in the contributions to it, greater or less. The supervision of the series fell to Hamilton; and it was so much under his control, both from the place of publication, and his priority and prominence in the plan or scheme of argument, that it cannot be supposed that any part of it had gone to press, without his inspection or such previous conference or correspondence with his associates, as insured his assent to what was submitted to the public. His intimacy with the whole work in the course of its publication must have been complete,—more so certainly than that of Jay, whose proportion of it was the least in quantity, and probably more so than Madison's. There can be no doubt, at the same time, that the whole work—passing under the signature of "Publius," and prepared by each of the writers with the common object of promoting the adoption of the Constitution by the people in the several States, had the united sanction of all of them. It therefore is, and ought to be regarded, in this sense, as their joint work.

That Hamilton was particularly appreciative of his separate part of it, or was particularly sensitive to the just distribution of public approbation between himself and his coadjutors, on that account, is believed to be without the least foundation in point of fact, whoever may have said or written it. His state of mind and feeling is believed to be just the reverse. After the work was consummated by the adoption of the Constitution, and especially after a great divergency had occurred between himself and Madison in regard to the administration of it, curiosity was probably awakened to discover their respective contributions to it; but it is seen, that when the revision of an edition was proposed to him in 1802, and a designation of the respective authors was requested of him for this object, he expressly declined assenting to the request, while he at the same time only conditionally favored a revision of it by some competent editor. He seemed indeed to doubt whether such an edition of it was desirable;* and when the new edition appeared, it was without any key to indicate the respective writers; and its preface, with the utmost delicacy to his known wishes, stated as to the papers of Jay and Madison, "that, as far as it has been practicable to discriminate their productions, they are not unequal in merit to those which are solely from the pen of Hamilton."

After the publication of this edition in 1802 by George F. Hopkins, the curiosity of personal friends doubtless often

---

* Mr. Hopkins relates, when Hamilton hesitated his consent, that he remarked to him, "*Heretofore* I have given the people *milk; hereafter* I will give them *meat;*" words indicating his formed purpose—to write a treatise upon government. Experience is teaching us the solemn lessons he did not live to inculcate.

solicited from Hamilton the same information as to the respective authors, but, except in the instances now seen, it was always met with the same reserve. The only instance in which he gave it under his own pen, was that previously stated, to his venerable and very confidential friend, the late Egbert Benson, who was a joint delegate with him to the Convention at Annapolis. This was probably in answer to Judge Benson's request, by leaving a small slip of paper at a morning call in a volume of his library. It is from this memorandum, made public after Hamilton's decease, we first obtain his representation of the authorship of the respective numbers of the Federalist.

No particular sanctity will be claimed for this brief memorandum. The pendency, at the time it was left in Judge Benson's office, of a personal controversy which might terminate his life, may have been his reason for then performing a promise which he might not afterwards be able to perform; but the performance may have been, and probably was, a mere incident to a visit to a personal friend made for other reasons. It were an unreasonable supposition that such a memorandum was intended in the mind of Hamilton to be invested with any of the characters of sanctity or dignity, which an ultimate act in the life of a man is commonly thought to impart. It was written and left, no doubt, in perfect good faith, as a true representation of the writer's knowledge or recollection, with the minute exception of a single figure which admits of explanation; but the entire memorandum will be regarded, and ought to be regarded, only as the averment of an upright and honorable man, meaning to state what he knew or believed to be true; and believing also that he had truly expressed what he knew.

The paper purports no more than to be a memorandum. It wants the essential forms of a record. It has neither expressed description nor signature. It is simply a collection of Arabic numerals in three lines, with the abbreviated word *numero*— No.—prefixed to each, the first line ending with the capital letter J; the second line ending with the capital letter M; and the third line with the capitals M and H jointly—a fourth line contains the words "all the rest by H."

The original cause of an apparent error of statement in Hamilton's memorandum, in his own copy of the Federalist, may have arisen from a mere slip of his pen or from a peculiarity in the formation of a single figure, writing with his usual rapidity, and especially of a figure which, in the cursive hand of many writers, looks much like another figure, that might embody an unobserved or supposed mistake. His private letters shew in his formation of three consecutive figures, that there is no break or raising of the pen from the paper, but that they are formed by a continuous movement of his hand. This may be regarded as the true solution of the only mistake supposed to exist in Hamilton's designation, and it is in reference to this supposed mistake that the succeeding observations are made. The printed numbers of the Federalist in "the Independent Journal" in which they first appeared, are in Roman characters. The numerals of the minute by Hamilton, copied by myself from his manuscript, and also in the minute left with Benson, are in Arabic characters. The minute prefixes the figures 2–3–4–5–54 before the name of Jay, implying, of course, that Jay was the writer of the papers of the Federalist numbered 2–3–4–5–54. Mr. Jay was incontestably the writer of numbers 2–3–4–5 and 64. The mistake is in the figure 5 instead of 6. In the *total* number of papers ascribed by Hamilton to Jay there is *no* mistake. Jay was but the author of five numbers. If the *topic* of number 64 had been adverted to, the mistake could not have occurred, for No. 64 is a paper on the power of making treaties—a subject from his previous services and then official station with which Jay was familiar, while the *topic* of number 54,—the apportionment of representation among the States—with the mixed basis of property and persons—persons free and persons regarded as property—was one with which Jay had no special relation, while, it will be seen, that Hamilton had in relation to it exerted a most important agency. Hamilton could not possibly have confounded these, but in bringing Roman numerals into Arabic, an erroneous glance of the eye, and either a slip or blur of the pen, might easily pervert a figure. As the memorandum does, in no part of it, allot the number 64 to either Jay or Madison, or to Madison and Hamilton jointly, and does allot all the *non* enumerated essays to Hamilton, it follows moreover that if the subjects of the two papers 54 and 64 had been the basis of enumeration, a double consciousness of the writer of the memorandum must have guided his pen aright—that of his being the author of No. 54, and of his not being the author of No. 64. It was the error of a figure simply. That such was the case, is shewn by a statement* in which it appears, that Hamilton did ascribe No. 64

---

* Statement by Judge Kent—more minutely referred to hereafter.

to Jay, retaining 54 to himself. The abbreviated copy by Hamilton of his original minute in the same formation of figures shows the haste in which it was made the day before he received the wound which terminated his life. The statement or allotment by Madison published in the National Intelligencer differs in this respect. It ascribes to himself both 54 and 64, to the latter of which numbers he subsequently relinquished his claim.

Having explained Hamilton's supposed single mistake in the ascription of the respective numbers, it is now proposed to proceed to a more minute investigation of the subject. But in what has been already adduced as evidence of error by Madison, or may be adduced in confirmation of Hamilton's accuracy, the editor deems it proper to disclaim any intention to impute premeditated error in either or in any of the statements which have appeared on this subject—nor does he claim to settle or to demonstrate any thing that will leave any imputation upon any one in regard to the subject. His long since declared intention to publish an edition of the Federalist, which would "state all the evidence known to exist to designate the respective contributions of its authors,"* gives the purport of this notice. As a question of mere literary interest, and also of comparative accuracy or probability in the respective sources of information, the subsequent remarks must pass for what they are worth. Not withholding, as will be seen, his own conviction on the subject, both from the evidence which exists and from a comparison of the numbers in question with those which are of the acknowledged authorship of either writer, he does not affect to regard what he may adduce as conclusive—or as taking from the reader the fullest liberty of forming from the same or any other sources his own free judgment.

As to number XVII claimed by Madison in "The Washington City Gazette," though disclaimed by him in his other distributions, a marked similarity, both of thought and of expression, will be seen with those of the brief of Hamilton's leading speech in the Federal convention.

In this number it is remarked; "*It is a known fact in human nature that its affections are commonly weak in proportion to the distance or diffusiveness of the object.*"†

---

* Hist. Rep. iii. 371; 1859.   † Federalist, page 154.

In this Brief,* *"Distance has a physical effect on men's minds;"* and in Hamilton's MSS. notes, commenting on an observation of Madison, he observes, *"The human mind is prone to limit its view to near and local objects."* In this number, "The variety of *more minute* interests"† is adverted to as giving influence to the local administrations. In Hamilton's MSS. notes a similar phraseology is found, connected with the same idea, "If more minute links are wanting others will supply them." In this number‡ it is stated, that "the operations of the National government will be less likely to inspire a *habitual sense of obligation;"* and the advantage of the States is said to consist in *"the ordinary administration of criminal and civil justice."* In this brief; among the "supports of government" is enumerated an *"§habitual sense of obligation."*

Number XVIII is stated in his list by Hamilton to have been a *joint* production with Madison—a particularity which shews the accuracy of his recollection. It *was* claimed, as his *sole* production, by Madison in all of his lists; until the publication of Hamilton's statement, that it was a *joint* production, being publicly urged, when it was in the list furnished by Madison to Gideon, first qualifiedly admitted by him also, to have been a *"joint* production."

The object or purport of this essay is, in continuation of the preceding number, to "show the tendency of Federal Governments, rather to anarchy among the members than tyranny in the head"—with farther examples." In this essay, it is stated; "‖ *Athens, as we learn from Demosthenes, was the arbiter of Greece seventy three years. The Lacedemonians next governed it twenty-nine years: at a subsequent period after the battle of Leuctra the Thebans had their turn of domination."* In Hamilton's brief;¶ are seen these notes: "Grecian Republics; Demosthenes says—Athens *seventy three years*—Lacedæmon *twenty seven—The bans after battle of Leuctra."* In this number this passage is also seen;** "The *Phocians having ploughed up some consecrated ground* belonging to the temple of Apollo, the Amphyctionic Council according to the superstition of the age imposed a fine on the sacrilegious offenders." "The latter *** invited the assistance of *Philip."* In Hamilton's brief†† are these notes; *"Phocians—consecrated ground—Philip,* &c."

---

* History of Republic of United States. iii. 276.

† Federalist, p. 155.   ‡ Ibid.   § Hist. Repub. iii. 277.

‖ Federalist, p. 159.   ¶ Hist. Repub. iii. 278.

** Federalist, p. 160.   †† Hist. Repub. 278.

In number (XIX) also claimed *solely* by Madison in all his four lists, though with the admission in Gideon's edition qualifiedly that it was a *joint* production, the same subject is treated; and there is seen a similar coincidence. In this number this example is cited;* "The first which presents itself is *the Germanic body.*" In Hamilton's brief,† "The *Germanic Empire.*" Subsequently in this number, this sentence is seen; "*Charlemagne* and his *immediate descendants*‡ possessed the reality." In Hamilton's brief;— "*Charlemagne* and *his successors.*"

Of this same number, the powers of "*the diet,*"§ and the council formed by "*the electors,*" are the subjects. In Hamilton's brief; "*Diet*—recesses—*Electors,* now seven, excluding others." In this same number‖—the example of "*the Swiss Cantons*" is adduced. In Hamilton's brief,¶ "*Swiss cantons.*" In this number it is stated**—"The *Protestant* and *Catholic cantons* have since had their *separate diets*—where all the most important concerns are adjusted, and which have left the general diet little other business than to take care of the *common bailiages.*" In the brief; "*two diets.*" In this number the separation resulting in *opposite alliances* with foreign powers—"of *Berne* and of Luzerne," is stated. In Hamilton's brief; "*opposite alliances*— *Berne—Luzerne.*" Some evidence as to Hamilton's title to a participation in these two numbers is also to be seen in the papers of "The Continentalist" published by him in the years 1781–82. Having therein briefly alluded to the examples of the contentions of the Grecian Republics—of *Sparta* and of "*Athens,*" and having also instanced the impotence of "the *Germanic Diet,*" he passes on to the example of "the *Helvetic league,*" adverts to "their powerful neighbours,"—and states that "the *Protestants and Catholics have had separate diets to manage almost all matters of importance; so that in fact the general diet is only kept up to regulate the affairs of the common bailiages.*" The coincidence of this passage with that previously quoted from the Federalist; and *near its close,* was not casual.

As to the number (XX). It is seen to be *claimed* by Madison in his two first lists, *not* claimed by him but *conceded* to Hamilton in his third list, and again qualifiedly claimed in his fourth list;—and that it, also in his list, is stated by Hamilton to have been a *joint*

---

* Federalist, p. 165.   † Hist. Rep. iii. 278.
‡ Ibid. p. 166.   § Federalist, 168.
‖ Federalist, p. 170.   ¶ Hist. Rep. iii. 278.
              ** Federalist, p. 171.

production. The analogy of this essay with Hamilton's brief, is less marked than in the previous instances; but by referring to his letter to Duane, the similarity in the train of thought is quite perceptible. In this number,* "the weight and influence" of the *Stadtholder* in "*The United Netherlands,*" from *his general* power and prerogatives, and "*his influence in the individual provinces,*" are stated to have been the only preventatives "of *anarchy;*" and it is added, "*the surrounding powers impose an absolute necessity of union to a certain degree.*" In Hamilton's letter to Duane† in 1780, as to "*the United Provinces.*" "*But the family of the Stadtholder, whose authority is interwoven with the whole Government, has been a strong link of union between them. Their physical necessities and the habits founded upon them have contributed to it.*" So in the "Continentalist,"‡ Hamilton observes of "*the United Provinces,*" "*The authority of the Stadtholder pervades the whole frame of the Republic, and is a kind of common link by which the provinces are bound together.*" "The *inconsiderableness of each province separately, and the imminent danger to which the whole would be exposed of being over-run by their neighbours,* in case of disunion, is a further preservation against the phrenzy of hostility." The closing paragraph of this number,§ stating the "*important truth*" resulting from these examples— that "a sovereignty over sovereignties, a government over governments, a *legislation for communities,* as contradistinguished from individuals, is a solecism in theory"—adds, "so in practice it is subversive of the order and ends of civil polity, by substituting *violence* in place of *law,* or the destructive *coercion* of the *sword,* in place of the mild and salutary *coercion* of the Magistracy." A coercion by the sword, it has been seen, was proposed by Madison in seventeen hundred and eighty. Hamilton in his brief,‖ enumerating among, "the supports of Government" force, remarks, "Force of two kinds—coercion of *laws*—coercion of *arms.* First does not exist—and the last *useless.* Attempt to use it, a war between the States;" and in Hamilton's brief, it is urged among the objections to the Confederation that it "*legislates upon communities.*"

The number Twenty one (XXI) *not* claimed by Madison in the first, second, and fourth of his enumerations, *is* claimed by him in his third. It is claimed by Hamilton in his list. In this number

* Federalist, p. 178.   † Hamilton's Works, i. 158.
‡ Continentalist, No. 2.   § Federalist, p. 176.
‖ Hist. Repub. iii. 276.

it is stated—"The next most palpable defect of the existing Confederation is the total want of a *sanction* to its laws." In Hamilton's brief, among the objections to the Confederation, is stated this, *"No sanction."* In this number, this passage is seen:* *"The wealth of nations depends upon an infinite variety of causes. Situation, soil, climate, the nature of the productions—the nature of the Government—the genius of the citizens—the degree of information they possess—the state of commerce, of arts, of industry—these circumstances and many more to complex, minute, or adventitious, to admit of a particular specification, occasion differences hardly conceivable in the relative opulence and riches of different countries. The consequence clearly is, that there can be no common measure of national wealth. There is no method of steering clear of this inconvenience but by authorizing the national Government to raise its own revenues in its own way."*

In a letter from Hamilton† to Clinton of February 24, 1783, this observation is to be seen. "The truth is, the ability of a country to pay taxes depends on *infinite combinations of physical and moral causes*, which can never be accommodated to any general rule; *climate, soil, productions*, advantages for navigation, *government, genius of the people*, progress of *arts*, and *industry*, and an *endless variety of circumstances*. The diversities are sufficiently great, in these States, to make an infinite difference in their *relative wealth*, the proportion of which can never be found by any *common measure whatever*. The *only possible way*, then, of making them contribute to the general expense, in an equal proportion to their means, is by *general taxes imposed under continental authority*."

The next Essay in question is number XLIX misprinted in the head of this number in the first or McLean edition of 1788—as "Number LXIX—that is 69 instead of 49. It is claimed by Hamilton in his list and by Madison in all of his lists, is ascribed to Madison in one of the Jefferson lists and to Hamilton in the other. In relation to this number Madison remarks "the paper number 49 also, in which Mr. Jefferson is painted in such strong colors was not likely to be even approved by Mr. Hamilton." To this observation, the counter remark is suggested by the essay, that its objections to Jefferson's project, pointed and studied as they are, were not to be expected from

---

* Federalist, p. 181.   † Hamilton's Works, i. 332.

Madison, his most intimate and perhaps most unquestioning friend. The contrast is to be observed between this and the preceding number 48 admitted to be Madison's. In 48, the allusion to Jefferson is simple commendation. In 49, there is seen indeed warm commendation, but followed by a careful, elaborate, and very explicitly stated disapproval throughout the essay. But the reason assigned by Madison for rejecting Hamilton's claim to this number, founded on a fact as existing at the time this essay was written, is not a fact. On the fifth of September, 1785, Jefferson writes, "I would advise him to apply to Colonel Hamilton, who was aid to General Washington, and is now very eminent at the bar, and much to be relied on." And on the 10th of October, 1792, Hamilton writes to General Pinckney of Jefferson—"that gentleman whom I *once very much esteemed,** but who does not permit me to retain that sentiment for him, is certainly a man of *sublimated* and *paradoxical* imagination, entertaining and propagating opinions inconsistent with dignified and orderly Government." As this and the following number relate to a topic as to which no similar project had ever come under Hamilton's view, no analogy was to be expected in his writings. It is a proposition quoted from Jefferson's "Notes on the State of Virginia,"† that, "whenever any two of the three branches of Government shall concur in opinion, each by the voices of two thirds of their whole number, that a Convention is necessary for altering the Constitution, or *correcting branches* of it, a Convention shall be called for the purpose." Could any project be more paradoxical" than this, or more "inconsistent with orderly government?" Could there be a project presented that would more be in conflict with Hamilton's urgency for a *stable* government?

Some passages in this number, are not without similitude to other of Hamilton's papers. "If it be true," this essay remarks,‡ "that all governments *rest on opinion;*" "The most rational government will not find it a superfluous advantage to *have the prejudices of the community on its side.*" "The *passions* ought to be *controuled and regulated* by the Government." In Hamilton's let-

* Hamilton's Works, v. 533.

† "Notes on the State of Virginia, written by Thomas Jefferson, Philadelphia, 1788,"—of which a copy, formerly in Hamilton's library, is in my possession.

‡ Federalist, p. 390.

ter to Duane,* urging a change of government, he remarks; "men are governed by *opinion.*" In his brief;† among the "*supports of government,*" is stated, an "*opinion of utility and necessity.*" "To effect any thing *passions must be turned towards general government.*" "The Government must be so constituted as to offer *strong motives*, in short, to *interest* all the *passions* of individuals."‡

---

* Hamilton's Works, i. 168.   † Hist. Repub. iii. 277, 278, 283.

‡ A statement has recently been made public taken from an *entry* by Chancellor Kent, in a *volume* of the Federalist of the edition of 1788. Nothing would more have grieved this distinguished and devoted friend of Hamilton during his life, and to his memory since his decease, as often manifested, and entitling him to the most respectful gratitude of the editor, who had the honor of his friendship, had he supposed that any minute of his would be used prejudicially. From a copy of this entry, in my possession, it appears that Hamilton represented "2, 8, 4, 5 and 64 as written by Mr. Jay—10–14, 37 to 49 both inclusive and 58 by James Madison, Junr.—numbers 18, 19, 20 by Messrs. Madison and Hamilton jointly—all the rest by Mr. Hamilton." "Mr. Hamilton told me that Mr. Madison wrote No. 48 and 49—from pa. 101 to 112 of vol. 2d—N.B. I showed the above mem, to Gen. Hamilton in my office in Albany, and he said that it was correct, himself seeing the correction above made." The note by Kent above quoted, that Nos. 2, 3, 4, 5 and 64 were Jay's, "has *no correction* in it. It stands exactly as it was written"* by Judge Kent; and as to the minute that this note or memorandum was shown to General Hamilton indicating the pages "from 101 to 112 of vol. 2d," it is certain that this minute was made some long time after the interview of Hamilton with Kent, for the reason that a letter of Judge Kent to William Coleman—dated Albany, May 12, 1817, states a number *differently*. "The note which I now possess"—that which states a number differently—"written in one of the volumes of the Federalist and which was there in February, 1804, and which I *am certain* received the correction and sanction of General Hamilton, I have annexed below." The corrections made by Judge Kent are these,—"The numbers 64, 49—48 and 49 have been written over other numbers—64 over 54—49 over 48—48 over 68—49 over 69." Here are two numbers 49, written over different numbers. The correction of 49 over 48 must have referred to the number 48 as printed in the "Packet," and when this number was referred to by its *topic*, Hamilton would of course ascribe it to Madison; for the 49 in the volume copy is the 48 of the "Packet," which Hamilton ascribes to Madison in his own list. The correction of the same number *twice* cannot be explained in any other way. The correction of 48 over 68—and the second correction of 49 over 69—are thus explained. They are corrections of misprints in the volumes of 1788 and carelessly repeated in the volumes of 1802 by the printer. The number 48 in both these editions is printed in Roman numerals as LXVIII—68—and the number 49 is printed also in both editions in Roman numerals as LXIX—69, but why 64 is written over 54, the

---

* James Kent to the editor, kindly giving exact transcripts of the entries in the volumes of his grandfather with explanatory statements. Feb. 5 and 11th, 1864.

In number L., claimed by Hamilton in his list and by Madison in all his lists, the same topic is pursued, and after some general observations, the precedent of Pennsylvania in her "Council of Censors" is canvassed. As to this, as well as to the scheme of Jefferson, an analogy in Hamilton's writings—for the same reason, that no such project had ever come before him, was *not* to be expected. In number Fifty one (LI.), claimed by Hamilton in his list and by Madison in all his lists, the necessity there stated, that, "in order to lay a due foundation for a separate and distinct exercise of the different powers of government, each department should have *a will of its own*," is seen to be a primary object in Hamilton's plan of a National Government,—read before the Federal Convention. In his brief, he notes.* "The general government must not only have a *strong soul*, but *strong organs* by which that soul is to operate." In his resolutions of 1783,† for a General Convention; he states among the great defects of the Confederation—"its confounding legislative, and executive powers, in *a single body*." In his brief, he pointedly remarks,‡ "the *want of checks*." This want was distinctly stated, as one of the chief sources of his solicitude; and in the structure of a Government, which he planned—he carried the principle as far as could be deemed wise—of drawing; as this essay approves,§ "all the appointments from the same fountain of authority—the people, through *channels having no communication whatever with one another*," adding with his own plan in his mind; "*Perhaps*, such a plan of constructing the several departments would be less difficult in practice than it may in contemplation appear." This Essay, after indicating the means of providing security against "a gradual concentration of power," proceeds, "ambition must be made to counteract ambition. The interest of the man must be connected with the constitutional rights of the place. It may be a reflection on human nature that

---

number LIV being accurately printed is not explained, nor explicable. Nor is the error of Judge Kent as to 53 to be explained in any similar way, for 53 is correctly printed in both editions—LIII. A list recently published as "Chancellor Kent's MSS. Notes," is merely a *copy* in the Chancellor's handwriting, and stated there as "copied from the newspaper extract" of the "list furnished by Mr. Madison himself," the *inaccuracy* of which it has been seen, was subsequently *admitted* by Madison in the Gideon edition of 1810. No weight can be attached to this mere copy of an erroneous list in Kent's hand, as being "Chancellor Kent's MSS. Notes."

* History of Repub. iii. 280. † Hamilton's Works, ii. 269.
‡ Hist. Rep. iii. 278 § Fed. p. 398.

such devices should be necessary to control the abuses of government. But what is *government itself* but the *greatest of all reflections* on *human nature*? If *men* were *angels, no government* would be necessary."*

This tone of thought and of expression warrant the belief that these sentences flowed from Hamilton's pen. They speak the independence of mind shown by him in the Federal Convention which gained him a large place in its confidence, and which he maintained in every stage of his responsible life. In the brief, of his great speech in that body, he quotes the pregnantly fallacious phrase—"*Vox populi—Vox Dei*,"—"The voice of the people is the voice of God"—and there meets it by a remark, equivalent to this—"*If men were angels, no government would be necessary*"—"Source of Government—*the unreasonableness of the people.*"†

In this essay it is also remarked; "*Different interests necessarily exist in different classes of citizens.*" So he had recently remarked in the New York legislature. Whence can this danger—"to the liberties of the people"—arise? "The members of Congress are annually chosen" (under the Confederation) "by the members of the several legislatures. They come together with *different habits, prejudices and interests.* They are, in fact, continually changing." It is observed in this Essay—"It is *of great importance* in a Republic, not only to guard the society against the oppression of its rulers; but to *guard one part of the society against the injustice of the other part.*" In his brief;‡ Hamilton observes, "*Society* naturally divides itself into two political divisions—the *few* and the *many*. If government in the hands of the *few*, they will tyrannize over the *many*; if in the hands of the *many* they will tyrannize over the *few*. It ought to be in the hands of both, and they *should be separated.*" The scheme of Charles Pinckney§ and the resolutions of Virginia submitted to the Federal Convention—wholly disregarded this principle—both deriving the Senate and the Executive from the more numerous branch of the legislature.

In this number, in the provision to fortify the Executive, it is stated—"An *absolute negative*, on the legislature, appears at first view to be the natural defence with which the executive magistrate should be armed. But, *perhaps* it would be neither altogether safe nor alone sufficient."‖ The analogy of this opinion

---

* Fed. 398.   † Hamilton's Works, ii. 414.

‡ Hist. Rep. iii. 280.   § Ibid. 260.   ‖ Federalist, 399.

with Hamilton's course in the Federal Convention cannot escape observation. He contended for the power of an *absolute* veto in the President, providing *effective checks* in the other provisions of his plan of a Constitution. Madison declared in the Convention, "To give such a prerogative," an absolute negative, "would certainly be *obnoxious* to the temper of this country—its present temper at least."* It is not probable, that, in respect to a Constitutional provision as to which he had avowed so earnest an objection, he would have thus qualified that opinion by a *"perhaps,"* while on the other hand, the doubt was clearly in Hamilton's mind, apprehending and indicating as he did, the dangers of the engrossing and controlling influence of the legislature.

From these "more general enquiries," the Federalist passes "to a more particular examination of the several parts of the government." The first topic was the plan of the House of Representatives as it related to "the qualifications of the electors and the elected." This is the subject of number fifty two (LII.) claimed by Hamilton in his list and by Madison in all his lists. That Hamilton would have preferred to treat of this subject may reasonably be inferred from the uniform current of his thoughts and from the marked position in which he stood in relation to it. He is seen to have argued in the first of his political essays with great force the right of representation. "The† right of Colonists to exercise a legislative power is *an inherent right.*" "The foundation of the English Constitution rests upon the principle; that no laws have any validity or binding force, *without the consent,* and *approbation* of the PEOPLE, given in the persons of their representatives, periodically elected by *themselves.*" "This constitutes the *democratical part* of the Government." "A‡ share in the sovereignty of the State," he subsequently wrote, "which is exercised by the citizens at large, in voting at elections, is one of the most important rights of the subject; and in a Republic ought to stand *foremost* in the estimation of the law. *It is that right by which we exist a free people.*" In conformity with this maxim, it is stated in this number, "The definition of the right of suffrage is very justly regarded as a *fundamental article of republican government.*"§ And in defence of this right he had very recently remarked in the legislature of New York. "The* qualifications both of *the electors*

---

* Madison Papers, ii. 786.   † Hamilton's Works, ii. 62, 1775.
‡ Hamilton's Works, ii. 315.   § Fed. p. 403.

and *the elected* ought to be *fundamental in a republican form of government*, not liable to be varied or added to by the legislature, and they should forever remain where the Constitution left them."

His theoretical opinions on this subject were the very opposite of those of Madison, whose birth and education were in a planting State, the Constitution whereof he had an agency in forming, and which limited the suffrage to persons having an interest in real estate. Viewing the subject on its *merits alone*, Madison remarked, "the freeholders of the country would be the safest depositories of American liberty."† Hamilton, on the contrary, duly measuring the tendencies of opposite interests, earnestly observed, "It is *essential* to the *democratic* rights of the community, that this branch be *directly elected by the people*."‡ The second article of his plan of a Constitution is seen to have embodied this principle;§ and in all his successively developed opinions, he has been seen seeking to limit the power of the State Governments, and to organize a National Government self existing and self supporting—a National Government deriving its power directly from the people, and acting directly upon them as individuals, a system equally important in the preservation of the Constitution, and, if temporarily suspended by civil war—in the restoration of its powers—the only theory consistent with the natural and constitutional rights of a free people.

The term of office of the Representatives in Congress is the next topic of this number. In respect to this, the Essay observes‖—"As it is essential to liberty, that the government in general should have a common interest with the people, so it is particularly essential that the branch of it under consideration should have an *immediate dependence* on, and an intimate sympathy with the people." So, in a recent speech on granting the power of levying an impost to the Confederation, he remarks— "The truth is, the security intended to the general liberty in the Confederation, consists in the frequent election, and in the rotation of the members of Congress, by which there is a constant and an effectual check upon them. This is the security which the people in every State enjoy against the usurpations of their internal governments; and it is the true source of security in a representative republic." A vindication of "biennial elections" is

---

* Hist. of Repub. iii. 207.   † Madison Papers, ii. 786.
‡ Secret Debates, 149.   § Hamilton's Works, ii. 396.
                    ‖ Federalist, p. 404.

drawn from the previous "history of this branch of the English Constitution"—from that of Ireland;—and from that of the several States when Colonies. When referring to Virginia, the author of this number* observes—"In Virginia, nevertheless, *if I have not been misinformed,* elections under the former Government were septennial." Such might be the language of a person, residing at a distance from that State with which the communications were then infrequent; probably without the means of recurring to her colonial records; who had passed his early life in the camp, and much of his after life under pressing professional engagements. But such an expression was not to be expected from Madison, a member of the Convention in 1775 which framed the first Constitution of that State,—in 1776 a member of her legislature—in 1777 a member of her "Council of State;" and in 1779 chosen one of her delegates to Congress—speaking of the term of office in her recent Colonial legislature.

In this number,† the change in England from triennial to septennial elections is justly disapproved. "The last change from *three* to *seven* years, is well known to have been introduced *pretty early in the present century under an alarm for the Hanoverian succession.*" Hamilton's previous language is equally explicit. "The *English Whigs, after* the Revolution," he remarks,‡ "from an overwhelming dread of Popery, and of the Pretender, from *triennial,* voted the Parliament *septennial.* They have been trying ever since to undo this false step in vain, and repenting the effects of their folly in the overgrown power of the new family."

Number Fifty three (LIII) is claimed by Hamilton in his list, and by Madison in all of his lists—is ascribed to Madison in one of the Jefferson lists, and to Hamilton in the other. It is a continuation of the subject last treated of in the preceding number—the *duration* of the term of office of the members of the House of Representatives. From what is shown, there can exist little doubt, that Madison was *not* the author of number fifty two. It is seen to have derived its defence of the provision for biennial elections from historical examples. In this succeeding number Fifty three (LIII), after an allusion to the periods established in certain of the United States, this subject is considered on broader grounds. "The natural alarm in the votaries of free government, of which the *frequency* of elections is the *corner*

* Fed. p. 407.   † Fed. p. 406.

‡ Hamilton's Works, ii. 289.—"Phocion," 1784.

stone,"* is here stated to have resulted from the instances in the
acts of the British Parliament, *prolonging* their term of office.
This "frequency of elections," he stated in the reference in the
preceding number—to have been—"the security of liberty;" and
this essay meets this objection to the Constitution decidedly, by
referring to "the important distinction so well understood in
America between a *Constitution established by the people*, and
unalterable by the Government, and a *law established* by the
government, and *alterable* by the *Government*."† This "important distinction" had been brought pressingly before Hamilton
by the violent bigotry and selfish proscription, shewn, in New
York in 1778, by the party whose leaders were now opposing
the adoption of the Constitution by that State. It was, while
opposing legislative discriminations violative of the Constitution
that he asserted its supremacy. "If the Constitution," he wrote,‡
"declares that persons possessing certain qualifications shall be
entitled to certain rights, while that Constitution remains in
force, the *Government*, which is the mere *creature* of the Constitution, can divest no citizen, who has the requisite qualifications, of his corresponding rights." "Happily for us in this country, the position is not to be controverted, that the Constitution
is the creature of the people; but it does not follow that they are
not bound by it, while they suffer it to continue in force; nor
does it follow that the legislature, which is, on the other hand, a
creature of the Constitution, can depart from it, on any presumption of the contrary sense of the people. The Constitution
is the compact made between the society at large and each individual." "All the authority of the legislature is delegated to them
under the Constitution; their rights and powers are there
defined; if they exceed them, it is a *treasonable usurpation* upon
the power and majesty of the people; and by the same rule that
they may take away from a single individual the rights he
claims under the Constitution, *they* may *erect* themselves into
perpetual dictators." "The second question," it is stated in this
number, is, "whether biennial elections be necessary or useful;"
and in reference to this, "the requisite knowledge" of the representative is considered. "Some knowledge of the affairs, and
even of the laws of all the States ought to be possessed by the
members from each of the States. How can foreign trade be
properly regulated by uniform laws without some acquaintance

---

* Federalist, p. 411.   † Ibid. 410.   ‡ Hamilton's Works, ii. 319, 322.

with the commerce, the ports, the usages, and the regulations of the different States? How can the trade between the different States be duly regulated, without some knowledge of their relative situations in these and other points? How can taxes be judiciously imposed and effectually collected, if they be not accommodated to the different laws and local circumstances relating to these objects in the different States? How can uniform regulations for the militia be duly provided without a similar knowledge of some internal circumstances by which the States are distinguished from each other? *These are the principal objects of federal legislation.*" ..... "A branch of knowledge which belongs to the acquirements of a federal representative, and which has not been mentioned, is that of foreign affairs." How much these observations are in accordance with the habitual themes of thought in Hamilton's mind is seen in his various writings and in the topics which he had selected for his own pen in the numbers of this work. They are summed up in a single sentence of one of his early concise productions, also entitled "Publius."* Speaking of the high office of a representative in Congress—"to form *useful alliances abroad*—to establish a *wise government at home*—to improve the *internal resources* and *finances* of the nation—would be the generous objects of his care." This number concludes by pointing briefly to the objections "of less importance," to annual elections. Hamilton had recently remarked in the Federal Convention. "There is a medium in every thing. I confess three years is not too long."† This was the term of office in his plan of a Constitution.

Number Fifty four (LIV) is ascribed by Hamilton in his list to Jay. Of the mistake in this ascription an explanation has been given, and from Hamilton's statement, designating the numbers by Madison and not including this, it is to be ascribed on Hamilton's authority to himself. Madison in all his lists claims this number to himself, although the minute of Rush previously quoted would indicate some uncertainty in his own mind. "The single number LIV," this minute states, "shows the name of 'Jay' in *manuscript*, near those initials over which the pen has been *again* drawn, leaving the manuscript initials 'J.M.' as before. In one of the Jefferson lists it is ascribed to Madison, in the other to Jay. In support of his claim to this number Madison remarks—"The paper No. 54 on the subject of the

---

* Hamilton's Works, ii. 161.　　　　† Secret Debates, 151.

Negroes, as comprized in the ratio of representation, was most
likely to be within the share executed by the southern member of the club." In a survey of all the circumstances connected
with the interesting subject of this paper, the probability is in
the opposite direction. The representation of three fifths of the
negroes was a reluctant concession to the Southern States,
"whose unfortunate situation," Hamilton subsequently remarked in the New York Convention, "it is to have a great
part of their population as well as property in blacks." The regulation complained of, he said, "was one result of the spirit of
accommodation which governed the Convention, and without
this indulgence no Union could possibly have been formed." But
imperative as this concession was, it was only the result of frequent negotiation in the Convention; and was a subject of sharp
animadversion when the plan of the Constitution was made
public. Of this animadversion, Hamilton was the especial object.
"The delegate from this State"—Hamilton—(it is charged upon
him) "acceded to it *alone* on the part of the State. With what
right they know best who deputed him; and as the legislature
are now convened, to them I refer him for the present, only
observing, that if he had not the most full and ample power for
what he did; (and I never heard it pretended that he had) I
cannot help thinking it a *most daring insult* offered to the
freemen and *freeholders* of this State, besides being an *unparalleled departure* from his duty to this State, as well as to the
United States."*

The peculiar form in which this subject is presented in this
essay is not a little confirmatory of the probability that it is the
production of a delegate to the General Convention from a
Northern State. It sustains the provision for the representation
of the colored people by stating the argument, as it *"might"* be
urged *"by one of our Southern brethren."* And at the close of
this hypothetical view, adds—*"Such* is the reasoning which an
advocate for the Southern interests *might* employ on this subject. And although it *may appear* to be a *little strained* in *some
points*, on the whole I *must confess*, that it fully *reconciles me*
to the scale of representation which the Convention have established." These qualifying expressions do not seem to be the natural or probable language of a delegate from Virginia. They are
the terms which would naturally and probably be used by a del-

---

* Expositor, No. 1, February 7, 1788.

egate from New York, aware of the force and extent of the Northern popular sentiment, jealous of the assuming temper of the Southern States, and especially jealous of the admission of any portion of the slave population, as the basis of representation, when the Southern field for the extension of slave labor was so disproportionately large, and the cession of a part of it to the Union had been so long, so tenaciously, and so offensively withheld.

If the probability be, that the vindication of this provision of the Constitution would more naturally have proceeded from the representative in the Convention of a Northern State? If it was to be expected, that the *sole* delegate from New York who signed the Constitution, must have felt the strong and difficult necessity of meeting and soothing, as to this *new* unexpected feature of the Constitution, the earnest prejudices of the freemen of this State at that time holding slaves, there is nothing in the opinions or in the political action of Hamilton at any time to diminish, but every thing to increase, this probability. In the earliest preserved production of his pen, when at the age of seventeen, writing "A Full Vindication" of the measures of Congress, warm with his great theme—"the natural rights of mankind" and the value of "civil liberty"—he declares, "All men have one common original, they participate in one common nature, and consequently have one common right. No reason can be assigned why one man should exercise any power or pre-eminence over his fellow creatures more than another, unless they have voluntarily vested him with it." "I consider civil liberty, in a genuine unadulterated sense, as the greatest of terrestrial blessings. I am convinced, that the WHOLE HUMAN race is *entitled* to it; and that it cannot be wrested from them without the *blackest* and *most aggravated guilt*."*—"Civil liberty is only natural liberty, modified and secured by the sanctions of civil society. It is not a thing in its own nature, precarious and *dependent* on *human will* and *caprice*, but it is conformable to the *constitution* of *man*, as well as necessary to the well being of Society." He meant "the WHOLE HUMAN RACE," and looked to the emancipation of the blacks as part of the great sacrifice to be laid by the American people on the Altar of Freedom. When urging upon the Continental Congress in 1779, the raising of several battalions of negroes with the assistance of the Government of

* Hamilton's Works, vol. i. p. 8.

South Carolina, and avowing his opinion, that "the negroes *will make very excellent soldiers*, with proper management," Hamilton uses words that cannot soon be unremembered. "The contempt," he writes to the President of Congress,* "we have been taught to entertain for the blacks, makes us fancy many things that are founded neither in reason nor experience; and an unwillingness to part with property of so valuable a kind, will furnish a thousand arguments to show the impracticability or pernicious tendency of a scheme which requires such sacrifices.... *An essential part of the plan is to give them their freedom with their swords.* This will secure their fidelity, animate their courage and I believe, will have a good influence upon those who remain by *opening* a door to their emancipation. This circumstance, I confess, has no small weight in inducing me to wish to success of the project, for the *dictates of humanity* and *true policy* equally interest me in favor of this unfortunate class of men." Fifteen days after the date of this letter, Congress met its suggestions by recommending to South Carolina (whence a delegate was present urging the measure) and to Georgia "immediately the raising three thousand able bodied negroes" to be commanded by white officers; by assuring a "provision for paying the proprietors of the enlisted negroes a full compensation;" and by declaring, that "every negro who shall well and faithfully serve as a soldier to the end of the present war, and shall then return his arms, be *emancipated;*" and receive a small reward.† The negro population of this country had rarely been a special subject of consideration during the several periods of the war of the Revolution, except in fixing the ratio of contribution by the several States. In the project of a Confederation, submitted by Franklin in 1775, he proposed that the ratio of contribution should be the number of "*male polls* between sixteen and sixty years of age." In the first draft of the Confederation, submitted in 1776, "the number of *inhabitants* of every age, sex, and quality, except Indians not paying taxes in any State," was proposed to be the rule. For this was substituted, a proposition made in 1777, that "the value of all land within each State granted to or surveyed for any person" should be the rule—which was adopted in "The Articles of Confederation." The dif-

---

* Hamilton's Works, i. 61. Ibid. 76, 77. Hamilton to John Jay, President of Congress, March 14, 1779.

† Secret Journals, i. 109.

ficulties of such a valuation led to a proposal, as the basis of contribution—of the proportion of numbers as early contemplated;
but, in this estimate, a compound of freemen and slaves was
suggested. The number of slaves to be embraced became the
disputed question. A vote was at last taken on the ratio "of free
inhabitants and three fifths of all other *inhabitants* of every sex
and condition, exception untaxed Indians;"* when owing to
Hamilton's temporary absence from Congress, the vote of New
York was lost. But, three days after, on *his* motion for a reconsideration, an amendment, offered by *him*, passed; declaring
that the supplies to Congress by the States should be "in proportion to the whole number of white and other free *inhabitants*
of every age, sex, and condition, including those bound to servitude for a term of years, and three fifths of *all other persons*,
not comprehended in the foregoing description, except Indians
not paying taxes in each State,"† the numbers to be triennially
taken. For the word "*inhabitants*," the word "*persons*" was thus
carefully substituted; and from this, it is seen, that the first
express recognition by Congress of the slaves as "*persons*" was
at the instance of Hamilton, a proud and memorable fact in his
history. This resolution was the *first* step towards—in fact, *laid
the basis* of—the recognition by the Constitution of the United
States, of the people of African descent within the United
States—as "*persons*," having representative rights, for Hamilton
then saw, as he subsequently declared in the New York Convention, that "representation and taxation go together, and one
uniform rule ought to apply to both." In the plan of a Constitution reported by the committee of detail, the measure of taxation, provided in the resolution of Hamilton passed in 1783, was
incorporated as that measure. In *his* plan of a Constitution, he
provided, that the direct and capitation taxes should be "proportioned in each State by the whole number of free persons,
except Indians not taxed, and by three fifths of all other persons," thus expunging the term "*white*;" and, in the plan
reported by the committee of revisal, this provision of his plan
of a Constitution, in its precise terms, was made; and became a
part of the Constitution of the United States, in apportioning
"the representatives and direct taxes among the several
States."‡ A final change in the provision of the Constitution

---

* Journal of Congress, viii. 166, March 28, 1783.
† Ibid. 171, April 1, 1783.   ‡ Art. 1. Sec. 2.

with respect to fugitives marks the sense of the general Convention. The plan last reported that "no person *legally held* to service or labor in one State, escaping to another, shall, in consequence of any regulations subsisting therein, be discharged from such service or labor," was so amended as to declare, instead of the terms—no person "*legally held* to service"—no person "held to service or labor in one State *under the laws thereof*." "The laws of a State might hold," but the Convention refrained from declaring, that such holding was "*legal*."

Nor are the facts which have been stated the only facts in evidence of Hamilton's view of the great and since momentous political problem—the condition of the people of African descent—the phrase habitually used by him when speaking in private of this "unfortunate race." In the same spirit of liberty which had asserted with pen and sword the Union and Independence of the whole people of the United States in their individual capacities, having retired from the cabinet of Washington retaining all his confidence, at his instance writing on the subject of the treaty of peace of 1783, Hamilton used these pregnant expressions to show that the freedom once proclaimed and promised to slaves never could be revoked. The last royal Governor of Virginia, Lord Dunmore, had proclaimed freedom to its slaves who should join his standard. England had freed and deported numbers of these slaves, She refused to pay for them. The Virginian member* of Washington's cabinet urged this as an objection to the ratification of the treaty with Great Britain of 1795, which made no provision for such payment. In answer to this objection, when commenting on this refusal, Hamilton remarked as to the freedom promised to the slave—"The grant was *irrevocable*. Nothing in the law of nations or in those of Great Britain will authorize the resumption of liberty once granted to a human being." ..... "In the interpretation of treaties things *odious* or *immoral* are not to be presumed. The abandonment of Negroes who had been induced to quit their masters on the faith of Official Proclamations promising them liberty, to fall again under the yoke of their masters and into slavery, is as *odious* and *immoral* a thing as *can be conceived*. It is odious not only as it imposes an *act of perfidy* on one of the contracting parties, but as it tends to bring back to servitude men once made free. The *general interests of humanity* conspire with the

---

* Edmund Randolph.

obligation which Great Britain had contracted towards the negroes to repel this construction of the treaty, if another can be found." The President of these United States has promised freedom to the slaves of rebels; by an "official Proclamation" he has granted to them that freedom. They are no longer slaves. "The grant" is "irrevocable." That Proclamation—the great event of modern history—is "a contract" which it were "an act of perfidy" not to perform. The wide door to Emancipation—the universal emancipation of the oppressed colored race from a cruel bondage, has been opened. That door never can be, never will be, closed. It has been opened by the law by which we exist as a nation—the righteous law of self-defence—the law of "common defence" proclaimed by the Constitution mandatorily to be "the supreme law of the land," a law acknowledged, interpreted, and recognized in its full extent by the most intelligent of its then adversaries in Virginia.

"It has been repeatedly said here," is the language of Patrick Henry, addressing the Convention of that State, called to consider the Constitution, "It has been repeatedly said here, that the great object of a National Government was national defence." "If they give power to the General Government for the general defence, the means must be commensurate to the end. All the means in the possession of the people must be given to the Government which is intrusted with the public defence.... If the Northern States shall be of opinion, that our Slaves are numberless, they may call forth every national resource. May Congress not say, that *every black man must fight?*.... Have they not power to provide for the general defence and welfare? May they not think that these call for *the abolition of slavery?* May they not pronounce all slaves free, and will they not be warranted by that power? This is no ambiguous implication or logical deduction. The paper" (the Constitution) "speaks to the point. They have the power in clear, unequivocal terms, and will clearly and certainly exercise it." It has been exercised under this very power of "common defence," and ere long the feet of no slave will stain our soil.

This number of the Federalist also relates to the apportionment of the members of the house of representatives among the several States by the same rule with that of direct taxes. Recognizing expressly the fitness of the number of the people being "the standard for regulating the proportion of those who are to represent the people of a State;" and adverting to it as the standard of contribution, this remark is to be noticed. "In the latter, it has reference to the *proportion of wealth,* of which *it is in no case a precise measure,* and in ordinary cases a very unfit one." This observation is in accordance with the opinions before expressed by Hamilton as to a subject which he had well examined. In his previously quoted letter to Governor Clinton in 1783, he remarks, "The proportion of the relative wealth in these States can never be found by *any common measure* whatever." *** "If a general standard must be fixed, numbers were preferable to land.** Both these measures have the common disadvantage of *being no* equal *representative of the wealth of the people,* but one is more simple, definite, and certain than the other." Still, it is remarked in this number; "notwithstanding the *imperfection* of the *rule,* as applied to the *relative wealth* and contributions of the States, it is evidently the least exceptionable among those that are practicable; and had too recently obtained the general sanction of America not to have found a ready preference with the Convention." The objection is then stated, "it does not follow from an admission of numbers for the measure of representation, or of slaves combined with free citizens as a ratio of taxation, that slaves ought to be included in the numerical rule of representation. Slaves are considered as *property,* not as *persons.* They ought therefore to be comprehended in estimates of taxation which are founded on property; and to be excluded from representation which is regulated by a census of *persons.*" Without denying this distinction, the answer is given, as expressing the views which would be preferred by the South—denying that slaves are considered merely as property and in no respect whatever as persons. "They partake of both these qualities, being considered by our laws, in some respects, as persons, and in other respects as property." "The Federal Constitution therefore decides with great propriety on the case of our slaves, when it views them in the mixed character of persons and property." "Would the Convention have been impartial or consistent, if they had rejected the slaves from the list of inhabitants, when the shares of representation were to be calculated, and inserted them on the lists when the tariff of contributions was to be adjusted? Could it be reasonably expected that the Southern States would concur in a system which considered their slaves in some degree as *men* when burdens were to be imposed, but refused to consider them in the same light when advantages were to be conferred? Might not some surprise also be expressed, that those who reproach the Southern States with the barbarous policy of considering as property a part of their human brethren, should themselves contend that the Government, to which all the States are to be parties, ought to consider this unfortunate race more completely in the unnatural light of property, than the very laws of which they complain?".... "Let the compromising expedient of the Constitution be mutually adopted, which regards them as inhabitants, but as debased by servitude below the equal level of free inhabitants, which regards the *slave* as divested of two fifths of the *man.*" Another reason is suggested, that "the votes, allowed in the federal legislature to the people of each State, ought to bear some proportion to the comparative wealth of the State." It may be seen, in the debates of the Convention of New York which soon followed, that one of the earliest urged objections taken was to "the three fifths" compromise, and the answer by Hamilton is almost in the words of this essay. "The best writers on Government have held that representation should be compounded of persons and property."**** "It will, however, be by no means admitted, that the slaves are considered altogether as property, they are *men* though degraded to the condition of slavery. They are *persons* known to the municipal laws of the States which they inhabit, as well as to the laws of nature. But representation and taxation go together, and one uniform rule should be applied to both. Would it be just to compute those slaves in the assessment of taxes and discard them from the estimate in the apportionment of representatives? Would it be just to impose a singular burthen without conferring some adequate advantage?"

The *number* of which the House of Representatives was to consist is the topic of the fifty fifth (LV) essay; claimed also by Hamilton in his list; and by Madison in all his lists. It is here stated;* "that no political problem is less *susceptible of a precise solution,* than that which relates to the *number* most *convenient* for a representative legislature, nor *is there any point* in which *the policy of the several States* is more *at variance.*" A marked coincidence with this passage is seen in another of Hamilton's briefs. It is there stated—"*nothing more difficult* than to *fix the degree of numbers requisite. Constitutions of States differ.*" In this number, it is also observed;† "that the *ratio* between the

---

* Federalist, p. 422

† Ibid. p. 423.

representatives and the people *ought not to be the same,* where
the latter are *very numerous,* as where they are *very few."* In
this brief, it is said; *"Ratio ought not to be the same* in a *large*
as in a *small* nation." In this number, it is remarked;* "In all
very numerous assemblies, of whatever characters composed,
passion never fails to wrest the sceptre from reason. Had every
Athenian been a Socrates; every Athenian assembly would still
have been a mob." So in Hamilton's manuscript notes;† "The
assembly when chosen will meet in one room, if they are drawn
from half the globe, and will be liable to all *the passions of popular assemblies."* In this number it is also observed; "At the
expiration of *twenty five years,* according to the computed rate
of increase, the number of representatives will amount *to two
hundred;* and of *fifty years* to *four hundred."*‡ In Hamilton's
brief, "The first Census 100—25 years, 200—50 years, 400."

In the Fifty Sixth (LVI) number; also claimed by Hamilton in
his list, and by Madison in all his lists, it is observed,§ "What
are to be the objects of federal legislation? Those which are of
most importance, and which seem most to require local knowledge, are *commerce, taxation,* and *the militia;"* (a repetition of
the same observation in number Fifty three), and it is added,‖
"the representatives of each State will not only bring with them,
a considerable knowledge of its laws, and a *local knowledge* of
their respective districts." In Hamilton's brief are found these
heads; *"Knowledge of local circumstances*—Objects to be considered. These—*Commerce—Taxation."* "As to *taxation—State
Systems."*

In essay number Fifty seven (LVII); also claimed by Hamilton in his list, and by Madison in all his lists, this passage is
seen;¶ "Let me now ask, what there is in the Constitution of the
House of Representatives, that violates the principles of Republican government, or favors the *elevation of the few* on the ruins
of the many?" "Who are to be the electors**—Not the rich more
than the poor." *"No qualification of wealth—of birth,"* &c. In
Hamilton's brief,—*"Elevation of few.* First—*No qualifications*
either for *electors or elected."* It is also stated in this number;**
"This cannot be said without maintaining, that *five or six thousand* citizens, are *less capable of choosing a fit* representative,
or more liable to be corrupted by an unfit one, than *five or six*

* Federalist, p. 424.   † Hamilton's MSS. vol. i. p. 66.
‡ Federalist, p. 425.   § Ibid. 430.
‖ Ibid. 431.   ¶ Ibid. 435.   ** Ibid. 438.

hundred." In Hamilton's brief; "*Five thousand not less fit to choose than five hundred—*not so *easily corrupted.*"

Nor ought this remark as to New York, to be unnoticed. "The members of Assembly, for the *cities* and *counties* of New York and Albany, are *elected* by very nearly as many *voters* as will be entitled to a representative in Congress, calculating on the number of sixty five representatives only."* The least reflection will pronounce, that it is not probable, but that it is indeed extremely improbable, that so minute a knowledge of such a matter as the number of voters in two distant localities of a distant State, should have been so positively stated—or even adverted to at all, by Madison—a resident of Virginia. That Hamilton was familiar with these facts is to be ascribed to his residence both in New York, and in Albany; and to the several questions which necessarily presented themselves to him during his very recent service in the legislature of New York.†

The Fifty eighth (LVIII) number, claimed by Hamilton in his list, and by Madison in all of his lists—answers a supposition "that the number of members of the House of Representatives, *will not be augmented* from time to time, as the progress of population may demand;"‡ and it is inferred, "that the larger States will be strenuous advocates for increasing the number and weight of that part of the legislature in which their influence predominates," from the fact that this branch of the legislature is a representation of citizens, and consequently the larger States will in it have most weight.

In Hamilton's brief this note is seen; "*Numbers will not be augmented;*" and the objection is answered, "*Large States to increase influence will be for increasing representatives.*" How solicitous his convictions were on the importance of an adequately large representation of the people in one branch of the legislature, may be seen in a report of a recent debate in the Federal Convention.§ Hamilton "expressed himself with great earnestness and anxiety in favor of the motion," to increase its numbers. "He avowed himself a friend to a vigorous government, but would declare at the same time, he held it essential that the popular branch of it should be on a broad foundation. He was seriously of opinion, that the House of Representatives

* Federalist, p. 439.

† He was in 1787, a member of the Committee of Ways and Means.—*Hist. Rep.* iii. 211.

‡ Federalist, 441.   § Madison Papers, iii. 1531.

9

was on so narrow a scale, as to be really dangerous; and to warrant a jealousy in the people, for their liberties. He remarked, that the connection between the President and Senate would tend to perpetuate him, by corrupt influence. It was the more necessary on this account, that a numerous representation in the other branch of the legislature should be established." The limitation in the Constitution, that "the number of representatives shall not exceed one for every thirty thousand," instead of forty thousand persons, was the last act of the convention previous to the vote for the adoption of the Constitution, and was made at the request of Washington from his seat as President of the body.

The Sixty second (LXII) and Sixty third (LXIII) essays, are the now remaining numbers in question. Hamilton claims them in his list, and Madison in all of his lists. These numbers treat of "the constitution of the Senate with regard to the qualifications of the members; the manner of appointing them; the equality of representation; the number of the Senators, and the duration of their appointments."

The first head of this subject is briefly noticed;—and the two others, admitted to have been the results of an unavoidable compromise between the larger and the smaller States, are not dwelt upon. The "number of the Senators and the duration of their appointments" are more fully discussed in the several points of view in which the utility of the second branch of the legislative department would present themselves. It may be observed, that Madison's original view was, that the second branch should be chosen by the first branch of the legislature. Hamilton from the outset contended for an independent body of men to be chosen by electors to be chosen by the people. Madison, however, felt the importance of its consisting "of a more select number, holding their appointments for a longer term" than the members of the other branch, and "going out in rotation," precautions the more necessary as he then thought of lodging in this branch a "negative on the State laws." Hamilton's plan of a Constitution was in accordance with his earliest opinion, and he is seen to have urged on the General Convention, as to the second branch of the legislature, that "their *duration* should be the earnest of *wisdom* and *stability*." Both these characteristics are considered in the discussion in these two numbers of this head of the subject—"the duration of the Senate?" "Without a select and *stable* member of the government,* the esteem of foreign powers will be" forfeited. This idea is expressed by him in the Convention. "Foreigners are jealous of our increasing greatness, and would rejoice in our distractions. Those who have had opportunities of conversing with foreigners respecting sovereigns in Europe, have discovered in them an anxiety for the preservation of our democratic Governments, probably for no other reason but to keep us weak. Unless your government is respectable, foreigners will invade your rights, and to maintain tranquillity it must be respectable—even to observe neutrality you must have a strong government." To maintain this tranquillity, his plan of government provided that, "the Senate shall exclusively possess the power of declaring war"—and that "no treaty shall be made without their advice and consent."

The value of a Senate in insuring the other important characteristic—"stability"—in the policy of a government is fully stated. "The objects of government may be divided into two general classes; the one depending on measures which have singly an *immediate* and *sensible* operation; the other depending on a *succession* of well chosen and *well connected* measures, which have a gradual and perhaps unobserved operation. The importance of the latter description to the collective and permanent welfare of every country needs no explanation. And yet it is evident, that an assembly elected for so short a term as to be unable to provide more than one or two links in a chain of measures, on which the general welfare may essentially depend, ought not to be answerable for the final result. The proper remedy for this defect, must be an additional body in the legislative department, which, having a sufficient *permanency* to provide for such objects as require a continued attention and a train of measures, may be justly and effectually answerable for the attainment of those objects." "The necessity of a Senate," it is stated, "is not less indicated by the propensity of all single and numerous assemblies to yield to the impulse of sudden and violent passions and to be seduced by *factious leaders* into intemperate and pernicious counsels." This objection to a single body has been quoted from Hamilton's MSS. notes, and the dangers from "factious leaders" is pointed to in his brief in the General Convention, that "*demagogues* will generally *prevail*." The importance of a Senate, as "a defence to the people against their own *temporary errors* and *delusions*" is also set forth in confor-

* Federalist, p. 474.

mity with the language of his brief. "There ought to be a principle in Government capable of *resisting the* popular current;" and
it is here added, "There are particular moments in public affairs,
when the people, stimulated by some *irregular passion*, or some
illicit advantage, or misled by the artful representations of interested men, will call for measures which they themselves will
afterwards be the most ready to lament and condemn." In his
brief,* it is stated—"Popular assemblies governed by a few individuals—the most popular branch will acquire an influence over
the other. The other may check in ordinary cases, in which there
is no *strong public passion*, but it will not in cases where there
is." Most happily for the people of this country, under the guid-
ance of Washington, with the systematic counsels of Hamilton,
the "irregular passions of the people misled by the artful representations of interested men," calling "for measures which they
themselves have afterwards been the most ready to lament and
condemn," were checked by "the interference of a temperate
and respectable body of citizens"—by the "wisdom and stability"
of the Senate of the United States.

Number Sixty four (LXIV.) is the last of the numbers as to
which there have been discrepant claims. In the second of Madison's lists, he claims this number to himself, reducing the contributions of Jay to *four* numbers, but, *after the publication of a
life of Jay*, which ascribes to him this number, as previously
stated; Madison relinquished this claim;† and in his other lists
adds it to the numbers by Jay. Hamilton in his list gives to Jay
his *full* number of *five* essays, but attributes to him, by a mistake of the pen as explained, *fifty four* instead of *sixty four*, of
which the evidence that Jay was the author has been recently
ascertained.‡ The enquiry may arise how it happened that, after

* Hamilton's Works, ii. 414.

† In the paper entitled The Federalist, by Madison, previously quoted, is
this passage—"He" (Hamilton) "ascribes to himself No. 64, written by Mr.
Jay, and to Mr. Jay No.   (the blank is there), written not by himself,
but by J. M. [See Life of Mr. Jay by Delaplaine."]

‡ In reply to a note of November 27th, 1863, addressed by me to Mr. John
Jay, a grandson of Governor Jay, stating, if there were "any family papers
relating to the Federalist which you would desire me to use in my edition,
you will oblige me by an early note." He answered, December 1, 1863, "The
other day I chanced upon a bundle of miscellaneous papers which contained
Jay's numbers of the Federalist, or three of them in his own hand, and these
I will get for you in a day or two." The draughts were of two of the early
papers and of No. 64.

so long an interval between the last of the numbers from the pen of Jay, he should have been the author of only one more number. That he offered to write this number, is not to be supposed. The probability is, its topic being the constitutional deposit and office of the treaty power, that it was written by him at the request of Hamilton, made in deference to his distinguished services as the chief negotiator of the treaty of peace with Great Britain, whose great conduct on that occasion Hamilton had defended in Congress.

The investigation of the authorship of the several essays having been finished, and the pledge "to state all the evidence known to exist to designate the respective contributions to it," being fulfilled, I will not in closing this paper withhold the renewed declaration of my conviction that the attribution by Hamilton of its numbers to the respective writers of them is, with one exception, entirely correct. This being so, it will be seen that the parts of each individual in the several topics of the work were these. Hamilton wrote the first essay, which, after an avowal of his solicitude for the adoption of the Constitution, and an indication of the apprehended sources of opposition to it, gives a programme of the work. The interesting particulars proposed to be discussed are stated—*"The utility of the* UNION *to your political prosperity: The insufficiency of the present confederation to preserve that Union: The necessity of a government at least equally energetic with the one proposed to the attainment of that object: The conformity of the proposed Constitution to the true principles of republican government: Its analogy to your own State Constitution: and lastly, the additional security which its adoption will afford to the preservation of that species of government,—to liberty and to property."*

It is seen; that Jay in the four succeeding numbers, exhibited "the dangers from *foreign* force and influence," and that his remaining number relates to the treaty power—these being the topics with which, as Embassador to Spain and to France, and as then Secretary of *foreign* affairs, he would be familiar. Madison took a larger and more varied part; some of his essays being supplementary to those by Hamilton—one, on the dangers of faction and the provisions against it, continued from a previous number by Hamilton—another on a distinct topic, being an answer to "an objection drawn from the extent of country"—a joint contribution with Hamilton in three numbers, on the subject of the tendency of Federal governments rather

to anarchy among the members than tyranny in the head; these
three numbers merely adducing historical examples to confirm
this view—two numbers, "concerning the difficulties which the
Convention must have experienced in the formation of a proper
plan;"—two numbers, shewing "the conformity of the plan to
republican principles, with an answer to an objection in respect
to the powers of the Constitution"—four numbers, giving "a
general view of the powers proposed to be vested in the
Union;"—two numbers, being "a discussion of the supposed danger from the powers of the Union to the State governments,
with an examination of the comparative means of influence of
the Federal and State governments"—and two; his last numbers, on "the meaning of the maxim which requires a separation of the departments of power with a view of the means of
giving efficacy in practice to that maxim"—in the whole, *three*
conjoint and *fourteen* other numbers. The residue, being the
great body of the work, is Hamilton's. His essays, beside a
delineation of its scope and leading topics, are directed to their
primary object—a comprehensive manifestation of the value of
the UNION—of the union of the People of the United States
under one firm National Government. They commence, with an
exposition of the causes which would induce the States, if disunited, to make war upon each other, followed by a detail of
the consequences which would attend such a situation;—the
"producing standing armies and other institutions unfriendly to
liberty"—and by an argued presentation of "the UTILITY of the
Union as a safeguard against domestic faction and *insurrection*"—of its "utility in respect to Commerce and a Navy," and
of "its tendency to promote the interests of revenue, and as
connected with it—that of economy." Then follows the great
topic, in contrast, so long the burthen of his thoughts and previous writings—a full exhibition of the "Defects of the Confederation, in relation to the Principle of legislation for the States
in their collective capacities," illustrated by examples to shew
"the tendency of Federal Governments rather to anarchy
among the members than to tyranny in the head"—a subject
commenced by Hamilton and jointly illustrated by Madison. Its
other *defects* are next pourtrayed; "the total want of a sanction
to its laws"—"the want of a mutual guarantee of the State governments"—"the principle of regulating the contributions of the
States to the common treasury by QUOTAS," with observations
to prove "the importance and advantage of authorizing the

national government to raise its own revenues in its own way"—"the want of a power to regulate commerce"—"the want of a direct and effective power of raising armies"—"the right of equal suffrage among the States," condemned by "every idea of proportion and every rule of fair representation," and exposing the government to be "obstructed at critical seasons"—the crowning defect—"the want of a Judiciary power"—the "improper organization of Congress—as a single body"—and the absence of "a ratification of the existing Federal system by the People." The exposure of these *defects* is naturally followed by a large and powerful argument of "the necessity of a government at least equally energetic," and by "an answer to the objection concerning standing armies," shewing the necessity of a government having within itself the means of national defence, and exhibiting "the securities to liberty provided in the Constitution, and those also resulting from the less frequent necessity of using force, than would be that of separate Confederacies; and from the checks to aggressions upon it in the power of the State Governments."

This discussion is appropriately succeeded by an argument of the necessary "power" in a Government charged with the common defence "of regulating the militia." The natural sequence to this argument is, the evincing the necessity of "the power of taxation to provide for the support of the national forces," by procuring revenue to the full extent of the national exigencies, leaving to the States "an independent and uncontrollable authority to raise their own revenues for the supply of their own wants," which involved an exposition of the interesting topic— the extent of the alienation under the Constitution of the "rights of State sovereignty,"—the great and tangent difficulty of that and of all future time until the Constitution, unless amended, shall expire,—and a refutation of the alleged conflict with State rights in the grant of power to the general government "to make all laws necessary and proper for carrying into execution the powers vested in it by the Constitution," and of the provision, "that the Constitution and the laws of the United States made in pursuance of it, and the treaties made by its authority shall be the supreme law of the land." A defence of the grant of a general power of taxation, as least burthensome to the people in its economical operation, and least likely to be carried to excess, closes the first original volume of the series, ending with its thirty sixth number.

Having next exhibited the impolicy of the project in Virginia and of the provision in Pennsylvania, for altering or *correcting breaches* of a Constitution by *occasional* or *periodical* conventions, Hamilton proceeds to show—instead of "exterior provisions for maintaining in practice the necessary partition of power among the several departments" of a government—that the true mode is "by so contriving its interior structure, as that its several constituent parts may, by their mutual relations, be the means of keeping each other in their proper places." The elucidation of this view, in the symmetrical stages of this discussion, led to "a more particular examination of the several parts of the government," beginning with the House of Representatives, followed by a view of the Constitution of the Senate—of that of the President, and closing with that of the judicial department—the last number relative thereto being an answer to "an objection raised against the Constitution with most success"—its "want of a constitutional provision for the trial by jury in civil cases." These examinations are much extended, and are pregnant with a practical philosophy, of which the conclusions are regarded in this country as maxims, and have served as early controlling guides in the formation of subsequent State Constitutions, since not always followed.

It has been seen, that "the commentary on the Executive branch of the Government" was completed by Hamilton and published on the fourth of April, 1788. The intelligence soon after received from South Carolina shewed that the policy resorted to in Massachusetts to induce there an unconditional adoption of the Constitution—the promise of subsequent amendments—had also been resorted to in that Southern State. One of the chief grounds of objection to be removed by such amendments was the want of a formal "bill of rights." This objection is answered in the last essay but one; by a recital of various provisions of the Constitution,—especially, "the establishment of the writ of *Habeas Corpus*—the prohibition of *ex post facto* laws, and of titles to nobility"—and by declaring that "the Constitution is in itself in every rational sense, and to every useful purpose—A BILL OF RIGHTS." The vindication of the Constitution is concluded by Hamilton with this brief summary—"The additional securities to republican government, to liberty and to property, to be derived from the adoption of the plan under consideration, consist chiefly in the restraints which the PRESERVATION of the UNION will impose on local factions and insurrections, and on the ambition of powerful individuals in single States, who might acquire credit and influence enough, from leaders and favorites, to become the DESPOTS of the people; in the diminution of the opportunities to foreign intrigue, which the dissolution of the Confederacy would invite and facilitate; in the prevention of extensive military establishments, which could not fail to grow out of wars between the States in a disunited situation; in the express guarantee of a republican form of Government to each; in the absolute and universal exclusion of titles of nobility; and in the precautions against the repetition of those practices on the part of the State governments, which have undermined the foundations of property and credit, have planted mutual distrust in the breasts of all classes of citizens, and have occasioned an almost universal prostration of morals."

Having "thus executed the task" of the Federalist, these Essays conclude with a decisive argument "of the extreme imprudence of insisting upon amendments *previous* to the adoption of the Constitution," thus "to prolong the precarious state of the national affairs, and to expose the Union to the jeopardy of successive experiments, in the chimerical pursuit of a perfect plan," and with a solemn appeal "against hazarding anarchy— CIVIL WAR—a perpetual alienation of the States from each other, and perhaps the military despotism of a victorious demagogue in the pursuit of what they are not likely to obtain, but from TIME and EXPERIENCE." "I dread the more," Hamilton declares in the last words of the Federalist, addressed to the People of the State of New York, "I dread the more the consequences of new attempts, because I KNOW that POWERFUL INDIVIDUALS, in this and other States, are enemies to a General National Government, in *every possible shape.*"

A critical analysis of this work is not within the province of this notice, but it cannot escape observation, in addition to the contributions of its other eminent writers, how much of its varied value must be ascribed to the varied properties of the mind of Hamilton—the headspring—as a scholar, a soldier, a jurist, a legislator, a political economist, and a statesman, each uniting its tributes in singular harmony to the great argument of the proposed grand result—the inducing the institution of a free, vigorous, yet moderate Government, to bind together in an indissoluble bond the people of the United States, by a Constitution ordained and established by themselves.

"A NATION without a NATIONAL GOVERNMENT is, in my view," he declared, "an awful spectacle. The establishment of a Constitution, in time of profound peace, by the voluntary consent of a whole people, is a PRODIGY, to the completion of which I look forward with trembling anxiety."

THE CONTINENTALIST.

NUMBER I.

JULY 12, 1781.

IT would be the extreme of vanity in us, not to be sensible, that we began this revolution with very vague and confined notions of the practical business of government. To the greater part of us it was a novelty; of those who under the former constitution had had opportunities of acquiring experience, a large proportion adhered to the opposite side, and the remainder can only be supposed to have possessed ideas adapted to the narrow colonial sphere, in which they had been accustomed to move, not of that enlarged kind suited to the government of an independent nation.

There were, no doubt, exceptions to these observations; men in all respects qualified for conducting the public affairs with skill and advantage; but their number was small—they were not always brought forward in our councils; and when they were, their influence was too commonly borne down by the prevailing torrent of ignorance and prejudice.

On a retrospect, however, of our transactions, under the disadvantages with which we commenced, it is perhaps more to be wondered at that we have done so well, than that we have not done better. There are, indeed, some traits in our conduct, as conspicuous for sound policy, as others for magnanimity. But, on the other hand, it must also be confessed, there have been many false steps, many chimerical projects and utopian speculations, in the management of our civil as well as of our military affairs. A part of these were the natural effects of the spirit of the times, dictated by our situation. An extreme jealousy of power is the attendant on all popular revolutions, and has seldom been without its evils. It is to this source we are to trace many of the fatal mistakes, which have so deeply endangered the common cause; particularly that defect which will be the object of these remarks—A want of power in Congress.

The present Congress, respectable for abilities and integrity, by experience convinced of the necessity of change, are preparing several important articles, to be submitted to the respective States, for augmenting the powers of the Confederation. But though there is hardly at this time a man of information in America, who will not acknowledge, as a general proposition, that in its present form, it is unequal, either to a vigorous prosecution of the war, or to the preservation of the Union in peace; yet when the principle comes to be applied to practice, there seems not to be the same agreement in the modes of remedying the defect; and it is to be feared from a disposition which appeared in some of the States, on a late occasion, that the salutary intentions of Congress may meet with more delay and opposition, than the critical posture of the States will justify.

It will be attempted to show, in a course of papers, what ought to be done, and the mischiefs of a contrary policy.

In the first stages of the controversy, it was excusable to err. Good intentions, rather than great skill, were to have been expected from us. But we have now had sufficient time for reflection, and experience as ample as unfortunate, to rectify our errors. To persist in them becomes disgraceful, and even criminal, and belies that character of good sense, and a quick discernment of our interests, which, in spite of our mistakes, we have been hitherto allowed. It will prove, that our sagacity is limited to interests of inferior moment, and that we are incapable of those enlightened and liberal views, necessary to make us a great and flourishing people.

History is full of examples, where in contests for liberty, a jealousy of power has either defeated the attempts to recover, or preserve it, in the first instance, or has afterwards subverted it by clogging government with too great precautions for its felicity, or by leaving too wide a door for sedition and popular licentiousness. In a government framed for durable liberty, not less regard must be paid to giving the magistrate a proper degree of authority, to make and execute the laws with vigor, than to guard against encroachments upon the rights of the community. As too much power leads to despotism, too little leads to anarchy, and both, eventually, to the ruin of the people. These are maxims well known, but never sufficiently attended to, in adjusting the frames of governments. Some momentary interest or passion is sure to give a wrong bias, and pervert the most favorable opportunities.

No friend to order or to rational liberty, can read without pain and disgust, the history of the Commonwealths of Greece. Generally speaking, they were a constant scene of the alternate tyranny of one part of the people over the other, or a few usurping demagogues over the whole. Most of them had been originally governed by kings, whose despotism (the natural disease of monarchy) had obliged their subjects to murder, expel, depose, or reduce them to a nominal existence, and institute popular governments. In these governments, that of Sparta excepted, the jealousy of power hindered the people from trusting out of their own hands a competent authority, to maintain the repose and stability of the commonwealth; whence originated the frequent revolutions and civil broils, with which they were distracted. This, and the want of a solid federal union to restrain the ambition and rivalship of the different cities, after a rapid succession of bloody wars, ended in their total loss of liberty, and subjugation to foreign powers.

In comparison of our governments with those of the ancient republics, we must, without hesitation, give the preference to our own; because every power with us is exercised by representation, not in tumultuary assemblies of the collective body of the people, where the art or impudence of the *Orator* or *Tribune*, rather than the utility or justice of the measure could seldom fail to govern. Yet, whatever may be the advantage on our side, in such a comparison, men who estimate the value of institutions, not from prejudices of the moment, but from experience and reason, must be persuaded that the same *jealousy of power* has prevented our reaping all the advantages, from the examples of other nations, which we ought to have done, and has rendered our Constitutions in many respects feeble and imperfect.

Perhaps the evil is not very great in respect to our State Constitutions; for notwithstanding their imperfections, they may, for some time, be made to operate in such a manner, as to answer the purposes of the common defence, and the maintenance of order; and they seem to have in themselves, and in the progress of society, among us, the seeds of improvement.

But this is not the case with respect to the Federal Government; if it is too weak at first, it will continually grow weaker. The ambition and local interests of the respective members, will be constantly undermining and usurping upon its prerogatives, till it comes to a dissolution; if a partial combination of some of the more powerful ones does not bring it to a more *speedy* and *violent end.*

THE CONTINENTALIST.

NUMBER II.

JULY 19, 1781.

IN a single state, where the sovereign power is exercised by delegation, whether it be a limited monarchy or a republic, the danger most
commonly is, that the sovereign will become too powerful for his con-
stitutents; in fœderal governments where different states are represented in a general council, the danger is on the other side—that the
members will be an overmatch for the common head; or in other words,
that it will not have sufficient influence and authority to secure the obedience of the several parts of the Confederacy.

In a single state, the sovereign has the whole legislative power as
well as the command of the national forces, of course an immediate con-
troul over the persons and property of the subjects,—every other
power is subordinate and dependent. If he undertakes to subvert the
constitution, it can only be preserved by a general insurrection of the
people. The magistrates of the provinces, counties, or towns, into which
the state is divided, having only an executive and police jurisdiction, can
take no decisive measures for counteracting the first indications of
tyranny; but must content themselves with the ineffectual weapon of
petition and remonstrance. They cannot raise money, levy troops, nor
form alliances. The leaders of the people must wait till their discontents
have ripened into a general revolt, to put them in a situation to confer
the powers, necessary for their defence. It will always be difficult for
this to take place; because the sovereign possessing the appearance and
forms of legal authority, having the forces and revenues of the state at
his command, and a large party among the people besides, which with
those advantages he can hardly fail to acquire—he will too often be able
to baffle the first motions of the discontented, and prevent that union
and concert essential to the success of their opposition.

The security therefore of the public liberty, must consist in such a
distribution of the sovereign power, as will make it morally impossible
for one part to gain an ascendency over the others, or for the whole to
unite in a scheme of usurpation.

In fœderal Governments, each member has a distinct sovereignty, makes and executes laws, imposes taxes, distributes justice, and exercises every other function of government. It has always within itself the means of revenue. And on an emergency can levy forces. If the common sovereign should meditate or attempt any thing unfavourable to the general liberty, each member having all the proper organs of power, can prepare for defence with celerity and vigour. Each can immediately sound the alarm to the others, and enter into leagues for mutual protection. If the combination is general, as is to be expected, the usurpers will soon find themselves without the means of recruiting their treasury, or their armies; and for want of continued supplies of men and money, must, in the end fall a sacrifice to the attempt. If the combination is not general, it will imply that some of the members are interested in that which is the cause of dissatisfaction to others, and this cannot be an attack upon the common liberty, but upon the interests of one part in favour of another part; and it will be a war between the members of the fœderal union with each other, not between them and the fœderal government. From the plainest principles of human nature, two inferences are to be drawn, one, that each member of a political confederacy, will be more disposed to advance its own authority upon the ruins of that of the confederacy, than to make any improper concession in its favour, or support it in unreasonable pretensions—the other, that the subjects of each member, will be more devoted in their attachments and obedience to their own particular governments, than to that of the union.

It is the temper of societies as well as of individuals to be impatient of constraint, and to prefer partial to general interest. Many cases may occur, where members of a confederacy have, or seem to have an advantage in things contrary to the good of the whole, or a disadvantage in others conducive to that end. The selfishness of every part will dispose each to believe, that the public burdens are unequally apportioned, and that itself is the victim. These, and other circumstances, will promote a disposition for abridging the authority of the fœderal government; and the ambition of men in office in each state, will make them glad to encourage it. They think their own consequence connected with the power of the government of which they are a part; and will endeavour to increase the one as the mean of increasing the other.

The particular governments will have more empire over the minds of their subjects than the general one, because their agency will be more direct, more uniform, and more apparent. The people will be habituated to look up to them as the arbiters and guardians of their personal concerns, by which the passions of the vulgar, if not of all men are most strongly affected; and in every differences with the confederated body will side with them against the common sovereign.

Experience confirms the truth of these principles.—The chief cities of Greece had once their council of Amphyctions, or States-general, with authority to decide and compose the differences of the several cities; and to transact many other important matters relative to the common interest and safety. At their first institution, they had great weight and

credit; but never enough to preserve effectually the balance and harmony of the confederacy; and in time their decrees only served as an
additional pretext to that side, whose pretensions they favoured. When
the cities were not engaged in foreign wars, they were at perpetual
variance among themselves. Sparta and Athens contended twenty seven
years for the precedence, or rather dominion of Greece, till the former
made herself mistress of the whole; and till in subsequent struggles,
having had recourse to the pernicious expedient of calling in the aid of
foreign enemies; the Macedonians first, and afterwards the Romans
became their masters.

The German diet had formerly more authority than it now has,
though like that of Greece never enough to hinder the great potentates
from disturbing the repose of the empire, and mutually wasting their
own territories and people.

The Helvetic league is another example. It is true it has subsisted
near five hundred years; but in that period the cantons have had
repeated and furious wars with each other, which would have made
them an easy prey to their more powerful neighbours, had not the
reciprocal jealousy of these prevented either from taking advantage of
their dissentions. This and their poverty have hitherto saved them from
total destruction, and kept them from feeling the miseries of foreign
conquest, added to those of civil war. The fœderal government is too
weak to hinder their renewal, whenever the ambition or fanaticism of
the principal cantons shall be disposed to rekindle the flame. For some
time past indeed, it has been in a great measure nominal; the Protestants and Catholics have had separate diets, to manage almost all matters of importance; so that in fact, the general diet is only kept up to
regulate the affairs of the common bailliages and preserve a semblance
of union; and even this, it is probable would cease, did not the extreme
weakness of the cantons, oblige them to a kind of coalition.

If the divisions of the United Provinces have not proceeded to equal
extremities, there are peculiar causes to be assigned. The authority of
the Stadt-holder pervades the whole frame of the republic, and is a kind
of common link by which the provinces are bound together. The jealousy of his progressive influence, in which more or less they all agree,
operates as a check upon their ill-humors against one another. The
inconsiderableness of each province separately, and the imminent danger to which the whole would be exposed of being overrun by their
neighbors, in case of disunion, is a further preservative against the
phrenzy of hostility; and their importance and even existence depending
entirely upon frugality, industry and commerce; peace, both at home
and abroad, is of necessity the predominant object of their policy.

THE CONTINENTALIST.

NUMBER III.

AUGUST 9, 1781.

THE situation of these states is very unlike that of the United Provinces. Remote as we are from Europe, in a little time we should fancy ourselves out of the reach of attempts from abroad, and in full liberty, at our leisure and convenience to try our strength at home. This might not happen at once; but if the FŒDERAL GOVERNMENT SHOULD LOSE ITS AUTHORITY it would CERTAINLY FOLLOW. Political societies, in close neighbourhood, must either be strongly united under one government or there will infallibly exist emulations and quarrels. This is in human nature; and we have no reason to think ourselves wiser, or better than other men. Some of the larger states, a small number of years hence, will be in themselves populous, rich and powerful, in all those circumstances calculated to inspire ambition and nourish ideas of separation and independence. Though it will ever be their true interest to preserve the union, their vanity and self importance, will be very likely to overpower that motive, and make them seek to place themselves at the head of particular confederacies, independent of the general one. A schism once introduced, competitions of boundary and rivalships of commerce will easily afford pretexts for war.

European powers may have many inducements for fomenting these divisions and playing us off against each other: But without such a disposition in them, if separations once take place, we shall, of course, embrace different interests and connections. The particular confederacies, leaguing themselves with rival nations, will naturally be involved in their disputes; into which they will be the more readily tempted by the hope of making acquisitions upon each other, and upon the colonies of the powers with whom they are respectively at enmity.

WE ALREADY SEE SYMPTOMS OF THE EVILS TO BE APPREHENDED. In the midst of a war for our existence as a nation; in the midst of dangers too serious to be trifled with, some of the states have evaded, or

10

refused, compliance with the demands of Congress in points of the greatest moment to the common safety. If they act such a part at this perilous juncture, what are we to expect in a time of peace and security? Is it not to be feared that the resolutions of Congress would soon become like the decisions of the Greek Amphyctions, or like the edicts of a German diet?

But as these evils are at a little distance, we may perhaps be insensible and short-sighted enough to disregard them. There are others that threaten our immediate safety. Our whole system is in disorder; our currency depreciated, till in many places it will hardly obtain a circulation at all—public credit at its lowest ebb—our army deficient in numbers and unprovided with every thing—the government in its present condition, unable to command the means to pay, clothe, or feed their troops—the enemy making an alarming progress in the southern states, lately in complete possession of two of them, though now in part rescued by the genius and exertions of a General without an army—a force under Cornwallis still formidable to Virginia.

We ought to blush to acknowledge that this is a true picture of our situation, when we reflect, that the enemy's whole force in the United States, including their American levies and the late reinforcement, is little more than fourteen thousand effective men;—that our population, by recent examination, has been found to be greater, than at the commencement of the war—that the quantity of our specie has also increased—that the country abounds with all the necessaries of life, and has a sufficiency of foreign commodities, with a considerable and progressive commerce—that we have beyond comparison a better stock of war-like materials, than when we began the contest, and an ally, as willing, as able, to supply our further wants. And that we have on the spot five thousand auxiliary troops, paid and subsisted by that ally, to assist in our defence.

Nothing but a GENERAL DISAFFECTION of the PEOPLE, or MISMANAGEMENT in their RULERS, can account for the figure we make, and for the distresses and perplexities we experience, contending against so small a force.

Our enemies themselves must now be persuaded that the first is not the cause, and we KNOW it is not. The most decided attachment of the people could alone have made them endure, without a convulsion, the successive shocks in our currency, added to the unavoidable inconveniences of war. There is perhaps not another nation in the world, that would have shown equal patience and perseverance in similar circumstances. The enemy have now tried the temper of almost every part of America; and they can hardly produce in their ranks a thousand men, who, without their arts and seductions, have voluntarily joined their standard. The miseries of a rigorous captivity, may perhaps have added half as many more to the number of the American levies, at this time in their armies. This small accession of force is the more extraordinary, as they have at some periods, been apparently in the full tide of success, while every thing wore an aspect tending to infuse despondency into the people of this country. This has been remarkably the case in the southern states.

They for a time had almost undisturbed possession of two of them; and Cornwallis, after overrunning a great part of a third; after two victorious battles, only brought with him into Virginia about two hundred tories—in the state where he thought himself so well established, that he presumptuously ventured to assure the minister, there was not a rebel left, a small body of continental troops, have been so effectually seconded by the militia of that vanquished country, as to have been able to capture a number of his troops more than equal to their own, and to repossess the principal part of the state.

As in the explanation of our embarrassments nothing can be alleged to the disaffection of the people, we must have recourse to the other cause—of IMPOLICY and MISMANAGEMENT in their RULERS.

Where the blame of this may lie is not so much the question as what are the proper remedies; yet it may not be amiss to remark that too large a share has fallen upon Congress. That body is no doubt chargeable with mistakes; but perhaps, its greatest has been too much readiness to make concessions of the powers implied in its original trust. This is partly to be attributed to an excessive complaisance to the spirit, which has evidently actuated a majority of the states,—a desire of monopolizing all power in themselves. Congress have been responsible for the administration of affairs, without the means of fulfilling that responsibility.

It would be too severe a reflection upon us to suppose, that a disposition to make the most of the friendship of others, and to exempt ourselves from a full share of the burthens of the war has had any part in the backwardness, which has appeared in many of the states, to confer powers and adopt measures adequate to the exigency. Such a sentiment would neither be wise, just, generous nor honourable; nor do I believe the accusation would be well founded, yet our conduct makes us liable to a suspicion of this sort. It is certain, however, that too sanguine expectations from Europe have unintentionally relaxed our efforts, by diverting a sense of danger, and begetting an opinion that the inequality of the contest would make every campaign the last.

We did not consider how difficult it must be to exhaust the resources of a nation circumstanced like that of Great Britain; whose government has always been distinguished for energy, and its people for enthusiasm. Nor did we in estimating the superiority of our friends make sufficient allowance for that want of concert, which will ever characterize the operations of allies, or for the immense advantage to the enemy, of having their forces, though inferior, under a single direction.

Finding the rest of Europe either friendly or pacific, we never calculated the contingencies with might alter that disposition: nor reflected that the death* of a single prince, the change or caprice of a single minister, was capable of giving a new face to the whole system.

We are at this time more sanguine than ever. The war with the Dutch, we believe, will give such an addition of force to our side as will make the superiority irresistible. No person can dispute this, if things remain in their present state; but the extreme disparity of the contest is the very reason, why this cannot be the case. The neutral powers will either effect a particular, or a general accommodation, or they will take their sides. There are three suppositions to be made; one, that there will be a compromise *between the united* provinces and England; for which we are certain the mediation of Austria and Russia have been offered—another a pacification between all the belligerent powers, for which we have reason to believe the same mediation has been offered—the third a rejection of the terms of mediation and a more general war.

Either of these suppositions is a motive for exertion—the first will place things in the same, probably in a worse situation, than before the declaration of the war against Holland. The composing of present differences may be accompanied with a revival of ancient connections: and at least would be productive of greater caution and restraint in a future intercourse with us.

The second, it is much to be dreaded, would hazard a dismemberment† of a part of these states; and we are bound in honor, in duty and

---

* The death of the Empress Queen has actually produced a change: Her politics, if not friendly to our connections, were at least pacific; and while she lived no hostile interference of the House of Austria was to be expected. The Emperor, her son, by her death, left more at liberty to pursue his inclinations, averse to the aggrandisement of France, of course afraid of the abasement of England, has given several indications of an unfriendly disposition. It should be weighty consideration with us, that among the potentates which we look upon as amicable, three of the principal ones are at a very advanced stage of life, The King of Spain, the King of Prussia, and the Empress of Russia. We know not what may be the politics of successors.

† Perhaps not expressly and directly, but virtually, under the plausible form of a new arrangement of limits.

If we are determined, as we ought to be with the concurrence of our allies, not to accept such a condition, then we ought to prepare for the third event, a more general and more obstinate war.

Should this take place a variety of new interests will be involved, and the affairs of America MAY CEASE TO BE OF PRIMARY IMPORTANCE. In proportion as the objects and operations of the war become complicated and extensive, the final success must become uncertain; and in proportion as the interests of others in our concerns may be weakened, or supplanted by more immediate interests of their own, ought our attention to ourselves, and exertions in our own behalf to be awakened and augmented.

We ought therefore, not only to strain every nerve for complying with the requisitions, to render the present campaign as decisive as possible; but we ought without delay, to ENLARGE THE POWERS OF CONGRESS. Every plan of which this is not the foundation will be illusory. The separate exertions of the states will never suffice.—Nothing but a well proportioned exertion of the resources of the whole, under the direction of a common council, with power sufficient to give efficacy to their resolutions, can preserve us from being a CONQUERED PEOPLE now, or can make us a HAPPY PEOPLE hereafter.

in interest, to employ every effort to dispossess the enemy of what they hold. A natural basis of the negociation with respect to this continent, will be, that each party shall retain what it possesses at the conclusion of the treaty, qualified perhaps by a cession of particular points for an equivalent elsewhere. It is too delicate to dwell on the motives to this apprehension; but if such a compromise sometimes terminates the disputes of nations originally independent, it will be less extraordinary where one party was originally under the dominion of the other.

THE CONTINENTALIST.

NUMBER IV.

AUGUST 30, 1781.

THE preceding numbers are chiefly intended to confirm an opinion, already pretty generally received, that it is necessary to augment the powers of the confederation. The principal difficulty yet remains to fix the public judgment definitively on the points which ought to compose that augmentation.

It may be pronounced with confidence that nothing short of the following articles can suffice.

1st—The Power of Regulating Trade, comprehending a right of granting bounties and premiums by way of encouragement, of imposing duties of every kind as well for revenue as regulation, of appointing all officers of the customs, and of laying embargoes in extraordinary emergencies.

2nd—A moderate—levied tax, throughout the United States, of a specific rate per pound or per acre,* granted to the Federal Government in perpetuity; and if Congress think proper, to be levied by their own collectors.

3d—A moderate capitation-tax† on every male inhabitant above fifteen years of age, exclusive of common soldiers, common seamen, day laborers, cottagers, and paupers, to be also vested in perpetuity, and with the same condition of collection.

4th—The disposal of all unlocated land for the benefit of the United States (so far as respects the profits of the first sale and the quit rents), the jurisdiction remaining to the respective States in whose limits they are contained.

5th—A certain proportion of the product of all mines discovered, or to be discovered, for the same duration, and with the same right of collection as in the second and third articles.

---

* Two pence an acre on cultivated, and a halfpenny on uncultivated land, would answer the purpose, and would be so moderate as not to be felt—a small tax on uncultivated land would have the good effect of obliging the proprietor either to cultivate it himself, or to dispose of it to some persons that would do it.

† Suppose a dollar, or even half a dollar per head.

6th—The appointment of all land (as well as naval) officers of every rank.

The three first articles are of IMMEDIATE NECESSITY; the three last would be of great present, but of much greater future utility; the whole combined would give solidity and permanency to the Union.

The great defect of the Confederation is, that it gives the United States no property; or, in other words, no revenue, nor the means of acquiring it, inherent in themselves and independent on the temporary pleasure of the different members. And power without revenue, in political society, is a name. While Congress continue altogether dependent on the occasional grants of the several States, for the means of defraying the expenses of the Federal Government, it can neither have dignity, vigor, nor credit. Credit supposes specific and permanent funds for the punctual payment of interest, with a moral certainty of the final redemption of the principal.

In our situation, it will probably require more, on account of the general diffidence which has been excited by the past disorders in our finances. It will perhaps be necessary, in the first instance, to appropriate funds for the redemption of the principal in a determinate period, as well as for the payment of interest.

It is essential that the property in such funds should be in the contractor himself, and the appropriation dependent on his own will.

If, instead of this, the possession or disposal of them is dependent on the voluntary or occasional concurrence of a number of different wills not under his absolute control, both the one and the other will be too precarious to be trusted. The most wealthy and best established nations are obliged to pledge their funds to obtain credit, and it would be the height of absurdity in us, in the midst of a revolution, to expect to have it on better terms. This credit being to be procured through Congress, the funds ought to be provided, declared, and vested in them.* It is a fact that verifies the want of specific funds—a circumstance which operates powerfully against our obtaining credit abroad is, not a distrust of our becoming independent, but of our continuing united; and with our present confederation the distrust is natural. Both foreigners and the thinking men among ourselves, would have much more confidence in the duration of the Union, if they were to see it supported on the foundation here proposed.

There are some among us ignorant enough to imagine, that the war may be carried on without credit, defraying the expenses of the year with what may be raised within the year. But this is for want of a knowledge of our real resources and expenses.

It may be demonstrated, that the whole amount of the revenue, which these States are capable of affording, will be deficient annually,

---

* It might, indeed, be a good restraint upon the spirit of running in debt, with which government are too apt to be infected, to make it a condition of the grants to Congress, that they shall be obliged, in all their loans, to appropriate funds for the payment of principal as well as interest, and such a restriction might be serviceable to public credit.

five or six millions of dollars for the support of civil government and of the war.

This is not a conjecture hazarded at random, but the result of experiment and calculation; nor can it appear surprising, when it is considered that the revenues of the United Provinces, equal to these States in population, beyond comparison superior in industry, commerce, and riches, do not exceed twenty five millions of guilders, or about nine millions and a half of dollars. In times of war, they have raised a more considerable sum, but it has been chiefly by gratuitious combinations of rich individuals, a resource we cannot employ, because there are few men of large fortunes in this country, and these for the most part in land. Taxes in the United Provinces are carried to an extreme which would be impracticable here. Not only the living are made to pay for every necessary of life, but even the dead are tributary to the public for the liberty of interment at particular hours. These considerations make it evident that we could not raise an equal amount of revenue in these States. Yet, in '76, when the currency was not depreciated, Congress emitted, for the expenses of the year, fourteen millions of dollars. It cannot be denied, that there was a want of order and economy in the expenditure of public money, nor that we had a greater military force to maintain at that time than we now have; but, on the other hand, allowing for the necessary increase in our different civil lists, and for the advanced prices of many articles, it can hardly be supposed possible to reduce our annual expense very much below that sum. This simple idea of the subject, without entering into details, may satisfy us, that the deficiency which has been stated is not to be suspected of exaggeration.

Indeed, nations the most powerful and opulent are obliged to have recourse to loans in time of war, and hence it is that most of the States of Europe are deeply immersed in debt. France is among the number, notwithstanding her immense population, wealth, and resources. England owes the enormous sum of two hundred millions sterling. The United Provinces with all their prudence and parsimony, owe a debt of the generality of fifty millions, besides the particular debts of each province. Almost all the other powers are more or less in the same circumstances.

While this teaches us how contracted and uninformed are the views of those who expect to carry on the war without running in debt. It ought to console us with respect to the amount of that which we now owe, or may have occasion to incur, in the remainder of the war. The whole, without burthening the people, may be paid off in twenty years after the conclusion of peace.

The principal part of the deficient five or six millions must be procured by loans from private persons at home and abroad. Every thing may be hoped from the generosity of France, which her means will permit, but she has full employment for her revenues and credit in the prosecution of the war on her own part. If we judge of the future by the past, the pecuniary succours from her must continue to be far short of our wants; and the contingency of a war on the continent of Europe makes it possible that they may diminish rather than increase.

We have in a less degree experienced the friendship of Spain in this article.

The government of the United Provinces, if disposed to do it, can give us no assistance. The resources of the Republic are chiefly mortgaged for former debts. Happily, it has extensive credit, but it will have occassion for the whole to supply its own exigencies.

Private men, either foreigners or natives, will not lend to a large amount, but on the usual security of funds properly established. This security Congress cannot give, till the several States vest them with revenue, or the means of revenue, for that purpose.

Congress have wisely appointed a Superintendent of their finances— a man of acknowledged abilities and integrity, as well as of great personal credit and pecuniary influence.

It was impossible, that the business of finance could be ably conducted by a body of men however well composed or well intentioned. Order in the future management of our moneyed concerns, a strict regard to the performance of public engagements, and of course the restoration of public credit, may be reasonably and confidently expected from Mr. Morris's administration, if he is furnished with materials upon which to operate; that is, if the Federal Government can acquire funds as the basis of his arrangements. He has very judiciously proposed a National Bank, which, by uniting the interest and influence of the moneyed men with the resources of Government, can alone give it that durable and extensive credit of which it stands in need. This is the best expedient he could have devised for relieving the public embarrassments; but to give success to the plan, it is essential that Congress should have it in their power to support him with unexceptionable funds. Had we begun the practice of funding four years ago, we should have avoided that depreciation of the currency which has been pernicious to the morals and to the credit of the nation; and there is no other method than this to prevent a continuance and multiplication of the evils flowing from that prolific source.

THE CONTINENTALIST.

NUMBER V.

APRIL 18, 1782.

[THE succeeding numbers of the Continentalist were written last fall, but accidentally got out of the possession of the writer. He has lately recovered them, and he gives them to the public more to finish the development of his plan, than from any hope that the temper of the times will adopt his ideas.]

THE vesting Congress with the power of regulating trade ought to have been a principal object of the confederation for a variety of reasons. It is as necessary for the purposes of commerce as of revenue. There are some who maintain that trade will regulate itself, and is not to be benefitted by the encouragements, or restraints of government. Such persons will imagine, that there is no need of a common directing power. This is one of those wild speculative paradoxes, which have grown into credit among us, contrary to the uniform practice and sense of the most enlightened nations.

Contradicted by the numerous institutions and laws, that exist every where for the benefit of trade, by the pains taken to cultivate particular branches and to discourage others, by the known advantages derived from those measures, and by the palpable evils that would attend their discontinuance—it must be rejected by every man acquainted with commercial history. Commerce, like other things, has its fixed principles, according to which it must be regulated: if these are understood and observed, it will be promoted by the attention of government, if unknown, or violated, it will be injured—but it is the same with every other part of administration.

To preserve the balance of trade in favour of a nation ought to be a leading aim of its policy. The avarice of individuals may frequently find its account in pursuing channels of traffic prejudicial to that balance, to which the government may be able to oppose effectual impediments. There may, on the other hand, be a possibility of opening new sources, which, though accompanied with great difficulties in the commencement, would in the event, amply reward the trouble and expense of bringing them to perfection. The undertaking may often exceed the influence and capitals of individuals, and may require no small assistance, as well from the revenue as from the authority of the state.

The contrary opinion, which has grown into a degree of vogue among us, has originated in the injudicious attempts made at different times to effect a REGULATION of PRICES. It became a cant phrase among the opposers of these attempts, that TRADE MUST REGULATE ITSELF: by which at first was only meant that it had its fundamental laws, agreeable to which its general operations must be directed; and that any violent attempts in opposition to these would commonly miscarry. In this sense the maxim was reasonable; but it has since been extended to militate against all interference by the sovereign; an extreme as little reconcileable with experience, or common sense, as the practice it was first framed to discredit.

The reasonings of a very ingenious and sensible writer,* by being misapprehended, have contributed to this mistake. The scope of his argument, is not, as by some supposed, that trade will hold a certain invariable course independent on the aid, protection, care or concern of government; but that it will, in the main, depend upon the comparative industry, moral and physical advantages of nations; and that though, for a while, from extraordinary causes, there may be a wrong balance against one of them, this will work its own cure, and things will ultimately return to their proper level. His object was to combat that excessive jealousy on this head, which has been productive of so many unnecessary wars, and with which the British nation is particularly infected; but it was no part of his design to insinuate that the regulating hand of government was either useless or hurtful. The nature of a government, its spirit, maxims and laws, with respect to trade, are among those constant moral causes, which influence its general results, and when it has by accident taken a wrong direction, assist in bringing it back to its natural course. This is every where admitted by all writers upon the subject; nor is there one who has asserted a contrary doctrine.

Trade may be said to have taken its rise in England under the auspices of Elizabeth; and its rapid progress there is in a great measure to be ascribed to the fostering care of government in that and succeeding reigns.

From a different spirit in the government, with superior advantages, France was much later in commercial improvements, nor would her trade have been at this time in so prosperous a condition, had it not been for the abilities and indefatigable endeavours of the great COLBERT. He laid the foundation of the French commerce, and taught the way to his successors to enlarge and improve it. The establishment of the woolen manufacture, in a kingdom, where nature seemed to have denied the means, is one among many proofs, how much may be effected in favour of commerce by the attention and patronage of a wise administration.

---

* Hume's Essay—Jealousy of Trade.

The number of useful edicts passed by Louis the 14th, and since his time, in spite of frequent interruptions from the jealous enmity of Great Britain, has advanced that of France to a degree which has excited the envy and astonishment of its neighbours.

The Dutch, who may justly be allowed a preeminence in the knowledge of trade, have ever made it an essential object of state. Their commercial regulations are more rigid and numerous, than those of any other country; and it is by a judicious and unremitted vigilance of government, that they have been able to extend their trafic to a degree so much beyond their natural and comparative advantages.

Perhaps it may be thought, that the power of regulation will be best placed in the governments of the several states, and that a general superintendence is unnecessary. If the states had distinct interests, were unconnected with each other, their own governments would then be the proper, and could be the only depositories of such a power; but as they are parts of a whole with a common interest in trade, as in other things, there ought to be a common direction in that as in other matters. It is easy to conceive, that many cases may occur, in which it would be beneficial to all the states to encourage, or suppress a particular branch of trade, while it would be detrimental to either to attempt it without the concurrence of the rest, and where the experiment would probably be left untried for fear of a want of that concurrence.

No mode can be so convenient as a source of revenue to the United States. It is agreed that imposts on trade, when not immoderate, or improperly laid, are one of the most eligible species of taxation. They fall in a great measure upon articles not of absolute necessity, and being partly transferred to the price of the commodity, are so far imperceptibly paid by the consumer. It is therefore that mode which may be exercised by the fœderal government with least exception or disgust Congress can easily possess all the information necessary to impose the duties with judgment, and the collection can without difficulty be made by their own officers.

They can have no temptation to abuse this power, because the motive of revenue will check its own extremes. Experience has shown that moderate duties are more productive than high ones. When they are low, a nation can trade abroad on better terms—its imports and exports will be larger—the duties will be regularly paid, and arising on a greater quantity of commodities, will yield more in the aggregate, than when they are so high as to operate either as a prohibition, or as an inducement to evade them by illicit practices.

It is difficult to assign any good reason why Congress should be more liable to abuse the powers with which they are intrusted than the state-assemblies. The frequency of the election of the members is a full security against a dangerous ambition, and the rotation established by the confederation makes it impossible for any state, by continuing the same men, who may put themselves at the head of a prevailing faction, to maintain for any length of time an undue influence in the national councils. It is to be presumed, that Congress will be in general better composed for abilities, and as well for integrity as any assembly on the continent.

But to take away any temptation from a cabal to load particular articles, which are the principal objects of commerce to particular states, with a too great proportion of duties, to ease the others in the general distribution of expense: let all the duties, whether for regulation or revenue, raised in each state, be credited to that state, and let it in like manner, be charged for all the bounties paid within itself for the encouragement of agriculture, manufactures or trade. This expedient will remove the temptation; for as the quotas of the respective states are to be determined by a standard of land, agreeable to the eighth article of the confederation, each will have so much the less to contribute otherwise, as it pays more on its commerce. An objection has been made in a late instance to this principle. It has been urged, that as the consumer pays the duty, those states which are not equally well situated for foreign commerce, and which consume a great part of the imports of their neighbours, will become contributers to a part of their taxes. This objection is rather specious than solid.

The maxim, that the consumer pays the duty, has been admitted in theory with too little reserve; frequently contradicted in practice. It is true, the merchant will be unwilling to let the duty be a deduction from his profits, if the state of the market will permit him to incorporate it with the price of his commodity. But this is often not practicable. It turns upon the quantity of goods at market in proportion to the demand. When the latter exceeds the former, and the competition is among the buyers, the merchant can easily increase his price, and make his customers pay the duty. When the reverse is the case, and the competition is among the sellers, he must then content himself with smaller profits and lose the value of the duty or at least a part of it. When a nation has a flourishing and well settled trade this more commonly happens than may be imagined, and it will, many times, be found that the duty is divided between the merchant and the consumer.

Besides this consideration which greatly diminishes the force of the objection, there is another which entirely destroys it. There is a strong reciprocal influence between the prices of all commodities in a state, by which they, sooner or later, attain a pretty exact balance and proportion to each other. If the immediate productions of the soil rise, the manufacturer will have more for his manufacture, the merchant for his goods; and the same will happen with whatever class the increase of price begins. If duties are laid upon the imports in one state, by which the prices of foreign articles are raised, the products of land and labour within that state will take a proportionate rise: and if a part of those articles are consumed in a neighbouring state, it will have the same influence there as at home. The importing state must allow an advanced price upon the commodities, which it receives in exchange from its neighbour, in a ratio to the increased price of the article it sells. To know then which is the gainer or loser, we must examine how the general balance of trade stands between them. If the importing state takes

more of the commodities of its neighbour than it gives in exchange, that
will be the loser by the reciprocal augmentation of prices, it will be the
gainer if it takes less, and neither will gain or lose if the barter is carried on upon equal terms. The balance of trade, and consequently the
gain, or loss, in this respect, will be governed more by the relative
industry and frugality of the parties, than by their relative advantages
for foreign commerce.

Between separate nations this reasoning will not apply with full
force, because a multitude of local and extraneous circumstances may
counteract the principle; but from the intimate connections of these
states, the similitude of governments, situations, customs, manners,
political and commercial causes will have nearly the same operation in
the intercourse between the states, as in that between the different
parts of the same state. If this should be controverted, the objection
drawn from the hypothesis of the consumer paying the duty must fall at
the same time: For as far as this is true it is as much confined in its
application to a state within itself as the doctrine of a reciprocal proportion of prices.

General principles in subjects of this nature ought always to be
advanced with caution: in an experimental analysis there are found such
a number of exceptions as tend to render them very doubtful: and in
questions which affect the existence and collective happiness of these
states, all nice and abstract distinctions should give way to plainer
interests, and to more obvious and simple rules of conduct.

But the objection which has been urged ought to have no weight on
another account. Which are the states that have not sufficient advantages for foreign commerce, and that will not in time be their own carriers? Connecticut and Jersey are the least maritime of the whole; yet
the sound which washes the coast of Connecticut, has an easy outlet to
the ocean, affords a number of harbours and bays, very commodious for
trading vessels. New London may be a receptacle for merchantmen of
almost any burthen: and the fine rivers with which the state is intersected, by facilitating the transportation of commodities to and from
every part, are extremely favourable both to its domestic and foreign
trade.

Jersey, by way of Amboy has a shorter communication with the
ocean, than the city of New York. Prince's bay, which may serve as an
out port to it, will admit and shelter in winter and summer vessels of
any size. Egg-harbour on its southern coast is not to be despised. The
Delaware may be made as subservient to its commerce as to that of
Pennsylvania, Gloucester, Burlington, and Trenton, being all conveniently situated on that river. The United Provinces with inferior
advantages of position to either of these states, have for centuries held
the first rank among commercial nations.

The want of large trading cities has been sometimes objected as an
obstacle to the commerce of these states; but this is a temporary deficiency that will repair itself with the increase of population and riches.
The reason that the states in question have hitherto carried on little

foreign trade, is that they have found it equally beneficial to purchase the commodities imported by their neighbours. If the imposts on trade should work an inconvenience to them, it will soon cease by making it their interest to trade abroad.

It is too much characteristic of our national temper to be ingenious in finding out and magnifying the minutest disadvantages, and to reject measures of evident utility, even of necessity, to avoid trivial and sometimes imaginary evils. We seem not to reflect, that in human society, there is scarcely any plan, however salutary to the whole and to every part, by the share each has in the common prosperity, but in one way, or another, and under particular circumstances, will operate more to the benefit of some parts than of others. Unless we can overcome this narrow disposition and learn to estimate measures by their general tendencies, we shall never be a great or a happy people, if we remain a people at all.

THE CONTINENTALIST.

NUMBER VI.

JULY 12, 1781.

LET us see what will be the consequences of not authorizing the Federal Government to regulate the trade of these States. Besides the want
of revenue and of power, besides the immediate risk to our independence, the dangers of all the future evils of a precarious Union, besides
the deficiency of a wholesome concert, and provident superintendence
to advance the general prosperity of trade, the direct consequence will
be that the landed interest and the laboring poor, will in the first place
fall a sacrifice to the trading interest; and the whole eventually to a bad
system of policy, made necessary by the want of such regulating power.

Each State will be afraid to impose duties on its commerce, lest the
other States, not doing the same, should enjoy greater advantages than
itself, by being able to afford native commodities cheaper abroad, and
foreign commodities cheaper at home.

A part of the evils resulting from this would be, a loss to the revenue
of those moderate duties, which, without being injurious to commerce,
are allowed to be the most agreeable species of taxes to the people.
Articles of foreign luxury, while they would contribute nothing to the
income of the State, being less dear by an exemption from duties, would
have a more extensive consumption.

Many branches of trade, hurtful to the common interest, would be
continued for want of proper checks and discouragements. As revenues
must be found to satisfy the public exigencies in peace and in war, too
great a proportion of taxes will fall directly upon land, and upon the
necessaries of life—the produce of that land.

The influence of these evils will be to render landed property fluctuating and less valuable—to oppress the poor by raising the prices of
necessaries—to injure commerce by encouraging the consumption of
foreign luxuries, by increasing the value of labor—by lessening the
quantity of home productions, enhancing their prices at foreign markets, of course obstructing their sale, and enabling other nations to sup-
plant us.

Particular caution ought at present to be observed in this country, not to burthen the soil itself and its productions with heavy impositions, because the quantity of unimproved land will invite the husbandmen to abandon old settlements for new; and the disproportion of our population for some time to come will necessarily make labor dear, to reduce which, and not to increase it, ought to be a capital object of our policy.

Easy duties, therefore, on commerce, especially on imports, ought to lighten the burthens which will unavoidably fall upon land. Though it may be said that, on the principle of a reciprocal influence of prices, whereon the taxes are laid in the first instance, they will in the end be borne by all classes, yet it is of the greatest importance that no one should sink under the immediate pressure.

The great art is to distribute the public burthens well, and not suffer them, either first or last, to fall too heavily on parts of the community; else, distress and disorder must ensue—a shock given to any part of the political machine vibrates through the whole.

As a sufficient revenue could not be raised from trade to answer the public purposes, other articles have been proposed. A moderate land and poll tax being of easy and unexpensive collection, and leaving nothing to discretion, are the simplest and best that could be devised.

It is to be feared, the avarice of many of the landholders will be opposed to a perpetual tax upon land, however moderate. They will ignorantly hope to shift the burthens of the national expense from themselves to others—a disposition as iniquitous as it is fruitless—the public necessities must be satisfied; this can only be done by the contributions of the whole society. Particular classes are neither able nor will be willing to pay for the protection and security of the others, and where so selfish a spirit discovers itself in any member, the rest of the community will unite to compel it to do its duty.

Indeed, many theorists in political economy have held, that all taxes, wherever they originate, fall upon land, and have therefore been of opinion, that it would be best to draw the whole revenue of the State immediately from that source, to avoid the expense of a more diversified collection, and the accumulations which will be heaped in their several stages, upon the primitive sums advanced in those stages which are imposed on our trade. But though it has been demonstrated that this theory has been carried to an extreme, impracticable in fact; yet it is evident, in tracing the matter, that a large part of all taxes, however remotely laid, will, by an insensible circulation come at last to settle upon land—the source of most of the materials employed in commerce.

It appears from a calculation made by the ablest master of political arithmetic, about sixty years ago, that the yearly product of all the lands in England amounted to £42,000,000 sterling; and the whole annual consumption at that period, of foreign as well as domestic commodities, did not exceed £49,000,000, and the surplus of the exportation above the importation £2,000,000, on which sums arise all the revenues in whatever shape, which go into the treasury.

It is easy to infer from this, how large a part of them must, directly or indirectly, be derived from land.

11

Nothing can be more mistaken, than the collision and rivalship which almost always subsist between the landing and trading interests, for the truth is they are so inseparably interwoven that one cannot be injured without injury nor benefited without benefit to the other. Oppress trade, lands sink in value; make it flourish, their value rises; incumber husbandry, trade declines, encourage agriculture, commerce revives. The progress of this mutual reaction might be easily delineated, but it is too obvious to every man, who turns his thoughts, however superficially, upon the subject, to require it. It is only to be regretted, that it is too often lost sight of, when the seductions of some immediate advantage or exemption tempt us to sacrifice the future to the present.

But perhaps the class is more numerous of those, who, not unwilling to bear their share of public burthens, are yet averse to the idea of perpetuity, as if there ever would arrive a period when the State would cease to want revenues; and taxes become unnecessary. It is of importance to unmask this delusion, and open the eyes of the people to the truth. It is paying too great a tribute to the idol of popularity, to flatter so injurious and so visionary an expectation. The error is too gross to be tolerated any where but in the cottage of the peasant. Should we meet with it in the Senate House, we must lament the ignorance or despise the hypocrisy on which it is ingrafted. Expense is in the present state of things entailed upon all governments; though, if we continue United, we shall be hereafter less exposed to wars by land than most other countries; yet while we have powerful neighbors on either extremity, and our frontier is embraced by savages, whose alliance they may without difficulty command, we cannot, in prudence, dispense with the usual precautions for our interior security. As a commercial people, maritime power must be a primary object of our attention, and a navy cannot be created or maintained without ample revenues. The nature of our popular institutions requires a numerous magistracy, for whom competent provision must be made, or we may be certain our affairs will always be committed to improper hands, and experience will teach us that no government costs so much as a bad one.

We may preach, till we are tired of the theme, the necessity of disinterestedness in republics, without making a single proselyte. The virtuous declaimer will neither persuade himself nor any other person to be content with a double mess of pottage, instead of a reasonable stipend for his services. We might as soon reconcile ourselves to the Spartan community of goods and wives, to their iron coin, their long beards, or their black broth. There is a total dissimilarity in the circumstances, as well as the manners of society among us, and it is as ridiculous to seek for models in the small ages of Greece and Rome, as it would be to go in quest of them among the Hottentots and Laplanders.

The public, for the different purposes that have been mentioned, must always have large demands upon its constituents, and the only question is, whether these shall be satisfied by annual grants, perpetually renewed by a perpetual grant, once for all, or by a compound of permanent and occasional supplies. The last is the wisest course. The Federal Government should neither be independent nor too much dependent. It should neither be raised above responsibility or control; nor should it want the means of maintaining its own weight, authority, dignity, and credit. To this end, permanent funds are indispensable; but they ought to be of such a nature, and so moderate in their amount as never to be inconvenient. Extraordinary supplies can be the objects of extraordinary emergencies; and in that salutary medium will consist our true wisdom.

It would seem as if no mode of taxation could be relished, but the worst of all modes, which now prevails by assessment. Every proposal for a specific tax is sure to meet with opposition. It has been objected to a poll tax at a fixed rate, that it will be unequal, and the rich will pay no more than the poor. In the form in which it has been offered in these papers the poor, properly speaking, are not comprehended, though it is true, that beyond the exclusion of the indigent, the tax has no reference to the proportion of property, but it should be remembered that it is impossible to devise any specific tax that will operate equally on the whole community. It must be the province of the Legislature to hold the scales with a judicious hand, and balance one by another. The rich must be made to pay for their luxuries, which is the only proper way of taxing their superior wealth.

Do we imagine that our assessments operate equally? Nothing can be more contrary to the fact. Wherever a discretionary power is lodged in any set of men over the property of their neighbors, they will abuse it. Their passions, prejudices, partialities, dislikes, will have the principal lead in measuring the abilities of those over whom their power extends; and assessors will ever be a set of petty tyrants, too unskillful, if honest, to be possessed of so delicate a trust; and too seldom honest to give them the excuse of want of skill.

The genius of liberty reprobates every thing arbitrary or discretionary in taxation. It exacts that every man, by a definite and general rule, should know what proportion of his property the State demands. Whatever liberty we may boast in theory, it cannot exist in fact while assessments continue.

The admission of them among us is a new proof, how often human conduct reconciles the most glaring opposites; in the present case, the most vicious practice of despotic governments, with the freest constitutions and the greatest love of liberty.

The establishment of permanent funds would not only answer the public purposes infinitely better than temporary supplies, but it would be the most effectual way of easing the people.

With this basis for procuring credit, the amount of present taxes might be greatly diminished. Large sums of money might be borrowed abroad, at a low interest, and introduced into the country, to defray the current expenses and pay the public debts; which would not only lessen the demand for immediate supplies, but would throw more money into circulation, and furnish the people with greater means of paying the taxes.

Though it be a just rule that we ought not to run in debt to avoid present expense, so far as our faculties extend; yet the propriety of doing it cannot be disputed, when it is apparent that these are incompetent to the public necessities. Efforts beyond our abilities can only tend to individual distress and national disappointment. The product of the three foregoing articles will be as little as can be required, to enable Congress to pay their debts, and restore order into their finances. In addition to them—

The disposal of the unlocated lands will hereafter be a valuable source of revenue, and an immediate one of credit. As it may be liable to the same condition with the duties on trade,—that is, the product of the sales within each State to be credited to that State, and as the rights of jurisdiction are not infringed, it seems to be susceptible of no reasonable objection.

Mines in every country constitute a branch of the revenue. In this, where nature has so richly impregnated the bowels of the earth, they may in time become a valuable one; and as they require the care and attention of government to bring them to perfection, this care and a share in the profits of it will very properly devolve upon Congress. All the precious metals should absolutely be the property of the Federal Government, and with respect to the others it should have a discretionary power of reserving, in the nature of a tax, such part as it may judge not inconsistent with the encouragement due to so important an object. This is rather a future than a present resource.

The reason of allowing Congress to appoint its own officers of the customs, collectors of the taxes, and military officers of every rank, is to create in the interior of each State, a mass of influence in favor of the Federal Government. The great danger has been shown to be, that it will not have power enough to defend itself, and preserve the Union, not that it will ever become formidable to the general liberty. A mere regard to the interests of the confederacy will never be a principle sufficiently active to crush the ambition and intrigues of different members. Force cannot effect it. A contest of arms will seldom be between the common sovereign, and a single refractory member, but between distinct combinations of the several parts against each other. A sympathy of situations will be apt to produce associates to the disobedient. The application of force is always disagreeable—the issue uncertain. It will be wise to obviate the necessity of it, by interesting such a number of individuals in each State, in support of the Federal Government, as will be counterpoised to the ambition of others, and will make it difficult for them to unite the people in opposition to the first and necessary measures of the Union.

There is something noble and magnificent in the perspective of a great Federal Republic, closely linked in the pursuit of a common interest, tranquil and prosperous at home—respectable abroad; but there is something proportionally diminutive and contemptible in the prospect of a number of petty States, with the appearance only of Union, jarring, jealous, and perverse, without any determined direction, fluctuating and unhappy at home, weak and insignificant by their dissensions in the eyes of other nations.

Happy America, if those to whom thou hast intrusted the guardianship of thy infancy, know how to provide for thy future repose, but miserable and undone, if their negligence or ignorance permits the spirit of discord to erect her banner on the ruins of thy tranquillity!

RESOLUTION FOR A GENERAL CONVENTION OF THE STATES.

PASSED BY THE LEGISLATURE OF NEW YORK, SUNDAY, JULY 21ST, 1782.

Resolved, That it appears to this Legislature—after full and solemn consideration of the several matters communicated by the Honorable the Committee of Congress, relative to the present posture of our affairs, foreign and domestic, and contained in a letter from the Secretary for Foreign Affairs, respecting the former, as well as of the representations, from time to time made by the Superintendent of the Finances of the United States, relative to his particular department— that the situation of these States is in a peculiar manner critical, and affords the strongest reason to apprehend, from a continuance of the present constitution of the continental Government, a subdivision of the public credit, and consequences highly dangerous to the safety and independence of these States.

Resolved, That while this Legislature are convinced by the before mentioned communications, that, notwithstanding the generous intentions of an Ally, from whom we have experienced, and doubtless shall still experience all possible support; exigencies may arise to prevent our receiving pecuniary succors hereafter, in any degree proportioned to our necessities. They are also convinced from facts within their own knowledge, that the provisions made by the respective States for carrying on the war, are not only inadequate to the end, but must continue to be so, while there is an adherence to the principles which now direct the operation of public measures.

Resolved, That it is also the opinion of this Legislature, that the present plan, instituted by Congress, for the administration of their Finances, is founded in wisdom and sound policy. That the salutary effects of it have already been felt in an extensive degree; and that after so many violent shocks sustained by the public credit, a failure in this system, for want of the support which the States are able to give, would be productive of evils too pernicious to be hazarded.

Resolved, That it appears to this Legislature, that the present British ministry, with a disposition not less hostile than that of their predecessors, taught by experience to avoid their errors; and assuming the appearance of moderation, are pursuing a scheme calculated to conciliate in Europe, and seduce in America. That the economical arrangements they appear to be adopting, are adapted to enlarging the credit of their Government, and multiplying its resources, at the same time that they serve to confirm the prepossessions and confidence of the people; and that the plan of a defensive war on this Continent, while they direct all their attention and resources to the augmentation of their Navy, is that which may be productive of consequences ultimately dangerous to the United States.

Resolved, That it is the opinion of this Legislature, that the present system of these States, exposes the common cause to a precarious issue, and leaves us at the mercy of events over which we have no influence —a conduct extremely unwise in any nation, and at all times; and to a change of which, we are impelled at this juncture, by reasons of peculiar and irresistible weight; and that it is the natural tendency of the weakness and disorders in our national measures, to spread diffidence and distrust among the people; and prepare their minds to receive the impressions the enemy wish to make.

Resolved, That the general state of European affairs, as far as they have come to the knowledge of this Legislature, affords, in their opinion, reasonable ground of confidence, and assures us, that with judicious, vigorous exertion on our part, we may rely on the final attainment of our object; but far from justifying indifference and security, calls upon us by every motive of honor, good faith, and patriotism, without delay, to unite in some system more effectual, for producing energy, harmony, and consistency of measures, than that which now exists; and more capable of putting the common cause out of the reach of contingencies.

Resolved, That in the opinion of this Legislature, the radical source of most of our embarrassments is, the WANT of SUFFICIENT POWER in Congress, to effectuate that ready and perfect co-operation of the different States, on which their immediate safety and future happiness depend—that experience has demonstrated the confederation to be defective in several essential points, particularly in not vesting the Federal Government either with a power of providing revenue for itself, or with ascertained and productive funds, secured by a sanction so solemn and general as would inspire the fullest confidence in them, and make them a substantial basis of credit—that these defects ought to be without loss of time repaired, the powers of Congress extended, a solid security established for the payment of debts already incurred; and competent means provided for future credit, and for supplying the current demands of the war.

Resolved, That it appears evidently to this Legislature, that the annual income of these States, admitting the best means were adopted for drawing out their resources, would fall far short of the annual expenditure; and that there would be a large deficiency to be supplied on the credit of the States, which, if it should be inconvenient for those powers to afford, on whose friendship we justly rely, must be sought for from individuals, to engage whom to lend, satisfactory securities must be pledged for the punctual payment of interest, and the final redemption of the principal.

Resolved, That it appears to this Legislature, that the foregoing important ends can never be attained by partial deliberations of the States *separately*; but that it is essential to the common welfare, that there should be as soon as possible a conference of the whole on the subject; and that it would be advisable for this purpose to propose to Congress to recommend, and to each State to adopt the measure of assembling A GENERAL CONVENTION OF THE STATES, specially authorized to revise and amend the Confederation, reserving a right to the respective Legislatures to ratify their determinations.

HAMILTON TO GOVERNOR CLINTON.

PHILADELPHIA, May 14, 1783.

The president of congress will of course have transmitted to your excellency the plan lately adopted by congress for funding the public debt. This plan was framed to accommodate it to the objections of some of the states; but this spirit of accommodation will only serve to render it less efficient, without making it more palatable. The opposition of the state of Rhode Island, for instance, is chiefly founded upon these two considerations: the merchants are opposed to any revenue from trade; and the state, depending almost wholly on commerce, wants to have credit for the amount of the duties.

Persuaded that the plan now proposed will have little more chance of success than a better one, and that if agreed to by all the states it will in a great measure fail in the execution, it received my negative.

My principal objections were—First, that it does not designate the funds (except the impost) on which the whole interest is to arise; and by which (selecting the capital articles of visible property) the collection would have been easy, the funds productive, and necessarily increasing with the increase of the country. Secondly, that the duration of the funds is not coextensive with the debt, but limited to twenty-five years, though there is a moral certainty that in that period the principal will not, by the present provision, be fairly extinguished. Thirdly, that the nomination and appointment of the collectors of the revenue are to reside in each state, instead of, at least, the nomination being in the United States; the consequence of which will be, that those states which have little interest in the funds, by having a small share of the public debt due to their own citizens, will take care to appoint such persons as are the least likely to collect the revenue.

The evils resulting from these defects will be, that in many instances the objects of the revenue will be improperly chosen, and will consist of a multitude of little articles, which will, on experiment, prove insufficient; that, for want of a vigorous collection in each state, the revenue will be unproductive in many, and will fall chiefly on those states which are governed by most liberal principles; that for want of an adequate security, the evidences of the public debt will not be transferable for any thing like their value. That this not admitting an incorporation of the creditors in the nature of banks, will deprive the public of the benefit of an increased circulation, and of course will disable the people from paying the taxes for want of a sufficient medium. I shall be happy to be mistaken in my apprehensions, but the experiment must determine.

I hope our state will consent to the plan proposed; because it is her interest, at all events, to promote the payment of the public debt in continental funds, independent of the general considerations of union and propriety. I am much mistaken, if the debts due from the United States to the citizens of the state of New-York do not considerably exceed its proportion of the necessary funds; of course it has an immediate interest that there should be a continental provision for them. But there are superior motives that ought to operate in every state—the obligations of national faith, honour, and reputation.

Individuals have been too long already sacrificed to the public convenience. It will be shocking, and, indeed, an eternal reproach to this country, if we begin the peaceable enjoyment of our independence by a violation of all the principles of honesty and true policy.

It is worthy of remark, that at least four-fifths of the domestic debt are due to the citizens of the states from Pennsylvania inclusively northward.

P. S.—It is particularly interesting that the state should have a representation here. Not only many matters are depending which require a full representation in congress, and there is now a thin one, but those matters are of a nature so particularly interesting to our state that we ought not to be without a voice in them. I wish two other gentlemen of the delegation may appear as soon as possible, for it would be very injurious to me to remain much longer. Having no future views in public life, I owe it to myself without delay to enter upon the care of my private concerns in earnest.

RESOLUTIONS FOR A GENERAL CONVENTION, 1783.

"WHEREAS, in the opinion of this congress, the confederation of the United States is defective in the following essential points.

"First, and generally, in confining the fœderal government within too narrow limits; withholding from it that efficacious authority and influence in all matters of general concern, which are indispensable to the harmony and welfare of the whole; embarrassing general provisions by unnecessary details and inconvenient exceptions incompatible with their nature, tending only to create jealousies and disputes respecting the proper bounds of the authority of the United States, and of that of the particular states, and a mutual interference of the one with the other.

"Secondly—In confounding legislative and executive powers in a *single* body; as that of determining on the number and quantity of force, land and naval, to be employed for the common defence, and of directing their operations when raised and equipped; with that of ascertaining and making requisitions for the necessary sums or quantities of money to be paid by the respective states into the common treasury, contrary to the most approved and well-founded maxims of free government, which require that the LEGISLATIVE, EXECUTIVE, and JUDICIAL authorities should be deposited *in distinct and separate hands*.

"Thirdly—In the want of a FEDERAL JUDICATURE, having cognizance of all matters of general concern in the last resort, especially those in which foreign nations and their subjects are interested; from which defect, by the interference of the local regulations of particular states militating, directly or indirectly, against the powers vested in the union, the national treaties will be liable to be infringed, the national faith to be violated, and the public tranquillity to be disturbed.

"Fourthly—In vesting the United States, in congress assembled, with the *power of general taxation*, comprehended in that 'of ascertaining the necessary sums of money to be raised for the common defence and of appropriating and applying the same for defraying the public expenses;' and yet rendering that power, so essential to the existence of the union, nugatory, by withholding from them all control over either the imposition or the collection of the taxes for raising the sums required, whence it happens that the inclinations, not the abilities, of the respective states are, in fact, the criterion of their contributions to the common expense, and the public burden has fallen, and will continue to fall, with very unequal weight.

"Fifthly—In fixing a rule for determining the proportion of each state towards the common expense, which, if practicable at all, must in the execution be attended with great expense, inequality, uncertainty, and difficulty.

"Sixthly—In authorizing congress 'to borrow money, or emit bills, on the credit of the United States,' without the power of establishing funds to secure the repayment of the money or the redemption of the bills emitted, from which must result one of these evils—either a want of sufficient credit in the first instance to borrow, or to circulate the bills emitted, whereby in great national exigencies the public safety may be endangered, or, in the second instance, frequent infractions of the public engagements, disappointments to lenders, repetitions of the calamities of depreciating paper, a continuance of the injustice and mischiefs of an unfunded debt, and, first or last, the annihilation of public credit. Indeed, in authorizing congress at all to emit an *unfunded* paper as the sign of value; a resource, which, though useful in the infancy of this country, indispensable in the commencement of the revolution, ought not to continue a formal part of the constitution, nor ever hereafter to be employed, being in its nature pregnant with abuses, and liable to be made the engine of imposition and fraud, holding out temptations equally pernicious to the integrity of government and to the morals of the people.

"Seventhly—In not making proper or competent provision for interior or exterior defence: for interior defence, by leaving it to the individual states to appoint all regimental officers of the land forces, to raise the men in their own way, to clothe, arm, and equip them, at the expense of the United States; from which circumstances have resulted, and will hereafter result, great confusion in the military department, continual disputes of rank, languid and disproportionate levies of men, an enormous increase of expense for want of system and uniformity in the manner of conducting them, and from the competitions of state bounties;—by an ambiguity in the fourth clause of the sixth article, susceptible of a construction which would devolve upon the particular states in time of peace the care of their own defence both by sea and land, and would preclude the United States from raising a single regiment or building a single ship before a declaration of war, or an actual commencement of hostilities; a principle dangerous to the confederacy in different respects, by leaving the United States at all times unprepared for the defence of their common rights, obliging them to begin to raise an army and to build and equip a navy at the moment they would have occasion to employ them, and by putting into the hands of a few states, who from their local situations are more immediately exposed, all the standing forces of the country, thereby not only leaving the care of the safety of the whole to a part, which will naturally be both unwilling and unable to make effectual provision at its particular expense, but also furnishing grounds of jealousy and distrust between the states, unjust in its operation to those states in whose hands they are, by throwing the exclusive burden of maintaining those forces upon them, while their neighbours immediately, and all the states ultimately, would share the benefits of their services; for exterior defence, in authorizing congress 'to build and equip a navy,' without providing any means of manning it, either by requisitions of the states, by the power of registering and drafting the sea-men in rotation, or by embargoes in cases of emergency, to induce them to accept employment on board the ships of war; the omission of all which leaves no other resource than voluntary enlistment; a resource which has been found ineffectual in every country, and for reasons of peculiar force, in this.

"Eighthly—In not vesting in the United States A GENERAL SUPERINTENDENCE OF TRADE, equally necessary in the view of *revenue* and *regulation*: of *revenue*, because duties on commerce, when moderate, *are* among the most agreeable and productive species of it which cannot without great disadvantages be imposed by particular states, while others refrain from doing it, but must be imposed in concert, and by laws operating upon the same principles, at the same moment, in all the states; otherwise those states which should not impose them would engross the commerce of such of their neighbours as did: of *regulation*, because by general prohibitions of particular articles, by a judicious arrangement of duties, sometimes by bounties on the manufacture or exportation of certain commodities, injurious branches of commerce might be discouraged, favourable branches encouraged, useful products and manufactures promoted; none of which advantages can be effectually attained by separate regulations without a general superintending power; because, also, it is essential to the due observance of the commercial stipulations of the United States with foreign powers, an interference with which will be unavoidable if the different states have the exclusive regulation of their own trade, and of course the construction of the treaties entered into.

"Ninthly—In defeating essential powers by provisoes and limitations inconsistent with their nature, as the power of making treaties with foreign nations, 'provided that no treaty of commerce shall be made whereby the legislative power of the respective states shall be restrained from imposing such imposts and duties on foreigners as their own people are subjected to, or from prohibiting the importation or exportation of any species of goods or commodities whatever;' a proviso susceptible of an interpretation which includes a constitutional possibility of defeating the treaties of commerce entered into by the United States. As also the power 'of regulating the trade, and managing all affairs with the Indians, not members of any states; *provided*, that the legislative right of any state within its own limits be not infringed or violated,' and others of a similar nature.

"Tenthly—In granting the United States the sole power 'of regulating the alloy and value of coin struck by their own authority, or by that of the respective states,' without the power of regulating foreign coin in circulation, though one is essential to the due exercise of the other, as there ought to be such proportions maintained between the national and foreign coin, as will give the former a preference in all internal negotiations; and without the latter power, the operations of government, in a matter of primary importance to the commerce and finances of the United States, will be exposed to numberless obstructions.

"Eleventhly—In requiring the assent of nine states to matters of principal importance, and of seven to all others, except adjournments from day to day, a rule destructive of vigour, consistency, or expedition, in the administration of affairs, tending to subject the *sense* of the majority to *that* of the minority, by putting it in the power of a small combination to retard and even to frustrate the most necessary measures, and to oblige the greater number, in cases which require speedy determinations, as happens in the most interesting concerns of the community, to come into the views of the smaller; the evils of which have been felt in critical conjunctures, and must always make the spirit of government a spirit of compromise and expedience, rather than of system and energy.

"Twelfthly—In vesting in the fœderal government the sole direction of the interests of the United States in their intercourse with foreign nations, without empowering it to pass ALL GENERAL LAWS in aid and support of the laws of nations; for the want of which authority, the faith of the United States may be broken, their reputation sullied, and their peace interrupted, by the negligence or misconception of any particular state.

"And whereas experience hath clearly manifested that the powers reserved to the union in the confederation, are unequal to the purpose of effectually drawing forth the resources of the respective members, for *the common welfare and defence*; whereby the United States have, upon several occasions, been exposed to the most critical and alarming situations; have wanted an army adequate to their defence, and proportioned to the abilities of the country; have on account of that deficiency seen essential posts reduced—others imminently endangered—whole states, and large parts of others, overrun and ravaged by small bodies of the enemy's forces; have been destitute of sufficient means of feeding, clothing, paying, and appointing that army, by which the troops, rendered less efficient for military operations, have been exposed to sufferings, which nothing but unparalleled patience, perseverance, and patriotism could have endured. Whereas, also, the United States have been too often compelled to make the administration of their affairs a succession of temporary expedients, inconsistent with order, economy, energy, or a scrupulous adherence to the public engagements, and now find themselves, at the close of a glorious struggle for independence, without any certain means of doing justice to those who have been its principal supporters—to an army which has bravely fought, and patiently suffered—to citizens who have cheerfully lent their money—and and to others who have in different ways contributed their property and their personal service to the common cause; obliged to rely for the only effectual mode of doing that justice by funding the debt on solid securities, on the precarious concurrence of thirteen distinct deliberatives, the dissent of either of which may defeat the plan, and leave these states, at this early period of their existence, involved in all the disgrace and mischiefs of violated faith and national bankruptcy. And whereas, notwithstanding we have, by the blessing of Providence, so far happily escaped the complicated dangers of such a situation, and now see the object of our wishes secured by an honourable peace, it would be unwise to hazard a repetition of the same dangers and embarrassments, in any future war in which these states may be engaged, or to continue this extensive empire under a government unequal to its protection and prosperity. And whereas, it is essential to the happiness and security of these states, that their union should be established on the most solid foundations, and it is manifest that this desirable object cannot be effected but by a GOVERNMENT, capable, both in peace and war, of making every member of the union contribute in just proportion to the common necessities, and of combining and directing the forces and wills of the several parts to a general end; to which purposes, in the opinion of congress, the present confederation is altogether inadequate. And whereas, on the spirit which may direct the councils and measures of these states, at the present juncture, may depend their future safety and welfare—Congress conceive it to be their duty, freely to state to their constituents the defects which, by experience, have been discovered in the present plan of the fœderal union, and solemnly to call their attention to a revisal and amendment of the same. Therefore resolved, That it be earnestly recommended to the several states to appoint a Convention, to meet at —— on the —— day of ——, with full powers to revise the confederation, and to adopt and propose such alterations as to them shall appear necessary, to be finally approved or rejected by the states respectively—and that a committee of —— be appointed to prepare an address upon the subject."

ANNAPOLIS CONVENTION.

ANNAPOLIS, September 14th, 1786.

"To the honourable the legislatures of Virginia, Delaware, Pennsylvania, New-Jersey, and New-York.

"The commissioners from the said states respectively assembled at Annapolis, humbly beg leave to report, That pursuant to their several appointments, they met at Annapolis, in the state of Maryland, on the eleventh day of September, instant, and having proceeded to a communication of their powers, they found that the states of New-York, Pennsylvania, and Virginia, had in substance, and nearly in the same terms, authorized their respective commissioners to meet such commissioners as were or might be appointed by the other states in the union, at such time and place as should be agreed upon by the said commissioners, to take into consideration the trade and commerce of the United States, to consider how far an uniform system in their commercial intercourse and regulations might be necessary to their common interest and permanent harmony, and to report to the several states such an act relative to this great object, as, when unanimously ratified by them, would enable the United States in congress assembled effectually to provide for the same.

"That the state of Delaware had given similar powers to their commissioners; with this difference only, that the act to be framed in virtue of these powers, is required to be reported 'to the United States in congress assembled, to be agreed to by them, and confirmed by the legislature of every state.'

"That the state of New-Jersey had enlarged the object of their appointment, empowering their commissioners 'to consider how far an uniform system in their commercial regulations, and *other* important matters, might be necessary to the common interest and permanent harmony of the several states; and to report such an act on the subject, as, when ratified by them, would enable the United States in congress assembled effectually to provide for the exigencies of the union.'

"That appointments of commissioners have also been made by the states of New-Hampshire, Massachusetts, Rhode Island, and North Carolina, none of whom, however, have attended. But that no information has been received by your commissioners of any appointment having been made by the states of Connecticut, Maryland, South Carolina, or Georgia. That the express terms of the powers to your commissioners supposing a deputation from all the states, and having for their object the trade and commerce of the United States, your commissioners did not conceive it advisable to proceed to the business of their mission under the circumstance of so partial and defective a representation.

"Deeply impressed, however, with the magnitude and importance of the object confided to them on this occasion, your commissioners cannot forbear to indulge an expression of their earnest and unanimous wish that speedy measures may be taken to effect a general meeting of the states in a future convention for the same, and such other purposes, as the situation of public affairs may be found to require.

"If in expressing this wish, or intimating any other sentiment, your commissioners should seem to exceed the strict bounds of their appointment, they entertain a full confidence that a conduct dictated by an anxiety for the welfare of the United States will not fail to receive a favourable construction. In this persuasion, your commissioners submit an opinion that the idea of extending the powers of their deputies to other objects than those of commerce, which had been adopted by the state of New-Jersey, was an improvement on the original plan, and will deserve to be incorporated into that of a future convention. They are the more naturally led to this conclusion, as, in the course of their reflections on the subject, they have been induced to think that the power of regulating trade is of such comprehensive extent, and will enter so far into the general system of the federal government, that to give it efficacy, and to obviate questions and doubts concerning its precise nature and limits, may require a correspondent adjustment of other parts of the federal system. That there are important defects in the system of the federal government, is acknowledged by the acts of all those states which have concurred in the present meeting; that the defects, upon a closer examination, may be found greater and more numerous than even these acts imply, is at least so far probable, from the embarrassments which characterize the present state of our national affairs foreign and domestic, as may reasonably be supposed to merit a deliberate and candid discussion in some mode which will unite the sentiments and councils of all the states.

"In the choice of the mode, your commissioners are of the opinion that a CONVENTION of deputies from the different states for the special and sole purpose of entering into this investigation, and digesting a plan of supplying such defects as may be discovered to exist, will be entitled to a preference, from considerations which will occur without being particularized. Your commissioners decline an enumeration of those national circumstances on which their opinion respecting the propriety of a future convention with those enlarged powers is founded, as it would be an intrusion of facts and observations, most of which have been frequently the subject of public discussion, and none of which can have escaped the penetration of those to whom they would in this instance be addressed.

"They are, however, of a nature so serious, as, in the view of your commissioners, to render the situation of the United States delicate and critical, calling for an exertion of the united virtue and wisdom of all the members of the confederacy. Under this impression, your commissioners with the most respectful deference beg leave to suggest their unanimous conviction, that it may effectually tend to advance the interests of the union, if the states by which they have been respectively delegated would concur themselves, and use their endeavours to procure the concurrence of the other states, in the appointment of commissioners to meet at Philadelphia on the second Monday in May next, to take into consideration the situation of the United States, to devise such further provisions as shall appear to them necessary to render the constitution of the federal government *adequate to the exigencies of the union*, and to report such an act for that purpose to the United States in congress assembled, as, when agreed to by them, and afterwards confirmed by the legislature of every state, will effectually provide for the same.

"Though your commissioners could not with propriety address these observations and sentiments to any but the states they have the honour to represent, they have nevertheless concluded from motives of respect, to transmit copies of this report to the United States in congress assembled, and to the executives of the other States."

SPEECH ON THE IMPOST GRANT.

The first objection (and that which is supposed to have the greatest force) against the principles of the bill, is, that it would be unconstitutional to delegate legislative power to Congress. If this objection be founded in truth, there is at once an end of the enquiry. God forbid that we should violate that Constitution which is the charter of our rights! But it is our duty to examine dispassionately whether it really stands in our way. If it does not, let us not erect an ideal barrier to a measure which the public good may require.

The first ground of the objection is deduced from that clause of the Constitution which declares "that no power shall be exercised over the people of this state but such as is granted by or derived from them."

This, it is plain, amounts to nothing more than a declaration of that fundamental maxim of republican governments, "that all power, mediately or immediately, is derived from the consent of the people," in opposition to those doctrines of despotism which uphold the divine right of kings, or lay the foundations of government in force, conquest, or necessity. It does not at all affect the question how far the legislature may go in granting power to the United States. A power conferred by the representatives of the people, if warranted by the Constitution under which they act, is a power derived from the people. This is not only a plain inference of reason, but the terms of the clause itself seem to have been calculated to let in the principle. The words, "derived from," are added to the words, "granted by," as if with design to distinguish an indirect derivation of power from an immediate grant of it. This explanation is even necessary to reconcile the Constitution to itself, and to give effect to all its parts, as I hope fully to demonstrate in its proper place.

The next clause of the Constitution relied upon, is that which declares that "the supreme legislative power *within this state* shall be vested in a Senate and Assembly." This, it is said, excludes the idea of any other legislative power operating *within the state*. But the more obvious construction of this clause, and that which best consists with the situation and views of the country at this time, with what has been done before and since the formation of our Constitution, and with those parts of the Constitution itself which acknowledge the Federal Government, is this—"In the distribution of the different parts of the sovereignty in the *particular* government of this state, the legislative authority shall reside in a Senate and Assembly," or, in other words, "the legislative authority of the particular Government of the State of New York shall be vested in a Senate and Assembly."

The framers of the Constitution could have had nothing more in view than to delineate the different departments of power in our own State government, and never could have intended to interfere with the formation of such a Constitution for the Union as the safety of the whole might require.

12

The justness of this construction will be further elucidated by that part of the Constitution which prescribes that "the supreme executive authority of *the state* shall be vested in a governor." If the former clause excludes the grant of legislative power, this must equally exclude the grant of executive power. And the consequence would be that there would be no Federal Government at all.

It will be of no avail to say that there is a difference in the two cases in the mode of expression; that, in one, the terms of description are "within the state," in the other, "of the state." In grammar, or good sense, the difference in the phrases constitutes no substantial difference in the meaning, or, if it does, it concludes against the objection; for the words, *within this state*, which are applied to the legislative power, have a certain precision that may be supposed to intend a distinction between that legislative power which is to operate *within the state* only, and that which is to operate upon this state in conjunction with the others. But I lay no stress on this observation. In my opinion the legislative power *"within this state"* or the legislative power "of this state," amount in substance to the same thing. And therefore (as has been already observed) if the Constitution prohibits the delegation of legislative power to the UNION, it equally prohibits the delegation of Executive power—and the CONFEDERACY must then be at an end; for without legislative or executive power, it becomes a nullity.

Unfortunately for the objection, if it proves anything it proves too much—It proves that the powers of the Union in their present form are an usurpation on the Constitution of this State. This will appear not only from the reasoning adduced, but from this further consideration,— that the United States are already possessed of *legislative* as well as *Executive* authority. The objects of Executive power are of three kinds, to make treaties with foreign nations, to make war and peace, to execute and interpret the laws. This description of the executive power will enable us the more readily to distinguish the legislative; which in general may be defined the power of prescribing rules for the community.

The United States are authorized to require from the several states as much money as they judge necessary for the general purposes of the union, and to limit the time within which it is to be raised: to call for such a number of troops as they deem requisite for the common defence in time of war—to establish rules in all cases of capture by sea or land—to regulate the alloy and value of coin, the standard of weights and measures, and to make all laws for the government of the army and navy of the union. All these are powers of the legislative kind, and are declared by the confederation to be binding upon all the states.

The first is nothing less than a power of taxing the states in gross though not in detail; and the last is the power of disposing of the liberty and lives of the citizens of this state, when in arms for the common defence. That the powers enumerated are all, or most of them of a legislative nature, will not be denied by the law members on the other side of the question. If the Constitution forbids the grant of legislative power to the UNION, all those authorities are illegal and unconstitutional, and ought to be resumed.

If, on the contrary, those authorities were properly granted, then it follows that the CONSTITUTION does not forbid the grant of legislative power, and the objection falls to the ground; for there is nothing in the Constitution permitting the grant of one kind of legislative authority, and forbidding that of another. The degree or nature of the powers of legislation which it might be proper to confer upon the federal government would in this case be a mere question of prudence and expediency to be determined by general considerations of utility and safety.

The principle of the objection under consideration would not only subvert the foundation of the UNION as now established—would not only render it impossible that any federal government could exist; but would defeat some of the provisions of the Constitution itself. This last idea deserves particular attention.

The nineteenth clause makes it the duty of the Governor "to correspond with the continental Congress." The twentieth provides "that the judges and chancellor shall hold no other office than delegate to the general Congress;" and the thirtieth directs "that delegates to *represent* this state in the general CONGRESS of the United States of America shall be annually appointed."

Now, Sir, I ask, if Congress were to have neither executive nor legislative authority, to what purpose were they to exist? To what purpose were delegates to be annually appointed to that body? To what purpose were these delegates to represent this state? Or how could they be said to represent it at all?

Is not the plain import of this part of the Constitution, that they were to *represent this state* in the general assembly of the UNITED STATES, for the purpose of managing the common concerns of the union? And does not this necessarily imply that they were to be clothed with such powers as should be found essential to that object? Does it amount to a constitutional warrant to the legislature to confer those powers of whatever kind they might be?

To answer these questions in the negative would be to charge the Constitution with the absurdity of proposing to itself an *end*, and yet prohibiting the means of accomplishing that end.

The words "to represent this state" are of great latitude, and are of themselves sufficient to convey any power necessary to the conduct and direction of its affairs in connection with the other parts of the confederacy.

In the interpretation of laws it is admitted to be a good rule to resort to the co-existing circumstances and collect from thence the intention of the framers of the law. Let us apply this rule to the present case.

In the commencement of the revolution delegates were sent to meet in Congress with large discretionary powers—In short, generally speaking, with full power "to take care of the republic." In the whole of this transaction the idea of an UNION of the colonies was carefully held up.—It pervaded all our public acts.

In the declaration of independence we find it continued and confirmed. That declaration, after setting forth its motives and causes, proceeds thus—"We, therefore, the representatives of the United States of
America in general Congress assembled, appealing to the Supreme
Judge of the world for the rectitude of our intentions, do in the name
and by the authority of the good people of these colonies, solemnly publish and declare, that these United Colonies are, and of right ought to
be, free and independent states; that they are absolved from all allegiance to the British Crown, and that all political connection between
them and the State of Great Britain is and ought to be totally dissolved;
and that as free and independent states they have full power to levy
war, conclude peace, contract alliances, establish commerce, and do all
other acts and things that independent states may of right do."

Hence we see that the UNION and INDEPENDENCE of these STATES
are blended and incorporated in one and the same act; which taken
together, clearly imports that the United States had in their origin full
power to do all acts and things which Independent States may of right
do; or, in other words, full power of sovereignty.

Accordingly, we find that upon the authority of that act only
approved by the several states, they did levy war, contract alliances,
and exercise other high powers of sovereignty even to the appointment
of a dictator, prior to the present confederation.

In this situation, and with this plenitude of power, our Constitution
knows and acknowledges the United States in Congress assembled, and
provides for the annual appointment of delegates to represent this state
in that body; which in substance amounts to a constitutional recognition
of the UNION with complete sovereignty.

A government may exist without any formal organization or precise
definition of its powers. However improper it might have been, that the
federal government should have continued to exist with such absolute
and undefined authority, this does not militate against the position that
it did possess such authority. It only proves the propriety of a more
regular formation to ascertain its limits. This was the object of the present confederation, which is, in fact, an abridgement of the original
sovereignty of the UNION.

It may be said, (for it has been said upon other occasions,) that
though the Constitution did consider the United States in the light I
have described, and left the legislature at liberty in the first instance to
have organized the FEDERAL GOVERNMENT in such a manner as they
thought proper, yet that liberty ceased with the establishment of the
present confederacy. The discretion of the legislature was then determined.

This, upon the face of it, is a subtilty, uncountenanced by a single
principle of government, or a single expression of the Constitution. It is
saying that a general authority given to the legislature for the permanent preservation and good of the community, has been exhausted and
spent by the exercise of a part of that authority. The position is the
more destitute of colour; because the confederation, by the express

terms of the compact, preserves and continues this power. The last clause of it authorises Congress to propose, and the states to agree to such alterations as might be afterwards found necessary or expedient.

We see, therefore, that the Constitution knows and acknowledges the United States in Congress; that it provides for the annual appointment of delegates to *represent this state* in that body without prescribing the objects or limits of that representation. That at the time our Constitution was framed, the UNION existed with full sovereignty; and that therefore the idea of sovereignty in the UNION is not incompatible with it. We see, further, that the doctrine contained in the objection against granting legislative power, would equally operate against granting executive power, would prove that the powers already vested in the union are illegal and unconstitutional, would render a confederacy of the states in any form impracticable, and would defeat all those provisions of our own Constitution which relate to the United States. I submit it to the committee, whether a doctrine pregnant with such consequences can be true— whether it is not as opposite to our Constitution as to the principles of national safety and prosperity—and whether it would not be lamentable if the zeal of opposition to a particular measure should carry us to the extreme of imposing upon the Constitution a sense foreign to it; which must embarrass the national councils upon future occasions, when all might agree in the utility and necessity of a different construction.

If the arguments I have used under this head are not well founded, let gentlemen *come forward and show their fallacy.* Let the subject have a fair and full examination, and let truth, on whatever side it may be, prevail!

Flattering myself it will appear to the committee that the Constitution at least offers us no impediment, I shall proceed to the topics of objection. The next that presents itself is a supposed danger to liberty from granting legislative power to Congress.

But before I enter upon this subject, to remove the aspersions thrown upon that body, I shall give a short history of some material facts relating to the origin and progress of the business. To excite the jealousies of the people, it has been industriously represented as an undue attempt to acquire an increase of power. It has been forgotten or intentionally overlooked, that, considering it in the strongest light as a proposal to alter the confederation, it is only exercising a power which the confederation has in direct terms reposed in Congress, who, as before observed, are by the 13th article, expressly authorised to propose alterations.

But so far was the measure from originating in improper views of that body, that, if I was rightly informed, it did not originate there at all. It was first suggested by a convention of the four Eastern states, and New York, at Hartford, and I believe was proposed there by the deputies of this state. A gentleman on our bench, unconnected with Congress, who now hears me, (I mean Judge Hobart,) was one of them. It was dictated by a principle which *bitter experience then* taught us, and which in peace or war will always be found true—that adequate supplies to the federal treasury can never flow from any system which requires the intervention of thirteen deliberatives between the *call* and the *execution*.

Congress agreed to the measure and recommended it. This state complied without hesitation. All parts of the government, senate, assembly, and council of revision concurred—neither the Constitution nor the public liberty presented any obstacle. The difficulties from these sources are a recent discovery.

So late as the first session of the legislature after the evacuation of this city, the Governor of the state in his speech to both houses, gave a decided countenance to the measure—this he does, though not in express terms, yet by implications not to be misunderstood.

The *leading opponents* of the impost, of the present day, have all of them at other times, either concurred in the measure in its most exceptionable form, and without the qualifications annexed to it by the proposed bill, or have by other instances of conduct contradicted their own hypothesis on the Constitution which professedly forms the main prop of their opposition.

The honorable member in my eye (   ) at the last session brought in a bill for granting to the United States the power of regulating the trade of the union. This surely includes more ample legislative authority than is comprehended in the mere power of levying a particular duty. It indeed goes to a prodigious extent much farther than on a superficial view can be imagined. Can we believe that the constitutional objection, if well founded, would so long have passed undiscovered and unnoticed? or is it fair to impute to Congress criminal motives for proposing a measure which was first recommended to them by five states, or from persisting in that measure, after the unequivocal experience they have had of the total inefficacy of the mode provided in the confederation for supplying the treasury of the union?

I leave the answer to these questions to the good sense and candor of the committee, and shall return to the examination of the question, how far the power proposed to be conferred upon Congress would be dangerous to the liberty of the people. And here I ask,

Whence can this danger arise? The members of Congress are annually chosen by the members of the several legislatures. They come together with different habits, prejudices, and interests. They are in fact continually changing. How is it possible for a body so composed to be formidable to the liberties of States, several of which are large empires in themselves?

The subversion of the liberty of these states could not be the business of a day. It would at least require time, premeditation, and concert. Can it be supposed that the members of a body so constituted would be unanimous in a scheme of usurpation? If they were not, would it not be discovered and disclosed? If we could even suppose this unanimity among one set of men, can we believe that all the new members who are yearly sent from one state or another would instantly enter into the same views? Would there not be found one honest man to warn his country of the danger?

Suppose the worst—suppose the combination entered into and continued. The execution would at least announce the design; and the means of defence would be easy. Consider the separate power of several of these states, and the situation of all. Consider the extent, populousness, and resources of Massachusetts, Virginia, Pennsylvania; I might add of New York, Connecticut, and other states. Where could Congress find means sufficient to subvert the government and liberties of either of these states! or rather, where find means sufficient to effect the conquest at all? If an attempt is made upon one, the others from a sense of common danger, would make common cause; and they could immediately unite and provide for their joint defence.

There is one consideration of immense force in this question not sufficiently attended to. It is this, that each state possesses in itself the full powers of government, and can at once in a regular and constitutional way, take measures for the preservation of its rights. In a single Kingdom or state, if the rulers attempt to establish a tyranny, the people can only defend themselves by a tumultuary insurrection; they must run to arms without concert or plan; while the usurpers clothed with the forms of legal authority can employ the forces of the state to suppress them in embryo; and before they can have time or opportunity to give system to their opposition. With us the case is widely different. Each state has a government completely organized in itself; and can at once enter into a regular plan of defence. With the forces of the community at its command it can immediately form connections with its neighbors, or even with foreign powers, if necessary.

In a contest of this kind, the body of the people will always be on the side of the state governments. This will not only result from their love of liberty and regard to their own safety; but from other strong principles of human nature. The state governments operate upon those immediate familiar personal concerns to which the sensibility of individuals is awake. The distribution of private justice belonging to them, they must always appear to the senses of the people as the immediate guardians of their rights—they will of course have the strongest hold on their attachment, respect and obedience. Another circumstance will contribute to the same end. Far the greatest number of offices and employments are in the gift of the states separately—the weight of official influence will therefore be in favor of the state governments; and with all these advantages they cannot fail to carry the people along with them in every contest with the general government in which they are not palpably in the wrong, and often when they are. What is to be feared from the efforts of Congress to establish a tyranny with the great body of the people under the direction of their state governments combined in opposition to their views? Must not their attempts recoil upon themselves, and terminate in their own ruin and disgrace? or rather, would not these considerations, if they were insensible to other motives, forever restrain them from making such attempts?

The causes taken notice of as securing the attachment of the people to their local governments, present us with another important truth—the natural imbecility of federal governments, and the danger that they will never be able to exercise power enough to manage the general affairs of the UNION. Though the States will have a common interest, yet they will also have a particular interest. For example, as a part of the Union, it will be the interest of every State to pay as little itself, and to let its neighbors pay as much as possible. Particular interests have always more influence upon men than general. The federal States, therefore, consulting their immediate advantage, may be considered as so many eccentric powers tending in a contrary direction to the government of the Union; and as they will generally carry the people along with them, the confederacy will be in continual danger of dissolution. This, Mr. Chairman, is the real rock upon which the happiness of this country is likely to split—this is the point to which our fears and cares should be directed; to guard against this, and not to terrify ourselves with imaginary dangers from the spectre of power in Congress, will be our true wisdom.

But let us examine a little more closely the measure under consideration. What does the bill before us require us to do? Merely to grant duties on imposts to the United States for the short period of twenty-five years—to be applied to the discharge of the principal and interest of the debts contracted for the support of the late war; the collection of which duties is to be made by officers appointed by the State, but accountable to Congress, according to such general regulations as the United States shall establish; subject to these important checks, that no citizen shall be carried out of the State for trial; that all prosecutions shall be in our own courts; that no excessive fines or penalties shall be imposed; and that a yearly account of the proceeds and application of the revenue shall be rendered to the legislature, on failure of which it reserves to itself a right of repealing its grant.

Is it possible for any measure to be better guarded? or is it possible that a grant for such precise objects, and with so many checks, can be dangerous to the public liberty?

Having now as I trust satisfactorily shown that the Constitution offers no obstacle to the measure, and that the liberty of the people cannot be endangered by it, it remains only to consider it in the view of revenue.

The sole question left for discussion is whether it be an eligible mode for supplying the Federal treasury or not?

The better to answer this question, it will be of use to examine how far the mode by quotas and requisitions has been found competent to the public exigencies.

The universal delinquency of the States during the war shall be passed over with the bare mention of it. The public embarrassments were a plausible apology for that delinquency, and it was hoped the peace would have produced greater punctuality. The experiment has disappointed that hope to a degree which confounds the least sanguine. A comparative view of the compliances of the several States, for the five last years, will furnish a striking result.

During that period, as appears by a statement on our files, New

Hampshire, North Carolina, South Carolina, and Georgia, have paid nothing. I say nothing, because the only actual payment is the trifling sum of about seven thousand dollars by New Hampshire. South Carolina indeed has credits, but these are merely by way of discount, on the supplies furnished by her during the war, in consideration of her peculiar sufferings and exertions, while the immediate theatre of it.

Connecticut and Delaware have paid about one-third of their requisitions. Massachusetts, Rhode Island, and Maryland, about one-half. Virginia, about three-fifths, Pennsylvania, nearly the whole, and New York, more than her quota.

These proportions are taken on the specie requisitions, the indents have been very partially paid, and in their present state are of little account.

The payments into the federal treasury have declined rapidly each year. The whole amount for three years past in specie has not exceeded 1,400,000 dollars, of which New York has paid one hundred per cent more than her proportion. This sum, little more than 400,000 dollars a year, it will readily be conceived, has been exhausted in the support of the civil establishments of the Union, and the necessary guards and garrisons at public arsenals, and on the frontiers; without any surplus for paying any part of the debt, foreign or domestic, principal or interest.

Things are continually growing worse, the last year in particular produced less than two hundred thousand dollars, and that from only two or three States. Several of the States have been so long unaccustomed to pay, that they seem no longer concerned even about the appearances of compliance.

Connecticut and New Jersey have almost formally declined paying any longer. The ostensible motive is the non-concurrence of this State in the impost system. The real one must be conjectured from the fact.

Pennsylvania, if I understand the scope of some late resolutions, means to discount the interest she pays upon her assumption to her own citizens; in which case there will be little coming from her to the United States. This seems to be bringing matters to a crisis.

The pecuniary support of the Federal government has of late devolved almost entirely upon Pennsylvania and New York. If Pennsylvania refuses to continue her aid, what will be the situation of New York? Are we willing to be the Atlas of the Union? or are we willing to see it perish?

This seems to be the alternative. Is there not a species of political knight-errantry in adhering pertinaciously to a system which throws the whole weight of the Confederation upon this STATE, or upon one or two more? Is it not our interest, on mere calculations of state policy, to promote a measure, which, operating under the same regulations in every State, must produce an equal, or nearly equal, effect everywhere, and oblige all the States to share the common burthen?

If the impost is granted to the United States, with the power of levying it, it must have a proportionate effect in all the States, for the same mode of collection everywhere will have nearly the same return everywhere.

What must be the final issue of the present state of things? Will the few States that now contribute be willing to contribute much longer? Shall we ourselves be long content with bearing the burthen singly? will not our zeal for a particular system soon give way to the pressure of so unequal a weight? and if all the States cease to pay, what is to become of the Union? It is sometimes asked, why do not Congress oblige the States to do their duty; but where are the means? Where are the fleets and armies, where the Federal treasury to support those fleets and armies, to enforce the requisitions of the Union? All methods short of coercion have repeatedly been tried in vain.

Let us now proceed to another most important inquiry. How are we to pay our foreign debt? This, I think, is estimated at about 7,000,000 of dollars; which will every year increase with the accumulations of interest. If we pay neither principal nor interest, we not only abandon all pretensions to character as a nation, but we endanger the public peace. However it may be in our power to evade the just demands of our domestic creditors, our foreign creditors must and will be paid.

They have power to enforce their demands, and sooner or later they may be expected to do it. It is not my intention to endeavour to excite the apprehensions of the committee, but I would appeal to their prudence. A discreet attention to the consequences of national measures is no impeachment of our firmness.

The foreign debt, I say, must sooner or later be paid, and the longer provision is delayed, the heavier it must fall at last.

We require about 1,600,000 dollars to discharge the interest and instalments of the present year, about a million annually upon an average for ten years more, and about 300,000 dollars for another ten years.

The product of the impost may be computed at about a million of dollars annually. It is an increasing fund. This fund would not only suffice for the discharge of the foreign debt, but important operations might be ingrafted upon it, towards the extinguishment of the domestic debt.

Is it possible to hesitate about the propriety of adopting a resource so easy in itself, and so extensive in its effects?

Here I expect I may be told there is no objection to employing this resource. The act of the last session does it. The only dispute is about the mode. We are willing to grant the *money*, but not the *power* required from us. Money will pay our debts; power may destroy our liberties.

It has been insinuated that nothing but a lust of power would have prevented Congress from accepting the grant in the shape it has already passed the legislature. This is a severe charge; if true, it ought undoubtedly to prevent our going a step further. But it is easy to show that Congress could not have accepted our grant without removing themselves further from the object than they now are. To gain one State they must have lost all the others. The grants of every State are accompanied with a condition, that similar grants be made by the other

States. It is not denied that our act is essentially different from theirs. Their acts give the United States the power of collecting the duty. Ours reserves it to the state, and makes it receivable in paper money.

The immediate consequences of accepting our grant would be a relinquishment of the grants of other States, they must take the matter up anew, and do the work over again, to accommodate it to our standard. In order to anchor one state, would it have been wise to set twelve, or at least eleven others, afloat?

It is said, that the States which have granted more would certainly be willing to grant less. They would easily accommodate their acts to that of New York, as more favorable to their own power and security.

But would Massachusetts and Virginia, which have no paper money of their own, accede to a plan that permitted other States to pay in paper, while they paid in specie? Would they consent that their citizens should pay *twenty* shillings in the pound, while the citizens of Rhode Island paid only *four*, the citizens of North Carolina *ten*, and of other States in different degrees of inequality, in proportion to the relative depreciation of their paper? Is it wise in this State to cherish a plan that gives such an advantage to the citizens of other States over its own?

The paper money of the State of New York, in most transactions, is equal to gold and silver; that of Rhode Island is depreciated to five for one; that of North Carolina to two for one; that of South Carolina may perhaps be worth fifteen shillings in the pound.

If the States pay the duties in paper, is it not evident that for every pound of that duty consumed by the citizen of New York, he would pay twenty shillings, while the citizen of South Carolina would pay fifteen shillings, of North Carolina, ten shillings, and Rhode Island, only four!

This consideration alone is sufficient to condemn the plan of our grant of last session, and to prove incontestably that the States which are averse to emitting a paper currency, or have it in their power to support one when emitted, would never come into it.

Again, would those States, which by their public acts demonstrate a conviction that the powers of the union require augmentation; which are conscious of energy in their own administration—would they be willing to concur in a plan which left the collection of the duties in the hands of each State, and of course subject to all the inequalities which a more or less vigorous system of collection would produce?

This too is an idea which ought to have great weight with us. We have better habits of government than are to be found in some of the States, and our constitution admits of more energy than the constitutions of most of the other States. The duties, therefore, would be more effectually collected with us than in such States, and they would have a similar effect to the depreciation of the money, in imposing a greater burthen on the citizens of this State.

If any State should incline to evade the payment of the duties, having the collection in its own hands, nothing would be easier than to effect it, and without materially sacrificing appearances.

It is manifest from this view of the subject, that we have the

strongest reasons as a State, to depart from our own act, and that it
would have been highly injudicious in Congress to have accepted it.

If there even had been a prospect of the concurrence of the other
States in the plan, how inadequate would it have been to the public exigencies, fettered with the embarrassments of a depreciating paper!

It is to no purpose to say, that the faith of the State was pledged by
the act to make the paper equal to gold and silver, and that the other
States would be obliged to do the same. What greater dependence can
be had on the faith of the States pledged to this measure, than on the
faith they pledged in the confederation, sanctioned by a solemn appeal
to heaven? If the obligation of faith in one case has had so little influence upon their conduct in respect to the requisitions of Congress, what
hope can there be that they would have greater influences in respect to
the deficiencies of the paper money?

There yet remains an important light in which to consider the subject
in the way of revenue. It is a clear point that we cannot carry the
duties upon imports to the same extent by separate arrangements as by
a general plan. We must regulate ourselves by what we find done in the
neighboring States. While Pennsylvania has only two and a half per
cent. on her importations, we cannot greatly exceed her. To go much
beyond it would injure our commerce in a variety of ways, and would
defeat itself—While the ports of Connecticut and New Jersey are open
to the introduction of goods free from duty, and the conveyance from
them to us is so easy—While they consider our imposts as an ungener-
ous advantage taken of them, which it would be laudable to elude, the
duties must be light, or they would be evaded. The facility to do it and
the temptation of doing it would be both so great, that we should collect perhaps less by an increase of the rates than we do now. Already
we experience the effects of this situation. But if the duties were to be
levied under a common direction, with the same precautions everywhere to guard against smuggling, they might be carried without prejudice to trade to a much more considerable height.

As things now are, we must adhere to the present standard of duties,
without any material alterations. Suppose this to produce fifty thousand
pounds a year. The duties to be granted to Congress ought, in proportion, to produce double that sum. To this it appears by a scheme now
before us, that additional duties might be imposed for the use of the
State, on certain enumerated articles, to the amount of thirty thousand
pounds. This would be an augmentation of our national revenue by indirect taxation to the extent of eighty thousand pounds a year; an
immense object in a single State, and which alone demonstrates the
good policy of the measure.

It is no objection to say that a great part of this fund will be dedicated to the use of the United States. Their exigencies must be supplied
in some way or other. The more is done towards it by means of the
impost, the less will be to be done in other modes. If we do not employ
that resource to the best account, we must find others in *direct* taxation. And to this are opposed all the habits and prejudices of the com-

munity. There is not a farmer in the state who would not pay a shilling in the voluntary consumption of articles on which a duty is paid, rather than a penny imposed immediately on his house and land.

There is but one objection to the measure under consideration that has come to my knowledge, which yet remains to be discussed. I mean the effect it is supposed to have upon our paper currency. It is said, the diversion of this fund would leave the credit of the paper without any effectual support.

Though I should not be disposed to put a consideration of this kind in competition with the safety of the UNION, yet I should be extremely cautious about doing anything that might affect the credit of our currency. The legislature having thought an emission of paper advisable, I consider it my duty as a representative of the people to take care of its credit. The farmers appeared willing to exchange their produce for it. The merchants on the other hand, had large debts outstanding. They supposed that giving a free circulation to the paper would enable their customers in the country to pay, and as they perceived that they would have it in their power to convert the money into produce, they naturally resolved to give it their support.

These causes combined to introduce the money into general circulation, and having once obtained credit, it will now be able to support itself.

The chief difficulty to have been apprehended in respect to the paper, was to overcome the diffidence which the still recent experience of depreciating paper had instilled into men's minds. This, it was to have been feared, would have shaken its credit at its outset; and if it had once began to sink, it would be no easy matter to prevent its total decline.

The event has however turned out otherwise, and the money has been fortunate enough to conciliate the general confidence. This point gained, there need be no apprehensions of its future fate, unless the government should do something to destroy that confidence.

The causes that first gave it credit still operate, and will in all probability continue so to do. The demand for money has not lessened, and the merchant has still the same inducement to countenance the circulation of the paper.

I shall not deny that the outlet which the payment of duties furnished to the merchant, was an additional motive to the reception of the paper. Nor is it proposed to take away this motive. There is now before the house a bill, one object of which is, the establishment of a state impost, on certain enumerated articles, in addition to that to be granted to the United States. It is computed on very good grounds that the additional duties would amount to about £30,000, and as they would be payable in paper currency, they would create a sufficient demand upon the merchant, to leave him in this respect, substantially the same inducement which he had before. Indeed, independent of this, the readiness of the trading people to take the money can never be doubted, while it will freely command the commodities of the country; for this to them is the most important use they can make of it.

But, besides the State Imposts, there must be other taxes; and these will all contribute to create a demand for the money; which is all we now mean, when we talk of funds for its support; for there are none appropriated for the REDEMPTION of the paper.

Upon the whole the additional duties will be a competent substitute for those now in existence; and the general good will of the community towards the paper, will be the best security for its credit.

Having now shown, Mr. Chairman, that there is no constitutional impediment to the adoption of the bill; that there is no danger to be apprehended to the public liberty from giving the power in question to the United States; that in the view of revenue the measure under consideration is not only expedient, but necessary. Let us turn our attention to the other side of this important subject. Let us ask ourselves what will be the consequence of rejecting the bill? What will be the situation of our national affairs if they are left much longer to float in the chaos in which they are now involved?

Can our NATIONAL CHARACTER be preserved without paying our debts? Can the UNION subsist without revenue? Have we realized the consequences which would attend its dissolution?

If these States are not united under a FEDERAL GOVERNMENT, they will infallibly have wars with each other; and their divisions will subject them to all the mischiefs of foreign influence and intrigue. The human passions will never want objects of hostility. The WESTERN territory is an obvious and fruitful source of contest. Let us also cast our eye upon the map of this State, intersected from one extremity to the other by a large navigable river. In the event of a rupture with them, what is to hinder our Metropolis from becoming a prey to our neighbors? Is it even supposable that they would suffer it to remain the nursery of wealth to a distinct community?

These subjects are delicate, but it is necessary to contemplate them, to teach us to form a true estimate of our situation.

Wars with each other would beget standing armies—a source of more real danger to our liberties than all the powers that could be conferred upon the representatives of the Union. And wars with each other would lead to opposite alliances with foreign powers, and plunge us into all the labyrinths of European politics.

The Romans in their progress to universal dominion when they conceived the project of subduing the refractory spirit of the Grecian Republics, which composed the famous Achaean league, began by sowing dissensions among them, and instilling jealousies of each other, and of the common head, and finished by making them a province of the ROMAN EMPIRE.

The application is easy; if there are any foreign enemies, if there are any domestic foes to this country, all their arts and artifices will be employed to effect a dissolution of the UNION. This cannot be better done than by sowing jealousies of the FEDERAL HEAD and cultivating in each state an undue attachment to its own power.

RESOLUTION FOR AN ACT BY CONGRESS RECOMMENDING THE HOLDING A CONVENTION.

FEBRUARY 17, 1787.

Resolved, If the Honorable the Senate concur, That the Delegates of this State in the Congress of the United States in America be, and they are hereby instructed to move in Congress for an Act recommending to the States composing the Union, that a Convention of Representatives from the said States respectively, be held and meet at a time and place to be mentioned in said recommendation, for the purpose of revising the Articles of Confederation and Perpetual Union between the United States of America, by such alterations and amendments as a majority of the Representatives in such Convention shall judge proper and necessary to render them adequate to the preservation and support of the Union.

RESOLUTION FOR THE APPOINTMENT BY NEW YORK OF DELEGATES TO THE GENERAL CONVENTION.

FEBRUARY 26, 1787.

Resolved, (if the Honorable the Senate concur herein,) That five Delegates be appointed on the part of this State to meet such Delegates as may be appointed on the part of the other States respectively, on the Second Monday of May next, at Philadelphia, for the sole and express purpose of revising the Articles of Confederation, and reporting to Congress and to the several Legislatures such alterations and provisions therein, as shall, when agreed to in Congress and confirmed by the several States, render the Federal Constitution adequate to the exigencies of Government and the preservation of the Union; and that, in case of such concurrence, the two Houses of the Legislature will meet on Thursday next, at such place as the Honorable the Senate shall think proper, for the purpose of electing the said delegates by joint ballot.

ARTICLES OF CONFEDERATION.

Articles of Confederation and perpetual Union between the States of New Hampshire, Massachusetts Bay, Rhode Island and Providence Plantations, Connecticut, New York, New Jersey, Pennsylvania, Delaware, Maryland, Virginia, North Carolina, South Carolina, and Georgia.

ARTICLE I. The style of this Confederacy shall be "The United States of America."

ART. II. Each State retains its sovereignty, freedom, and independence, and every power, jurisdiction, and right, which is not by this Confederation expressly delegated to the United States, in Congress assembled.

ART. III. The said States hereby severally enter into a firm league of friendship with each other, for their common defence, the security of their liberties, and their mutual and general welfare, binding themselves to assist each other, against all force offered to, or attacks made upon them, or any of them, on account of religion, sovereignty, trade, or any other pretence whatever.

ART. IV. The better to secure and perpetuate mutual friendship and intercourse among the people of the different States in this Union, the free inhabitants of each of these States, paupers, vagabonds, and fugitives from justice excepted, shall be entitled to all the privileges and immunities of free citizens in the several States, and the people of each State shall have free ingress and regress to and from any other State, and shall enjoy therein all the privileges of trade and commence, subject to the same duties, impositions, and restrictions as the inhabitants thereof respectively, provided that such restrictions shall not extend so far as to prevent the removal of property imported into any State, to any other State of which the owner is an inhabitant; provided also, that no imposition, duties or restriction shall be laid by any State, on the property of the United States, or either of them.

If any person guilty of or charged with treason, felony, or other high misdemeanor in any State, shall flee from justice, and be found in any of the United States, he shall upon demand of the governor or executive power of the State from which he fled, be delivered up and removed to the State having jurisdiction of his offence.

Full faith and credit shall be given in each of these States to the records, acts, and judicial proceedings of the Courts and magistrates of every other State.

ART. V. For the more convenient management of the general interests of the United States, delegates shall be annually appointed in such manner as the legislature of each State shall direct, to meet in Congress on the first Monday in November, in every year, with a power reserved to each State, to recall its delegates, or any of them, at any time within the year, and to send others in their stead, for the remainder of the year.

No State shall be represented in Congress by less than two, nor by more than seven members; and no person shall be capable of being a delegate for more than three years in any term of six years, nor shall any person, being a delegate, be capable of holding any office under the United States, for which he or another for his benefit receives any salary, fees, or emolument of any kind.

Each State shall maintain its own delegates in a meeting of the States, and while they act as members of the committee of the States.

In determining questions in the United States, in Congress assembled, each State shall have one vote.

Freedom of speech and debate in Congress shall not be impeached or questioned in any Court or place out of Congress, and the members of Congress shall be protected, in their persons from arrests and imprisonments, during the time of their going to and from, and attendance on Congress, except for treason, felony, or breach of the peace.

ART. VI. No State, without the consent of the United States in Congress assembled, shall send any embassy to, or receive any embassy from, or enter into any conference, agreement, alliance, or treaty with any king, prince, or State; nor shall any person holding any office of profit or trust under the United States, or any of them, accept of any present, emolument, office, or title of any kind whatever from any king, prince, or foreign State; nor shall the United States in Congress assembled, or any of them, grant any title of nobility.

No two or more States shall enter into any treaty, confederation, or alliance whatever between them, without the consent of the United States in Congress assembled, specifying accurately the purposes for which the same is to be entered into, and how long it shall continue.

No State shall lay any imposts or duties, which may interfere with any stipulations in treaties entered into by the United States in Congress assembled, with any king, prince, or State, in pursuance of any treaties already proposed by Congress, to the Courts of France and Spain.

No vessels of war shall be kept up in time of peace by any State, except such number only as shall be deemed necessary by the United States, in Congress assembled, for the defence of such State or its trade; nor shall any body of forces be kept up by any State, in time of peace, except such number only as in the judgment of the United States, in Congress assembled, shall be deemed requisite to garrison the forts necessary for the defence of such State; but every State shall always keep up a well regulated and disciplined militia, sufficiently armed and accoutred, and shall provide and constantly have ready for use, in public stores, a due number of field pieces and tents, and a proper quantity of arms, ammunition, and camp equipage.

No State shall engage in any war without the consent of the United States in Congress assembled, unless such State be actually invaded by enemies, or shall have received certain advice of a resolution being formed by some nation of Indians to invade such State, and the danger is so imminent as not to admit of a delay till the United States in Congress assembled can be consulted; nor shall any State grant commissions to any ships or vessels of war, nor letters of marque or reprisal, except it be after a declaration of war by the United States in Congress assembled, and then only against the kingdom or State, and the subjects thereof, against which war has been so declared, and under such regulations as shall be established by the United States in Congress assembled, unless such State be infested by pirates, in which case vessels of war may be fitted out for that occasion, and kept so long as the danger shall continue, or until the United States in Congress assembled shall determine otherwise.

ART. VII. When land forces are raised by any State for the common defence, all officers of or under the rank of Colonel shall be appointed by the legislature of each State respectively, by whom such forces shall be raised, or in such manner as such State shall direct; and all vacancies shall be filled up by the State which first made the appointment.

ART. VIII. All charges of war and all other expenses that shall be incurred for the common defence or general welfare, and allowed by the United States in Congress assembled, shall be defrayed out of a common treasury, which shall be supplied by the several States, in proportion to the value of all land within each State, granted to or surveyed for any person, and such land and the buildings and improvements thereon shall be estimated according to such mode as the United States in Congress assembled shall from time to time direct and appoint.

13

The taxes for paying that proportion shall be laid and levied by the authority and direction of the legislatures of the several States within the time agreed upon by the United States in Congress assembled.

ART. IX. The United States in Congress assembled shall have the sole and exclusive right and power of determining on peace and war, except in the cases mentioned in the sixth article—of sending and receiving ambassadors—entering into treaties and alliances, provided that no treaty of commerce shall be made whereby the legislative power of the respective States shall be restrained from imposing such imposts and duties on foreigners as their own people are subjected to, or from prohibiting the exportation or importation of any species of goods or commodities whatsoever—of establishing rules for deciding, in all cases, what captures on land or water shall be legal, and in what manner prizes taken by land or naval forces in the service of the United States shall be divided or appropriated—of granting letters of marque and reprisal in times of peace—appointing Courts for the trial of piracies and felonies committed on the high seas, and establishing courts for receiving and determining finally appeals in all cases of captures, provided that no member of Congress shall be appointed a judge of any of the said Courts.

The United States in Congress assembled shall also be the last resort on appeal in all disputes and differences now subsisting or that hereafter may arise between two or more States concerning boundary, jurisdiction, or any other cause whatever; which authority shall always be exercised in the manner following:—Whenever the legislative or executive authority or lawful agent of any State in controversy with another shall present a petition to Congress stating the matter in question and praying for a hearing, notice thereof shall be given by order of Congress to the legislative or executive authority of the other State in controversy, and a day assigned for the appearance of the parties by their lawful agents, who shall then be directed to appoint, by joint consent, commissioners or judges to constitute a court for hearing and determining the matter in question; but if they cannot agree, Congress shall name three persons out of each of the United States, and from the list of such persons each party shall alternately strike out one, the petitioners beginning, until the number shall be reduced to thirteen; and from that number not less than seven nor more than nine names, as Congress shall direct, shall, in the presence of Congress be drawn out by lot, and the persons whose names shall be so drawn, or any five of them, shall be commissioners or judges, to hear and finally determine the controversy, so always as a major part of the Judges who shall hear the cause shall agree in the determination; and if either party shall neglect to attend at the day appointed, without showing reasons, which Congress shall judge sufficient, or, being present, shall refuse to strike, the Congress shall proceed to nominate three persons out of each State, and the secretary of Congress shall strike in behalf of such party absent or refusing; and the judgment and sentence of the Court to be appointed, in the manner before prescribed, shall be final and conclusive; and if any of the parties shall refuse to submit to the authority of such court, or to appear or defend their claim or cause, the Court shall nevertheless proceed to pronounce sentence or judgment, which shall in like manner be final and decisive, the judgment or sentence and other proceedings being in either case transmitted to Congress, and lodged among the acts of Congress for the security of the parties concerned: provided that every commissioner, before he sits in judgment, shall take an oath, to be administered by one of the judges of the Supreme or Superior Court of the State where the cause shall be tried, *"well and truly to hear and determine the matter in question according to the best of his judgment, without favour, affection, or hope of reward:"* provided also that no State shall be deprived of territory for the benefit of the United States.

All controversies concerning the private right of soil, claimed under different grants of two or more States, whose jurisdictions as they may respect such lands and the

States which passed such grants are adjusted, the said grants or either of them being at the same time claimed to have originated antecedent to such settlement of jurisdiction, shall, on the petition of either party to the Congress of the United States, be finally determined as near as may be in the same manner as is before prescribed for deciding disputes respecting territorial jurisdiction between different States.

The United States in Congress assembled shall also have the sole and exclusive right and power of regulating the alloy and value of coin struck by their own authority, or by that of the respective States—fixing the standard of weights and measures throughout the United States—regulating the trade and managing all affairs with the Indians, not members of any of the States, provided that the legislative right of any State within its own limits be not infringed or violated—establishing and regulating and regulating post-offices from one State to another, throughout all the United States, and exacting such postage on the papers passing through the same as may be requisite to defray the expenses of the said office—appointing all officers of the land forces in the service of the United States, excepting regimental officers—appointing all the officers of the naval forces, and commissioning all officers whatever in the service of the United States—making rules for the government and regulation of the said land and naval forces, and directing their operations.

The United States in Congress assembled shall have authority to appoint a committee, to sit in the recess of Congress, to be denominated "A Committee of the States," and to consist of one delegate from each State; and to appoint such other committees and civil officers as may be necessary for managing the general affairs of the United States under their direction—to appoint one of their number to preside, provided that no person be allowed to serve in the office of president more than one year in any term of three years; to ascertain the necessary sums of money to be raised for the service of the United States, and to appropriate and apply the same for defraying the public expenses—to borrow money, or emit bills on the credit of the United States, transmitting every half-year to the respective States an account of the sums of money so borrowed or emitted—to build and equip a navy—to agree upon the number of land forces, and to make requisitions from each State for its quota, in proportion to the number of white inhabitants in such State; which requisition shall be binding, and thereupon the legislature of each State shall appoint the regimental officers, raise the men, and clothe, arm, and equip them in a soldier-like manner, at the expense of the United States, and the officers and men so clothed, armed, and equipped shall march to the place appointed, and within the time agreed on by the United States in Congress assembled; but if the United States in Congress assembled shall, on consideration of circumstances, judge proper that any State should not raise men, or should raise a smaller number than its quota, and that any other State should raise a greater number of men than the quota thereof, such extra number shall be raised, officered, clothed, armed, and equipped in the same manner as the quota of such State, unless the legislature of such State shall judge that such extra number cannot be safely spared out of the same, in which case they shall raise, officer, clothe, arm, and equip as many of such extra number as they judge can be safely spared. And the officers and men so clothed, armed, and equipped shall march to the place appointed, and within the time agreed on by the United States in Congress assembled.

The United States in Congress assembled shall never engage in a war, nor grant letters of marque and reprisal in time of peace, nor enter into any treaties or alliances, nor coin money, nor regulate the value thereof, nor ascertain the sums and expenses necessary for the defence and welfare of the United States, or any of them, nor emit bills, nor borrow money on the credit of the United States, nor appropriate money, nor agree upon the number of vessels of war to be built or purchased, or the number of land or sea forces to be raised, nor appoint a commander in chief of the army or navy, unless nine States assent to the same; nor shall a question on any other point, except for adjourning from day to day, be determined, unless by the votes of a majority of the United States in Congress assembled.

The Congress of the United States shall have power to adjourn to any time within the year, and to any place within the United States, so that no period of adjournment be for a longer duration than the space of six months, and shall publish the journal of their proceedings monthly, except such parts thereof relating to treaties, alliances, or military operations, as in their judgment require secrecy, and the yeas and nays of the delegates of each State on any question shall be entered on the journal, when it is desired by any delegate; and the delegates of a State, or any of them, at his or their request, shall be furnished with a transcript of the said journal, except such parts as are above excepted, to lay before the legislatures of the several States.

ART. X. The Committee of the States, or any nine of them, shall be authorized to execute, in the recess of Congress, such of the powers of Congress as the United States in Congress assembled, by the consent of nine States, shall from time to time think expedient to vest them with: provided that no power be delegated to the said Committee, for the exercise of which, by the Articles of Confederation, the voice of nine States in the Congress of the United States assembled is requisite.

ART. XI. Canada, acceding to this Confederation, and joining in the measures of the United States, shall be admitted into and entitled to all the advantages of this Union; but no other colony shall be admitted into the same, unless such admission be agreed to by nine States.

ART. XII. All bills of credit emitted, moneys borrowed, and debts contracted by or under the authority of Congress, before the assembling of the United States in pursuance of the present Confederation, shall be deemed and considered as a charge against the United States, for payment and satisfaction where of the said United States and the public faith are hereby solemnly pledged.

ART. XIII. Every State shall abide by the determinations of the United States in Congress assembled, on all questions which by this Confederation are submitted to them. And the Articles of this Confederation shall be inviolably observed by every State, and the Union shall be perpetual; nor shall any alteration at any time hereafter be made in any of them; unless such alteration be agreed to in a Congress of the United States, and be afterwards confirmed by the legislatures of every State.

AND WHEREAS it hath pleased the Great Governor of the world to incline the hearts of the legislatures we respectively represent in Congress to approve of and to authorize us to ratify the said articles of Confederation and perpetual Union, KNOW YE, That we the undersigned delegates, by virtue of the power and authority to us given for that purpose, do by these presents, in the name and in behalf of our respective constituents, fully and entirely ratify and confirm each and every of the said Articles of Confederation and perpetual Union, and all and singular the matters and things therein contained: and we do further solemnly plight and engage the faith of our respective constituents that they shall abide by the determinations of the United States in Congress assembled, on all questions which by the said Confederation are submitted to them. And that the Articles thereof shall be inviolably observed by the States we respectively represent, and that the Union shall be perpetual.

HAMILTON'S FIRST PLAN OF GOVERNMENT.

The People of the United States of America do ordain and establish this Constitution for the Government of themselves and their Posterity.

ARTICLE I.

SECTION 1. The Legislative power shall be vested in two distinct bodies of men, one to be called the Assembly, the other the Senate, subject to the negative hereinafter mentioned.

SEC. 2. The Executive power, with the qualifications hereinafter specified, shall be vested in a President of the United States.

SEC. 3. The supreme Judicial authority, except in the cases otherwise provided for in this Constitution, shall be vested in a court to be called the Supreme Court, to consist of not less than six, nor more than twelve judges.

ARTICLE II.

SEC. 1. The Assembly shall consist of persons to be called Representatives, who shall be chosen, except in the first instance, by the free male citizens and inhabitants of the several States comprehended in the Union, all of whom of the age of twenty-one years and upwards shall be entitled to an equal vote.

SEC. 2. But the first Assembly shall be chosen in the manner prescribed in the last Article, and shall consist of one hundred members, of whom New Hampshire shall have five, Massachusetts thirteen, Rhode Island two, Connecticut seven, New York nine, New Jersey six, Pennsylvania twelve, Delaware two, Maryland eight, Virginia sixteen, North Carolina eight, South Carolina eight, Georgia four.

SEC. 3. The Legislature shall provide for the future elections of Representatives, apportioning them in each State, from time to time, as nearly as may be to the number of persons described in the 4th Section of the VIIth Article, so as that the whole number of Representatives shall never be less than one hundred, nor more than   hundred. There shall be a census taken for this purpose within three years, after the first meeting of the Legislature, and within every successive period of ten years. The term for which Representatives shall be elected shall be determined by the Legislature; but shall not exceed three years. There shall be a general election at least once in three years; and the time of service of all the members in each Assembly shall begin (except in filling vacancies) on the same day, and shall always end on the same day.

SEC. 4. Forty members shall make a house sufficient to proceed to business. But this number may be increased by the Legislature, yet so as never to exceed a majority of the whole number of Representatives.

SEC. 5. The Assembly shall choose its President and other officers; shall judge of the qualifications and elections of its own members; punish them for improper conduct in their capacity of Representatives not extending to life or limb, and shall exclusively possess the power of impeachment, except in the case of the President of the

United States; but no impeachment of a member of the Senate shall be by less than two-thirds of the Representatives present.

SEC. 6. Representatives may vote by proxy, but no Representative present shall be proxy for more than one who is absent.

SEC. 7. Bills for raising revenue and bills for appropriating monies for the support of fleets and armies and for paying the salaries of the officers of government shall originate in the Assembly, but may be altered and amended by the Senate.

SEC. 8. The acceptance of an office under the United States by a Representative shall vacate his seat in the Assembly.

ARTICLE III.

SEC. 1. The Senate shall consist of persons to be chosen, except in the first instance, by Electors elected for that purpose by the citizens and inhabitants of the several States, comprehended in the Union, who shall have in their own right, or in the right of their wives, an estate in land for not less than life, or a term of years, whereof; at the time of giving their votes, there shall be at least fourteen years unexpired.

SEC. 2. But the first Senate shall be chosen in the manner prescribed in the last Article, and shall consist of forty members to be called Senators, of whom New Hampshire shall have   ; Massachusetts   ; Rhode Island   ; Connecticut ; New York   ; New Jersey   ; Pennsylvania   ; Delaware   ; Maryland   ; Virginia   ; North Carolina   ; South Carolina   ; Georgia .

SEC. 3. The Legislature shall provide for the future elections of Senators; for which purpose the States respectively, which have more than one Senator, shall be divided into convenient districts to which the Senators shall be apportioned: a State having but one Senator shall be itself a district. On the death, resignation, or removal from office of a Senator, his place shall be supplied by a new election in the District from which he came. Upon each election there shall be not less than six, nor more than twelve electors chosen in a District.

SEC. 4. The number of Senators shall never be less than forty, nor shall any State, if the same shall not hereafter be divided, ever have less than the number allotted to it in the second Section of this Article. But the Legislature may increase the whole number of Senators, in the same proportion to the whole number of Representatives, as forty is to one hundred, and such increase beyond the present number shall be apportioned to the respective States, in a ratio to the respective numbers of their Representatives.

SEC. 5. If States shall be divided, or if a new arrangement of the boundaries of two or more States shall take place, the Legislature shall apportion the number of Senators (in elections succeeding such division or arrangement) to which the constituent parts were entitled, according to the change of situation, having regard to the number of persons described in the 4th Section of the VIIth Article.

SEC. 6. The Senators shall hold their places during good behaviour, removeable only by conviction on impeachment for some crime or misdemeanour. They shall continue to exercise their offices, when impeached, until a conviction shall take place. Sixteen Senators attending in person shall be sufficient to make a house to transact business. But the Legislature may increase this number, yet so as never to exceed a majority of the whole number of Senators. The Senators may vote by proxy, but no Senator who is present shall be proxy for more than two who are absent.

SEC. 7. The Senate shall choose its President and other officers, shall judge of the qualifications and elections of its members, and shall punish them for improper conduct in their capacity of Senators; but such punishment shall not extend to life or limb, nor to expulsion. In the absence of their President, they may choose a temporary President. The President shall only have a casting vote when the House is equally divided.

SEC. 8. The Senate shall exclusively possess the power of declaring war. No treaty shall be made without their advice and consent, which shall also be necessary to the appointment of all officers, except such for which a different provision is made in this Constitution.

ARTICLE IV.

SEC. 1. The President of the United States of America (except in the first instance) shall be elected in the manner following.

The Judges of the Supreme Court shall, within sixty days after a vacancy shall happen, cause public notice to be given in each State of such vacancy, appointing therein three several days for the several purposes following, to wit—

A day for commencing the election of Electors for the purposes hereinafter specified—to be called the first Electors, which day shall not be less than forty, nor more than sixty days after the day of the publication of the notice in each State; another day for the meeting of the Electors not less than forty, nor more than ninety days, from the day for commencing their election; another day for the meeting of Electors, to be chosen by the first Electors, for the purpose hereinafter specified, and to be called the second Electors, which day shall not be less than forty, nor more than sixty days, after the day for the meeting of the first Electors.

SEC. 2. After notice of a vacancy shall have been given, there shall be chosen in each State a number of persons, as the first Electors in the preceding Section mentioned, equal to the whole number of the Representatives and Senators of such State in the Legislature of the United States; which Electors shall be chosen by the citizens of such State, having an estate of inheritance, or for three lives in land, or a clear personal estate of the value of one thousand Spanish milled dollars of the present standard.

SEC. 3. These first Electors shall meet in their respective States at the time appointed, at one place, and shall proceed to vote by ballot for a President, who shall not be one of their own number, unless the Legislature upon experiment should hereafter direct otherwise.

They shall cause two lists to be made of the name or names of the person or persons voted for, which they or the major part of them shall sign and certify. They shall then proceed each to nominate openly in the presence of the others two persons as for second Electors, and out of the persons who shall have the four highest numbers of nominations; they shall afterwards by ballot by plurality of votes choose two, who shall be the second Electors, to each of whom shall be delivered one of the lists before mentioned. These second Electors shall not be any of the persons voted for as President.

A copy of the same list, signed and certified in like manner, shall be transmitted by the first Electors to the seat of the government of the United States, under a sealed cover directed to the President of the Assembly, which, after the meeting of the second Electors, shall be opened for the inspection of the two houses of the Legislature.

SEC. 4. These second Electors shall meet precisely on the day appointed (and not on another day) at one place. The Chief Justice of the Supreme Court, or if there be no Chief Justice, the Judge Senior in office in such court, or if there be no one Judge Senior in office, some other Judge of that court, by the choice of the rest of the Judges, or of a majority of them, shall attend at the same place, and shall preside at the meeting, but shall have no vote. Two-thirds of the whole number of the Electors shall constitute a sufficient meeting for the execution of their trust. At this meeting the lists delivered to the respective Electors shall be produced and inspected, and if there be any person who has a majority of the whole number of the votes given by the first Electors, he shall be the President of the United States. But if there be no such person, the second Electors so met shall proceed to vote by ballot for one of the *persons* named in the lists, *who* shall have the three highest numbers of the votes of the first Electors, and if upon the first or any succeeding ballot, on the day of the meeting, either of those persons shall have a number of votes equal to a majority of the whole number of second Electors chosen, he shall be the President. But if no such choice be made on the day appointed for the meeting, either by reason of the non-attendance of the second Electors, or their not agreeing or any other matter, the person having the greatest number of votes of the first Electors shall be the President.

SEC. 5. If it should happen that the Chief Justice or some other Judge of the Supreme Court should not attend in due time, the second Electors shall proceed to the execution of their trust without him.

SEC. 6. If the Judges should neglect to cause the notice required by the first Section of this Article to be given within the time therein limited, they may nevertheless cause it to be afterwards given; but their neglect, if wilful, is hereby declared to be an offence for which they may be impeached, and if convicted, they shall be punished as in other cases of conviction on impeachment.

SEC. 7. The Legislature shall by permanent laws provide such further regulations as may be necessary for the more orderly election of the President, not contravening the provisions herein contained.

SEC. 8. The President, before he shall enter upon the execution of his office, shall take an oath or affirmation faithfully to execute the same, and to the utmost of his judgment and power to protect the rights of the people, and preserve the Constitution inviolate. This oath or affirmation shall be administered by the President of the Senate for the time being, in the presence of both houses of the Legislature.

SEC. 9. The Senate and the Assembly shall always convene in session on the day appointed for the meeting of the second Electors, and shall continue sitting till the President take the oath or affirmation of office. He shall hold his office during good behaviour, removeable only by conviction upon an impeachment for some crime or misdemeanour.

SEC. 10. The President at the beginning of every meeting of the Legislature, as soon as they shall be ready to proceed to business, shall convene them together at the place where the Senate shall sit, and shall communicate to them all such matters as may be necessary for their information, or as may require their consideration. He may by message during the session communicate all other matters which may appear to him proper. He may, whenever in his opinion the public business shall require it, convene the Senate and Assembly, or either of them, and may prorogue them for a time not exceeding forty days at one prorogation, and if they should disagree about their adjournment, he may adjourn them to such time as he shall think proper. He shall have a right to negative all bills, resolutions or acts of the two houses of the Legislature about to be passed into laws. He shall take care that the laws be faithfully executed. He shall be the Commander in Chief of the army and navy of the United States, and of the militia within the several States, and shall have the direction of war when commenced; but he shall not take the actual command in the field of an army, without the consent of the Senate and Assembly.

All treaties, conventions, and agreements with foreign nations shall be made by him, by and with the advice and consent of the Senate. He shall have the appointment of the principal or chief officer of each of the departments of war, naval affairs, finance and foreign affairs, and shall have the nomination, and by and with the consent of the Senate the appointment of all other officers to be appointed under the authority of the United States, except such for whom different provision is made by this Constitution, and provided that this shall not be construed to prevent the Legislature from appointing by name in their laws persons to special and particular trusts created in such laws, nor shall be construed to prevent principals in offices merely ministerial from constituting deputies. In the recess of the Senate he may fill vacancies in offices by appointments, to continue in force until the end of the next session of the Senate, and he shall commission all officers. He shall have power to pardon all offences, except treason, for which he may grant reprieves until the opinion of the Senate and Assembly can be had, and with their concurrence may pardon the same.

SEC. 11. He shall receive a fixed compensation for his services, to be paid to him at stated times, and not to be increased nor diminished during his continuance in office.

SEC. 12. If he depart out of the United States without the consent of the Senate and Assembly, he shall thereby abdicate his office.

SEC. 13. He may be impeached for any crime or misdemeanour by the two houses of the Legislature, two-thirds of each house concurring, and if convicted shall be removed from office. He may be afterwards tried and punished in the ordinary course of law. His impeachment shall operate as a suspension from office until the determination thereof.

SEC. 14. The President of the Senate shall be Vice President of the United States. On the death, resignation, impeachment, removal from office, or absence from the United States of the President thereof, the Vice President shall exercise all the powers by this Constitution vested in the President until another shall be appointed, or until he shall return within the United States, if his absence was with the consent of the Senate and Assembly.

ARTICLE V.

SEC. 1. There shall be a Chief Justice of the Supreme Court, who, together with the other Judges thereof, shall hold their offices during good behaviour, removeable only by conviction on impeachment for some crime or misdemeanour. Each Judge shall have a competent salary, to be paid to him at stated times, and not to be diminished during his continuance in office.

The Supreme Court shall have original jurisdiction in all causes in which the United States shall be a party; in all controversies between the United States and a particular State, or between two or more States, except such as relate to a claim of territory, between the United States and one or more States, which shall determined in the mode prescribed in the VI. Article; in all cases affecting foreign ministers, consuls, and agents, and an appellate jurisdiction both as to law and fact, in all cases which shall concern the citizens of foreign nations, in all questions between the citizens of different States, and in all others in which the fundamental rights of this Constitution are involved, subject to such exceptions as are herein contained, and to such regulations as the Legislature shall provide.

The Judges of all courts which may be constituted by the Legislature shall also hold their places during good behaviour, removeable only by conviction on impeachment for some crime or misdemeanour; and shall have competent salaries, to be paid at stated times, and not to be diminished during their continuance in office. But nothing herein contained shall be construed to prevent the Legislature from abolishing such courts themselves.

All crimes, except upon impeachment, shall be tried by a jury of twelve men, and if they shall have been committed within any State shall be tried within such State, and all civil causes arising under this Constitution of the like kind with those which have been heretofore triable by jury in the respective States, shall in like manner be tried by jury, unless in special cases the Legislature shall think proper to make different provision, to which provision the concurrence of two-thirds of both houses shall be necessary.

SEC. 2. Impeachments of the President and Vice President of the United States, members of the Senate, the Governors and Presidents of the several States, the principal or chief officers of the departments enumerated in the tenth Section of the fourth Article, ambassadors and other like public ministers, the Judges of the Supreme Court, generals, and admirals of the navy, shall be tried by a court to consist of the Judges of the Supreme Court and the Chief Justice or first or senior Judge of the Superior Court of law in each State, of whom twelve shall constitute a court. A majority of the Judges present may convict. All other persons shall be tried on impeachment by a court to consist of the Judges of the Supreme Court and six Senators drawn by lot; a majority of whom may convict.

Impeachments shall clearly specify the particular offence for which the party accused is to be tried, and judgment on conviction upon the trial thereof shall be either of removal from office singly, or removal from office and disqualification for holding any future office or place of trust; but no judgment on impeachment shall prevent prosecution and punishment in the ordinary course of law, provided that no Judge concerned in such conviction shall sit as Judge on the second trial. The Legislature may remove the disabilities incurred by conviction on impeachment.

ARTICLE VI.

Controversies about the right of territory between the United States and particular States shall be determined by a court to be constituted in manner following.

The State or States claiming in opposition to the United States as parties shall nominate a number of persons equal to double the number of the Judges of the Supreme Court for the time being, of whom none shall be citizens by birth of the States which are parties, nor inhabitants thereof when nominated, and of whom not more than two shall have their actual residence in one State. Out of the persons so nominated the Senate shall elect one-half, who, together with the Judges of the Supreme Court, shall form the court.

Two-thirds of the whole number may hear and determine the controversy by plurality of voices. The States concerned may at their option claim a decision by the Supreme Court only. All the members of the court hereby instituted shall, prior to the hearing of the cause, take an oath impartially, and according to the best of their judgments and consciences, to hear and determine the controversy.

ARTICLE VII.

SEC. 1. The Legislature of the United States shall have power to pass all laws which they shall judge necessary to the common defence and safety, and to the general welfare of the Union. But no bill, resolution, or act of the Senate and Assembly shall have the force of a law until it shall have received the assent of the President, or of the Vice President when exercising the powers of the President, and if such assent shall not have been given within ten days after such bill, resolution, or other act shall have been presented for that purpose, the same shall not be a law. No bill, resolution, or other act not assented to shall be revived in the same session of the Legislature. The mode of signifying such assent shall be by signing the bill, act, or resolution, and returning it so signed to either house of the Legislature.

SEC. 2. The enacting style of all laws shall be: "Be it enacted by the people of the United States of America."

SEC. 3. No bill of attainder shall be passed, nor any *ex post facto* law; nor shall any title of nobility be granted by the United States or by either of them; nor shall any person holding an office or place of trust under the United States, without the permission of the Legislature accept any present, emolument, office, or title from a foreign prince or state; nor shall any religious sect or denomination, or religious test for any office or place be ever established by law.

SEC. 4. Taxes on lands, houses, and other real estate, and capitation taxes, shall be proportioned in each State by the whole number of free persons, except Indians not taxed and by three-fifths of all other persons.

SEC. 5. The two houses of the Legislature may by joint ballot appoint a Treasurer of the United States. Neither house (in the session of both houses) without the consent of the other shall adjourn for more than three days at a time. The Senators and Representatives in attending, going to and coming from the session of their respective houses shall be privileged from arrests, except for crimes and breaches of the peace. The place of meeting shall always be at the seat of Government, which shall be fixed by law.

SEC. 6. The laws of the United States and the treaties which have been made under the Articles of the Confederation, and which shall be made under this Constitution, shall be the supreme law of the land, and shall be so construed by the courts of the several States.

SEC. 7. The Legislature shall convene at least once in each year, which, unless otherwise provided for by law, shall be the first Monday in December.

SEC. 8. The members of the two houses of the Legislature shall receive a reasonable compensation for their services, to be paid out of the treasury of the United States and ascertained by law. The law for making such provision shall be passed with the concurrence of the first Assembly, and shall extend to succeeding Assemblies, and no succeeding Assembly shall concur in an alteration of such provision, so as to increase its own compensation; but there shall be always a law in existence for making such provision.

ARTICLE VIII.

SEC. 1. The Governor or President of each State shall be appointed under the authority of the United States, and shall have a right to negative all laws about to be passed in the State of which he shall be Governor or President, subject to such qualifications and regulations as the Legislature of the United States shall prescribe. He shall in other respects have the same powers only which the Constitution of the State does or shall allow to its Governor or President, except as to the appointment of officers of the militia.

SEC. 2. Each Governor or President of a State shall hold his office until a successor be actually appointed, unless he die or resign, or be removed from office by conviction on impeachment. There shall be no appointment of such Governor or President in the recess of the Senate.

The Governors and Presidents of the several States, at the time of the ratification of this Constitution, shall continue in office in the same manner and with the same powers as if they had been appointed pursuant to the first Section of this Article.

The officers of militia in the several States may be appointed under the authority of the United States; the Legislature whereof may authorize the Governors or Presidents of States to make such appointments, with such restrictions as they shall think proper.

ARTICLE IX.

SEC. 1. No person shall be eligible to the office of President of the United States unless he be now a citizen of one of the States, or hereafter be born a citizen of the United States.

SEC. 2. No person shall be eligible as a Senator or Representative unless at the time of his election he be a citizen and inhabitant of the State in which he is chosen, provided that he shall not be deemed to be disqualified by a temporary absence from the State.

SEC. 3. No person entitled by this Constitution to elect or be elected President of the United States, or a Senator or Representative in the Legislature thereof, shall be disqualified but by the conviction of some offence for which the law shall have previously ordained the punishment of disqualification. But the Legislature may by law provide that persons holding offices under the United States or either of them shall not be eligible to a place in the Assembly or Senate, and shall be during their continuance in office suspended from sitting in the Senate.

SEC. 4. No person having an office or place of trust under the United States shall without permission of the Legislature accept any present, emolument, office, or title from any foreign prince or state.

SEC. 5. The citizens of each State shall be entitled to the rights, privileges, and immunities of citizens in every other State, and full faith and credit shall be given in each State to the public acts, records, and judicial proceedings of another.

SEC. 6. Fugitives from justice from one State who shall be found in another shall be delivered up on the application of the State from which they fled.

SEC. 7. No new State shall be erected within the limits of another, or by the junction of two or more States, without the concurrent consent of the Legislature of the United States and of the States concerned. The Legislature of the United States may admit new States into the Union.

SEC. 8. The United States are hereby declared to be bound to guarantee to each State a republican form of Government, and to protect each State as well against domestic violence as foreign invasion.

SEC. 9. All treaties, contracts, and engagements of the United States of America, under the Articles of Confederation and perpetual Union, shall have equal validity under this Constitution.

SEC. 10. No State shall enter into a treaty, alliance, or contract with another or with a foreign power without the consent of the United States.

SEC. 11. The members of the Legislature of the United States and of each State, and all officers executive and judicial of the one and of the other, shall take an oath or affirmation to support the Constitution of the United States.

SEC. 12. This Constitution may receive such alteration and amendments as may be proposed by the Legislature of the United States, with the concurrence of two-thirds of the members of both houses, and ratified by the Legislatures of or by conventions of deputies chosen by the people in two-thirds of the States composing the Union.

ARTICLE X.

This Constitution shall be submitted to the consideration of conventions in the several States, the members whereof shall be chosen by the people of such States respectively under the direction of their respective Legislatures. Each convention which shall ratify the same shall appoint the first Representatives and Senators from such State, acording to the rule prescribed in the   Section of the   Article. The Representatives so appointed shall continue in office for one year only. Each convention so ratifying shall give notice thereof to the Congress of the United States, transmitting at the same time a list of the Representatives and Senators chosen. When the Constitution shall have been duly ratified, Congress shall give notice of a day and place for the meeting of the Senators and Representatives from the several States, and when these or a majority of them shall have assembled according to such notice, they shall by joint ballot by plurality of votes elect a President of the United States, and the Constitution, thus organized, shall be carried into effect.

THE FEDERAL CONSTITUTION,

AS AGREED UPON

BY THE CONVENTION,

SEPTEMBER 17, 1787.

𝔚e the 𝔓eople *of the United States, in order to form a more perfect Union, establish Justice, insure domestic Tranquillity, provide for the common Defence, promote the general Welfare, and secure the Blessings of Liberty to ourselves and our posterity, do ordain and establish this CONSTITUTION for the United States of America.*

ARTICLE I.

SECTION 1. ALL legislative powers herein granted shall be vested in a congress of the United States, which shall consist of a senate and house of representatives.

SECT. 2. The house of representatives shall be composed of members chosen every second year by the people of the several states, and the electors in each state shall have the qualifications requisite for electors of the most numerous branch of the state legislature.

No person shall be a representative who shall not have attained to the age of twenty-five years, and been seven years a citizen of the United States, and who shall not, when elected, be an inhabitant of that state in which he shall be chosen.

Representatives and direct taxes shall be apportioned among the several states which may be included within this union, according to their respective numbers, which shall be determined by adding to the whole number of free persons, including those bound to service for a term of years, and excluding Indians not taxed, three-fifths of all other persons. The actual enumeration shall be made within three years after the first meeting of the congress of the United States, and within every subsequent term of ten years, in such manner as they shall by law direct. The number of representatives shall not exceed one for every thirty thousand, but each state shall have at least one representative; and until such enumeration shall be made, the state of New-Hampshire shall be entitled to choose three, Massachusetts eight, Rhode-Island and Providence Plantations one, Connecticut five, New-York six, New-Jersey four, Pennsylvania eight, Delaware one, Maryland six, Virginia ten, North-Carolina five, South-Carolina five, and Georgia three.

When vacancies happen in the representation from any state, the executive authority thereof shall issue writs of election to fill such vacancies.

The house of representatives shall choose their speaker and other officers; and shall have the sole power of impeachment.

SECT. 3. The senate of the United States shall be composed of two senators from each state, chosen by the legislature thereof, for six years; and each senator shall have one vote.

Immediately after they shall be assembled in consequence of the first election, they shall be divided as equally as may be into three classes. The seats of the senators of the first class shall be vacated at the expiration of the second year, the second class at the expiration of the fourth year, and the third class at the expiration of the sixth year, so that one third may be chosen every second year; and if vacancies happen by resignation or otherwise, during the recess of the legislature of any state, the executive thereof may make temporary appointments until the next meeting of the legislature, which shall then fill such vacancies.

No person shall be a Senator who shall not have attained to the age of thirty years, and been nine years a citizen of the United States, and who shall not, when elected, be an inhabitant of that state for which he shall be chosen.

The vice-president of the United States shall be president of the senate, but shall have no vote, unless they be equally divided.

The senate shall choose their other officers, and also a president *pro tempore*, in the absence of the vice-president, or when he shall exercise the office of president of the United States.

The senate shall have the sole power to try all impeachments. When sitting for that purpose they shall be on oath or affirmation. When the president of the United States is tried, the chief justice shall preside. And no person shall be convicted without the concurrence of two-thirds of the members present.

Judgment in cases of impeachment shall not extend further than to removal from office, and disqualification to hold and enjoy any office of honour, trust, or profit, under the United States; but the party convicted shall, nevertheless, be liable and subject to indictment, trial, judgment, and punishment, according to law.

SECT. 4. The times, places, and manner of holding elections for senators and representatives, shall be prescribed in each state by the legislature thereof: but the congress may at any time by law make or alter such regulations, except as to the places of choosing senators.

The congress shall assemble at least once in every year, and such meeting shall be on the first Monday in December, unless they shall by law appoint a different day.

SECT. 5. Each house shall be the judge of the elections, returns, and qualifications of its own members; and a majority of each shall constitute a quorum to do business: but a smaller number may adjourn from day to day, and may be authorized to compel the attendance of absent members, in such manner, and under such penalties, as each house may provide.

Each house may determine the rules of its proceedings, punish its members for disorderly behaviour, and, with the concurrence of two-thirds, expel a member.

Each house shall keep a journal of its proceedings, and from time to time publish the same, excepting such parts as may in their judgment require secresy; and the yeas and nays of the members of either house on any question shall, at the desire of one-fifth of those present, be entered on the journal.

Neither house, during the session of congress, shall, without the consent of the other, adjourn for more than three days, nor to any other place than that in which the two houses shall be sitting.

SECT. 6. The senators and representatives shall receive a compensation for their services, to be ascertained by law, and paid out of the treasury of the United States. They shall in all cases, except treason, felony, and breach of the peace, be privileged from arrest during their attendance at the session of their respective houses, and in going to and returning from the same, and for any speech or debate in either house, they shall not be questioned in any other place.

No senator or representative shall, during the time for which he was elected, be appointed to any civil office under the authority of the United States, which shall have been created, or the emoluments whereof shall have been increased during such time;

and no person, holding any office under the United States, shall be a member of either house during his continuance in office.

SECT. 7. All bills for raising revenue shall originate in the house of representatives; but the senate may propose or concur with amendments as on other bills.

Every bill which shall have passed the house of representatives and the senate shall, before it become a law, be presented to the president of the United States; if he approve, he shall sign it; but if not, he shall return it, with his objections, to that house in which it shall have originated, who shall enter the objections at large on their journal, and proceed to reconsider it. If after such reconsideration two-thirds of that house shall agree to pass the bill, it shall be sent, together with the objections, to the other house, by which it shall likewise be reconsidered, and if approved by two-thirds of that house, it shall become a law. But in all such cases the votes of both houses shall be determined by yeas and nays, and the names of the persons voting for and against the bill shall be entered on the journal of each house respectively. If any bill shall not be returned by the president within ten days (Sundays excepted) after it shall have been presented to him, the same shall be a law, in like manner as if he had signed it, unless the congress by their adjournment prevent its return, in which case it shall not be a law.

Every order, resolution, or vote, to which the concurrence of the senate and house of representatives may be necessary (except on a question of adjournment) shall be presented to the president of the United States; and before the same shall take effect, shall be approved by him, or, being disapproved by him, shall be repassed by two-thirds of the senate and house of representatives, according to the rules and limitations prescribed in the case of a bill.

SECT. 8. The congress shall have power,

To lay and collect taxes, duties, imposts, and excises, to pay the debts and provide for the common defence and general welfare of the United States; but all duties, imposts, and excises, shall be uniform throughout the United States:

To borrow money on the credit of the United States:

To regulate commerce with foreign nations, and among the several states, and with the Indian tribes:

To establish an uniform rule of naturalization, and uniform laws on the subjects of bankruptcies throughout the United States:

To coin money, regulate the value thereof, and of foreign coin, and fix the standard of weights and measures:

To provide for the punishment of counterfeiting the securities and current coin of the United States:

To establish post-offices and post-roads:

To promote the progress of science and useful arts, by securing for limited times to authors and inventors the exclusive right to their respective writings and discoveries:

To constitute tribunals inferior to the supreme court:

To define and punish piracies and felonies committed on the high seas, and offences against the law of nations:

To declare war, grant letters of marque and reprisal, and make rules concerning captures on land and water:

To raise and support armies, but no appropriation of money to that use shall be for a longer term than two years:

To provide and maintain a navy:

To make rules for the government and regulation of the land and naval forces:

To provide for calling forth the militia to execute the laws of the union, suppress insurrections, and repel invasions:

To provide for organizing, arming, and disciplining the militia, and for governing such parts of them as may be employed in the service of the United States, reserving to the states respectively, the appointment of the officers, and the authority of training the militia according to the discipline prescribed by congress:

To exercise exclusive legislation in all cases whatsoever, over such district (not exceeding ten miles square) as may, by cession of particular states, and the acceptance of congress, become the seat of the government of the United States, and to exercise like authority over all places purchased by the consent of the legislature of the state in which the same shall be, for the erection of forts, magazines, arsenals, dockyards, and other needful buildings: And,

To make all laws which shall be necessary and proper for carrying into execution the foregoing powers, and all other powers vested by this constitution in the government of the United States, or in any department or officer thereof.

SECT. 9. The migration or importation of such persons as any of the states now existing shall think proper to admit, shall not be prohibited by the congress prior to the year one thousand eight hundred and eight, but a tax or duty may be imposed on such importation, not exceeding ten dollars for each person.

The privilege of the writ of *habeas corpus* shall not be suspended, unless when in cases of rebellion or invasion the public safety may require it.

No bill of attainder or *ex post facto* law shall be passed.

No capitation, or other direct tax shall be laid, unless in proportion to the *census* or enumeration herein before directed to be taken.

No tax or duty shall be laid on articles exported from any state. No preference shall be given by any regulation of commerce or revenue to the ports of one state over those of another; nor shall vessels bound to, or from, one state, be obliged to enter, clear, or pay duties in another.

No money shall be drawn from the treasury, but in consequence of appropriations made by law; and a regular statement and account of the receipts and expenditure of all public money shall be published from time to time.

No title of nobility shall be granted by the United States: And no person holding any office of profit or trust under them, shall, without the consent of the congress, accept of any present, emolument, office, or title, of any kind whatever, from any king, prince, or foreign state.

SECT. 10. No state shall enter into any treaty, alliance, or confederation; grant letters of marque and reprisal; coin money; emit bills of credit; make any thing but gold and silver coin a tender in payment of debts; pass any bill of attainder, *ex post facto* law, or law impairing the obligation of contracts; or grant any title of nobility.

No state shall, without the consent of the congress, lay any imposts or duties on imports or exports, except what may be absolutely necessary for executing its inspection laws; and the net proceeds of all duties and imposts, laid by any state on imports or exports, shall be for the use of the treasury of the United States; and all such laws shall be subject to the revision and control of the congress. No state shall, without the consent of congress, lay any duties of tonnage, keep troops, or ships of war, in time of peace, enter into any agreement or compact with another state, or with a foreign power, or engage in war, unless actually invaded, or in such imminent danger as will not admit of delay.

ARTICLE II.

SECT. 1. The executive power shall be vested in a president of the United States of America. He shall hold his office during the term of four years, and together with the vice-president, chosen for the same term, be elected as follows:

Each state shall appoint, in such manner as the legislature thereof may direct, a number of electors, equal to the whole number of senators and representatives to which the state may be entitled in the congress: but no senator or representative, or person holding an office of trust or profit under the United States, shall be appointed an elector.

The electors shall meet in their respective states, and vote by ballot for two persons, of whom one at least shall not be an inhabitant of the same state with themselves. And they shall make a list of all the persons voted for, and of the number of votes for each; which list they shall sign and certify, and transmit sealed to the seat of the government of the United States, directed to the president of the senate. The president of the senate shall, in the presence of the senate and house of representatives, open all the certificates, and the votes shall then be counted. The person having the greatest number of votes shall be the president, if such number be a majority of the whole number of electors appointed; and if there be more than one who have such majority, and have an equal number of votes, then the house of representatives shall immediately choose by ballot one of them for president; and if no person have a majority, then from the five highest on the list the said house shall in like manner choose the president. But in choosing the president, the votes shall be taken by states, the representation from each state having one vote; a quorum for this purpose shall consist of a member or members from two-thirds of the states, and a majority of all the states shall be necessary to a choice. In every case, after the choice of the president, the person having the greatest number of votes of the electors shall be the vice-president. But if there should remain two or more who have equal votes, the senate shall choose from them by ballot the vice-president.

The congress may determine the time of choosing the electors, and the day on which they shall give their votes; which day shall be the same throughout the United States.

No person except a natural born citizen, or a citizen of the United States, at the time of the adoption of this constitution, shall be eligible to the office of president; neither shall any person be eligible to that office who shall not have attained to the age of thirty-five years, and been fourteen years a resident within the United States.

In case of removal of the president from office, or of his death, resignation, or inability to discharge the powers and duties of the said office, the same shall devolve on the vice-president, and the congress may by law provide for the case of removal, death, resignation, or inability, both of the president and vice-president, declaring what officer shall then act as president, and such officer shall act accordingly, until the disability be removed, or a president shall be elected.

The president shall, at stated times, receive for his services a compensation, which shall neither be increased or diminished during the period for which he shall have been elected, and he shall not receive within that period any other emolument from the United States, or any of them.

Before he enter into the execution of his office, he shall take the following oath or affirmation:

"I do solemnly swear (or affirm) that I will faithfully execute the office of president of the United States, and will to the best of my ability, preserve, protect, and defend the constitution of the United States."

SECT. 2. The president shall be commander in chief of the army and navy of the United States; and of the militia of the several states, when called into the actual service of the United States; he may require the opinion, in writing, of the principal officer in each of the executive departments, upon any subject relating to the duties of their respective offices, and he shall have power to grant reprieves and pardons for offences against the United States, except in cases of impeachment.

He shall have power, by and with the advice and consent of the senate, to make treaties, provided two-thirds of the senators present concur; and he shall nominate, and by and with the advice and consent of the senate, shall appoint ambassadors, other public ministers and consuls, judges of the supreme court, and all other officers of the United States, whose appointments are not herein otherwise provided for, and which shall be established by law. But the congress may by law vest the appointment

14

of such inferior officers, as they think proper, in the president alone, in the courts of law, or in the heads of departments.

The president shall have power to fill up all vacancies that may happen during the recess of the senate, by granting commissions which shall expire at the end of their next session.

SECT. 3. He shall from time to time give to the congress information of the state of the union, and recommend to their consideration such measures as he shall judge necessary and expedient; he may, on extraordinary occasions, convene both houses, or either of them, and in case of disagreement between them, with respect to the time of adjournment, he may adjourn them to such time as he shall think proper; he shall receive ambassadors and other public ministers; he shall take care that the laws be faithfully executed, and shall commission all the officers of the United States.

SECT. 4. The president, vice-president, and all civil officers of the United States shall be removed from office on impeachment for, and conviction of, treason, bribery, or other high crimes and misdemeanors.

ARTICLE III.

SECT. 1. The judicial power of the United States shall be vested in one supreme court, and in such inferior courts as the congress may from time to time ordain and establish. The judges, both of the supreme and inferior court, shall hold their offices during good behaviour, and shall at stated times, receive for their services a compensation, which shall not be diminished during their continuance in office.

SECT. 2. The judicial power shall extend to all cases in law and equity, arising under this constitution, the laws of the United States, and treaties made, or which shall be made, under their authority; to all cases affecting ambassadors, other public ministers and consuls; to all cases of admiralty and maritime jurisdiction; to controversies to which the United States shall be a party; to controversies between two or more states; between a state and citizens of another state; between citizens of different states; between citizens of the same state claiming lands under grants of different states; and between a state, or the citizens thereof, and foreign states, citizens or subjects.

In all cases affecting ambassadors, other public ministers and consuls, and those in which a state shall be party, the supreme court shall have original jurisdiction. In all the other cases before mentioned, the supreme court shall have appellate jurisdiction, both as to law and fact, with such exceptions, and under such regulations, as the congress shall make.

The trial of all crimes, except in cases of impeachment, shall be by jury; and such trial shall be held in the state where the said crimes shall have been committed; but when not committed within any state, the trial shall be at such place or places as the congress may by law have directed.

SECT. 3. Treason against the United States, shall consist only in levying war against them, or in adhering to their enemies, giving them aid and comfort. No person shall be convicted of treason unless on the testimony of two witnesses to the same overt act, or on confession in open court.

The Congress shall have power to declare the punishment of treason, but no attainder of treason shall work corruption of blood, or forfeiture, except during the life of the person attained.

ARTICLE IV.

SECT. 1. Full faith and credit shall be given in each state to the public acts, records, and judicial proceedings of every other state. And the congress may by general laws prescribe the manner in which such acts, records, and proceedings shall be proved, and the effect thereof.

SECT. 2. The citizens of each state shall be entitled to all privileges and immunities of citizens in the several states.

A person charged in any state with treason, felony, or other crime, who shall flee from justice, and be found in another state, shall, on demand of the executive authority of the state from which he fled, be delivered up, to be removed to the state having jurisdiction of the crime.

No person held to service or labour in one state, under the laws thereof, escaping into another, shall, in consequence of any law or regulation therein, be discharged from such service or labour, but shall be delivered up on claim of the party to whom such service or labour may be due.

SECT. 3. New states may be admitted by the congress into this union; but no new state shall be formed or erected within the jurisdiction of any other state, nor any state be formed by the junction of two or more states, or parts of states, without the consent of the legislatures of the states concerned, as well as of the congress.

The congress shall have power to dispose of and make all needful rules and regulations respecting the territory or other property belonging to the United States; and nothing in this constitution shall be so construed as to prejudice any claims of the United States, or of any particular state.

SECT. 4. The United States shall guarantee to every state in this Union, a republican form of government, and shall protect each of them against invasion; and on application of the legislature, or of the executive (when the legislature cannot be convened) against domestic violence.

ARTICLE V.

The congress, whenever two-thirds of both houses shall deem it necessary, shall propose amendments to this constitution, or, on the application of the legislatures of two-thirds of the several states, shall call a convention for proposing amendments, which, in either case, shall be valid to all intents and purposes, as part of this constitution, when ratified by the legislatures of three-fourths of the several states, or by conventions in three-fourths thereof, as the one or the other mode of ratification may be proposed by the congress: Provided, that no amendment which may be made prior to the year one thousand eight hundred and eight, shall in any manner affect the first and fourth clauses in the ninth section of the first article; and that no state, without its consent, shall be deprived of its equal suffrage in the senate.

ARTICLE VI.

All debts contracted and engagements entered into, before the adoption of this constitution, shall be as valid against the United States under this constitution, as under the confederation.

This constitution, and the laws of the United States which shall be made in pursuance thereof; and all treaties made, or which shall be made, under the authority of the United States, shall be the supreme law of the land; and the judges in every state shall be bound thereby, any thing in the constitution or laws of any state to the contrary notwithstanding.

The senators and representatives before mentioned, and the members of the several state legislatures, and all executive and judicial officers, both of the United States and of the several states, shall be bound by oath or affirmation to support this constitution; but no religious test shall ever be required as a qualification to any office or public trust under the United States.

ARTICLE VII.

The ratification of the convention of nine states, shall be sufficient for the establishment of this constitution between the states so ratifying the same.

DONE in convention, by the unanimous consent of the states present, the seventeenth day of September, in the year of our Lord one thousand seven hundred and eighty-seven, and of the independence of the United States of America the twelfth. In witness whereof, we have hereunto subscribed our names.

GEORGE WASHINGTON, PRESIDENT, *and Deputy from Virginia.*

NEW-HAMPSHIRE ... { JOHN LANGDON, NICHOLAS GILMAN.

MASSACHUSETTS. ... { NATHANIEL GORHAM, RUFUS KING.

CONNECTICUT. ..... { WILLIAM SAMUEL JOHNSON, ROGER SHERMAN.

NEW-YORK .... { ALEXANDER HAMILTON.

NEW-JERSEY .... { WILLIAM LIVINGSTON, DAVID BREARLY, WILLIAM PATERSON, JONATHAN DAYTON.

PENNSYLVANIA .... { BENJAMIN FRANKLIN, THOMAS MIFFLIN, ROBERT MORRIS, GEORGE CLYMER, THOMAS FITZSIMONS, JARED INGERSOLL, JAMES WILSON, GOUVERNEUR MORRIS.

DELAWARE .... { GEORGE READ, GUNNING BEDFORD, junior, JOHN DICKINSON, RICHARD BASSETT, JACOB BROOM.

MARYLAND .... { JAMES M'HENRY, DANIEL OF ST. THOMAS JENIFER, DANIEL CARROL.

VIRGINIA. .... { JOHN BLAIR, JAMES MADISON, junior.

NORTH-CAROLINA... { WILLIAM BLOUNT, RICHARD DOBBS SPAIGHT, HUGH WILLIAMSON.

SOUTH-CAROLINA ... { JOHN RUTLEDGE, CHS. COTESWORTH PINCKNEY, CHARLES PINCKNEY, PIERCE BUTLER.

GEORGIA .... { WILLIAM FEW, ABRAHAM BALDWIN.

Attest.   WILLIAM JACKSON, *Secretary.*

IN CONVENTION.

MONDAY, September 17, 1787.

PRESENT, *The State of New-Hampshire, Massachusetts, Connecticut, Mr. Hamilton from New-York, New-Jersey, Pennsylvania, Delaware, Maryland, Virginia, North-Carolina, South-Carolina and Georgia.*

Resolved, That the preceding constitution be laid before the United States in congress assembled, and that it is the opinion of this convention, that it should afterwards be submitted to a convention of delegates, chosen in each state by the people thereof, under the recommendation of its legislature, for their assent and ratification; and that each convention assenting to, and ratifying the same, should give notice thereof to the United States in congress assembled.

Resolved, That it is the opinion of this convention, that as soon as the conventions of nine states shall have ratified this constitution, the United States in congress assembled should fix a day on which electors should be appointed by the states which shall have ratified the same, and a day on which the electors should assemble to vote for the president, and the time and place for commencing proceedings under this constitution. That after such publication the electors should be appointed, and the senators and representatives elected: That the electors should meet on the day fixed for the election of the president, and should transmit their votes certified, signed, sealed, and directed, as the constitution requires, to the secretary of the United States in congress assembled; that the senators and representatives should convene at the time and place assigned; that the senators should appoint a president of the senate, for the sole purpose of receiving, opening, and counting the votes for president; and that after he shall be chosen, the congress, together with the president, should without delay proceed to execute this constitution.

By the unanimous order of the Convention.

GEORGE WASHINGTON, *President.*

WILLIAM JACKSON, *Secretary.*

AMENDMENTS TO THE CONSTITUTION.

The first *ten* amendments were proposed in Congress during its *first* session, and on the 15th of December, 1791, were ratified. The *eleventh* amendment was proposed during the *first* session of the *third* congress, and was announced by the President of the United States in a message to it, of date January 8th, 1798, as having been ratified. The *twelfth* amendment originated with Hamilton,* and was proposed during the first session of the eighth Congress, and was adopted in 1804.

ARTICLE THE FIRST.

CONGRESS shall make no law respecting the establishment of religion, or prohibiting the free exercise thereof; or abridging the freedom of speech, or of the press; or the right of the people peaceably to assemble, and to petition the government for a redress of grievances.

ARTICLE THE SECOND.

A well regulated militia being necessary to the security of a free state, the right of the people to keep and bear arms shall not be infringed.

ARTICLE THE THIRD.

No soldier shall, in time of peace, be quartered in any house without the consent of the owner; nor in time of war, but in a manner to be prescribed by law.

ARTICLE THE FOURTH.

The right of the people to be secure in their persons, houses, papers, and effects, against unreasonable searches and seizures, shall not be violated, and no warrants shall issue, but upon probable cause, supported by oath or affirmation, and particularly describing the place to be searched, and the persons or things to be seized.

ARTICLE THE FIFTH.

No person shall be held to answer for a capital or otherwise infamous crime, unless on a presentment or indictment of a grand jury, except in cases arising in the land or naval forces, or in the militia when in actual service in time of war or public danger; nor shall any person be subject for the same offence to be twice put in jeopardy of life or limb; nor shall be compelled in any criminal case to be witness against himself; nor be deprived of life, liberty, or property, without due process of law; nor shall private property be taken for public use without just compensation.

ARTICLE THE SIXTH.

In all criminal prosecutions the accused shall enjoy the right to a speedy and public trial, by an impartial jury of the state and district wherein the crime shall have been committed, which district shall have been previously ascertained by law, and to be informed of the nature and cause of the accusation; to be confronted with the witnesses against him; to have compulsory process for obtaining witnesses in his favour, and to have the assistance of counsel for his defence.

ARTICLE THE SEVENTH.

In suits at common law, where the value in controversy shall exceed twenty dollars, the right of trial by jury shall be preserved; and no fact tried by a jury, shall be otherwise re-examined in any court of the United States than according to the rules of the common law.

ARTICLE THE EIGHTH.

Excessive bail shall not be required, nor excessive fines imposed, nor cruel and unusual punishments inflicted.

ARTICLE THE NINTH.

The enumeration in the constitution of certain rights, shall not be construed to deny or disparage others retained by the people.

ARTICLE THE TENTH.

The powers not delegated to the United States by the constitution, nor prohibited by it to the states, are reserved to the states respectively, or to the people.

ARTICLE THE ELEVENTH.

The judicial power of the United States shall not be construed to extend to any suit in law or equity, commenced or prosecuted against one of the United States by citizens of another state, or by citizens or subjects of any foreign state.

* Hist. Rep. VII., 566.

ARTICLE XII.

The electors shall meet in their respective states, and vote by ballot for president and vice-president, one of whom, at least, shall not be an inhabitant of the same state with themselves; they shall name in their ballots the person voted for as president, and in distinct ballots the person voted for as vice-president; and they shall make distinct lists of all persons voted for as president, and of all persons voted for as vice-president, and of the number of votes for each, which lists they shall sign and certify, and transmit sealed to the seat of the government of the United States, directed to the president of the senate; the president of the senate shall, in the presence of the senate and house of representatives, open all the certificates, and the votes shall then be counted: the person having the greatest number of votes for president, shall be the president, if such number be a majority of the whole number of electors appointed; and if no person have such majority, then from the persons having the highest numbers, not exceeding three, on the list of those voted for as president, the house of representatives shall choose immediately, by ballot, the president. But in choosing the president, the votes shall be taken by states, the representation from each state having one vote; a quorum for this purpose shall consist of a member or members from two thirds of the states, and a majority of all the states shall be necessary to a choice. And if the house of representatives shall not choose a president whenever the right of choice shall devolve upon them, before the fourth day of March next following, then the vice-president shall act as president as in the case of the death or other constitutional disability of the president.

The person having the greatest number of votes as vice-president, shall be the vice-president, if such number be a majority of the whole number of electors appointed: and if no person have a majority, then from the two highest numbers on the list, the senate shall choose the vice-president: a quorum for the purpose shall consist of two thirds of the whole number of senators, and a majority of the whole number shall be necessary to a choice.

But no person constitutionally ineligible to the office of president, shall be eligible to that of vice-president of the United States.

IN CONVENTION.

SEPTEMBER 17th, 1787.

SIR: We have now the honor to submit to the consideration of the United States in Congress assembled, that Constitution which has appeared to us the most advisable. The friends of our country have long seen and desired, that the power of making war, peace, and treaties; that of levying money and regulating commerce, and the correspondent executive and judicial authorities should be fully and effectually vested in the general government of the Union; but the impropriety of delegating such extensive trusts to one body of men is evident. Hence results the necessity of a different organization. It is obviously impracticable, in the federal government of these States, to secure all rights of independent sovereignty to each, and yet provide for the interest and safety of all. Individuals entering into society must give up a share of liberty to preserve the rest. The magnitude of the sacrifice must depend as well on situation and circumstance as on the object to be obtained. It is at all times difficult to draw with precision the line between those rights which must be surrendered, and those which may be reserved; and on the present occasion this difficulty was increased by a difference among the several states as to their situation, extent, habits, and particular interests.

In all our deliberations on this subject we kept steadily in our view, that which appears to us the greatest interest of every true American, the consolidation of our union, in which is involved our prosperity, felicity, safety, perhaps our national existence. This important consideration, seriously and deeply impressed on our minds, led each state in the convention to be less rigid on points of inferior magnitude than might have been otherwise expected; and thus the Constitution, which we now present, is the result of a spirit of amity, and of that mutual deference and concession which the peculiarity of our political situation rendered indispensable.

That it will meet the full and entire approbation of every state is not perhaps to be expected; but each will doubtless consider, that had her interests alone been consulted, the consequences might have been particularly disagreeable or injurious to others; that it is liable to as few exceptions as could reasonably have been expected, we hope and believe; that it may promote the lasting welfare of that country so dear to us all, and secure her freedom and happiness, is our most ardent wish. With great respect, we have the honor to be, sir, your excellency's most obedient and humble servants,

By unanimous order of the convention.   Go: WASHINGTON, President.

His excellency the President of Congress.

THE FEDERALIST.

NUMBER I.

NEW YORK, OCTOBER 27, 1787.

HAMILTON.

INTRODUCTION.

AFTER full experience of the insufficiency of the existing Federal Government, you are invited to deliberate upon a new Constitution for the United States of America.

The subject speaks its own importance; comprehending in its consequences, nothing less than the existence of the UNION—the safety and welfare of the parts of which it is composed—the the fate of an empire, in many respects, the most interesting in the world. It has been frequently remarked, that, it seems to have been reserved to the people of this country, to decide by their conduct and example, the important question, whether societies of men are really capable or not, of establishing good government from reflection and choice, or whether they are for ever destined to depend, for their political constitutions, on accident and force. If there be any truth in the remark, the crisis, at which we are arrived, may with propriety be regarded as the period when that decision is to be made; and a wrong election of the part we shall act, may, in this view, deserve to be considered as the general misfortune of mankind.

This idea, by adding the inducements of philanthropy to those of patriotism, will heighten the solicitude, which all considerate and good men must feel for the event. Happy will it be if our

choice should be directed by a judicious estimate of our true
interests, uninfluenced by considerations foreign to the public
good. But this is more ardently to be wished for, than seriously
to be expected. The plan offered to our deliberations, affects too
many particular interests, innovates upon too many local institutions, not to involve in its discussion a variety of objects
extraneous to its merits; and of views, passions, and prejudices,
little favourable to the discovery of truth.

Among the most formidable of the obstacles, which the new
constitution will have to encounter, may readily be distinguished
the obvious interest of a certain class of men in every state, to
resist all changes which may hazard a diminution of the power,
emolument, and consequence, of the offices they hold under the
state establishments: and the perverted ambition of another
class of men, who will either hope to aggrandize themselves by
the confusions of their country, or will flatter themselves with
fairer prospects of elevation from the subdivision of the empire
into several partial confederacies, than from its union under one
government.

It is not, however, my design to dwell upon observations of
this nature. I am aware that it would be disingenuous to resolve
indiscriminately the opposition of any set of men into interested
or ambitious views, merely because their situations might subject them to suspicion. Candour will oblige us to admit, that
even such men may be actuated by upright intentions; and it
cannot be doubted, that much of the opposition which has
already shown itself, or that may hereafter make its appearance,
will spring from sources, blameless at least, if not respectable—
the honest errors of minds led astray by preconceived jealousies
and fears. So numerous indeed, and so powerful are the causes,
which serve to give a false bias to the judgment, that we, upon
many occasions, see wise and good men on the wrong as well as
on the right side of questions, of the first magnitude to society.
This circumstance, if duly attended to, would always furnish a
lesson of moderation to those who are engaged in any controversy, however well persuaded of being in the right. And a fur-

ther reason for caution, in this respect, might be drawn from the reflection, that we are not always sure, that those who advocate the truth are actuated by purer principles than their antagonists. Ambition, avarice, personal animosity, party opposition, and many other motives, not more laudable than these, are apt to operate as well upon those who support, as upon those who oppose, the right side of a question. Were there not even these inducements to moderation, nothing could be more illjudged than that intolerant spirit, which has, at all times, characterized political parties. For, in politics as in religion, it is equally absurd to aim at making proselytes by fire and sword. Heresies in either can rarely be cured by persecution.

And yet, just as these sentiments must appear to candid men, we have already sufficient indications, that it will happen in this, as in all former cases of great national discussion. A torrent of angry and malignant passions will be let loose. To judge from the conduct of the opposite parties, we shall be led to conclude, that they will mutually hope to evince the justness of their opinions, and to increase the number of their converts, by the loudness of their declamations, and by the bitterness of their invectives. An enlightened zeal for the energy and efficiency of government, will be stigmatized as the offspring of a temper fond of power, and hostile to the principles of liberty. An overscrupulous jealousy of danger to the rights of the people, which is more commonly the fault of the head than of the heart, will be represented as mere pretence and artifice; the stale bait for popularity at the expense of public good. It will be forgotten, on the one hand, that jealousy is the usual concomitant of violent love, and that the noble enthusiasm of liberty is too apt to be infected with a spirit of narrow and illiberal distrust. On the other hand, it will be equally forgotten, that the vigour of government is essential to the security of liberty; that, in the contemplation of a sound and well informed judgment, their interests can never be separated; and that a dangerous ambition more often lurks behind the specious mask of zeal for the rights of the people, than under the forbidding appearances of zeal for the firmness and efficiency of government. History will teach us, that the former has been found a much more certain road to the introduction of despotism than the latter; and that of those men who have overturned the liberties of republics, the greatest number have begun their career, by paying an obsequious court to the people, commencing demagogues and ending tyrants.

In the course of the preceding observations it has been my aim, fellow citizens, to put you upon your guard against all attempts, from whatever quarter, to influence your decision in a matter of the utmost moment to your welfare, by any impressions other than those which may result from the evidence of truth. You will, no doubt, at the same time, have collected from the general scope of them, that they proceed from a source not unfriendly to the new constitution. Yes, my countrymen, I own to you, that, after having given it an attentive consideration, I am clearly of opinion, it is your interest to adopt it. I am convinced, that this is the safest course for your liberty, your dignity, and your happiness. I affect not reserves, which I do not feel. I will not amuse you with an appearance of deliberation, when I have decided. I frankly acknowledge to you my convictions, and I will freely lay before you the reasons on which they are founded. The consciousness of good intentions disdains ambiguity. I shall not, however, multiply professions on this head. My motives must remain in the depository of my own breast: my arguments will be open to all, and may be judged of by all. They shall at least be offered in a spirit, which will not disgrace the cause of truth.

I propose, in a series of papers, to discuss the following interesting particulars... *The utility of the UNION to your political prosperity... The insufficiency of the present confederation to preserve that Union... The necessity of a government, at least equally energetic with the one proposed, to the attainment of this object... The conformity of the proposed constitution to the true principles of republican government... Its analogy to your own state constitution... and lastly, The additional security, which its adoption will afford to the preservation of that species of government, to liberty, and to property.*

In the progress of this discussion, I shall endeavour to give a satisfactory answer to all the objections which shall have made their appearance, that may seem to have any claim to attention.

It may perhaps be thought superfluous to offer arguments to prove the utility of the UNION; a point, no doubt, deeply engraved on the hearts of the great body of the people in every state, and one which, it may be imagined, has no adversaries. But the fact is, that we already hear it whispered in the private circles of those who oppose the new constitution, that the Thirteen States are of too great extent for any general system, and that we must of necessity resort to separate confederacies of distinct portions of the whole.* This doctrine will, in all probability, be gradually propagated, till it has votaries enough to countenance its open avowal. For nothing can be more evident, to those who are able to take an enlarged view of the subject, than the alternative of an adoption of the constitution, or a dismemberment of the Union. It may therefore be essential to examine particularly the advantages of that Union, the certain evils, and the probable dangers, to which every state will be exposed from its dissolution. This shall accordingly be done.

PUBLIUS.

* The same idea, tracing the arguments to their consequences, is held out in several of the late publications against the new constitution.

THE FEDERALIST.

NUMBER II.

NEW YORK, OCTOBER 31, 1787.

JAY.

CONCERNING DANGERS FROM FOREIGN FORCE AND INFLUENCE.

WHEN the people of America reflect, that the question now submitted to their determination, is one of the most important that has engaged, or can well engage, their attention, the propriety of their taking a very comprehensive, as well as a very serious, view of it, must be evident.

Nothing is more certain than the indispensable necessity of government; and it is equally undeniable, that whenever and however it is instituted, the people must cede to it some of their natural rights, in order to vest it with requisite powers. It is well worthy of consideration therefore, whether it would conduce more to the interest of the people of America, that they should, to all general purposes, be one nation, under one federal government, than that they should divide themselves into separate confederacies, and give to the head of each, the same kind of powers which they are advised to place in one national government.

It has until lately been a received and uncontradicted opinion, that the prosperity of the people of America depended on their continuing firmly united; and the wishes, prayers, and efforts, of our best and wisest citizens, have been constantly directed to that object. But politicians now appear, who insist that this opinion is erroneous, and that instead of looking for safety and happiness in union, we ought to seek it in a division of the states into distinct confederacies or sovereignties. However extraordinary this new doctrine may appear, it nevertheless has its advocates; and certain characters who were formerly much opposed to it, are at present of the number. Whatever may be the arguments or inducements, which have wrought this change in the sentiments and declarations of these gentlemen, it certainly would not be wise in the people at large to adopt these new political tenets, without being fully convinced that they are founded in truth and sound policy.

It has often given me pleasure to observe, that independent America was not composed of detached and distant territories, but that one connected, fertile, wide-spreading country, was the portion of our western sons of liberty. Providence has in a particular manner blessed it with a variety of soils and productions, and watered it with innumerable streams, for the delight and accommodation of its inhabitants. A succession of navigable waters forms a kind of chain round its borders, as if to bind it together; while the most noble rivers in the world, running at convenient distances, present them with highways for the easy communication of friendly aids, and the mutual transportation and exchange of their various commodities.

With equal pleasure I have as often taken notice, that Providence has been pleased to give this one connected country to one united people; a people descended from the same ancestors, speaking the same language, professing the same religion, attached to the same principles of government, very similar in their manners and customs, and who, by their joint counsels, arms and efforts, fighting side by side throughout a long and bloody war, have nobly established their general liberty and independence.

This country and this people seem to have been made for each other; and it appears as if it was the design of Providence, that an inheritance so proper and convenient for a band of brethren, united to each other by the strongest ties, should never be split into a number of unsocial, jealous, and alien sovereignties.

Similar sentiments have hitherto prevailed among all orders and denominations of men among us. To all general purposes, we have uniformly been one people. Each individual citizen every where enjoying the same national rights, privileges, and protection. As a nation, we have made peace and war: as a nation, we have vanquished our common enemies: as a nation, we have formed alliances, and made treaties, and entered into various compacts and conventions with foreign states.

A strong sense of the value and blessings of Union induced the people, at a very early period, to institute a federal government to preserve and perpetuate it. They formed it almost as soon as they had a political existence; nay, at a time, when their habitations were in flames, when many of them were bleeding in the field; and when the progress of hostility and desolation left little room for those calm and mature inquiries and reflections, which must ever precede the formation of a wise and well balanced government for a free people. It is not to be wondered at that a government instituted in times so inauspicious should on experiment be found greatly deficient, and inadequate to the purpose it was intended to answer.

This intelligent people perceived and regretted these defects. Still continuing no less attached to union, than enamoured of liberty, they observed the danger, which immediately threatened the former and more remotely the latter; and being persuaded that ample security for both, could only be found in a national government more wisely framed, they, as with one voice, convened the late Convention at Philadelphia, to take that important subject under consideration.

This Convention, composed of men who possessed the confidence of the people, and many of whom had become highly distinguished by their patriotism, virtue, and wisdom, in times which tried the souls of men, undertook the arduous task. In the mild season of peace, with minds unoccupied by other subjects, they passed many months in cool uninterrupted and daily consultations: And finally, without having been awed by power, or influenced by any passion, except love for their country, they presented and recommended to the people the plan produced by their joint and very unanimous counsels.

Admit, for so is the fact, that this plan is only *recommended*, not imposed, yet, let it be remembered, that it is neither recommended to *blind* approbation, nor to *blind* reprobation; but to that sedate and candid consideration, which the magnitude and importance of the subject demand, and which it certainly ought to receive. But, as has been already remarked, it is more to be wished than expected that it may be so considered and examined. Experience on a former occasion teaches us not to be too sanguine in such hopes. It is not yet forgotten, that well grounded apprehensions of imminent danger induced the people of America to form the memorable Congress of 1774. That body recommended certain measures to their constituents, and the event proved their wisdom; yet it is fresh in our memories how soon the press began to teem with pamphlets and weekly papers against those very measures. Not only many of the officers of government who obeyed the dictates of personal interest, but others from a mistaken estimate of consequences, from the undue influence of ancient attachments, or whose ambition aimed at objects which did not correspond with the public good, were indefatigable in their endeavours to persuade the people to reject the advice of that patriotic Congress. Many indeed were deceived and deluded, but the great majority reasoned and decided judiciously; and happy they are in reflecting that they did so.

They considered that the Congress was composed of many wise and experienced men. That being convened from different parts of the country, they brought with them and communicated to each other a variety of useful information. That in the course of the time they passed together in inquiring into and discussing the true interests of their country, they must have acquired very accurate knowledge on that head. That they were individually interested in the public liberty and prosperity, and therefore that it was not less their inclination than their duty, to recommend such measures only, as after the most mature deliberation they really thought prudent and advisable.

These and similar considerations then induced the people to rely greatly on the judgment and integrity of the Congress; and they took their advice, notwithstanding the various arts and endeavours used to deter and dissuade them from it. But if the people at large had reason to confide in the men of that Congress, few of whom had then been fully tried or generally known, still greater reason have they now to respect the judgment and advice of the Convention; for it is well known, that some of the most distinguished members of that Congress, who have been since tried and justly approved for patriotism and abilities, and who have grown old in acquiring political information, were also members of this Convention, and carried into it their accumulated knowledge and experience.

It is worthy of remark, that not only the first, but every succeeding Congress, as well as the late Convention, have invariably joined with the people in thinking that the prosperity of America depended on its Union. To preserve and perpetuate it, was the great object of the people in forming that Convention; and it is also the great object of the plan which the Convention has advised them to adopt. With what propriety therefore, or for what good purposes, are attempts at this particular period made, by some men, to depreciate the importance of the Union? or why is it suggested that three or four confederacies would be better than one? I am persuaded in my own mind, that the people have always thought right on this subject, and that their universal and uniform attachment to the cause of the Union, rests on great and weighty reasons.

They who promote the idea of substituting a number of distinct confederacies in the room of the plan of the Convention, seem clearly to foresee that the rejection of it would put the continuance of the Union in the utmost jeopardy: that certainly would be the case; and I sincerely wish that it may be as clearly foreseen by every good citizen, that whenever the dissolution of the Union arrives, America will have reason to exclaim in the words of the Poet, "FAREWELL! A LONG FAREWELL, TO ALL MY GREATNESS!"

PUBLIUS.

15

THE FEDERALIST.

NUMBER III.

NEW YORK, NOVEMBER 3, 1787.

JAY.

THE SAME SUBJECT CONTINUED.

IT is not a new observation that the people of any country (if like the Americans, intelligent and well informed) seldom adopt, and steadily persevere for many years, in any erroneous opinion respecting their interests. That consideration naturally tends to create great respect for the high opinion which the people of America have so long and uniformly entertained of the importance of their continuing firmly united under one federal government, vested with sufficient powers for all general and national purposes.

The more attentively I consider and investigate the reasons which appear to have given birth to this opinion, the more I become convinced that they are cogent and conclusive.

Among the many objects to which a wise and free people find it necessary to direct their attention, that of providing for their *safety* seems to be the first. The *safety* of the people doubtless has relation to a great variety of circumstances and considerations, and consequently affords great latitude to those who wish to define it precisely and comprehensively.

At present I mean only to consider it as it respects security for the preservation of peace and tranquility, as well against dangers from *foreign arms and influence*, as against dangers arising from domestic causes. As the former of these comes first in order, it is proper it should be the first discussed. Let us therefore proceed to examine whether the people are not right in their opinion, that a cordial Union under an efficient national Government, affords them the best security that can be devised against *hostilities* from abroad.

The number of wars which have happened, or may happen in the world, will always be found to be in proportion to the number and weight of the causes, whether *real* or *pretended*, which *provoke* or *invite* them. If this remark be just, it becomes useful to inquire, whether so many *just* causes of war are likely to be given by *united* America, as by *disunited* America; for if it should turn out that united America will probably give the fewest, then it will follow that, in this respect, the Union tends most to preserve the people in a state of peace with other nations.

The *just* causes of war for the most part arise either from violations of treaties, or from direct violence. America has already formed treaties with no less than six foreign nations, and all of them, except Prussia, are maritime, and therefore able to annoy and injure us: She has also extensive commerce with Portugal, Spain, and Britain; and with respect to the two latter, has the additional circumstance of neighbourhood to attend to.

It is of high importance to the peace of America, that she observe the law of nations towards all these powers; and to me it appears evident, that this will be more perfectly and punctually done by one national government, than it could be either by thirteen separate states, or by three or four distinct confederacies. For this opinion various reasons may be assigned.

When once an efficient national government is established, the best men in the country will not only consent to serve, but will also generally be appointed to manage it; for although town, or county, or other contracted influence, may place men in state assemblies, or senates, or courts of justice, or executive departments; yet more general and extensive reputation for talents and other qualifications, will be necessary to recommend men to offices under the national government, especially as it will have the widest field for choice, and never experience that want of proper persons, which is not uncommon in some of the states. Hence it will result, that the administration, the political councils, and the judicial decisions, of the national government, will be more wise, systematical and judicious, than those of individual states, and consequently more satisfactory with respect to the other nations, as well as more *safe* with respect to ourselves.

Under the national government, treaties and articles of treaties, as well as the laws of nations, will always be expounded in one sense, and executed in the same manner; whereas adjudications on the same points and questions, in thirteen states, or in three or four confederacies, will not always accord or be consistent; and that as well from the variety of independent courts and judges, appointed by different and independent governments, as from the different local laws and interests which may affect and influence them. The wisdom of the Convention in committing such questions to the jurisdiction and judgment of courts appointed by, and responsible only to one national government, cannot be too much commended.

The prospect of present loss or advantage, may often tempt the governing party in one or two states to swerve from good faith and justice; but those temptations not reaching the other states, and consequently having little or no influence on the national government, the temptations will be fruitless, and good faith and justice be preserved. The case of the treaty of peace with Britain, adds great weight to this reasoning.

If even the governing party in a state should be disposed to resist such temptations, yet as such temptations may, and commonly do, result from circumstances peculiar to the state, and may affect a great number of the inhabitants, the governing party may not always be able, if willing, to prevent the injustice meditated, or to punish the aggressors. But the national government, not being affected by those local circumstances, will neither be induced to commit the wrong themselves, nor want power or inclination to prevent, or punish its commission by others.

So far therefore as either designed or accidental violations of treaties and of the laws of nations afford *just* causes of war, they are less to be apprehended under one general government, than under several lesser ones; and in that respect, the former most favours the *safety* of the people.

As to those just causes of war which proceed from direct and unlawful violence, it appears equally clear to me, that one good national government affords vastly more security against dangers of that sort, than can be derived from any other quarter.

Such violences are more frequently occasioned by the passions and interests of a part than of the whole, of one or two states than of the union. Not a single Indian war has yet been produced by aggressions of the present federal government, feeble as it is; but there are several instances of Indian hostilities having been provoked by the improper conduct of individual states, who either unable or unwilling to restrain or punish offences, have given occasion to the slaughter of many innocent inhabitants.

The neighbourhood of Spanish and British territories, bordering on some states, and not on others, naturally confines the causes of quarrel more immediately to the borderers. The bordering states, if any, will be those who, under the impulse of sudden irritations, and a quick sense of apparent interest or injury, will be most likely by direct violence, to excite war with those nations; and nothing can so effectually obviate that danger, as a national government, whose wisdom and prudence will not be diminished by the passions which actuate the parties immediately interested.

But not only fewer just causes of war will be given by the national government, but it will also be more in their power to accommodate and settle them amicably. They will be more temperate and cool, and in that respect, as well as in others, will be more in a capacity to act with circumspection than the offending state. The pride of states, as well as of men, naturally disposes them to justify all their actions, and opposes their acknowledging, correcting, or repairing their errors and offences. The national government in such cases will not be affected by this pride; but will proceed with moderation and candour to consider and decide on the means most proper to extricate them from the difficulties which threaten them.

Besides, it is well known that acknowledgments, explanations, and compensations, are often accepted as satisfactory from a strong united nation, which would be rejected as unsatisfactory if offered by a state or confederacy of little consideration or power.

In the year 1685, the state of Genoa having offended Louis XIVth, endeavoured to appease him. He demanded that they should send their *Doge* or chief magistrate, accompanied by four of their Senators, to *France*, to ask his pardon and receive his terms. They were obliged to submit to it for the sake of peace. Would he on any occasion either have demanded or have received the like humiliation from Spain, or Britain, or any other powerful nation?

PUBLIUS.

THE FEDERALIST.

NUMBER IV.

NEW YORK, NOVEMBER 7, 1787.

JAY.

THE SAME SUBJECT CONTINUED.

MY last paper assigned several reasons why the safety of the people would be best secured by Union against the danger it may be exposed to by *just* causes of war given to other nations; and those reasons show that such causes would not only be more rarely given, but would also be more easily accommodated by a national government, than either by the state governments, or the proposed confederacies.

But the safety of the people of America against dangers from foreign force, depends not only on their forbearing to give just causes of war to other nations, but also on their placing and continuing themselves in such a situation as not to invite hostility or insult; for it need not be observed, that there are pretended as well as just causes of war.

It is too true, however disgraceful it may be to human nature, that nations in general will make war whenever they have a prospect of getting any thing by it; nay, that absolute monarchs will often make war when their nations are to get nothing by it, but for purposes and objects merely personal, such as, a thirst for military glory, revenge for personal affronts, ambition, or private compacts to aggrandize or support their particular families, or partizans. These, and a variety of motives, which affect only the mind of the sovereign, often lead him to engage in wars not sanctioned by justice, or the voice and interests of his people. But independent of these inducements to war, which are most prevalent in absolute monarchies, but which well deserve our attention, there are others which affect nations as often as kings; and some of them will, on examination, be found to grow out of our relative situation and circumstances.

With France and with Britain we are rivals in the fisheries, and can supply their markets cheaper than they can themselves, notwithstanding any efforts to prevent it by bounties on their own, or duties on foreign fish.

With them, and with most other European nations, we are rivals in navigation, and the carrying trade; and we shall deceive ourselves if we suppose that any of them will rejoice to see these flourish in our hands: for as our carrying trade cannot increase, without in some degree diminishing their's, it is more their interest and will be more their policy, to restrain than to promote it.

In the trade to China and India, we interfere with more than one nation, inasmuch as it enables us to partake in advantages which they had in a manner monopolized, and as we thereby supply ourselves with commodities which we used to purchase from them.

The extension of our own commerce in our own vessels, cannot give pleasure to any nations who possess territories on or near this continent, because the cheapness and excellence of our productions, added to the circumstance of vicinity, and the enterprise and address of our merchants and navigators, will give us a greater share in the advantages which those territories afford, than consists with the wishes or policy of their respective sovereigns.

Spain thinks it convenient to shut the Mississippi against us on the one side, and Britain excludes us from the St. Lawrence on the other; nor will either of them permit the other waters, which are between them and us, to become the means of mutual intercourse and traffic.

From these, and like considerations, which might, if consistent with prudence, be more amplified and detailed, it is easy to see that jealousies and uneasinesses may gradually slide into the minds and cabinets of other nations; and that we are not to expect they should regard our advancement in union, in power and consequence by land and by sea, with an eye of indifference and composure.

The people of America are aware that inducements to war may arise out of these circumstances, as well as from others not so obvious at present; and that whenever such inducements may find fit time and opportunity for operation, pretences to colour and justify them will not be wanting. Wisely therefore do they consider union and a good national government, as necessary to put and keep them in such a situation, as, instead of inviting war, will tend to repress and discourage it. That situation consists in the best possible state of defence, and necessarily depends on the government, the arms, and the resources of the country.

As the safety of the whole is the interest of the whole, and cannot be provided for without government, either one or more, or many, let us inquire whether one good government is not, relative to the object in question, more competent than any other given number whatever.

One government can collect and avail itself of the talents and experience of the ablest men, in whatever part of the Union they may be found. It can move on uniform principles of policy. It can harmonize, assimilate, and protect the several parts and members, and extend the benefit of its foresight and precautions to each. In the formation of treaties it will regard the interest of the whole, and the particular interests of the parts as connected with that of the whole. It can apply the resources and power of the whole to the defence of any particular part, and that more easily and expeditiously than state governments, or separate confederacies, can possibly do, for want of concert and unity of system. It can place the militia under one plan of discipline, and by putting their officers in a proper line of subordination to the chief magistrate, will in a manner consolidate them into one corps, and thereby render them more efficient than if divided into thirteen, or into three or four distinct independent bodies.

What would the militia of Britain be, if the English militia obeyed the government of England, if the Scotch militia obeyed the government of Scotland, and if the Welch militia obeyed the government of Wales? Suppose an invasion: would those three governments (if they agreed at all) be able with all their respective forces, to operate against the enemy so effectually as the single government of Great Britain would?

We have heard much of the fleets of Britain; and if we are wise, the time may come, when the fleets of America may engage attention. But if one national government had not so regulated the navigation of Britain as to make it a nursery for seamen—if one national government had not called forth all the national means and materials for forming fleets, their prowess and their thunder would never have been celebrated. Let England have its navigation and fleet; let Scotland have its navigation and fleet; let Wales have its navigation and fleet; let Ireland have its navigation and fleet; let those four of the constituent parts of the British empire be under four independent governments, and it is easy to perceive how soon they would each dwindle into comparative insignificance.

Apply these facts to our own case. Leave America divided into thirteen, or, if you please, into three or four independent governments, what armies could they raise and pay, what fleets could they ever hope to have? If one was attacked, would the others fly to its succour, and spend their blood and money in its defence? Would there be no danger of their being flattered into neutrality by specious promises, or seduced by a too great fondness for peace to decline hazarding their tranquillity and present safety for the sake of neighbours, of whom perhaps they have been jealous, and whose importance they are content to see diminished? Although such conduct would not be wise, it would nevertheless be natural. The history of the states of Greece, and of other countries, abound with such instances; and it is not improbable that what has so often happened, would, under similar circumstances, happen again.

But admit that they might be willing to help the invaded state or confederacy. How, and when, and in what proportion, shall aids of men and money be afforded? Who shall command the allied armies, and from which of the associates shall he receive his orders? Who shall settle the terms of peace? and in case of disputes, what umpire shall decide between them, and compel acquiescence? Various difficulties and inconveniences would be inseparable from such a situation; whereas one government, watching over the general and common interests, combining and directing the powers and resources of the whole, would be free from all these embarrassments, and conduce far more to the safety of the people.

But whatever may be our situation, whether firmly united under one national government, or split into a number of confederacies, certain it is, that foreign nations will know and view it exactly as it is; and they will act towards us accordingly. If they see that our national government is efficient and well administered—our trade prudently regulated—our militia properly organized and disciplined—our resources and finances discreetly managed—our credit re-established—our people free, contented, and united; they will be much more disposed to cultivate our friendship, than to provoke our resentment. If, on the other hand, they find us either destitute of an effectual government, (each state doing right or wrong, as to its rulers may seem convenient) or split into three or four independent, and probably discordant, republics or confederacies, one inclining to Britain, another to France, and a third to Spain, and perhaps played off against each other by the three, what a poor pitiful figure will America make in their eyes! How liable would she become, not only to their contempt, but to their outrage; and how soon would dear bought experience proclaim, that when a people or family so divide, it never fails to be against themselves.

PUBLIUS

THE FEDERALIST.

NUMBER V.

NEW YORK, NOVEMBER 10, 1787.

JAY.

THE SAME SUBJECT CONTINUED.

QUEEN Ann, in her letter of the 1st July, 1706, to the Scotch Parliament, makes some observations on the importance of the *Union* then forming between England and Scotland, which merit our attention.

I shall present the public with one or two extracts from it. "An entire and perfect union will be the solid foundation of lasting peace: It will secure your religion, liberty, and property; remove the animosities amongst yourselves, and the jealousies and differences betwixt our two kingdoms. It must increase your strength, riches, and trade; and by this union the whole island, being joined in affection and free from all apprehensions of different interests, will be *enabled to resist all its enemies.*" "We most earnestly recommend to you calmness and unanimity in this great and weighty affair, that the union may be brought to a happy conclusion, being the only *effectual* way to secure our present and future happiness; and disappoint the designs of our and your enemies, who will doubtless, on this occasion, *use their utmost endeavours to prevent or delay this union.*"

It was remarked in the preceding paper, that weakness and divisions at home, would invite dangers from abroad; and that nothing would tend more to secure us from them than union, strength, and good government within ourselves. This subject is copious, and cannot easily be exhausted.

The history of Great-Britain is the one with which we are in general the best acquainted, and it gives us many useful lessons. We may profit by their experience, without paying the price which it cost them. Although it seems obvious to common sense, that the people of such an island should be but one nation, yet we find that they were for ages divided into three, and that those three were almost constantly embroiled in quarrels and wars with one another. Notwithstanding their true interest, with respect to the continental nations, was really the same, yet by the arts and policy, and practices of those nations, their mutual jealousies were perpetually kept enflamed, and for a long series of years they were far more inconvenient and troublesome, than they were useful and assisting to each other.

Should the people of America divide themselves into three or four nations, would not the same thing happen? Would not similar jealousies arise, and be in like manner cherished? Instead of their being "joined in affection, and free from all apprehension of different interests," envy and jealousy would soon extinguish confidence and affection, and the partial interests of each confederacy, instead of the general interests of all America, would be the only objects of their policy and pursuits. Hence, like most other *bordering* nations, they would always be either involved in disputes and war, or live in the constant apprehension of them.

The most sanguine advocates for three or four confederacies, cannot reasonably suppose that they would long remain exactly on an equal footing in point of strength, even if it was possible to form them so at first: but admitting that to be practicable, yet what human contrivance can secure the continuance of such equality? Independent of those local circumstances, which tend to beget and increase power in one part, and to impede its progress in another, we must advert to the effects of that superior policy and good management which would probably distinguish the government of one above the rest, and by which their relative equality in strength and consideration would be destroyed. For it cannot be presumed, that the same degree of sound policy, prudence, and foresight, would uniformly be observed by each of these confederacies, for a long succession of years.

Whenever, and from whatever causes it might happen, and happen it would, that any one of these nations or confederacies should rise on the scale of political importance much above the degree of her neighbours, that moment would those neighbours behold her with envy and with fear. Both those passions would lead them to countenance, if not to promote, whatever might promise to diminish her importance; and would also restrain them from measures calculated to advance, or even to secure her prosperity.—Much time would not be necessary to enable her to discern these unfriendly dispositions. She would soon begin, not only to lose confidence in her neighbours, but also to feel a disposition equally unfavourable to them. Distrust naturally creates distrust; and by nothing is good will and kind conduct more speedily changed, than by invidious jealousies and uncandid imputations, whether expressed or implied.

The North is generally the region of strength, and many local circumstances render it probable, that the most northern of the proposed confederacies would, at a period not very far distant, be unquestionably more formidable than any of the others. No sooner would this become evident, than the *Northern Hive* would excite the same ideas and sensations in the more Southern parts of America, which it formerly did in the Southern parts of Europe: Nor does it appear to be a rash conjecture, that its young swarms might often be tempted to gather honey in the more blooming fields and milder air of their luxurious and more delicate neighbours.

They who well consider the history of similar divisions and confederacies, will find abundant reasons to apprehend, that those in contemplation would in no other sense be neighbours, than as they would be borderers; that they would neither love nor trust one another, but on the contrary, would be a prey to discord, jealousy, and mutual injuries; in short, that they would place us exactly in the situation in which some nations doubtless wish to see us—in which we should be *formidable only to each other*.

From these considerations, it appears that those persons are greatly mistaken, who suppose that alliances offensive and defensive might be formed between these confederacies, which would produce that combination and union of wills, of arms, and of resources, which would be necessary to put and keep them in a formidable state of defence against foreign enemies.

When did the independent states into which Britain and Spain were formerly divided, combine in such alliances, or unite their forces against a foreign enemy? The proposed confederacies will be *distinct nations*. Each of them would have to regulate its commerce with foreigners by distinct treaties; and as their productions and commodities are different, and proper for different markets, so would those treaties be essentially different. Different commercial concerns must create different interests, and of course different degrees of political attachment to, and connection with, different foreign nations. Hence it might and probably would happen, that the foreign nation with whom the *Southern* confederacy might be at war, would be the one, with whom the *Northern* confederacy would be the most desirous of preserving peace and friendship. An alliance so contrary to their immediate interest would not therefore be easy to form, nor if formed, would it be observed and fulfilled with perfect good faith.

Nay, it is far more probable that in America, as in Europe, neighbouring nations, acting under the impulse of opposite interests, and unfriendly passions, would frequently be found taking different sides. Considering our distance from Europe, it would be more natural for these confederacies to apprehend danger from one another, than from distant nations, and therefore that each of them should be more desirous to guard against the others, by the aid of foreign alliances, than to guard against foreign dangers by alliances between themselves. And here let us not forget how much more easy it is to receive foreign fleets into our ports, and foreign armies into our country, than it is to persuade or compel them to depart. How many conquests did the Romans and others make in the character of allies, and what innovations did they under the same character introduce into the governments of those whom they pretended to protect?

Let candid men judge then whether the division of America into any given number of independent sovereignties, would tend to secure us against the hostilities and improper interference of foreign nations.

PUBLIUS.

16

THE FEDERALIST.

NUMBER VI.

NEW YORK, NOVEMBER 14, 1787.

HAMILTON.

CONCERNING DANGERS FROM WAR BETWEEN THE STATES.

THE three last numbers of this work have been dedicated to an enumeration of the dangers to which we should be exposed, in a state of disunion, from the arms and arts of foreign nations. I shall now proceed to delineate dangers of a different, and, perhaps, still more alarming kind, those which will in all probability flow from dissentions between the states themselves, and from domestic factions and convulsions. These have been already in some instances slightly anticipated; but they deserve a more particular and more full investigation.

If these states should either be wholly disunited, or only united in partial confederacies, a man must be far gone in Utopian speculations, who can seriously doubt that the subdivisions into which they might be thrown, would have frequent and violent contests with each other. To presume a want of motives for such contests, as an argument against their existence, would be to forget that men are ambitious, vindictive, and rapacious. To look for a continuation of harmony between a number of independent unconnected sovereignties, situated in the same neighbourhood, would be to disregard the uniform course of human events, and to set at defiance the accumulated experience of ages.

The causes of hostility among nations are innumerable. There are some which have a general and almost constant operation upon the collective bodies of society. Of this description are the love of power, or the desire of preeminence and dominion—the jealousy of power, or the desire of equality and safety. There are others which have a more circumscribed, though an equally operative influence, within their spheres: such are the rivalships and competitions of commerce between commercial nations. And there are others, not less numerous than either of the former, which take their origin entirely in private passions; in the attachments, enmities, interests, hopes, and fears, of leading individuals in the communities of which they are members. Men of this class, whether the favourites of a king or of a people, have in too many instances abused the confidence they possessed; and assuming the pretext of some public motive, have not scrupled to sacrifice the national tranquillity to personal advantage, or personal gratification.

The celebrated Pericles, in compliance with the resentments of a prostitute,* at the expense of much of the blood and treasure of his countrymen, attacked, vanquished, and destroyed the city of the *Samnians*. The same man, stimulated by private pique against the *Magarensians*, another nation of Greece, or to avoid a prosecution with which he was threatened as an accomplice in a supposed theft of the statuary *Phidias*, or to get rid of the accusations prepared to be brought against him for dissipating the funds of the state in the purchase of popularity, or from a combination of all these causes, was the primitive author of that famous and fatal war, distinguished in the Grecian annals by the name of the *Peloponnesian* war; which, after various vicissitudes, intermissions, and renewals, terminated in the ruin of the Athenian commonwealth.

The ambitious cardinal, who was prime minister to Henry VIIIth, permitting his vanity to aspire to the triple-crown, entertained hopes of succeeding in the acquisition of that splendid prize by the influence of the emperor Charles Vth. To secure

---

* ASPASIA, vide PLUTARCH'S life of Pericles.

the favour and interest of this enterprising and powerful monarch, he precipitated England into a war with France, contrary to the plainest dictates of policy, and at the hazard of the safety and independence, as well of the kingdom over which he presided by his counsels, as of Europe in general. For if there ever was a sovereign who bid fair to realize the project of universal monarchy, it was the emperor Charles Vth, of whose intrigues Wolsey was at once the instrument and the dupe.

The influence which the bigotry of one female,* the petulances of another,† and the cabals of a third,‡ had in the contemporary policy, ferments, and pacifications, of a considerable part of Europe, are topics that have been too often descanted upon not to be generally known.

To multiply examples of the agency of personal considerations in the production of great national events, either foreign or domestic, according to their direction, would be an unnecessary waste of time. Those who have but a superficial acquaintance with the sources from which they are to be drawn, will themselves recollect a variety of instances; and those who have a tolerable knowledge of human nature, will not stand in need of such lights, to form their opinion either of the reality or extent of that agency. Perhaps, however, a reference, tending to illustrate the general principle, may with propriety be made to a case which has lately happened among ourselves. If SHAYS had had not been a *desperate debtor*, it is much to be doubted whether Massachusetts would have been plunged into a civil war.

But notwithstanding the concurring testimony of experience, in this particular, there are still to be found visionary, or designing men, who stand ready to advocate the paradox of perpetual peace between the states, though dismembered and alienated from each other. The genius of republics, say they, is pacific; the spirit of commerce has a tendency to soften the manners of men, and to extinguish those inflammable humours which have so often kindled into wars. Commercial republics, like ours, will

---

* Madame de Maintenon.   † Duchess of Marlborough.
‡ Madame de Pompadour.

never be disposed to waste themselves in ruinous contentions with each other. They will be governed by mutual interest, and will cultivate a spirit of mutual amity and concord.

We may ask these projectors in politics, whether it is not the true interest of all nations to cultivate the same benevolent and philosophic spirit? If this be their true interest, have they in fact pursued it? Has it not, on the contrary, invariably been found, that momentary passions, and immediate interests, have a more active and imperious control over human conduct, than general or remote considerations of policy, utility, or justice? Have republics in practice been less addicted to war than monarchies? Are not the former administered by men as well as the latter? Are there not aversions, predilections, rivalships, and desires of unjust acquisition, that affect nations, as well as kings? Are not popular assemblies frequently subject to the impulses of rage, resentment, jealousy, avarice, and of other irregular and violent propensities? Is it not well known, that their determinations are often governed by a few individuals in whom they place confidence, and that they are of course liable to be tinctured by the passions and views of those individuals? Has commerce hitherto done any thing more than change the objects of war? Is not the love of wealth as domineering and enterprising a passion as that of power or glory? Have there not been as many wars founded upon commercial motives, since that has become the prevailing system of nations, as were before occasioned by the cupidity of territory or dominion? Has not the spirit of commerce, in many instances, administered new incentives to the appetite both for the one and for the other?—Let experience, the least fallible guide of human opinions, be appealed to for an answer to these inquiries.

Sparta, Athens, Rome, and Carthage, were all republics; two of them, Athens and Carthage, of the commercial kind. Yet were they as often engaged in wars, offensive and defensive, as the neighbouring monarchies of the same times. Sparta was little better than a well regulated camp; and Rome was never sated of carnage and conquest.

Carthage, though a commercial republic, was the aggressor in the very war that ended in her destruction. Hannibal had carried her arms into the heart of Italy, and even to the gates of Rome, before Scipio, in turn, gave him an overthrow in the territories of Carthage, and made a conquest of the commonwealth.

Venice, in latter times, figured more than once in wars of ambition; till becoming an object of terror to the other Italian states, Pope Julius the Second found means to accomplish that formidable league,* which gave a deadly blow to the power and pride of that haughty republic.

The provinces of Holland, till they were overwhelmed in debts and taxes, took a leading and conspicuous part in the wars of Europe. They had furious contests with England for the dominion of the sea; and were among the most persevering and most implacable of the opponents of Lewis XIV.

In the government of Britain the representatives of the people compose one branch of the national legislature. Commerce has been for ages the predominant pursuit of that country. Yet few nations have been more frequently engaged in war; and the wars, in which that kingdom has been engaged, have in numerous instances proceeded from the people. There have been, if I may so express it, almost as many popular as royal wars. The cries of the nation and the importunities of their representatives have, upon various occasions, dragged their monarchs into war, or continued them in it, contrary to their inclinations, and sometimes contrary to the real interests of the state. In that memorable struggle for superiority, between the rival houses of *Austria* and *Bourbon*, which so long kept Europe in a flame, it is well known that the antipathies of the English against the French, seconding the ambition, or rather the avarice, of a favourite leader, † protracted the war beyond the limits marked

---

* THE LEAGUE OF CAMBRAY, comprehending the Emperor, the King of France, the King of Aragon, and most of the Italian Princes and States.

† The Duke of Marlborough.

out by sound policy, and for a considerable time in opposition to the views of the court.

The wars of these two last mentioned nations have in a great measure grown out of commercial considerations;—the desire of supplanting, and the fear of being supplanted either in particular branches of traffic, or in the general advantages of trade and navigation; and sometimes even the more culpable desire of sharing in the commerce of other nations, without their consent.

The last war but two between Britain and Spain, sprang from the attempts of the English merchants, to prosecute an illicit trade with the Spanish main. These unjustifiable practices on their part, produced severities on the part of the Spaniards, towards the subjects of Great Britain, which were not more justifiable; because they exceeded the bounds of a just retaliation, and were chargeable with inhumanity and cruelty. Many of the English who were taken on the Spanish coasts, were sent to dig in the mines of Potosi; and by the usual progress of a spirit of resentment, the innocent were after a while confounded with the guilty in indiscriminate punishment. The complaints of the merchants kindled a violent flame throughout the nation, which soon after broke out in the house of commons, and was communicated from that body to the ministry. Letters of reprisal were granted, and a war ensued; which, in its consequences, overthrew all the alliances that but twenty years before had been formed, with sanguine expectations of the most beneficial fruits.

From this summary of what has taken place in other countries, whose situations have borne the nearest resemblance to our own, what reason can we have to confide in those reveries, which would seduce us into the expectation of peace and cordiality between the members of the present confederacy, in a state of separation? Have we not already seen enough of the fallacy and extravagance of those idle theories which have amused us with promises of an exemption from the imperfections, the weaknesses, and the evils incident to society in every shape? Is

it not time to awake from the deceitful dream of a golden age,
and to adopt as a practical maxim for the direction of our political conduct, that we, as well as the other inhabitants of the
globe, are yet remote from the happy empire of perfect wisdom
and perfect virtue?

Let the point of extreme depression to which our national dignity and credit have sunk; let the inconveniences felt every
where from a lax and ill administration of government; let the
revolt of a part of the state of North Carolina; the late menacing disturbances in Pennsylvania, and the actual insurrections
and rebellions in Massachusetts, declare!

So far is the general sense of mankind from corresponding
with the tenets of those, who endeavour to lull asleep our apprehensions of discord and hostility between the states, in the
event of disunion, that it has from long observation of the
progress of society become a sort of axiom in politics, that vicinity, or nearness of situation, constitutes nations natural enemies.
An intelligent writer expresses himself on this subject to this
effect: "NEIGHBOURING NATIONS (says he) are naturally ENEMIES
of each other, unless their common weakness forces them to
league in a CONFEDERATE REPUBLIC, and their constitution prevents the differences that neighbourhood occasions, extinguish-
ing that secret jealousy, which disposes all states to aggrandize
themselves at the expense of their neighbours."* This passage,
at the same time, points out the EVIL and suggests the REMEDY.

PUBLIUS.

---

* Vide, Principes des Négotiations par l'Abbé de Mably.

THE FEDERALIST.

NUMBER VII.

NEW YORK, NOVEMBER 17, 1787.

HAMILTON.

THE SUBJECT CONTINUED, AND PARTICULAR CAUSES ENUMERATED.

IT is sometimes asked, with an air of seeming triumph, what inducements the states could have, if disunited, to make war upon each other? It would be a full answer to this question to say,—precisely the same inducements which have, at different times, deluged in blood all the nations in the world. But unfortunately for us, the question admits of a more particular answer. There are causes of difference within our immediate contemplation, of the tendency of which, even under the restraints of a federal constitution, we have had sufficient experience to enable us to form a judgment of what might be expected, if those restraints were removed.

Territorial disputes have at all times been found one of the most fertile sources of hostility among nations. Perhaps the greatest proportion of the wars that have desolated the earth have sprung from this origin. This cause would exist, among us, in full force. We have a vast tract of unsettled territory within the boundaries of the United States. There still are discordant and undecided claims between several of them; and the dissolution of the union would lay a foundation for similar claims between them all. It is well known, that they have heretofore had serious and animated discussions concerning the right to the lands which were ungranted at the time of the revolution, and which usually went under the name of crown-lands. The states within the limits of whose colonial governments they were comprised, have claimed them as their property; the others have contended that the rights of the crown in this article devolved upon the union; especially as to all that part of the Western territory which, either by actual possession, or through the submission of the Indian proprietors, was subject to the jurisdiction of the King of Great-Britain, till it was relinquished by the treaty of peace. This, it has been said, was at all events an acquisition to the confederacy by compact with a foreign power. It has been the prudent policy of Congress to appease this controversy, by prevailing upon the states to make cessions to the United States for the benefit of the whole. This has been so far accomplished, as under a continuation of the union, to afford a decided prospect of an amicable termination of the dispute. A dismemberment of the confederacy however would revive this dispute, and would create others on the same subject. At present, a large part of the vacant Western territory is by cession at least, if not by any anterior right, the common property of the union. If that were at an end, the states which have made cessions, on a principle of federal compromise, would be apt, when the motive of the grant had ceased, to reclaim the lands as a reversion. The other states would no doubt insist on a proportion, by right of representation. Their argument would be, that a grant once made, could not be revoked; and that the justice of their participating in territory acquired or secured, by the joint efforts of the confederacy, remained undiminished. If, contrary to probability, it should be admitted by all the states, that each had a right to a share of this common stock, there would still be a difficulty to be surmounted, as to a proper rule of apportionment. Different principles would be set up by different states for this purpose; and as they would affect the opposite interests of the parties, they might not easily be susceptible of a pacific adjustment.

In the wide field of Western territory, therefore, we perceive an ample theatre for hostile pretensions, without any umpire or common judge to interpose between the contending parties. To reason from the past to the future, we shall have good ground to apprehend, that the sword would sometimes be appealed to as the arbiter of their differences. The circumstances of the dispute between Connecticut and Pennsylvania, respecting the lands at Wyoming, admonish us not to be sanguine in expecting an easy accommodation of such differences. The articles of confederation obliged the parties to submit the matter to the decision of a federal court. The submission was made, and the court decided in favour of Pennsylvania. But Connecticut gave strong indications of dissatisfaction with that determination; nor did she appear to be entirely resigned to it, till by negotiation and management something like an equivalent was found for the loss she supposed herself to have sustained. Nothing here said, is intended to convey the slightest censure on the conduct of that State. She no doubt sincerely believed herself to have been injured by the decision; and states, like individuals, acquiesce with great reluctance in determinations to their disadvantage.

Those who had an opportunity of seeing the inside of the transactions, which attended the progress of the controversy between this state and the district of Vermont, can vouch the opposition we experienced, as well from states not interested, as from those which were interested in the claim; and can attest the danger to which the peace of the confederacy might have been exposed, had this state attempted to assert its rights by force. Two motives preponderated in that opposition; one, a jealousy entertained of our future power; another, the interest of certain individuals of influence in the neighbouring states, who had obtained grants of lands under the actual government of that district. Even the states which brought forward claims, in contradiction to ours, seemed more solicitous to dismember this state, than to establish their own pretensions. These were New-Hampshire, Massachusetts, and Connecticut. New-Jersey and Rhode-Island, upon all occasions, discovered a warm zeal for the independence of Vermont; and Maryland, until alarmed by the appearance of a connection between Canada and that place, entered deeply into the same views. These being small states, saw with an unfriendly eye the perspective of our growing greatness. In a review of these transactions, we may trace some of the causes which would be likely to embroil the states with each other, if it should be their unpropitious destiny to become disunited.

The competitions of commerce would be another fruitful source of contention. The states less favourably circumstanced, would be desirous of escaping from the disadvantages of local situation, and of sharing in the advantages of their more fortunate neighbours. Each state, or separate confederacy, would pursue a system of commercial polity peculiar to itself. This would occasion distinctions, preferences, and exclusions, which would beget discontent. The habits of intercourse, on the basis of equal privileges, to which we have been accustomed from the earliest settlement of the country, would give a keener edge to those causes of discontent, than they would naturally have, independent of this circumstance. *We should be ready to denominate injuries, those things which were in reality the justifiable acts of independent sovereignties consulting a distinct interest.* The spirit of enterprise, which characterizes the commercial part of America, has left no occasion of displaying itself unimproved. It is not at all probable, that this unbridled spirit would pay much respect to those regulations of trade, by which particular states might endeavour to secure exclusive benefits to their own citizens. The infractions of these regulations on one side, the efforts to prevent and repel them on the other, would naturally lead to outrages, and these to reprisals and wars.

The opportunities, which some states would have of rendering others tributary to them, by commercial regulations, would be impatiently submitted to by the tributary states. The relative situation of New-York, Connecticut, and New-Jersey, would afford an example of this kind. New-York, from the necessities of revenue, must lay duties on her importations. A great part of these duties must be paid by the inhabitants of the two other states, in the capacity of consumers of what we import. New-York would neither be willing, nor able to forego this advantage. Her citizens would not consent that a duty paid by them should be remitted in favour of the citizens of her neighbours; nor would it be practicable, if there were not this impediment in the way, to distinguish the customers in our own markets.

Would Connecticut and New-Jersey long submit to be taxed by New-York for her exclusive benefit? Should we be long permitted to remain in the quiet and undisturbed enjoyment of a metropolis, from the possession of which we derived an advantage so odious to our neighbours, and, in their opinion, so oppressive? Should we be able to preserve it against the incumbent weight of Connecticut on the one side, and the co-operating pressure of New-Jersey on the other? These are questions that temerity alone will answer in the affirmative.

The public debt of the Union would be a further cause of collision between the separate states or confederacies. The apportionment, in the first instance, and the progressive extinguishment, afterwards, would be alike productive of ill humour and animosity. How would it be possible to agree upon a rule of apportionment, satisfactory to all? There is scarcely any, that can be proposed, which is entirely free from real objections. These, as usual, would be exaggerated by the adverse interest of the parties. There are even dissimilar views among the states, as to the general principle of discharging the public debt. Some of them, either less impressed with the importance of national credit, or because their citizens have little, if any, immediate interest in the question, feel an indifference, if not a repugnance, to the payment of the domestic debt, at any rate. These would be inclined to magnify the difficulties of a distribution. Others of them, a numerous body of whose citizens are creditors of the public, beyond the proportion of the state in the total amount of the national debt, would be strenuous for some equitable and effectual provision. The procrastinations of the former, would excite the resentments of the latter. The settlement of a rule, would in the mean time be postponed, by real differences of opinion, and affected delays. The citizens of the states interested, would clamour; foreign powers would urge, for the satisfaction of their just demands; and the peace of the states would be exposed to the double contingency of external invasion, and internal contention.

But suppose the difficulties of agreeing upon a rule surmounted, and the apportionment made. Still there is great room to suppose, that the rule agreed upon would, in the experiment, be found to bear harder upon some states than upon others. Those which were sufferers by it, would naturally seek for a mitigation of the burthen. The others would as naturally be disinclined to a revision, which was likely to end in an increase of their own incumbrances. Their refusal would afford to the complaining states a pretext for withholding their contributions, too plausible not to be embraced with avidity; and the non-compliance of these states with their engagements, would be a ground of bitter dissention and altercation. If even the rule adopted should in practice justify the equality of its principle, still delinquencies in payment, on the part of some of the states, would result from a diversity of other causes—the real deficiency of resources; the mismanagement of their finances; accidental disorders in the administration of the government; and in addition to the rest, the reluctance with which men commonly part with money for purposes, that have outlived the exigencies which produced them, and interfere with the supply of immediate wants. Delinquencies from whatever causes would be productive of complaints, recriminations, and quarrels. There is, perhaps, nothing more likely to disturb the tranquillity of nations, than their being bound to mutual contributions for any common object, which does not yield an equal and coincident benefit. For it is an observation as true, as it is trite, that there is nothing men differ so readily about, as the payment of money.

Laws in violation of private contracts, as they amount to aggressions on the rights of those states, whose citizens are injured by them, may be considered as another probable source of hostility. We are not authorized to expect, that a more liberal, or more equitable spirit would preside over the legislations of the individual states hereafter, if unrestrained by any additional checks, than we have heretofore seen, in too many instances, disgracing their several codes. We have observed the disposition to retaliation excited in Connecticut, in consequence of the enormities perpetrated by the legislature of Rhode-Island; and we may reasonably infer, that in similar cases, under other circumstances, a war, not of *parchment*, but of the sword, would chastise such atrocious breaches of moral obligation and social justice.

The probability of incompatible alliances between the different states or confederacies, and different foreign nations, and the effects of this situation upon the peace of the whole, have been sufficiently unfolded in some preceding papers. From the view they have exhibited of this part of the subject, this conclusion is to be drawn, that America, if not connected at all, or only by the feeble tie of a simple league offensive and defensive, would, by the operation of such opposite and jarring alliances, be gradually entangled in all the pernicious labyrinths of European politics and wars; and by the destructive contentions of the parts into which she was divided, would be likely to become a prey to the artifices and machinations of powers equally the enemies of them all. *Divide et impera* must be the motto of every nation that either hates or fears us.

PUBLIUS.

THE FEDERALIST.

NUMBER VIII.

NEW YORK, NOVEMBER 21, 1787.

HAMILTON.

THE EFFECTS OF INTERNAL WAR IN PRODUCING STANDING ARMIES, AND OTHER INSTITUTIONS UNFRIENDLY TO LIBERTY.

ASSUMING it therefore as an established truth, that, in case of disunion, the several states, or such combinations of them as might happen to be formed out of the wreck of the general confederacy, would be subject to those vicissitudes of peace and war, of friendship and enmity with each other, which have fallen to the lot of all neighbouring nations not united under one government, let us enter into a concise detail of some of the consequences that would attend such a situation.

War between the states, in the first periods of their separate existence, would be accompanied with much greater distresses than it commonly is in those countries, where regular military establishments have long obtained. The disciplined armies always kept on foot on the continent of Europe, though they bear a malignant aspect to liberty and economy, have, notwithstanding, been productive of the signal advantage of rendering sudden conquests impracticable, and of preventing that rapid desolation, which used to mark the progress of war, prior to their introduction. The art of fortification has contributed to the same ends. The nations of Europe are encircled with chains of fortified places, which mutually obstruct invasion. Campaigns are wasted in reducing two or three frontier garrisons, to gain admittance into an enemy's country. Similar impediments occur at every step, to exhaust the strength, and delay the progress of an invader. Formerly, an invading army would penetrate into the heart of a neighbouring country, almost as soon as intelligence of its approach could be received; but now, a comparatively small force of disciplined troops, acting on the defensive, with the aid of posts, is able to impede, and finally to frustrate, the enterprises of one much more considerable. The history of war, in that quarter of the globe, is no longer a history of nations subdued, and empires overturned; but of towns taken and retaken, of battles that decide nothing, of retreats more beneficial than victories, of much effort and little acquisition.

In this country, the scene would be altogether reversed. The jealousy of military establishments, would postpone them as long as possible. The want of fortifications, leaving the frontiers of one state open to another, would facilitate inroads. The populous states would, with little difficulty, over-run their less populous neighbours. Conquests would be as easy to be made, as difficult to be retained. War, therefore, would be desultory and predatory. Plunder and devastation ever march in the train of irregulars. The calamities of individuals would make the principal figure in the events, which would characterize our military exploits.

This picture is not too highly wrought; though, I confess, it would not long remain a just one. Safety from external danger, is the most powerful director of national conduct. Even the ardent love of liberty will, after a time, give way to its dictates. The violent destruction of life and property incident to war; the continual effort and alarm attendant on a state of continual danger, will compel nations the most attached to liberty, to resort for repose and security to institutions which have a tendency to destroy their civil and political rights. To be more safe, they, at length, become willing to run the risk of being less free.

17

The institutions chiefly alluded to, are STANDING ARMIES, and the correspondent appendages of military establishment. Standing armies, it is said, are not provided against in the new constitution; and it is thence inferred that they would exist under it.* This inference, from the very form of the proposition, is, at best, problematical and uncertain. But STANDING ARMIES, it may be replied, must inevitably result from a dissolution of the confederacy. Frequent war, and constant apprehension, which require a state of as constant preparation, will infallibly produce them. The weaker states, or confederacies, would first have recourse to them, to put themselves upon an equality with their more potent neighbours. They would endeavour to supply the inferiority of population and resources, by a more regular and effective system of defence, by disciplined troops, and by fortifications. They would, at the same time, be obliged to strengthen the executive arm of government; in doing which, their constitutions would acquire a progressive direction towards monarchy. It is of the nature of war to increase the executive, at the expense of the legislative authority.

The expedients which have been mentioned would soon give the states, or confederacies, that made use of them, a superiority over their neighbours. Small states, or states of less natural strength, under vigorous governments, and with the assistance of disciplined armies, have often triumphed over large states, or states of greater natural strength, which have been destitute of these advantages. Neither the pride, nor the safety, of the more important states, or confederacies, would permit them long to submit to this mortifying and adventitious superiority. They would quickly resort to means similar to those by which it had been effected, to reinstate themselves in their lost pre-eminence. Thus we should in a little time see established

* This objection will be fully examined in its proper place; and it will be shown, that the only rational precaution which could have been taken on this subject, has been taken; and a much better one than is to be found in any constitution that has been heretofore framed in America, most of which contain no guard at all on this subject.

in every part of this country, the same engines of despotism which have been the scourge of the old world. This, at least, would be the natural course of things; and our reasonings will be likely to be just, in proportion as they are accommodated to this standard.

These are not vague inferences deduced from speculative defects in a constitution, the whole power of which is lodged in the hands of the people, or their representatives and delegates; they are solid conclusions, drawn from the natural and necessary progress of human affairs.

It may perhaps be asked, by way of objection, why did not standing armies spring up out of the contentions which so often distracted the ancient republics of Greece? Different answers equally satisfactory, may be given to this question. The industrious habits of the people of the present day, absorbed in the pursuits of gain, and devoted to the improvements of agriculture and commerce, are incompatible with the condition of a nation of soldiers, which was the true condition of the people of those republics. The means of revenue, which have been so greatly multiplied by the increase of gold and silver, and of the arts of industry, and the science of finance, which is the offspring of modern times, concurring with the habits of nations, have produced an entire revolution in the system of war, and have rendered disciplined armies, distinct from the body of the citizens, the inseparable companion of frequent hostility.

There is a wide difference also, between military establishments in a country which, by its situation, is seldom exposed to invasions, and in one which is often subject to them, and always apprehensive of them. The rulers of the former can have no good pretext, if they are even so inclined, to keep on foot armies so numerous as must of necessity be maintained in the latter. These armies being, in the first case, rarely, if at all, called into activity for interior defence, the people are in no danger of being broken to military subordination. The laws are not accustomed to relaxations, in favour of military exigencies; the civil state remains in full vigour, neither corrupted nor confounded

with the principles or propensities of the other state. The smallness of the army forbids competition with the natural strength
of the community, and the citizens, not habituated to look up to
the military power for protection, or to submit to its oppressions, neither love nor fear the soldiery: They view them with a
spirit of jealous acquiescence in a necessary evil, and stand
ready to resist a power which they suppose may be exerted to
the prejudice of their rights.

The army under such circumstances, though it may usefully
aid the magistrate to suppress a small faction, or an occasional
mob, or insurrection, will be utterly incompetent to the purpose
of enforcing encroachments against the united efforts of the
great body of the people.

But in a country, where the perpetual menacings of danger
oblige the government to be always prepared to repel it, her
armies must be numerous enough for instant defence. The continual necessity for his services enhances the importance of the
soldier, and proportionably degrades the condition of the citizen.
The military state becomes elevated above the civil. The inhabitants of territories often the theatre of war, are unavoidably
subjected to frequent infringements on their rights, which serve
to weaken their sense of those rights; and by degrees, the people are brought to consider the soldiery not only as their pro-
tectors, but as their superiors. The transition from this disposition to that of considering them as masters, is neither remote
nor difficult: But it is very difficult to prevail upon a people
under such impressions, to make a bold, or effectual resistance,
to usurpations, supported by the military power.

The kingdom of Great Britain falls within the first description. An insular situation, and a powerful marine, guarding it in
a great measure against the possibility of foreign invasion,
supersede the necessity of a numerous army within the kingdom. A sufficient force to make head against a sudden descent
till the militia could have time to rally and embody, is all that
has been deemed requisite. No motive of national policy has
demanded, nor would public opinion have tolerated a larger

number of troops upon its domestic establishment. This peculiar felicity of situation* has, in a great degree, contributed to preserve the liberty, which that country to this day enjoys, in spite of the prevalent venality and corruption. If Britain had been situated on the continent, and had been compelled, as she would have been, by that situation, to make her military establishments at home co-extensive with those of the other great powers of Europe, she, like them, would in all probability, at this day be a victim to the absolute power of a single man. It is possible, though not easy, for the people of that island to be enslaved from other causes; but it cannot be by the prowess of an army so inconsiderable as that which has been usually kept up within the kingdom.

If we are wise enough to preserve the union, we may for ages enjoy an advantage similar to that of an insulated situation. Europe is at a great distance from us. Her colonies in our vicinity, will be likely to continue too much disproportioned in strength, to be able to give us any dangerous annoyance. Extensive military establishments cannot, in this position, be necessary to our security. But if we should be disunited, and the integral parts should either remain separated, or which is most probable, should be thrown together into two or three confederacies, we should be in a short course of time, in the predicament of the continental powers of Europe. Our liberties would be a prey to the means of defending ourselves against the ambition and jealousy of each other.

This is an idea not superficial nor futile, but solid and weighty. It deserves the most serious and mature consideration of every prudent and honest man, of whatever party: If such men will make a firm and solemn pause, and meditate dispassionately on its vast importance; if they will contemplate it in all its attitudes, and trace it to all its consequences, they will not hesitate to part with trivial objections to a constitution, the

---

* The recent prodigious aggrandizement of France has, probably, altered the situation of Great-Britain in this respect: it will be happy if the alteration has no tendency inauspicious to British liberty.

rejection of which would in all probability put a final period to the Union. The airy phantoms that now flit before the distempered imaginations of some of its adversaries, would then quickly give place to the more substantial prospects of dangers, real, certain, and extremely formidable.

PUBLIUS.

THE FEDERALIST.

NUMBER IX.

NEW YORK, NOVEMBER 21, 1787.

HAMILTON.

THE UTILITY OF THE UNION AS A SAFEGUARD AGAINST DOMESTIC FACTION AND INSURRECTION.

A FIRM union will be of the utmost moment to the peace and liberty of the states, as a barrier against domestic faction and insurrection.

It is impossible to read the history of the petty republics of Greece and Italy, without feeling sensations of horror and disgust at the distractions with which they were continually agitated, and at the rapid succession of revolutions, by which they were kept perpetually vibrating between the extremes of tyranny and anarchy. If they exhibit occasional calms, these only serve as shortlived contrasts to the furious storms that are to succeed. If now and then intervals of felicity open themselves to view, we behold them with a mixture of regret arising from the reflection, that the pleasing scenes before us are soon to be overwhelmed by the tempestuous waves of sedition and party rage. If momentary rays of *glory* break forth from the gloom, while they *dazzle* us with a transient and fleeting brilliancy, they at the same time admonish us to lament, that the vices of government should pervert the direction, and tarnish the lustre, of those bright talents and exalted endowments, for which the favoured soils that produced them have been so justly celebrated.

From the disorders that disfigure the annals of those republics, the advocates of despotism have drawn arguments, not only against the forms of republican government, but against the very principles of civil liberty. They have decried all free government, as inconsistent with the order of society, and have indulged themselves in malicious exultation over its friends and partizans. Happily for mankind, stupendous fabrics reared on the basis of liberty, which have flourished for ages, have in a few glorious instances refuted their gloomy sophisms. And, I trust, America will be the broad and solid foundation of other edifices not less magnificent, which will be equally permanent monuments of their error.

But it is not to be denied, that the portraits they have sketched of republican government, were too just copies of the originals from which they were taken. If it had been found impracticable, to have devised models of a more perfect structure, the enlightened friends of liberty would have been obliged to abandon the cause of that species of government as indefensible. The science of politics, however, like most other sciences, has received great improvement. The efficacy of various principles is now well understood, which were either not known at all, or imperfectly known to the ancients. The regular distribution of power into distinct departments; the introduction of legislative balances and checks; the institution of courts composed of judges, holding their offices during good behaviour; the representation of the people in the legislature, by deputies of their own election; these are either wholly new discoveries, or have made their principal progress towards perfection in modern times. They are means, and powerful means, by which the excellencies of republican government may be retained, and its imperfections lessened or avoided. To this catalogue of circumstances, that tend to the amelioration of popular systems of civil government, I shall venture, however novel it may appear to some, to add one more, on a principle, which has been made the foundation of an objection to the new constitution; I mean the ENLARGEMENT of the ORBIT within which such systems are to

revolve, either in respect to the dimensions of a single state, or
to the consolidation of several smaller states into one great confederacy. The latter is that which immediately concerns the
object under consideration. It will, however, be of use to examine the principle in its application to a single state, which shall
be attended to in another place.

The utility of a confederacy, as well to suppress faction, and
to guard the internal tranquillity of states, as to increase their
external force and security, is in reality not a new idea. It has
been practised upon in different countries and ages, and has
received the sanction of the most approved writers on the
subjects of politics. The opponents of the PLAN proposed have
with great assiduity cited and circulated the observations of
Montesquieu on the necessity of a contracted territory for a
republican government. But they seem not to have been
apprised of the sentiments of that great man expressed in
another part of his work, nor to have adverted to the consequences of the principle to which they subscribe with such
ready acquiescence.

When Montesquieu recommends a small extent for republics,
the standards he had in view were of dimensions, far short of
the limits of almost every one of these states. Neither Virginia,
Massachusetts, Pennsylvania, New-York, North-Carolina, nor
Georgia, can by any means be compared with the models from
which he reasoned, and to which the terms of his description
apply. If we therefore receive his ideas on this point, as the criterion of truth, we shall be driven to the alternative, either of
taking refuge at once in the arms of monarchy, or of splitting
ourselves into an infinity of little, jealous, clashing, tumultuous
commonwealths, the wretched nurseries of unceasing discord,
and the miserable objects of universal pity or contempt. Some of
the writers, who have come forward on the other side of the
question, seem to have been aware of the dilemma; and have
even been bold enough to hint at the division of the larger
states, as a desirable thing. Such an infatuated policy, such a
desperate expedient, might, by the multiplication of petty

offices, answer the views of men, who possess not qualifications to extend their influence beyond the narrow circles of personal intrigue; but it could never promote the greatness or happiness of the people of America.

Referring the examination of the principle itself to another place, as has been already mentioned, it will be sufficient to remark here, that in the sense of the author who has been most emphatically quoted upon the occasion, it would only dictate a reduction of the SIZE of the more considerable MEMBERS of the union; but would not militate against their being all comprehended in one confederate government. And this is the true question, in the discussion of which we are at present interested.

So far are the suggestions of Montesquieu from standing in opposition to a general union of the states, that he explicitly treats of a CONFEDERATE REPUBLIC as the expedient for extending the sphere of popular government, and reconciling the advantages of monarchy with those of republicanism.

"It is very probable," says he,* "that mankind would have been obliged, at length, to live constantly under the government of a SINGLE PERSON, had they not contrived a kind of constitution, that has all the internal advantages of a republican, together with the external force of a monarchical government. I mean a CONFEDERATE REPUBLIC.

"This form of government is a convention, by which several smaller *states* agree to become members of a larger *one*, which they intend to form. It is a kind of assemblage of societies, that constitute a new one, capable of increasing by means of new associations, till they arrive to such a degree of power as to be able to provide for the security of the united body.

"A republic of this kind, able to withstand an external force, may support itself without any internal corruption. The form of this society prevents all manner of inconveniences.

* Spirit of Laws, Vol. I. Book IX. Chap. I.

"If a single member should attempt to usurp the supreme authority, he could not be supposed to have an equal authority and credit in all the confederate states. Were he to have too great influence over one, this would alarm the rest. Were he to subdue a part, that which would still remain free might oppose him with forces, independent of those which he had usurped, and overpower him before he could be settled in his usurpation.

"Should a popular insurrection happen in one of the confederate states, the others are able to quell it. Should abuses creep into one part, they are reformed by those that remain sound. The state may be destroyed on one side, and not on the other; the confederacy may be dissolved, and the confederates preserve their sovereignty.

"As this government is composed of small republics, it enjoys the internal happiness of each, and with respect to its external situation, it is possessed, by means of the association, of all the advantages of large monarchies."

I have thought it proper to quote at length these interesting passages, because they contain a luminous abridgment of the principal arguments in favour of the union, and must effectually remove the false impressions, which a misapplication of the other parts of the work was calculated to produce. They have, at the same time, an intimate connection with the more immediate design of this paper; which is to illustrate the tendency of the union to repress domestic faction and insurrection.

A distinction, more subtle than accurate, has been raised between a *confederacy* and a *consolidation* of the states. The essential characteristic of the first, is said to be the restriction of its authority to the members in their collective capacities, without reaching to the individuals of whom they are composed. It is contended that the national council ought to have no concern with any object of internal administration. An exact equality of suffrage between the members, has also been insisted upon as a leading feature of a confederate government. These positions are, in the main, arbitrary; they are supported neither by principle nor precedent. It has indeed happened, that governments of this kind have generally operated in the manner which the distinction taken notice of supposes to be inherent in their nature; but there have been in most of them extensive exceptions to the practice, which serve to prove, as far as example will go, that there is no absolute rule on the subject. And it will be clearly shown, in the course of this investigation, that, as far as the principle contended for has prevailed, it has been the cause of incurable disorder and imbecility in the government.

The definition of a *confederate republic* seems simply to be, "an assemblage of societies," or an association of two or more states into one state. The extent, modifications, and objects, of the federal authority, are mere matters of discretion. So long as the separate organization of the members be not abolished, so long as it exists by a constitutional necessity for local purposes, though it should be in perfect subordination to the general authority of the union, it would still be, in fact and in theory, an association of states, or a confederacy. The proposed constitution, so far from implying an abolition of the state governments, makes them constituent parts of the national sovereignty, by allowing them a direct representation in the senate, and leaves in their possession certain exclusive, and very important, portions of the sovereign power. This fully corresponds, in every rational import of the terms, with the idea of a federal government.

In the Lycian confederacy, which consisted of twenty-three CITIES, or republics, the largest were entitled to *three* votes in the COMMON COUNCIL, those of the middle class to *two*, and the smallest to *one*. The COMMON COUNCIL had the appointment of all the judges and magistrates of the respective CITIES. This was certainly the most delicate species of interference in their internal administration; for if there be any thing that seems exclusively appropriated to the local jurisdictions, it is the appointment of their own officers. Yet Montesquieu, speaking of this association, says, "Were I to give a model of an excellent confederate republic, it would be that of Lycia." Thus we perceive, that the distinctions insisted upon, were not within the contemplation of this enlightened writer; and we shall be led to conclude, that they are the novel refinements of an erroneous theory.

PUBLIUS.

THE FEDERALIST.

NUMBER X.

NEW YORK, NOVEMBER 24, 1787.

MADISON.

THE SAME SUBJECT CONTINUED.

AMONG the numerous advantages promised by a well constructed union, none deserves to be more accurately developed
than its tendency to break and control the violence of faction.
The friend of popular governments, never finds himself so much
alarmed for their character and fate, as when he contemplates
their propensity to this dangerous vice. He will not fail, therefore, to set a due value on any plan which, without violating
the principles to which he is attached, provides a proper cure
for it. The instability, injustice, and confusion, introduced into
the public councils, have, in truth, been the mortal diseases
under which popular governments have everywhere perished;
as they continue to be the favourite and fruitful topics from
which the adversaries to liberty derive their most specious
declamations. The valuable improvements made by the American constitutions on the popular models, both ancient and modern, cannot certainly be too much admired; but it would be an
unwarrantable partiality, to contend that they have as effectually obviated the danger on this side, as was wished and
expected. Complaints are every where heard from our most
considerate and virtuous citizens, equally the friends of public
and private faith, and of public and personal liberty, that our

governments are too unstable; that the public good is disregarded in the conflicts of rival parties; and that measures are too often decided, not according to the rules of justice, and the rights of the minor party, but by the superiour force of an interested and overbearing majority. However anxiously we may wish that these complaints had no foundation, the evidence of known facts will not permit us to deny that they are in some degree true. It will be found, indeed, on a candid review of our situation, that some of the distresses under which we labour, have been erroneously charged on the operation of our governments; but it will be found, at the same time, that other causes will not alone account for many of our heaviest misfortunes; and, particularly, for that prevailing and increasing distrust of public engagements, and alarm for private rights, which are echoed from one end of the continent to the other. These must be chiefly, if not wholly, effects of the unsteadiness and injustice, with which a factious spirit has tainted our public administrations.

By a faction, I understand a number of citizens, whether amounting to a majority or minority of the whole, who are united and actuated by some common impulse of passion, or of interest, adverse to the rights of other citizens, or to the permanent and aggregate interests of the community.

There are two methods of curing the mischiefs of faction: The one, by removing its causes; the other, by controlling its effects.

There are again two methods of removing the causes of faction: The one, by destroying the liberty which is essential to its existence; the other, by giving to every citizen the same opinions, the same passions, and the same interests.

It could never be more truly said, than of the first remedy, that it was worse than the disease. Liberty is to faction what air is to fire, an aliment, without which it instantly expires. But it could not be a less folly to abolish liberty, which is essential to political life, because it nourishes faction, than it would be to wish the annihilation of air, which is essential to animal life, because it imparts to fire its destructive agency.

The second expedient is as impracticable, as the first would be unwise. As long as the reason of man continues fallible, and he is at liberty to exercise it, different opinions will be formed. As long as the connection subsists between his reason and his self-love, his opinions and his passions will have a reciprocal influence on each other; and the former will be objects to which the latter will attach themselves. The diversity in the faculties of men, from which the rights of property originate, is not less an insuperable obstacle to an uniformity of interests. The protection of these faculties is the first object of government. From the protection of different and unequal faculties of acquiring property, the possession of different degrees and kinds of property immediately results; and from the influence of these on the sentiments and views of the respective proprietors, ensues a division of the society into different interests and parties.

The latent causes of faction are thus sown in the nature of man; and we see them every where brought into different degrees of activity, according to the different circumstances of civil society. A zeal for different opinions concerning religion, concerning government, and many other points, as well of speculation as of practice; an attachment to different leaders, ambitiously contending for pre-eminence and power; or to persons of other descriptions, whose fortunes have been interesting to the human passions, have, in turn, divided mankind into parties, inflamed them with mutual animosity, and rendered them much more disposed to vex and oppress each other, than to co-operate for their common good. So strong is this propensity of mankind, to fall into mutual animosities, that where no substantial occasion presents itself, the most frivolous and fanciful distinctions have been sufficient to kindle their unfriendly passions, and excite their most violent conflicts. But the most common and durable source of factions, has been the various and unequal distribution of property. Those who hold, and those who are without property, have ever formed distinct interests in society. Those who are creditors, and those who are debtors, fall under a like discrimination. A landed interest, a manufacturing interest, a mercantile interest, a moneyed interest, with many lesser interests, grow up of necessity in civilized nations, and divide them into different classes, actuated by different sentiments and views. The regulation of these various and interfering interests forms the principal task of modern legislation, and involves the spirit of party and faction in the necessary and ordinary operations of government.

No man is allowed to be a judge in his own cause; because his interest will certainly bias his judgment, and, not improbably, corrupt his integrity. With equal, nay, with greater reason, a body of men are unfit to be both judges and parties at the same time; yet what are many of the most important acts of legislation, but so many judicial determinations, not indeed concerning the rights of single persons, but concerning the rights of large bodies of citizens? and what are the different classes of legislators, but advocates and parties to the causes which they determine? Is a law proposed concerning private debts? It is a question to which the creditors are parties on one side, and the debtors on the other. Justice ought to hold the balance between them. Yet the parties are, and must be, themselves the judges: and the most numerous party, or, in other words, the most powerful faction, must be expected to prevail. Shall domestic manufactures be encouraged, and in what degree, by restrictions on foreign manufactures? are questions which would be differently decided by the landed and the manufacturing classes; and probably by neither with a sole regard to justice and the public good. The apportionment of taxes, on the various descriptions of property, is an act which seems to require the most exact impartiality; yet there is, perhaps, no legislative act, in which greater opportunity and temptation are given to a predominant party, to trample on the rules of justice. Every shilling, with which they overburden the inferiour number, is a shilling saved to their own pockets.

It is in vain to say, that enlightened statesmen will be able to adjust these clashing interests, and render them all subservient to the public good. Enlightened statesmen will not always be at the helm: nor, in many cases, can such an adjustment be made at all, without taking into view indirect and remote considerations, which will rarely prevail over the immediate interest which one party may find in disregarding the rights of another, or the good of the whole.

The inference to which we are brought is, that the *causes* of faction cannot be removed; and that relief is only to be sought in the means of controlling its *effects*.

If a faction consists of less than a majority, relief is supplied by the republican principle, which enables the majority to defeat its sinister views, by regular vote. It may clog the administration, it may convulse the society; but it will be unable to execute and mask its violence under the forms of the constitution. When a majority is included in a faction, the form of popular government, on the other hand, enables it to sacrifice to its ruling passion or interest, both the public good and the rights of other citizens. To secure the public good, and private rights, against the danger of such a faction, and at the same time to preserve the spirit and the form of popular government, is then the great object to which our inquiries are directed. Let me add, that it is the great desideratum, by which alone this form of government can be rescued from the opprobrium under which it has so long laboured, and be recommended to the esteem and adoption of mankind.

By what means is this object attainable? Evidently by one of two only. Either the existence of the same passion or interest in a majority, at the same time must be prevented; or the majority, having such coexistent passion or interest, must be rendered, by their number and local situation, unable to concert and carry into effect schemes of oppression. If the impulse and the opportunity be suffered to coincide, we well know, that neither moral nor religious motives can be relied on as an adequate control. They are not found to be such on the injustice and violence of individuals, and lose their efficacy in proportion to the number combined together; that is, in proportion as their efficacy becomes needful.

From this view of the subject, it may be concluded, that a pure democracy, by which I mean a society consisting of a small number of citizens, who assemble and administer the government in person, can admit of no cure from the mischiefs of faction. A common passion or interest will, in almost every case, be felt by a majority of the whole; a communication and concert, results from the form of government itself; and there is nothing to check the inducements to sacrifice the weaker party, or an obnoxious individual. Hence it is, that such democracies have ever been spectacles of turbulence and contention; have ever been found incompatible with personal security, or the rights of property; and have, in general, been as short in their lives, as they have been violent in their deaths. Theoretic politicians, who have patronized this species of government, have erroneously supposed, that by reducing mankind to a perfect equality in their political rights, they would, at the same time, be perfectly equalized and assimilated in their possessions, their opinions, and their passions.

A republic, by which I mean a government in which the scheme of representation takes place, opens a different prospect, and promises the cure for which we are seeking. Let us examine the points in which it varies from pure democracy, and we shall comprehend both the nature of the cure and the efficacy which it must derive from the union.

The two great points of difference, between a democracy and a republic, are, first, the delegation of the government, in the latter, to a small number of citizens elected by the rest; secondly, the greater number of citizens, and greater sphere of country, over which the latter may be extended.

The effect of the first difference is, on the one hand, to refine and enlarge the public views, by passing them through the medium of a chosen body of citizens, whose wisdom may best discern the true interest of their country, and whose patriotism and love of justice, will be least likely to sacrifice it to temporary or partial considerations. Under such a regulation, it may well happen, that the public voice, pronounced by the representatives of the people, will be more consonant to the public good, than if pronounced by the people themselves, convened for the purpose. On the other hand, the effect may be inverted. Men of factious tempers, of local prejudices, or of sinister designs, may be intrigue, by corruption, or by other means, first obtain the suffrages, and then betray the interests of the people. The question resulting is, whether small or extensive republics are most favourable to the election of proper guardians of the public weal; and it is clearly decided in favour of the latter by two obvious considerations.

In the first place, it is to be remarked, that however small the republic may be, the representatives must be raised to a certain number, in order to guard against the cabals of a few; and that however large it may be, they must be limited to a certain number, in order to guard against the confusion of a multitude. Hence, the number of representatives in the two cases not being in proportion to that of the constituents, and being proportionally greatest in the small republic, it follows, that if the proportion of fit characters be not less in the large than in the small republic, the former will present a greater option, and consequently a greater probability of a fit choice.

In the next place, as each representative will be chosen by a greater number of citizens in the large than in the small republic, it will be more difficult for unworthy candidates to practice with success the vicious arts, by which elections are too often carried; and the suffrages of the people being more free, will be more likely to centre in men who possess the most attractive merit, and the most diffusive and established characters.

It must be confessed, that in this, as in most other cases, there is a mean, on both sides of which inconveniences will be found to lie. By enlarging too much the number of electors, you render the representative too little acquainted with all their local circumstances and lesser interests; as by reducing it too much, you render him unduly attached to these, and too little fit to comprehend and pursue great and national objects. The federal constitution forms a happy combination in this respect; the great and aggregate interests being referred to the national, the local and particular to the state legislatures.

The other point of difference is, the greater number of citizens, and extent of territory, which may be brought within the compass of republican, than of democratic government; and it is this circumstance principally which renders factious combinations less to be dreaded in the former, than in the latter. The smaller the society, the fewer probably will be the distinct parties and interests composing it; the fewer the distinct parties and interests, the more frequently will a majority be found of the same party; and the smaller the number of individuals composing a majority, and the smaller the compass within which they are placed, the more easily will they concert and execute their plans of oppression. Extend the sphere, and you take in a greater variety of parties and interests; you make it less probable that a majority of the whole will have a common motive to invade the rights of other citizens; or if such a common motive exists, it will be more difficult for all who feel it to discover their own strength, and to act in unison with each other. Besides other impediments, it may be remarked, that where there is a consciousness of unjust or dishonourable purposes, communication is always checked by distrust, in proportion to the number whose concurrence is necessary.

Hence, it clearly appears, that the same advantage, which a republic has over a democracy, in controlling the effects of faction, is enjoyed by a large over a small republic—is enjoyed by the union over the states composing it. Does this advantage consist in the substitution of representatives, whose enlightened views and virtuous sentiments render them superior to local prejudices, and to schemes of injustice? It will not be denied, that the representation of the union will be most likely to possess these requisite endowments. Does it consist in the greater security afforded by a greater variety of parties, against the event of any one party being able to outnumber and oppress the rest? In an equal degree does the increased variety of parties, comprised within the union, increase this security. Does it, in fine, consist in the greater obstacles opposed to the concert and accomplishment of the secret wishes of an unjust and interested majority? Here, again, the extent of the union gives it the most palpable advantage.

The influence of factious leaders may kindle a flame within their particular states, but will be unable to spread a general conflagration through the other states; a religious sect may degenerate into a political faction in a part of the confederacy; but the variety of sects dispersed over the entire face of it, must secure the national councils against any danger from that source: a rage for paper money, for an abolition of debts, for an equal division of property, or for any other improper or wicked project, will be less apt to pervade the whole body of the union, than a particular member of it; in the same proportion as such a malady is more likely to taint a particular county or district, than an entire state.

In the extent and proper structure of the union, therefore, we behold a republican remedy for the diseases most incident to republican government. And according to the degree of pleasure and pride we feel in being republicans, ought to be our zeal in cherishing the spirit, and supporting the character of federalists.

PUBLIUS.

THE FEDERALIST.

NUMBER XI.

NEW YORK, NOVEMBER 24, 1787.

HAMILTON.

THE UTILITY OF THE UNION IN RESPECT TO COMMERCE AND A NAVY.

THE importance of the union, in a commercial light, is one of those points, about which there is least room to entertain a difference of opinion, and which has in fact commanded the most general assent of men, who have any acquaintance with the subject. This applies as well to our intercourse with foreign countries, as with each other.

There are appearances to authorize a supposition, that the adventurous spirit, which distinguishes the commercial character of America, has already excited uneasy sensations in several of the maritime powers of Europe. They seem to be apprehensive of our too great interference in that carrying trade, which is the support of their navigation, and the foundation of their naval strength. Those of them, which have colonies in America, look forward, with painful solicitude, to what this country is capable of becoming. They foresee the dangers, that may threaten their American dominions from the neighbourhood of states, which have all the dispositions, and would possess all the means, requisite to the creation of a powerful marine. Impressions of this kind will naturally indicate the policy of fostering divisions among us, and of depriving us, as far as possible, of an ACTIVE COMMERCE in our own bottoms. This would answer then the threefold purpose of preventing our interference in their navigation, of monopolizing the profits of our trade, and of clipping the wings, on which we might soar to a dangerous greatness. Did not prudence forbid the detail, it would not be 'difficult to trace, by facts, the workings of this policy to the cabinets of ministers. If we continue united, we may, in a variety of ways, counteract a policy so unfriendly to our prosperity. By prohibitory regulations, extending at the same time throughout the states, we may oblige foreign countries to bid against each other, for the privileges of our markets. This assertion will not appear chimerical to those who are able to appreciate the importance, to any manufacturing nation, of the markets of three millions of people—increasing in rapid progression; for the most part, exclusively addicted to agriculture, and likely from local circumstances to remain in this disposition; and the immense difference there would be to the trade and navigation of such a nation, between a direct communication in its own ships, and an indirect conveyance of its products and returns, to and from America, in the ships of another country. Suppose, for instance, we had a government in America, capable of excluding Great Britain (with whom we have at present no treaty of commerce) from all our ports; what would be the probable operation of this step upon her politics? Would it not enable us to negociate, with the fairest prospect of success, for commercial privileges of the most valuable and extensive kind, in the dominions of that kingdom? When these questions have been asked, upon other occasions, they have received a plausible, but not a solid or satisfactory answer. It has been said, that prohibitions on our part would produce no change in the system of Britain; because she could prosecute her trade with us, through the medium of the Dutch, who would be her immediate customers and pay-masters for those articles which were wanted for the supply of our markets. But would not her navigation be materially injured, by the loss of the important advantage of being her own carrier in that trade?

Would not the principal part of its profits be intercepted by the Dutch, as a compensation for their agency and risk? Would not the mere circumstance of freight occasion a considerable deduction? Would not so circuitous an intercourse facilitate the competitions of other nations, by enhancing the price of British commodities in our markets, and by transferring to other hands the management of this interesting branch of the British commerce?

A mature consideration of the objects, suggested by these questions, will justify a belief, that the real disadvantages to Great Britain, from such a state of things, conspiring with the prepossessions of a great part of the nation in favour of the American trade, and with the importunities of the West-India islands, would produce a relaxation in her present system, and would let us into the enjoyment of privileges in the markets of those islands and elsewhere, from which our trade would derive the most substantial benefits. Such a point gained from the British government, and which could not be expected without an equivalent in exemptions and immunities in our markets, would be likely to have a correspondent effect on the conduct of other nations, who would not be inclined to see themselves altogether supplanted in our trade.

A further resource for influencing the conduct of European nations towards us, in this respect, would arise from the establishment of a federal navy. There can be no doubt, that the continuance of the union, under an efficient government, would put it in our power, at a period not very distant, to create a navy, which, if it could not vie with those of the great maritime powers, would at least be of respectable weight, if thrown into the scale of either of two contending parties. This would be more particularly the case, in relation to operations in the West-Indies. A few ships of the line, sent opportunely to the reinforcement of either side, would often be sufficient to decide the fate of a campaign, on the event of which, interests of the greatest magnitude were suspended. Our position is, in this respect, a very commanding one. And if to this consideration we add that of the usefulness of supplies from this country, in the prosecution of military operations in the West-Indies, it will readily be perceived, that a situation so favourable, would enable us to bargain with great advantage for commercial privileges. A price would be set not only upon our friendship, but upon our neutrality. By a steady adherence to the union, we may hope, ere long, to become the arbiter of Europe in America; and to be able to incline the balance of European competitions in this part of the world, as our interest may dictate.

But in the reverse of this eligible situation, we shall discover, that the rivalships of the parts would make them checks upon each other, and would frustrate all the tempting advantages, which nature has kindly placed within our reach. In a state so insignificant, our commerce would be a prey to the wanton intermeddlings of all nations at war with each other; who, having nothing to fear from us, would, with little scruple or remorse, supply their wants by depredations on our property, as often as it fell in their way. The rights of neutrality will only be respected, when they are defended by an adequate power. A nation, despicable by its weakness, forfeits even the privilege of being neutral.

Under a vigorous national government, the natural strength and resources of the country, directed to a common interest, would baffle all the combinations of European jealousy to restrain our growth. This situation would even take away the motive to such combinations, by inducing an impracticability of success. An active commerce, an extensive navigation, a flourishing marine, would then be the inevitable offspring of moral and physical necessity. We might defy the little arts of little politicians to control, or vary, the irresistible and unchangeable course of nature.

But in a state of disunion, these combinations might exist, and might operate with success. It would be in the power of the maritime nations, availing themselves of our universal impotence, to prescribe the conditions of our political existence; and as they have a common interest in being our carriers, and still more in preventing us from becoming theirs, they would, in all probability, combine to embarrass our navigation in such a manner, as would in effect destroy it, and confine us to a PASSIVE COMMERCE. We should thus be compelled to content ourselves with the first price of our commodities, and to see the profits of our trade snatched from us, to enrich our enemies and persecutors. That unequalled spirit of enterprise, which signalizes the genius of the American merchants and navigators, and which is in itself an inexhaustible mine of national wealth, would be stifled and lost; and poverty and disgrace would overspread a country, which, with wisdom, might make herself the admiration and envy of the world.

There are rights of great moment to the trade of America, which are rights of the union: I allude to the fisheries, to the navigation of the Lakes, and to that of the Mississippi. The dissolution of the confederacy would give room for delicate questions, concerning the future existence of these rights; which the interest of more powerful partners would hardly fail to solve to our disadvantage. The disposition of Spain, with regard to the Mississippi, needs no comment. France and Britain are concerned with us in the fisheries; and view them as of the utmost moment to their navigation. They, of course, would hardly remain long indifferent to that decided mastery, of which experience has shown us to be possessed, in this valuable branch of traffic; and by which we are able to undersell those nations in their own markets. What more natural, than that they should be disposed to exclude from the lists such dangerous competitors?

This branch of trade ought not to be considered as a partial benefit. All the navigating states may in different degrees advantageously participate in it; and under circumstances of a greater extension of mercantile capacity, would not be unlikely to do it. As a nursery of seamen, it now is, or when time shall have more nearly assimilated the principles of navigation in the several states, will become an universal resource. To the establishment of a navy, it must be indispensable.

To this great national object, a NAVY, union will contribute in

various ways. Every institution will grow and flourish in proportion to the quantity and extent of the means concentered
towards its formation and support. A navy of the United States,
as it would embrace the resources of all, is an object far less
remote than a navy of any single state, or partial confederacy,
which would only embrace the resources of a part. It happens,
indeed, that different portions of confederated America, possess
each some peculiar advantage for this essential establishment.
The more southern states furnish in greater abundance certain
kinds of naval stores—tar, pitch, and turpentine. Their wood, for
the construction of ships, is also of a more solid and lasting texture. The difference in the duration of the ships of which the
navy might be composed, if chiefly constructed of southern
wood, would be of signal importance, either in the view of naval
strength, or of national economy. Some of the southern and of
the middle states, yield a greater plenty of iron and of better
quality. Seamen must chiefly be drawn from the northern hive.
The necessity of naval protection to external or maritime commerce, and the conduciveness of that species of commerce, to
the prosperity of a navy, are points too manifest to require a
particular elucidation. They, by a kind of reaction, mutually beneficial, promote each other.

An unrestrained intercourse between the states themselves,
will advance the trade of each, by an interchange of their respective productions, not only for the supply of reciprocal wants, but
for exportation to foreign markets. The veins of commerce in
every part will be replenished, and will acquire additional motion
and vigour from a free circulation of the commodities of every
part. Commercial enterprise will have much greater scope, from
the diversity in the productions of different states. When the staple of one fails, from a bad harvest or unproductive crop, it can
call to its aid the staple of another. The variety, not less than the
value, of products for exportation, contributes to the activity of
foreign commerce. It can be conducted upon much better terms,
with a large number of materials of a given value, than with a
small number of materials of the same value; arising from the

competitions of trade, and from the fluctuations of markets. Particular articles may be in great demand at certain periods, and unsaleable at others; but if there be a variety of articles, it can scarcely happen that they should all be at one time in the latter predicament; and on this account, the operations of the merchant would be less liable to any considerable obstruction or stagnation. The speculative trader will at once perceive the force of these observations; and will acknowledge, that the aggregate balance of the commerce of the United States, would bid fair to be much more favourable than that of the Thirteen States, without union, or with partial unions.

It may perhaps be replied to this, that whether the states are united, or disunited, there would still be an intimate intercourse between them, which would answer the same ends: But this intercourse would be fettered, interrupted, and narrowed, by a multiplicity of causes; which in the course of these papers have been amply detailed. An unity of commercial, as well as political interests, can only result from an unity of government.

There are other points of view, in which this subject might be placed, of a striking and animating kind. But they would lead us too far into the regions of futurity, and would involve topics not proper for newspaper discussion. I shall briefly observe, that our situation invites, and our interests prompt us, to aim at an ascendant in the system of American affairs. The world may politically, as well as geographically, be divided into four parts, each having a distinct set of interests. Unhappily for the other three, Europe, by her arms and by her negociations; by force and by fraud, has, in different degrees, extended her dominion over them all. Africa, Asia, and America, have successively felt her domination. The superiority she has long maintained, has tempted her to plume herself as the mistress of the world, and to consider the rest of mankind as created for her benefit. Men, admired as profound philosophers, have, in direct terms, attributed to her inhabitants a physical superiority; and have gravely asserted that all animals, and with them the human species, degenerate in America—that even dogs cease to bark,

after having breathed a while in our atmosphere.* Facts have
too long supported these arrogant pretensions of the European:
It belongs to us to vindicate the honour of the human race, and
to teach that assuming brother moderation. Union will enable us
to do it. Disunion will add another victim to his triumphs. Let
Americans disdain to be the instruments of European greatness!
Let the Thirteen States, bound together in a strict and indissoluble union, concur in erecting one great American system, superior to the control of all transatlantic force or influence, and able
to dictate the terms of the connection between the old and the
new world!

PUBLIUS.

* Recherches philosophiques sur les Américains.

THE FEDERALIST.

NUMBER XII.

NEW YORK, NOVEMBER 28, 1787.

HAMILTON.

THE UTILITY OF THE UNION IN RESPECT TO REVENUE.

THE effects of union, upon the commercial prosperity of the states, have been sufficiently delineated. Its tendency to promote the interests of revenue, will be the subject of our present inquiry.

A prosperous commerce is now perceived and acknowledged, by all enlightened statesmen, to be the most useful, as well as the most productive, source of national wealth; and has accordingly become a primary object of their political cares. By multiplying the means of gratification, by promoting the introduction and circulation of the precious metals, those darling objects of human avarice and enterprise, it serves to vivify and invigorate all the channels of industry, and to make them flow with greater activity and copiousness. The assiduous merchant, the laborious husbandman, the active mechanic, and the industrious manufacturer—all orders of men, look forward with eager expectation, and growing alacrity, to this pleasing reward of their toils. The often-agitated question between agriculture and commerce, has, from indubitable experience, received a decision, which has silenced the rivalships that once subsisted between them, and has proved, to the entire satisfaction of their friends, that their interests are intimately blended and interwoven. It has been found, in various countries, that in proportion as commerce has flourished, land has risen in value. And how could it have happened otherwise? Could that which procures a freer vent for the products of the earth; which furnishes new incitements to the cultivators of land; which is the most powerful instrument in increasing the quantity of money in a state—could that, in fine, which is the faithful handmaid of labour and industry, in every shape, fail to augment the value of that article, which is the prolific parent of far the greatest part of the objects, upon which they are exerted? It is astonishing, that so simple a truth should ever have had an adversary; and it is one, among a multitude of proofs, how apt a spirit of ill informed jealousy, or of too great abstraction and refinement, is to lead men astray from the plainest paths of reason and conviction.

The ability of a country to pay taxes, must always be proportioned, in a great degree, to the quantity of money in circulation, and to the celerity with which it circulates. Commerce, contributing to both these objects, must of necessity render the payment of taxes easier, and facilitate the requisite supplies to the treasury. The hereditary dominions of the emperor of Germany, contain a great extent of fertile, cultivated, and populous territory, a large proportion of which is situated in mild and luxuriant climates. In some parts of this territory are to be found, the best gold and silver mines in Europe. And yet, from the want of the fostering influence of commerce, that monarch can boast but slender revenues. He has several times been compelled to owe obligations to the pecuniary succours of other nations, for the preservation of his essential interests; and is unable, upon the strength of his own resources, to sustain a long or continued war.

But it is not in this aspect of the subject alone, that union will be seen to conduce to the purposes of revenue. There are other points of view, in which its influence will appear more immediate and decisive. It is evident from the state of the country, from the habits of the people, from the experience we have had on the point itself, that it is impracticable to raise any very considerable sums by direct taxation. Tax laws have in vain been multiplied; new methods to enforce the collection have in vain been tried; the public expectation has been uniformly disappointed, and the treasuries of the states have remained empty. The popular system of administration, inherent in the nature of popular government, coinciding with the real scarcity of money, incident to a languid and mutilated state of trade, has hitherto defeated every experiment for extensive collections, and has at length taught the different legislatures the folly of attempting them.

No person, acquainted with what happens in other countries, will be surprised at this circumstance. In so opulent a nation as that of Britain, where direct taxes, from superior wealth, must be much more tolerable, and, from the vigour of the government, much more practicable, than in America, far the greatest part of the national revenue is derived from taxes of the indirect kind; from imposts, and from excises. Duties on imported articles, form a large branch of this latter description.

In America, it is evident, that we must a long time depend for the means of revenue, chiefly on such duties. In most parts of it, excises must be confined within a narrow compass. The genius of the people will illy brook the inquisitive and peremptory spirit of excise laws. The pockets of the farmers, on the other hand, will reluctantly yield but scanty supplies, in the unwelcome shape of impositions on their houses and lands; and personal property is too precarious and invisible a fund to be laid hold of in any other way, than by the imperceptible agency of taxes on consumption.

If these remarks have any foundation, that state of things which will best enable us to improve and extend so valuable a resource, must be the best adapted to our political welfare. And it cannot admit of a serious doubt, that this state of things must rest on the basis of a general union. As far as this would be conducive to the interests of commerce, so far it must tend to the extension of the revenue to be drawn from that source. As far

19

as it would contribute to render regulations for the collection of the duties more simple and efficacious, so far it must serve to answer the purposes of making the same rate of duties more productive, and of putting it into the power of the government to increase the rate, without prejudice to trade.

The relative situation of these states; the number of rivers with which they are intersected, and of bays that wash their shores; the facility of communication in every direction; the affinity of language and manners; the familiar habits of intercourse; all these are circumstances that would conspire to render an illicit trade between them a matter of little difficulty; and would ensure frequent evasions of the commercial regulations of each other. The separate states, or confederacies, would be driven by mutual jealousy to avoid the temptations to that kind of trade, by the lowness of their duties. The temper of our governments, for a long time to come, would not permit those rigorous precautions, by which the European nations guard the avenues into their respective countries, as well by land as by water, and which, even there, are found insufficient obstacles to the adventurous stratagems of avarice.

In France, there is an army of patrols (as they are called) constantly employed to secure her fiscal regulations against the inroads of the dealers in contraband. Mr. Neckar computes the number of these patrols at upwards of twenty thousand. This proves the immense difficulty in preventing that species of traffic, where there is an inland communication, and shows, in a strong light, the disadvantages, with which the collection of duties in this country would be incumbered, if by disunion the states should be placed in a situation with respect to each other, resembling that of France with respect to her neighbours. The arbitrary and vexatious powers with which the patrols are necessarily armed, would be intolerable in a free country.

If, on the contrary, there be but one government, pervading all the states, there will be, as to the principal part of our commerce, but ONE SIDE to guard, the ATLANTIC COAST. Vessels arriving directly from foreign countries, laden with valuable cargoes, goes, would rarely choose to expose themselves to the complicated and critical perils, which would attend attempts to unlade prior to their coming into port. They would have to dread both the dangers of the coast, and of detection, as well after, as before their arrival at the places of their final destination. An ordinary degree of vigilance, would be competent to the prevention of any material infractions upon the rights of the revenue. A few armed vessels, judiciously stationed and employed, might at small expense be made useful sentinels of the laws. And the government, having the same interest to provide against violations every where, the co-operation of its measures in each state, would have a powerful tendency to render them effectual. Here also we should preserve, by union, an advantage which nature holds out to us, and which would be relinquished by separation. The United States lie at a great distance from Europe, and at a considerable distance from all other places, with which they would have extensive connections of foreign trade. The passage from them to us in a few hours, or in a single night, as between the coasts of France and Britain, and of other neighbouring nations, would be impracticable. This is a prodigious security against a direct contraband with foreign countries; but a circuitous contraband to one state, through the medium of another, would be both easy and safe. The difference between a direct importation from abroad, and an indirect importation, through the channel of an adjoining state, in small parcels, according to time and opportunity, with the additional facilities of inland communication, must be palpable to every man of discernment.

It is, therefore, evident, that one national government would be able, at much less expense, to extend the duties on imports, beyond comparison, further, than would be practicable to the states separately, or to any partial confederacies: Hitherto I believe it may safely be asserted, that these duties have not upon an average exceeded in any state three per cent. In France they are estimated at about fifteen per cent. and in Britain the proportion is still greater. There seems to be nothing to hinder their being increased in this country, to at least treble their present amount. The single article of ardent spirits, under federal regulation, might be made to furnish a considerable revenue. According to the ratio of importation into this state, the whole quantity imported into the United States may, at a low computation, be estimated at four millions of gallons; which at a shilling per gallon, would produce two hundred thousand pounds. That article would well bear this rate of duty; and if it should tend to diminish the consumption of it, such an effect would be equally favourable to the agriculture, to the economy, to the morals, and to the health of society. There is, perhaps, nothing so much a subject of national extravagance, as this very article.

What will be the consequence, if we are not able to avail ourselves of the resource in question in its full extent? A nation cannot long exist without revenue. Destitute of this essential support, it must resign its independence, and sink into the degraded condition of a province. This is an extremity to which no government will of choice accede. Revenue therefore must be had at all events. In this country, if the principal part be not drawn from commerce, it must fall with oppressive weight upon land. It has been already intimated that excises, in their true signification, are too little in unison with the feelings of the people, to admit of great use being made of that mode of taxation: nor indeed, in the states where almost the sole employment is agriculture, are the objects proper for excise sufficiently numerous, to permit very ample collections in that way. Personal estate, as before remarked, from the difficulty of tracing it, cannot be subjected to large contributions, by any other means than by taxes on consumption. In populous cities, it may be enough the subject of conjecture, to occasion the oppression of individuals, without much aggregate benefit to the state; but beyond these circles, it must, in a great measure, escape the eye and the hand of the tax gatherer. As the necessities of the state, nevertheless, must be satisfied in some mode, the defect of other resources must throw the principal weight of the public burthens on the possessors of land. And, as on the other hand, the wants of the government can never obtain an adequate supply, unless all the sources of revenue are open to its demands, the finances of the community, under such embarrassments, cannot be put into a situation consistent with its respectability or its security. Thus we shall not even have the consolations of a full treasury, to atone for the oppression of that valuable class of citizens, who are employed in the cultivation of the soil. But public and private distress will keep pace with each other in gloomy concert; and unite in deploring the infatuation of those counsels which led to disunion.

PUBLIUS.

THE FEDERALIST.

NUMBER XIII.

NEW YORK, NOVEMBER 28, 1787.

HAMILTON.

THE SAME SUBJECT CONTINUED, WITH A VIEW TO ECONOMY.

As connected with the subject of revenue, we may with propriety consider that of economy. The money saved from one object, may be usefully applied to another; and there will be so much the less to be drawn from the pockets of the people. If the states be united under one government, there will be but one national civil list to support; if they are divided into several confederacies, there will be as many different national civil lists to be provided for; and each of them, as to the principal departments, co-extensive with that which would be necessary for a government of the whole. The entire separation of the states into thirteen unconnected sovereignties, is a project too extravagant, and too replete with danger, to have many advocates. The ideas of men who speculate upon the dismemberment of the empire, seem generally turned towards three confederacies; one consisting of the four northern, another of the four middle, and a third of the five southern states. There is little probability that there would be a greater number. According to this distribution, each confederacy would comprise an extent of territory larger than that of the kingdom of Great Britain. No well informed man will suppose that the affairs of such a confederacy can be properly regulated by a government, less comprehensive in its organs or institutions, than that which has been proposed by the convention. When the dimensions of a state attain to a certain magnitude, it requires the same energy of government, and the same forms of administration, which are requisite in one of much greater extent. This idea admits not of precise demonstration, because there is no rule by which we can measure the momentum of civil power, necessary to the government of any given number of individuals; but when we consider that the Island of Britain, nearly commensurate with each of the supposed confederacies, contains about eight millions of people, and when we reflect upon the degree of authority required to direct the passions of so large a society to the public good, we shall see no reason to doubt, that the like portion of power would be sufficient to perform the same task in a society far more numerous. Civil power, properly organized and exerted, is capable of diffusing its force to a very great extent; and can, in a manner, reproduce itself in every part of a great empire, by a judicious arrangement of subordinate institutions.

The supposition, that each confederacy into which the states would be likely to be divided, would require a government not less comprehensive than the one proposed, will be strengthened by another conjecture, more probable than that which presents us with three confederacies, as the alternative to a general union. If we attend carefully to geographical and commercial considerations, in conjunction with the habits and prejudices of the different states, we shall be led to conclude, that, in case of disunion, they will most naturally league themselves under two governments. The four eastern states, from all the causes that form the links of national sympathy and connection, may with certainty be expected to unite. New-York, situated as she is, would never be unwise enough to oppose a feeble and unsupported flank to the weight of that confederacy. There are obvious reasons, that would facilitate her accession to it. New-Jersey is too small a state to think of being a frontier, in opposition to this still more powerful combination; nor do there appear to be any obstacles to her admission into it. Even Pennsylvania would have strong inducements to join the northern league. An active foreign commerce, on the basis of her own navigation, is her true policy, and coincides with the opinions and dispositions of her citizens. The more southern states, from various circumstances, may not think themselves much interested in the encouragement of navigation. They may prefer a system, which would give unlimited scope to all nations, to be the carriers, as well as the purchasers, of their commodities. Pennsylvania may not choose to confound her interests in a connection so adverse to her policy. As she must, at all events, be a frontier, she may deem it most consistent with her safety, to have her exposed side turned towards the weaker power of the southern, rather than towards the stronger power of the northern confederacy. This would give her the fairest chance to avoid being the FLANDERS of America. Whatever may be the determination of Pennsylvania, if the northern confederacy includes New-Jersey, there is no likelihood of more than one confederacy to the south of that state.

Nothing can be more evident than that the Thirteen States will be able to support a national government, better than one half, or one third, or any number less than the whole. This reflection must have great weight in obviating that objection to the proposed plan, which is founded on the principle of expense; an objection however, which, when we come to take a nearer view of it, will appear in every light to stand on mistaken ground.

If, in addition to the consideration of a plurality of civil lists, we take into view the number of persons who must necessarily be employed to guard the inland communication, between the different confederacies, against illicit trade, and who in time will infallibly spring up out of the necessities of revenue; and if we also take into view the military establishments, which it has been shown would unavoidably result from the jealousies and conflicts of the several nations, into which the states would be divided, we shall clearly discover that a separation would be not less injurious to the economy, than to the tranquillity, commerce, revenue, and liberty, of every part.

PUBLIUS.

THE FEDERALIST.

NUMBER XIV.

NEW YORK, DECEMBER 1, 1777.

MADISON.

AN OBJECTION DRAWN FROM THE EXTENT OF COUNTRY
ANSWERED.

WE have seen the necessity of the union, as our bulwark against foreign danger; as the conservator of peace among ourselves; as the guardian of our commerce, and other common interests; as the only substitute for those military establishments which have subverted the liberties of the old world; and as the proper antidote for the diseases of faction, which have proved fatal to other popular governments, and of which alarming symptoms have been betrayed by our own. All that remains, within this branch of our inquiries, is to take notice of an objection, that may be drawn from the great extent of country which the union embraces. A few observations, on this subject, will be the more proper, as it is perceived, that the adversaries of the new constitution are availing themselves of a prevailing prejudice, with regard to the practicable sphere of republican administration, in order to supply, by imaginary difficulties, the want of those solid objections, which they endeavour in vain to find.

The errour which limits republican government to a narrow district, has been unfolded and refuted in preceding papers. I remark here only, that it seems to owe its rise and prevalence chiefly to the confounding of a republic with a democracy; and applying to the former, reasonings drawn from the nature of the latter. The true distinction between these forms, was also adverted to on a former occasion. It is, that in a democracy, the people meet and exercise the government in person: in a republic, they assemble and administer it by their representatives and agents. A democracy, consequently, must be confined to a small spot. A republic may be extended over a large region.

To this accidental source of the errour, may be added the artifice of some celebrated authors, whose writings have had a great share in forming the modern standard of political opinions. Being subjects, either of an absolute, or limited monarchy, they have endeavoured to heighten the advantages, or palliate the evils, of those forms, by placing in comparison with them the vices and defects of the republican, and by citing, as specimens of the latter, the turbulent democracies of ancient Greece, and modern Italy. Under the confusion of names, it has been an easy task to transfer to a republic observations applicable to a democracy only; and, among others, the observation, that it can never be established but among a small number of people, living within a small compass of territory.

Such a fallacy may have been the less perceived, as most of the popular governments of antiquity were of the democratic species; and even in modern Europe, to which we owe the great principle of representation, no example is seen of a government wholly popular, and founded, at the same time, wholly on that principle. If Europe has the merit of discovering this great mechanical power in government, by the simple agency of which, the will of the largest political body may be concentered, and its force directed to any object, which the public good requires; America can claim the merit of making the discovery the basis of unmixed and extensive republics. It is only to be lamented, that any of her citizens should wish to deprive her of the additional merit of displaying its full efficacy in the establishment of the comprehensive system now under her consideration.

As the natural limit of a democracy is that distance from the central point, which will just permit the most remote citizens to assemble as often as their public functions demand, and will include no greater number than can join in those functions: so the natural limit of a republic, is that distance from the centre, which will barely allow the representatives of the people to meet as often as may be necessary for the administration of public affairs. Can it be said, that the limits of the United States exceed this distance? It will not be said by those who recollect, that the Atlantic coast is the longest side of the union; that during the term of thirteen years, the representatives of the states have been almost continually assembled; and that the members, from the most distant states, are not chargeable with greater intermissions of attendance, than those from the states in the neighbourhood of Congress.

That we may form a juster estimate with regard to this interesting subject, let us resort to the actual dimensions of the union. The limits, as fixed by the treaty of peace, are, on the east the Atlantic, on the south the latitude of thirty-one degrees, on the west the Mississippi, and on the north an irregular line running in some instances beyond the forty-fifth degree, in others falling as low as the forty-second. The southern shore of lake Erie lies below that latitude. Computing the distance between the thirty-first and forty-fifth degrees, it amounts to nine hundred and seventy-three common miles; computing it from thirty-one to forty-two degrees, to seven hundred sixty-four miles and a half. Taking the mean for the distance, the amount will be eight hundred sixty-eight miles and three fourths. The mean distance from the Atlantic to the Mississippi, does not probably exceed seven hundred and fifty miles. On a comparison of this extent, with that of several countries in Europe, the practicability of rendering our system commensurate to it, appears to be demonstrable. It is not a great deal larger than Germany, where a diet, representing the whole empire, is continually assembled; or than Poland before the late dismemberment, where another national diet was the depository of the supreme power. Passing by France and Spain, we find that in Great Britain, inferiour as it may be in size, the representatives of the northern extremity of the island, have as far to travel to the national council, as will be required of those of the most remote parts of the union.

Favourable as this view of the subject may be, some observations remain, which will place it in a light still more satisfactory.

In the first place, it is to be remembered, that the general government is not to be charged with the whole power of making and administering laws; its jurisdiction is limited to certain enumerated objects, which concern all the members of the republic, but which are not to be attained by the separate provisions of any. The subordinate governments, which can extend their care to all those other objects, which can be separately provided for, will retain their due authority and activity. Were it proposed by the plan of the convention, to abolish the governments of the particular states, its adversaries would have some ground for their objection; though it would not be difficult to show, that if they were abolished, the general government would be compelled, by the principle of self-preservation, to reinstate them in their proper jurisdiction.

A second observation to be made is, that the immediate object of the federal constitution, is to secure the union of the thirteen primitive states, which we know to be practicable; and to add to them such other states, as may arise in their own bosoms, or in their neighbourhoods, which we cannot doubt to be equally practicable. The arrangements that may be necessary for those angles and fractions of our territory, which lie on our north western frontier, must be left to those whom further discoveries and experience will render more equal to the task.

Let it be remarked, in the third place, that the intercourse throughout the union will be daily facilitated by new improvements. Roads will every where be shortened, and kept in better order; accommodations for travellers will be multiplied and meliorated; an interiour navigation on our eastern side, will be opened throughout, or nearly throughout, the whole extent of the Thirteen States. The communication between the western and Atlantic districts, and between different parts of each, will be rendered more and more easy, by those numerous canals, with which the beneficence of nature has intersected our country, and which art finds it so little difficult to connect and complete.

A fourth, and still more important consideration, is, that as almost every state will, on one side or other, be a frontier, and will thus find, in a regard to its safety, an inducement to make some sacrifices for the sake of the general protection: so the states which lie at the greatest distance from the heart of the union, and which of course may partake least of the ordinary circulation of its benefits, will be at the same time immediately contiguous to foreign nations, and will consequently stand, on particular occasions, in greatest need of its strength and resources. It may be inconvenient for Georgia, or the states forming our western or north eastern borders, to send their representatives to the seat of government; but they would find it more so to struggle alone against an invading enemy, or even to support alone the whole expense of those precautions, which may be dictated by the neighbourhood of continual danger. If they should derive less benefit therefore from the union in some respects, than the less distant states, they will derive greater benefit from it in other respects, and thus the proper equilibrium will be maintained throughout.

I submit to you, my fellow-citizens, these considerations, in full confidence that the good sense which has so often marked your decisions, will allow them their due weight and effect; and that you will never suffer difficulties, however formidable in appearance, or however fashionable the errour on which they may be founded, to drive you into the gloomy and perilous scenes into which the advocates for disunion would conduct you. Hearken not to the unnatural voice, which tells you that the people of America, knit together as they are by so many chords of affection, can no longer live together as members of the same

family; can no longer continue the mutual guardians of their
mutual happiness; can no longer be fellow-citizens of one great,
respectable, and flourishing empire. Hearken not to the voice,
which petulantly tells you, that the form of government recommended for your adoption, is a novelty in the political world;
that it has never yet had a place in the theories of the wildest
projectors; that it rashly attempts what it is impossible to
accomplish. No, my countrymen, shut your ears against this
unhallowed language. Shut your hearts against the poison which
it conveys. The kindred blood which flows in the veins of American citizens, the mingled blood which they have shed in defence
of their sacred rights, consecrate their union, and excite horrour
at the idea of their becoming aliens, rivals, enemies. And if novelties are to be shunned, believe me, the most alarming of all
novelties, the most wild of all projects, the most rash of all
attempts, is that of rending us in pieces, in order to preserve
our liberties, and promote our happiness. But why is the experiment of an extended republic to be rejected, merely because it
may comprise what is new? Is it not the glory of the people of
America, that whilst they have paid a decent regard to the opinions of former times and other nations, they have not suffered a
blind veneration for antiquity, for custom, or for names, to over-
rule the suggestions of their own good sense, the knowledge of
their own situation, and the lessons of their own experience? To
this manly spirit, posterity will be indebted for the possession,
and the world for the example, of the numerous innovations displayed on the American theatre, in favour of private rights and
public happiness. Had no important step been taken by the
leaders of the revolution, for which a precedent could not be discovered; no government established of which an exact model did
not present itself, the people of the United States might, at this
moment, have been numbered among the melancholy victims of
misguided councils; must at best have been labouring under the
weight of some of those forms which have crushed the liberties
of the rest of mankind. Happily for America, happily, we trust,
for the whole human race, they pursued a new and more noble

course. They accomplished a revolution which has no parallel in the annals of human society. They reared the fabrics of governments which have no model on the face of the globe. They formed the design of a great confederacy, which it is incumbent on their successors to improve and perpetuate. If their works betray imperfections, we wonder at the fewness of them. If they erred most in the structure of the union, this was the work most difficult to be executed; this is the work which has been new modelled by the act of your convention, and it is that act on which you are now to deliberate and to decide.

PUBLIUS.

THE FEDERALIST.

NUMBER XV.

NEW YORK, DECEMBER 1, 1787.

HAMILTON.

CONCERNING THE DEFECTS OF THE PRESENT CONFEDERATION,
IN RELATION TO THE PRINCIPLE OF LEGISLATION FOR
THE STATES IN THEIR COLLECTIVE CAPACITIES.

IN the course of the preceding papers, I have endeavoured, my fellow citizens, to place before you, in a clear and convincing light, the importance of union to your political safety and happiness. I have unfolded to you a complication of dangers to which you would be exposed, should you permit that sacred knot, which binds the people of America together, to be severed or dissolved by ambition or by avarice, by jealousy or by misrepresentation. In the sequel of the inquiry, through which I propose to accompany you, the truths intended to be inculcated will receive further confirmation from facts and arguments hitherto unnoticed. If the road, over which you will still have to pass, should in some places appear to you tedious or irksome, you will recollect, that you are in quest of information on a subject the most momentous, which can engage the attention of a free people; that the field through which you have to travel is in itself spacious, and that the difficulties of the journey have been unnecessarily increased by the mazes with which sophistry has beset the way. It will be my aim to remove the obstacles to your progress, in as compendious a manner as it can be done, without sacrificing utility to dispatch.

In pursuance of the plan, which I have laid down for the discussion of the subject, the point next in order to be examined, is the "insufficiency of the present confederation to the preservation of the union."

It may perhaps be asked, what need there is of reasoning or proof to illustrate a position, which is neither controverted nor doubted; to which the understandings and feelings of all classes of men assent; and which in substance is admitted by the opponents as well as by the friends of the new constitution? It must in truth be acknowledged, that however these may differ in other respects, they in general appear to harmonize in the opinion, that there are material imperfections in our national system, and that something is necessary to be done to rescue us from impending anarchy. The facts that support this opinion, are no longer objects of speculation. They have forced themselves upon the sensibility of the people at large, and have at length extorted from those, whose mistaken policy has had the principal share in precipitating the extremity at which we are arrived, a reluctant confession of the reality of many of those defects in the scheme of our federal government, which have been long pointed out and regretted by the intelligent friends of the union.

We may indeed, with propriety, be said to have reached almost the last stage of national humiliation. There is scarcely any thing that can wound the pride, or degrade the character, of an independent people, which we do not experience. Are there engagements, to the performance of which we are held by every tie respectable among men? These are the subjects of constant and unblushing violation. Do we owe debts to foreigners, and to our own citizens, contracted in a time of imminent peril, for the preservation of our political existence? These remain without any proper or satisfactory provision for their discharge. Have we valuable territories and important posts in the possession of a foreign power, which, by express stipula-

20

tions, ought long since to have been surrendered? These are still retained, to the prejudice of our interest not less than of our rights. Are we in a condition to resent, or to repel the aggression? We have neither troops, nor treasury, nor government.* Are we even in a condition to remonstrate with dignity? The just imputations on our own faith, in respect to the same treaty, ought first to be removed. Are we entitled, by nature and compact, to a free participation in the navigation of the Mississippi? Spain excludes us from it. Is public credit an indispensable resource in time of public danger? We seem to have abandoned its cause as desperate and irretrievable. Is commerce of importance to national wealth? Ours is at the lowest point of declension. Is respectability in the eyes of foreign powers, a safeguard against foreign encroachments? The imbecility of our government even forbids them to treat with us: Our ambassadors abroad are the mere pageants of mimic sovereignty. Is a violent and unnatural decrease in the value of land, a symptom of national distress? The price of improved land, in most parts of the country, is much lower than can be accounted for by the quantity of waste land at market, and can only be fully explained by that want of private and public confidence, which are so alarmingly prevalent among all ranks, and which have a direct tendency to depreciate property of every kind. Is private credit the friend and patron of industry? That most useful kind which relates to borrowing and lending, is reduced within the narrowest limits, and this still more from an opinion of insecurity than from a scarcity of money. To shorten an enumeration of particulars which can afford neither pleasure nor instruction, it may in general be demanded, what indication is there of national disorder, poverty, and insignificance, that could befal a community so peculiarly blessed with natural advantages as we are, which does not form a part of the dark catalogue of our public misfortunes?

This is the melancholy situation to which we have been

* I mean for the union.

brought by those very maxims and counsels, which would now deter us from adopting the proposed constitution; and which, not content with having conducted us to the brink of a precipice, seem resolved to plunge us into the abyss that awaits us below. Here, my countrymen, impelled by every motive that ought to influence an enlightened people, let us make a firm stand for our safety, our tranquillity, our dignity, our reputation. Let us at last break the fatal charm which has too long seduced us from the paths of felicity and prosperity.

It is true, as has been before observed, that facts too stubborn to be resisted, have produced a species of general assent to the abstract proposition, that there exist material defects in our national system; but the usefulness of the concession, on the part of the old adversaries of federal measures, is destroyed by a strenuous opposition to a remedy, upon the only principles that can give it a chance of success. While they admit that the government of the United States is destitute of energy, they contend against conferring upon it those powers which are requisite to supply that energy. They seem still to aim at things repugnant and irreconcilable; at an augmentation of federal authority, without a diminution of state authority; at sovereignty in the union, and complete independence in the members. They still, in fine, seem to cherish with blind devotion the political monster of an *imperium in imperio*. This renders a full display of the principal defects of the confederation necessary, in order to show, that the evils we experience do not proceed from minute or partial imperfections, but from fundamental errors in the structure of the building, which cannot be amended, otherwise than by an alteration in the very elements and main pillars of the fabric.

The great, and radical vice, in the construction of the existing confederation, is in the principle of LEGISLATION for STATES or GOVERNMENTS, in their CORPORATE, or COLLECTIVE CAPACITIES, and as contradistinguished from the INDIVIDUALS of whom they consist. Though this principle does not run through all the powers delegated to the union; yet it pervades and governs those on which the efficacy of the rest depends: Except, as to the rule of apportionment, the United States have an indefinite discretion to make requisitions for men and money; but they have no authority to raise either, by regulations extending to the individual citizens of America. The consequence of this is, that, though in theory, their resolutions concerning those objects, are laws, constitutionally binding on the members of the union, yet, in practice, they are mere recommendations, which the states observe or disregard at their option.

It is a singular instance of the capriciousness of the human mind, that, after all the admonitions we have had from experience on this head, there should still be found men, who object to the new constitution, for deviating from a principle which has been found the bane of the old; and which is, in itself, evidently incompatible with the idea of a GOVERNMENT; a principle, in short, which, if it is to be executed at all, must substitute the violent and sanguinary agency of the sword, to the mild influence of the magistracy.

There is nothing absurd or impracticable, in the idea of a league or alliance between independent nations, for certain defined purposes precisely stated in a treaty; regulating all the details of time, place, circumstance, and quantity; leaving nothing to future discretion; and depending for its execution on the good faith of the parties. Compacts of this kind, exist among all civilized nations, subject to the usual vicissitudes of peace and war; of observance and non-observance, as the interests or passions of the contracting powers dictate. In the early part of the present century, there was an epidemical rage in Europe for this species of compacts; from which the politicians of the times fondly hoped for benefits which were never realized. With a view to establishing the equilibrium of power, and the peace of that part of the world, all the resources of negociation were exhausted, and triple and quadruple alliances were formed; but they were scarcely formed before they were broken, giving an instructive, but afflicting, lesson to mankind, how little dependence is to be placed on treaties which have no other sanction than the obligations of good faith; and which oppose general considerations of peace and justice, to the impulse of any immediate interest or passion.

If the particular states in this country are disposed to stand in a similar relation to each other, and to drop the project of a general DISCRETIONARY SUPERINTENDENCE, the scheme would indeed be pernicious, and would entail upon us all the mischiefs which have been enumerated under the first head; but it would have the merit of being, at least, consistent and practicable. Abandoning all views towards a confederate government, this would bring us to a simple alliance, offensive and defensive; and would place us in a situation to be alternately friends and enemies of each other, as our mutual jealousies and rivalships, nourished by the intrigues of foreign nations, should prescribe to us.

But if we are unwilling to be placed in this perilous situation; if we still adhere to the design of a national government, or, which is the same thing, of a superintending power, under the direction of a common council, we must resolve to incorporate into our plan those ingredients, which may be considered as forming the characteristic difference between a league and a government; we must extend the authority of the union to the persons of the citizens—the only proper objects of government.

Government implies the power of making laws. It is essential to the idea of a law, that it be attended with a sanction; or, in other words, a penalty or punishment for disobedience. If there be no penalty annexed to disobedience, the resolutions or commands which pretend to be laws, will in fact amount to nothing more than advice or recommendation. This penalty, whatever it may be, can only be inflicted in two ways; by the agency of the courts and ministers of justice, or by military force; by the COERCION of the magistracy, or by the COERCION of arms. The first kind can evidently apply only to men; the last kind must of necessity be employed against bodies politic, or communities or states. It is evident, that there is no process of a court by which their observance of the laws can, in the last resort, be enforced.

Sentences may be denounced against them for violations of their duty; but these sentences can only be carried into execution by the sword. In an association, where the general authority is confined to the collective bodies of the communities that compose it, every breach of the laws must involve a state of war, and military execution must become the only instrument of civil obedience. Such a state of things can certainly not deserve the name of government, nor would any prudent man choose to commit his happiness to it.

There was a time when we were told that breaches, by the states, of the regulations of the federal authority were not to be expected; that a sense of common interest would preside over the conduct of the respective members, and would beget a full compliance with all the constitutional requisitions of the union. This language, at the present day, would appear as wild as a great part of what we now hear from the same quarter will be thought, when we shall have received further lessons from that best oracle of wisdom, experience. It at all times betrayed an ignorance of the true springs by which human conduct is actuated, and belied the original inducements to the establishment of civil power. Why has government been instituted at all? Because the passions of men will not conform to the dictates of reason and justice, without constraint. Has it been found that bodies of men act with more rectitude or greater disinterestedness than individuals? The contrary of this has been inferred by all accurate observers of the conduct of mankind; and the inference is founded upon obvious reasons. Regard to reputation, has a less active influence, when the infamy of a bad action is to be divided among a number, than when it is to fall singly upon one. A spirit of faction, which is apt to mingle its poison in the deliberations of all bodies of men, will often hurry the persons, of whom they are composed, into improprieties and excesses, for which they would blush in a private capacity.

In addition to all this, there is, in the nature of sovereign power, an impatience of control, which disposes those who are invested with the exercise of it, to look with an evil eye upon all external attempts to restrain or direct its operations. From this spirit it happens, that in every political association which is formed upon the principle of uniting in a common interest a number of lesser sovereignties, there will be found a kind of eccentric tendency in the subordinate or inferior orbs, by the operation of which, there will be a perpetual effort in each to fly off from the common centre. This tendency is not difficult to be accounted for. It has its origin in the love of power. Power controlled or abridged is almost always the rival and enemy of that power by which it is controlled or abridged. This simple proposition will teach us how little reason there is to expect, that the persons entrusted with the administration of the affairs of the particular members of a confederacy, will at all times be ready, with perfect good humour, and an unbiassed regard to the public weal, to execute the resolutions or decrees of the general authority. The reverse of this results from the constitution of man.

If therefore the measures of the confederacy cannot be executed, without the intervention of the particular administrations, there will be little prospect of their being executed at all. The rulers of the respective members, whether they have a constitutional right to do it or not, will undertake to judge of the propriety of the measures themselves. They will consider the conformity of the thing proposed or required to their immediate interests or aims; the momentary conveniences or inconveniences that would attend its adoption. All this will be done; and in a spirit of interested and suspicious scrutiny, without that knowledge of national circumstances and reasons of state, which is essential to a right judgment, and with that strong predilection in favour of local objects, which can hardly fail to mislead the decision. The same process must be repeated in every member of which the body is constituted; and the execution of the plans, framed by the councils of the whole, will always fluctuate on the discretion of the ill-informed and prejudiced opinion of every part. Those who have been conversant in the proceedings of popular assemblies; who have seen how difficult it often is, when there is no exterior pressure of circumstances, to bring them to harmonious resolutions on important points, will readily conceive how impossible it must be to induce a number of such assemblies, deliberating at a distance from each other, at different times, and under different impressions, long to co-operate in the same views and pursuits.

In our case, the concurrence of thirteen distinct sovereign wills is requisite under the confederation, to the complete execution of every important measure, that proceeds from the union. It has happened, as was to have been foreseen. The measures of the union have not been executed; the delinquences of the states have, step by step, matured themselves to an extreme, which has at length arrested all the wheels of the national government, and brought them to an awful stand. Congress at this time scarcely possess the means of keeping up the forms of administration, till the states can have time to agree upon a more substantial substitute for the present shadow of a federal government. Things did not come to this desperate extremity at once. The causes which have been specified, produced at first only unequal and disproportionate degrees of compliance with the requisitions of the union. The greater deficiencies of some states furnished the pretext of example, and the temptation of interest to the complying, or at least delinquent states. Why should we do more in proportion than those who are embarked with us in the same political voyage? Why should we consent to bear more than our proper share of the common burthen? These were suggestions which human selfishness could not withstand, and which even speculative men, who looked forward to remote consequences, could not without hesitation combat. Each state, yielding to the persuasive voice of immediate interest or convenience, has successively withdrawn its support, till the frail and tottering edifice seems ready to fall upon our heads, and to crush us beneath its ruins.

PUBLIUS.

THE FEDERALIST.

NUMBER XVI.

NEW YORK, DECEMBER 5, 1787.

HAMILTON.

THE SAME SUBJECT CONTINUED, IN RELATION TO THE SAME PRINCIPLES.

THE tendency of the principle of legislation for states or communities in their political capacities, as it has been exemplified by the experiment we have made of it, is equally attested by the events which have befallen all other governments of the confederate kind, of which we have any account, in exact proportion to its prevalence in those systems. The confirmations of this fact will be worthy of a distinct and particular examination. I shall content myself with barely observing here, that of all the confederacies of antiquity which history has handed down to us, the Lycian and Achæan leagues, as far as there remain vestiges of them, appear to have been most free from the fetters of that mistaken principle, and were accordingly those which have best deserved, and have most liberally received, the applauding suffrages of political writers.

This exceptionable principle may, as truly as emphatically, be styled the parent of anarchy: it has been seen that delinquencies in the members of the union are its natural and necessary offspring; and that whenever they happen, the only constitutional remedy is force, and the immediate effect of the use of it, civil war.

It remains to inquire how far so odious an engine of government, in its application to us, would even be capable of answering its end. If there should not be a large army, constantly at the disposal of the national government, it would either not be able to employ force at all, or when this could be done, it would amount to a war between different parts of the confederacy, concerning the infractions of a league; in which the strongest combination would be most likely to prevail, whether it consisted of those who supported, or of those who resisted, the general authority. It would rarely happen that the delinquency to be redressed would be confined to a single member, and if there were more than one, who had neglected their duty, similarity of situation would induce them to unite for common defence. Independent of this motive of sympathy, if a large and influential state should happen to be the aggressing member, it would commonly have weight enough with its neighbours, to win over some of them as associates to its cause. Specious arguments of danger to the general liberty could easily be contrived; plausible excuses for the deficiencies of the party, could, without difficulty, be invented, to alarm the apprehensions, inflame the passions, and conciliate the good will even of those states which were not chargeable with any violation, or omission of duty. This would be the more likely to take place, as the delinquencies of the larger members might be expected sometimes to proceed from an ambitious premeditation in their rulers, with a view to getting rid of all external control upon their designs of personal aggrandizement; the better to effect which, it is presumable they would tamper beforehand with leading individuals in the adjacent states. If associates could not be found at home, recourse would be had to the aid of foreign powers, who would seldom be disinclined to encouraging the dissensions of a confederacy, from the firm union of which they had so much to fear. When the sword is once drawn, the passions of men observe no bounds of moderation. The suggestions of wounded pride, the instigations of irritated resentment, would be apt to carry the states, against which the arms of the union were exerted, to any extremes necessary to avenge the affront, or to avoid the disgrace of submission. The first war of this kind would probably terminate in a dissolution of the union.

This may be considered as the violent death of the confederacy. Its more natural death is what we now seem to be on the point of experiencing, if the federal system be not speedily renovated in a more substantial form. It is not probable, considering the genius of this country, that the complying states would often be inclined to support the authority of the union, by engaging in a war against the non-complying states. They would always be more ready to pursue the milder course of putting themselves upon an equal footing with the delinquent members, by an imitation of their example. And the guilt of all would thus become the security of all. Our past experience has exhibited the operation of this spirit in its full light. There would in fact be an insuperable difficulty in ascertaining when force could with propriety be employed. In the article of pecuniary contribution, which would be the most usual source of delinquency, it would often be impossible to decide whether it had proceeded from disinclination, or inability. The pretence of the latter would always be at hand. And the case must be very flagrant in which its fallacy could be detected with sufficient certainly to justify the harsh expedient of compulsion. It is easy to see that this problem alone, as often as it should occur, would open a wide field to the majority that happened to prevail in the national council, for the exercise of factious views, of partiality, and of oppression.

It seems to require no pains to prove that the states ought not to prefer a national constitution, which could only be kept in motion by the instrumentality of a large army, continually on foot to execute the ordinary requisitions or decrees of the government. And yet this is the plain alternative involved by those who wish to deny it the power of extending its operations to individuals. Such a scheme, if practicable at all, would instantly degenerate into a military despotism; but it will be found in every light impracticable. The resources of the union would not be equal to the maintenance of an army considerable enough to confine the larger states within the limits of their duty; nor would the means ever be furnished of forming such an army in the first instance. Whoever considers the populousness and strength of several of these states singly at the present juncture, and looks forward to what they will become, even at the distance of half a century, will at once dismiss as idle and visionary any scheme, which aims at regulating their movements by laws, to operate upon them in their collective capacities, and to be executed by a coercion applicable to them in the same capacities. A project of this kind is little less romantic than the monstertaming spirit, attributed to the fabulous heroes and demigods of antiquity.

Even in those confederacies, which have been composed of members smaller than many of our counties, the principle of legislation for sovereign states, supported by military coercion, has never been found effectual. It has rarely been attempted to be employed, but against the weaker members; and in most instances attempts to coerce the refractory and disobedient, have been the signals of bloody wars; in which one half of the confederacy has displayed its banners against the other.

The result of these observations to an intelligent mind must be clearly this, that if it be possible at any rate to construct a federal government capable of regulating the common concerns, and preserving the general tranquility, it must be founded, as to the objects committed to its care, upon the reverse of the principle contended for by the opponents of the proposed constitution. It must carry its agency to the persons of the citizens. It must stand in need of no intermediate legislations; but must itself be empowered to employ the arm of the ordinary magistrate to execute its own resolutions. The majesty of the national authority must be manifested through the medium of the courts of justice. The government of the union, like that of each state, must be able to address itself immediately to the hopes and fears of individuals; and to attract to its support, those passions, which have the strongest influence upon the human heart. It must, in short, possess all the means, and have a right to resort to all the methods, of executing the powers with which it is entrusted, that are possessed and exercised by the governments of the particular states.

To this reasoning it may perhaps be objected, that if any state should be disaffected to the authority of the union, it could at any time obstruct the execution of its laws, and bring the matter to the same issue of force, with the necessity of which the opposite scheme is reproached.

The plausibility of this objection will vanish the moment we advert to the essential difference between a mere NON-COMPLI-ANCE and a DIRECT and ACTIVE RESISTANCE. If the interposition of the state legislatures be necessary to give effect to a measure of the union, they have only NOT TO ACT, or TO ACT EVA-SIVELY, and the measure is defeated. This neglect of duty may be disguised under affected but unsubstantial provisions so as not to appear, and of course not to excite any alarm in the people for the safety of the constitution. The state leaders may even make a merit of their surreptitious invasions of it, on the ground of some temporary convenience, exemption, or advantage.

But if the execution of the laws of the national government should not require the intervention of the state legislatures; if they were to pass into immediate operation upon the citizens themselves, the particular governments could not interrupt their progress without an open and violent exertion of an unconstitutional power. No omission, nor evasions, would answer the end. They would be obliged to act, and in such a manner, as would leave no doubt that they had encroached on the national rights. An experiment of this nature would always be hazardous in the face of a constitution in any degree competent to its own defence, and of a people enlightened enough to distinguish between a legal exercise and an illegal usurpation of authority. The success of it would require not merely a factious majority in the legislature, but the concurrence of the courts of justice, and of the body of the people. If the judges were not embarked in a conspiracy with the legislature, they would pronounce the resolutions of such a majority to be contrary to the supreme law of the land, unconstitutional and void. If the people were not tainted with the spirit of their state representatives, they, as the natural guardians of the constitution, would throw their weight into the national scale, and give it a decided preponderancy in the contest. Attempts of this kind would not often be made with levity or rashness; because they could seldom be made without danger to the authors; unless in cases of a tyrannical exercise of the federal authority.

If opposition to the national government should arise from the disorderly conduct of refractory, or seditious individuals, it could be overcome by the same means which are daily employed against the same evil, under the state governments. The magistracy, being equally the ministers of the law of the land, from whatever source it might emanate, would, doubtless, be as ready to guard the national as the local regulations, from the inroads of private licentiousness. As to those partial commotions and insurrections, which sometimes disquiet society, from the intrigues of an inconsiderable faction, or from sudden or occasional ill humours, that do not infect the great body of the community, the general government could command more extensive resources, for the suppression of disturbances of that kind, than would be in the power of any single member. And as to those mortal feuds, which, in certain conjunctures, spread a conflagration through a whole nation, or through a very large proportion of it, proceeding either from weighty causes of discontent, given by the government, or from the contagion of some violent popular paroxism, they do not fall within any ordinary rules of calculation. When they happen, they commonly amount to revolutions, and dismemberments of empire. No form of government can always either avoid or control them. It is in vain to hope to guard against events too mighty for human foresight or precaution; and it would be idle to object to a government, because it could not perform impossibilities.

PUBLIUS.

THE FEDERALIST.

NUMBER XVII.

NEW YORK, DECEMBER 5, 1787.

HAMILTON.

THE SUBJECT CONTINUED, AND ILLUSTRATED BY EXAMPLES, TO
SHOW THE TENDENCY OF FEDERAL GOVERNMENTS, RATHER TO
ANARCHY AMONG THE MEMBERS, THAN TYRANNY IN THE
HEAD.

An objection, of a nature different from that which has been
stated and answered in my last address, may, perhaps, be urged
against the principle of legislation for the individual citizens of
America. It may be said, that it would tend to render the government of the union too powerful, and to enable it to absorb
those residuary authorities, which it might be judged proper to
leave with the states for local purposes. Allowing the utmost latitude to the love of power, which any reasonable man can
require, I confess I am at a loss to discover what temptation the
persons entrusted with the administration of the general government, could ever feel to divest the states of the authorities of
that description. The regulation of the mere domestic police of a
state, appears to me to hold out slender allurements to ambition.
Commerce, finance, negociation, and war, seem to comprehend
all the objects which have charms for minds governed by that
passion; and all the powers necessary to those objects, ought, in
the first instance, to be lodged in the national depository. The
administration of private justice between the citizens of the
same state; the supervision of agriculture, and of other concerns

of a similar nature; all those things, in short, which are proper to be provided for by local legislation, can never be desirable cares of a general jurisdiction. It is therefore improbable, that there should exist a disposition in the federal councils, to usurp the powers with which they are connected; because the attempt to exercise them, would be as troublesome as it would be nugatory; and the possession of them, for that reason, would contribute nothing to the dignity, to the importance, or to the splendour, of the national government.

But let it be admitted, for argument sake, that mere wantonness, and lust of domination, would be sufficient to beget that disposition; still it may be safely affirmed, that the sense of the constituent body of the national representatives, or, in other words, of the people of the several states, would control the indulgence of so extravagant an appetite. It will always be far more easy for the state governments to encroach upon the national authorities, than for the national government to encroach upon the state authorities. The proof of this proposition turns upon the greater degree of influence which the state governments, if they administer their affairs with uprightness and prudence, will generally possess over the people; a circumstance which at the same time teaches us, that there is an inherent and intrinsic weakness in all federal constitutions; and that too much pains cannot be taken in their organization, to give them all the force which is compatible with the principles of liberty.

The superiority of influence in favor of the particular governments, would result partly from the diffusive construction of the national government; but chiefly from the nature of the objects to which the attention of the state administrations would be directed.

It is a known fact in human nature, that its affections are commonly weak in proportion to the distance or diffusiveness of the object. Upon the same principle that a man is more attached to his family than to his neighbourhood, to his neighbourhood than to the community at large, the people of each state would be apt to feel a stronger bias towards their local governments, than towards the government of the union, unless the force of that principle should be destroyed by a much better administration of the latter.

This strong propensity of the human heart, would find powerful auxiliaries in the objects of state regulation.

The variety of more minute interests, which will necessarily fall under the superintendence of the local administrations, and which will form so many rivulets of influence, running through every part of the society, cannot be particularized, without involving a detail too tedious and uninteresting, to compensate for the instruction it might afford.

There is one transcendent advantage belonging to the province of the state governments, which alone suffices to place the matter in a clear and satisfactory light—I mean the ordinary administration of criminal and civil justice. This, of all others, is the most powerful, most universal, and most attractive source of popular obedience and attachment. It is this, which, being the immediate and visible guardian of life and property; having its benefits and its terrors in constant activity before the public eye; regulating all those personal interests, and familiar concerns, to which the sensibility of individuals is more immediately awake; contributes, more than any other circumstance, to impress upon the minds of the people affection, esteem, and reverence towards the government. This great cement of society, which will diffuse itself almost wholly through the channels of the particular governments, independent of all other causes of influence, would insure them so decided an empire over their respective citizens, as to render them at all times a complete counterpoise, and not unfrequently dangerous rivals to the power of the union.

The operations of the national government, on the other hand, falling less immediately under the observation of the mass of the citizens, the benefits derived from it will chiefly be perceived, and attended to by speculative men. Relating to more general interests, they will be less apt to come home to the feelings of the people; and, in proportion, less likely to inspire a habitual sense of obligation, and an active sentiment of attachment.

The reasoning on this head has been abundantly exemplified by the experience of all federal constitutions, with which we are acquainted, and of all others, which have borne the least analogy to them.

Though the ancient feudal systems were not, strictly speaking, confederacies, yet they partook of the nature of that species of association. There was a common head, chieftain, or sovereign, whose authority extended over the whole nation; and a number of subordinate vassals, or feudatories, who had large portions of land allotted to them, and numerous trains of *inferior* vassals or retainers, who occupied and cultivated that land upon the tenure of fealty, or obedience to the persons of whom they held it. Each principal vassal was a kind of sovereign within his particular demesnes. The consequences of this situation were a continual opposition to the authority of the sovereign, and frequent wars between the great barons, or chief feudatories themselves. The power of the head of the nation was commonly too weak either to preserve the public peace, or to protect the people against the oppressions of their immediate lords. This period of European affairs is emphatically styled by historians, the times of feudal anarchy.

When the sovereign happened to be a man of vigorous and warlike temper and of superior abilities, he would acquire a personal weight and influence, which answered for the time the purposes of a more regular authority. But in general, the power of the barons triumphed over that of the prince; and in many instances his dominion was entirely thrown off, and the great fiefs were erected into independent principalities or states. In those instances in which the monarch finally prevailed over his vassals, his success was chiefly owing to the tyranny of those vassals over their dependants. The barons, or nobles, equally the enemies of the sovereign and the oppressors of the common people, were dreaded and detested by both; till mutual danger and mutual interest effected an union between them fatal to the power of the aristocracy. Had the nobles, by a conduct of clemency and justice, preserved the fidelity and devotion of their retainers and followers, the contests between them and the prince must almost always have ended in their favour, and in the abridgement or subversion of the royal authority.

This is not an assertion founded merely in speculation or conjecture. Among other illustrations of its truth which might be cited, Scotland will furnish a cogent example. The spirit of clanship which was at an early day introduced into that kingdom, uniting the nobles and their dependants by ties equivalent to those of kindred, rendered the aristocracy a constant overmatch for the power of the monarch, till the incorporation with England subdued its fierce and ungovernable spirit, and reduced it within those rules of subordination, which a more rational and a more energetic system of civil polity had previously established in the latter kingdom.

The separate governments in a confederacy may aptly be compared with the feudal baronies; with this advantage in their favour, that from the reasons already explained, they will generally possess the confidence and good will of the people; and with so important a support, will be able effectually to oppose all encroachments of the national government. It will be well if they are not able to counteract its legitimate and necessary authority. The points of similitude consist in the rivalship of power, applicable to both, and in the CONCENTRATION of large portions of the strength of the community into particular DEPOSITORIES, in one case at the disposal of individuals, in the other case, at the disposal of political bodies.

A concise review of the events that have attended confederate governments, will further illustrate this important doctrine; an inattention to which has been the great source of our political mistakes, and has given our jealousy a direction to the wrong side. This review shall form the subject of some ensuing papers.

PUBLIUS.

THE FEDERALIST.

NUMBER XVIII.

NEW YORK, DECEMBER 8, 1787.

HAMILTON AND MADISON.

THE SUBJECT CONTINUED, WITH FARTHER EXAMPLES.

AMONG the confederacies of antiquity, the most considerable was that of the Grecian republics, associated under the Amphyctionic council. From the best transmitted accounts of this celebrated institution, it bore a very instructive analogy to the present confederation of the American states.

The members retained the character of independent and sovereign states, and had equal votes in the federal council. This council had a general authority to propose and resolve whatever it judged necessary for the common welfare of Greece; to declare and carry on war; to decide, in the last resort, all controversies between the members; to fine the aggressing party; to employ the whole force of the confederacy against the disobedient; to admit new members. The Amphyctions were the guardians of religion, and of the immense riches belonging to the temple of Delphos, where they had the right of jurisdiction in controversies between the inhabitants and those who came to consult the oracle. As a further provision for the efficacy of the federal powers, they took an oath mutually to defend and protect the united cities, to punish the violaters of this oath, and to inflict vengeance on sacrilegious despoilers of the temple.

In theory, and upon paper, this apparatus of powers, seems amply sufficient for all general purposes. In several material instances, they exceed the power enumerated in the articles of confederation. The Amphyctions had in their hands the superstition of the times, one of the principal engines by which government was then maintained; they had a declared authority to use coercion against refractory cities, and were bound by oath to exert this authority on the necessary occasions.

Very different, nevertheless, was the experiment from the theory. The powers, like those of the present congress, were administered by deputies appointed wholly by the cities in their political capacities; and exercised over them in the same capacities. Hence the weakness, the disorders, and finally the destruction of the confederacy. The more powerful members, instead of being kept in awe and subordination, tyrannized successively over all the rest. Athens, as we learn from Demosthenes, was the arbiter of Greece seventy-three years. The Lacedemonians next governed it twenty-nine years; at a subsequent period, after the battle of Leuctra, the Thebans had their turn of domination.

It happened but too often, according to Plutarch, that the deputies of the strongest cities, awed and corrupted those of the weakest, and that judgment went in favour of the most powerful party.

Even in the midst of defensive and dangerous wars with Persia and Macedon, the members never acted in concert, and were more or fewer of them, eternally the dupes, or the hirelings, of the common enemy. The intervals of foreign war, were filled up by domestic vicissitudes, convulsions, and carnage.

After the conclusion of the war with Xerxes, it appears that the Lacedemonians required that a number of the cities should be turned out of the confederacy for the unfaithful part they had acted. The Athenians, finding that the Lacedemonians would lose fewer partizans by such a measure than themselves, and would become masters of the public deliberations, vigorously opposed and defeated the attempt. This piece of history proves at once the inefficiency of the union; the ambition and jealousy of its most powerful members, and the dependent and degraded condition of the rest. The smaller members, though entitled by the theory of their system, to revolve in equal pride and majesty around the common centre, had in fact become satellites of the orbs of primary magnitude.

Had the Greeks, says the abbé Milot, been as wise as they were courageous, they would have been admonished by experience of the necessity of a closer union, and would have availed themselves of the peace which followed their success against the Persian arms, to establish such a reformation. Instead of this obvious policy, Athens and Sparta, inflated with the victories and the glory they had acquired, became first rivals, and then enemies; and did each other infinitely more mischief than they had suffered from Xerxes. Their mutual jealousies, fears, hatreds, and injuries, ended in the celebrated Peloponnesian war; which itself ended in the ruin and slavery of the Athenians, who had begun it.

As a weak government, when not at war, is ever agitated by internal dissentions; so these never fail to bring on fresh calamities from abroad. The Phocians having ploughed up some consecrated ground belonging to the temple of Apollo, the Amphyctionic council, according to the superstition of the age, imposed a fine on the sacrilegious offenders. The Phocians, being abetted by Athens and Sparta, refused to submit to the decree. The Thebans, with others of the cities, undertook to maintain the authority of the Amphyctions, and to avenge the violated god. The latter being the weaker party, invited the assistance of Philip of Macedon, who secretly fostered the contest. Philip gladly seized the opportunity of executing the designs he had long planned against the liberties of Greece. By his intrigues and bribes, he won over to his interests the popular leaders of several cities; by their influence and votes, gained admission into the Amphyctionic council; and by his arts and his arms, made himself master of the confederacy.

Such were the consequences of the fallacious principle, on

which this interesting establishment was founded. Had Greece, says a judicious observer on her fate, been united by a stricter confederation, and persevered in her union, she would never have worn the chains of Macedon; and might have proved a barrier to the vast projects of Rome.

The Achæan league, as it is called, was another society of Grecian republics, which supplies us with valuable instruction.

The union here was far more intimate, and its organization much wiser, than in the preceding instance. It will accordingly appear, that though not exempt from a similar catastrophe, it by no means equally deserved it.

The cities composing this league, retained their municipal jurisdiction, appointed their own officers, and enjoyed a perfect equality. The senate in which they were represented, had the sole and exclusive right of peace and war; of sending and receiving ambassadors; of entering into treaties and alliances; of appointing a chief magistrate or pretor, as he was called,—who commanded their armies; and who, with the advice and consent of ten of the senators, not only administered the government in the recess of the senate, but had a great share in its deliberations, when assembled. According to the primitive constitution, there were two pretors associated in the administration, but on trial, a single one was preferred.

It appears that the cities had all the same laws and customs, the same weights and measures, and the same money. But how far this effect proceeded from the authority of the federal council, is left in uncertainty. It is said only, that the cities were in a manner compelled to receive the same laws and usages. When Lacedemon was brought into the league, by Philopœmen, it was attended with an abolition of the institutions and laws of Lycurgus, and an adoption of those of the Achæans. The Amphyctionic confederacy, of which she had been a member, left her in the full exercise of her government and her legislation. This circumstance alone proves a very material difference in the genius of the two systems.

It is much to be regretted that the monuments which remain

of this curious political fabric are so imperfect. Could its interior structure and regular operation be ascertained, it is probable that more light would be thrown by it on the science of federal government, than by any of the like experiments with which we are acquainted.

One important fact seems to be witnessed by all the historians who take notice of Achæan affairs. It is, that as well after the renovation of the league by Aratus, as before its dissolution by the arts of Macedon, there was infinitely more of moderation and justice in the administration of its government, and less of violence and sedition in the people, than were to be found in any of the cities exercising *singly* all the prerogatives of sovereignty. The abbé Mably in his observations on Greece, says that the popular government, which was so tempestuous elsewhere, caused no disorders in the members of the Achæan republic, *because it was there tempered by the general authority and laws of the confederacy.*

We are not to conclude too hastily, however, that faction did not in a certain degree agitate the particular cities; much less, that a due subordination and harmony reigned in the general system. The contrary is sufficiently displayed in the vicissitudes and fate of the republic.

Whilst the Amphyctionic confederacy remained, that of the Achæans, which comprehended the less important cities only, made little figure on the theatre of Greece. When the former became a victim to Macedon, the latter was spared by the policy of Philip and Alexander. Under the successors of these princes, however, a different policy prevailed. The arts of division were practised among the Achæans; each city was seduced into a separate interest; the union was dissolved. Some of the cities fell under the tyranny of Macedonian garrisons: others under that of usurpers springing out of their own confusions. Shame and oppression ere long awakened their love of liberty. A few cities re-united. Their example was followed by others, as opportunities were found of cutting off their tyrants. The league soon embraced almost the whole Peloponnesus. Macedon saw its progress; but was hindered by internal dissentions from stopping it. All Greece caught the enthusiasm, and seemed ready to unite in one confederacy, when the jealousy and envy in Sparta and Athens, of the rising glory of the Achæans, threw a fatal damp on the enterprise. The dread of the Macedonian power induced the league to court the alliance of the kings of Egypt and Syria; who, as successors of Alexander, were rivals of the king of Macedon. This policy was defeated by Cleomenes, king of Sparta, who was led by his ambition to make an unprovoked attack on his neighbours the Achæans; and who, as an enemy to Macedon, had interest enough with the Egyptian and Syrian princes, to effect a breach of their engagements with the league. The Achæans were now reduced to the dilemma of submitting to Cleomenes, or of supplicating the aid of Macedon, its former oppressor. The latter expedient was adopted. The contest of the Greeks always afforded a pleasing opportunity to that powerful neighbour, of intermeddling in their affairs. A Macedonian army quickly appeared: Cleomenes was vanquished. The Achæans soon experienced, as often happens, that a victorious and powerful ally, is but another name for a master. All that their most abject compliances could obtain from him, was a toleration of the exercise of their laws. Philip, who was now on the throne of Macedon, soon provoked, by his tyrannies, fresh combinations among the Greeks. The Achæans, though weakened by internal dissentions, and by the revolt of Messene, one of its members, being joined by the Etolians and Athenians, erected the standard of opposition. Finding themselves, though thus supported, unequal to the undertaking, they once more had recourse to the dangerous expedient of introducing the succour of foreign arms. The Romans, to whom the invitation was made, eagerly embraced it. Philip was conquered: Macedon subdued. A new crisis ensued to the league. Dissentions broke out among its members. These the Romans fostered. Callicrates, and other popular leaders, became mercenary instruments for inveigling their countrymen. The more effectually to nourish discord and disorder, the Romans had, to the astonishment of those who

confided in their sincerity, already proclaimed universal liberty*
throughout Greece. With the same insidious views, they now
seduced the members from the league, by representing to their
pride, the violation it committed on their sovereignty. By these
arts, this union, the last hope of Greece, the last hope of ancient
liberty, was torn into pieces; and such imbecility and distraction
introduced, that the arms of Rome found little difficulty in completing the ruin which their arts had commenced. The Achæans
were cut to pieces; and Achaia loaded with chains, under which
it is groaning at this hour.

I have thought it not superfluous to give the outlines of this
important portion of history; both because it teaches more than
one lesson; and because, as a supplement to the outlines of the
Achæan constitution, it emphatically illustrates the tendency of
federal bodies, rather to anarchy among the members, than to
tyranny in the head.

PUBLIUS.

* This was but another name more specious, for the independence of the
members on the federal head.

THE FEDERALIST.

NUMBER XIX.

NEW YORK, DECEMBER 8, 1787.

HAMILTON AND MADISON.

THE SUBJECT CONTINUED, WITH FARTHER EXAMPLES.

THE examples of ancient confederacies, cited in my last paper, have not exhausted the source of experimental instruction on this subject. There are existing institutions, founded on a similar principle, which merit particular consideration. The first which presents itself is the Germanic body.

In the early ages of Christianity, Germany was occupied by seven distinct nations, who had no common chief. The Franks, one of the number, having conquered the Gauls, established the kingdom which has taken its name from them. In the ninth century, Charlemagne, its warlike monarch, carried his victorious arms in every direction; and Germany became a part of his vast dominions. On the dismemberment, which took place under his sons, this part was erected into a separate and independent empire. Charlemagne and his immediate descendants possessed the reality, as well as the ensigns and dignity of imperial power. But the principal vassals, whose fiefs had become hereditary, and who composed the national diets, which Charlemagne had not abolished, gradually threw off the yoke, and advanced to sovereign jurisdiction and independence. The force of imperial sovereignty was insufficient to restrain such powerful dependants; or to preserve the unity and tranquillity of the empire.

The most furious private wars, accompanied with every species
of calamity, were carried on between the different princes and
states. The imperial authority, unable to maintain the public
order, declined by degrees, till it was almost extinct in the anarchy, which agitated the long interval between the death of the
last emperor of the Suabian, and the accession of the first
emperor of the Austrian lines. In the eleventh century, the
emperors enjoyed full sovereignty: In the fifteenth, they had little more than the symbols and decorations of power.

Out of this feudal system, which has itself many of the important features of a confederacy, has grown the federal system,
which constitutes the Germanic empire. Its powers are vested in
a diet representing the component members of the confederacy;
in the emperor who is the executive magistrate, with a negative
on the decrees of the diet; and in the imperial chamber and aulic
council, two judiciary tribunals having supreme jurisdiction in
controversies which concern the empire, or which happen among
its members.

The diet possesses the general power of legislating for the
empire; of making war and peace; contracting alliances; assess-
ing quotas of troops and money; constructing fortresses; regulating coin; admitting new members; and subjecting disobedient
members to the ban of the empire, by which the party is
degraded from his sovereign rights, and his possessions forfeited. The members of the confederacy are expressly restricted
from entering into compacts, prejudicial to the empire, from
imposing tolls and duties on their mutual intercourse, without
the consent of the emperor and diet; from altering the value of
money; from doing injustice to one another; or from affording
assistance or retreat to disturbers of the public peace. And the
ban is denounced against such as shall violate any of these
restrictions. The members of the diet, as such, are subject in all
cases to be judged by the emperor and diet, and in their private
capacities, by the aulic council and imperial chamber.

The prerogatives of the emperor are numerous. The most
important of them are, his exclusive right to make propositions

to the diet; to negative its resolutions; to name ambassadors; to confer dignities and titles; to fill vacant electorates; to found universities; to grant privileges not injurious to the states of the empire; to receive and apply the public revenues; and generally to watch over the public safety. In certain cases, the electors form a council to him. In quality of emperor, he possesses no territory within the empire; nor receives any revenue for his support. But his revenues and dominions, in other qualities, constitute him one of the most powerful princes in Europe.

From such a parade of constitutional powers, in the representatives and head of this confederacy, the natural supposition would be, that it must form an exception to the general character which belongs to its kindred systems.—Nothing would be farther from the reality. The fundamental principle, on which it rests, that the empire is a community of sovereigns; that the diet is a representation of sovereigns; and that the laws are addressed to sovereigns; renders the empire a nerveless body; incapable of regulating its own members; insecure against external dangers; and agitated with unceasing fermentations in its own bowels.

The history of Germany, is a history of wars between the emperor and the princes and states; of wars among the princes and states themselves; of the licentiousness of the strong, and the oppression of the weak; of foreign intrusions, and foreign intrigues; of requisitions of men and money disregarded, or partially complied with; of attempts to enforce them, altogether abortive, or attended with slaughter and desolation, involving the innocent with the guilty; of general imbecility, confusion, and misery.

In the sixteenth century, the emperor, with one part of the empire on his side, was seen engaged against the other princes and states. In one of the conflicts, the emperor himself was put to flight, and very near being made prisoner by the elector of Saxony. The late king of Prussia was more than once pitted against his imperial sovereign; and commonly proved an overmatch for him. Controversies and wars among the members themselves, have been so common, that the German annals are crowded with the bloody pages which describe them. Previous to the peace of Westphalia, Germany was desolated by a war of thirty years, in which the emperor, with one half of the empire, was on one side; and Sweden, with the other half, on the opposite side. Peace was at length negociated, and dictated by foreign powers; and the articles of it, to which foreign powers are parties, made a fundamental part of the Germanic constitution.

If the nation happens, on any emergency, to be more united by the necessity of self-defence, its situation is still deplorable. Military preparations must be preceded by so many tedious discussions, arising from the jealousies, pride, separate views, and clashing pretensions, of sovereign bodies, that before the diet can settle the arrangements, the enemy are in the field; and before the federal troops are ready to take it, are retiring into winter quarters.

The small body of national troops, which has been judged necessary in time of peace, is defectively kept up, badly paid, infected with local prejudices, and supported by irregular and disproportionate contributions to the treasury.

The impossibility of maintaining order, and dispensing justice among these sovereign subjects, produced the experiment of dividing the empire into nine or ten circles or districts; of giving them an interior organization; and of charging them with the military execution of the laws against delinquent and contumacious members. This experiment has only served to demonstrate more fully, the radical vice of the constitution. Each circle is the miniature picture of the deformities of this political monster. They either fail to execute their commissions, or they do it with all the devastation and carnage of civil war. Sometimes whole circles are defaulters; and then they increase the mischief which they were instituted to remedy.

We may form some judgment of this scheme of military coercion, from a sample given by Thuanus. In Donawerth, a free and imperial city, of the circle of Suabia, the abbé de St. Croix enjoyed certain immunities which had been reserved to him. In the exercise of these, on some public occasion, outrages were committed on him, by the people of the city. The consequence was, that the city was put under the ban of the empire; and the duke of Bavaria, though director of another circle, obtained an appointment to enforce it. He soon appeared before the city, with a corps of ten thousand troops; and finding it a fit occasion, as he had secretly intended from the beginning, to revive an antiquated claim, on the pretext that his ancestors had suffered the place to be dismembered from his territory;* he took possession of it in his own name; disarmed and punished the inhabitants, and re-annexed the city to his domains.

It may be asked, perhaps, what has so long kept this disjointed machine from falling entirely to pieces? The answer is obvious. The weakness of most of the members, who are unwilling to expose themselves to the mercy of foreign powers; the weakness of most of the principal members, compared with the formidable powers all around them; the vast weight and influence which the emperor derives from his separate and hereditary dominions; and the interest he feels in preserving a system with which his family pride is connected, and which constitutes him the first prince in Europe; these causes support a feeble and precarious union; whilst the repellent quality, incident to the nature of sovereignty, and which time continually strengthens, prevents any reform whatever, founded on a proper consolidation. Nor is it to be imagined, if this obstacle could be surmounted, that the neighbouring powers would suffer a revolution to take place, which would give to the empire the force and pre-eminence to which it is entitled. Foreign nations have long considered themselves as interested in the changes made by events in this constitution; and have, on various occasions, betrayed their policy of perpetuating its anarchy and weakness.

If more direct examples were wanting, Poland, as a govern-

* Pfeffel, Nouvel abreg. chronol. de l'hist. &c. d'Allemagne, says the pretext was to indemnify himself for the expense of the expedition.

ment over local sovereigns, might not improperly be taken notice of. Nor could any proof, more striking, be given of the calamities flowing from such institutions.—Equally unfit for self-government, and self-defence, it has long been at the mercy of its powerful neighbours; who have lately had the mercy to disburden it of one third of its people and territories.

The connection among the Swiss cantons, scarcely amounts to a confederacy; though it is sometimes cited as an instance of the stability of such institutions.

They have no common treasury; no common troops even in war; no common coin; no common judicatory, nor any other common mark of sovereignty.

They are kept together by the peculiarity of their topographical position; by their individual weakness and insignificancy; by the fear of powerful neighbours, to one of which they were formerly subject; by the few sources of contention among a people of such simple and homogeneous manners; by their joint interest in their dependent possessions; by the mutual aid they stand in need of, for suppressing insurrections and rebellions; an aid expressly stipulated, and often required and afforded; and by the necessity of some regular and permanent provision for accommodating disputes among the cantons. The provision is, that the parties at variance shall each choose four judges out of the neutral cantons, who, in case of disagreement, choose an umpire. This tribunal, under an oath of impartiality, pronounces definitive sentence, which all the cantons are bound to enforce. The competency of this regulation may be estimated by a clause in their treaty of 1683, with Victor Amadeus of Savoy; in which he obliges himself to interpose as mediator in disputes between the cantons; and to employ force, if necessary, against the contumacious party.

So far as the peculiarity of their case will admit of comparison with that of the United States, it serves to confirm the principle intended to be established. Whatever efficacy the union may have had in ordinary cases, it appears that the moment a cause of difference sprang up, capable of trying its strength, it failed.

The controversies on the subject of religion, which in three instances have kindled violent and bloody contests, may be said in fact to have served the league. The Protestant and Catholic cantons, have since had their separate diets; where all the most important concerns are adjusted, and which have left the general diet little other business than to take care of the common bailages.

That separation had another consequence, which merits attention. It produced opposite alliances with foreign powers; of Bern, as the head of the Protestant association, with the United Provinces; and of Luzerne, as the head of the Catholic association, with France.

PUBLIUS.

22

THE FEDERALIST.

NUMBER XX.

NEW YORK, DECEMBER 12, 1787.

HAMILTON AND MADISON.

THE SAME SUBJECT CONTINUED, WITH FARTHER EXAMPLES.

THE United Netherlands are a confederacy of republics, or rather of aristocracies, of a very remarkable texture; yet confirming all the lessons derived from those which we have already reviewed.

The union is composed of seven co-equal and sovereign states, and each state or province is a composition of equal and independent cities. In all important cases, not only the provinces, but the cities, must be unanimous.

The sovereignty of the union is represented by the states general, consisting usually of about fifty deputies appointed by the provinces. They hold their seats, some for life, some for six, three, and one years. From two provinces they continue in appointment during pleasure.

The states general have authority to enter into treaties and alliances; to make war and peace; to raise armies and equip fleets; to ascertain quotas and demand contributions. In all these cases, however, unanimity and the sanction of their constituents are requisite. They have authority to appoint and receive ambassadors; to execute treaties and alliances already formed; to provide for the collection of duties on imports and exports; to regulate the mint, with a saving to the provincial rights; to govern as sovereigns the dependent territories. The provinces are restrained, unless with the general consent, from entering into foreign treaties; from establishing imposts injurious to others, or charging their neighbours with higher duties than their own subjects. A council of state, a chamber of accounts, with five colleges of admiralty, aid and fortify the federal administration.

The executive magistrate of the union is the stadtholder, who is now an hereditary prince. His principal weight and influence in the republic are derived from his independent title; from his great patrimonial estates; from his family connections with some of the chief potentates of Europe; and more than all, perhaps, from his being stadtholder in the several provinces, as well as for the union, in which provincial quality, he has the appointment of town magistrates under certain regulations, executes provincial decrees, presides when he pleases in the provincial tribunals; and has throughout the power of pardon.

As stadtholder of the union, he has, however, considerable prerogatives.

In his political capacity, he has authority to settle disputes between the provinces, when other methods fail; to assist at the deliberations of the states general, and at their particular conferences; to give audience to foreign ambassadors, and to keep agents for his particular affairs at foreign courts.

In his military capacity, he commands the federal troops; provides for garrisons, and in general regulates military affairs; disposes of all appointments from colonels to ensigns, and of the governments and posts of fortified towns.

In his marine capacity, he is admiral general, and superintends and directs every thing relative to naval forces, and other naval affairs; presides in the admiralties in person or by proxy; appoints lieutenant admirals and other officers; and establishes councils of war, whose sentences are not executed till he approves them.

His revenue, exclusive of his private income, amounts to

300,000 florins. The standing army which he commands consists of about 40,000 men.

Such is the nature of the celebrated Belgic confederacy, as delineated on parchment. What are the characters which practice has stampt upon it? Imbecility in the government; discord among the provinces; foreign influence and indignities; a precarious existence in peace, and peculiar calamities from war.

It was long ago remarked by Grotius, that nothing but the hatred of his countrymen to the house of Austria, kept them from being ruined by the vices of their constitution.

The union of Utrecht, says another respectable writer, reposes an authority in the states general, seemingly sufficient to secure harmony, but the jealousy in each province renders the practice very different from the theory.

The same instrument, says another, obliges each province to levy certain contributions; but this article never could, and probably never will, be executed; because the inland provinces, who have little commerce, cannot pay an equal quota.

In matters of contribution, it is the practice to wave the articles of the constitution. The danger of delay obliges the consenting provinces to furnish their quotas, without waiting for the others; and then to obtain reimbursement from the others, by deputations, which are frequent, or otherwise, as they can. The great wealth and influence of the province of Holland, enable her to effect both these purposes.

It has more than once happened that the deficiencies have been ultimately to be collected at the point of the bayonet; a thing practicable, though dreadful, in a confederacy, where one of the members exceeds in force all the rest; and where several of them are too small to meditate resistance: But utterly impracticable in one composed of members, several of which are equal to each other in strength and resources, and equal singly to a vigorous and persevering defence.

Foreign ministers, says Sir William Temple, who was himself a foreign minister, elude matters taken *ad referendum*, by tampering with the provinces and cities. In 1726, the treaty of Hanover was delayed by these means a whole year. Instances of a like nature are numerous and notorious.

In critical emergencies, the states general are often compelled to overleap their constitutional bounds. In 1688, they concluded a treaty of themselves, at the risk of their heads. The treaty of Westphalia in 1648, by which their independence was formally and finally recognized, was concluded without the consent of Zealand. Even as recently as the last treaty of peace with Great Britain, the constitutional principle of unanimity was departed from. A weak constitution must necessarily terminate in dissolution, for want of proper powers, or from the usurpation of powers requisite for the public safety. Whether the usurpation, when once begun, will stop at the salutary point, or go forward to the dangerous extreme, must depend on the contingencies of the moment. Tyranny has perhaps oftener grown out of the assumptions of power, called for, on pressing exigencies, by a defective constitution, than out of the full exercise of the largest constitutional authorities.

Notwithstanding the calamities produced by the stadtholdership, it has been supposed, that without his influence in the individual provinces, the causes of anarchy manifest in the confederacy, would long ago have dissolved it. "Under such a government, says the abbé Mably, the union could never have subsisted, if the provinces had not a spring within themselves, capable of quickening their tardiness, and compelling them to the same way of thinking. This spring is the stadtholder." It is remarked by Sir William Temple, "that in the intermissions of the stadtholdership, Holland, by her riches and her authority, which drew the others into a sort of dependence, supplied the place."

These are not the only circumstances which have controlled the tendency to anarchy and dissolution. The surrounding powers impose an absolute necessity of union to a certain degree, at the same time that they nourish, by their intrigues, the consti-

tutional vices, which keep the republic in some measure always
at their mercy.

The true patriots have long bewailed the fatal operation of
these vices, and have made no less than four regular experiments by *extraordinary assemblies*, convened for the special
purpose, to apply a remedy. As many times, has their laudable
zeal found it impossible to *unite the public councils* in reforming the known, the acknowledged, the fatal evils of the existing constitution. Let us pause, my fellow-citizens, for one
moment, over this melancholy and monitory lesson of history;
and with the tear that drops for the calamities brought on
mankind by their adverse opinions and selfish passions, let our
gratitude mingle an ejaculation to Heaven, for the propitious
concord which has distinguished the consultations for our
political happiness.

A design was also conceived, of establishing a general tax to
be administered by the federal authority. This also had its
adversaries and failed.

This unhappy people seem to be now suffering, from popular
convulsions, from dissentions among the states, and from the
actual invasion of foreign arms, the crisis of their destiny. All
nations have their eyes fixed on the awful spectacle. The first
wish prompted by humanity is, that this severe trial may issue
in such a revolution of their government, as will establish their
union, and render it the parent of tranquillity, freedom, and happiness: The next, that the asylum under which, we trust, the
enjoyment of these blessings will speedily be secured in this
country, may receive and console them for the catastrophe of
their own.

I make no apology for having dwelt so long on the contemplation of these federal precedents. Experience is the oracle of
truth; and where its responses are unequivocal, they ought to be
conclusive and sacred. The important truth, which it unequivocally pronounces in the present case, is, that a sovereignty over
sovereigns, a government over governments, a legislation for

communities, as contradistinguished from individuals; as it is a solecism in theory, so in practice, it is subversive of the order and ends of civil polity, by substituting *violence* in the place of *law*, or the destructive *coercion* of the *sword*, in the place of the mild and salutary *coercion* of the *magistracy*.

PUBLIUS.

THE FEDERALIST.

NUMBER XXI.

NEW YORK, DECEMBER 12, 1787.

HAMILTON.

FURTHER DEFECTS OF THE PRESENT CONSTITUTION.

HAVING in the three last numbers taken a summary review of the principal circumstances and events, which depict the genius and fate of other confederate governments; I shall now proceed in the enumeration of the most important of those defects, which have hitherto disappointed our hopes from the system established among ourselves. To form a safe and satisfactory judgment of the proper remedy, it is absolutely necessary that we should be well acquainted with the extent and malignity of the disease.

The next most palpable defect of the existing confederation, is the total want of a SANCTION to its laws. The United States, as now composed, have no power to exact obedience, or punish disobedience to their resolutions, either by pecuniary mulcts, by a suspension or divestiture of privileges, or by any other constitutional means. There is no express delegation of authority to them to use force against delinquent members; and if such a right should be ascribed to the federal head, as resulting from the nature of the social compact between the states, it must be by inference and construction, in the face of that part of the second article, by which it is declared, "that each state shall retain every power, jurisdiction, and right, not *expressly* delegated to the United States in Congress assembled." The want of such a right involves, no doubt, a striking absurdity; but we are reduced to the dilemma, either of supposing that deficiency, preposterous as it may seem, or of contravening or explaining away a provision, which has been of late a repeated theme of the eulogies of those who oppose the new constitution; and the omission of which, in that plan, has been the subject of much plausible animadversion, and severe criticism. If we are unwilling to impair the force of this applauded provision, we shall be obliged to conclude, that the United States afford the extraordinary spectacle of a government, destitute even of the shadow of constitutional power, to enforce the execution of its own laws. It will appear, from the specimens which have been cited, that the American confederacy, in this particular, stands discriminated from every other institution of a similar kind, and exhibits a new and unexampled phenomenon in the political world.

The want of a mutual guarantee of the state governments, is another capital imperfection in the federal plan. There is nothing of this kind declared in the articles that compose it: and to imply a tacit guarantee from considerations of utility, would be a still more flagrant departure from the clause which has been mentioned, than to imply a tacit power of coercion, from the like considerations. The want of a guarantee, though it might in its consequences endanger the union, does not so immediately attack its existence, as the want of a constitutional sanction to its laws.

Without a guarantee, the assistance to be derived from the union, in repelling those domestic dangers, which may sometimes threaten the existence of the state constitutions, must be renounced. Usurpation may rear its crest in each state, and trample upon the liberties of the people; while the national government could legally do nothing more than behold its encroachments with indignation and regret. A successful faction may erect a tyranny on the ruins of order and law, while no succour could constitutionally be afforded by the union to the friends and supporters of the government. The tempestuous situation, from which Massachusetts has scarcely emerged, evinces, that dangers of this kind are not merely speculative. Who can determine what might have been the issue of her late convulsions, if the mal-contents had been headed by a Cæsar or by a Cromwell? Who can predict what effect a despotism, established in Massachusetts, would have upon the liberties of New-Hampshire or Rhode-Island; of Connecticut or New-York?

The inordinate pride of state importance, has suggested to some minds an objection to the principle of a guarantee in the federal government; as involving an officious interference in the domestic concerns of the members. A scruple of this kind would deprive us of one of the principal advantages to be expected from union; and can only flow from a misapprehension of the nature of the provision itself. It could be no impediment to reforms of the state constitutions by a majority of the people in a legal and peaceable mode. This right would remain undiminished. The guarantee could only operate against changes to be effected by violence. Towards the prevention of calamities of this kind, too many checks cannot be provided. The peace of society, and the stability of government, depend absolutely on the efficacy of the precautions adopted on this head. Where the whole power of the government is in the hands of the people, there is the less pretence for the use of violent remedies, in partial or occasional distempers of the state. The natural cure for an ill administration, in a popular or representative constitution, is, a change of men. A guarantee by the national authority, would be as much directed against the usurpations of rulers, as against the ferments and outrages of faction and sedition in the community.

The principle of regulating the contributions of the states to the common treasury by QUOTAS, is another fundamental error in the confederation. Its repugnancy to an adequate supply of the national exigencies, has been already pointed out, and has sufficiently appeared from the trial which has been made of it. I speak of it now solely, with a view to equality among the states. Those who have been accustomed to contemplate the circumstances, which produce and constitute national wealth, must be satisfied that there is no common standard, or barometer, by which the degrees of it can be ascertained. Neither the value of lands, nor the numbers of the people, which have been successively proposed as the rule of state contributions, has any pretension to being a just representative. If we compare the wealth of the United Netherlands with that of Russia or Germany, or even of France; and if we at the same time compare the total value of the lands, and the aggregate population of the contracted territory of that republic, with the total value of the lands, and the aggregate population of the immense regions of either of those kingdoms, we shall at once discover, that there is no comparison between the proportion of either of these two objects, and that of the relative wealth of those nations. If the like parallel were to be run between several of the American states, it would furnish a like result. Let Virginia be contrasted with North-Carolina, Pennsylvania with Connecticut, or Maryland with New-Jersey, and we shall be convinced that the respective abilities of those states, in relation to revenue, bear little or no analogy to their comparative stock in lands, or to their comparative population. The position may be equally illustrated, by a similar process between the counties of the same state. No man acquainted with the state of New-York will doubt, that the active wealth of King's county bears a much greater proportion to that of Montgomery, than it would appear to do, if we should take either the total value of the lands, or the total numbers of the people as a criterion.

The wealth of nations depends upon an infinite variety of causes. Situation, soil, climate, the nature of the productions, the nature of the government, the genius of the citizens; the degree of information they possess; the state of commerce, of arts, of industry; these circumstances, and many more too complex, minute, or adventitious, to admit of a particular specification, occasion differences hardly conceivable in the relative opulence and riches of different countries. The consequence clearly is, that there can be no common measure of national wealth; and of course, no general or stationary rule, by which the ability of a state to pay taxes can be determined. The attempt, therefore, to regulate the contributions of the members of a confederacy, by any such rule, cannot fail to be productive of glaring inequality, and extreme oppression.

This inequality would of itself be sufficient in America to work the eventual destruction of the union, if any mode of enforcing a compliance with its requisitions could be devised. The suffering states would not long consent to remain associated upon a principle which distributed the public burthens with so unequal a hand; and which was calculated to impoverish and oppress the citizens of some states, while those of others would scarcely be conscious of the small proportion of the weight they were required to sustain. This, however, is an evil inseparable from the principle of quotas and requisitions.

There is no method of steering clear of this inconvenience, but by authorizing the national government to raise its own revenues in its own way. Imposts, excises, and in general all duties upon articles of consumption, may be compared to a fluid, which will in time find its level with the means of paying them. The amount to be contributed by each citizen will in a degree be at his own option, and can be regulated by an attention to his resources. The rich may be extravagant, the poor can be frugal. And private oppression may always be avoided, by a judicious selection of objects proper for such impositions. If inequalities should arise in some states from duties on particular objects, these will, in all probability, be counterbalanced by proportional inequalities in other states, from the duties on other objects. In the course of time and things, an equilibrium, as far as it is attainable, in so complicated a subject, will be established every where. Or if inequalities should still exist, they would neither be so great in their degree, so uniform in their operation, nor so odious in their appearance, as those which would necessarily spring from quotas, upon any scale that can possibly be devised.

It is a signal advantage of taxes on articles of consumption, that they contain in their own nature a security against excess. They prescribe their own limit; which cannot be exceeded without defeating the end proposed—that is, an extension of the revenue. When applied to this object, the saying is as just as it is witty, that "in political arithmetic, two and two do not always make four." If duties are too high, they lessen the consumption—the collection is eluded; and the product to the treasury is not so great as when they are confined within proper and moderate bounds.

This forms a complete barrier against any material oppression of the citizens, by taxes of this class, and is itself a natural limitation of the power of imposing them.

Impositions of this kind usually fall under the denomination of indirect taxes, and must for a long time constitute the chief part of the revenue raised in this country. Those of the direct kind, which principally relate to lands and buildings, may admit of a rule of apportionment. Either the value of land, or the number of the people may serve as a standard. The state of agriculture, and the populousness of a country, are considered as having a near relation to each other. And as a rule for the purpose intended, numbers in the view of simplicity and certainty, are entitled to a preference. In every country it is an Herculean task to obtain a valuation of the land; in a country imperfectly settled and progressive in improvement, the difficulties are increased almost to impracticability. The expense of an accurate valuation, is in all situations a formidable objection. In a branch of taxation where no limits to the discretion of the government are to be found in the nature of the thing, the establishment of a fixed rule, not incompatible with the end, may be attended with fewer inconveniences than to leave that discretion altogether at large.

PUBLIUS.

THE FEDERALIST.

NUMBER XXII.

NEW YORK, DECEMBER 15, 1787.

HAMILTON.

THE SAME SUBJECT CONTINUED, AND CONCLUDED.

IN addition to the defects of the existing federal system, enumerated in the last number, there are others of not less importance, which concur in rendering that system altogether unfit for the administration of the affairs of the union.

The want of a power to regulate commerce, is by all parties allowed to be of the number. The utility of such a power has been anticipated under the first head of our inquiries; and for this reason, as well as from the universal conviction entertained upon the subject, little need be added in this place. It is indeed evident, on the most superficial view, that there is no object, either as it respects the interests of trade or finance, that more strongly demands a federal superintendance. The want of it has already operated as a bar to the formation of beneficial treaties with foreign powers; and has given occasions of dissatisfaction between the states. No nation acquainted with the nature of our political association would be unwise enough to enter into stipulations with the United States, conceding on their part privileges of importance, while they were apprised that the engagements on the part of the union, might at any moment be violated by its members; and while they found, from experience, that they might enjoy every advantage they desired in our markets, without granting us any return, but such as their momentary convenience might suggest. It is not therefore to be wondered at, that Mr. Jenkinson, in ushering into the house of commons a bill for regulating the temporary intercourse between the two countries, should preface its introduction by a declaration, that similar provisions in former bills had been found to answer every purpose to the commerce of Great Britain, and that it would be prudent to persist in the plan until it should appear whether the American government was likely or not to acquire greater consistency.*

Several states have endeavoured, by separate prohibitions, restrictions, and exclusions, to influence the conduct of that kingdom in this particular; but the want of concert, arising from the want of a general authority, and from clashing and dissimilar views in the states, has hitherto frustrated every experiment of the kind; and will continue to do so, as long as the same obstacles to an uniformity of measures continue to exist.

The interfering and unneighbourly regulations of some states, contrary to the true spirit of the union, have, in different instances, given just cause of umbrage and complaint to others; and it is to be feared that examples of this nature, if not restrained by a national control, would be multiplied and extended till they became not less serious sources of animosity and discord, than injurious impediments to the intercourse between the different parts of the confederacy. "The commerce of the German empire,† is in continual trammels, from the multiplicity of the duties which the several princes and states exact upon the merchandizes passing through their territories; by means of which the fine streams and navigable rivers with which Germany is so happily watered, are rendered almost useless." Though the genius of the people of this country might never permit this description to be strictly applicable to us, yet we may reasonably expect, from the gradual conflicts of state

* This, as nearly as I can recollect, was the sense of this speech on introducing the last bill.

† Encyclopedia, article Empire.

regulations, that the citizens of each, would at length come to be considered and treated by the others in no better light than that of foreigners and aliens.

The power of raising armies, by the most obvious construction of the articles of the confederation, is merely a power of making requisitions upon the states for quotas of men. This practice, in the course of the late war, was found replete with obstructions to a vigorous, and to an economical system of defence. It gave birth to a competition between the states, which created a kind of auction for men. In order to furnish the quotas required of them, they outbid each other, till bounties grew to an enormous and insupportable size. The hope of a still further increase, afforded an inducement to those who were disposed to serve, to procrastinate their enlistment; and disinclined them from engaging for any considerable periods. Hence slow and scanty levies of men, in the most critical emergencies of our affairs—short enlistments at an unparalleled expense—continual fluctuations in the troops, ruinous to their discipline, and subjecting the public safety frequently to the perilous crisis of a disbanded army. Hence also, those oppressive expedients for raising men, which were upon several occasions practised, and which nothing but the enthusiasm of liberty, would have induced the people to endure.

This method of raising troops, is not more unfriendly to economy and vigour, than it is to an equal distribution of the burthen. The states near the seat of war, influenced by motives of self-preservation, made efforts to furnish their quotas, which even exceeded their abilities, while those at a distance from danger were, for the most part, as remiss as the others were diligent, in their exertions. The immediate pressure of this inequality, was not, in this case, as in that of the contributions of money, alleviated by the hope of a final liquidation. The states which did not pay their proportions of money, might at least be charged with their deficiencies; but no account could be formed of the deficiencies in the supplies of men. We shall not, however, see much reason to regret the want of this hope, when we consider how little prospect there is, that the most delinquent states ever will be able to make compensation for their pecuniary failures. The system of quotas and requisitions, whether it be applied to men or money, is, in every view, a system of imbecility in the union, and of inequality and injustice among the members.

The right of equal suffrage among the states, is another exceptionable part of the confederation. Every idea of proportion, and every rule of fair representation, conspire to condemn a principle, which gives to Rhode-Island an equal weight in the scale of power with Massachusetts, or Connecticut, or New-York; and to Delaware, an equal voice in the national deliberations with Pennsylvania, or Virginia, or North-Carolina. Its operation contradicts that fundamental maxim of republican government, which requires that the sense of the majority should prevail. Sophistry may reply, that sovereigns are equal, and that a majority of the votes of the states, will be a majority of confederated America. But this kind of logical legerdemain, will never counteract the plain suggestions of justice and common sense. It may happen, that this majority of states is a small minority of the people of America;* and two thirds of the people of America, could not long be persuaded, upon the credit of artificial distinctions and syllogistic subtleties, to submit their interests to the management and disposal of one third. The larger states would, after a while, revolt from the idea of receiving the law from the smaller. To acquiesce in such a privation of their due importance in the political scale, would be, not merely to be insensible to the love of power, but even to sacrifice the desire of equality. It is neither rational to expect the first, nor just to require the last: Considering how peculiarly the safety and welfare of the smaller states depend on union, they ought readily to renounce a pretension, which, if not relinquished, would prove fatal to its duration.

* New-Hampshire, Rhode-Island, New-Jersey, Delaware, Georgia, South-Carolina, and Maryland, are a majority of the whole number of the States, but they do not contain one third of the people.

23

It may be objected to this, that not seven, but nine states, or two thirds of the whole number, must consent to the most important resolutions; and it may be thence inferred, that nine states would always comprehend a majority of the inhabitants of the union. But this does not obviate the impropriety of an equal vote, between states of the most unequal dimensions and populousness; nor is the inference accurate in point of fact; for we can enumerate nine states, which contain less than a majority of the people;* and it is constitutionally possible, that these nine may give the vote. Besides, there are matters of considerable moment determinable by a bare majority; and there are others, concerning which doubts have been entertained, which, if interpreted in favour of the sufficiency of a vote of seven states, would extend its operation to interests of the first magnitude. In addition to this, it is to be observed, that there is a probability of an increase in the number of states, and no provision for a proportional augmentation of the ratio of votes.

But this is not all; what, at first sight, may seem a remedy, is, in reality, a poison. To give a minority a negative upon the majority, which is always the case, where more than a majority is requisite to a decision, is, in its tendency, to subject the sense of the greater number to that of the lesser. Congress, from the non-attendance of a few states, have been frequently in the situation of a Polish diet, where a single VETO has been sufficient to put a stop to all their movements. A sixtieth part of the union, which is about the proportion of Delaware and Rhode-Island, has several times been able to oppose an entire bar to its operations. This is one of those refinements, which, in practice, has an effect the reverse of what is expected from it in theory. The necessity of unanimity in public bodies, or of something approaching towards it, has been founded upon a supposition that it would contribute to security. But its real operation is, to embarrass the administration, to destroy the energy of government, and to substitute the pleasure, caprice, or artifices of an

* Add New-York and Connecticut to the foregoing seven, and they will still be less than a majority.

insignificant, turbulent, or corrupt junto, to the regular deliberations and decisions of a respectable majority. In those emergencies of a nation, in which the goodness or badness, the weakness or strength of its government, is of the greatest
importance, there is commonly a necessity for action. The public
business must, in some way or other, go forward. If a pertina-
cious minority can control the opinion of a majority, respecting
the best mode of conducting it, the majority, in order that something may be done, must conform to the views of the minority;
and thus the sense of the smaller number, will over-rule that of
the greater, and give a tone to the national proceedings. Hence
tedious delays; continual negociation and intrigue; contemptible
compromises of the public good. And yet, in such a system, it is
even fortunate when such compromises can take place: For,
upon some occasions, things will not admit of accommodation;
and then the measures of government must be injuriously suspended, or fatally defeated. It is often, by the impracticability of
obtaining the concurrence of the necessary number of votes,
kept in a state of inaction. Its situation must always savour of
weakness; sometimes border upon anarchy.

It is not difficult to discover, that a principle of this kind gives
greater scope to foreign corruption, as well as to domestic faction, than that which permits the sense of the majority to
decide; though the contrary of this has been presumed. The mistake has proceeded from not attending with due care to the mischiefs that may be occasioned, by obstructing the progress of
government at certain critical seasons. When the concurrence of
a large number is required by the constitution to the doing of
any national act, we are apt to rest satisfied that all is safe,
because nothing improper will be likely *to be done*; but we forget how much good may be prevented, and how much ill may be
produced, by the power of hindering that which it is necessary
to do, and of keeping affairs in the same unfavourable posture in
which they may happen to stand at particular periods.

Suppose, for instance, we were engaged in a war, in conjunction with one foreign nation, against another. Suppose the

necessity of our situation demanded peace, and that the interest or ambition of our ally led him to seek the prosecution of the war, with views that might justify us in making separate terms. In such a state of things, this ally of ours would evidently find it much easier by his bribes and his intrigues, to tie up the hands of government from making peace, where two thirds of all the votes were requisite to that object, than where a simple majority would suffice. In the first case, he would have to corrupt a smaller, in the last a greater number. Upon the same principle, it would be much easier for a foreign power with which we were at war, to perplex our councils and embarrass our exertions. And in a commercial view, we may be subjected to similar inconveniences. A nation with which we might have a treaty of commerce, could with much greater facility prevent our forming a connection with her competitor in trade; though such a connection should be ever so beneficial to ourselves.

Evils of this description ought not to be regarded as imaginary. One of the weak sides of republics, among their numerous advantages, is, that they afford too easy an inlet to foreign corruption. An hereditary monarch, though often disposed to sacrifice his subjects to his ambition, has so great a personal interest in the government, and in the external glory of the nation, that it is not easy for a foreign power to give him an equivalent, for what he would sacrifice by treachery to the state. The world has accordingly been witness to few examples of this species of royal prostitution, though there have been abundant specimens of every other kind.

In republics, persons elevated from the mass of the community, by the suffrages of their fellow-citizens, to stations of great pre-eminence and power, may find compensations for betraying their trust, which to any but minds actuated by superior virtue, may appear to exceed the proportion of interest they have in the common stock, and to over-balance the obligations of duty. Hence it is, that history furnishes us with so many mortifying examples of the prevalency of foreign corruption in republican governments. How much this contributed to the ruin of the ancient commonwealths, has been already disclosed. It is well known that the deputies of the United Provinces have, in various instances, been purchased by the emissaries of the neighbouring kingdoms. The earl of Chesterfield, if my memory serves me right, in a letter to his court, intimates that his success in an important negociation, must depend on his obtaining a major's commission for one of those deputies. And in Sweden, the rival parties were alternately bought by France and England, in so barefaced and notorious a manner, that it excited universal disgust in the nation, and was a principal cause that the most limited monarch in Europe, in a single day, without tumult, violence, or opposition, became one of the most absolute and uncontroled.

A circumstance, which crowns the defects of the confederation, remains yet to be mentioned—the want of a judiciary power. Laws are a dead letter, without courts to expound and define their true meaning and operation. The treaties of the United States, to have any force at all, must be considered as part of the law of the land. Their true import, as far as respects individuals, must, like all other laws, be ascertained by judicial determinations. To produce uniformity in these determinations, they ought to be submitted in the last resort, to one SUPREME TRIBUNAL. And this tribunal ought to be instituted under the same authority which forms the treaties themselves. These ingredients are both indispensable. If there is in each state a court of final jurisdiction, there may be as many different final determinations on the same point, as there are courts. There are endless diversities in the opinions of men. We often see not only different courts, but the judges of the same court, differing from each other. To avoid the confusion which would unavoidably result from the contradictory decisions of a number of independent judicatories, all nations have found it necessary to establish one tribunal paramount to the rest, possessing a general superintendance, and authorized to settle and declare in the last resort an uniform rule of civil justice.

This is the more necessary where the frame of the government is so compounded, that the laws of the whole are in danger of being contravened by the laws of the parts. In this case, if the particular tribunals are invested with a right of ultimate decision, besides the contradictions to be expected from difference of opinion, there will be much to fear from the bias of local views and prejudices, and from the interference of local regulations. As often as such an interference should happen, there would be reason to apprehend, that the provisions of the particular laws might be preferred to those of the general laws, from the deference with which men in office naturally look up to that authority to which they owe their official existence. The treaties of the United States, under the present constitution, are liable to the infractions of thirteen different legislatures, and as many different courts of final jurisdiction, acting under the authority of those legislatures. The faith, the reputation, the peace of the whole union, are thus continually at the mercy of the prejudices, the passions, and the interests of every member of which these are composed. Is it possible that foreign nations can either respect or confide in such a government? Is it possible that the people of America will longer consent to trust their honour, their happiness, their safety, on so precarious a foundation?

In this review of the confederation, I have confined myself to the exhibition of its most material defects; passing over those imperfections in its details, by which even a considerable part of the power intended to be conferred upon it, has been in a great measure rendered abortive. It must be by this time evident to all men of reflection, who are either free from erroneous prepossessions, or can divest themselves of them, that it is a system so radically vicious and unsound, as to admit not of amendment, but by an entire change in its leading features and characters.

The organization of congress, is itself utterly improper for the exercise of those powers, which are necessary to be deposited in the union. A single assembly may be a proper receptacle of those slender, or rather fettered authorities, which have been heretofore delegated to the federal head; but it would be inconsistent with all the principles of good government, to intrust it with those additional powers which even the moderate and more rational adversaries of the proposed constitution admit, ought to reside in the United States. If that plan should not be adopted; and if the necessity of union should be able to withstand the ambitious aims of those men, who may indulge magnificent schemes of personal aggrandizement from its dissolution; the probability would be, that we should run into the project of conferring supplementary powers upon congress, as they are now constituted. And either the machine, from the intrinsic feebleness of its structure, will moulder into pieces in spite of our illjudged efforts to prop it; or by successive augmentations of its force and energy, as necessity might prompt, we shall finally accumulate in a single body, all the most important prerogatives of sovereignty; and thus entail upon our posterity, one of the most execrable forms of government that human infatuation ever contrived. Thus we should create in reality that very tyranny, which the adversaries of the new constitution either are, or affect to be, solicitous to avert.

It has not a little contributed to the infirmities of the existing federal system, that it never had a ratification by the PEOPLE. Resting on no better foundation than the consent of the several legislatures, it has been exposed to frequent and intricate questions concerning the validity of its powers; and has, in some instances, given birth to the enormous doctrine of a right of legislative repeal. Owing its ratification to the law of a state, it has been contended, that the same authority might repeal the law by which it was ratified. However gross a heresy it may be, to maintain that a *party* to a *compact* has a right to revoke that *compact*, the doctrine itself has had respectable advocates. The possibility of a question of this nature, proves the necessity of laying the foundations of our national government deeper, than in the mere sanction of delegated authority. The fabric of American empire ought to rest on the solid basis of THE CONSENT OF THE PEOPLE. The streams of national power ought to flow immediately from that pure original fountain of all legitimate authority.

PUBLIUS.

THE FEDERALIST.

NUMBER XXIII.

NEW YORK, DECEMBER 19, 1787.

HAMILTON.

THE NECESSITY OF A GOVERNMENT, AT LEAST EQUALLY ENER-
GETIC WITH THE ONE PROPOSED.

THE necessity of a constitution, at least equally energetic with
the one proposed, to the preservation of the union, is the point,
at the examination of which we are now arrived.

This inquiry will naturally divide itself into three branches.
The objects to be provided for by a federal government. The
quantity of power necessary to the accomplishment of those
objects. The persons upon whom that power ought to operate.
Its distribution and organization, will more properly claim our
attention under the succeeding head.

The principal purposes to be answered by union, are these:
The common defence of the members; the preservation of the
public peace, as well against internal convulsions as external
attacks; the regulation of commerce with other nations, and
between the states; the superintendance of our intercourse,
political and commercial, with foreign countries.

The authorities essential to the care of the common defence
are these: To raise armies; to build and equip fleets; to prescribe
rules for the government of both; to direct their operations; to
provide for their support. These powers ought to exist without
limitation; because it is impossible to foresee or to define the

extent and variety of national exigencies, and the correspondent extent and variety of the means which may be necessary to satisfy them. The circumstances that endanger the safety of nations are infinite; and for this reason, no constitutional shackles can wisely be imposed on the power to which the care of it is committed. This power ought to be co-extensive with all the possible combinations of such circumstances; and ought to be under the direction of the same councils, which are appointed to preside over the common defence.

This is one of those truths, which, to a correct and unprejudiced mind, carries its own evidence along with it; and may be obscured, but cannot be made plainer by argument or reasoning. It rests upon axioms, as simple as they are universal—the *means* ought to be proportioned to the *end*; the persons from whose agency the attainment of any *end* is expected, ought to possess the *means* by which it is to be attained.

Whether there ought to be a federal government intrusted with the care of the common defence, is a question, in the first instance, open to discussion; but the moment it is decided in the affirmative, it will follow, that, that government ought to be cloathed with all the powers requisite to the complete execution of its trust. And unless it can be shown, that the circumstances which may affect the public safety, are reducible within certain determinate limits; unless the contrary of this position can be fairly and rationally disputed, it must be admitted as a necessary consequence, that there can be no limitation of that authority, which is to provide for the defence and protection of the community, in any matter essential to its efficacy; that is, in any matter essential to the *formation*, *direction*, or *support* of the NATIONAL FORCES.

Defective as the present confederation has been proved to be, this principle appears to have been fully recognized by the framers of it; though they have not made proper or adequate provision for its exercise. Congress have an unlimited discretion to make requisitions of men and money; to govern the army and navy; to direct their operations. As their requisitions are made constitutionally binding upon the states, who are in fact under the most solemn obligations to furnish the supplies required of them, the intention evidently was, that the United States should command whatever resources were by them judged requisite to the "common defence and general welfare." It was presumed, that a sense of their true interests, and a regard to the dictates of good faith, would be found sufficient pledges for the punctual performance of the duty of the members to the federal head.

The experiment has however demonstrated, that this expectation was ill founded and illusory; and the observations made under the last head will, I imagine, have sufficed to convince the impartial and discerning, that there is an absolute necessity for an entire change in the first principles of the system. That if we are in earnest about giving the union energy and duration, we must abandon the vain project of legislating upon the states in their collective capacities; we must extend the laws of the federal government to the individual citizens of America; we must discard the fallacious scheme of quotas and requisitions, as equally impracticable and unjust. The result from all this is, that the union ought to be invested with full power to levy troops; to build and equip fleets; and to raise the revenues which will be required for the formation and support of an army and navy, in the customary and ordinary modes practised in other governments.

If the circumstances of our country are such, as to demand a compound, instead of a simple; a confederate, instead of a sole government, the essential point which will remain to be adjusted, will be to discriminate the OBJECTS, as far as it can be done, which shall appertain to the different provinces or departments of power: allowing to each, the most ample authority for fulfilling THOSE which may be committed to its charge. Shall the union be constituted the guardian of the common safety? Are fleets, and armies, and revenues, necessary to this purpose? The government of the union must be empowered to pass all laws, and to make all regulations which have relation to them. The same must be the case in respect to commerce, and to every other matter to which its jurisdiction is permitted to extend. Is the administration of justice, between the citizens of the same state, the proper department of the local governments? These must possess all the authorities which are connected with this object, and with every other that may be allotted to their particular cognizance and direction. Not to confer in each case a degree of power, commensurate to the end, would be to violate the most obvious rules of prudence and propriety, and improvidently to trust the great interests of the nation to hands which are disabled from managing them with vigour and success.

Who so likely to make suitable provisions for the public defence, as that body to which the guardianship of the public safety is confided? Which, as the centre of information, will best understand the extent and urgency of the dangers that threaten; as the representative of the WHOLE, will feel itself most deeply interested in the preservation of every part; which, from the responsibility implied in the duty assigned to it, will be most sensibly impressed with the necessity of proper exertions; and which, by the extension of its authority throughout the states, can alone establish uniformity and concert in the plans and measures, by which the common safety is to be secured? Is there not a manifest inconsistency in devolving upon the federal government the care of the general defence, and leaving in the state governments the *effective* powers, by which it is to be provided for? Is not a want of co-operation the infallible consequence of such a system? And will not weakness, disorder, an undue distribution of the burthens and calamities of war, an unnecessary and intolerable increase of expense, be its natural and inevitable concomitants? Have we not had unequivocal experience of its effects in the course of the revolution, which we have just achieved?

Every view we may take of the subject as candid inquirers after truth, will serve to convince us, that it is both unwise and dangerous to deny the federal government an unconfined authority, in respect to all those objects which are intrusted to its management. It will indeed deserve the most vigilant and careful attention of the people, to see that it be modelled in such a manner as to admit of its being safely vested with the requisite powers. If any plan, which has been, or may be, offered to our consideration, should not, upon a dispassionate inspection, be found to answer this description, it ought to be rejected. A government, the constitution of which renders it unfit to be intrusted with all the powers which a free people *ought to delegate to any government*, would be an unsafe and improper depository of the NATIONAL INTERESTS. Wherever THESE can with propriety be confided, the coincident powers may safely accompany them. This is the true result of all just reasoning upon the subject. And the adversaries of the plan, promulgated by the convention, would have given a better impression of their candour, if they had confined themselves to showing, that the internal structure of the proposed government, was such as to render it unworthy of the confidence of the people. They ought not to have wandered into inflammatory declamations and unmeaning cavils, about the extent of the powers. The POWERS are not too extensive for the OBJECTS of federal administration, or, in other words, for the management of our NATIONAL INTERESTS; nor can any satisfactory argument be framed, to show that they are chargeable with such an excess. If it be true, as has been insinuated by some of the writers on the other side, that the difficulty arises from the nature of the thing, and that the extent of the country will not permit us to form a government, in which such ample powers can safely be reposed, it would prove that we ought to contract our views, and resort to the expedient of separate confederacies, which will move within more practicable spheres. For the absurdity must continually stare us in the face, of confiding to a government the direction of the most essential national concerns, without daring to trust it with the authorities which are indispensable to their proper and efficient management. Let us not attempt to reconcile contradictions, but firmly embrace a rational alternative.

I trust, however, that the impracticability of one general system cannot be shown. I am greatly mistaken, if any thing of weight has yet been advanced of this tendency; and I flatter myself, that the observations, which have been made in the course of these papers, have served to place the reverse of that position in as clear a light as any matter, still in the womb of time and experience, is susceptible of. This, at all events, must be evident, that the very difficulty itself, drawn from the extent of the country, is the strongest argument in favour of an energetic government; for any other can certainly never preserve the union of so large an empire. If we embrace, as the standard of our political creed, the tenets of those, who oppose the adoption of the proposed constitution, we cannot fail to verify the gloomy doctrines, which predict the impracticability of a national system, pervading the entire limits of the present confederacy.

PUBLIUS.

THE FEDERALIST.

NUMBER XXIV.

NEW YORK, DECEMBER 19, 1787.

HAMILTON.

THE SUBJECT CONTINUED, WITH AN ANSWER TO AN OBJECTION
CONCERNING STANDING ARMIES.

To the powers proposed to be conferred upon the federal government, in respect to the creation and direction of the national forces, I have met with but one specific objection; which is, that proper provision has not been made against the existence of standing armies in time of peace: An objection which I shall now endeavour to show, rests on weak and unsubstantial foundations.

It has indeed been brought forward in the most vague and general form, supported only by bold assertions, without the appearance of argument; without even the sanction of theoretical opinions, in contradiction to the practice of other free nations, and to the general sense of America, as expressed in most of the existing constitutions. The propriety of this remark will appear, the moment it is recollected that the objection under consideration turns upon a supposed necessity of restraining the LEGISLATIVE authority of the nation, in the article of military establishments; a principle unheard of, except in one or two of our state constitutions, and rejected in all the rest.

A stranger to our politics, who was to read our newspapers at the present juncture, without having previously inspected the plan reported by the convention, would be naturally led to one of two conclusions: either that it contained a positive injunction, that standing armies should be kept up in time of peace; or, that it vested in the EXECUTIVE the whole power of levying troops, without subjecting his discretion in any shape to the control of the legislature.

If he came afterwards to peruse the plan itself, he would be surprised to discover, that neither the one nor the other was the case; that the whole power of raising armies was lodged in the *legislature*, not in the *executive*; that this legislature was to be a popular body, consisting of the representatives of the people periodically elected; and that instead of the provision he had supposed in favour of standing armies, there was to be found in respect to this object, an important qualification even of the legislative discretion, in that clause which forbids the appropriation of money for the support of an army for any longer period than two years: A precaution which, upon a nearer view of it, will appear to be a great and real security against military establishments without evident necessity.

Disappointed in his first surmise, the person I have supposed would be apt to pursue his conjectures a little further. He would naturally say to himself, it is impossible that all this vehement and pathetic declamation can be without some colourable pretext. It must needs be that this people, so jealous of their liberties, have, in all the preceding models of the constitutions which they have established, inserted the most precise and rigid precautions on this point, the omission of which in the new plan, has given birth to all this apprehension and clamour.

If, under this impression, he proceeded to pass in review the several state constitutions, how great would be his disappointment to find that *two only* of them* contained an interdiction of

---

* This statement of the matter is taken from the printed collections of state constitutions. Pennsylvania and North-Carolina, are the two which contain the interdiction in these words: "As standing armies in time of peace are dangerous to liberty, THEY OUGHT NOT to be kept up." This is, in truth, rather a CAUTION than a PROHIBITION. New-Hampshire, Massachusetts,

standing armies in time of peace; that the other eleven had either observed a profound silence on the subject, or had in express terms admitted the right of the legislature to authorize their existence.

Still, however, he would be persuaded that there must be some plausible foundation, for the cry raised on this head. He would never be able to imagine, while any source of information remained unexplored, that it was nothing more than an experiment upon the public credulity, dictated either by a deliberate intention to deceive, or by the overflowings of a zeal too intemperate to be ingenuous. It would probably occur to him, that he would be likely to find the precautions he was in search of, in the primitive compact between the states. Here, at length, he would expect to meet with a solution of the enigma. No doubt, he would observe to himself, the existing confederation must contain the most explicit provisions against military establishments in time of peace; and a departure from this model in a favourite point, has occasioned the discontent, which appears to influence these political champions.

If he should now apply himself to a careful and critical survey of the articles of confederation, his astonishment would not only be increased, but would acquire a mixture of indignation, at the unexpected discovery, that these articles, instead of containing the prohibition he looked for, and though they had, with jealous circumspection, restricted the authority of the state legislatures in this particular, had not imposed a single restraint on that of the United States. If he happened to be a man of quick sensibility, or ardent temper, he could now no longer refrain from pronouncing

Delaware, and Maryland, have in each of their bills of rights a clause to this effect: "Standing armies are dangerous to liberty, and ought not to be raised or kept up WITHOUT THE CONSENT OF THE LEGISLATURE;" which is a formal admission of the authority of the legislature. New-York has no bill of rights, and her constitution says not a word about the matter. No bills of rights appear annexed to the constitutions of the other states, and their constitutions are equally silent. I am told, however, that one or two states have bills of rights, which do not appear in this collection; but that those also recognize the right of the legislative authority in this respect.

24

these clamours to be, the dishonest artifices of a sinister and unprincipled opposition, to a plan which ought at least to receive a fair and candid examination from all sincere lovers of their country! How else, he would say, could the authors of them have been tempted to vent such loud censures upon that plan, about a point, in which it seems to have conformed itself to the general sense of America as declared in its different forms of government, and in which it has even superadded a new and powerful guard unknown to any of them? If, on the contrary, he happened to be a man of calm and dispassionate feelings, he would indulge a sigh for the frailty of human nature, and would lament, that in a matter so interesting to the happiness of millions, the true merits of the question should be perplexed, and obscured by expedients so unfriendly to an impartial and right determination. Even such a man could hardly forbear remarking, that a conduct of this kind, has too much the appearance, of an intention to mislead the people by alarming their passions, rather than to convince them by arguments addressed to their understandings.

But however little this objection may be countenanced, even by precedents among ourselves, it may be satisfactory to take a nearer view of its intrinsic merits. From a close examination, it will appear, that restraints upon the discretion of the legislature, in respect to military establishments, would be improper to be imposed; and if imposed, from the necessities of society, would be unlikely to be observed.

Though a wide ocean separates the United States from Europe, yet there are various considerations that warn us against an excess of confidence or security. On one side of us, stretching far into our rear, are growing settlements subject to the dominion of Britain. On the other side, and extending to meet the British settlements, are colonies and establishments subject to the dominion of Spain. This situation, and the vicinity of the West-India islands, belonging to these two powers, create between them, in respect to their American possessions, and in relation to us, a common interest. The savage tribes on our western frontier, ought to be regarded as our natural enemies;

their natural allies: because they have most to fear from us, and most to hope from them. The improvements in the art of navigation, have, as to the facility of communication, rendered distant nations, in a great measure, neighbours. Britain and Spain, are among the principal maritime powers of Europe. A future concert of views between these nations, ought not to be regarded as improbable. The increasing remoteness of consanguinity, is every day diminishing the force of the family compact between France and Spain. And politicians have ever, with great reason, considered the ties of blood, as feeble and precarious links of political connection. These circumstances, combined, admonish us not to be too sanguine in considering ourselves as entirely out of the reach of danger.

Previous to the revolution, and ever since the peace, there has been a constant necessity for keeping small garrisons on our western frontier. No person can doubt, that these will continue to be indispensable, if it should only be to guard against the ravages and depredations of the Indians. These garrisons must either be furnished by occasional detachments from the militia, or by permanent corps in the pay of the government. The first is impracticable; and if practicable, would be pernicious. The militia, in times of profound peace, would not long, if at all, submit to be dragged from their occupations and families, to perform that most disagreeable duty. And if they could be prevailed upon, or compelled to do it, the increased expense of a frequent rotation of service, and the loss of labour, and disconcertion of the industrious pursuits of individuals, would form conclusive objections to the scheme. It would be as burthensome and injurious to the public, as ruinous to private citizens. The latter resource of permanent corps in the pay of government, amounts to a standing army in time of peace; a small one, indeed, but not the less real for being small.

Here is a simple view of the subject, that shows us at once the impropriety of a constitutional interdiction of such establishments, and the necessity of leaving the matter to the discretion and prudence of the legislature.

In proportion to our increase in strength, it is probable, nay, it may be said certain, that Britain and Spain would augment their military establishments in our neighbourhood. If we should not be willing to be exposed, in a naked and defenceless condition, to their insults or encroachments, we should find it expedient to increase our frontier garrisons, in some ratio to the force by which our western settlements might be annoyed. There are, and will be, particular posts, the possession of which will include the command of large districts of territory, and facilitate future invasions of the remainder. It may be added, that some of those posts will be keys to the trade with the Indian nations. Can any man think it would be wise, to leave such posts in a situation to be at any instant seized by one or the other of two neighbouring and formidable powers? To act this part, would be to desert all the usual maxims of prudence and policy.

If we mean to be a commercial people, or even to be secure on our Atlantic side, we must endeavour, as soon as possible, to have a navy. To this purpose, there must be dock-yards and arsenals; and, for the defence of these, fortifications, and probably garrisons. When a nation has become so powerful by sea, that it can protect its dock-yards by its fleets, this supersedes the necessity of garrisons for that purpose; but where naval establishments are in their infancy, moderate garrisons will, in all likelihood, be found an indispensable security against descents for the destruction of the arsenals and dock-yards, and sometimes of the fleet itself.

PUBLIUS.

THE FEDERALIST.

NUMBER XXV.

NEW YORK, DECEMBER 22, 1787.

HAMILTON.

THE SUBJECT CONTINUED, WITH THE SAME VIEW.

IT may perhaps be urged, that the objects enumerated in the preceding number ought to be provided by the state governments, under the direction of the union. But this would be an inversion of the primary principle of our political association; as it would in practice transfer the care of the common defence from the federal head to the individual members: A project oppressive to some states, dangerous to all, and baneful to the confederacy.

The territories of Britain, Spain, and of the Indian nations in our neighbourhood, do not border on particular states; but encircle the union from MAINE to GEORGIA. The danger, though in different degrees, is therefore common. And the means of guarding against it, ought, in like manner, to be the objects of common councils, and of a common treasury. It happens that some states, from local situation, are more directly exposed. NEW-YORK is of this class. Upon the plan of separate provisions, New-York would have to sustain the whole weight of the establishments requisite to her immediate safety, and to the mediate, or ultimate protection of her neighbours. This would neither be equitable as it respected New-York, nor safe as it respected the other states. Various inconveniences would attend such a

system. The states, to whose lot it might fall to support the necessary establishments, would be as little able as willing, for a
considerable time to come, to bear the burthen of competent
provisions. The security of all, would thus be subjected to the
parsimony, improvidence, or inability of a part. If from the
resources of such part becoming more abundant, its provisions
should be proportionally enlarged, the other states would
quickly take the alarm at seeing the whole military force of the
union in the hands of two or three of its members; and those
probably amongst the most powerful. They would each choose to
have some counterpoise: and pretences could easily be contrived. In this situation, military establishments, nourished by
mutual jealousy, would be apt to swell beyond their natural or
proper size; and being at the separate disposal of the members,
they would be engines for the abridgment, or demolition, of the
national authority.

Reasons have been already given to induce a supposition, that
the state governments will too naturally be prone to a rivalship
with that of the union, the foundation of which will be the love
of power; and that in any contest between the federal head and
one of its members, the people will be most apt to unite with
their local government: If in addition to this immense advantage, the ambition of the members should be stimulated by the
separate and independent possession of military forces, it would
afford too strong a temptation, and too great facility to them to
make enterprises upon, and finally to subvert, the constitutional
authority of the union. On the other hand, the liberty of the people would be less safe in this state of things, than in that which
left the national forces in the hands of the national government.
As far as an army may be considered as a dangerous weapon of
power, it had better be in those hands, of which the people are
most likely to be jealous, than in those of which they are least
likely to be so. For it is a truth which the experience of all ages
has attested, that the people are commonly most in danger,
when the mean of injuring their rights are in the possession of
those of whom they entertain the least suspicion.

The framers of the existing confederation, fully aware of the danger to the union from the separate possession of military forces by the states, have in express terms, prohibited them from having either ships or troops, unless with the consent of congress. The truth is, that the existence of a federal government and military establishments, under state authority, are not less at variance with each other, than a due supply of the federal treasury, and the system of quotas and requisitions.

There are other views besides those already presented, in which the impropriety of restraints on the discretion of the national legislature will be equally manifest. The design of the objection, which has been mentioned, is to preclude standing armies in time of peace; though we have never been informed how far it is desired the prohibition should extend; whether to raising armies, as well as to *keeping them up*, in a season of tranquillity, or not. If it be confined to the latter, it will have no precise signification, and it will be ineffectual for the purpose intended. When armies are once raised, what shall be denominated "keeping them up," contrary to the sense of the constitution? What time shall be requisite to ascertain the violation? Shall it be a week, a month, a year? Or shall we say, they may be continued as long as the danger which occasioned their being raised continues? This would be to admit that they might be kept up *in time of peace*, against threatening or impending danger; which would be at once to deviate from the literal meaning of the prohibition, and to introduce an extensive latitude of construction. Who shall judge of the continuance of the danger? This must undoubtedly be submitted to the national government, and the matter would then be brought to this issue, that the national government, to provide against apprehended danger, might, in the first instance, raise troops, and might afterwards keep them on foot, as long as they supposed the peace or safety of the community was in any degree of jeopardy. It is easy to perceive, that a discretion so latitudinary as this, would afford ample room for eluding the force of the provision.

The utility of a provision of this kind, can only be vindicated on the hypothesis of a probability, at least possibility, of combination between the executive and legislature, in some scheme of usurpation. Should this at any time happen, how easy would it be to fabricate pretences of approaching danger? Indian hostilities instigated by Spain or Britain, would always be at hand. Provocations to produce the desired appearances, might even be given to some foreign power, and appeased again by timely concessions. If we can reasonably presume such a combination to have been formed, and that the enterprize is warranted by a sufficient prospect of success: the army when once raised, from whatever cause, or on whatever pretext, may be applied to the execution of the project.

If to obviate this consequence, it should be resolved to extend the prohibition to the *raising* of armies in time of peace, the United States would then exhibit the most extraordinary spectacle, which the world has yet seen—that of a nation incapacitated by its constitution to prepare for defence, before it was actually invaded. As the ceremony of a formal denunciation of war has of late fallen into disuse, the presence of an enemy within our territories must be waited for, as the legal warrant to the government to begin its levies of men for the protection of the state. We must receive the blow, before we could even prepare to return it. All that kind of policy by which nations anticipate distant danger, and meet the gathering storm, must be abstained from, as contrary to the genuine maxims of a free government. We must expose our property and liberty to the mercy of foreign invaders, and invite them by our weakness, to seize the naked and defenceless prey, because we are afraid that rulers, created by our choice, dependent on our will, might endanger that liberty, by an abuse of the means necessary to its preservation.

Here I expect we shall be told, that the militia of the country is its natural bulwark, and would at all times be equal to the national defence. This doctrine, in substance, had like to have lost us our independence. It cost millions to the United States, that might have been saved. The facts, which from our own experience forbid a reliance of this kind, are too recent to permit us to be the dupes of such a suggestion. The steady operations of war against a regular and disciplined army, can only be successfully conducted by a force of the same kind. Considerations of economy, not less than of stability and vigour, confirm this position. The American militia, in the course of the late war, have, by their valour on numerous occasions, erected eternal monuments to their fame; but the bravest of them feel and know, that the liberty of their country could not have been established by their efforts alone, however great and valuable they were. War, like most other things, is a science to be acquired and perfected by diligence, by perseverance, by time, and by practice.

All violent policy, as it is contrary to the natural and experienced course of human affairs, defeats itself. Pennsylvania at this instant affords an example of the truth of this remark. The bill of rights of that state declares, that standing armies are dangerous to liberty, and ought not to be kept up in time of peace. Pennsylvania nevertheless, in a time of profound peace, from the existence of partial disorders in one or two of her counties, has resolved to raise a body of troops; and in all probability, will keep them up as long as there is any appearance of danger to the public peace. The conduct of Massachusetts affords a lesson on the same subject, though on different ground. That state (without waiting for the sanction of congress, as the articles of the confederation require) was compelled to raise troops to quell a domestic insurrection, and still keeps a corps in pay to prevent a revival of the spirit of revolt. The particular constitution of Massachusetts opposed no obstacle to the measure; but the instance is still of use to instruct us, that cases are likely to occur under our governments, as well as under those of other nations, which will sometimes render a military force in time of peace, essential to the security of the society, and that it is therefore improper, in this respect, to control the legislative discretion. It also teaches us, in its application to the United States, how little the rights of a feeble government are likely to be respected, even by its own constituents. And it teaches us, in addition to the rest, how unequal are parchment provisions, to a struggle with public necessity.

It was a fundamental maxim with the Lacedemonian commonwealth, that the post of admiral should not be conferred twice on the same person. The Peloponnesian confederates, having suffered a severe defeat at sea from the Athenians, demanded Lysander, who had before served with success in that capacity, to command the combined fleets. The Lacedemonians, to gratify their allies, and yet preserve the semblance of an adherence to their ancient institutions, had recourse to the flimsy subterfuge of investing Lysander with the real power of admiral, under the nominal title of vice-admiral. This instance is selected from among a multitude that might be cited, to confirm the truth already advanced and illustrated by domestic examples; which is, that nations pay little regard to rules and maxims, calculated in their very nature to run counter to the necessities of society. Wise politicians will be cautious about fettering the government with restrictions, that cannot be observed; because they know, that every breach of the fundamental laws, though dictated by necessity, impairs that sacred reverence, which ought to be maintained in the breast of rulers towards the constitution of a country, and forms a precedent for other breaches, where the same plea of necessity does not exist at all, or is less urgent and palpable.

PUBLIUS.

THE FEDERALIST.

NUMBER XXVI.

NEW YORK, DECEMBER 22, 1787.

HAMILTON.

THE SUBJECT CONTINUED, WITH THE SAME VIEW.

It was a thing hardly to have been expected, that in a popular revolution, the minds of men should stop, at that happy mean, which marks the salutary boundary between POWER and PRIVILEGE, and combines the energy of government with the security of private rights. A failure in this delicate and important point, is the great source of the inconveniences we experience; and if we are not cautious to avoid a repetition of the error, in our future attempts to rectify and ameliorate our system, we may travel from one chimerical project to another; we may try change after change; but we shall never be likely to make any material change for the better.

The idea of restraining the legislative authority, in the means of providing for the national defence, is one of those refinements, which owe their origin to a zeal for liberty more ardent than enlightened. We have seen, however, that it has not had thus far an extensive prevalency; that even in this country, where it made its first appearance, Pennsylvania and North-Carolina, are the only two states by which it has been in any degree patronized; and that all the others have refused to give it the least countenance. They wisely judged that confidence must be placed somewhere; that the necessity of doing it, is

implied in the very act of delegating power: and that it is better
to hazard the abuse of that confidence than to embarrass the
government and endanger the public safety, by impolitic restrictions on the legislative authority. The opponents of the proposed
constitution, combat in this respect the general decision of
America; and instead of being taught by experience, the propriety of correcting any extremes, into which we may have heretofore run; they appear disposed to conduct us into others still
more dangerous, and more extravagant. As if the tone of government had been found too high, or too rigid, the doctrines
they teach are calculated to induce us to depress, or to relax it,
by expedients which upon other occasions, have been condemned or forborne. It may be affirmed without the imputation
of invective, that if the principles they inculcate on various
points, could so far obtain as to become the popular creed, they
would utterly unfit the people of this country for any species of
government whatever. But a danger of this kind is not to be
apprehended. The citizens of America have too much discernment to be argued into anarchy. And I am much mistaken, if
experience has not wrought a deep and solemn conviction in the
public mind, that greater energy of government is essential to
the welfare and prosperity of the community.

It may not be amiss in this place, concisely to remark the origin and progress of the idea, which aims at the exclusion of military establishments in time of peace. Though in speculative
minds, it may arise from a contemplation of the nature and tendency of such institutions, fortified by the events that have happened in other ages and countries; yet, as a national sentiment,
it must be traced to those habits of thinking which we derive
from the nation, from which the inhabitants of these states have
in general sprung.

In England, for a long time after the Norman conquest, the
authority of the monarch was almost unlimited. Inroads were
gradually made upon the prerogative, in favour of liberty, first
by the barons, and afterwards by the people, till the greatest
part of its most formidable pretensions became extinct. But it

was not till the revolution in 1688, which elevated the prince of
Orange to the throne of Great Britain, that English liberty was
completely triumphant. As incident to the undefined power of
making war, an acknowledged prerogative of the crown, Charles
II. had, by his own authority, kept on foot in time of peace a
body of 5,000 regular troops. And this number James II.
increased to 30,000; who were paid out of his civil list. At the
revolution, to abolish the exercise of so dangerous an authority,
it became an article of the bill of rights then framed, that "raising or keeping a standing army within the kingdom in time of
peace, *unless with the consent of parliament*, was against law."

In that kingdom, when the pulse of liberty was at its highest
pitch, no security against the danger of standing armies was
thought requisite, beyond a prohibition of their being raised or
kept up by the mere authority of the executive magistrate. The
patriots, who effected that memorable revolution, were too temperate, and too well informed, to think of any restraint on the
legislative discretion. They were aware, that a certain number
of troops for guards and garrisons, were indispensable; that no
precise bounds could be set to the national exigencies; that a
power equal to every possible contingency must exist somewhere in the government; and that when they referred the exercise of that power to the judgment of the legislature, they had
arrived at the ultimate point of precaution, which was reconcileable with the safety of the community.

From the same source, the people of America may be said to
have derived an hereditary impression of danger to liberty, from
standing armies in time of peace. The circumstances of a revolution, quickened the public sensibility on every point connected
with the security of popular rights; and in some instances raised
the warmth of our zeal beyond the degree, which consisted with
the due temperature of the body politic. The attempts of two of
the states, to restrict the authority of the legislature in the article of military establishments, are of the number of these
instances. The principles, which had taught us to be jealous of
the power of an hereditary monarch, were, by an injudicious

excess, extended to the representatives of the people in their popular assemblies. Even in some of the states, where this error was not adopted, we find unnecessary declarations, that standing armies ought not to be kept up, in time of peace, *without the consent of the legislature*; I call them unnecessary, because the reason, which had introduced a similar provision into the English bill of rights, is not applicable to any of the state constitutions. The power of raising armies at all, under those constitutions, can by no construction be deemed to reside any where else, than in the legislatures themselves; and it was superfluous, if not absurd, to declare, that a matter should not be done without the consent of a body, which alone had the power of doing it. Accordingly, in some of those constitutions, and among others, in that of the state of New-York, which has been justly celebrated, both in Europe and America, as one of the best of the forms of government established in this country, there is a total silence upon the subject.

It is remarkable, that even in the two states, which seem to have meditated an interdiction of military establishments in time of peace, the mode of expression made use of is rather monitory, than prohibitory. It is not said, that standing armies *shall not be* kept up, but that they *ought not* to be kept up in time of peace. This ambiguity of terms appears to have been the result of a conflict between jealousy and conviction, between the desire of excluding such establishments at all events, and the persuasion that an absolute exclusion would be unwise and unsafe.

Can it be doubted that such a provision, whenever the situation of public affairs was understood to require a departure from it, would be interpreted by the legislature into a mere admonition, and would be made to yield to the actual or supposed necessities of the state? Let the fact already mentioned with respect to Pennsylvania, decide. What then, it may be asked, is the use of such a provision, if it cease to operate, the moment there is an inclination to disregard it?

Let us examine whether there be any comparison, in point of

efficacy, between the provision alluded to, and that which is contained in the new constitution, for restraining the appropriations of money for military purposes, to the period of two years. The former, by aiming at too much, is calculated to effect nothing; the latter, by steering clear of an imprudent extreme, and by being perfectly compatible with a proper provision for the exigencies of the nation, will have a salutary and powerful operation.

The legislature of the United States will be *obliged*, by this provision, once at least in every two years, to deliberate upon the propriety of keeping a military force on foot; to come to a new resolution on the point; and to declare their sense of the matter, by a formal vote in the face of their constituents. They are not *at liberty* to vest in the executive department, permanent funds for the support of an army; if they were even incautious enough to be willing to repose in it so improper a confidence. As the spirit of party, in different degrees, must be expected to infect all political bodies, there will be, no doubt, persons in the national legislature willing enough to arraign the measures, and criminate the views of the majority. The provision for the support of a military force, will always be a favourable topic for declamation. As often as the question comes forward, the public attention will be roused and attracted to the subject, by the party in opposition: And if the majority should be really disposed to exceed the proper limits, the community will be warned of the danger, and will have an opportunity of taking measures to guard against it. Independent of parties in the national legislature itself, as often as the period of discussion arrived, the state legislatures, who will always be not only vigilant, but suspicious and jealous guardians of the rights of the citizens, against encroachments from the federal government, will constantly have their attention awake to the conduct of the national rulers, and will be ready enough, if any thing improper appears, to sound the alarm to the people, and not only to be the VOICE, but if necessary, the ARM of their discontent.

Schemes to subvert the liberties of a great community,

require time to mature them for execution. An army, so large as seriously to menace those liberties, could only be formed by progressive augmentations; which would suppose, not merely a temporary combination between the legislature and executive, but a continued conspiracy for a series of time. Is it probable that such a combination would exist at all? Is it probable that it would be persevered in, and transmitted through all the successive variations in the representative body, which biennial elections would naturally produce in both houses? Is it presumable, that every man, the instant he took his seat in the national senate, or house of representatives, would commence a traitor to his constituents, and to his country? Can it be supposed, that there would not be found one man, discerning enough to detect so atrocious a conspiracy, or bold or honest enough to apprise his constituents of their danger.? If such presumptions can fairly be made, there ought at once to be an end of all delegated authority. The people should resolve to recal all the powers they have heretofore parted with; and to divide themselves into as many states as there are counties, in order that they may be able to manage their own concerns in person.

If such suppositions could even be reasonably made, still the concealment of the design, for any duration, would be impracticable. It would be announced, by the very circumstance of augmenting the army to so great an extent, in time of profound peace. What colourable reason could be assigned, in a country so situated, for such vast augmentations of the military force? It is impossible that the people could be long deceived; and the destruction of the project, and of the projectors, would quickly follow the discovery.

It has been said, that the provision, which limits the appropriation of money for the support of an army to the period of two years, would be unavailing; because the executive, when once possessed of a force large enough to awe the people into submission, would find resources in that very force, sufficient to enable him to dispense with supplies from the votes of the legislature. But the question again recurs: Upon what pretence could he be put in possession of a force of that magnitude, in time of peace? If we suppose it to have been created in consequence of some domestic insurrection or foreign war, then it becomes a case not within the principle of the objection; for this is levelled against the power of keeping up troops in time of peace. Few persons will be so visionary, as seriously to contend that military forces ought not to be raised to quell a rebellion, or resist an invasion; and if the defence of the community, under such circumstances, should make it necessary to have an army, so numerous as to hazard its liberty, this is one of those calamities for which there is neither preventative nor cure. It cannot be provided against, by any possible form of government: It might even result from a simple league offensive and defensive; if it should ever be necessary for the confederates or allies, to form an army for common defence.

But it is an evil infinitely less likely to attend us in an united, than in a disunited state; nay, it may be safely asserted, that it is an evil altogether unlikely to attend us in the latter situation. It is not easy to conceive a possibility, that dangers so formidable can assail the whole union, as to demand a force considerable enough to place our liberties in the least jeopardy; especially if we take into view the aid to be derived from the militia, which ought always to be counted upon, as a valuable and powerful auxiliary. But in a state of disunion, as has been fully shown in another place, the contrary of this supposition would become not only probable, but almost unavoidable.

PUBLIUS.

THE FEDERALIST.

NUMBER XXVII.

NEW YORK, DECEMBER 26, 1787.

HAMILTON.

THE SUBJECT CONTINUED, WITH THE SAME VIEW.

IT has been urged, in different shapes, that a constitution of the kind proposed by the convention, cannot operate, without the aid of a military force to execute its laws. This, however, like most other things that have been alleged on that side, rests on mere general assertion, unsupported by any precise or intelligible designation of the reasons upon which it is founded. As far as I have been able to divine the latent meaning of the objectors, it seems to originate in a pre-supposition, that the people will be disinclined to the exercise of federal authority, in any matter of an internal nature. Waving any exception that might be taken to the inaccuracy, or in explicitness, of the distinction between internal and external, let us inquire what ground there is to pre-suppose that disinclination in the people. Unless we presume, at the same time, that the powers of the general government will be worse administered than those of the state governments, there seems to be no room for the presumption of ill will, disaffection, or opposition in the people. I believe it may be laid down as a general rule, that their confidence in, and their obedience to, a government, will commonly be proportioned to the goodness or badness of its administration. It must be admitted, that there are exceptions to this rule;

but these exceptions depend so entirely on accidental causes, that they cannot be considered as having any relation to the intrinsic merits or demerits of a constitution. These can only be judged of by general principles and maxims.

Various reasons have been suggested, in the course of these papers, to induce a probability, that the general government will be better administered, than the particular governments; the principal of which are, that the extension of the spheres of election will present a greater option, or latitude of choice, to the people; that, through the medium of the state legislatures, who are select bodies of men, and who are to appoint the members of the national senate, there is reason to expect, that this branch will generally be composed with peculiar care and judgment; that these circumstances promise greater knowledge, and more comprehensive information, in the national councils; and that, on account of the extent of the country from which will be drawn those to whose direction they will be committed, they will be less apt to be tainted by the spirit of faction, and more out of the reach of those occasional ill humours, or temporary prejudices and propensities, which, in smaller societies, frequently contaminate the public deliberations, beget injustice and oppression towards a part of the community, and engender schemes, which, though they gratify a momentary inclination or desire, terminate in general distress, dissatisfaction, and disgust. Several additional reasons of considerable force, will occur, to fortify that probability, when we come to survey, with a more critical eye, the interior structure of the edifice which we are invited to erect. It will be sufficient here to remark, that, until satisfactory reasons can be assigned to justify an opinion, that the federal government is likely to be administered in such a manner, as to render it odious or contemptible to the people, there can be no reasonable foundation for the supposition, that the laws of the union will meet with any greater obstruction from them, or will stand in need of any other methods to enforce their execution, than the laws of the particular members.

The hope of impunity, is a strong incitement to sedition, the dread of punishment, a proportionably strong discouragement to it. Will not the government of the union, which, if possessed of a due degree of power, can call to its aid the collective resources of the whole confederacy, be more likely to repress the *former* sentiment, and to inspire the *latter*, than that of a single state, which can only command the resources within itself? A turbulent faction in a state, may easily suppose itself able to contend with the friends to the government in that state; but it can hardly be so infatuated, as to imagine itself equal to the combined efforts of the union. If this reflection be just, there is less danger of resistance from irregular combinations of individuals, to the authority of the confederacy, than to that of a single member.

I will, in the first place, hazard an observation, which will not be the less just, because to some it may appear new; which is, that the more the operations of the national authority are intermingled in the ordinary exercise of government, the more the citizens are accustomed to meet with it in the common occurrences of their political life; the more it is familiarized to their sight, and to their feelings; the further it enters into those objects, which touch the most sensible cords, and put in motion the most active springs of the human heart; the greater will be the probability, that it will conciliate the respect and attachment of the community. Man is very much a creature of habit. A thing that rarely strikes his senses, will have but a transient influence upon his mind. A government continually at a distance and out of sight, can hardly be expected to interest the sensations of the people. The inference is, that the authority of the union, and the affections of the citizens towards it, will be strengthened, rather than weakened, by its extension to what are called matters of internal concern; and that it will have less occasion to recur to force, in proportion to the familiarity and comprehensiveness of its agency. The more it circulates through those channels and currents, in which the passions of mankind naturally flow, the less will it require the aid of the violent and perilous expedients of compulsion.

One thing, at all events, must be evident, that a government like the one proposed, would bid much fairer to avoid the necessity of using force, than the species of league contended for by most of its opponents; the authority of which should only operate upon the states in their political or collective capacities. It has been shown, that in such a confederacy, there can be no sanction for the laws but force; that frequent delinquencies in the members, are the natural offspring of the very frame of the government; and that as often as these happen, they can only be redressed, if at all, by war and violence.

The plan reported by the convention, by extending the authority of the federal head to the individual citizens of the several states, will enable the government to employ the ordinary magistracy of each, in the execution of its laws. It is easy to perceive, that this will tend to destroy, in the common apprehension, all distinction between the sources from which they might proceed; and will give the federal government the same advantage for securing a due obedience to its authority, which is enjoyed by the government of each state; in addition to the influence on public opinion, which will result from the important consideration, of its having power to call to its assistance and support the resources of the whole union. It merits particular attention in this place, that the laws of the confederacy, as to the *enumerated* and *legitimate* objects of its jurisdiction, will become the SUPREME LAW of the land; to the observance of which, all officers, legislative, executive, and judicial, in each state, will be bound by the sanctity of an oath. Thus the legislatures, courts, and magistrates, of the respective members, will be incorporated into the operations of the national government, *as far as its just and constitutional authority extends*; and will be rendered auxiliary to the enforcement of its laws.* Any man, who will pursue, by his own reflections, the consequences of this situation, will perceive, that if its powers are administered with

* The sophistry which has been employed, to show that this will tend to the destruction of the state governments will, in its proper place, be fully detected.

a common share of prudence, there is good ground to calculate upon a regular and peaceable execution of the laws of the union. If we will arbitrarily suppose the contrary, we may deduce any inferences we please from the supposition; for it is certainly possible, by an injudicious exercise of the authorities of the best government that ever was, or ever can be instituted, to provoke and precipitate the people into the wildest excesses. But though the adversaries of the proposed constitution should presume, that the national rulers would be insensible to the motives of public good, or to the obligations of duty; I would still ask them, how the interests of ambition, or the views of encroachment, can be promoted by such a conduct?

PUBLIUS.

THE FEDERALIST.

NUMBER XXVIII.

NEW YORK, DECEMBER 26, 1787.

HAMILTON.

THE SAME SUBJECT CONTINUED.

THAT there may happen cases, in which the national government may be under the necessity of resorting to force, cannot be denied. Our own experience has corroborated the lessons taught by the examples of other nations; that emergencies of this sort will sometimes exist in all societies, however constituted; that seditions and insurrections are, unhappily, maladies as inseparable from the body politic, as tumours and eruptions from the natural body; that the idea of governing at all times by the simple force of law, (which we have been told is the only admissible principle of republican government) has no place but in the reveries of those political doctors, whose sagacity disdains the admonitions of experimental instruction.

Should such emergencies at any time happen under the national government, there could be no remedy but force. The means to be employed, must be proportioned to the extent of the mischief. If it should be a slight commotion in a small part of a state, the militia of the residue would be adequate to its suppression: and the natural presumption is, that they would be ready to do their duty. An insurrection, whatever may be its immediate cause, eventually endangers all government: Regard to the public peace, if not to the rights of the union, would engage the citizens, to whom the contagion had not communicated itself, to oppose the insurgents: And if the general government should be found in practice conducive to the prosperity and felicity of the people, it were irrational to believe that they would be disinclined to its support.

If, on the contrary, the insurrection should pervade a whole state, or a principal part of it, the employment of a different kind of force might become unavoidable. It appears that Massachusetts found it necessary to raise troops for suppressing the disorders within that state; that Pennsylvania, from the mere apprehension of commotions among a part of her citizens, has thought proper to have recourse to the same measure. Suppose the state of New-York had been inclined to re-establish her lost jurisdiction over the inhabitants of Vermont; could she have hoped for success in such an enterprise, from the efforts of the militia alone? Would she not have been compelled to raise, and to maintain, a more regular force for the execution of her design? If it must then be admitted, that the necessity of recurring to a force different from the militia, in cases of this extraordinary nature, is applicable to the state governments themselves, why should the possibility, that the national government might be under a like necessity in similar extremities, be made an objection to its existence? Is it not surprising that men, who declare an attachment to the union in the abstract, should urge, as an objection to the proposed constitution, what applies with ten-fold weight to the plan for which they contend; and what, as far as it has any foundation in truth, is an inevitable consequence of civil society upon an enlarged scale? who would not prefer that possibility, to the unceasing agitations, and frequent revolutions, which are the continual scourges of petty republics?

Let us pursue this examination in another light. Suppose, in lieu of one general system, two or three, or even four confederacies were to be formed, would not the same difficulty oppose itself to the operations of either of these confederacies? Would not each of them be exposed to the same casualties; and, when these happened, be obliged to have recourse to the same expedients for upholding its authority, which are objected to a government for all the states? Would the militia, in this supposition, be more ready or more able to support the federal authority, than in the case of a general union? All candid and intelligent men must, upon due consideration, acknowledge, that the principle of the objection is equally applicable to either of the two cases; and that whether we have one government for all the states, or different governments for different parcels of them, or as many unconnected governments as there are states, there might sometimes be a necessity, to make use of a force constituted differently from the militia, to preserve the peace of the community, and to maintain the just authority of the laws against those violent invasions of them, which amount to insurrections and rebellions.

Independent of all other reasonings upon the subject, it is a full answer to those who require a more peremptory provision against military establishments in time of peace, to say, that the whole power of the proposed government is to be in the hands of the representatives of the people. This is the essential, and, after all, the only efficacious security for the rights and privileges of the people, which is attainable in civil society.*

If the representatives of the people betray their constituents, there is then no resource left but in the exertion of that original right of self-defence, which is paramount to all positive forms of government; and which, against the usurpation of the national rulers, may be exerted with an infinitely better prospect of success, than against those of the rulers of an individual state. In a single state, if the persons intrusted with supreme power become usurpers, the different parcels, subdivisions, or districts, of which it consists, having no distinct government in each, can take no regular measures for defence. The citizens must rush tumultuously to arms, without concert, without system, without resource; except in their courage and despair. The usurpers,

* Its full efficacy will be examined hereafter.

cloathed with the forms of legal authority, can too often crush the opposition in embryo. The smaller the extent of territory, the more difficult will it be for the people to form a regular, or systematic plan of opposition; and the more easy will it be to defeat their early efforts. Intelligence can be more speedily obtained of their preparations and movements; and the military force in the possession of the usurpers, can be more rapidly directed against the part where the opposition has begun. In this situation, there must be a peculiar coincidence of circumstances, to ensure success to the popular resistance.

The obstacles to usurpation, and the facilities of resistance, increase with the increased extent of the state; provided the citizens understand their rights, and are disposed to defend them. The natural strength of the people in a large community, in proportion to the artificial strength of the government, is greater than in a small; and of course more competent to a struggle with the attempts of the government to establish a tyranny. But in a confederacy, the people, without exaggeration, may be said to be entirely the masters of their own fate. Power being almost always the rival of power; the general government will, at all times, stand ready to check the usurpations of the state governments; and these will have the same disposition towards the general government. The people, by throwing themselves into either scale, will infallibly make it preponderate. If their rights are invaded by either, they can make use of the other, as the instrument of redress. How wise will it be in them, by cherishing the union, to preserve to themselves an advantage which can never be too highly prized!

It may safely be received as an axiom in our political system, that the state governments will, in all possible contingencies, afford complete security against invasions of the public liberty by the national authority. Projects of usurpation, cannot be masked under pretences, so likely to escape the penetration of select bodies of men, as of the people at large. The legislatures will have better means of information, they can discover the danger at a distance; and possessing all the organs of civil power, and the confidence of the people, they can at once adopt a regular plan of opposition, in which they can combine all the resources of the community. They can readily communicate with each other in the different states; and unite their common forces, for the protection of their common liberty.

The great extent of the country, is a further security. We have already experienced its utility, against the attacks of a foreign enemy. And it would have precisely the same effect against the enterprises of ambitious rulers in the national councils. If the federal army should be able to quell the resistance of one state, the distant states would have it in their power to make head with fresh forces. The advantages obtained in one place must be abandoned, to subdue the opposition in others; and the moment the part which had been reduced to submission was left to itself, its efforts would be renewed, and its resistance revive.

We should recollect, that the extent of the military force, must, at all events, be regulated by the resources of the country. For a long time to come, it will not be possible to maintain a large army; and as the means of doing this, increase, the population, and the natural strength of the community will proportionably increase. When will the time arrive, that the federal government can raise and maintain an army capable of erecting a despotism over the great body of the people of an immense empire; who are in a situation, through the medium of their state governments, to take measures for their own defence with all the celerity, regularity, and system, of independent nations? The apprehension may be considered as a disease, for which there can be found no cure in the resources of argument and reasoning.

PUBLIUS.

THE FEDERALIST.

NUMBER XXIX.

NEW YORK, JANUARY 11, 1788.

HAMILTON.

CONCERNING THE MILITIA.

THE power of regulating the militia, and of commanding its services in times of insurrection and invasion, are natural incidents to the duties of superintending the common defence, and of watching over the internal peace of the confederacy.

It requires no skill in the science of war to discern, that uniformity in the organization and discipline of the militia, would be attended with the most beneficial effects, whenever they were called into service for the public defence. It would enable them to discharge the duties of the camp, and of the field, with mutual intelligence and concert; an advantage of peculiar moment in the operations of an army; And it would fit them much sooner to acquire the degree of proficiency in military functions, which would be essential to their usefulness. This desirable uniformity can only be accomplished, by confiding the regulation of the militia, to the direction of the national authority. It is therefore with the most evident propriety, that the plan of the convention proposes to empower the union "to provide for organizing, arming, and disciplining the militia, and for governing such part of them as may be employed in the service of the United States, *reserving to the states respectively the appointment of the officers, and the authority of training the militia according to the discipline prescribed by Congress."*

Of the different grounds, which have been taken in opposition to this plan, there is none that was so little to have been expected, or is so untenable in itself, as the one from which this particular provision has been attacked. If a well regulated militia be the most natural defence of a free country, it ought certainly to be under the regulation, and at the disposal of that body, which is constituted the guardian of the national security. If standing armies are dangerous to liberty, an efficacious power over the militia, in the same body, ought, as far as possible, to take away the inducement and the pretext, to such unfriendly institutions. If the federal government can command the aid of the militia in those emergencies, which call for the military arm in support of the civil magistrate, it can the better dispense with the employment of a different kind of force. If it cannot avail itself of the former, it will be obliged to recur to the latter. To render an army unnecessary, will be a more certain method of preventing its existence, than a thousand prohibitions upon paper.

In order to cast an odium upon the power of calling forth the militia to execute the laws of the union, it has been remarked, that there is no where any provision in the proposed constitution for requiring the aid of the POSSE COMITATUS, to assist the magistrate in the execution of his duty; whence it has been inferred, that military force was intended to be his only auxiliary. There is a striking incoherence in the objections which have appeared, and sometimes even from the same quarter, not much calculated to inspire a very favourable opinion of the sincerity or fair dealing of their authors. The same persons who tell us in one breath, that the powers of the federal government will be despotic and unlimited, inform us in the next, that it has not authority sufficient even to call out the POSSE COMITATUS. The latter, fortunately, is as much short of the truth, as the former exceeds it. It would be as absurd to doubt, that a right to pass all laws *necessary* and *proper* to execute its declared powers, would include that of requiring the assistance of the citizens to the officers who may be intrusted with the execution of those laws; as it would be to believe, that a right to enact laws necessary and proper for the imposition and collection of taxes, would involve that of varying the rules of descent, and of the alienation of landed property, or of abolishing the trial by jury in cases relating to it. It being therefore evident, that the supposition of a want of power to require the aid of the POSSE COMITATUS is entirely destitute of colour, it will follow, that the conclusion which has been drawn from it, in its application to the authority of the federal government over the militia, is as uncandid, as it is illogical. What reason could there be to infer, that force was intended to be the sole instrument of authority, merely because there is a power to make use of it when necessary? What shall we think of the motives which could induce men of sense to reason in this extraordinary manner? How shall we prevent a conflict between charity and conviction?

By a curious refinement upon the spirit of republican jealousy, we are even taught to apprehend danger from the militia itself, in the hands of the federal government. It is observed, that select corps may be formed, composed of the young and the ardent, who may be rendered subservient to the views of arbitrary power. What plan for the regulation of the militia, may be pursued by the national government, is impossible to be foreseen. But so far from viewing the matter in the same light with those who object to select corps as dangerous, were the constitution ratified, and were I to deliver my sentiments to a member of the federal legislature on the subject of a militia establishment, I should hold to him in substance the following discourse:

"The project of disciplining all the militia of the United States, is as futile as it would be injurious, if it were capable of being carried into execution. A tolerable expertness in military movements, is a business that requires time and practice. It is not a day, nor a week, nor even a month that will suffice for the attainment of it. To oblige the great body of the yeomanry, and of the other classes of the citizens, to be under arms for the purpose of going through military exercises and evolutions, as often as might be necessary, to acquire the degree of perfection which would entitle them to the character of a well regulated militia, would be a real grievance to the people, and a serious public inconvenience and loss. It would form an annual deduction from the productive labour of the country, to an amount, which, calculating upon the present numbers of the people, would not fall far short of a million of pounds. To attempt a thing which would abridge the mass of labour and industry to so considerable an extent, would be unwise; and the experiment, if made, could not succeed, because it would not long be endured. Little more can reasonably be aimed at, with respect to the people at large, than to have them properly armed and equipped; and in order to see that this be not neglected, it will be necessary to assemble them once or twice in the course of a year.

"But, though the scheme of disciplining the whole nation must be abandoned as mischievous or impracticable; yet it is a matter of the utmost importance, that a well digested plan should, as soon as possible, be adopted for the proper establishment of the militia. The attention of the government ought particularly to be directed to the formation of a select corps of moderate size, upon such principles as will really fit it for service in case of need. By thus circumscribing the plan, it will be possible to have an excellent body of well trained militia, ready to take the field whenever the defence of the state shall require it. This will not only lessen the call for military establishments; but if circumstances should at any time oblige the government to form an army of any magnitude, that army can never be formidable to the liberties of the people, while there is a large body of citizens, little, if at all, inferior to them in discipline and the use of arms, who stand ready to defend their own rights, and those of their fellow citizens. This appears to me the only substitute that can be devised for a standing army; and the best possible security against it, if it should exist."

Thus differently from the adversaries of the proposed constitution should I reason on the same subject; deducing arguments of safety, from the very sources which they represent as fraught with danger and perdition. But how the national legislature may reason on the point, is a thing which neither they nor I can foresee.

There is something so far fetched, and so extravagant, in the idea of danger to liberty from the militia, that one is at a loss whether to treat it with gravity or with raillery; whether to consider it as a mere trial of skill, like the paradoxes of rhetoricians; as a disingenuous artifice, to instil prejudices at any price; or as the serious offspring of political fanaticism. Where, in the name of common sense, are our fears to end, if we may not trust our sons, our brothers, our neighbours, our fellow citizens? What shadow of danger can there be from men, who are daily mingling with the rest of their countrymen; and who participate with them in the same feelings, sentiments, habits and interests? What reasonable cause of apprehension can be inferred from a power in the union to prescribe regulations for the militia, and to command its services when necessary; while the particular states are to have the *sole and exclusive appointment of the officers?* If it were possible seriously to indulge a jealousy of the militia, upon any conceivable establishment under the federal government, the circumstance of the officers being in the appointment of the states, ought at once to extinguish it. There can be no doubt, that this circumstance will always secure to them a preponderating influence over the militia.

In reading many of the publications against the constitution, a man is apt to imagine that he is perusing some ill written tale or romance; which, instead of natural and agreeable images, exhibits to the mind nothing but frightful and distorted shapes—

"Gorgons, Hydras, and Chimeras dire;"

discoloring and disfiguring whatever it represents, and transforming every thing it touches into a monster.

A sample of this is to be observed in the exaggerated and improbable suggestions, which have taken place respecting the power of calling for the services of the militia. That of New-Hampshire is to be marched to Georgia, of Georgia to New-Hampshire, of New-York to Kentucky, and of Kentucky to Lake Champlain. Nay, the debts due to the French and Dutch, are to be paid in militia-men, instead of Louis d'ors and ducats. At one moment, there is to be a large army to lay prostrate the liberties of the people; at another moment, the militia of Virginia are to be dragged from their homes, five or six hundred miles, to tame the republican contumacy of Massachusetts; and that of Massachusetts is to be transported an equal distance, to subdue the refractory haughtiness of the aristocratic Virginians. Do the persons, who rave at this rate, imagine, that their art or their eloquence can impose any conceits or absurdities upon the people of America for infallible truths?

If there should be an army to be made use of as the engine of despotism, what need of the militia? If there should be no army, whither would the militia, irritated at being required to undertake a distant and distressing expedition, for the purpose of rivetting the chains of slavery upon a part of their countrymen, direct their course, but to the seat of the tyrants, who had meditated so foolish, as well as so wicked a project; to crush them in their imagined entrenchments of power, and make them an example of the just vengeance of an abused and incensed people? Is this the way in which usurpers stride to dominion over a numerous and enlightened nation? Do they begin by exciting the detestation of the very instruments of their intended usurpations? Do they usually commence their career by wanton and disgustful acts of power, calculated to answer no end, but to draw upon themselves universal hatred and execration? Are suppositions of this sort, the sober admonitions of discerning patriots to a discerning people? Or are they the inflammatory ravings of chagrined incendiaries, or distempered enthusiasts? If we were even to suppose the national rulers actuated by the most ungovernable ambition, it is impossible to believe that they would employ such preposterous means to accomplish their designs.

In times of insurrection, or invasion, it would be natural and proper, that the militia of a neighbouring state should be marched into another, to resist a common enemy, or to guard the republic against the violences of faction or sedition. This was frequently the case, in respect to the first object, in the course of the late war; and this mutual succour is, indeed, a principal end of our political association. If the power of affording it be placed under the direction of the union, there will be no danger of a supine and listless inattention to the dangers of a neighbour, till its near approach had superadded the incitements of self-preservation, to the too feeble impulses of duty and sympathy.

PUBLIUS.

THE FEDERALIST.

NUMBER XXX.

NEW YORK, DECEMBER 29, 1787.

HAMILTON.

CONCERNING TAXATION.

IT has been already observed, that the federal government ought to possess the power of providing for the support of the national forces; in which proposition was intended to be included the expense of raising troops, of building and equipping fleets, and all other expenses in any wise connected with military arrangements and operations. But these are not the only objects to which the jurisdiction of the union, in respect to revenue, must necessarily be impowered to extend. It must embrace a provision for the support of the national civil list; for the payment of the national debts contracted, or that may be contracted; and, in general, for all those matters which will call for disbursements out of the national treasury. The conclusion is, that there must be interwoven in the frame of the government, a general power of taxation in one shape or another.

Money is with propriety considered as the vital principle of the body politic; as that which sustains its life and motion, and enables it to perform its most essential functions. A complete power, therefore, to procure a regular and adequate supply of revenue, as far as the resources of the community will permit may be regarded as an indispensable ingredient in every constitution. From a deficiency in this particular, one of two evils must ensue; either the people must be subjected to continual plunder, as a substitute for a more eligible mode of supplying the public wants, or the government must sink into a fatal atrophy, and in a short course of time perish.

In the Ottoman or Turkish empire, the sovereign, though in other respects absolute master of the lives and fortunes of his subjects, has no right to impose a new tax. The consequence is, that he permits the bashaws or governors of provinces to pillage the people at discretion; and, in turn, squeezes out of them the sums of which he stands in need, to satisfy his own exigencies, and those of the state. In America, from a like cause, the government of the union has gradually dwindled into a state of decay, approaching nearly to annihilation. Who can doubt, that the happiness of the people in both countries would be promoted by competent authorities in the proper hands, to provide the revenues which the necessities of the public might require?

The present confederation, feeble as it is, intended to repose in the United States, an unlimited power of providing for the pecuniary wants of the union. But proceeding upon an erroneous principle, it has been done in such a manner, as entirely to have frustrated the intention. Congress, by the articles which compose that compact (as has been already stated) are authorized to ascertain and call for any sums of money necessary, in their judgment, to the service of the United States; and their requisitions, if conformable to the rule of apportionment, are, in every constitutional sense, obligatory upon the states. These have no right to question the propriety of the demand: no discretion beyond that of devising the ways and means of furnishing the sums demanded. But though this be strictly and truly the case; though the assumption of such a right would be an infringement of the articles of union: though it may seldom or never have been avowedly claimed; yet in practice it has been constantly exercised, and would continue to be so, as long as the revenues of the confederacy should remain dependent on the intermediate agency of its members. What the consequences of the system have been, is within the knowledge of every man, the least conversant in our public affairs, and has been abundantly unfolded in different parts of these inquiries. It is this which has chiefly contributed to reduce us to a situation, that affords ample cause of mortification to ourselves, and of triumph to our enemies.

What remedy can there be for this situation, but in a change of the system, which has produced it? in a change of the fallacious and delusive system of quotas and requisitions? What substitute can there be imagined for this *ignis fatuus* in finance, but that of permitting the national government to raise its own revenues by the ordinary methods of taxation, authorized in every well ordered constitution of civil government? Ingenious men may declaim with plausibility on any subject; but no human ingenuity can point out any other expedient to rescue us from the inconveniences and embarrassments, naturally resulting from defective supplies of the public treasury.

The more intelligent adversaries of the new constitution, admit the force of this reasoning; but they qualify their admission, by a distinction between what they call *internal*, and *external* taxations. The former they would reserve to the state governments; the latter, which they explain into commercial imposts, or rather duties on imported articles, they declare themselves willing to concede to the federal head. This distinction, however, would violate that fundamental maxim of good sense and sound policy, which dictates that every POWER ought to be proportionate to its OBJECT; and would still leave the general government in a kind of tutelage to the state governments, inconsistent with every idea of vigour or efficiency. Who can pretend that commercial imposts are, or would be, alone equal to the present and future exigencies of the union? Taking into the account the existing debt, foreign and domestic, upon any plan of extinguishment, which a man, moderately impressed with the importance of public justice and public credit could approve, in addition to the establishments, which all parties will acknowledge to be necessary, we could not reasonably ably flatter ourselves, that this resource alone, upon the most improved scale, would even suffice for its present necessities. Its future necessities admit not of calculation or limitation; and upon the principle more than once adverted to, the power of making provision for them as they arise, ought to be equally unconfined. I believe it may be regarded as a position, warranted by the history of mankind, that *in the usual progress of things, the necessities of a nation, in every stage of its existence, will be found at least equal to its resources.*

To say that deficiencies may be provided for by requisitions upon the states, is on the one hand to acknowledge that this system cannot be depended upon; and on the other hand, to depend upon it for every thing beyond a certain limit. Those who have carefully attended to its vices and deformities, as they have been exhibited by experience, or delineated in the course of these papers, must feel an invincible repugnancy to trusting the national interests, in any degree, to its operation. Whenever it is brought into activity, its inevitable tendency, must be to enfeeble the union, and sow the seeds of discord and contention between the federal head and its members, and between the members themselves. Can it be expected that the deficiencies would be better supplied in this mode, than the total wants of the union have heretofore been supplied, in the same mode? It ought to be recollected, that if less will be required from the states, they will have proportionably less means to answer the demand. If the opinions of those who contend for the distinction which has been mentioned, were to be received as evidence of truth, one would be led to conclude, that there was some known point in the economy of national affairs, at which it would be safe to stop, and to say: Thus far, the ends of public happiness will be promoted by supplying the wants of government, and all beyond this is unworthy of our care or anxiety. How is it possible that a government, half supplied and always necessitous, can fulfill the purposes of its institution; can provide for the security, advance the prosperity, or support the reputation of the commonwealth? How can it ever possess either energy or stability, dignity or credit, confidence at home, or respectability abroad? How can its administration be any thing else than a succession of expedients temporizing, impotent, disgraceful? How will it be able to avoid a frequent sacrifice of its engagements to immediate necessity? How can it undertake or execute any liberal or enlarged plans of public good?

Let us attend to what would be the effects of this situation, in the very first war in which we should happen to be engaged. We will presume, for argument sake, that the revenue arising from the import duties answers the purposes of a provision for the public debt, and of a peace establishment for the union. Thus circumstanced, a war breaks out. What would be the probable conduct of the government in such an emergency? Taught by experience, that proper dependence could not be placed on the success of requisitions; unable, by its own authority, to lay hold of fresh resources, and urged by considerations of national danger, would it not be driven to the expedient of diverting the funds already appropriated, from their proper objects, to the defence of the state? It is not easy to see how a step of this kind could be avoided; and if it should be taken, it is evident that it would prove the destruction of public credit at the very moment that it was become essential to the public safety. To imagine that at such a crisis credit might be dispensed with, would be the extreme of infatuation. In the modern system of war, nations the most wealthy, are obliged to have recourse to large loans. A country so little opulent as ours, must feel this necessity in a much stronger degree. But who would lend to a government, that prefaced its overtures for borrowing, by an act which demonstrated that no reliance could be placed on the steadiness of its measures for paying? The loans it might be able to procure, would be as limited in their extent, as burthensome in their conditions. They would be made upon the same principles that usurers commonly lend to bankrupt and fraudulent debtors—with a sparing hand, and at enormous premiums.

It may perhaps be imagined, that from the scantiness of the

resources of the country, the necessity of diverting the established funds in the case supposed, would exist; though the national government should possess an unrestrained power of taxation. But two considerations will serve to quiet all apprehensions on this head; one is, that we are sure the resources of the community in their full extent, will be brought into activity for the benefit of the union; the other is, that whatever deficiencies there may be, can without difficulty be supplied by loans.

The power of creating by its own authority, new funds from new objects of taxation, would enable the national government to borrow, as far as its necessities might require. Foreigners, as well as the citizens of America, could then reasonably repose confidence in its engagements; but to depend upon a government, that must itself depend upon thirteen other governments, for the means of fulfilling its contracts, when once its situation is clearly understood, would require a degree of credulity, not often to be met with in the pecuniary transactions of mankind, and little reconcileable with the usual sharp-sightedness of avarice.

Reflections of this kind may have trifling weight with men, who hope to see the halcyon scenes of the poetic or fabulous age realized in America; but to those who believe we are likely to experience a common portion of the vicissitudes and calamities, which have fallen to the lot of other nations, they must appear entitled to serious attention. Such men must behold the actual situation of their country with painful solicitude, and deprecate the evils which ambition or revenge might, with too much facility, inflict upon it.

PUBLIUS.

THE FEDERALIST.

NUMBER XXXI.

NEW YORK, JANUARY 1, 1788.

HAMILTON.

THE SAME SUBJECT CONTINUED.

IN disquisitions of every kind, there are certain primary truths, or first principles, upon which all subsequent reasonings must depend. These contain an internal evidence, which, antecedent to all reflection or combination, commands the assent of the mind. Where it produces not this effect, it must proceed either from some disorder in the organs of perception, or from the influence of some strong interest, or passion, or prejudice. Of this nature are the maxims in geometry, that the whole is greater than its part; that things equal to the same, are equal to one another; that two straight lines cannot inclose a space; and that all right angles are equal to each other. Of the same nature, are these other maxims in ethics and politics, that there cannot be an effect without a cause; that the means ought to be proportioned to the end; that every power ought to be commensurate with its object; that there ought to be no limitation of a power destined to effect a purpose, which is itself incapable of limitation. And there are other truths in the two latter sciences, which, if they cannot pretend to rank in the class of axioms, are such direct inferences from them, and so obvious in themselves, and so agreeable to the natural and unsophisticated dictates of common sense, that they challenge the assent of a sound and unbiassed mind, with a degree of force and conviction almost equally irresistible.

The objects of geometrical inquiry, are so entirely abstracted from those pursuits which stir up and put in motion the unruly passions of the human heart, that mankind, without difficulty, adopt not only the more simple theorems of the science, but even those abstruse paradoxes which, however they may appear susceptible of demonstration, are at variance with the natural conceptions which the mind, without the aid of philosophy, would be led to entertain upon the subject. The INFINITE DIVISIBILITY of matter, or in other words, the INFINITE divisibility of a FINITE thing, extending even to the minutest atom, is a point agreed among geometricians; though not less incomprehensible to common sense, than any of those mysteries in religion, against which the batteries of infidelity have been so industriously levelled.

But in the sciences of morals and politics, men are found far less tractable. To a certain degree, it is right and useful that this should be the case. Caution and investigation are a necessary armour against error and imposition. But this untractableness may be carried too far, and may degenerate into obstinacy, perverseness, or disingenuity. Though it cannot be pretended, that the principles of moral and political knowledge have, in general, the same degree of certainty with those of the mathematics; yet they have much better claims in this respect, than, to judge from the conduct of men in particular situations, we should be disposed to allow them. The obscurity is much oftener in the passions and prejudices of the reasoner, than in the subject. Men, upon too many occasions, do not give their own understandings fair play; but yielding to some untoward bias, they entangle themselves in words, and confound themselves in subtleties.

How else could it happen (if we admit the objectors to be sincere in their opposition) that positions so clear as those which manifest the necessity of a general power of taxation in the government of the union, should have to encounter any adversaries among men of discernment? Though these positions have been elsewhere fully stated, they will perhaps not be improperly recapitulated in this place, as introductory to an examination of what may have been offered by way of objection to them. They are in substance as follow:

A government ought to contain in itself every power requisite to the full accomplishment of the objects committed to its care, and to the complete execution of the trusts for which it is responsible; free from every other control, but a regard to the public good and to the sense of the people.

As the duties of superintending the national defence, and of securing the public peace against foreign or domestic violence, involve a provision for casualties and dangers, to which no possible limits can be assigned, the power of making that provision ought to know no other bounds than the exigencies of the nation, and the resources of the community.

As revenue is the essential engine by which the means of answering the national exigencies must be procured, the power of procuring that article in its full extent, must necessarily be comprehended in that of providing for those exigencies.

As theory and practice conspire to prove, that the power of procuring revenue is unavailing, when exercised over the states in their collective capacities, the federal government must of necessity be invested with an unqualified power of taxation in the ordinary modes.

Did not experience evince the contrary, it would be natural to conclude, that the propriety of a general power of taxation in the national government might safely be permitted to rest on the evidence of these propositions, unassisted by any additional arguments or illustrations. But we find, in fact, that the antagonists of the proposed constitution, so far from acquiescing in their justness or truth, seem to make their principal and most zealous effort against this part of the plan. It may therefore be satisfactory to analize the arguments with which they combat it.

Those of them which have been most laboured with that view,

seem in substance to amount to this: "It is not true, because the exigencies of the union may not be susceptible of limitation, that its power of laying taxes ought to be unconfined. Revenue is as requisite to the purposes of the local administrations, as to those of the union; and the former are at least of equal importance with the latter, to the happiness of the people. It is therefore as necessary, that the state governments should be able to command the means of supplying their wants, as, that the national government should possess the like faculty, in respect to the wants of the union. But an indefinite power of taxation in the *latter* might, and probably would, in time, deprive the *former* of the means of providing for their own necessities; and would subject them entirely to the mercy of the national legislature. As the laws of the union are to become the supreme law of the land; as it is to have power to pass all laws that may be NECESSARY for carrying into execution, the authorities with which it is proposed to vest it; the national government might at any time abolish the taxes imposed for state objects, upon the pretence of an interference with its own. It might allege a necessity of doing this, in order to give efficacy to the national revenues: And thus all the resources of taxation might, by degrees, become the subjects of federal monopoly, to the entire exclusion and destruction of the state governments."

This mode of reasoning, appears sometimes to turn upon the supposition of usurpation in the national government; at other times, it seems to be designed only as a deduction from the constitutional operation of its intended powers. It is only in the latter light, that it can be admitted to have any pretensions to fairness. The moment we launch into conjectures, about the usurpations of the federal government, we get into an unfathomable abyss, and fairly put ourselves out of the reach of all reasoning. Imagination may range at pleasure, till it gets bewildered amidst the labyrinths of an enchanted castle, and knows not on which side to turn to escape from the apparitions which itself has raised. Whatever may be the limits, or modifications, of the powers of the union, it is easy to imagine an endless train of possible dangers; and by indulging an excess of jealousy and timidity, we may bring ourselves to a state of absolute scepticism and irresolution. I repeat here what I have observed in substance in another place, that all observations, founded upon the danger of usurpation, ought to be referred to the composition and structure of the government, not to the nature and extent of its powers. The state governments, by their original constitutions, are invested with complete sovereignty. In what does our security consist against usurpations from that quarter? Doubtless in the manner of their formation, and in a due dependence of those who are to administer them upon the people. If the proposed construction of the federal government be found, upon an impartial examination of it, to be such as to afford, to a proper extent, the same species of security, all apprehensions on the score of usurpation ought to be discarded.

It should not be forgotten, that a disposition in the state governments, to encroach upon the rights of the union, is quite as probable as a disposition in the union to encroach upon the rights of the state governments. What side would be likely to prevail in such a conflict, must depend on the means which the contending parties could employ, towards insuring success. As in republics, strength is always on the side of the people; and as there are weighty reasons to induce a belief, that the state governments will commonly possess most influence over them, the natural conclusion is, that such contests will be most apt to end to the disadvantage of the union; and that there is greater probability of encroachments by the members upon the federal head, than by the federal head upon the members. But it is evident, that all conjectures of this kind, must be extremely vague and fallible; and that it is by far the safest course to lay them altogether aside; and to confine our attention wholly to the nature and extent of the powers, as they are delineated in the constitution. Every thing beyond this, must be left to the prudence and firmness of the people; who, as they will hold the scales in their own hands, it is to be hoped, will always take care to preserve the constitutional equilibrium between the general and the state governments. Upon this ground, which is evidently the true one, it will not be difficult to obviate the objections, which have been made to an indefinite power of taxation in the United States.

PUBLIUS.

THE FEDERALIST.

NUMBER XXXII.

NEW YORK, JANUARY 4, 1788.

HAMILTON.

THE SAME SUBJECT CONTINUED.

ALTHOUGH I am of opinion that there would be no real danger of the consequences to the state governments, which seem to be apprehended from a power in the union to control them in the levies of money; because I am persuaded that the sense of the people, the extreme hazard of provoking the resentments of the state governments, and a conviction of the utility and necessity of local administrations, for local purposes, would be a complete barrier against the oppressive use of such a power: Yet I am willing here to allow, in its full extent, the justness of the reasoning, which requires, that the individual states should possess an independent and uncontrolable authority to raise their own revenues for the supply of their own wants. And making this concession, I affirm that (with the sole exception of duties on imports and exports) they would, under the plan of the convention, retain that authority in the most absolute and unqualified sense; and that an attempt on the part of the national government to abridge them in the exercise of it, would be a violent assumption of power, unwarranted by any article or clause of its constitution.

An entire consolidation of the states into one complete national sovereignty, would imply an entire subordination of the parts; and whatever powers might remain in them, would be altogether dependent on the general will. But as the plan of the convention aims only at a partial union or consolidation, the state governments would clearly retain all the rights of sovereignty which they before had, and which were not, by that act, *exclusively* delegated to the United States. This exclusive delegation, or rather this alienation of state sovereignty, would only exist in three cases; where the constitution in express terms granted an exclusive authority to the union; where it granted, in one instance, an authority to the union; and in another, prohibited the states from exercising the like authority; and where it granted an authority to the union, to which a similar authority in the states would be absolutely and totally *contradictory* and *repugnant*. I use these terms to distinguish this last case from another which might appear to resemble it; but which would, in fact, be essentially different: I mean where the exercise of a concurrent jurisdiction, might be productive of occasional interferences in the *policy* of any branch of administration, but would not imply any direct contradiction or repugnancy in point of constitutional authority. These three cases of exclusive jurisdiction in the federal government, may be exemplified by the following instances: The last clause but one in the eighth section of the first article, provides expressly, that congress shall exercise "*exclusive legislation*" over the district to be appropriated as the seat of government. This answers to the first case. The first clause of the same section impowers congress "*to lay and collect taxes, duties, imposts, and excises;*" and the second clause of the tenth section of the same article declares, that "*no state shall*, without the consent of congress, *lay any imposts or duties on imports or exports*, expect for the purpose of executing its inspection laws." Hence would result an exclusive power in the union to lay duties on imports and exports, with the particular exception mentioned; but this power is abridged by another clause, which declares, that no tax or duty shall be laid on articles exported from any state; in consequence of which qualification, it now only extends to the *duties on imports*. This answers to the second case. The third will be found in that clause which declares, that congress shall have power "to establish an UNIFORM RULE of naturalization throughout the United States." This must necessarily be exclusive; because if each state had power to prescribe a DISTINCT RULE, there could be no UNIFORM RULE.

A case which may perhaps be thought to resemble the latter, but which is in fact widely different, affects the question immediately under consideration. I mean the power of imposing taxes on all articles other than exports and imports. This, I contend, is manifestly a concurrent and coequal authority in the United States and in the individual states. There is plainly no expression in the granting clause, which makes that power *exclusive* in the union. There is no independent clause or sentence which prohibits the states from exercising it. So far is this from being the case, that a plain and conclusive argument to the contrary is deducible, from the restraint laid upon the states in relation to duties on imports and exports. This restriction implies an admission, that if it were not inserted, the states would possess the power it excludes, and it implies a further admission, that as to all other taxes, the authority of the states remains undiminished. In any other view it would be both unnecessary and dangerous; it would be unnecessary, because if the grant to the union of the power of laying such duties, implied the exclusion of the states, or even their subordination in this particular, there could be no need of such a restriction; it would be dangerous, because the introduction of it leads directly to the conclusion which has been mentioned, and which, if the reasoning of the objectors be just, could not have been intended; I mean that the states, in all cases to which the restriction did not apply, would have a concurrent power of taxation with the union. The restriction in question amounts to what lawyers call a NEGATIVE PREGNANT; that is, a *negation* of one thing, and an *affirmance* of another; a negation of the authority of the states to impose taxes on imports and exports, and an affirmance of their authority to impose them on all other articles. It would be mere

27

sophistry to argue that it was meant to exclude them *absolutely* from the imposition of taxes of the former kind, and to leave them at liberty to lay others *subject to the control* of the national legislature. The restraining or prohibitory clause only says, that they shall not, *without the consent of congress*, lay such duties; and if we are to understand this in the sense last mentioned, the constitution would then be made to introduce a formal provision, for the sake of a very absurd conclusion; which is, that the states, *with the consent* of the national legislature, might tax imports and exports; and that they might tax every other article, *unless controled* by the same body. If this was the intention, why was it not left, in the first instance, clause, conferring a general power of taxation upon the union? It is evident that this could not have been the intention, and that it will not bear a construction of the kind.

As to a supposition of repugnancy between the power of taxation in the states and in the union, it cannot be supported in that sense which would be requisite to work an exclusion of the states. It is indeed possible, that a tax might be laid on a particular article by a state, which might render it *inexpedient* that a further tax should be laid on the same article by the union; but it would not imply a constitutional inability to impose a further tax. The quantity of the imposition, the expediency or inexpediency of an increase on either side, would be mutually questions of prudence; but there would be involved no direct contradiction of power. The particular policy of the national and of the state system of finance, might now and then not exactly coincide, and might require reciprocal forbearances. It is not however a mere possibility of inconvenience in the exercise of powers, but an immediate constitutional repugnancy, that can by implication alienate and extinguish a pre-existing right of sovereignty.

The necessity of a concurrent jurisdiction in certain cases, results from the division of the sovereign power; and the rule that all authorities, of which the states are not explicitly divested in favour of the union, remain with them in full vigour, is not only a theoretical consequence of that division, but is clearly admitted by the whole tenor of the instrument which contains the articles of the proposed constitution. We there find, that notwithstanding the affirmative grants of general authorities, there has been the most pointed care in those cases where it was deemed improper that the like authorities should reside in the states, to insert negative clauses prohibiting the exercise of them by the states. The tenth section of the first article consists altogether of such provisions. This circumstance is a clear indication of the sense of the convention, and furnishes a rule of interpretation out of the body of the act, which justifies the position I have advanced, and refutes every hypothesis to the contrary.

PUBLIUS.

THE FEDERALIST.

NUMBER XXXIII.

NEW YORK, JANUARY 4, 1788.

HAMILTON.

THE SAME SUBJECT CONTINUED.

THE residue of the argument against the provisions of the constitution, in respect to taxation, is ingrafted upon the following clauses: The last clause of the eighth section of the first article, authorizes the national legislature "to make all laws which shall be *necessary* and *proper*, for carrying into execution *the powers* by that constitution vested in the government of the United States, or in any department or officer thereof;" and the second clause of the sixth article declares, that "the constitution and the laws of the United States made *in pursuance thereof*, and the treaties made by their authority, shall be the *supreme law* of the land; any thing in the constitution or laws of any state to the contrary notwithstanding."

These two clauses have been the sources of much virulent invective, and petulant declamation, against the proposed constitution; they have been held up to the people in all the exaggerated colours of misrepresentation, as the pernicious engines by which their local governments were to be destroyed, and their liberties exterminated—as the hideous monster whose devouring jaws would spare neither sex nor age, nor high nor low, nor sacred nor profane; and yet, strange as it may appear, after all this clamour, to those who may not have happened to contemplate them in the same light, it may be affirmed with perfect confidence, that the constitutional operation of the intended government would be precisely the same, if these clauses were entirely obliterated, as if they were repeated in every article. They are only declaratory of a truth, which would have resulted by necessary and unavoidable implication from the very act of constituting a federal government, and vesting it with certain specified powers. This is so clear a proposition, that moderation itself can scarcely listen to the railings which have been so copiously vented against this part of the plan, without emotions that disturb its equanimity.

What is a power, but the ability or faculty of doing a thing? What is the ability to do a thing, but the power of employing the *means* necessary to its execution? What is a LEGISLATIVE power, but a power of making LAWS? What are the *means* to execute a LEGISLATIVE power, but LAWS? What is the power of laying and collecting taxes, but a *legislative power*, or a power of *making laws*, to lay and collect taxes? What are the proper means of executing such a power, but *necessary* and *proper* laws?

This simple train of inquiry furnishes us at once with a test of the true nature of the clause complained of. It conducts us to this palpable truth, that a power to lay and collect taxes, must be a power to pass all laws *necessary* and *proper* for the execution of that power: and what does the unfortunate and calumniated provision in question do, more than declare the same truth; to wit, that the national legislature to whom the power of laying and collecting taxes had been previously given, might, in the execution of that power, pass all laws *necessary* and *proper* to carry it into effect? I have applied these observations thus particularly to the power of taxation, because it is the immediate subject under consideration, and because it is the most important of the authorities proposed to be conferred upon the union. But the same process will lead to the same result, in relation to all other powers declared in the constitution. And it is *expressly* to execute these powers, that the sweeping clause, as it has been affectedly called, authorizes the national legislature to pass all *necessary* and *proper* laws. If there be any thing exceptionable, it must be sought for in the specific powers, upon which this general declaration is predicated. The declaration itself, though it may be chargeable with tautology or redundancy, is at least perfectly harmless.

But SUSPICION may ask, why then was it introduced? The answer is, that it could only have been done for greater caution, and to guard against all cavilling refinements in those who might hereafter feel a disposition to curtail and evade the legitimate authorities of the union. The convention probably foresaw, what it has been a principal aim of these papers to inculcate, that the danger which most threatens our political welfare, is, that the state governments will finally sap the foundations of the union; and might therefore think it necessary, in so cardinal a point, to leave nothing to construction. Whatever may have been the inducement to it, the wisdom of the precaution is evident from the cry which has been raised against it; as that very cry betrays a disposition to question the great and essential truth which it is manifestly the object of that provision to declare.

But it may be again asked, who is to judge of the *necessity* and *propriety* of the laws to be passed for executing the powers of the union? I answer, first, that this question arises as well and as fully upon the simple grant of those powers, as upon the declaratory clause: and I answer, in the second place, that the national government, like every other, must judge, in the first instance, of the proper exercise of its powers; and its constituents in the last. If the federal government should overpass the just bounds of its authority, and make a tyrannical use of its powers; the people, whose creature it is, must appeal to the standard they have formed, and take such measures to redress the injury done to the constitution, as the exigency may suggest and prudence justify. The propriety of a law, in a constitutional light, must always be determined by the nature of the powers upon which it is founded. Suppose, by some forced construction of its authority (which indeed cannot easily be imagined) the federal legislature should attempt to vary the law of descent in any state; would it not be evident, that in making such an attempt, it had exceeded its jurisdiction, and infringed upon that of the state? Suppose, again, that upon the pretence of an interference with its revenues, it should undertake to abrogate a land tax, imposed by the authority of a state; would it not be equally evident, that this was an invasion of that concurrent jurisdiction in respect to this species of tax, which the constitution plainly supposes to exist in the state governments? If there ever should be a doubt on this head, the credit of it will be entirely due to those reasoners, who, in the imprudent zeal of their animosity to the plan of the convention, have laboured to envelope it in a cloud, calculated to obscure the plainest and simplest truths.

But it is said, that the laws of the union are to be the *supreme law* of the land. What inference can be drawn from this, or what would they amount to, if they were not to be supreme? It is evident they would amount to nothing. A LAW, by the very meaning of the term, includes supremacy. It is a rule, which those to whom it is prescribed are bound to observe. This results from every political association. If individuals enter into a state of society, the laws of that society must be the supreme regulator of their conduct. If a number of political societies enter into a larger political society, the laws which the latter may enact, pursuant to the powers intrusted to it by its constitution, must necessarily be supreme over those societies, and the individuals of whom they are composed. It would otherwise be a mere treaty, dependent on the good faith of the parties, and not a government; which is only another word for POLITICAL POWER AND SUPREMACY. But it will not follow from this doctrine, that acts of the larger society which are *not pursuant* to its constitutional powers, but which are invasions of the residuary authorities of the smaller societies, will become the supreme law of the land. These will be merely acts of usurpation, and will deserve to be treated as such. Hence we perceive, that the clause which declares the supremacy of the laws of the union, like the one we have just before considered, only declares a truth, which flows immediately and necessarily from the institution of a federal government. It will not, I presume, have escaped observation, that it *expressly* confines this supremacy to laws made *pursuant to the constitution*; which I mention merely as an instance of caution in the convention; since that limitation would have been to be understood, though it had not been expressed.

Though a law, therefore, laying a tax for the use of the United States would be supreme in its nature, and could not legally be opposed or controled; yet, a law abrogating or preventing the collection of a tax laid by the authority of a state, (unless upon imports and exports) would not be the supreme law of the land, but an usurpation of a power, not granted by the constitution. As far as an improper accumulation of taxes, on the same object, might tend to render the collection difficult or precarious, this would be a mutual inconvenience, not arising from a superiority or defect of power on either side, but from an injudicious exercise of power by one or the other, in a manner equally disadvantageous to both. It is to be hoped and presumed, however, that mutual interests would dictate a concert in this respect, which would avoid any material inconvenience. The inference from the whole is—that the individual states would, under the proposed constitution, retain an independent and uncontrolable authority to raise revenue to any extent of which they may stand in need, by every kind of taxation, except duties on imports and exports. It will be shown in the next paper, that this *concurrent jurisdiction* in the article of taxation, was the only admissible substitute for an entire subordination, in respect to this branch of power, of state authority to that of the union.

PUBLIUS.

THE FEDERALIST.

NUMBER XXXIV.

NEW YORK, JANUARY 4, 1788.

HAMILTON.

THE SAME SUBJECT CONTINUED.

I FLATTER myself it has been clearly shown in my last number, that the particular states, under the proposed constitution, would have CO-EQUAL authority with the union in the article of revenue, except as to duties on imports. As this leaves open to the states far the greatest part of the resources of the community, there can be no colour for the assertion, that they would not possess means as abundant as could be desired, for the supply of their own wants, independent of all external control. That the field is sufficiently wide, will more fully appear, when we come to develope the inconsiderable share of the public expenses, for which it will fall to the lot of the state governments to provide.

To argue upon abstract principles, that this co-ordinate authority cannot exist, would be to set up theory and supposition against fact and reality. However proper such reasonings might be, to show that a thing *ought not to exist*, they are wholly to be rejected, when they are made use of to prove that it does not exist, contrary to the evidence of the fact itself. It is well known, that in the Roman republic, the legislative authority in the last resort, resided for ages in two different political bodies; not as branches of the same legislature, but as distinct

and independent legislatures; in each of which an opposite interest prevailed; in one, the Patrician; in the other, the Plebeian.
Many arguments might have been adduced, to prove the unfitness of two such seemingly contradictory authorities, each having power to *annul* or *repeal* the acts of the other. But a man
would have been regarded as frantic, who should have
attempted at Rome to disprove their existence. It will readily be
understood, that I allude to the COMITIA CENTURIATA and the
COMITIA TRIBUTIA. The former, in which the people voted by centuries, was so arranged as to give a superiority to the Patrician
interest: In the latter, in which numbers prevailed, the Plebeian
interests had an entire predominancy. And yet these two legislatures co-existed for ages, and the Roman republic attained to
the pinnacle of human greatness.

In the case particularly under consideration, there is no such
contradiction as appears in the example cited; there is no power
on either side to annul the acts of the other. And in practice,
there is little reason to apprehend any inconvenience; because,
in a short course of time, the wants of the states will naturally
reduce themselves within *a very narrow compass*; and in the
interim, the United States will, in all probability, find it convenient to abstain wholly from those objects to which the particular states would be inclined to resort.

To form a more precise judgment of the true merits of this
question, it will be well to advert to the proportion between
the objects that will require a federal provision in respect to
revenue, and those which will require a state provision. We
shall discover that the former are altogether unlimited; and that
the latter are circumscribed within very moderate bounds. In
pursuing this inquiry, we must bear in mind, that we are not
to confine our view to the present period, but to look forward
to remote futurity. Constitutions of civil government, are
not to be framed upon a calculation of existing exigencies; but
upon a combination of these, with the probable exigencies of
ages, according to the natural and tried course of human affairs.
Nothing, therefore, can be more fallacious, than to infer the

extent of any power proper to be lodged in the national government, from an estimate of its immediate necessities. There ought to be a CAPACITY to provide for future contingencies, as they may happen; and as these are illimitable in their nature, so it is impossible safely to limit that capacity. It is true, perhaps, that a computation might be made, with sufficient accuracy to answer the purpose, of the quantity of revenue requisite to discharge the subsisting engagements of the union, and to maintain those establishments, which, for some time to come, would suffice in time of peace. But would it be wise, or would it not rather be the extreme of folly, to stop at this point, and to leave the government intrusted with the care of the national defence, in a state of absolute incapacity to provide for the protection of the community, against future invasions of the public peace, by foreign war or domestic convulsions? If we must be obliged to exceed this point where can we stop short of an indefinite power of providing for emergencies as they may arise? Though it be easy to assert, in general terms, the possibility of forming a rational judgment of a due provision against probable dangers; yet we may safely challenge those who make the assertion, to bring forward their data, and may affirm, that they would be found as vague and uncertain as any that could be produced to establish the probable duration of the world. Observations, confined to the mere prospects of internal attacks, can deserve no weight; though even these will admit of no satisfactory calculations: But if we mean to be a commercial people, it must form a part of our policy to be able one day to defend that commerce. The support of a navy, and of naval wars, would involve contingencies that must baffle all the efforts of political arithmetic.

Admitting that we ought to try the novel and absurd experiment in politics, of tying up the hands of government from offensive war, founded upon reasons of state: Yet, certainly, we ought not to disable it from guarding the community against the ambition or enmity of other nations. A cloud has been for some time hanging over the European world. If it should break forth into a storm, who can insure us, that in its progress, a part of its fury would not be spent upon us? No reasonable man would hastily pronounce that we are entirely out of its reach. Or if the combustible materials that now seem to be collecting, should be dissipated without coming to maturity; or if a flame should be kindled without extending to us; what security can we have that our tranquillity will long remain undisturbed from some other cause, or from some other quarter? Let us recollect, that peace or war will not always be left to our option; that however moderate or unambitious we may be, we cannot count upon the moderation, or hope to extinguish the ambition, of others. Who could have imagined, at the conclusion of the last war, that France and Britain, wearied and exhausted as they both were, would already have looked with so hostile an aspect upon each other? To judge from the history of mankind, we shall be compelled to conclude, that the fiery and destructive passions of war, reign in the human breast with much more powerful sway, than the mild and beneficent sentiments of peace; and that to model our political systems upon speculations of lasting tranquillity, would be to calculate on the weaker springs of the human character.

What are the chief sources of expense in every government? What has occasioned that enormous accumulation of debts with which several of the European nations are oppressed? The answer plainly is, wars and rebellions; the support of those institutions which are necessary to guard the body politic against these two most mortal diseases of society. The expenses arising from those institutions which relate to the mere domestic police of a state, to the support of its legislative, executive, and judiciary departments, with their different appendages, and to the encouragement of agriculture and manufactures, (which will comprehend almost all the objects of state expenditure) are insignificant in comparison with those which relate to the national defence.

In the kingdom of Great Britain, where all the ostentatious apparatus of monarchy is to be provided for, not above a fifteenth part of the annual income of the nation is appropriated to the class of expenses last mentioned; the other fourteen fifteenths are absorbed in the payment of the interest of debts, contracted for carrying on the wars in which that country has been engaged, and in the maintenance of fleets and armies. If, on the one hand, it should be observed, that the expenses incurred in the prosecution of the ambitious enterprises and vain-glorious pursuits of a monarchy, are not a proper standard by which to judge of those which might be necessary in a republic; it ought, on the other hand, to be remarked, that there should be as great a disproportion, between the profusion and extravagance of a wealthy kingdom in its domestic administration, and the frugality and economy, which, in that particular, become the modest simplicity of republican government. If we balance a proper deduction from one side, against that which it is supposed ought to be made from the other, the proportion may still be considered as holding good.

But let us take a view of the large debt which we have ourselves contracted in a single war, and let us only calculate on a common share of the events which disturb the peace of nations, and we shall instantly perceive, without the aid of any elaborate illustration, that there must always be an immense disproportion between the objects of federal and state expenditure. It is true, that several of the states, separately, are incumbered with considerable debts, which are an excrescence of the late war. But this cannot happen again, if the proposed system be adopted; and when these debts are discharged, the only call for revenue of any consequence, which the state governments will continue to experience, will be for the mere support of their respective civil lists; to which, if we add all contingencies, the total amount in every state, ought to fall considerably short of a million of dollars.

If it cannot be denied to be a just principle, that in framing a constitution of government for a nation, we ought, in those provisions which are designed to be permanent, to calculate, not on temporary, but on permanent causes of expense; our attention

would be directed to a provision in favour of the state governments, for an annual sum of about 1,000,000 of dollars; while the
exigencies of the union could be susceptible of no limits, even in
imagination. In this view of the subject, by what logic can it be
maintained, that the local governments ought to command, in
perpetuity, an *exclusive* source of revenue for any sum beyond
that which has been stated? To extend its power further, in
exclusion of the authority of the union, would be to take the
resources of the community out of those hands which stood in
need of them for the public welfare, in order to put them into
other hands, which could have no just or proper occasion for
them.

Suppose, then, the convention had been inclined to proceed
upon the principle of a repartition of the objects of revenue,
between the union and its members, in *proportion* to their comparative necessities; what particular fund could have been
selected for the use of the states, that would not either have
been too much or too little; too little for their present, too much
for their future wants? As to the line of separation between
external and internal taxes, this would leave to the states, at a
rough computation, the command of two thirds of the resources
of the community, to defray from a tenth to a twentieth of its
expenses; and to the union, one third of the resources of the
community, to defray from nine tenths to nineteen twentieths of
its expenses. If we desert this boundary, and content ourselves
with leaving to the states an exclusive power of taxing houses
and lands, there would still be a great disproportion between
the *means* and the *end*; the possession of one third of the
resources of the community, to supply, at most, one tenth of its
wants. If any fund could have been selected, and appropriated,
equal to, and not greater than, the object, it would have been
inadequate to the discharge of the existing debts of the particular states, and would have left them dependent on the union for
a provision for this purpose.

The preceding train of observations, will justify the position
which has been elsewhere laid down, that "A CONCURRENT JURIS-

DICTION in the article of taxation, was the only admissible substitute for an entire subordination, in respect to this branch of power, of state authority to that of the union." Any separation of the objects of revenue that could have been fallen upon, would have amounted to a sacrifice of the great INTERESTS of the union, to the POWER of the individual states. The convention thought the concurrent jurisdiction preferable to that subordination; and it is evident, that it has at least the merit of reconciling an indefinite constitutional power of taxation in the federal government, with an adequate and independent power in the states, to provide for their own necessities. There remain a few other lights, in which this important subject of taxation will claim a further consideration.

PUBLIUS.

THE FEDERALIST.

NUMBER XXXV.

NEW YORK, JANUARY 8, 1788.

HAMILTON.

THE SAME SUBJECT CONTINUED.

BEFORE we proceed to examine any other objections to an indefinite power of taxation in the union, I shall make one general remark; which is, that if the jurisdiction of the national government, in the article of revenue, should be restricted to particular objects, it would naturally occasion an undue proportion of the public burthens to fall upon those objects. Two evils would spring from this source—the oppression of particular branches of industry, and an unequal distribution of the taxes, as well among the several states, as among the citizens of the same state.

Suppose, as has been contended for, the federal power of taxation were to be confined to duties on imports; it is evident that the government, for want of being able to command other resources, would frequently be tempted to extend these duties to an injurious excess. There are persons who imagine that this can never be the case; since the higher they are, the more it is alleged they will tend to discourage an extravagant consumption, to produce a favourable balance of trade, and to promote domestic manufactures. But all extremes are pernicious in various ways. Exorbitant duties on imported articles, serve to beget a general spirit of smuggling; which is always prejudicial to the fair trader, and eventually to the revenue itself: They tend to render other classes of the community tributary, in an improper degree, to the manufacturing classes, to whom they give a premature monopoly of the markets: They sometimes force industry out of its most natural channels into others, in which it flows with less advantage. And in the last place, they oppress the merchant, who is often obliged to pay them himself, without any retribution from the consumer. When the demand is equal to the quantity of goods at market, the consumer generally pays the duty; but when the markets happen to be overstocked, a great proportion falls upon the merchant, and sometimes not only exhausts his profits, but breaks in upon his capital. I am apt to think, that a division of the duty, between the seller and the buyer, more often happens than is commonly imagined. It is not always possible to raise the price of a commodity, in exact proportion to every additional imposition laid upon it. The merchant, especially in a country of small commercial capital, is often under a necessity of keeping prices down, in order to a more expeditious sale.

The maxim, that the consumer is the payer, is so much oftener true than the reverse of the proposition, that it is far more equitable that the duties on imports should go into a common stock, than that they should redound to the exclusive benefit of the importing states. But it is not so generally true, as to render it equitable, that those duties should form the only national fund. When they are paid by the merchant, they operate as an additional tax upon the importing state; whose citizens pay their proportion of them in the character of consumers. In this view, they are productive of inequality among the states; which inequality would be increased with the increased extent of the duties. The confinement of the national revenues to this species of imposts, would be attended with inequality, from a different cause, between the manufacturing and the non-manufacturing states. The states which can go furthest towards the supply of their own wants, by their own manufactures, will not, according to their numbers or wealth, consume so great a proportion of imported articles, as those states which are not in the same favourable situation; they would not, therefore, in this mode alone, contribute to the public treasury in a ratio to their abilities. To make them do this, it is necessary that recourse be had to excises; the proper objects of which are particular kinds of manufactures. New-York is more deeply interested in these considerations, than such of her citizens, as contend for limiting the power of the union to external taxation, may be aware of. New-York is an importing state, and from a greater disproportion between her population and territory, is less likely, than some other states, speedily to become in any considerable degree a manufacturing state. She would of course suffer, in a double light, from restraining the jurisdiction of the union to commercial imposts.

So far as these observations tend to inculcate a danger of the import duties being extended to an injurious extreme, it may be observed, conformably to a remark made in another part of these papers, that the interest of the revenue itself would be a sufficient guard against such an extreme. I readily admit that this would be the case, as long as other resources were open; but if the avenues to them were closed, HOPE, stimulated by necessity, might beget experiments, fortified by rigorous precautions and additional penalties; which, for a time, might have the intended effect, till there had been leisure to contrive expedients to elude these new precautions. The first success would be apt to inspire false opinions; which it might require a long course of subsequent experience to correct. Necessity, especially in politics, often occasions false hopes, false reasonings, and a system of measures correspondently erroneous. But even if this supposed excess should not be a consequence of the limitation of the federal power of taxation, the inequalities spoken of would still ensue, though not in the same degree, from the other causes that have been noticed. Let us now return to the examination of objections.

One which, if we may judge from the frequency of its repetition, seems most to be relied on, is, that the house of represen-

tatives is not sufficiently numerous for the reception of all the
different classes of citizens; in order to combine the interests
and feelings of every part of the community, and to produce a
due sympathy between the representative body and its constituents. This argument presents itself under a very specious
and seducing form; and is well calculated to lay hold of the prejudices of those to whom it is addressed. But when we come to
dissect it with attention, it will appear to be made up of nothing
but fair sounding words. The object it seems to aim at, is in the
first place impracticable, and in the sense in which it is contended for, is unnecessary. I reserve for another place, the discussion of the question which relates to the sufficiency of the
representative body in respect to numbers; and shall content
myself with examining here the particular use which has been
made of a contrary supposition, in reference to the immediate
subject of our inquiries.

The idea of an actual representation of all classes of the people, by persons of each class, is altogether visionary. Unless it
were expressly provided in the constitution, that each different
occupation should send one or more members, the thing would
never take place in practice. Mechanics and manufacturers will
always be inclined, with few exceptions, to give their votes to
merchants, in preference to persons of their own professions or
trades. Those discerning citizens are well aware, that the
mechanic and manufacturing arts furnish the materials of mercantile enterprise and industry. Many of them, indeed, are
immediately connected with the operations of commerce. They
know that the merchant is their natural patron and friend; and
they are aware, that however great the confidence they may
justly feel in their own good sense, their interests can be more
effectually promoted by the merchant than by themselves. They
are sensible that their habits of life have not been such as to
give them those acquired endowments, without which, in a
deliberative assembly, the greatest natural abilities are for the
most part useless; and that the influence and weight, and superior acquirements of the merchants, render them more equal to

a contest with any spirit which might happen to infuse itself into the public councils, unfriendly to the manufacturing and trading interests. These considerations, and many others that might be mentioned, prove, and experience confirms it, that artizans and manufacturers, will commonly be disposed to bestow their votes upon merchants and those whom they recommend. We must therefore consider merchants as the natural representatives of all these classes of the community.

With regard to the learned professions, little need be observed; they truly form no distinct interest in society; and according to their situation and talents, will be indiscriminately the objects of the confidence and choice of each other, and of other parts of the community.

Nothing remains but the landed interest; and this, in a political view, and particularly in relation to taxes, I take to be perfectly united, from the wealthiest landlord, down to the poorest tenant. No tax can be laid on land which will not affect the proprietor of thousands of acres, as well as the proprietor of a single acre. Every land-holder will therefore have a common interest to keep the taxes on land as low as possible; and common interest may always be reckoned upon as the surest bond of sympathy. But if we even could suppose a distinction of interests between the opulent land-holder, and the middling farmer, what reason is there to conclude, that the first would stand a better chance of being deputed to the national legislature than the last? If we take fact as our guide, and look into our own senate and assembly, we shall find that moderate proprietors of land prevail in both; nor is this less the case in the senate, which consists of a smaller number than in the assembly, which is composed of a greater number. Where the qualifications of the electors are the same, whether they have to choose a small or a large number, their votes will fall upon those in whom they have most confidence; whether these happen to be men of large fortunes, or of moderate property, or of no property at all.

It is said to be necessary that all classes of citizens should have some of their own number in the representative body, in order that their feelings and interests may be the better understood and attended to. But we have seen that this will never happen under any arrangement that leaves the votes of the people free. Where this is the case, the representative body, with too few exceptions to have any influence on the spirit of the government, will be composed of land-holders, merchants, and men of the learned professions. But where is the danger that the interests and feelings of the different classes of citizens will not be understood, or attended to by these three descriptions of men? Will not the land-holder know and feel whatever will promote or injure the interests of landed property? and will he not, from his own interest in that species of property, be sufficiently prone to resist every attempt to prejudice or encumber it? Will not the merchant understand and be disposed to cultivate, as far as may be proper, the interests of the mechanic and manufacturing arts, to which his commerce is so nearly allied? Will not the man of the learned profession, who will feel a neutrality to the rivalships among the different branches of industry, be likely to prove an impartial arbiter between them, ready to promote either, so far as it shall appear to him conducive to the general interests of the community?

If we take into the account the momentary humours or dispositions which may happen to prevail in particular parts of the society, and to which a wise administration will never be inattentive, is the man whose situation leads to extensive inquiry and information less likely to be a competent judge of their nature, extent, and foundation, than one whose observation does not travel beyond the circle of his neighbours and acquaintances? Is it not natural that a man who is a candidate for the favour of the people, and who is dependent on the suffrages of his fellow citizens for the continuance of his public honours, should take care to inform himself of their dispositions and inclinations, and should be willing to allow them their proper degree of influence upon his conduct? This dependence, and the necessity of being bound himself, and his posterity, by the laws to which he gives his assent, are the true, and they are the strong cords of sympathy between the representative and the constituent.

There is no part of the administration of government that requires extensive information, and a thorough knowledge of the principles of political economy, so much as the business of taxation. The man who understands those principles best, will be least likely to resort to oppressive expedients, or to sacrifice any particular class of citizens to the procurement of revenue. It might be demonstrated that the most productive system of finance will always be the least burthensome. There can be no doubt that, in order to a judicious exercise of the power of taxation, it is necessary that the person in whose hands it is, should be acquainted with the general genius, habits, and modes of thinking, of the people at large, and with the resources of the country. And this is all that can be reasonably meant by a knowledge of the interests and feelings of the people. In any other sense, the proposition has either no meaning, or an absurd one. And in that sense, let every considerate citizen judge for himself, where the requisite qualification is most likely to be found.

PUBLIUS.

THE FEDERALIST.

NUMBER XXXVI.

NEW YORK, JANUARY 8, 1788.

HAMILTON.

THE SAME SUBJECT CONTINUED.

WE have seen that the result of the observations, to which the foregoing number has been principally devoted, is, that from the natural operation of the different interests and views of the various classes of the community, whether the representation of the people be more or less numerous, it will consist almost entirely of proprietors of land, of merchants, and of members of the learned professions, who will truly represent all those different interests and views. If it should be objected, that we have seen other descriptions of men in the local legislatures; I answer, that it is admitted there are exceptions to the rule, but not in sufficient number to influence the general complexion or character of the government. There are strong minds in every walk of life, that will rise superior to the disadvantages of situation, and will command the tribute due to their merit, not only from the classes to which they particularly belong, but from the society in general. The door ought to be equally open to all; and I trust, for the credit of human nature, that we shall see examples of such vigorous plants flourishing in the soil of federal, as well as of state legislation; but occasional instances of this sort, will not render the reasoning, founded upon the general course of things, less conclusive.

The subject might be placed in several other lights, that would all lead to the same result; and in particular it might be asked, what greater affinity or relation of interest can be conceived between the carpenter and blacksmith, and the linen manufacturer or stocking weaver, than between the merchant and either of them? It is notorious, that there are often as great rivalships between different branches of the mechanic or manufacturing arts, as there are between any of the departments of labour and industry; so that unless the representative body were to be far more numerous, than would be consistent with any idea of regularity or wisdom in its deliberations, it is impossible that what seems to be the spirit of the objection we have been considering, should ever be realized in practice. But I forbear to dwell longer on a matter, which has hitherto worn too loose a garb to admit even of an accurate inspection of its real shape or tendency.

There is another objection of a somewhat more precise nature, which claims our attention. It has been asserted that a power of internal taxation in the national legislature, could never be exercised with advantage, as well from the want of a sufficient knowledge of local circumstances, as from an interference between the revenue laws of the union, and of the particular states. The supposition of a want of proper knowledge, seems to be entirely destitute of foundation. If any question is depending in a state legislature, respecting one of the counties, which demands a knowledge of local details, how is it acquired? No doubt, from the information of the members of the county. Cannot the like knowledge be obtained in the national legislature, from the representatives of each state? And is it not to be presumed, that the men who will generally be sent there, will be possessed of the necessary degree of intelligence, to be able to communicate that information? Is the knowledge of local circumstances, as applied to taxation, a minute topographical acquaintance with all the mountains, rivers, streams, highways, and bye-paths in each state? or is it a general acquaintance with its situation, and resources—with the state of its agriculture, commerce, manufactures—with the nature of its products and consumptions—with the different degrees and kinds of its wealth, property and industry?

Nations in general, even under governments of the more popular kind, usually commit the administration of their finances to single men, or to boards composed of a few individuals, who digest and prepare, in the first instance, the plans of taxation; which are afterwards passed into law by the authority of the sovereign or legislature. Inquisitive, and enlightened statesmen, are every where deemed best qualified, to make a judicious selection of the objects proper for revenue: which is a clear indication, as far as the sense of mankind can have weight in the question, of the species of knowledge of local circumstances, requisite to the purposes of taxation.

The taxes intended to be comprised under the general denomination of internal taxes, may be subdivided into those of the *direct*, and those of the *indirect* kind. Though the objection be made to both, yet the reasoning upon it seems to be confined to the former branch. And indeed as to the latter, by which must be understood duties and excises on articles of consumption, one is at a loss to conceive, what can be the nature of the difficulties apprehended. The knowledge relating to them, must evidently be of a kind, that will either be suggested by the nature of the article itself, or can easily be procured from any well informed man, especially of the mercantile class. The circumstances that may distinguish its situation in one state, from its situation in another, must be few, simple, and easy to be comprehended. The principal thing to be attended to, would be to avoid those articles which had been previously appropriated to the use of a particular state; and there could be no difficulty in ascertaining the revenue system of each. This could always be known from the respective codes of laws, as well as from the information of the members of the several states.

The objection, when applied to real property, or to houses and lands, appears to have, at first sight, more foundation; but even in this view, it will not bear a close examination. Land taxes are commonly laid in one of two modes, either by *actual* valuations, permanent or periodical, or by occasional assessments, at the discretion, or according to the best judgment of certain officers, whose duty it is to make them. In either case, the EXECUTION of the business, which alone requires the knowledge of local details, must be confided to discreet persons in the character of commissioners or assessors, elected by the people, or appointed by the government for the purpose. All that the law can do, must be to name the persons, or to prescribe the manner of their election or appointment, to fix their numbers and qualifi- cations; and to draw the general outlines of their powers and duties. And what is there in all this, that cannot as well be per- formed by the national legislature, as by the state legislature? The attention of either, can only reach to general principles; local details, as already observed, must be referred to those who are to execute the plan.

But there is a simple point of view, in which this matter may be placed, that must be altogether satisfactory. The national leg- islature can make use of the *system of each state within that state*. The method of laying and collecting this species of taxes in each state, can, in all its parts, be adopted and employed by the federal government.

Let it be recollected, that the proportion of these taxes is not to be left to the discretion of the national legislature: but it is to be determined by the numbers of each state, as described in the second section of the first article. An actual census, or enumeration of the people, must furnish the rule; a circumstance which effectually shuts the door to partiality or oppression. The abuse of this power of taxation seems to have been provided against with guarded circumspection. In addition to the precaution just mentioned, there is a provision that "all duties, imposts, and excises, shall be UNIFORM throughout the United States."

It has been very properly observed, by different speakers and writers on the side of the constitution, that if the exercise of the power of internal taxation by the union, should be judged beforehand upon mature consideration, or should be discovered on experiment, to be really inconvenient, the federal government may forbear the use of it, and have recourse to requisitions in its stead. By way of answer to this, it has been triumphantly asked, why not in the first instance omit that ambiguous power, and rely upon the latter resource? Two solid answers may be given; the first is, that the actual exercise of the power, may be found both *convenient*, and *necessary*; for it is impossible to prove in theory, or otherwise than by the experiment, that it cannot be advantageously exercised. The contrary indeed, appears most probable. The second answer is, that the existence of such a power in the constitution, will have a strong influence in giving efficacy to requisitions. When the states know that the union can supply itself without their agency, it will be a powerful motive for exertion on their part.

As to the interference of the revenue laws of the union, and of its members; we have already seen that there can be no clashing or repugnancy of authority. The laws cannot, therefore, in a legal sense, interfere with each other; and it is far from impossible to avoid an interference even in the policy of their different systems. An effectual expedient for this purpose will be, mutually to abstain from those objects, which either side may have first had recourse to. As neither can *control* the other, each will have an obvious and sensible interest in this reciprocal forbearance. And where there is an *immediate* common interest, we may safely count upon its operation. When the particular debts of the states are done away, and their expenses come to be limited within their natural compass, the possibility almost of interference will vanish. A small land tax will answer the purposes of the states, and will be their most simple, and most fit resource.

Many spectres have been raised out of this power of internal taxation, to excite the apprehensions of the people—double sets of revenue officers—a duplication of their burthens by double taxations, and the frightful forms of odious and oppressive poll-taxes, have been played off with all the ingenious dexterity of political legerdemain.

As to the first point, there are two cases in which there can be no room for double sets of officers; one, where the right of imposing the tax is exclusively vested in the union, which applies to the duties on imports: the other, where the object has not fallen under any state regulation or provisions, which may be applicable to a variety of objects. In other cases, the probability is, that the United States will either wholly abstain from the objects pre-occupied for local purposes, or will make use of the state officers, and state regulations, for collecting the additional imposition. This will best answer the views of revenue, because it will save expense in the collection, and will best avoid any occasion of disgust to the state governments and to the people. At all events, here is a practicable expedient for avoiding such an inconvenience; and nothing more can be required than to show, that evils predicted do not necessarily result from the plan.

As to any argument derived from a supposed system of influence, it is a sufficient answer to say, that it ought not to be presumed; but the supposition is susceptible of a more precise answer. If such a spirit should infest the councils of the union, the most certain road to the accomplishment of its aim would be, to employ the state officers as much as possible, and to attach them to the union by an accumulation of their emoluments. This would serve to turn the tide of state influence into the channels of the national government, instead of making federal influence flow in an opposite and adverse current. But all suppositions of this kind are invidious, and ought to be banished from the consideration of the great question before the people. They can answer no other end than to cast a mist over the truth.

As to the suggestion of double taxation, the answer is plain.

The wants of the union are to be supplied in one way or another; if by the authority of the federal government, then it will not remain to be done by that of the state governments. The quantity of taxes to be paid by the community, must be the same in either case; with this advantage, if the provision is to be made by the union,—that the capital resource of commercial imposts, which is the most convenient branch of revenue, can be prudently improved to a much greater extent under federal, than under state regulation, and of course will render it less necessary to recur to more inconvenient methods; and with this further advantage, that as far as there may be any real difficulty in the exercise of the power of internal taxation, it will impose a disposition to greater care in the choice and arrangement of the means; and must naturally tend to make it a fixed point of policy in the national administration, to go as far as may be practicable in making the luxury of the rich tributary to the public treasury, in order to diminish the necessity of those impositions, which might create dissatisfaction in the poorer and most numerous classes of the society. Happy it is when the interest which the government has in the preservation of its own power, coincides with a proper distribution of the public burthens, and tends to guard the least wealthy part of the community from oppression!

As to poll taxes, I, without scruple, confess my disapprobation of them; and though they have prevailed from an early period in those states,* which have uniformly been the most tenacious of their rights, I should lament to see them introduced into practice under the national government. But does it follow, because there is a power to lay them, that they will actually be laid? Every state in the union has power to impose taxes of this kind; and yet in several of them they are unknown in practice. Are the state governments to be stigmatized as tyrannies, because they possess this power? If they are not, with what propriety

* The New-England States.

can the like power justify such a charge against the national
government, or even be urged as an obstacle to its adoption? As
little friendly as I am to this species of imposition, I still feel a
thorough conviction, that the power of having recourse to it,
ought to exist in the federal government. There are certain
emergencies of nations, in which expedients, that in the ordinary
state of things ought to be forborne, become essential to the
public weal. And the government, from the possibility of such
emergencies, ought ever to have the option of making use of
them. The real scarcity of objects in this country, which may be
considered as productive sources of revenue, is a reason peculiar
to itself, for not abridging the discretion of the national councils
in this respect. There may exist certain critical and tempestuous
conjunctures of the state, in which a poll tax may become an
inestimable resource. And as I know nothing to exempt this portion of the globe from the common calamities that have befallen
other parts of it, I acknowledge my aversion to every project
that is calculated to disarm the government of a single weapon,
which in any possible contingency might be usefully employed
for the general defence and security.

I have now gone through the examination of those powers,
proposed to be conferred upon the federal government, which
relate more peculiarly to its energy, and to its efficiency for
answering the great and primary objects of union. There are
others which, though omitted here, will, in order to render the
view of the subject more complete, be taken notice of under the
next head of our inquiries. I flatter myself the progress already
made, will have sufficed to satisfy the candid and judicious part
of the community, that some of the objections which have been
most strenuously urged against the constitution, and which were
most formidable in their first appearance, are not only destitute
of substance, but if they had operated in the formation of the
plan, would have rendered it incompetent to the great ends of
public happiness and national prosperity. I equally flatter
myself, that a further and more critical investigation of the sys-

tem, will serve to recommend it still more to every sincere and disinterested advocate for good government; and will leave no doubt with men of this character, of the propriety and expediency of adopting it. Happy will it be for ourselves, and most honourable for human nature, if we have wisdom and virtue enough, to set so glorious an example to mankind.

PUBLIUS.

THE FEDERALIST.

NUMBER XXXVII.

NEW YORK, JANUARY 15, 1788.

MADISON.

CONCERNING THE DIFFICULTIES WHICH THE CONVENTION MUST
HAVE EXPERIENCED IN THE FORMATION OF A PROPER PLAN.

IN reviewing the defects of the existing confederation, and
showing that they cannot be supplied by a government of less
energy than that before the public, several of the most important principles of the latter fell of course under consideration.
But as the ultimate object of these papers is, to determine
clearly and fully the merits of this constitution, and the expediency of adopting it, our plan cannot be completed without taking
a more critical and thorough survey of the work of the convention; without examining it on all its sides; comparing it in all its
parts, and calculating its probable effects.

That this remaining task may be executed under impressions
conducive to a just and fair result, some reflections must in this
place be indulged, which candour previously suggests.

It is a misfortune, inseparable from human affairs, that public
measures are rarely investigated with that spirit of moderation,
which is essential to a just estimate of their real tendency to
advance, or obstruct, the public good; and that this spirit is
more apt to be diminished than promoted, by those *occasions*
which require an unusual exercise of it. To those who have been
led by experience to attend to this consideration, it could not

appear surprising, that the act of the convention which recommends so many important changes and innovations, which may be viewed in so many lights and relations, and which touches the springs of so many passions and interests, should find or excite dispositions unfriendly, both on one side and on the other, to a fair discussion and accurate judgment of its merits. In some, it has been too evident from their own publications, that they have scanned the proposed constitution, not only with a predisposition to censure, but with a predetermination to condemn; as the language held by others, betrays an opposite predetermination or bias, which must render their opinions also of little moment in the question. In placing, however, these different characters on a level, with respect to the weight of their opinions, I wish not to insinuate that there may not be a material difference in the purity of their intentions. It is but just to remark in favour of the latter description, that as our situation is universally admitted to be peculiarly critical, and to require indispensably, that something should be done for our relief, the predetermined patron of what has been actually done, may have taken his bias from the weight of these considerations, as well as from considerations of a sinister nature. The predetermined adversary, on the other hand, can have been governed by no venial motive whatever. The intentions of the first may be upright, as they may on the contrary be culpable. The views of the last cannot be upright, and must be culpable. But the truth is, that these papers are not addressed to persons falling under either of these characters. They solicit the attention of those only, who add to a sincere zeal for the happiness of their country, a temper favourable to a just estimate of the means of promoting it.

Persons of this character will proceed to an examination of the plan submitted by the convention, not only without a disposition to find or to magnify faults; but will see the propriety of reflecting, that a faultless plan was not to be expected. Nor will they barely make allowances for the errours which may be chargeable on the fallibility to which the convention, as a body of men, were liable; but will keep in mind, that they themselves also are but men, and ought not to assume an infallibility in rejudging the fallible opinions of others.

With equal readiness will it be perceived, that besides these inducements to candour, many allowances ought to be made for the difficulties inherent in the very nature of the undertaking referred to the convention.

The novelty of the undertaking immediately strikes us. It has been shown in the course of these papers, that the existing confederation is founded on principles which are fallacious; that we must consequently change this foundation, and with it the superstructure resting upon it. It has been shown, that the other confederacies which could be consulted as precedents, have been vitiated by the same erroneous principles, and can therefore furnish no other light than that of beacons, which give warning of the course to be shunned, without pointing out that which ought to be pursued. The most that the convention could do in such a situation, was to avoid the errours suggested by the past experience of other countries, as well as of our own; and to provide a convenient mode of rectifying their own errours as future experience may unfold them.

Among the difficulties encountered by the convention, a very important one must have lain, in combining the requisite stability and energy in government, with the inviolable attention due to liberty, and to the republican form. Without substantially accomplishing this part of their undertaking, they would have very imperfectly fulfilled the object of their appointment, or the expectation of the public: yet that it could not be easily accomplished, will be denied by no one who is unwilling to betray his ignorance of the subject. Energy in government is essential to that security against external and internal dangers, and to that prompt and salutary execution of the laws, which enter into the very definition of good government. Stability in government is essential to national character, and to the advantages annexed to it, as well as to that repose and confidence in the minds of the people, which are among the chief blessings of civil society. An irregular and mutable legislation is not more an evil in itself, than it is odious to the people; and it may be pronounced with assurance, that the people of this country, enlightened as they are, with regard to the nature, and interested, as the great body of them are, in the effects of good government, will never be satisfied, till some remedy be applied to the vicissitudes and uncertainties, which characterize the state administrations. On comparing, however, these valuable ingredients with the vital principles of liberty, we must perceive at once the difficulty of mingling them together in their due proportions. The genius of republican liberty seems to demand on one side, not only that all power should be derived from the people; but that those entrusted with it should be kept in dependence on the people, by a short duration of their appointments; and that even during this short period, the trust should be placed not in a few, but in a number of hands. Stability, on the contrary, requires, that the hands, in which power is lodged, should continue for a length of time the same. A frequent change of men will result from a frequent return of elections; and a frequent change of measures, from a frequent change of men: whilst energy of government requires not only a certain duration of power, but the execution of it by a single hand.

How far the convention may have succeeded in this part of their work, will better appear on a more accurate view of it. From the cursory view here taken, it must clearly appear to have been an arduous part.

Not less arduous must have been the task of marking the proper line of partition, between the authority of the general, and that of the state governments. Every man will be sensible of this difficulty, in proportion as he has been accustomed to contemplate and discriminate objects, extensive and complicated in their nature. The faculties of the mind itself have never yet been distinguished and defined, with satisfactory precision, by all the efforts of the most acute and metaphysical philosophers. Sense, perception, judgment, desire, volition, memory, imagination, are found to be separated, by such delicate shades and minute gradations, that their boundaries have eluded the most subtle investigations, and remain a pregnant source of ingenious disquisition and controversy. The boundaries between the great kingdoms of nature, and, still more, between the various provinces, and lesser portions, into which they are subdivided, afford another illustration of the same important truth. The most sagacious and laborious naturalists have never yet succeeded, in tracing with certainty the line which separates the district of vegetable life, from the neighbouring region of unorganized matter, or which marks the termination of the former, and the commencement of the animal empire. A still greater obscurity lies in the distinctive characters, by which the objects in each of these great departments of nature have been arranged and assorted.

When we pass from the works of nature, in which all the delineations are perfectly accurate, and appear to be otherwise only from the imperfection of the eye which surveys them, to the institutions of man, in which the obscurity arises as well from the object itself, as from the organ by which it is contemplated; we must perceive the necessity of moderating still further our expectations and hopes from the efforts of human sagacity. Experience has instructed us, that no skill in the science of government has yet been able to discriminate and define, with sufficient certainty, its three great provinces, the legislative, executive, and judiciary; or even the privileges and powers of the different legislative branches. Questions daily occur in the course of practice, which prove the obscurity which reigns in these subjects, and which puzzle the greatest adepts in political science.

The experience of ages, with the continued and combined labours of the most enlightened legislators and jurists, have been equally unsuccessful in delineating the several objects and limits of different codes of laws, and different tribunals of justice. The precise extent of the common law, the statute law, the maritime law, the ecclesiastical law, the law of corporations, and other local laws and customs, remain still to be clearly and finally established in Great Britain, where accuracy in such subjects has been more industriously pursued than in any other part of the world. The jurisdiction of her several courts, general and local, of law, of equity, of admiralty, &c., is not less a source of frequent and intricate discussions, sufficiently denoting the indeterminate limits by which they are respectively circumscribed. All new laws, though penned with the greatest technical skill, and passed on the fullest and most mature deliberation, are considered as more or less obscure and equivocal, until their meaning be liquidated and ascertained by a series of particular discussions and adjudications. Besides the obscurity arising from the complexity of objects, and the imperfection of the human faculties, the medium through which the conceptions of men are conveyed to each other, adds a fresh embarrassment. The use of words is to express ideas. Perspicuity therefore requires, not only that the ideas should be distinctly formed, but that they should be expressed by words distinctly and exclusively appropriated to them. But no language is so copious as to supply words and phrases for every complex idea, or so correct as not to include many, equivocally denoting different ideas. Hence it must happen, that however accurately objects may be discriminated in themselves, and however accurately the discrimination may be conceived, the definition of them may be rendered inaccurate, by the inaccuracy of the terms in which it is delivered. And this unavoidable inaccuracy must be greater or less, according to the complexity and novelty of the objects defined. When the Almighty himself condescends to address mankind in their own language, his meaning, luminous as it must be, is rendered dim and doubtful, by the cloudy medium through which it is communicated.

Here, then, are three sources of vague and incorrect definitions; indistinctness of the object, imperfection of the organ of perception, inadequateness of the vehicle of ideas. Any one of these must produce a certain degree of obscurity. The convention, in delineating the boundary between the federal and state jurisdictions, must have experienced the full effect of them all.

To the difficulties already mentioned, may be added the interfering pretensions of the larger and smaller states. We cannot err, in supposing that the former would contend for a participation in the government, fully proportioned to their superiour wealth and importance; and that the latter would not be less tenacious of the equality at present enjoyed by them. We may well suppose, that neither side would entirely yield to the other, and consequently that the struggle could be terminated only by compromise. It is extremely probable also, that after the ratio of representation had been adjusted, this very compromise must have produced a fresh struggle between the same parties, to give such a turn to the organization of the government, and to the distribution of its powers, as would increase the importance of the branches, in forming which they had respectively obtained the greatest share of influence. There are features in the constitution which warrant each of these suppositions; and as far as either of them is well founded, it shows that the convention must have been compelled to sacrifice theoretical propriety, to the force of extraneous considerations.

Nor could it have been the large and small states only, which would marshal themselves in opposition to each other on various points. Other combinations, resulting from a difference of local position and policy, must have created additional difficulties. As every state may be divided into different districts, and its citizens into different classes, which give birth to contending interests and local jealousies; so the different parts of the United States are distinguished from each other, by a variety of circumstances, which produce a like effect on a larger scale. And although this variety of interests, for reasons sufficiently explained in a former paper, may have a salutary influence on the administration of the government, when formed; yet every one must be sensible of the contrary influence, which must have been experienced in the task of forming it.

Would it be wonderful, if under the pressure of all these difficulties, the convention should have been forced into some deviations from that artificial structure and regular symmetry, which an abstract view of the subject might lead an ingenious theorist to bestow on a constitution planned in his closet, or in his imagination? The real wonder is that so many difficulties should have been surmounted; and surmounted with an unanimity almost as unprecedented, as it must have been unexpected. It is impossible for any man of candour to reflect on this circumstance, without partaking of the astonishment. It is impossible, for the man of pious reflection, not to perceive in it a finger of that Almighty Hand, which has been so frequently and signally extended to our relief in the critical stages of the revolution.

We had occasion, in a former paper, to take notice of the repeated trials which have been unsuccessfully made in the United Netherlands, for reforming the baneful and notorious vices of their constitution. The history of almost all the great councils and consultations, held among mankind for reconciling their discordant opinions, assuaging their mutual jealousies, and adjusting their respective interests, is a history of factions, contentions, and disappointments; and may be classed among the most dark and degrading pictures, which display the infirmities and depravities of the human character. If, in a few scattered instances, a brighter aspect is presented, they serve only as exceptions to admonish us of the general truth; and by their lustre to darken the gloom of the adverse prospect, to which they are contrasted. In revolving the causes from which these exceptions result, and applying them to the particular instance before us, we are necessarily led to two important conclusions. The first is, that the convention must have enjoyed, in a very singular degree, an exemption from the pestilential influence of party animosities; the diseases most incident to deliberative bodies, and most apt to contaminate their proceedings. The second conclusion is, that all the deputations composing the convention were either satisfactorily accommodated by the final act; or were induced to accede to it, by a deep conviction of the necessity of sacrificing private opinions and partial interests to the public good; and by a despair of seeing this necessity diminished by delays, or by new experiments.

PUBLIUS.

THE FEDERALIST.

NUMBER XXXVIII.

NEW YORK, JANUARY 15, 1788.

MADISON.

THE SUBJECT CONTINUED, AND THE INCOHERENCE OF THE OBJECTIONS TO THE PLAN EXPOSED.

It is not a little remarkable, that in every case reported by ancient history, in which government has been established with deliberation and consent, the task of framing it has not been committed to an assembly of men; but has been performed by some individual citizen, of preeminent wisdom and approved integrity.

Minos, we learn, was the primitive founder of the government of Crete; as Zaleucus was of that of the Locrians. Theseus first, and after him Draco and Solon, instituted the government of Athens. Lycurgus was the lawgiver of Sparta. The foundation of the original government of Rome was laid by Romulus: and the work completed by two of his elective successors, Numa, and Tullus Hostilius. On the abolition of royalty, the consular administration was substituted by Brutus, who stepped forward with a project for such a reform, which, he alleged, had been prepared by Servius Tullius, and to which his address obtained the assent and ratification of the senate and people. This remark is applicable to confederate governments also. Amphyction, we are told, was the author of that which bore his name. The Achæan league received its first birth from Achæus, and its second from Aratus.

What degree of agency these reputed lawgivers might have in their respective establishments, or how far they might be clothed with the legitimate authority of the people, cannot, in every instance, be ascertained. In some, however, the proceeding was strictly regular. Draco appears to have been entrusted by the people of Athens, with indefinite powers to reform its government and laws. And Solon, according to Plutarch, was in a manner compelled, by the universal suffrage of his fellow-citizens, to take upon him the sole and absolute power of new modelling the constitution. The proceedings under Lycurgus were less regular; but as far as the advocates for a regular reform could prevail, they all turned their eyes towards the single efforts of that celebrated patriot and sage, instead of seeking to bring about a revolution, by the intervention of a deliberative body of citizens.

Whence could it have proceeded, that a people, jealous as the Greeks were of their liberty, should so far abandon the rules of caution, as to place their destiny in the hands of a single citizen? Whence could it have proceeded that the Athenians, a people who would not suffer an army to be commanded by fewer than ten generals, and who required no other proof of danger to their liberties than the illustrious merit of a fellow-citizen, should consider one illustrious citizen as a more eligible depository of the fortunes of themselves and their posterity, than a select body of citizens, from whose common deliberations more wisdom, as well as more safety, might have been expected? These questions cannot be fully answered, without supposing that the fears of discord and disunion among a number of counsellors, exceeded the apprehension of treachery or incapacity in a single individual. History informs us likewise, of the difficulties with which these celebrated reformers had to contend; as well as of the expedients which they were obliged to employ, in order to carry their reforms into effect. Solon, who seems to have indulged a more temporizing policy, confessed that he had not given to his countrymen the government best suited to their happiness, but most tolerable to their prejudices. And Lycurgus, more true to his object, was under the necessity of mixing a portion of violence with the authority of superstition; and of securing his final success, by a voluntary renunciation, first of his country, and then of his life.

If these lessons teach us, on one hand, to admire the improvement made by America on the ancient mode of preparing and establishing regular plans of government; they serve not less on the other, to admonish us of the hazards and difficulties incident to such experiments, and of the great imprudence of unnecessarily multiplying them.

Is it an unreasonable conjecture, that the errours which may be contained in the plan of the convention, are such as have resulted, rather from the defect of antecedent experience on this complicated and difficult subject, than from a want of accuracy or care in the investigation of it; and, consequently, such as will not be ascertained until an actual trial shall have pointed them out? This conjecture is rendered probable, not only by many considerations of a general nature, but by the particular case of the articles of confederation.

It is observable, that among the numerous objections and amendments suggested by the several states, when these articles were submitted for their ratification, not one is found, which alludes to the great and radical errour, which on actual trial has discovered itself. And if we except the observations which New Jersey was led to make, rather by her local situation, than by her peculiar foresight, it may be questioned whether a single suggestion was of sufficient moment to justify a revision of the system. There is abundant reason nevertheless to suppose, that immaterial as these objections were, they would have been adhered to with a very dangerous inflexibility in some states, had not a zeal for their opinions and supposed interests been stifled by the more powerful sentiment of self-preservation. One state, we may remember, persisted for several years in refusing her concurrence, although the enemy remained the whole period at our gates, or rather in the very bowels of our country. Nor was her pliancy in the end effected by a less motive, than the fear of being chargeable with protracting the public calamities, and endangering the event of the contest. Every candid reader will make the proper reflections on these important facts.

A patient, who finds his disorder daily growing worse, and that an efficacious remedy can no longer be delayed without extreme danger; after coolly revolving his situation, and the characters of different physicians, selects and calls in such of them as he judges most capable of administering relief, and best entitled to his confidence. The physicians attend: the case of the patient is carefully examined—a consultation is held: they are unanimously agreed, that the symptoms are critical; but that the case, with proper and timely relief, is so far from being desperate, that it may be made to issue in an improvement of his constitution. They are equally unanimous in prescribing the remedy, by which this happy effect is to be produced. The prescription is no sooner made known, however, than a number of persons interpose, and, without denying the reality or danger of the disorder, assure the patient that the prescription will be poison to his constitution, and forbid him under pain of certain death, to make use of it. Might not the patient reasonably demand, before he ventured to follow this advice, that the authors of it should at least agree among themselves on some other remedy to be substituted? And if he found them differing as much from one another, as from his first counsellors, would he not act prudently, in trying the experiment unanimously recommended by the latter, rather than in hearkening to those who could neither deny the necessity of a speedy remedy, nor agree in proposing one?

Such a patient, and in such a situation, is America at this moment. She has been sensible of her malady. She has obtained a regular and unanimous advice from men of her own deliberate choice. And she is warned by others against following this advice, under pain of the most fatal consequences. Do the monitors deny the reality of her danger? No. Do they deny the necessity of some speedy and powerful remedy? No. Are they agreed, are any two of them agreed, in their objections to the remedy proposed, or in the proper one to be substituted? Let them speak for themselves.

This one tells us, that the proposed constitution ought to be rejected, because it is not a confederation of the states, but a government over individuals. Another admits, that it ought to be a government over individuals, to a certain extent, but by no means to the extent proposed. A third does not object to the government over individuals, or to the extent proposed, but to the want of a bill of rights. A fourth concurs in the absolute necessity of a bill of rights, but contends that it ought to be declaratory, not of the personal rights of individuals, but of the rights reserved to the states in their political capacity. A fifth is of opinion, that a bill of rights of any sort would be superfluous and misplaced, and that the plan would be unexceptionable, but for the fatal power of regulating the times and places of election. An objector in a large state exclaims loudly against the unreasonable equality of representation in the senate. An objector in a small state is equally loud against the dangerous inequality in the house of representatives. From this quarter, we are alarmed with the amazing expense, from the number of persons who are to administer the new government. From another quarter, and sometimes from the same quarter, on another occasion, the cry is, that the congress will be but a shadow of a representation, and that the government would be far less objectionable, if the number and the expense were doubled. A patriot in a state that does not import or export, discerns insuperable objections against the power of direct taxation. The patriotic adversary in a state of great exports and imports, is not less dissatisfied that the whole burthen of taxes may be thrown on consumption. This politician discovers in the constitution a direct and irresistible tendency to monarchy: that is equally sure, it will end in aristocracy. Another is puzzled to say which of these shapes it will ultimately assume, but sees clearly it must be one or other of them: whilst a fourth is not wanting, who with no less confidence affirms, that the constitution is so far from having a bias towards either of these dangers, that the weight on that side will not be sufficient to keep it upright and firm against its opposite propensities. With another class of adversaries to the constitution, the language is, that the legislative, executive, and judiciary departments, are intermixed in such a manner, as to contradict all the ideas of regular government, and all the requisite precautions in favour of liberty. Whilst this objection circulates in vague and general expressions, there are not a few who lend their sanction to it. Let each one come forward with his particular explanation, and scarcely any two are exactly agreed on the subject. In the eyes of one, the junction of the senate with the president, in the responsible function of appointing to offices, instead of vesting this executive power in the executive alone, is the vicious part of the organization. To another, the exclusion of the house of representatives, whose numbers alone could be a due security against corruption and partiality in the exercise of such a power, is equally obnoxious. With another, the admission of the president into any share of a power, which must ever be a dangerous engine in the hands of the executive magistrate, is an unpardonable violation of the maxims of republican jealousy. No part of the arrangement, according to some, is more inadmissible than the trial of impeachments by the senate, which is alternately a member both of the legislative and executive departments, when this power so evidently belonged to the judiciary department. We concur fully, reply others, in the objection to this part of the plan, but we can never agree that a reference of impeachments to the judiciary authority would be an amendment of the errour: our principal dislike to the organization, arises from the extensive powers already lodged in that department. Even among the zealous patrons of a council of state, the most irreconcilable variance is discovered, concerning the mode in which it ought to be constituted. The demand of one gentleman is, that the council should consist of a small number, to be appointed by the most numerous branch of the legislature. Another would prefer a larger number, and considers it as a fundamental condition, that the appointment should be made by the president himself.

As it can give no umbrage to the writers against the plan of the federal constitution, let us suppose, that as they are the most zealous, so they are also the most sagacious, of those who think the late convention were unequal to the task assigned them, and that a wiser and better plan might and ought to be substituted. Let us further suppose, that their country should concur, both in this favourable opinion of their merits, and in their unfavourable opinion of the convention; and should accordingly proceed to form them into a second convention, with full powers, and for the express purpose of revising and remoulding the work of the first. Were the experiment to be seriously made, though it requires some effort to view it seriously even in fiction, I leave it to be decided by the sample of opinions just exhibited, whether, with all their enmity to their predecessors, they would, in any one point, depart so widely from their example, as in the discord and ferment that would mark their own deliberations; and whether the constitution, now before the public, would not stand as fair a chance for immortality, as Lycurgus gave to that of Sparta, by making its change to depend on his own return from exile and death, if it were to be immediately adopted, and were to continue in force, not until a BETTER, but until ANOTHER should be agreed upon by this new assembly of lawgivers.

It is a matter both of wonder and regret, that those who raise so many objections against the new constitution, should never call to mind the defects of that which is to be exchanged for it. It is not necessary that the former should be perfect: it is sufficient that the latter is more imperfect. No man would refuse to give brass for silver or gold, because the latter had some alloy in it. No man would refuse to quit a shattered and tottering habitation, for a firm and commodious building, because the latter had not a porch to it; or because some of the rooms might be a little larger or smaller, or the ceiling a little higher or lower than his fancy would have planned them.

But waving illustrations of this sort, is it not manifest, that most of the capital objections urged against the new system, lie with tenfold weight against the existing confederation? Is an indefinite power to raise money dangerous in the hands of a federal government? The present congress can make requisitions to any amount they please; and the states are constitutionally bound to furnish them. They can emit bills of credit as long as they will pay for the paper; they can borrow both abroad and at home, as long as a shilling will be lent. Is an indefinite power to raise troops dangerous? The confederation gives to congress that power also: and they have already begun to make use of it. Is it improper and unsafe to intermix the different powers of government in the same body of men? Congress, a single body of men, are the sole depository of all the federal powers. Is it particularly dangerous to give the keys of the treasury, and the command of the army, into the same hands? The confederation places them both in the hands of congress. Is a bill of rights essential to liberty? The confederation has no bill of rights. Is it an objection against the new constitution, that it empowers the senate, with the concurrence of the executive, to make treaties which are to be the laws of the land? The existing congress, without any such control, can make treaties which they themselves have declared, and most of the states have recognized, to be the supreme law of the land. Is the importation of slaves permitted by the new constitution for twenty years? By the old it is permitted forever.

I shall be told, that however dangerous this mixture of powers may be in theory, it is rendered harmless by the dependence of congress on the states for the means of carrying them into practice: that however large the mass of powers may be, it is in fact a lifeless mass. Then, say I, in the first place, that the confederation is chargeable with the still greater folly, of declaring certain powers in the federal government to be absolutely necessary, and at the same time rendering them absolutely nugatory; and, in the next place, that if the union is to continue, and no better government be substituted, effective powers must either be granted to, or assumed by, the existing congress; in either of which events, the contrast just stated will hold good. But this is not all. Out of this lifeless mass, has already grown an excrescent power, which tends to realize all the dangers that can be apprehended from a defective construction of the supreme government of the union. It is now no longer a point of speculation and hope, that the western territory is a mine of vast wealth to the United States: and although it is not of such a nature as to extricate them from their present distresses, or for some time to come to yield any regular supplies for the public expenses; yet must it hereafter be able, under proper management, both to effect a gradual discharge of the domestic debt, and to furnish, for a certain period, liberal tributes to the federal treasury. A very large proportion of this fund has been already surrendered by individual states; and it may with reason be expected, that the remaining states will not persist in withholding similar proofs of their equity and generosity. We may calculate, therefore, that a rich and fertile country, of an area equal to the inhabited extent of the United States, will soon become a national stock. Congress have assumed the administration of this stock. They have begun to render it productive. Congress have undertaken to do more:—they have proceeded to form new states; to erect temporary governments; to appoint officers for them; and to prescribe the conditions on which such states shall be admitted into the confederacy. All this has been done: and done without the least colour of constitutional authority. Yet no blame has been whispered: no alarm has been sounded. A GREAT and INDEPENDENT fund of revenue is passing into the hands of a SINGLE BODY of men, who can RAISE TROOPS to an INDEFINITE NUMBER, and appropriate money to their support for an INDEFINITE PERIOD OF TIME. And yet there are men, who have not only been silent spectators of this prospect, but who are advocates for the system which exhibits it; and, at the same time, urge against the new system the objections which we have heard. Would they not act with more consistency, in urging the establishment of the latter, as no less necessary to guard the union against the future powers and resources of a body constructed like the existing congress, than to save it from the dangers threatened by the present impotency of that assembly?

I mean not, by any thing here said, to throw censure on the measures which have been pursued by congress. I am sensible they could not have done otherwise. The public interest, the necessity of the case, imposed upon them the task of overleaping their constitutional limits. But is not the fact an alarming proof of the danger resulting from a government, which does not possess regular powers commensurate to its objects? A dissolution, or usurpation, is the dreadful dilemma to which it is continually exposed.

PUBLIUS.

THE FEDERALIST.

NUMBER XXXIX.

NEW YORK, JANUARY 18, 1788.

MADISON.

THE CONFORMITY OF THE PLAN TO REPUBLICAN PRINCIPLES: AN OBJECTION IN RESPECT TO THE POWERS OF THE CONVENTION, EXAMINED.

THE last paper having concluded the observations, which were meant to introduce a candid survey of the plan of government reported by the convention, we now proceed to the execution of that part of our undertaking.

The first question that offers itself is, whether the general form and aspect of the government be strictly republican? It is evident that no other form would be reconcilable with the genius of the people of America; with the fundamental principles of the revolution; or with that honourable determination which animates every votary of freedom, to rest all our political experiments on the capacity of mankind for self-government. If the plan of the convention, therefore, be found to depart from the republican character, its advocates must abandon it as no longer defensible.

What, then, are the distinctive characters of the republican form? Were an answer to this question to be sought, not by recurring to principles, but in the application of the term by political writers, to the constitutions of different states, no satisfactory one would ever be found. Holland, in which no particle

of the supreme authority is derived from the people, has passed
almost universally under the denomination of a republic. The
same title has been bestowed on Venice, where absolute power
over the great body of the people is exercised, in the most absolute manner, by a small body of hereditary nobles. Poland, which
is a mixture of aristocracy and of monarchy in their worst
forms, has been dignified with the same appellation. The government of England, which has one republican branch only, combined with a hereditary aristocracy and monarchy, has, with
equal impropriety, been frequently placed on the list of
republics. These examples, which are nearly as dissimilar to
each other as to a genuine republic, show the extreme inaccuracy with which the term has been used in political disquisitions.

If we resort, for a criterion, to the different principles on
which different forms of government are established, we may
define a republic to be, or at least may bestow that name on, a
government which derives all its powers directly or indirectly
from the great body of the people, and is administered by persons holding their offices during pleasure, for a limited period,
or during good behaviour. It is *essential* to such a government,
that it be derived from the great body of the society, not from
an inconsiderable proportion, or a favoured class of it; otherwise
a handful of tyrannical nobles, exercising their oppressions by a
delegation of their powers, might aspire to the rank of republicans, and claim for their government the honourable title of
republic. It is *sufficient* for such a government, that the persons
administering it be appointed, either directly or indirectly, by
the people; and that they hold their appointments by either of
the tenures just specified; otherwise every government in the
United States, as well as every other popular government that
has been or can be well organized or well executed, would be
degraded from the republican character. According to the constitution of every state in the union, some or other of the officers of government are appointed indirectly only by the people.
According to most of them, the chief magistrate himself is so
appointed. And according to one, this mode of appointment is

extended to one of the coordinate branches of the legislature. According to all the constitutions also, the tenure of the highest offices is extended to a definite period, and in many instances, both within the legislative and executive departments, to a period of years. According to the provisions of most of the constitutions, again, as well as according to the most respectable and received opinions on the subject, the members of the judiciary department are to retain their offices by the firm tenure of good behaviour.

On comparing the constitution planned by the convention, with the standard here fixed, we perceive at once, that it is, in the most rigid sense, conformable to it. The house of representatives, like that of one branch at least of all the state legislatures, is elected immediately by the great body of the people. The senate, like the present congress, and the senate of Maryland, derives its appointment indirectly from the people. The president is indirectly derived from the choice of the people, according to the example in most of the states. Even the judges, with all other officers of the union, will, as in the several states, be the choice, though a remote choice, of the people themselves. The duration of the appointments is equally conformable to the republican standard, and to the model of the state constitutions. The house of representatives is periodically elective, as in all the states; and for the period of two years, as in the state of South Carolina. The senate is elective, for the period of six years; which is but one year more than the period of the senate of Maryland; and but two more than that of the senates of New York and Virginia. The president is to continue in office for the period of four years; as in New York and Delaware, the chief magistrate is elected for three years, and in South Carolina for two years. In the other states the election is annual. In several of the states, however, no explicit provision is made for the impeachment of the chief magistrate. And in Delaware and Virginia, he is not impeachable till out of office. The president of the United States is impeachable at any time during his continuance in office. The tenure by which the judges are to hold their places, is, as it unquestionably ought to be, that of good behaviour. The tenure of the ministerial offices generally, will be a subject of legal regulation, conformably to the reason of the case, and the example of the state constitutions.

Could any further proof be required of the republican complexion of this system, the most decisive one might be found in its absolute prohibition of titles of nobility, both under the federal and the state governments; and in its express guarantee of the republican form to each of the latter.

But it was not sufficient, say the adversaries of the proposed constitution, for the convention to adhere to the republican form. They ought, with equal care, to have preserved the *federal* form, which regards the union as a *confederacy* of sovereign states; instead of which, they have framed a *national* government, which regards the union as a *consolidation* of the states. And it is asked, by what authority this bold and radical innovation was undertaken? The handle which has been made of this objection requires, that it should be examined with some precision.

Without inquiring into the accuracy of the distinction on which the objection is founded, it will be necessary to a just estimate of its force, first, to ascertain the real character of the government in question; secondly, to inquire how far the convention were authorized to propose such a government; and thirdly, how far the duty they owed to their country, could supply any defect of regular authority.

First. In order to ascertain the real character of the government, it may be considered in relation to the foundation on which it is to be established; to the sources from which its ordinary powers are to be drawn; to the operation of those powers; to the extent of them; and to the authority by which future changes in the government are to be introduced.

On examining the first relation, it appears, on one hand, that the constitution is to be founded on the assent and ratification of the people of America, given by deputies elected for the special purpose; but on the other, that this assent and ratification is to be given by the people, not as individuals composing one entire nation, but as composing the distinct and independent states to which they respectively belong. It is to be the assent and ratification of the several states, derived from the supreme authority in each state—the authority of the people themselves. The act, therefore, establishing the constitution, will not be a *national*, but a *federal* act.

That it will be a federal, and not a national act, as these terms are understood by the objectors, the act of the people, as forming so many independent states, not as forming one aggregate nation, is obvious from this single consideration, that it is to result neither from the decision of a *majority* of the people of the union, nor from that of a *majority* of the states. It must result from the *unanimous* assent of the several states that are parties to it, differing no otherwise from their ordinary assent than in its being expressed, not by the legislative authority, but by that of the people themselves. Were the people regarded in this transaction as forming one nation, the will of the majority of the whole people of the United States would bind the minority; in the same manner as the majority in each state must bind the minority; and the will of the majority must be determined either by a comparison of the individual votes, or by considering the will of the majority of the states, as evidence of the will of a majority of the people of the United States. Neither of these rules has been adopted. Each state, in ratifying the constitution, is considered as a sovereign body, independent of all others, and only to be bound by its own voluntary act. In this relation, then, the new constitution will, if established, be a *federal*, and not a *national* constitution.

The next relation is, to the sources from which the ordinary powers of government are to be derived. The house of representatives will derive its powers from the people of America, and the people will be represented in the same proportion, and on the same principle, as they are in a legislature of a particular state. So far the government is *national*, not *federal*. The senate, on the other hand, will derive its powers from the states, as political and coequal societies; and these will be represented on the principle of equality in the senate, as they now are in the existing congress. So far the government is *federal*, not *national*. The executive power will be derived from a very compound source. The immediate election of the president is to be made by the states in their political characters. The votes allotted to them are in a compound ratio, which considers them partly as distinct and coequal societies; partly as unequal members of the same society. The eventual election, again, is to be made by that branch of the legislature which consists of the national representatives; but in this particular act, they are to be thrown into the form of individual delegations, from so many distinct and coequal bodies politic. From this aspect of the government, it appears to be of a mixed character, presenting at least as many *federal* as *national* features.

The difference between a federal and national government, as it relates to the *operation of the government*, is, by the adversaries of the plan of the convention, supposed to consist in this, that in the former, the powers operate on the political bodies composing the confederacy, in their political capacities; in the latter, on the individual citizens composing the nation, in their individual capacities. On trying the constitution by this criterion, it falls under the *national*, not the *federal* character; though perhaps not so completely as has been understood. In several cases, and particularly in the trial of controversies to which states may be parties, they must be viewed and proceeded against in their collective and political capacities only. But the operation of the government on the people in their individual capacities, in its ordinary and most essential proceedings, will, on the whole, in the sense of its opponents, designate it, in this relation, a *national* government.

But if the government be national, with regard to the *operation* of its powers, it changes its aspect again, when we contemplate it in relation to the *extent* of its powers. The idea of a national government involves in it, not only an authority over the individual citizens, but an indefinite supremacy over all persons and things, so far as they are objects of lawful government. Among a people consolidated into one nation, this supremacy is completely vested in the national legislature. Among communities united for particular purposes, it is vested partly in the general, and partly in the municipal legislatures. In the former case, all local authorities are subordinate to the supreme; and may be controled, directed, or abolished by it at pleasure. In the latter, the local or municipal authorities form distinct and independent portions of the supremacy, no more subject within their respective spheres, to the general authority, than the general authority is subject to them within its own sphere. In this relation, then, the proposed government cannot be deemed a *national* one; since its jurisdiction extends to certain enumerated objects only, and leaves to the several states a residuary and inviolable sovereignty over all other objects. It is true, that in controversies relating to the boundary between the two jurisdictions, the tribunal which is ultimately to decide, is to be established under the general government. But this does not change the principle of the case. The decision is to be impartially made, according to the rules of the constitution; and all the usual and most effectual precautions are taken to secure this impartiality. Some such tribunal is clearly essential to prevent an appeal to the sword, and a dissolution of the compact; and that it ought to be established under the general, rather than under the local governments; or, to speak more properly, that it could be safely established under the first alone, is a position not likely to be combated.

If we try the constitution by its last relation, to the authority by which amendments are to be made, we find it neither wholly *national*, nor wholly *federal*. Were it wholly national, the supreme and ultimate authority would reside in the *majority* of the people of the union; and this authority would be competent at all times, like that of a majority of every national society, to alter or abolish its established government. Were it wholly federal on the other hand, the concurrence of each state in the union would be essential to every alteration that would be binding on all. The mode provided by the plan of the convention, is not founded on either of these principles. In requiring more than a majority, and particularly, in computing the proportion by *states*, not by *citizens*, it departs from the *national*, and advances towards the *federal* character. In rendering the concurrence of less than the whole number of states sufficient, it loses again the *federal*, and partakes of the *national* character.

The proposed constitution, therefore, even when tested by the rules laid down by its antagonists, is, in strictness, neither a national nor a federal constitution; but a composition of both. In its foundation it is federal, not national; in the sources from which the ordinary powers of the government are drawn, it is partly federal, and partly national: in the operation of these powers, it is national, not federal; in the extent of them again, it is federal, not national; and finally in the authoritative mode of introducing amendments, it is neither wholly federal, nor wholly national.

PUBLIUS.

THE FEDERALIST.

NUMBER XL.

NEW YORK, JANUARY 18, 1788.

MADISON.

THE SAME OBJECTION FURTHER EXAMINED.

THE *second* point to be examined is, whether the convention were authorized to frame, and propose this mixed constitution.

The powers of the convention ought, in strictness, to be determined, by an inspection of the commissions given to the members by their respective constituents. As all of these, however, had reference, either to the recommendation from the meeting at Annapolis, in September, 1786, or to that from congress, in February, 1787, it will be sufficient to recur to these particular acts.

The act from Annapolis recommends the "appointment of commissioners to take into consideration the situation of the United States; to devise *such further provisions*, as shall appear to them necessary to render the constitution of the federal government *adequate to the exigencies of the union*; and to report such an act for that purpose, to the United States in congress assembled, as, when agreed to by them, and afterwards confirmed by the legislature of every state, will effectually provide for the same."

The recommendatory act of congress is in the words following: "Whereas, there is provision in the articles of confederation and perpetual union, for making alterations therein, by the assent of a congress of United States, and of the legislatures of the several states; and whereas experience hath evinced, that there are defects in the present confederation; as a mean to remedy which, several of the states, and *particularly the state of New York*, by express instructions to their delegates in congress, have suggested a convention for the purposes expressed in the following resolution; and such convention appearing to be the most probable mean of establishing in these states *a firm national government:*"

"Resolved, That in the opinion of congress, it is expedient, that on the 2d Monday in May next, a convention of delegates, who shall have been appointed by the several states, be held at Philadelphia, for the sole and express purpose *of revising the articles of confederation*, and reporting to congress and the several legislatures, such *alterations and provisions therein*, as shall, when agreed to in congress, and confirmed by the states, render the federal constitution *adequate to the exigencies of government, and the preservation of the union.*"

From these two acts, it appears, 1st, that the object of the convention was to establish, in these states, *a firm national government*; 2d, that this government was to be such as would be *adequate to the exigencies of government*, and *the preservation of the union*; 3d, that these purposes were to be effected by *alterations and provisions in the articles of confederation*, as it is expressed in the act of congress; or by *such further provisions as should appear necessary*, as it stands in the recommendatory act from Annapolis; 4th, that the alterations and provisions were to be reported to congress, and to the states, in order to be agreed to by the former and confirmed by the latter.

From a comparison, and fair construction, of these several modes of expression, is to be deduced the authority under which the convention acted. They were to frame a *national government*, adequate to the *exigencies of government*, and *of the union*; and to reduce the articles of confederation into such form, as to accomplish these purposes.

There are two rules of construction dictated by plain reason, as well as founded on legal axioms. The one is, that every part of the expression ought, if possible, to be allowed some meaning, and be made to conspire to some common end. The other is, that where the several parts cannot be made to coincide, the less important should give way to the more important part: the means should be sacrificed to the end, rather than the end to the means.

Suppose, then, that the expressions defining the authority of the convention, were irreconcilably at variance with each other; that a *national* and *adequate government* could not possibly, in the judgment of the convention, be effected by *alterations* and *provisions* in the *articles of confederation*; which part of the definition ought to have been embraced, and which rejected? Which was the more important; which the less important part? Which the end; which the means? Let the most scrupulous expositors of delegated powers; let the most inveterate objectors against those exercised by the convention, answer these questions. Let them declare, whether it was of most importance to the happiness of the people of America, that the articles of confederation should be disregarded, and an adequate government be provided, and the union preserved; or that an adequate government should be omitted, and the articles of confederation preserved. Let them declare, whether the preservation of these articles was the end, for securing which a reform of the government was to be introduced as the means; or whether the establishment of a government, adequate to the national happiness, was the end at which these articles themselves originally aimed, and to which they ought, as insufficient means, to have been sacrificed.

But is it necessary to suppose, that these expressions are absolutely irreconcilable to each other; that no *alterations* or *provisions* in the *articles of the confederation*, could possibly mould them into a national and adequate government: into such a government as has been proposed by the convention?

No stress, it is presumed, will, in this case, be laid on the *title*; a change of that could never be deemed an exercise of ungranted power. *Alterations* in the body of the instrument are expressly authorized. *New provisions* therein are also expressly authorized. Here then is a power to change the title; to insert new articles; to alter old ones. Must it of necessity be admitted, that this power is infringed, so long as a part of the old articles remain? Those who maintain the affirmative, ought at least to mark the boundary between authorized and usurped innovations; between that degree of change which lies within the compass of *alterations and further provisions*, and that which amounts to a *transmutation* of the government. Will it be said, that the alterations ought not to have touched the substance of the confederation? The states would never have appointed a convention, with so much solemnity, nor described its objects with so much latitude, if some *substantial* reform had not been in contemplation. Will it be said, that the *fundamental principles* of the confederation were not within the purview of the convention, and ought not to have been varied? I ask, what are these principles? Do they require, that in the establishment of the constitution, the states should be regarded as distinct and independent sovereigns? They are so regarded by the constitution proposed. Do they require, that the members of the government should derive their appointment from the legislatures, not from the people of the states? One branch of the new government is to be appointed by these legislatures; and under the confederation, the delegates to congress *may all* be appointed immediately by the people; and in two states* are actually so appointed. Do they require, that the powers of the government should act on the states, and not immediately on individuals? In some instances, as has been shown, the powers of the new government will act on the states in their collective characters. In some instances also, those of the existing government act immediately on individuals. In cases of capture; of piracy; of the post-office; of coins, weights, and measures; of trade with the Indians; of claims under grants of land, by different states; and, above all, in the case of trials by courts-martial in the army and navy,

---

* Connecticut and Rhode Island.

by which death may be inflicted without the intervention of a jury, or even of a civil magistrate; in all these cases, the powers of the confederation operate immediately on the persons and interests of individual citizens. Do these fundamental principles require, particularly, that no tax should be levied, without the intermediate agency of the states? The confederation itself, authorizes a direct tax, to a certain extent, on the post-office. The power of coinage, has been so construed by congress, as to levy a tribute immediately from that source also. But pretermitting these instances, was it not an acknowledged object of the convention, and the universal expectation of the people, that the regulation of trade should be submitted to the general government, in such a form as would render it an immediate source of general revenue? Had not congress repeatedly recommended this measure, as not inconsistent with the fundamental principles of the confederation? Had not every state, but one; had not New York herself, so far complied with the plan of congress, as to recognize the *principle* of the innovation? Do these principles, in fine, require that the powers of the general government should be limited, and that, beyond this limit, the states should be left in possession of their sovereignty and independence? We have seen, that in the new government, as in the old, the general powers are limited; and that the states, in all unenumerated cases, are left in the enjoyment of their sovereign and independent jurisdiction.

Truth is, that the great principles of the constitution proposed by the convention, may be considered less, as absolutely new, than as the expansion of principles which are found in the articles of confederation. The misfortune under the latter system has been, that these principles are so feeble and confined, as to justify all the charges of inefficiency which have been urged against it; and to require a degree of enlargement, which gives to the new system the aspect of an entire transformation of the old.

In one particular, it is admitted, that the convention have departed from the tenor of their commission. Instead of reporting a plan requiring the confirmation *of all the states*, they have reported a plan, which is to be confirmed, and may be carried into effect, by *nine states only*. It is worthy of remark, that this objection, though the most plausible, has been the least urged in the publications which have swarmed against the convention. The forbearance can only have proceeded from an irresistible conviction of the absurdity of subjecting the fate of twelve states to the perverseness or corruption of a thirteenth; from the example of inflexible opposition given by a *majority* of one sixtieth of the people of America, to a measure approved and called for by the voice of twelve states, comprising fifty-nine six-tieths of the people; an example still fresh in the memory and indignation of every citizen who has felt for the wounded honour and prosperity of his country. As this objection, therefore, has been in a manner waved by those who have criticised the powers of the convention, I dismiss it without further observation.

The *third* point to be inquired into is, how far considerations of duty arising out of the case itself, could have supplied any defect of regular authority.

In the preceding inquiries, the powers of the convention have been analyzed and tried with the same rigour, and by the same rules, as if they had been real and final powers, for the establishment of a constitution for the United States. We have seen, in what manner they have borne the trial, even on that supposition. It is time now to recollect, that the powers were merely advisory and recommendatory; that they were so meant by the states, and so understood by the convention; and that the latter have accordingly planned and proposed a constitution, which is to be of no more consequence than the paper on which it is written, unless it be stamped with the approbation of those to whom it is addressed. This reflection places the subject in a point of view altogether different, and will enable us to judge with propriety of the course taken by the convention.

Let us view the ground on which the convention stood. It may be collected from their proceedings, that they were deeply and unanimously impressed with the crisis, which had led their country, almost with one voice, to make so singular and solemn an experiment, for correcting the errours of a system, by which this crisis had been produced; that they were no less deeply and unanimously convinced, that such a reform as they have proposed, was absolutely necessary to effect the purposes of their appointment. It could not be unknown to them, that the hopes and expectations of the great body of citizens, throughout this great empire, were turned with the keenest anxiety, to the event of their deliberations. They had every reason to believe, that the contrary sentiments agitated the minds and bosoms of every external and internal foe to the liberty and prosperity of the United States. They had seen in the origin and progress of the experiment, the alacrity with which the *proposition*, made by a single state (Virginia) towards a partial amendment of the confederation had been attended to and promoted. They had seen the *liberty assumed* by a *very few* deputies, from a *very few* states, convened at Annapolis, of recommending a great and critical object, wholly foreign to their commission, not only justified by the public opinion, but actually carried into effect, by twelve out of the thirteen states. They had seen, in a variety of instances, assumptions by congress, not only of recommendatory, but of operative powers, warranted in the public estimation, by occasions and objects infinitely less urgent than those by which their conduct was to be governed. They must have reflected, that in all great changes of established governments, forms ought to give way to substance; that a rigid adherence in such cases to the former, would render nominal and nugatory, the transcendant and precious right of the people to "abolish or alter their governments as to them shall seem most likely to effect their safety and happiness:"* since it is impossible for the people spontaneously and universally, to move in concert towards their object: and it is therefore essential, that such changes be instituted by some *informal and unauthorized propositions*, made by some patriotic and respectable citizen, or

* Declaration of Independence.

number of citizens. They must have recollected, that it was by this irregular and assumed privilege, of proposing to the people plans for their safety and happiness, that the states were first united against the danger with which they were threatened by their ancient government; that committees and congresses were formed for concentrating their efforts, and defending their rights: and that *conventions* were *elected* in *the several states*, for establishing the constitutions under which they are now governed. Nor could it have been forgotten, that no little ill-timed scruples, no zeal for adhering to ordinary forms, were anywhere seen, except in those who wished to indulge, under these masks, their secret enmity to the substance contended for. They must have borne in mind, that as the plan to be framed and proposed, was to be submitted to *the people themselves*, the disapprobation of this supreme authority would destroy it for ever: its approbation blot out all antecedent errours and irregularities. It might even have occurred to them, that where a disposition to cavil prevailed, their neglect to execute the degree of power vested in them, and still more their recommendation of any measure whatever not warranted by their commission, would not less excite animadversion, than a recommendation at once of a measure fully commensurate to the national exigencies.

Had the convention, under all these impressions, and in the midst of all these considerations, instead of exercising a manly confidence in their country, by whose confidence they had been so peculiarly distinguished, and of pointing out a system capable, in their judgment, of securing its happiness, taken the cold and sullen resolution of disappointing its ardent hopes, of sacrificing substance to forms, of committing the dearest interests of their country to the uncertainties of delay, and the hazard of events; let me ask the man, who can raise his mind to one elevated conception, who can awaken in his bosom one patriotic emotion, what judgment ought to have been pronounced by the impartial world, by the friends of mankind, by every virtuous citizen, on the conduct and character of this assembly? Or if there be a man whose propensity to condemn is susceptible of no control, let me then ask, what sentence he has in reserve for the twelve states who *usurped the power* of sending deputies to the convention, a body utterly unknown to their constitutions; for congress, who recommended the appointment of this body, equally unknown to the confederation; and for the state of New York, in particular, who first urged, and then complied with this unauthorized interposition?

But that the objectors may be disarmed of every pretext, it shall be granted for a moment, that the convention were neither authorized by their commission, nor justified by circumstances, in proposing a constitution for their country: does it follow that the constitution ought, for that reason alone, to be rejected? If, according to the noble precept, it be lawful to accept good advice even from an enemy, shall we set the ignoble example, of refusing such advice even when it is offered by our friends? The prudent inquiry, in all cases, ought surely to be not so much *from whom* the advice comes, as whether the advice be *good*.

The sum of what has been here advanced and proved is, that the charge against the convention of exceeding their powers, except in one instance little urged by the objectors, has no foundation to support it; that if they had exceeded their powers, they were not only warranted, but required, as the confidential servants of their country, by the circumstances in which they were placed, to exercise the liberty which they assumed; and that finally, if they had violated both their powers and their obligations, in proposing a constitution, this ought nevertheless to be embraced, if it be calculated to accomplish the views and happiness of the people of America. How far this character is due to the constitution, is the subject under investigation.

PUBLIUS.

THE FEDERALIST.

NUMBER XLI.

NEW YORK, JANUARY 22, 1788.

MADISON.

GENERAL VIEW OF THE POWERS PROPOSED TO BE VESTED IN THE UNION.

THE constitution proposed by the convention, may be considered under two general points of view. The FIRST relates to the sum or quantity of power which it vests in the government, including the restraints imposed on the states. The SECOND, to the particular structure of the government, and the distribution of this power among its several branches.

Under the first view of the subject, two important questions arise:—1. Whether any part of the powers transferred to the general government be unnecessary or improper?—2. Whether the entire mass of them be dangerous to the portion of jurisdiction left in the several states?

Is the aggregate power of the general government greater than ought to have been vested in it? This is the first question.

It cannot have escaped those, who have attended with candour to the arguments employed against the extensive powers of the government, that the authors of them have very little considered, how far these powers were necessary means of attaining a necessary end. They have chosen rather to dwell on the inconveniencies which must be unavoidably blended with all political advantages; and on the possible abuses which must be incident to every power or trust, of which a beneficial use can be made. This method of handling the subject, cannot impose on the good sense of the people of America. It may display the subtlety of the writer; it may open a boundless field of rhetoric and declamation; it may inflame the passions of the unthinking, and may confirm the prejudices of the misthinking: but cool and candid people will at once reflect, that the purest of human blessings must have a portion of alloy in them; that the choice must always be made, if not of the lesser evil, at least of the GREATER, not the PERFECT good; and that in every political institution, a power to advance the public happiness, involves a discretion which may be misapplied and abused. They will see, therefore, that in all cases where power is to be conferred, the point first to be decided is, whether such a power be necessary to the public good; as the next will be, in case of an affirmative decision, to guard as effectually as possible against a perversion of the power to the public detriment.

That we may form a correct judgment on this subject, it will be proper to review the several powers conferred on the government of the union; and that this may be the more conveniently done, they may be reduced into different classes as they relate to the following different objects: 1. Security against foreign danger; 2. Regulation of the intercourse with foreign nations; 3. Maintenance of harmony and proper intercourse among the states; 4. Certain miscellaneous objects of general utility; 5. Restraint of the states from certain injurious acts; 6. Provisions for giving due efficacy to all these powers.

The powers falling within the first class, are those of declaring war, and granting letters of marque; of providing armies and fleets; of regulating and calling forth the militia; of levying and borrowing money.

Security against foreign danger, is one of the primitive objects of civil society. It is an avowed and essential object of the American union. The powers requisite for attaining it, must be effectually confided to the federal councils.

Is the power of declaring war necessary? No man will answer

this question in the negative. It would be superfluous, therefore, to enter into a proof of the affirmative. The existing confederation establishes this power in the most ample form.

Is the power of raising armies, and equipping fleets necessary? This is involved in the foregoing power. It is involved in the power of self-defence.

But was it necessary to give an INDEFINITE POWER of raising TROOPS, as well as providing fleets; and of maintaining both in PEACE, as well as in WAR?

The answer to these questions has been too far anticipated in another place, to admit an extensive discussion of them in this place. The answer indeed seems to be so obvious and conclusive, as scarcely to justify such a discussion in any place. With what colour of propriety, could the force necessary for defence be limited, by those who cannot limit the force of offence? If a federal constitution could chain the ambition, or set bounds to the exertions of all other nations, then indeed might it prudently chain the discretion of its own government, and set bounds to the exertions for its own safety.

How could a readiness for war in time of peace be safely prohibited, unless we could prohibit, in like manner, the preparations and establishments of every hostile nation? The means of security can only be regulated by the means and danger of attack. They will in fact be ever determined by these rules, and by no others. It is in vain to oppose constitutional barriers to the impulse of self-preservation. It is worse than in vain: because it plants in the constitution itself necessary usurpations of power, every precedent of which is a germ of unnecessary and multiplied repetitions. If one nation maintains constantly a disciplined army, ready for the service of ambition or revenge, it obliges the most pacific nations, who may be within the reach of its enterprises, to take corresponding precautions. The fifteenth century was the unhappy epoch of military establishments in time of peace. They were introduced by Charles VII of France. All Europe has followed, or been forced into the example. Had the example not been followed by other nations, all Europe must long ago have worn the chains of a universal monarch. Were every nation, except France, not to disband its peace establishment, the same event might follow. The veteran legions of Rome were an overmatch for the undisciplined valour of all other nations, and rendered her mistress of the world.

Not the less true is it, that the liberties of Rome proved the final victim to her military triumphs; and that the liberties of Europe, as far as they ever existed, have, with few exceptions, been the price of her military establishments. A standing force, therefore, is a dangerous, at the same time that it may be a necessary, provision. On the smaller scale, it has its inconveniences. On an extensive scale, its consequences may be fatal. On any scale, it is an object of laudable circumspection and precaution. A wise nation will combine all these considerations; and whilst it does not rashly preclude itself from any resource which may become essential to its safety, will exert all its prudence in diminishing both the necessity and the danger of resorting to one which may be inauspicious to its liberties.

The clearest marks of this prudence are stamped on the proposed constitution. The union itself, which it cements and secures, destroys every pretext for a military establishment which could be dangerous. America united, with a handful of troops, or without a single soldier, exhibits a more forbidding posture to foreign ambition, than America disunited with a hundred thousand veterans ready for combat. It was remarked, on a former occasion, that the want of this pretext had saved the liberties of one nation in Europe. Being rendered by her insular situation, and her maritime resources, impregnable to the armies of her neighbours, the rulers of Great Britain have never been able, by real or artificial dangers, to cheat the public into an extensive peace establishment. The distance of the United States from the powerful nations of the world, gives them the same happy security. A dangerous establishment can never be necessary or plausible, so long as they continue a united people.

But let it never for a moment be forgotten, that they are indebted for this advantage to their union alone. The moment of its dissolution will be the date of a new order of things. The fears of the weaker, or the ambition of the stronger states, or confederacies, will set the same example in the new as Charles VII did in the old world. The example will be followed here, from the same motives which produced universal imitation there. Instead of deriving from our situation the precious advantage which Great Britain has derived from hers, the face of America will be but a copy of that of the continent of Europe. It will present liberty everywhere crushed between standing armies, and perpetual taxes. The fortunes of disunited America, will be even more disastrous than those of Europe. The sources of evil in the latter are confined to her own limits. No superior powers of another quarter of the globe intrigue among her rival nations, inflame their mutual animosities, and render them the instruments of foreign ambition, jealousy, and revenge. In America, the miseries springing from her internal jealousies, contentions, and wars, would form a part only of her lot. A plentiful addition of evils, would have their source in that relation in which Europe stands to this quarter of the earth, and which no other quarter of the earth bears to Europe.

This picture of the consequences of disunion cannot be too highly coloured, or too often exhibited. Every man who loves peace; every man who loves his country; every man who loves liberty, ought to have it ever before his eyes, that he may cherish in his heart a due attachment to the union of America, and be able to set a due value on the means of preserving it.

Next to the effectual establishment of the union, the best possible precaution against danger from standing armies, is a limitation of the term for which revenue may be appropriated to their support. This precaution the constitution has prudently added. I will not repeat here the observations, which I flatter myself have placed this subject in a just and satisfactory light. But it may not be improper to take notice of an argument against this part of the constitution, which has been drawn from the policy and practice of Great Britain. It is said, that the continuance of an army in that kingdom, requires an annual vote of the legislature: whereas the American constitution has lengthened this critical period to two years. This is the form in which the comparison is usually stated to the public: but is it a just form? is it a fair comparison? Does the British constitution restrain the parliamentary discretion to one year? Does the American impose on the congress appropriations for two years? On the contrary, it cannot be unknown to the authors of the fallacy themselves, that the British constitution fixes no limit whatever to the discretion of the legislature, and that the American ties down the legislature to two years, as the longest admissible term.

Had the argument from the British example been truly stated, it would have stood thus: the term for which supplies may be appropriated to the army establishment, though unlimited by the British constitution, has nevertheless in practice been limited by parliamentary discretion to a single year. Now, if in Great Britain, where the house of commons is elected for seven years; where so great a proportion of the members are elected by so small a proportion of the people; where the electors are so corrupted by the representatives, and the representatives so corrupted by the crown, the representative body can possess a power to make appropriations to the army for an indefinite term, without desiring, or without daring, to extend the term beyond a single year; ought not suspicion herself to blush, in pretending that the representatives of the United States, elected FREELY by the WHOLE BODY of the people, every SECOND YEAR, cannot be safely entrusted with a discretion over such appropriations, expressly limited to the short period of TWO YEARS!

A bad cause seldom fails to betray itself. Of this truth, the management of the opposition to the federal government, is an unvaried exemplification. But among all the blunders which have been committed, none is more striking than the attempt to enlist on that side, the prudent jealousy entertained by the people, of standing armies. The attempt has awakened fully the public attention to that important subject; and has led to investigations which must terminate in a thorough and universal conviction, not only that the constitution has provided the most effectual guards against danger from that quarter, but that nothing short of a constitution fully adequate to the national defence, and the preservation of the union, can save America from as many standing armies, as it may be split into states or confederacies; and from such a progressive augmentation of these establishments in each, as will render them as burthensome to the properties, and ominous to the liberties of the people, as any establishment that can become necessary, under a united and efficient government, must be tolerable to the former and safe to the latter.

The palpable necessity of the power to provide and maintain a navy, has protected that part of the constitution against a spirit of censure, which has spared few other parts. It must indeed be numbered among the greatest blessings of America, that as her union will be the only source of her maritime strength, so this will be a principal source of her security against danger from abroad. In this respect, our situation bears another likeness to the insular advantage of Great Britain. The batteries most capable of repelling foreign enterprises on our safety, are happily such as can never be turned by a perfidious government against our liberties.

The inhabitants of the Atlantic frontier, are all of them deeply interested in this provision for naval protection. If they have hitherto been suffered to sleep quietly in their beds; if their property has remained safe against the predatory spirit of licentious adventurers; if their maritime towns have not yet been compelled to ransom themselves from the terrours of a conflagration, by yielding to the exactions of daring and sudden invaders, these instances of good fortune are not to be ascribed to the capacity of the existing government for the protection of those from whom it claims allegiance, but to causes that are fugitive and fallacious. If we except perhaps Virginia and Maryland, which are peculiarly vulnerable on their eastern frontiers, no part of the union ought to feel more anxiety on this subject than New-York. Her sea-coast is extensive. A very important district of the state, is an island. The state itself is penetrated by a large navigable river for more than fifty leagues. The great emporium of its commerce, the great reservoir of its wealth, lies every moment at the mercy of events, and may be almost regarded as a hostage for ignominious compliances with the dictates of a foreign enemy; or even with the rapacious demands of pirates and barbarians. Should a war be the result of the precarious situation of European affairs, and all the unruly passions attending it be let loose on the ocean, our escape from insults and depredations, not only on that element, but every part of the other bordering on it, will be truly miraculous. In the present condition of America, the states more immediately exposed to these calamities have nothing to hope from the phantom of a general government which now exists; and if their single resources were equal to the task of fortifying themselves against the danger, the objects to be protected would be almost consumed by the means of protecting them.

The power of regulating and calling forth the militia, has been already sufficiently vindicated and explained.

The power of levying and borrowing money, being the sinew of that which is to be exerted in the national defence, is properly thrown into the same class with it. This power, also, has been examined already with much attention, and has, I trust, been clearly shown to be necessary, both in the extent and form given to it by the constitution. I will address one additional reflection only, to those who contend that the power ought to have been restrained to external taxation—by which they mean, taxes on articles imported from other countries. It cannot be doubted, that this will always be a valuable source of revenue; that for a considerable time, it must be a principal source; that at this moment, it is an essential one. But we may form very mistaken ideas on this subject, if we do not call to mind in our calculations, that the extent of revenue drawn from foreign com-

merce, must vary with the variations, both in the extent and the
kind of imports; and that these variations do not correspond
with the progress of population, which must be the general measure of the public wants. As long as agriculture continues the
sole field of labour, the importation of manufactures must
increase as the consumers multiply. As soon as domestic manufactures are begun by the hands not called for by agriculture,
the imported manufactures will decrease as the numbers of people increase. In a more remote stage, the imports may consist in
a considerable part of raw materials, which will be wrought into
articles for exportation, and will, therefore, require rather the
encouragement of bounties, than to be loaded with discouraging
duties. A system of government, meant for duration, ought to
contemplate these revolutions, and be able to accommodate
itself to them.

Some, who have not denied the necessity of the power of taxation, have grounded a very fierce attack against the constitution, on the language in which it is defined. It has been urged
and echoed, that the power "to lay and collect taxes, duties,
imposts, and excises, to pay the debts, and provide for the common defence and general welfare of the United States," amounts
to an unlimited commission to exercise every power, which may
be alleged to be necessary for the common defence or general
welfare. No stronger proof could be given of the distress under
which these writers labour for objections, than their stooping to
such a misconstruction.

Had no other enumeration or definition of the powers of the
congress been found in the constitution, than the general expressions just cited, the authors of the objection might have had some
colour for it; though it would have been difficult to find a reason
for so awkward a form of describing an authority to legislate in
all possible cases. A power to destroy the freedom of the press,
the trial by jury, or even to regulate the course of descents,
or the forms of conveyances, must be very singularly expressed
by the terms "to raise money for the general welfare."

But what colour can the objection have, when a specification of the objects alluded to by these general terms, immediately follows; and is not even separated by a longer pause than a semicolon? If the different parts of the same instrument ought to be so expounded, as to give meaning to every part which will bear it; shall one part of the same sentence be excluded altogether from a share in the meaning; and shall the more doubtful and indefinite terms be retained in their full extent, and the clear and precise expressions be denied any signification whatsoever? For what purpose could the enumeration of particular powers be inserted, if these and all others were meant to be included in the preceding general power? Nothing is more natural or common, than first to use a general phrase, and then to explain and qualify it by a recital of particulars. But the idea of an enumeration of particulars, which neither explain nor qualify the general meaning, and can have no other effect than to confound and mislead, is an absurdity, which, as we are reduced to the dilemma of charging either on the authors of the objection or on the authors of the constitution, we must take the liberty of supposing, had not its origin with the latter.

The objection here is the more extraordinary, as it appears, that the language used by the convention is a copy from the articles of confederation. The objects of the union among the states, as described in article third, are, "their common defence, security of their liberties, and mutual and general welfare." The terms of article eighth are still more identical: "All charges of war, and all other expenses, that shall be incurred for the common defence or general welfare, and allowed by the United States in congress, shall be defrayed out of a common treasury," &c. A similar language again occurs in article ninth. Construe either of these articles by the rules which would justify the construction put on the new constitution, and they vest in the existing congress a power to legislate in all cases whatsoever. But what would have been thought of that assembly, if, attaching themselves to these general expressions, and disregarding the specifications which ascertain and limit their import, they had exercised an unlimited power of providing for the common

defence and general welfare? I appeal to the objectors themselves, whether they would in that case have employed the same
reasoning in justification of congress, as they now make use of
against the convention. How difficult it is for errour to escape
its own condemnation!

PUBLIUS.

THE FEDERALIST.

NUMBER XLII.

NEW YORK, JANUARY 22, 1788.

MADISON.

THE SAME VIEW CONTINUED.

THE *second* class of powers, lodged in the general government, consists of those which regulate the intercourse with foreign nations, to wit: to make treaties; to send and receive ambassadors, other public ministers and consuls; to define and punish piracies and felonies committed on the high seas, and offences against the law of nations; to regulate foreign commerce, including a power to prohibit, after the year 1808, the importation of slaves, and to lay an intermediate duty of ten dollars per head, as a discouragement to such importations.

This class of powers forms an obvious and essential branch of the federal administration. If we are to be one nation in any respect, it clearly ought to be in respect to other nations.

The powers to make treaties, and to send and receive ambassadors, speak their own propriety. Both of them are comprised in the articles of confederation; with this difference only, that the former is disembarrassed by the plan of the convention of an exception, under which treaties might be substantially frustrated by regulations of the states; and that a power of appointing and receiving "other public ministers and consuls," is expressly and very properly added to the former provision concerning ambassadors. The term ambassador, if taken strictly, as

seems to be required by the second of the articles of confederation, comprehends the highest grade only of public ministers;
and excludes the grades which the United States will be most
likely to prefer, where foreign embassies may be necessary. And
under no latitude of construction will the term comprehend consuls. Yet it has been found expedient, and has been the practice
of congress, to employ the inferiour grades of public ministers;
and to send and receive consuls.

It is true, that where treaties of commerce stipulate for the
mutual appointment of consuls, whose functions are connected
with commerce, the admission of foreign consuls may fall within
the power of making commercial treaties; and that where no
such treaties exist, the mission of American consuls into foreign
countries may *perhaps* be covered under the authority, given by
the ninth article of the confederation, to appoint all such civil
officers as may be necessary for managing the general affairs of
the United States. But the admission of consuls into the United
States, where no previous treaty has stipulated it, seems to
have been nowhere provided for. A supply of the omission is one
of the lesser instances, in which the convention have improved
on the model before them. But the most minute provisions
become important, when they tend to obviate the necessity or
the pretext for gradual and unobserved usurpations of power. A
list of the cases, in which congress have been betrayed, or
forced, by the defects of the confederation, into violations of
their chartered authorities, would not a little surprise those who
have paid no attention to the subject; and would be no inconsiderable argument in favour of the new constitution, which seems
to have provided no less studiously for the lesser, than the more
obvious and striking defects of the old.

The power to define and punish piracies and felonies committed on the high seas, and offences against the law of nations,
belongs with equal propriety to the general government; and is
a still greater improvement on the articles of confederation.

These articles contain no provision for the case of offences
against the law of nations: and consequently leave it in the

power of any indiscreet member to embroil the confederacy with foreign nations.

The provision of the federal articles on the subject of piracies and felonies, extends no farther than to the establishment of courts for the trial of these offences. The definition of piracies might, perhaps, without inconveniency, be left to the law of nations; though a legislative definition of them is found in most municipal codes. A definition of felonies on the high seas, is evidently requisite. Felony is a term of loose signification, even in the common law of England; and of various import in the statute law of that kingdom. But neither the common, nor the statute law of that, or of any other nation, ought to be a standard for the proceedings of this, unless previously made its own by legislative adoption. The meaning of the term, as defined in the codes of the several states, would be as impracticable, as the former would be a dishonourable and illegitimate guide. It is not precisely the same in any two of the states; and varies in each with every revision of its criminal laws. For the sake of certainty and uniformity, therefore, the power of defining felonies in this case, was in every respect necessary and proper.

The regulation of foreign commerce, having fallen within several views which have been taken of this subject, has been too fully discussed to need additional proofs here of its being properly submitted to the federal administration.

It were doubtless to be wished, that the power of prohibiting the importation of slaves, had not been postponed until the year 1808, or rather, that it had been suffered to have immediate operation. But it is not difficult to account, either for this restriction on the general government, or for the manner in which the whole clause is expressed. It ought to be considered as a great point gained in favour of humanity, that a period of twenty years may terminate for ever within these states, a traffic which has so long and so loudly upbraided the barbarism of modern policy; that within that period, it will receive a considerable discouragement from the federal government, and may be totally abolished, by a concurrence of the few states which continue the unnatural traffic, in the prohibitory example which has been given by so great a majority of the union. Happy would it be for the unfortunate Africans, if an equal prospect lay before them, of being redeemed from the oppressions of their European brethren!

Attempts have been made to pervert this clause into an objection against the constitution, by representing it on one side, as a criminal toleration of an illicit practice: and on another, as calculated to prevent voluntary and beneficial emigrations from Europe to America. I mention these misconstructions, not with a view to give them an answer, for they deserve none; but as specimens of the manner and spirit, in which some have thought fit to conduct their opposition to the proposed government.

The powers included in the *third* class, are those which provide for the harmony and proper intercourse among the states.

Under this head, might be included the particular restraints imposed on the authority of the states, and certain powers of the judicial department; but the former are reserved for a distinct class, and the latter will be particularly examined, when we arrive at the structure and organization of the government. I shall confine myself to a cursory review of the remaining powers comprehended under this third description, to wit: to regulate commerce among the several states and the Indian tribes; to coin money, regulate the value thereof, and of foreign coin; to provide for the punishment of counterfeiting the current coin and securities of the United States; to fix the standard of weights and measures; to establish an uniform rule of naturalization, and uniform laws of bankruptcy; to prescribe the manner in which the public acts, records, and judicial proceedings of each state shall be proved, and the effect they shall have in other states; and to establish post-offices and post-roads.

The defect of power in the existing confederacy, to regulate the commerce between its several members, is in the number of those which have been clearly pointed out by experience. To the proofs and remarks which former papers have brought into view on this subject, it may be added, that without this supplemental provision, the great and essential power of regulating foreign commerce, would have been incomplete and ineffectual. A very material object of this power was the relief of the states which import and export through other states, from the improper contributions levied on them by the latter. Were these at liberty to regulate the trade between state and state, it must be foreseen, that ways would be found out, to load the articles of import and export, during the passage through their jurisdiction, with duties which would fall on the makers of the latter, and the consumers of the former. We may be assured, by past experience, that such a practice would be introduced by future contrivances; and both by that and a common knowledge of human affairs, that it would nourish unceasing animosities, and not improbably terminate in serious interruptions of the public tranquillity. To those who do not view the question through the medium of passion or of interest, the desire of the commercial states to collect, in any form, an indirect revenue from their uncommercial neighbours, must appear not less impolitic than it is unfair; since it would stimulate the injured party, by resentment as well as interest, to resort to less convenient channels for their foreign trade. But the mild voice of reason, pleading the cause of an enlarged and permanent interest, is but too often drowned before public bodies as well as individuals, by the clamours of an impatient avidity for immediate and immoderate gain.

The necessity of a superintending authority over the reciprocal trade of confederated states, has been illustrated by other examples as well as our own. In Switzerland, where the union is so very slight, each canton is obliged to allow to merchandises, a passage through its jurisdiction into other cantons, without an augmentation of the tolls. In Germany, it is a law of the empire, that the princes and states shall not lay tolls or customs on bridges, rivers, or passages, without the consent of the emperor and diet; though it appears from a quotation in an antecedent paper, that the practice in this, as in many other instances in that confederacy, has not followed the law, and has produced there the mischiefs which have been foreseen here. Among the restraints imposed by the union of the Netherlands on its members, one is, that they shall not establish imposts disadvantageous to their neighbours, without the general permission.

The regulation of commerce with the Indian tribes, is very properly unfettered from two limitations in the articles of confederation, which render the provision obscure and contradictory. The power is there restrained to Indians, not members of any of the states, and is not to violate or infringe the legislative right of any state within its own limits. What description of Indians are to be deemed members of a state, is not yet settled; and has been a question of frequent perplexity and contention in the federal councils. And how the trade with Indians, though not members of a state, yet residing within its legislative jurisdiction, can be regulated by an external authority, without so far intruding on the internal rights of legislation, is absolutely incomprehensible. This is not the only case, in which the articles of confederation have inconsiderately endeavoured to accomplish impossibilities; to reconcile a partial sovereignty in the union, with complete sovereignty in the states; to subvert a mathematical axiom, by taking away a part, and letting the whole remain.

All that need be remarked on the power to coin money, regulate the value thereof, and of foreign coin, is, that by providing for this last case, the constitution has supplied a material omission in the articles of confederation. The authority of the existing congress is restrained to the regulation of coin *struck* by their own authority, or that of the respective states. It must be seen at once, that the proposed uniformity in the *value* of the current coin, might be destroyed by subjecting that of foreign coin to the different regulations of the different states.

The punishment of counterfeiting the public securities, as well as the current coin, is submitted of course to that authority which is to secure the value of both.

The regulation of weights and measures is transferred from

the articles of confederation, and is founded on like considerations with the preceding power of regulating coin.

The dissimilarity in the rules of naturalization has long been remarked as a fault in our system, and as laying a foundation for intricate and delicate questions. In the fourth article of the confederation, it is declared, "that the *free inhabitants* of each of these states, paupers, vagabonds, and fugitives from justice excepted, shall be entitled to all privileges and immunities of *free citizens* in the several states; and *the people* of each state shall, in every other, enjoy all the privileges of trade and commerce," &c. There is a confusion of language here, which is remarkable. Why the terms *free inhabitants* are used in one part of the article, *free citizens* in another, and *people* in another; or what was meant by superadding to "all privileges and immunities of free citizens"—"all the privileges of trade and commerce," cannot easily be determined. It seems to be a construction scarcely avoidable, however, that those who come under the denomination of *free inhabitants* of a state, although not citizens of such state, are entitled, in every other state, to all the privileges of *free citizens* of the latter; that is, to greater privileges than they may be entitled to in their own state: so that it may be in the power of a particular state, or rather every state is laid under a necessity, not only to confer the rights of citizenship in other states upon any whom it may admit to such rights within itself, but upon any whom it may allow to become inhabitants within its jurisdiction. But were an exposition of the term "inhabitants" to be admitted, which would confine the stipulated privileges to citizens alone, the difficulty is diminished only, not removed. The very improper power would still be retained by each state, of naturalizing aliens in every other state. In one state, residence for a short term confers all the rights of citizenship: in another, qualifications of greater importance are required. An alien, therefore legally incapacitated for certain rights in the latter, may, by previous residence only in the former, elude his incapacity; and thus the law of one state be preposterously rendered paramount to the law of another, within the jurisdiction of the other.

We owe it to mere casualty, that very serious embarrassments on this subject have been hitherto escaped. By the laws of several states, certain descriptions of aliens, who had rendered themselves obnoxious, were laid under interdicts inconsistent, not only with the rights of citizenship, but with the privileges of residence. What would have been the consequence, if such persons, by residence, or otherwise, had acquired the character of citizens under the laws of another state, and then asserted their rights as such, both to residence and citizenship, within the state proscribing them? Whatever the legal consequences might have been, other consequences would probably have resulted of too serious a nature, not to be provided against. The new constitution has accordingly, with great propriety, made provision against them, and all others proceeding from the defect of the confederation on this head, by authorizing the general government to establish an uniform rule of naturalization throughout the United States.

The power of establishing uniform laws of bankruptcy, is so intimately connected with the regulation of commerce, and will prevent so many frauds where the parties or their property may lie, or be removed into different states, that the expediency of it seems not likely to be drawn into question.

The power of prescribing, by general laws, the manner in which the public acts, records, and judicial proceedings of each state, shall be proved, and the effect they shall have in other states, is an evident and valuable improvement on the clause relating to this subject in the articles of confederation. The meaning of the latter is extremely indeterminate; and can be of little importance under any interpretation which it will bear. The power here established, may be rendered a very convenient instrument of justice, and be particularly beneficial on the borders of contiguous states, where the effects liable to justice may be suddenly and secretly translated in any stage of the process, within a foreign jurisdiction.

The power of establishing post-roads must, in every view, be a harmless power; and may perhaps, by judicious management, become productive of great public conveniency. Nothing which tends to facilitate the intercourse between the states, can be deemed unworthy of the public care.

PUBLIUS.

THE FEDERALIST.

NUMBER XLIII.

NEW YORK, JANUARY 25, 1788.

MADISON.

THE SAME VIEW CONTINUED.

THE *fourth* class comprises the following miscellaneous powers.

1. A power to "promote the progress of science and useful arts, by securing for a limited time, to authors and inventors, the exclusive right to their respective writings and discoveries."

The utility of this power will scarcely be questioned. The copyright of authors has been solemnly adjudged in Great Britain, to be a right at common law. The right to useful inventions, seems with equal reason to belong to the inventors. The public good fully coincides in both cases with the claims of individuals. The states cannot separately make effectual provision for either of the cases, and most of them have anticipated the decision of this point, by laws passed at the instance of congress.

2. "To exercise exclusive legislation in all cases whatsoever, over such district, (not exceeding ten miles square,) as may, by cession of particular states, and the acceptance of congress, become the seat of the government of the United States; and to exercise like authority over all places purchased by the consent of the legislature of the states, in which the same shall be, for the erection of forts, magazines, arsenals, dock-yards, and other needful buildings."

The indispensable necessity of complete authority at the seat of government, carries its own evidence with it. It is a power exercised by every legislature of the union, I might say of the world, by virtue of its general supremacy. Without it, not only the public authority might be insulted and its proceedings be interrupted with impunity, but a dependence of the members of the general government on the state comprehending the seat of the government, for protection in the exercise of their duty, might bring on the national councils an imputation of awe or influence, equally dishonourable to the government and dissatisfactory to the other members of the confederacy. This consideration has the more weight, as the gradual accumulation of public improvements at the stationary residence of the government, would be both too great a public pledge to be left in the hands of a single state, and would create so many obstacles to a removal of the government, as still further to abridge its necessary independence. The extent of this federal district is sufficiently circumscribed to satisfy every jealousy of an opposite nature. And as it is to be appropriated to this use with the consent of the state ceding it; as the state will no doubt provide in the compact for the rights, and the consent of the citizens inhabiting it; as the inhabitants will find sufficient inducements of interest, to become willing parties to the cession; as they will have had their voice in the election of the government, which is to exercise authority over them; as a municipal legislature for local purposes, derived from their own suffrages, will of course be allowed them; and as the authority of the legislature of the state, and of the inhabitants of the ceded part of it, to concur in the cession, will be derived from the whole people of the state, in their adoption of the constitution, every imaginable objection seems to be obviated.

The necessity of a like authority over forts, magazines, &c., established by the general government, is not less evident. The public money expended on such places, and the public property deposited in them, require, that they should be exempt from the authority of the particular state. Nor would it be proper for the

places on which the security of the entire union may depend,
to be in any degree dependent on a particular member of
it. All objections and scruples are here also obviated, by requiring the concurrence of the states concerned in every such
establishment.

3. "To declare the punishment of treason, but no attainder of
treason shall work corruption of blood, or forfeiture, except during the life of the person attainted."

As treason may be committed against the United States, the
authority of the United States ought to be enabled to punish it;
but as newfangled and artificial treasons have been the great
engines by which violent factions, the natural offspring of free
governments, have usually wreaked their alternate malignity on
each other, the convention have, with great judgment, opposed
a barrier to this peculiar danger, by inserting a constitutional
definition of the crime, fixing the proof necessary for conviction
of it, and restraining the congress, even in punishing it, from
extending the consequences of guilt beyond the person of its
author.

4. "To admit new states into the union; but no new state shall
be formed or erected within the jurisdiction of any other state;
nor any state be formed by the junction of two or more states,
or parts of states, without the consent of the legislatures of the
states concerned, as well as of the congress."

In the articles of confederation, no provision is found on this
important subject. Canada was to be admitted of right, on her
joining in the measures of the United States; and the other
colonies, by which were evidently meant, the other British
colonies, at the discretion of nine states. The eventual establishment of *new states*, seems to have been overlooked by the compilers of that instrument. We have seen the inconvenience of
this omission, and the assumption of power into which congress
have been led by it. With great propriety, therefore, has the
new system supplied the defect. The general precaution, that no
new states shall be formed, without the concurrence of the federal authority, and that of the states concerned, is consonant to

the principles which ought to govern such transactions. The particular precaution against the erection of new states, by the partition of a state without its consent, quiets the jealousy of the larger states; as that of the smaller is quieted by a like precaution, against a junction of states without their consent.

5. "To dispose of, and make all needful rules and regulations, respecting the territory or other property, belonging to the United States, with a proviso, that nothing in the constitution shall be so construed, as to prejudice any claims of the United States, or of any particular state."

This is a power of very great importance, and required by considerations, similar to those which show the propriety of the former. The proviso annexed, is proper in itself, and was probably rendered absolutely necessary by jealousies and questions concerning the western territory sufficiently known to the public.

6. "To guaranty to every state in the union a republican form of government; to protect each of them against invasion; and, on application of the legislature or of the executive, (when the legislature cannot be convened,) against domestic violence."

In a confederacy founded on republican principles, and composed of republican members, the superintending government ought clearly to possess authority to defend the system against aristocratic or monarchical innovations. The more intimate the nature of such an union may be, the greater interest have the members in the political institutions of each other; and the greater right to insist, that the forms of government under which the compact was entered into, should be *substantially* maintained.

But a right implies a remedy; and where else could the remedy be deposited, than where it is deposited by the constitution? Governments of dissimilar principles and forms have been found less adapted to a federal coalition of any sort, than those of a kindred nature. "As the confederate republic of Germany," says Montesquieu, "consists of free cities, and petty states, subject to different princes, experience shows us, that it is more imperfect, than that of Holland and Switzerland." "Greece was undone," he adds, "as soon as the king of Macedon obtained a seat among the Amphyctions." In the latter case, no doubt, the disproportionate force, as well as the monarchical form of the new confederate, had its share of influence on the events.

It may possibly be asked, what need there could be of such a precaution, and whether it may not become a pretext for alterations in the state governments, without the concurrence of the states themselves. These questions admit of ready answers. If the interposition of the general government should not be needed, the provision for such an event will be a harmless superfluity only in the constitution. But who can say, what experiments may be produced by the caprice of particular states, by the ambition of enterprising leaders, or by the intrigues and influence of foreign powers? To the second question it may be answered, that if the general government should interpose by virtue of this constitutional authority, it will be of course bound to pursue the authority. But the authority extends no farther than to a *guaranty* of a republican form of government, which supposes a preexisting government of the form which is to be guaranteed. As long, therefore, as the existing republican forms are continued by the states, they are guaranteed by the federal constitution. Whenever the states may choose to substitute other republican forms, they have a right to do so, and to claim the federal guaranty for the latter. The only restriction imposed on them is, that they shall not exchange republican for anti-republican constitutions; a restriction which, it is presumed, will hardly be considered as a grievance.

A protection against invasion is due, from every society, to the parts composing it. The latitude of the expression here used seems to secure each state, not only against foreign hostility, but against ambitious or vindictive enterprises of its more powerful neighbours. The history, both of ancient and modern confederacies, proves, that the weaker members of the union ought not to be insensible to the policy of this article.

Protection against domestic violence is added with equal propriety. It has been remarked, that even among the Swiss cantons, which, properly speaking, are not under one government,
provision is made for this object: and the history of that league
informs us, that mutual aid is frequently claimed and afforded;
and as well by the most democratic, as the other cantons. A
recent and well-known event among ourselves has warned us to
be prepared for emergencies of a like nature.

At first view, it might seem not to square with the republican
theory, to suppose, either that a majority have not the right, or
that a minority will have the force, to subvert a government;
and consequently, that the federal interposition can never be
required, but when it would be improper. But theoretic reasoning, in this, as in most other cases, must be qualified by the
lessons of practice. Why may not illicit combinations, for purposes of violence, be formed as well by a majority of a state,
especially a small state, as by a majority of a county, or a district of the same state; and if the authority of the state ought in
the latter case to protect the local magistracy, ought not the
federal authority in the former to support the state authority?
Besides, there are certain parts of the state constitutions, which
are so interwoven with the federal constitution, that a violent
blow cannot be given to the one, without communicating the
wound to the other. Insurrections in a state will rarely induce a
federal interposition, unless the number concerned in them bear
some proportion to the friends of government. It will be much
better, that the violence in such cases should be repressed by
the superintending power, than that the majority should be left
to maintain their cause by a bloody and obstinate contest. The
existence of a right to interpose, will generally prevent the
necessity of exerting it.

Is it true, that force and right are necessarily on the same
side in republican governments? May not the minor party possess such a superiority of pecuniary resources, of military talents and experience, or of secret succours from foreign powers,

as will render it superiour also in an appeal to the sword? May
not a more compact and advantageous position turn the scale on
the same side, against a superiour number so situated as to be
less capable of a prompt and collected exertion of its strength?
Nothing can be more chimerical than to imagine, that in a trial
of actual force, victory may be calculated by the rules which
prevail in a census of the inhabitants, or which determine the
event of an election! May it not happen, in fine, that the minority of *citizens* may become a majority of *persons*, by the accession of alien residents, of a casual concourse of adventurers, or
of those whom the constitution of the state has not admitted to
the rights of suffrage? I take no notice of an unhappy species
of population abounding in some of the states, who, during
the calm of regular government, are sunk below the level of
men; but who, in the tempestuous scenes of civil violence,
may emerge into the human character, and give a superiority of strength to any party with which they may associate
themselves.

In cases where it may be doubtful on which side justice lies,
what better umpires could be desired by two violent factions,
flying to arms and tearing a state to pieces, than the representatives of confederate states, not heated by the local flame? To
the impartiality of judges, they would unite the affection of
friends. Happy would it be, if such a remedy for its infirmities
could be enjoyed by all free governments; if a project equally
effectual, could be established for the universal peace of
mankind!

Should it be asked, what is to be the redress for an insurrection pervading all the states, and comprising a superiority of the
entire force, though not a constitutional right? The answer must
be, that such a case, as it would be without the compass of
human remedies, so it is fortunately not within the compass of
human probability; and that it is a sufficient recommendation
of the federal constitution, that it diminishes the risk of a calamity, for which no possible constitution can provide a cure.

Among the advantages of a confederate republic, enumerated by Montesquieu, an important one is, "that should a popular insurrection happen in one of the states, the others are able to quell it. Should abuses creep into one part, they are reformed by those that remain sound."

7. "To consider all debts contracted, and engagements entered into, before the adoption of this constitution, as being no less valid against the United States under this constitution, than under the confederation."

This can only be considered as a declaratory proposition; and may have been inserted, among other reasons, for the satisfaction of the foreign creditors of the United States, who cannot be strangers to the pretended doctrine, that a change in the political form of civil society, has the magical effect of dissolving its moral obligations.

Among the lesser criticisms which have been exercised on the constitution, it has been remarked, that the validity of engagements ought to have been asserted in favour of the United States, as well as against them; and in the spirit which usually characterizes little critics, the omission has been transformed and magnified into a plot against the national rights. The authors of this discovery may be told, what few others need be informed of, that as engagements are in their nature reciprocal, an assertion of their validity on one side, necessarily involves a validity on the other side; and that as the article is merely declaratory, the establishment of the principle in one case, is sufficient for every case. They may be further told, that every constitution must limit its precautions to dangers that are not altogether imaginary; and that no real danger can exist that the government would *dare*, with, or even without, this constitutional declaration before it, to remit the debts justly due to the public, on the pretext here condemned.

8. "To provide for amendments to be ratified by three fourths of the states, under two exceptions only."

That useful alterations will be suggested by experience, could not but be foreseen. It was requisite, therefore, that a mode for introducing them should be provided. The mode preferred by the convention seems to be stamped with every mark of propriety. It guards equally against that extreme facility, which would render the constitution too mutable; and that extreme difficulty, which might perpetuate its discovered faults. It moreover equally enables the general and the state governments to originate the amendment of errours, as they may be pointed out by the experience on one side, or on the other. The exception in favour of the equality of suffrage in the senate, was probably meant as a palladium to the residuary sovereignty of the states, implied and secured by that principle of representation in one branch of the legislature; and was probably insisted on by the states particularly attached to that equality. The other exception must have been admitted on the same considerations which produced the privilege defended by it.

9. "The ratification of the conventions of nine states, shall be sufficient for the establishment of this constitution between the states ratifying the same."

This article speaks for itself. The express authority of the people alone could give due validity to the constitution. To have required the unanimous ratification of the thirteen states, would have subjected the essential interests of the whole, to the caprice or corruption of a single member. It would have marked a want of foresight in the convention, which our own experience would have rendered inexcusable.

Two questions of a very delicate nature present themselves on this occasion: 1. On what principle the confederation, which stands in the solemn form of a compact among the states, can be superseded without the unanimous consent of the parties to it: 2. What relation is to subsist between the nine or more states ratifying the constitution, and the remaining few who do not become parties to it?

The first question is answered at once by recurring to the absolute necessity of the case; to the great principle of self-preservation; to the transcendent law of nature and of nature's God, which declares that the safety and happiness of society are the objects at which all political institutions aim, and to which all such institutions must be sacrificed. *Perhaps*, also, an answer may be found without searching beyond the principles of the compact itself. It has been heretofore noted among the defects of the confederation, that in many of the states, it had received no higher sanction than a mere legislative ratification. The principle of reciprocality seems to require, that its obligation on the other states should be reduced to the same standard. A compact between independent sovereigns, founded on acts of legislative authority, can pretend to no higher validity than a league or treaty between the parties. It is an established doctrine on the subject of treaties, that all the articles are mutually conditions of each other; that a breach of any one article is a breach of the whole treaty; and that a breach, committed by either of the parties, absolves the others, and authorizes them, if they please, to pronounce the compact violated and void. Should it unhappily be necessary to appeal to these delicate truths, for a justification for dispensing with the consent of particular states to a dissolution of the federal pact, will not the complaining parties find it a difficult task to answer the *multiplied* and *important* infractions, with which they may be confronted? The time has been, when it was incumbent on us all to veil the ideas which this paragraph exhibits. The scene is now changed, and with it the part which the same motives dictate.

The second question is not less delicate: and the flattering prospect of its being merely hypothetical, forbids an over curious discussion of it. It is one of those cases which must be left to provide for itself. In general, it may be observed, that although no political relation can subsist between the assenting and dissenting states, yet the moral relations will remain uncancelled. The claims of justice, both on one side and on the other, will be in force, and must be fulfilled; the rights of humanity must in all cases be duly and mutually respected; whilst considerations of a common interest, and above all, the remembrance of the endearing scenes which are past, and the anticipation of a speedy triumph over the obstacles to reunion, will, it is hoped, not urge in vain *moderation* on one side, and *prudence* on the other.

PUBLIUS.

THE FEDERALIST.

NUMBER XLIV.

NEW YORK, JANUARY 25, 1788.

MADISON.

THE SAME VIEW CONTINUED AND CONCLUDED.

A *fifth* class of provisions in favour of the federal authority, consists of the following restrictions on the authority of the several states.

1. "No state shall enter into any treaty, alliance or confederation; grant letters of marque and reprisal; coin money; emit bills of credit; make any thing but gold and silver a legal tender in payment of debts; pass any bill of attainder, *ex post facto* law, or law impairing the obligation of contracts; or grant any title of nobility."

The prohibition against treaties, alliances, and confederations, makes a part of the existing articles of union; and, for reasons which need no explanation, is copied into the new constitution. The prohibition of letters of marque, is another part of the old system, but is somewhat extended in the new. According to the former, letters of marque could be granted by the states after a declaration of war: according to the latter, these licenses must be obtained, as well during the war, as previous to its declaration, from the government of the United States. This alteration is fully justified, by the advantage of uniformity in all points which relate to foreign powers; and of immediate responsibility to the nation in all those, for whose conduct the nation itself is to be responsible.

The right of coining money, which is here taken from the states, was left in their hands by the confederation, as a concurrent right with that of congress, under an exception in favour of the exclusive right of congress to regulate the alloy and value. In this instance, also, the new provision is an improvement on the old. Whilst the alloy and value depended on the general authority, a right of coinage in the particular states could have no other effect than to multiply expensive mints, and diversify the forms and weights of the circulating pieces. The latter inconveniency defeats one purpose for which the power was originally submitted to the federal head: and as far as the former might prevent an inconvenient remittance of gold and silver to the central mint for recoinage, the end can be as well attained by local mints established under the general authority.

The extension of the prohibition to bills of credit, must give pleasure to every citizen, in proportion to his love of justice, and his knowledge of the true springs of public prosperity. The loss which America has sustained since the peace, from the pestilent effects of paper money on the necessary confidence between man and man; on the necessary confidence in the public councils; on the industry and morals of the people, and on the character of republican government, constitutes an enormous debt against the states, chargeable with this unadvised measure, which must long remain unsatisfied; or rather an accumulation of guilt, which can be expiated no otherwise than by a voluntary sacrifice on the altar of justice, of the power which has been the instrument of it. In addition to these persuasive considerations, it may be observed, that the same reasons which show the necessity of denying to the states the power of regulating coin prove, with equal force, that they ought not to be at liberty to substitute a paper medium, in the place of coin. Had every state a right to regulate the value of its coin, there might be as many different currencies as states; and thus, the intercourse among them would be impeded: retrospective alterations in its value might be made, and thus the citizens of other states be injured and animosities be kindled among the states themselves. The subjects of foreign powers might suffer from the same cause, and hence the union be discredited and embroiled by the indiscretion of a single member. No one of these mischiefs is less incident to a power in the states to emit paper money, than to coin gold or silver. The power to make any thing but gold and silver a tender in payment of debts, is withdrawn from the states, on the same principle with that of issuing a paper currency.

Bills of attainder, *ex post facto* laws, and laws impairing the obligation of contracts, are contrary to the first principles of the social compact, and to every principle of sound legislation. The two former are expressly prohibited by the declarations prefixed to some of the state constitutions, and all of them are prohibited by the spirit and scope of these fundamental charters. Our own experience has taught us, nevertheless, that additional fences against these dangers ought not to be omitted. Very properly, therefore, have the convention added this constitutional bulwark in favour of personal security and private rights; and I am much deceived, if they have not, in so doing, as faithfully consulted the genuine sentiments, as the undoubted interests of their constituents. The sober people of America are weary of the fluctuating policy which has directed the public councils. They have seen with regret and with indignation, that sudden changes, and legislative interferences, in cases affecting personal rights, become jobs in the hands of enterprising and influential speculators; and snares to the more industrious and less informed part of the community. They have seen, too, that one legislative interference is but the first link of a long chain of repetitions; every subsequent interference being naturally produced by the effects of the preceding. They very rightly infer, therefore, that some thorough reform is wanting, which will banish speculations on public measures, inspire a general prudence and industry, and give a regular course to the business of society. The prohibition with respect to titles of nobility, is copied from the articles of confederation, and needs no comment.

2. "No state shall, without the consent of the congress lay any imposts or duties on imports or exports, except what may be absolutely necessary for executing its inspection laws, and the neat produce of all duties and imposts laid by any state on imports or exports, shall be for the use of the treasury of the United States; and all such laws shall be subject to the revision and control of the congress. No state shall, without the consent of congress, lay any duty on tonnage, keep troops or ships of war in time of peace; enter into any agreement or compact with another state, or with a foreign power, or engage in war unless actually invaded, or in such imminent danger as will not admit of delay."

The restraint on the power of the states over imports and exports, is enforced by all the arguments which prove the necessity of submitting the regulation of trade to the federal councils. It is needless, therefore, to remark further on this head, than that the manner in which the restraint is qualified, seems well calculated at once to secure to the states a reasonable discretion in providing for the conveniency of their imports and exports, and to the United States a reasonable check against the abuse of this discretion. The remaining particulars of this clause, fall within reasonings which are either so obvious, or have been so fully developed, that they may be passed over without remark.

The sixth and last class, consists of the several powers and provisions, by which efficacy is given to all the rest.

1. "Of these the first is, the power to make all laws which shall be necessary and proper for carrying into execution the foregoing powers, and all other powers vested by this constitution in the government of the United States, or in any department or officer thereof."

Few parts of the constitution have been assailed with more intemperance than this; yet on a fair investigation of it, as has been elsewhere shown, no part can appear more completely invulnerable. Without the *substance* of this power, the whole constitution would be a dead letter. Those who object to the article, therefore, as a part of the constitution, can only mean that the *form* of the provision is improper, But have they considered, whether a better form could have been substituted?

There are four other possible methods, which the convention might have taken on this subject. They might have copied the second article of the existing confederation, which would have prohibited the exercise of any power not *expressly* delegated: they might have attempted a positive enumeration of the powers comprehended under the general terms "necessary and proper:" they might have attempted a negative enumeration of them, by specifying the powers excepted from the general definition: they might have been altogether silent on the subject; leaving these necessary and proper powers, to construction and inference.

Had the convention taken the first method of adopting the second article of confederation, it is evident that the new congress would be continually exposed, as their predecessors have been, to the alternative of construing the term *"expressly"* with so much rigour, as to disarm the government of all real authority whatever, or with so much latitude as to destroy altogether the force of the restriction. It would be easy to show, if it were necessary, that no important power, delegated by the articles of confederation, has been or can be executed by congress without recurring more or less to the doctrine of *construction* or *implication.* As the powers delegated under the new system are more extensive, the government which is to administer it would find itself still more distressed with the alternative of betraying the public interest by doing nothing; or of violating the constitution by exercising powers indispensably necessary and proper; but, at the same time, not *expressly* granted.

Had the convention attempted a positive enumeration of the powers necessary and proper for carrying their other powers into effect; the attempt would have involved a complete digest of laws on every subject to which the constitution relates; accommodated too not only to the existing state of things, but to all the possible changes which futurity may produce: for in every new application of a general power, the *particular powers*, which are the means of attaining the *object* of the general power, must always necessarily vary with that object; and be often properly varied whilst the object remains the same.

Had they attempted to enumerate the particular powers or means not necessary or proper for carrying the general powers into execution, the task would have been no less chimerical; and would have been liable to this further objection; that every defect in the enumeration, would have been equivalent to a positive grant of authority. If, to avoid this consequence, they had attempted a partial enumeration of the exceptions, and described the residue by the general terms, *not necessary or proper*; it must have happened that the enumeration would comprehend a few of the excepted powers only; that these would be such as would be least likely to be assumed or tolerated, because the enumeration would of course select such as would be least necessary or proper, and that the unnecessary and improper powers included in the residuum, would be less forcibly excepted, than if no partial enumeration had been made.

Had the constitution been silent on this head, there can be no doubt that all the particular powers requisite as means of executing the general powers would have resulted to the government, by unavoidable implication. No axiom is more clearly established in law, or in reason, than that wherever the end is required, the means are authorized; wherever a general power to do a thing is given, every particular power necessary for doing it is included. Had this last method, therefore, been pursued by the convention, every objection now urged against their plan, would remain in all its plausibility; and the real inconveniency would be incurred of not removing a pretext which may be seized on critical occasions, for drawing into question the essential powers of the union.

If it be asked, what is to be the consequence, in case the congress shall misconstrue this part of the constitution, and exercise powers not warranted by its true meaning; I answer the same as if they should misconstrue or enlarge any other power vested in them; as if the general power had been reduced to particulars, and any one of these were to be violated; the same in short, as if the state legislatures should violate their respective constitutional authorities. In the first instance, the success of the usurpation will depend on the executive and judiciary departments, which are to expound and give effect to the legislative acts; and in the last resort, a remedy must be obtained from the people, who can, by the election of more faithful representatives, annual the acts of the usurpers. The truth is, that this ultimate redress may be more confided in against unconstitutional acts of the federal, than of the state legislatures, for this plain reason, that as every such act of the former, will be an invasion of the rights of the latter, these will be ever ready to mark the innovation, to sound the alarm to the people, and to exert their local influence in effecting a change of federal representatives. There being no such intermediate body between the state legislatures and the people, interested in watching the conduct of the former, violations of the state constitutions are more likely to remain unnoticed and unredressed.

2. "This constitution, and the laws of the United States which shall be made in pursuance thereof, and all treaties made, or which shall be made, under the authority of the United States, shall be the supreme law of the land, and the judges in every state shall be bound thereby, any thing in the constitution or laws of any state to the contrary notwithstanding."

The indiscreet zeal of the adversaries to the constitution, has betrayed them into an attack on this part of it also, without which it would have been evidently and radically defective. To be fully sensible of this, we need only suppose for a moment, that the supremacy of the state constitutions had been left complete, by a saving clause in their favour.

In the first place, as these constitutions invest the state legislatures with absolute sovereignty, in all cases not excepted by the existing articles of confederation, all the authorities contained in the proposed constitution, so far as they exceed those enumerated in the confederation, would have been annulled, and the new congress would have been reduced to the same impotent condition with their predecessors.

In the next place, as the constitutions of some of the states do not even expressly and fully recognise the existing powers of the confederacy, an express saving of the supremacy of the former would, in such states, have brought into question every power contained in the proposed constitution.

In the third place, as the constitutions of the states differ much from each other, it might happen that a treaty or national law of great and equal importance to the states, would interfere with some, and not with other constitutions, and would consequently be valid in some of the states, at the same time that it would have no effect in others.

In fine, the world would have seen for the first time, a system of government founded on an inversion of the fundamental principles of all government; it would have seen the authority of the whole society everywhere subordinate to the authority of the parts; it would have seen a monster, in which the head was under the direction of the members.

3. "The senators and representatives, and the members of the several state legislatures; and all executive and judicial officers, both of the United States and the several states, shall be bound by oath or affirmation, to support this constitution."

It has been asked, why it was thought necessary, that the state magistracy should be bound to support the federal constitution, and unnecessary that a like oath should be imposed on the officers of the United States, in favour of the state constitutions?

Several reasons might be assigned for the distinctions. I content myself with one, which is obvious and conclusive. The members of the federal government will have no agency in carrying the state constitutions into effect. The members and officers of the state governments, on the contrary, will have an essential agency in giving effect to the federal constitution. The election of the president and senate will depend, in all cases, on the legislatures of the several states. And the election of the house of representatives will equally depend on the same authority in the first instance; and will, probably, for ever be conducted by the officers, and according to the laws of the states.

4. Among the provisions for giving efficacy to the federal powers, might be added those which belong to the executive and judiciary departments: but as these are reserved for particular examination in another place, I pass them over in this.

We have now reviewed, in detail, all the articles composing the sum or quantity of power, delegated by the proposed constitution to the federal government; and are brought to this undeniable conclusion, that no part of the power is unnecessary or improper, for accomplishing the necessary objects of the union. The question therefore, whether this amount of power shall be granted or not, resolves itself into another question, whether or not a government commensurate to the exigencies of the union, shall be established; or, in other words, whether the union itself shall be preserved.

PUBLIUS.

THE FEDERALIST.

NUMBER XLV.

NEW YORK, JANUARY 29, 1788.

MADISON.

A FURTHER DISCUSSION OF THE SUPPOSED DANGER FROM THE
POWERS OF THE UNION, TO THE STATE GOVERNMENTS.

HAVING shown, that no one of the powers transferred to the
federal government is unnecessary or improper, the next question to be considered is, whether the whole mass of them will be
dangerous to the portion of authority left in the several states.

The adversaries to the plan of the convention, instead of considering in the first place, what degree of power was absolutely
necessary for the purposes of the federal government, have
exhausted themselves in a secondary inquiry into the possible
consequences of the proposed degree of power to the governments of the particular states. But if the union, as has been
shown, be essential to the security of the people of America
against foreign danger; if it be essential to their security
against contentions and wars among the different states; if it
be essential to guard them against those violent and oppressive
factions, which imbitter the blessings of liberty, and against
those military establishments which must gradually poison its
very fountain; if, in a word, the union be essential to the happiness of the people of America, is it not preposterous, to urge
as an objection to a government, without which the objects of
the union cannot be attained, that such a government may dero-

gate from the importance of the governments of the individual
states? Was then the American revolution effected, was the
American confederacy formed, was the precious blood of thousands spilt, and the hard-earned substance of millions lavished,
not that the people of America should enjoy peace, liberty, and
safety; but that the governments of the individual states, that
particular municipal establishments, might enjoy a certain
extent of power, and be arrayed with certain dignities and
attributes of sovereignty? We have heard of the impious doctrine in the old world, that the people were made for kings, not
kings for the people. Is the same doctrine to be revived in the
new, in another shape, that the solid happiness of the people is
to be sacrificed to the views of political institutions of a different form? It is too early for politicians to presume on our
forgetting that the public good, the real welfare of the great
body of the people, is the supreme object to be pursued; and
that no form of government whatever has any other value, than
as it may be fitted for the attainment of this object. Were the
plan of the convention adverse to the public happiness, my
voice would be, Reject the plan. Were the union itself inconsistent with the public happiness, it would be, Abolish the
union. In like manner, as far as the sovereignty of the states
cannot be reconciled to the happiness of the people, the voice
of every good citizen must be, Let the former be sacrificed to
the latter. How far the sacrifice is necessary, has been shown.
How far the unsacrificed residue will be endangered, is the
question before us.

Several important considerations have been touched in the
course of these papers, which discountenance the supposition,
that the operation of the federal government will by degrees
prove fatal to the state governments. The more I revolve the
subject, the more fully I am persuaded, that the balance is much
more likely to be disturbed by the preponderancy of the last
than of the first scale.

We have seen, in all the examples of ancient and modern confederacies, the strongest tendency continually betraying itself

in the members, to despoil the general government of its authorities, with a very ineffectual capacity in the latter to defend itself against the encroachments. Although in most of these examples, the system has been so dissimilar from that under consideration, as greatly to weaken any inference concerning the latter, from the fate of the former; yet as the states will retain, under the proposed constitution, a very extensive portion of active sovereignty, the inference ought not to be wholly disregarded. In the Achæan league, it is probable that the federal head had a degree and species of power, which gave it a considerable likeness to the government framed by the convention. The Lycian confederacy, as far as its principles and form are transmitted, must have borne a still greater analogy to it. Yet history does not inform us, that either of them ever degenerated, or tended to degenerate, into one consolidated government. On the contrary, we know that the ruin of one of them proceeded from the incapacity of the federal authority to prevent the dissensions, and finally the disunion of the subordinate authorities. These cases are the more worthy of our attention, as the external causes by which the component parts were pressed together, were much more numerous and powerful than in our case; and consequently, less powerful ligaments within would be sufficient to bind the members to the head, and to each other.

In the feudal system, we have seen a similar propensity exemplified. Notwithstanding the want of proper sympathy in every instance between the local sovereigns and the people, and the sympathy in some instances between the general sovereign and the latter; it usually happened that the local sovereigns prevailed in the rivalship for encroachments. Had no external dangers enforced internal harmony and subordination; and particularly, had the local sovereigns possessed the affections of the people, the great kingdoms in Europe would at this time consist of as many independent princes, as there were formerly feudatory barons.

The state governments will have the advantage of the federal

government, whether we compare them in respect to the immediate dependence of the one on the other; to the weight of personal influence which each side will possess; to the powers
respectively vested in them; to the predilection and probable
support of the people; to the disposition and faculty of resisting
and frustrating the measures of each other.

The state governments may be regarded as constituent and
essential parts of the federal government; whilst the latter is
nowise essential to the operation or organization of the former.
Without the intervention of the state legislatures, the president
of the United States cannot be elected at all. They must in all
cases have a great share in his appointment, and will, perhaps,
in most cases, of themselves determine it. The senate will be
elected absolutely and exclusively by the state legislatures.
Even the house of representatives, though drawn immediately
from the people, will be chosen very much under the influence
of that class of men, whose influence over the people obtains for
themselves an election into the state legislatures. Thus, each of
the principal branches of the federal government will owe its
existence more or less to the favour of the state governments,
and must consequently feel a dependence, which is much more
likely to beget a disposition too obsequious, than too overbearing towards them. On the other side, the component parts of the
state governments will in no instance be indebted for their
appointment to the direct agency of the federal government, and
very little, if at all, to the local influence of its members.

The number of individuals employed under the constitution
of the United States, will be much smaller than the number
employed under the particular states. There will consequently
be less of personal influence on the side of the former than of
the latter. The members of the legislative, executive, and judiciary departments of thirteen and more states; the justices of
peace, officers of militia, ministerial officers of justice, with all
the county, corporation, and town officers, for three millions
and more of people, intermixed, and having particular acquaintance with every class and circle of people, must exceed beyond

all proportion, both in number and influence, those of every description who will be employed in the administration of the federal system. Compare the members of the three great departments, of the thirteen states, excluding from the judiciary department the justices of peace, with the members of the corresponding departments of the single government of the union; compare the militia officers of three millions of people, with the military and marine officers of any establishment which is within the compass of probability, or, I may add, of possibility; and in this view alone, we may pronounce the advantage of the states to be decisive. If the federal government is to have collectors of revenue, the state governments will have theirs also. And as those of the former will be principally on the seacoast, and not very numerous, whilst those of the latter will be spread over the face of the country, and will be very numerous, the advantage in this view also lies on the same side. It is true that the confederacy is to possess, and may exercise the power of collecting internal as well as external taxes throughout the states: but it is probable that this power will not be resorted to, except for supplemental purposes of revenue; that an option will then be given to the states to supply their quotas by previous collections of their own; and that the eventual collection, under the immediate authority of the union, will generally be made by the officers, and according to the rules appointed by the several states. Indeed, it is extremely probable, that in other instances, particularly in the organization of the judicial power, the officers of the states will be clothed with the correspondent authority of the union. Should it happen, however, that separate collectors of internal revenue should be appointed under the federal government, the influence of the whole number would not bear a comparison with that of the multitude of state officers in the opposite scale. Within every district, to which a federal collector would be allotted, there would not be less than thirty or forty, or even more officers, of different descriptions, and many of them persons of character and weight, whose influence would lie on the side of the state.

The powers delegated by the proposed constitution to the federal government, are few and defined. Those which are to remain in the state governments, are numerous and indefinite. The former will be exercised principally on external objects, as war, peace, negotiation, and foreign commerce; with which last the power of taxation will, for the most part, be connected. The powers reserved to the several states will extend to all the objects, which, in the ordinary course of affairs, concern the lives, liberties, and properties of the people; and the internal order, improvement, and prosperity of the state.

The operations of the federal government will be most extensive and important in times of war and danger; those of the state governments in times of peace and security. As the former periods will probably bear a small proportion to the latter, the state governments will here enjoy another advantage over the federal government. The more adequate indeed the federal powers may be rendered to the national defence, the less frequent will be those scenes of danger which might favour their ascendancy over the governments of the particular states.

If the new constitution be examined with accuracy and candour, it will be found that the change which it proposes, consists much less in the addition of NEW POWERS to the union, than in the invigoration of its ORIGINAL POWERS. The regulation of commerce, it is true, is a new power; but that seems to be an addition which few oppose, and from which no apprehensions are entertained. The powers relating to war and peace, armies and fleets, treaties and finance, with the other more considerable powers, are all vested in the existing congress by the articles of confederation. The proposed change does not enlarge these powers; it only substitutes a more effectual mode of administering them. The change relating to taxation, may be regarded as the most important: and yet the present congress have as complete authority to REQUIRE of the states indefinite supplies of money for the common defence and general welfare, as the future congress will have to require them of individual citizens; and the latter will be no more bound than the states themselves have been, to pay the quotas respectively taxed on them. Had the states complied punctually with the articles of confederation, or could their compliance have been enforced by as peaceable means as may be used with success towards single persons, our past experience is very far from countenancing an opinion, that the state governments would have lost their constitutional pow- ers, and have gradually undergone an entire consolidation. To maintain that such an event would have ensued, would be to say at once, that the existence of the state governments is incom- patible with any system whatever, that accomplishes the essen- tial purposes of the union.

PUBLIUS.

THE FEDERALIST.

NUMBER XLVI.

NEW YORK, JANUARY 29, 1788.

MADISON.

THE SUBJECT OF THE LAST PAPER RESUMED; WITH AN EXAMI-
NATION OF THE COMPARATIVE MEANS OF INFLUENCE OF THE
FEDERAL AND STATE GOVERNMENTS.

RESUMING the subject of the last paper, I proceed to inquire,
whether the federal government or the state governments, will
have the advantage with regard to the predilection and support
of the people.

Notwithstanding the different modes in which they are
appointed, we must consider both of them as substantially
dependent on the great body of the citizens of the United
States. I assume this position here as it respects the first,
reserving the proofs for another place. The federal and state
governments are in fact but different agents and trustees of the
people, instituted with different powers, and designated for different purposes. The adversaries of the constitution seem to
have lost sight of the people altogether, in their reasonings on
this subject; and to have viewed these different establishments,
not only as mutual rivals and enemies, but as uncontrolled by
any common superiour, in their efforts to usurp the authorities
of each other. These gentlemen must here be reminded of their
errour. They must be told, that the ultimate authority, wherever the derivative may be found, resides in the people alone;

and that it will not depend merely on the comparative ambition or address of the different governments, whether either, or which of them, will be able to enlarge its sphere of jurisdiction at the expense of the other. Truth, no less than decency, requires, that the event, in every case, should be supposed to depend on the sentiments and sanction of their common constituents.

Many considerations, besides those suggested on a former occasion, seem to place it beyond doubt, that the first and most natural attachment of the people will be to the governments of their respective states. Into the administration of these, a greater number of individuals will expect to rise. From the gift of these, a greater number of offices and emoluments will flow. By the superintending care of these, all the more domestic and personal interests of the people will be regulated and provided for. With the affairs of these, the people will be more familiarly and minutely conversant: and with the members of these, will a greater proportion of the people have the ties of personal acquaintance and friendship, and of family and party attachments. On the side of these, therefore, the popular bias may well be expected most strongly to incline.

Experience speaks the same language in this case. The federal administration, though hitherto very defective, in comparison with what may be hoped under a better system, had, during the war, and particularly whilst the independent fund of paper emissions was in credit, an activity and importance as great as it can well have, in any future circumstances whatever. It was engaged, too, in a course of measures which had for their object the protection of every thing that was dear, and the acquisition of every thing that could be desirable to the people at large. It was, nevertheless, invariably found, after the transient enthusiasm for the early congresses was over, that the attention and attachment of the people were turned anew to their own particular governments; that the federal council was at no time the idol of popular favour; and that opposition to proposed enlargements of its powers and importance, was the side usually taken by the men, who wished to build their political consequence on the prepossessions of their fellow-citizens.

If, therefore, as has been elsewhere remarked, the people should in future become more partial to the federal than to the state governments, the change can only result from such manifest and irresistible proofs of a better administration, as will overcome all their antecedent propensities. And in that case, the people ought not surely to be precluded from giving most of their confidence where they may discover it to be most due: but even in that case, the state governments could have little to apprehend, because it is only within a certain sphere, that the federal power can, in the nature of things, be advantageously administered.

The remaining points, on which I propose to compare the federal and state governments, are the disposition and faculty they may respectively possess, to resist and frustrate the measures of each other.

It has been already proved, that the members of the federal will be more dependent on the members of the state governments, than the latter will be on the former. It has appeared also, that the prepossessions of the people, on whom both will depend, will be more on the side of the state governments, than of the federal government. So far as the disposition of each, towards the other, may be influenced by these causes, the state governments must clearly have the advantage. But in a distinct and very important point of view, the advantage will lie on the same side. The prepossessions, which the members themselves will carry into the federal government, will generally be favourable to the states; whilst it will rarely happen, that the members of the state governments will carry into the public councils a bias in favour of the general government. A local spirit will infallibly prevail much more in the members of the congress, than a national spirit will prevail in the legislatures of the particular states. Every one knows, that a great proportion of the errours committed by the state legislatures, proceeds from the disposition of the members to sacrifice the comprehensive and permanent interests of the state, to the particular and separate views of the counties or districts in which they reside. And if they do not sufficiently enlarge their policy, to embrace the collective welfare of their particular state, how can it be imagined, that they will make the aggregate prosperity of the union, and the dignity and respectability of its government, the objects of their affections and consultations? For the same reason, that the members of the state legislatures will be unlikely to attach themselves sufficiently to national objects, the members of the federal legislature will be likely to attach themselves too much to local objects. The states will be to the latter, what counties and towns are to the former. Measures will too often be decided according to their probable effect, not on the national prosperity and happiness, but on the prejudices, interests, and pursuits of the governments and people of the individual states. What is the spirit that has in general characterized the proceedings of congress? A perusal of their journals, as well as the candid acknowledgements of such as have had a seat in that assembly, will inform us, that the members have but too frequently displayed the character, rather of partisans of their respective states, than of impartial guardians of a common interest; that where, on one occasion, improper sacrifices have been made of local considerations to the aggrandizement of the federal government, the great interests of the nation have suffered on an hundred, from an undue attention to the local prejudices, interests, and views of the particular states. I mean not by these reflections to insinuate, that the new federal government will not embrace a more enlarged plan of policy, than the existing government may have pursued; much less, that its views will be as confined as those of the state legislatures: but only that it will partake sufficiently of the spirit of both, to be disinclined to invade the rights of the individual states, or the prerogatives of their governments. The motives on the part of the state governments, to augment their prerogatives by defalcations from the federal government, will be overruled by no reciprocal predispositions in the members.

Were it admitted, however, that the federal government may feel an equal disposition with the state governments to extend its power beyond the due limits, the latter would still have the advantage in the means of defeating such encroachments. If an act of a particular state, though unfriendly to the national government, be generally popular in that state, and should not too grossly violate the oaths of the state officers, it is executed immediately, and, of course, by means on the spot, and depending on the state alone. The opposition of the federal government, or the interposition of federal officers, would but inflame the zeal of all parties on the side of the state; and the evil could not be prevented or repaired, if at all, without the employment of means which must always be resorted to with reluctance and difficulty. On the other hand, should an unwarrantable measure of the federal government be unpopular in particular states, which would seldom fail to be the case, or even a warrantable measure be so, which may sometimes be the case, the means of opposition to it are powerful and at hand. The disquietude of the people; their repugnance, and perhaps refusal, to cooperate with the officers of the union; the frowns of the executive magistracy of the state; the embarrassments created by legislative devices, which would often be added on such occasions, would oppose, in any state, difficulties not to be despised; would form, in a large state, very serious impediments; and where the sentiments of several adjoining states happened to be in unison, would present obstructions which the federal government would hardly be willing to encounter.

But ambitious encroachments of the federal government, on the authority of the state governments, would not excite the opposition of a single state, or of a few states only. They would be signals of general alarm. Every government would espouse the common cause. A correspondence would be opened. Plans of resistance would be concerted. One spirit would animate and conduct the whole. The same combination, in short, would result from an apprehension of the federal, as was produced by the dread of a foreign yoke; and unless the projected innovations should be voluntarily renounced, the same appeal to a trial of force would be made in the one case, as was made in the other. But what degree of madness could ever drive the federal government to such an extremity? In the contest with Great Britain, one part of the empire was employed against the other. The more numerous part invaded the rights of the less numerous part. The attempt was unjust and unwise; but it was not in speculation absolutely chimerical. But what would be the contest, in the case we are supposing? Who would be the parties? A few representatives of the people would be opposed to the people themselves; or rather one set of representatives would be contending against thirteen sets of representatives, with the whole body of their common constituents on the side of the latter.

The only refuge left for those who prophesy the downfal of the state governments, is the visionary supposition, that the federal government may previously accumulate a military force for the projects of ambition. The reasonings contained in these papers must have been employed to little purpose indeed, if it could be necessary now to disprove the reality of this danger. That the people and the states should, for a sufficient period of time, elect an uninterrupted succession of men ready to betray both; that the traitors should, throughout this period, uniformly and systematically pursue some fixed plan for the extension of the military establishment; that the governments and the people of the states should silently and patiently behold the gathering storm, and continue to supply the materials, until it should be prepared to burst on their own heads, must appear to every one more like the incoherent dreams of a delirious jealousy, or the misjudged exaggerations of a counterfeit zeal, than like the sober apprehensions of genuine patriotism. Extravagant as the supposition is, let it however be made. Let a regular army, fully equal to the resources of the country, be formed; and let it be entirely at the devotion of the federal government; still it would not be going too far to say, that the state governments, with the people on their side, would be able to repel the danger. The highest number to which, according to the best computation, a standing army can be carried in any country, does not exceed one hundredth part of the whole number of souls; or one twenty-fifth part of the number able to bear arms. This proportion would not yield, in the United States, an army of more than twenty-five or thirty thousand men. To these would be opposed a militia amounting to near half a million of citizens with arms in their hands, officered by men chosen from among themselves, fighting for their common liberties, and united and conducted by governments possessing their affections and confidence. It may well be doubted, whether a militia thus circumstanced, could ever be conquered by such a proportion of regular troops. Those, who are best acquainted with the late successful resistance of this country against the British arms, will be most inclined to deny the possibility of it. Besides the advantage of being armed, which the Americans possess over the people of almost every other nation, the existence of subordinate governments, to which the people are attached, and by which the militia officers are appointed, forms a barrier against the enterprises of ambition, more insurmountable than any which a simple government of any form can admit of. Notwithstanding the military establishments in the several kingdoms of Europe, which are carried as far as the public resources will bear, the governments are afraid to trust the people with arms. And it is not certain, that with this aid alone, they would not be able to shake off their yokes. But were the people to possess the additional advantages of local governments chosen by themselves, who could collect the national will, and direct the national force, and of officers appointed out of the militia, by these governments, and attached both to them and to the militia, it may be affirmed with the greatest assurance, that the throne of every tyranny in Europe would be speedily overturned in spite of the legions which surround it. Let us not insult the free and gallant citizens of America with the suspicion, that they would be less able to defend the rights of which they would be in actual possession, than the debased subjects of arbitrary power would be to rescue theirs from the hands of their oppressors. Let us rather no longer insult them with the supposition, that they can ever reduce themselves to the necessity of making the experiment, by a blind and tame submission to the long train of insidious measures which must precede and produce it.

The argument under the present head may be put into a very concise form, which appears altogether conclusive. Either the mode in which the federal government is to be constructed, will render it sufficiently dependent on the people, or it will not. On the first supposition, it will be restrained by that dependence from forming schemes obnoxious to their constituents. On the other supposition, it will not possess the confidence of the people, and its schemes of usurpation will be easily defeated by the state governments; which will be supported by the people.

On summing up the considerations stated in this and the last paper, they seem to amount to the most convincing evidence, that the powers proposed to be lodged in the federal government, are as little formidable to those reserved to the individual states, as they are indispensably necessary to accomplish the purposes of the union; and that all those alarms which have been sounded, of a meditated and consequential annihilation of the state governments, must, on the most favourable interpretation, be ascribed to the chimerical fears of the authors of them.

PUBLIUS.

THE FEDERALIST.

NUMBER XLVII.

NEW YORK, FEBRUARY 1, 1788.

MADISON.

THE MEANING OF THE MAXIM, WHICH REQUIRES A SEPARATION OF
THE DEPARTMENTS OF POWER, EXAMINED AND ASCERTAINED.

HAVING reviewed the general form of the proposed government, and the general mass of power allotted to it; I proceed to
examine the particular structure of this government, and the
distribution of this mass of power among its constituent parts.

One of the principal objections inculcated by the more
respectable adversaries to the constitution, is its supposed violation of the political maxim, that the legislative, executive, and
judiciary departments, ought to be separate and distinct. In the
structure of the federal government, no regard, it is said, seems
to have been paid to this essential precaution in favour of liberty. The several departments of power are distributed and
blended in such a manner, as at once to destroy all symmetry
and beauty of form; and to expose some of the essential parts of
the edifice to the danger of being crushed by the disproportionate weight of other parts.

No political truth is certainly of greater intrinsic value, or is
stamped with the authority of more enlightened patrons of liberty, than that on which the objection is founded. The accumulation of all powers, legislative, executive, and judiciary, in the

same hands, whether of one, a few, or many, and whether hereditary, self-appointed, or elective, may justly be pronounced the very definition of tyranny. Were the federal constitution, therefore, really chargeable with this accumulation of power, or with a mixture of powers, having a dangerous tendency to such an accumulation, no further arguments would be necessary to inspire a universal reprobation of the system. I persuade myself, however, that it will be made apparent to every one, that the charge cannot be supported, and that the maxim on which it relies has been totally misconceived and misapplied. In order to form correct ideas on this important subject, it will be proper to investigate the sense in which the preservation of liberty requires, that the three great departments of power should be separate and distinct.

The oracle who is always consulted and cited on this subject, is the celebrated Montesquieu. If he be not the author of this invaluable precept in the science of politics, he has the merit at least of displaying and recommending it most effectually to the attention of mankind. Let us endeavour, in the first place, to ascertain his meaning on this point.

The British constitution was to Montesquieu, what Homer has been to the didactic writers on epic poetry. As the latter have considered the work of the immortal bard, as the perfect model from which the principles and rules of the epic art were to be drawn, and by which all similar works were to be judged: so this great political critic appears to have viewed the constitution of England as the standard, or to use his own expression, as the mirror of political liberty: and to have delivered, in the form of elementary truths, the several characteristic principles of that particular system. That we may be sure then not to mistake his meaning in this case, let us recur to the source from which the maxim was drawn.

On the slightest view of the British constitution, we must perceive, that the legislative, executive, and judiciary departments, are by no means totally separate and distinct from each other. The executive magistrate forms an integral part of the al authority. He alone has the prerogative of making treaties with foreign sovereigns, which, when made, have, under certain limitations, the force of legislative acts. All the members of the judiciary department are appointed by him; can be removed by him on the address of the two houses of parliament, and form, when he pleases to consult them, one of his constitutional councils. One branch of the legislative department, forms also a great constitutional council to the executive chief; as, on another hand, it is the sole depository of judicial power in cases of impeachment, and is invested with the supreme appellate jurisdiction in all other cases. The judges again are so far connected with the legislative department, as often to attend and participate in its deliberations, though not admitted to a legislative vote.

From these facts, by which Montesquieu was guided, it may clearly be inferred, that in saying, "there can be no liberty, where the legislative and executive powers are united in the same person, or body of magistrates;" or, "if the power of judging, be not separated from the legislative and executive powers," he did not mean that these departments ought to have no *partial agency* in, or no *control* over the acts of each other. His meaning, as his own words import, and still more conclusively as illustrated by the example in his eye, can amount to no more than this, that where the *whole* power of one department is exercised by the same hands which possess the *whole* power of another department, the fundamental principles of a free constitution are subverted. This would have been the case in the constitution examined by him, if the king, who is the sole executive magistrate, had possessed also the complete legislative power, or the supreme administration of justice; or if the entire legislative body had possessed the supreme judiciary, or the supreme executive authority. This, however, is not among the vices of that constitution. The magistrate, in whom the whole executive power resides, cannot of himself make a law, though he can put a negative on every law; nor administer justice in person, though he has the appointment of those who do administer it.

The judges can exercise no executive prerogative, though they are shoots from the executive stock; nor any legislative function, though they may be advised with by the legislative councils. The entire legislature can perform no judiciary act; though by the joint act of two of its branches, the judges may be removed from their offices; and though one of its branches is possessed of the judicial power in the last resort. The entire legislature again can exercise no executive prerogative, though one of its branches* constitutes the supreme executive magistracy; and another, on the impeachment of a third, can try and condemn all the subordinate officers in the executive department.

The reasons on which Montesquieu grounds his maxim, are a further demonstration of his meaning. "When the legislative and executive powers are united in the same person or body," says he, "there can be no liberty, because apprehensions may arise lest *the same* monarch or senate should *enact* tyrannical laws, to *execute* them in a tyrannical manner." Again, "Were the power of judging joined with the legislative, the life and liberty of the subject would be exposed to arbitrary control, for *the judge* would then be *the legislator*. Were it joined to the executive power, *the judge* might behave with all the violence of *an oppressor*." Some of these reasons are more fully explained in other passages; but briefly stated as they are here, they sufficiently establish the meaning which we have put on this celebrated maxim of this celebrated author.

If we look into the constitutions of the several states, we find, that notwithstanding the emphatical, and, in some instances, the unqualified terms in which this axiom has been laid down, there is not a single instance in which the several departments of power have been kept absolutely separate and distinct. New Hampshire, whose constitution was the last formed, seems to have been fully aware of the impossibility and inexpediency of avoiding any mixture whatever of these departments; and has qualified the doctrine by declaring, "that the legislative, execu-

* The king.

tive, and judiciary powers, ought to be kept as separate from, and independent of each other, *as the nature of a free government will admit; or as is consistent with that chain of connexion, that binds the whole fabric of the constitution in one indissoluble bond of unity and amity.*" Her constitution accordingly mixes these departments in several respects. The senate, which is a branch of the legislative department, is also a judicial tribunal for the trial of impeachments. The president, who is the head of the executive department, is the presiding member also of the senate; and, besides an equal vote in all cases, has a casting vote in case of a tie. The executive head is himself eventually elective every year by the legislative department; and his council is every year chosen by and from the members of the same department. Several of the officers of state are also appointed by the legislature. And the members of the judiciary department are appointed by the executive department.

The constitution of Massachusetts has observed a sufficient, though less pointed caution, in expressing this fundamental article of liberty. It declares, "that the legislative department shall never exercise the executive and judicial powers, or either of them: the executive shall never exercise the legislative and judicial powers, or either of them: the judicial shall never exercise the legislative and executive powers, or either of them." This declaration corresponds precisely with the doctrine of Montesquieu, as it has been explained, and is not in a single point violated by the plan of the convention. It goes no farther than to prohibit any one of the entire departments from exercising the powers of another department. In the very constitution to which it is prefixed, a partial mixture of powers has been admitted. The executive magistrate has a qualified negative on the legislative body; and the senate, which is a part of the legislature, is a court of impeachment for members both of the executive and judiciary departments. The members of the judiciary department, again, are appointable by the executive department, and removeable by the same authority, on the address of the two legislative branches. Lastly, a number of the officers of

government are annually appointed by the legislative department. As the appointment to offices, particularly executive
offices, is in its nature an executive function, the compilers of
the constitution have, in this last point at least, violated the rule
established by themselves.

I pass over the constitutions of Rhode Island and Connecticut,
because they were formed prior to the revolution; and even
before the principle under examination had become an object of
political attention.

The constitution of New York contains no declaration on this
subject; but appears very clearly to have been framed with an
eye to the danger of improperly blending the different departments. It gives, nevertheless, to the executive magistrate a partial control over the legislative department; and, what is more,
gives a like control to the judiciary department, and even blends
the executive and judiciary departments in the exercise of this
control. In its council of appointment, members of the legislative
are associated with the executive authority, in the appointment
of officers, both executive and judiciary. And its court for the
trial of impeachments and correction of errours, is to consist of
one branch of the legislature and the principal members of the
judiciary department.

The constitution of New Jersey has blended the different
powers of government more than any of the preceding. The governour, who is the executive magistrate, is appointed by the legislature; is chancellor and ordinary, or surrogate of the state; is
a member of the supreme court of appeals, and president with a
casting vote of one of the legislative branches. The same legislative branch acts again as executive council of the governour,
and with him constitutes the court of appeals. The members of
the judiciary department are appointed by the legislative
department, and removeable by one branch of it on the impeachment of the other.

According to the constitution of Pennsylvania,* the president,

* The constitutions of these states have been since altered.

who is head of the executive department, is annually elected by a vote in which the legislative department predominates. In conjunction with an executive council, he appoints the members of the judiciary department, and forms a court of impeachment for trial of all officers, judiciary as well as executive. The judges of the supreme court, and justices of the peace seem also to be removeable by the legislature; and the executive power of pardoning in certain cases to be referred to the same department. The members of the executive council are made EX OFFICIO justices of peace throughout the state.

In Delaware,* the chief executive magistrate is annually elected by the legislative department. The speakers of the two legislative branches are vice-presidents in the executive department. The executive chief, with six others, appointed three by each of the legislative branches, constitute the supreme court of appeals: he is joined with the legislative department in the appointment of the other judges. Throughout the states, it appears that the members of the legislature may at the same time be justices of the peace. In this state, the members of one branch of it are EX OFFICIO justices of the peace; as are also the members of the executive council. The principal officers of the executive department are appointed by the legislative; and one branch of the latter forms a court of impeachments. All officers may be removed on address of the legislature.

Maryland has adopted the maxim in the most unqualified terms; declaring that the legislative, executive, and judicial powers of government, ought to be for ever separate and distinct from each other. Her constitution, notwithstanding, makes the executive magistrate appointable by the legislative department; and the members of the judiciary by the executive department.

The language of Virginia is still more pointed on this subject. Her constitution declares, "that the legislative, executive, and judiciary departments, shall be separate and distinct; so that

* The constitutions of these states have been since altered.

neither exercise the powers properly belonging to the other; nor shall any person exercise the powers of more than one of them at the same time; except that the justices of county courts shall be eligible to either house of assembly." Yet we find not only this express exception, with respect to the members of the inferiour courts; but that the chief magistrate, with his executive council, are appointable by the legislature; that two members of the latter, are triennially displaced at the pleasure of the legislature; and that all the principal officers, both executive and judiciary, are filled by the same department. The executive prerogative of pardoning, also, is in one case vested in the legislative department.

The constitution of North Carolina which declares, "that the legislative, executive, and supreme judicial powers of government, ought to be for ever separate and distinct from each other," refers at the same time, to the legislative department, the appointment not only of the executive chief, but all the principal officers within both that and the judiciary department.

In South Carolina, the constitution makes the executive magistracy eligible by the legislative department. It gives to the latter, also, the appointment of the members of the judiciary department, including even justices of the peace and sheriffs; and the appointment of officers in the executive department, down to captains in the army and navy of the state.

In the constitution of Georgia, where it is declared, "that the legislative, executive, and judiciary departments shall be separate and distinct, so that neither exercise the powers properly belonging to the other," we find that the executive department is to be filled by appointments of the legislature; and the executive prerogative of pardoning to be finally exercised by the same authority. Even justices of the peace are to be appointed by the legislature.

In citing these cases in which the legislative, executive, and judiciary departments, have not been kept totally separate and distinct, I wish not to be regarded as an advocate for the particular organizations of the several state governments. I am fully aware, that among the many excellent principles which they exemplify, they carry strong marks of the haste, and still stronger of the inexperience, under which they were framed. It is but too obvious, that in some instances, the fundamental principle under consideration, has been violated by too great a mixture, and even an actual consolidation of the different powers; and that in no instance has a competent provision been made for maintaining in practice the separation delineated on paper. What I have wished to evince is, that the charge brought against the proposed constitution, of violating a sacred maxim of free government, is warranted neither by the real meaning annexed to that maxim by its author, nor by the sense in which it has hitherto been understood in America. This interesting subject will be resumed in the ensuing paper.

PUBLIUS.

THE FEDERALIST.

NUMBER XLVIII.

NEW YORK, FEBRUARY 1, 1788.

MADISON.

THE SAME SUBJECT CONTINUED, WITH A VIEW TO THE MEANS
OF GIVING EFFICACY IN PRACTICE TO THAT MAXIM.

It was shown in the last paper, that the political apothegm
there examined, does not require that the legislative, executive,
and judiciary departments, should be wholly unconnected with
each other. I shall undertake in the next place to show, that
unless these departments be so far connected and blended, as to
give to each a constitutional control over the others, the degree
of separation which the maxim requires, as essential to a free
government, can never in practice be duly maintained.

It is agreed on all sides, that the powers properly belonging
to one of the departments ought not to be directly and completely administered by either of the other departments. It is
equally evident, that neither of them ought to possess, directly
or indirectly, an overruling influence over the others in the
administration of their respective powers. It will not be denied,
that power is of an encroaching nature, and that it ought to be
effectually restrained from passing the limits assigned to it.
After discriminating, therefore, in theory, the several classes of
power, as they may in their nature be legislative, executive, or
judiciary; the next, and most difficult task, is to provide some
practical security for each, against the invasion of the others.

What this security ought to be, is the great problem to be solved.

Will it be sufficient to mark, with precision, the boundaries of these departments, in the constitution of the government, and to trust to these parchment barriers against the encroaching spirit of power? This is the security which appears to have been principally relied on by the compilers of most of the American constitutions. But experience assures us, that the efficacy of the provision has been greatly overrated; and that some more adequate defence is indispensably necessary for the more feeble, against the more powerful members of the government. The legislative department is everywhere extending the sphere of its activity, and drawing all power into its impetuous vortex.

The founders of our republics have so much merit for the wisdom which they have displayed, that no task can be less pleasing than that of pointing out the errours into which they have fallen. A respect for truth, however, obliges us to remark, that they seem never for a moment to have turned their eyes from the danger to liberty, from the overgrown and all-grasping prerogative of an hereditary magistrate, supported and fortified by an hereditary branch of the legislative authority. They seem never to have recollected the danger from legislative usurpations, which, by assembling all power in the same hands, must lead to the same tyranny as is threatened by executive usurpations.

In a government where numerous and extensive prerogatives are placed in the hands of an hereditary monarch, the executive department is very justly regarded as the source of danger, and watched with all the jealousy which a zeal for liberty ought to inspire. In a democracy, where a multitude of people exercise in person the legislative functions, and are continually exposed, by their incapacity for regular deliberation and concerted measures, to the ambitious intrigues of their executive magistrates, tyranny may well be apprehended on some favourable emergency, to start up in the same quarter. But in a representative republic, where the executive magistracy is carefully limited, both in the extent and the duration of its power; and where the legislative power is exercised by an assembly, which is inspired by a supposed influence over the people, with an intrepid confidence in its own strength; which is sufficiently numerous to feel all the passions which actuate a multitude; yet not so numerous as to be incapable of pursuing the objects of its passions, by means which reason prescribes; it is against the enterprising ambition of this department, that the people ought to indulge all their jealousy and exhaust all their precautions.

The legislative department derives a superiority in our governments from other circumstances. Its constitutional powers being at once more extensive, and less susceptible of precise limits, it can, with the greater facility, mask, under complicated and indirect measures, the encroachments which it makes on the co-ordinate departments. It is not unfrequently a question of real nicety in legislative bodies, whether the operation of a particular measure will, or will not extend beyond the legislative sphere. On the other side, the executive power being restrained within a narrower compass, and being more simple in its nature; and the judiciary being described by landmarks, still less uncertain, projects of usurpation by either of these departments would immediately betray and defeat themselves. Nor is this all: as the legislative department alone has access to the pockets of the people, and has in some constitutions full discretion, and in all a prevailing influence over the pecuniary rewards of those who fill the other departments; a dependence is thus created in the latter, which gives still greater facility to encroachments of the former.

I have appealed to our own experience for the truth of what I advance on this subject. Were it necessary to verify this experience by particular proofs, they might be multiplied without end. I might collect vouchers in abundance from the records and archives of every state in the union. But as a more concise, and at the same time equally satisfactory evidence, I will refer to the example of two states, attested by two unexceptionable authorities.

The first example is that of Virginia, a state which, as we have seen, has expressly declared in its constitution, that the three great departments ought not to be intermixed. The authority in support of it is Mr. Jefferson, who, besides his other advantages for remarking the operation of the government, was himself the chief magistrate of it. In order to convey fully the ideas with which his experience had impressed him on this subject, it will be necessary to quote a passage of some length from his very interesting "Notes on the state of Virginia," p. 195. "All the powers of government, legislative, executive, and judiciary, result to the legislative body. The concentrating these in the same hands, is precisely the definition of despotic government. It will be no alleviation that these powers will be exercised by a plurality of hands, and not by a single one. One hundred and seventy-three despots would surely be as oppressive as one. Let those who doubt it, turn their eyes on the republic of Venice. As little will it avail us, that they are chosen by ourselves. An *elective despotism* was not the government we fought for; but one which should not only be founded on free principles, but in which the powers of government should be so divided and balanced among several bodies of magistracy, as that no one could transcend their legal limits, without being effectually checked and restrained by the others. For this reason, that convention which passed the ordinance of government, laid its foundation on this basis, that the legislative, executive, and judiciary departments should be separate and distinct, so that no person should exercise the powers of more than one of them at the same time. *But no barrier was provided between these several powers.* The judiciary and executive members were left dependent on the legislative for their subsistence in office, and some of them for their continuance in it. If, therefore, the legislature assumes executive and judiciary powers, no opposition is likely to be made; nor, if made, can be effectual; because in that case, they may put their proceedings into the form of an act of assembly, which will render them obligatory on the other branches. They have accordingly, in many instances *decided rights*, which should have been left to *judiciary controversy*; and *the direction of the executive, during the whole time of their session, is becoming habitual and familiar.*"

The other state, which I shall take for an example, is Pennsylvania; and the other authority the council of censors which assembled in the years 1783 and 1784. A part of the duty of this body, as marked out by the constitution, was "to inquire, whether the constitution had been preserved inviolate in every part; and whether the legislative and executive branches of government had performed their duty as guardians of the people, or assumed to themselves, or exercised other or greater powers than they are entitled to by the constitution." In the execution of this trust, the council were necessarily led to a comparison of both the legislative and executive proceedings, with the constitutional powers of these departments; and from the facts enumerated, and to the truth of most of which both sides in the council subscribed, it appears, that the constitution had been flagrantly violated by the legislature in a variety of important instances.

A great number of laws had been passed, violating, without any apparent necessity, the rule requiring that all bills of a public nature shall be previously printed for the consideration of the people; although this is one of the precautions chiefly relied on by the constitution against improper acts of the legislature.

The constitutional trial by jury had been violated; and powers assumed, which had not been delegated by the constitution.

Executive powers had been usurped.

The salaries of the judges, which the constitution expressly requires to be fixed, had been occasionally varied; and cases belonging to the judiciary department frequently drawn within legislative cognizance and determination.

Those who wish to see the several particulars falling under each of these heads, may consult the journals of the council, which are in print. Some of them, it will be found, may be imputable to peculiar circumstances connected with the war: but the greater part of them may be considered as the spontaneous shoots of an ill-constituted government.

It appears also, that the executive department had not been innocent of frequent breaches of the constitution. There are three observations, however, which ought to be made on this head: *First*, A great proportion of the instances were either immediately produced by the necessities of the war, or recommended by congress, or the commander in chief; *Second*, In most of the other instances, they conformed either to the declared or the known sentiments of the legislative department: *Third*, The executive department of Pennsylvania is distinguished from that of the other states, by the number of members composing it. In this respect, it has as much affinity to a legislative assembly, as to an executive council. And being at once exempt from the restraint of an individual responsibility for the acts of the body, and deriving confidence from mutual example and joint influence; unauthorized measures would of course be more freely hazarded, than where the executive department is administered by a single hand, or by a few hands.

The conclusion which I am warranted in drawing from these observations is, that a mere demarkation on parchment of the constitutional limits of the several departments, is not a sufficient guard against those encroachments which lead to a tyrannical concentration of all the powers of government in the same hands.

PUBLIUS.

THE FEDERALIST.

NUMBER XLIX.

FEBRUARY 5, 1788.

HAMILTON.

THE SAME SUBJECT CONTINUED, WITH THE SAME VIEW.

THE author of the "Notes on the state of Virginia," quoted in the last paper, has subjoined to that valuable work, the draught of a constitution, which had been prepared in order to be laid before a convention expected to be called in 1783, by the legislature, for the establishment of a constitution for that commonwealth. The plan, like every thing from the same pen, marks a turn of thinking original, comprehensive, and accurate; and is the more worthy of attention, as it equally displays a fervent attachment to republican government, and an enlightened view of the dangerous propensities against which it ought to be guarded. One of the precautions which he proposes, and on which he appears ultimately to rely as a palladium to the weaker departments of power, against the invasions of the stronger, is perhaps altogether his own, and as it immediately relates to the subject of our present inquiry, ought not to be overlooked.

His proposition is, "that whenever any two of the three branches of government shall concur in opinion, each by the voices of two thirds of their whole number, that a convention is necessary for altering the constitution, or *correcting breaches of it*, a convention shall be called for the purpose."

As the people are the only legitimate fountain of power, and it is from them that the constitutional charter, under which the several branches of government hold their power, is derived; it seems strictly consonant to the republican theory, to recur to the same original authority, not only whenever it may be necessary to enlarge, diminish, or new-model the powers of government; but also, whenever any one of the departments may commit encroachments on the chartered authorities of the others. The several departments being perfectly co-ordinate by the terms of their common commission, neither of them, it is evident, can pretend to an exclusive or superior right of settling the boundaries between their respective powers; and how are the encroachments of the stronger to be prevented, or the wrongs of the weaker to be redressed, without an appeal to the people themselves; who, as the grantors of the commission, can alone declare its true meaning, and enforce its observance?

There is certainly great force in this reasoning, and it must be allowed to prove, that a constitutional road to the decision of the people, ought to be marked out, and kept open, for certain great and extraordinary occasions. But there appear to be insuperable objections against the proposed recurrence to the people, as a provision in all cases for keeping the several departments of power within their constitutional limits.

In the first place, the provision does not reach the case of a combination of two of the departments, against a third. If the legislative authority, which possesses so many means of operating on the motives of the other departments, should be able to gain to its interest either of the others, or even one third of its members, the remaining department could derive no advantage from this remedial provision. I do not dwell, however, on this objection, because it may be thought to lie rather against the modification of the principle, than against the principle itself.

In the next place, it may be considered as an objection inherent in the principle, that, as every appeal to the people would carry an implication of some defect in the government, frequent appeals would, in a great measure, deprive the government of that veneration which time bestows on every thing, and without which perhaps the wisest and freest governments would not possess the requisite stability. If it be true that all governments rest on opinion, it is no less true, that the strength of opinion in each individual, and its practical influence on his conduct, depend much on the number which he supposes to have entertained the same opinion. The reason of man, like man himself, is timid and cautious, when left alone; and acquires firmness and confidence, in proportion to the number with which it is associated. When the examples, which fortify opinion, are ancient, as well as numerous, they are known to have a double effect. In a nation of philosophers, this consideration ought to be disregarded. A reverence for the laws, would be sufficiently inculcated by the voice of an enlightened reason. But a nation of philosophers, is as little to be expected, as the philosophical race of kings wished for by Plato. And in every other nation, the most rational government will not find it a superfluous advantage to have the prejudices of the community on its side.

The danger of disturbing the public tranquillity, by interesting too strongly the public passions, is a still more serious objection against a frequent reference of constitutional questions, to the decision of the whole society. Notwithstanding the success which has attended the revisions of our established forms of government, and which does so much honour to the virtue and intelligence of the people of America, it must be confessed, that the experiments are of too ticklish a nature to be unnecessarily multiplied. We are to recollect, that all the existing constitutions were formed in the midst of a danger which repressed the passions most unfriendly to order and concord; of an enthusiastic confidence of the people in their patriotic leaders, which stifled the ordinary diversity of opinions on great national questions; of an universal ardour for new and opposite forms, produced by an universal resentment and indignation against the ancient government; and whilst no spirit of party, connected with the changes to be made, or the abuses to be reformed, could mingle its leaven in the operation. The future situations in which we must expect to be usually placed, do not present any equivalent security against the danger which is apprehended.

But the greatest objection of all is, that the decisions which would probably result from such appeals, would not answer the purpose of maintaining the constitutional equilibrium of the government. We have seen that the tendency of republican governments is, to an aggrandizement of the legislative, at the expense of the other departments. The appeals to the people, therefore, would usually be made by the executive and judiciary departments. But whether made by one side or the other, would each side enjoy equal advantages on the trial? Let us view their different situations. The members of the executive and judiciary departments, are few in number, and can be personally known to a small part only of the people. The latter, by the mode of their appointment, as well as by the nature and permanency of it, are too far removed from the people to share much in their prepossessions. The former are generally the objects of jealousy; and their administration is always liable to be discoloured and rendered unpopular. The members of the legislative department, on the other hand, are numerous. They are distributed and dwell among the people at large. Their connexions of blood, of friendship, and of acquaintance, embrace a great proportion of the most influential part of the society. The nature of their public trust implies a personal weight with the people, and that they are more immediately the confidential guardians of their rights and liberties. With these advantages, it can hardly be supposed, that the adverse party would have an equal chance for a favourable issue.

But the legislative party would not only be able to plead their cause most successfully with the people: They would probably be constituted themselves the judges. The same influence which had gained them an election into the legislature, would gain them a seat in the convention. If this should not be the case with all, it would probably be the case with many, and pretty certainly with those leading characters, on whom everything depends in such bodies. The convention, in short, would be composed chiefly of men who had been, who actually were, or who expected to be, members of the department whose conduct was arraigned. They would consequently be parties to the very question to be decided by them.

It might, however, sometimes happen, that appeals would be made under circumstances less adverse to the executive and judiciary departments. The usurpations of the legislature might be so flagrant and so sudden, as to admit of no specious colouring. A strong party among themselves might take side with the other branches. The executive power might be in the hands of a peculiar favourite of the people. In such a posture of things, the public decision might be less swayed by prepossessions in favour of the legislative party. But still it could never be expected to turn on the true merits of the question. It would inevitably be connected with the spirit, of parties pre-existing, or springing out of the question itself. It would be connected with persons of distinguished character, and extensive influence in the community. It would be pronounced by the very men who had been agents in, or opponents of the measures, to which the decision would relate. The *passions*, therefore, not the *reason*, of the public, would sit in judgment. But it is the reason of the public alone, that ought to control and regulate the government. The passions ought to be controled and regulated by the government.

We found in the last paper, that mere declarations in the written constitution, are not sufficient to restrain the several departments within their legal limits. It appears in this, that occasional appeals to the people, would be neither a proper, nor an effectual provision, for that purpose. How far the provisions of a different nature contained in the plan above quoted, might be adequate, I do not examine. Some of them are unquestionably founded on sound political principles, and all of them are framed with singular ingenuity and precision.

PUBLIUS.

THE FEDERALIST.

NUMBER L.

NEW YORK, FEBRUARY 5, 1788.

HAMILTON.

THE SAME SUBJECT CONTINUED, WITH THE SAME VIEW.

It may be contended, perhaps, that instead of *occasional* appeals to the people, which are liable to the objections urged against them, *periodical* appeals are the proper and adequate means of *preventing and correcting infractions of the constitution.*

It will be attended to, that in the examination of these expedients, I confine myself to their aptitude for *enforcing* the constitution, by keeping the several departments of power within their due bounds; without particularly considering them, as provisions for *altering* the constitution itself. In the first view, appeals to the people at fixed periods, appear to be nearly as ineligible, as appeals on particular occasions as they emerge. If the periods be separated by short intervals, the measures to be reviewed and rectified, will have been of recent date, and will be connected with all the circumstances which tend to vitiate and pervert the result of occasional revisions. If the periods be distant from each other, the same remark will be applicable to all recent measures; and in proportion as the remoteness of the others may favour a dispassionate review of them, this advantage is inseparable from inconveniences which seem to counterbalance it. In the first place, a distant prospect of public censure would be a very feeble restraint on power from those excesses, to which it might be urged by the force of present motives. Is it to be imagined, that a legislative assembly, consisting of a hundred or two hundred members, eagerly bent on some favourite object, and breaking through the restraints of the constitution in pursuit of it, would be arrested in their career, by considerations drawn from a censorial revision of their conduct at the future distance of ten, fifteen, or twenty years? In the next place, the abuses would often have completed their mischievous effects, before the remedial provision would be applied. And in the last place, where this might not be the case, they would be of long standing, would have taken deep root, and would not easily be extirpated.

The scheme of revising the constitution, in order to correct recent breaches of it, as well as for other purposes, has been actually tried in one of the states. One of the objects of the council of censors, which met in Pennsylvania, in 1783 and 1784, was, as we have seen, to inquire "whether the constitution had been violated; and whether the legislative and executive departments had encroached on each other." This important and novel experiment in politics, merits, in several points of view, very particular attention. In some of them it may, perhaps, as a single experiment, made under circumstances somewhat peculiar, be thought to be not absolutely conclusive. But, as applied to the case under consideration, it involves some facts which I venture to remark, as a complete and satisfactory illustration of the reasoning which I have employed.

First. It appears, from the names of the gentlemen who composed the council, that some, at least, of its most active and leading members, had also been active and leading characters in the parties which pre-existed in the state.

Second. It appears that the same active and leading members of the council, had been active and influential members of the legislative and executive branches, within the period to be reviewed; and even patrons or opponents of the very measures to be thus brought to the test of the constitution. Two of the members had been vice-presidents of the state, and several others members of the executive council within the seven preceding years. One of them had been speaker, and a number of others, distinguished members of the legislative assembly, within the same period.

Third. Every page of their proceedings witnesses the effect of all these circumstances on the temper of their deliberations. Throughout the continuance of the council, it was split into two fixed and violent parties. The fact is acknowledged and lamented by themselves. Had this not been the case, the face of their proceedings exhibit a proof equally satisfactory. In all questions, however unimportant in themselves, or unconnected with each other, the same names stand invariably contrasted on the opposite columns. Every unbiassed observer, may infer without danger of mistake, and at the same time, without meaning to reflect on either party, or any individuals of either party, that unfortunately *passion*, not *reason*, must have presided over their decisions. When men exercise their reason coolly and freely, on a variety of distinct questions, they inevitably fall into different opinions on some of them. When they are governed by a common passion, their opinions, if they are so to be called, will be the same.

Fourth. It is at least problematical, whether the decisions of this body do not, in several instances, misconstrue the limits prescribed for the legislative and executive departments, instead of reducing and limiting them within their constitutional places.

Fifth. I have never understood that the decisions of the council on constitutional questions, whether rightly or erroneously formed, have had any effect in varying the practice founded on legislative constructions. It even appears, if I mistake not, that in one instance, the contemporary legislature denied the constructions of the council, and actually prevailed in the contest.

This censorial body, therefore, proves at the same time, by its researches, the existence of the disease; and by its example, the inefficacy of the remedy.

This conclusion cannot be invalidated by alleging, that the state in which the experiment was made, was at that crisis, and had been for a long time before, violently heated and distracted by the rage of party. Is it to be presumed, that at any future septennial epoch, the same state will be free from parties? Is it to be presumed that any other state, at the same, or any other given period, will be exempt from them? Such an event ought to be neither presumed nor desired; because an extinction of parties necessarily implies either an universal alarm for the public safety, or an absolute extinction of liberty.

Were the precaution taken of excluding from the assemblies elected by the people to revise the preceding administration of the government, all persons who should have been concerned in the government within the given period, the difficulties would not be obviated. The important task would probably devolve on men, who with inferior capacities, would in other respects be little better qualified. Although they might not have been personally concerned in the administration, and therefore not immediately agents in the measures to be examined; they would probably have been involved in the parties connected with these measures, and have been elected under their auspices.

PUBLIUS.

THE FEDERALIST.

NUMBER LI.

NEW YORK, FEBRUARY 8, 1788.

HAMILTON.

THE SAME SUBJECT CONTINUED, WITH THE SAME VIEW, AND
CONCLUDED.

To what expedient then shall we finally resort, for maintaining in practice the necessary partition of power among the several departments, as laid down in the constitution? The only answer that can be given is, that as all these exterior provisions are found to be inadequate, the defect must be supplied, by so contriving the interior structure of the government, as that its several constituent parts may, by their mutual relations, be the means of keeping each other in their proper places. Without presuming to undertake a full development of this important idea, I will hazard a few general observations, which may perhaps place it in a clearer light, and enable us to form a more correct judgment of the principles and structure of the government planned by the convention.

In order to lay a due foundation for that separate and distinct exercise of the different powers of government, which, to a certain extent, is admitted on all hands to be essential to the preservation of liberty, it is evident that each department should have a will of its own; and consequently should be so constituted, that the members of each should have as little agency as possible in the appointment of the members of the others.

Were this principle rigorously adhered to, it would require that all the appointments for the supreme executive, legislative, and judiciary magistracies, should be drawn from the same fountain of authority, the people, through channels, having no communication whatever with one another. Perhaps such a plan of constructing the several departments, would be less difficult in practice, than it may in contemplation appear. Some difficulties, however, and some additional expense, would attend the execution of it. Some deviations, therefore, from the principle must be admitted. In the constitution of the judiciary department in particular, it might be inexpedient to insist rigorously on the principle; first, because peculiar qualifications being essential in the members, the primary consideration ought to be to select that mode of choice, which best secures these qualifications; secondly, because the permanent tenure by which the appointments are held in that department, must soon destroy all sense of dependence on the authority conferring them.

It is equally evident, that the members of each department should be as little dependent as possible on those of the others, for the emoluments annexed to their offices. Were the executive magistrate, or the judges, not independent of the legislature in this particular, their independence in every other, would be merely nominal.

But the great security against a gradual concentration of the several powers in the same department, consists in giving to those who administer each department, the necessary constitutional means, and personal motives, to resist encroachments of the others. The provision for defence must in this, as in all other cases, be made commensurate to the danger of attack. Ambition must be made to counteract ambition. The interest of the man, must be connected with the constitutional rights of the place. It may be a reflection on human nature, that such devices should be necessary to control the abuses of government. But what is government itself, but the greatest of all reflections on human nature? If men were angels, no government would be necessary.

If angels were to govern men, neither external nor internal controls on government would be necessary. In framing a government, which is to be administered by men over men, the great difficulty lies in this: You must first enable the government to control the governed; and in the next place, oblige it to control itself. A dependence on the people is, no doubt, the primary control on the government; but experience has taught mankind the necessity of auxiliary precautions.

This policy of supplying by opposite and rival interests, the defect of better motives, might be traced through the whole system of human affairs, private as well as public. We see it particularly displayed in all the subordinate distributions of power; where the constant aim is, to divide and arrange the several offices in such a manner, as that each may be a check on the other; that the private interest of every individual, may be a centinel over the public rights. These inventions of prudence cannot be less requisite in the distribution of the supreme powers of the state.

But it is not possible to give to each department an equal power of self-defence. In republican government, the legislative authority necessarily predominates. The remedy for this inconveniency is, to divide the legislature into different branches; and to render them by different modes of election, and different principles of action, as little connected with each other, as the nature of their common functions, and their common dependence on the society, will admit. It may even be necessary to guard against dangerous encroachments, by still further precautions. As the weight of the legislative authority requires that it should be thus divided, the weakness of the executive may require, on the other hand, that it should be fortified. An absolute negative on the legislature, appears, at first view, to be the natural defence with which the executive magistrate should be armed. But perhaps it would be neither altogether safe, nor alone sufficient. On ordinary occasions, it might not be exerted with the requisite firmness; and on extraordinary occasions, it might be perfidiously abused. May not this defect of an absolute negative be supplied by some qualified connexion between this weaker department, and the weaker branch of the stronger department, by which the latter may be led to support the constitutional rights of the former, without being too much detached from the rights of its own department?

If the principles on which these observations are founded be just, as I persuade myself they are, and they be applied as a criterion to the several state constitutions, and to the federal constitution, it will be found, that if the latter does not perfectly correspond with them, the former are infinitely less able to bear such a test.

There are moreover two considerations particularly applicable to the federal system of America, which place it in a very interesting point of view.

First. In a single republic, all the power surrendered by the people, is submitted to the administration of a single government; and the usurpations are guarded against, by a division of the government into distinct and separate departments. In the compound republic of America, the power surrendered by the people, is first divided between two distinct governments, and then the portion allotted to each subdivided among distinct and separate departments. Hence a double security arises to the rights of the people. The different governments will control each other; at the same time that each will be controled by itself.

Second. It is of great importance in a republic, not only to guard the society against the oppression of its rulers; but to guard one part of the society against the injustice of the other part. Different interests necessarily exist in different classes of citizens. If a majority be united by a common interest, the rights of the minority will be insecure. There are but two methods of providing against this evil: The one by creating a will in the community independent of the majority, that is, of the society itself; the other by comprehending in the society so many separate descriptions of citizens, as will render an unjust combination of a majority of the whole very improbable, if not impracticable. The first method prevails in all governments possessing an hereditary or self-appointed authority. This, at best, is but a precarious security; because a power independent of the society, may as well espouse the unjust views of the major, as the rightful interests of the minor party, and may possibly be turned against both parties. The second method, will be exemplified in the federal republic of the United States. Whilst all authority in it will be derived from, and dependent on the society, the society itself will be broken into so many parts, interests, and classes of citizens, that the rights of individuals, or of the minority, will be in little danger from interested combinations of the majority. In a free government, the security for civil rights must be the same as that for religious rights. It consists in the one case in the multiplicity of interests, and in the other, in the multiplicity of sects. The degree of security in both cases will depend on the number of interests and sects; and this may be presumed to depend on the extent of country and number of people comprehended under the same government. This view of the subject, must particularly recommend a proper federal system, to all the sincere and considerate friends of republican government: since it shows, that in exact proportion, as the territory of the union may be formed into more circumscribed confederacies, or states, oppressive combinations of a majority will be facilitated, the best security under the republican form, for the rights of every class of citizens, will be diminished; and consequently, the stability and independence of some member of the government, the only other security must be proportionably increased. Justice is the end of government. It is the end of civil society. It ever has been, and ever will be pursued, until it be obtained, or until liberty be lost in the pursuit. In a society, under the forms of which the stronger faction can readily unite and oppress the weaker, anarchy may as truly be said to reign, as in a state of nature where the weaker individual is not secured against the violence of the stronger: And as in the latter state even the stronger individuals are prompted by the uncertainty of their condition, to submit to a government, which may protect the weak, as well as themselves: so in the former state, will the more powerful factions be gradually induced by a like motive, to wish for a government which will protect all parties, the weaker as well as the more powerful. It can be little doubted, that if the state of Rhode-Island was separated from the confederacy, and left to itself, the insecurity of rights under the popular form of government within such narrow limits, would be displayed by such reiterated oppressions of factious majorities, that some power altogether independent of the people, would soon be called for by the voice of the very factions whose misrule had proved the necessity of it. In the extended republic of the United States, and among the great variety of interests, parties, and sects, which it embraces, a coalition of a majority of the whole society could seldom take place upon any other principles, than those of justice and the general good: Whilst there being thus less danger to a minor from the will of the major party, there must be less pretext also, to provide for the security of the former, by introducing into the government a will not dependent on the latter: or, in other words, a will independent of the society itself. It is no less certain than it is important, notwithstanding the contrary opinions which have been entertained, that the larger the society, provided it lie within a practicable sphere, the more duly capable it will be of self-government. And happily for the republican cause, the practicable sphere may be carried to a very great extent, by a judicious modification and mixture of the federal principle.

PUBLIUS.

THE FEDERALIST.

NUMBER LII.

NEW YORK, FEBRUARY 8, 1788.

HAMILTON.

CONCERNING THE HOUSE OF REPRESENTATIVES, WITH A VIEW TO THE QUALIFICATIONS OF THE ELECTORS AND ELECTED, AND THE TIME OF SERVICE OF THE MEMBERS.

FROM the more general inquiries pursued in the four last papers, I pass on to a more particular examination of the several parts of the government. I shall begin with the house of representatives.

The first view to be taken of this part of the government, relates to the qualifications of the electors, and the elected.

Those of the former, are to be the same, with those of the electors of the most numerous branch of the state legislatures. The definition of the right of suffrage, is very justly regarded as a fundamental article of republican government. It was incumbent on the convention, therefore, to define and establish this right in the constitution. To have left it open for the occasional regulation of the congress, would have been improper for the reason just mentioned. To have submitted it to the legislative discretion of the states, would have been improper for the same reason; and for the additional reason, that it would have rendered too dependent on the state governments, that branch of the federal government, which ought to be dependent on the people alone. To have reduced the different qualifications in the

different states to one uniform rule, would probably have been
as dissatisfactory to some of the states, as it would have been
difficult to the convention. The provision made by the convention appears, therefore, to be the best that lay within their
option. It must be satisfactory to every state; because it is conformable to the standard already established, or which may be
established by the state itself. It will be safe to the United
States; because, being fixed by the state constitutions, it is not
alterable by the state governments, and it cannot be feared that
the people of the states will alter this part of their constitutions,
in such a manner as to abridge the rights secured to them by
the federal constitution.

The qualifications of the elected, being less carefully and
properly defined, by the state constitutions, and being at the
same time more susceptible of uniformity, have been very properly considered and regulated by the convention. A representative of the United States, must be of the age of twenty-five
years; must have been seven years a citizen of the United
States; must, at the time of his election, be an inhabitant of the
state he is to represent, and during the time of his service,
must be in no office under the United States. Subject to these
reasonable limitations, the door of this part of the federal government is open to merit of every description, whether native
or adoptive, whether young or old, and without regard to
poverty or wealth, or to any particular profession of religious
faith.

The term for which the representatives are to be elected,
falls under a second view which may be taken of this branch.
In order to decide on the propriety of this article, two questions must be considered; first, whether biennial elections will,
in this case, be safe; secondly, whether they be necessary or
useful.

First. As it is essential to liberty, that the government in general should have a common interest with the people; so it is particularly essential, that the branch of it under consideration
should have an immediate dependence on, and an intimate sym-

pathy with, the people. Frequent elections, are unquestionably the only policy, by which this dependence and sympathy can be effectually secured. But what particular degree of frequency may be absolutely necessary for the purpose, does not appear to be susceptible of any precise calculation—and must depend on a variety of circumstances, with which it may be connected. Let us consult experience, the guide that ought always to be followed, whenever it can be found.

The scheme of representation, as a substitute for a meeting of the citizens in person, being but imperfectly known to ancient polity; it is in more modern times only that we are to expect instructive examples. And even here, in order to avoid a research too vague and diffusive, it will be proper to confine ourselves to the few examples which are best known, and which bear the greatest analogy to our particular case. The first to which this character ought to be applied, is the house of commons in Great Britain. The history of this branch of the English constitution, anterior to the date of Magna Charta, is too obscure to yield instruction. The very existence of it, has been made a question among political antiquaries. The earliest records of subsequent date prove, that parliaments were to *sit* only, every year; not that they were to be *elected* every year. And even these annual sessions, were left so much at the discretion of the monarch, that under various pretexts, very long and dangerous intermissions were often contrived by royal ambition. To remedy this grievance, it was provided by a statute in the reign of Charles IId, that the intermissions should not be protracted beyond a period of three years. On the accession of William IIId, when a revolution took place in the government, the subject was still more seriously resumed, and it was declared to be among the fundamental rights of the people, that parliaments ought to be held *frequently*. By another statute which passed a few years later in the same reign, the term "frequently," which had alluded to the triennial period settled in the time of Charles IId, is reduced to a precise meaning, it being expressly enacted, that a new parliament shall be called within three years after the determination of the former. The last change, from three to seven years, is well known to have been introduced pretty early in the present century, under an alarm for the Hanoverian succession. From these facts it appears, that the greatest frequency of elections which has been deemed necessary in that kingdom, for binding the representatives to their constituents, does not exceed a triennial return of them. And if we may argue from the degree of liberty retained even under septennial elections, and all the other vicious ingredients in the parliamentary constitution, we cannot doubt that a reduction of the period from seven to three years, with some other necessary reforms, would so far extend the influence of the people over their representatives as to satisfy us, that biennial elections under the federal system, cannot possibly be dangerous to the requisite dependence of the house of representatives on their constituents.

Elections in Ireland, till of late, were regulated entirely by the discretion of the crown, and were seldom repeated, except on the accession of a new prince, or some other contingent event. The parliament which commenced with George IId, was continued throughout his whole reign, a period of about thirty-five years. The only dependence of the representative on the people, consisted in the right of the latter to supply occasional vacancies, by the election of new members, and in the chance of some event which might produce a general new election. The ability also of the Irish parliament to maintain the rights of their constituents, so far as the disposition might exist, was extremely shackled by the control of the crown, over the subjects of their deliberation. Of late, these shackles, if I mistake not, have been broken; and octennial parliaments have besides been established. What effect may be produced by this partial reform, must be left to further experience. The example of Ireland, from this view of it, can throw but little light on the subject. As far as we can draw any conclusion from it, it must be, that if the people of that country have been able, under all these disadvantages, to retain any liberty whatever, the advantage of biennial elections would secure to them every degree of liberty, which might depend on a due connexion, between their representatives and themselves.

Let us bring our inquiries nearer home. The example of these states, when British colonies, claims particular attention; at the same time that it is so well known, as to require little to be said on it. The principle of representation, in one branch of the legislature at least, was established in all of them. But the periods of election were different. They varied, from one to seven years. Have we any reason to infer, from the spirit and conduct of the representatives of the people, prior to the revolution, that biennial elections would have been dangerous to the public liberties? The spirit, which every where displayed itself, at the commencement of the struggle, and which vanquished the obstacles to independence, is the best of proof, that a sufficient portion of liberty had been every where enjoyed, to inspire both a sense of its worth, and a zeal for its proper enlargement. This remark holds good, as well with regard to the then colonies, whose elections were least frequent, as to those whose elections were most frequent. Virginia was the colony which stood first in resisting the parliamentary usurpations of Great Britain; it was the first also in espousing, by public act, the resolution of independence. In Virginia, nevertheless, if I have not been misinformed, elections under the former government were septennial. This particular example is brought into view, not as a proof of any peculiar merit, for the priority in those instances was probably accidental; and still less of any advantage in *septennial* elections, for when compared with a greater frequency, they are inadmissible; but merely as a proof, and I conceive it to be a very substantial proof, that the liberties of the people can be in no danger from *biennial* elections.

The conclusion resulting from these examples, will be not a little strengthened, by recollecting three circumstances. The first is, that the federal legislature will possess a part only, of that supreme legislative authority which is vested completely in the British parliament; and which, with a few exceptions, was exercised by the colonial assemblies, and the Irish legislature. It is a received and well founded maxim, that, where no other circumstances affect the case, the greater the power is, the shorter ought to be its duration; and, conversely, the smaller the power, the more safely may its duration be protracted. In the second place, it has, on another occasion, been shown, that the federal legislature will not only be restrained by its dependence on the people, as other legislative bodies are; but that it will be moreover watched and controled by the several collateral legislatures, which other legislative bodies are not. And in the third place, no comparison can be made between the means that will be possessed by the more permanent branches of the federal government, for seducing, if they should be disposed to seduce, the house of representatives from their duty to the people; and the means of influence over the popular branch, possessed by the other branches of governments above cited. With less power, therefore, to abuse, the federal representatives can be less tempted on one side, and will be doubly watched on the other.

PUBLIUS.

THE FEDERALIST.

NUMBER LIII.

NEW YORK, FEBRUARY 12, 1788.

HAMILTON.

THE SAME SUBJECT CONTINUED, WITH A VIEW OF THE TERM OF
SERVICE OF THE MEMBERS.

I SHALL here, perhaps, be reminded of a current observation, "that where annual elections end, tyranny begins." If it be true, as has often been remarked, that sayings which become proverbial, are generally founded in reason, it is not less true, that, when once established, they are often applied to cases to which the reason of them does not extend. I need not look for a proof beyond the instance before us. What is the reason on which this proverbial observation is founded? No man will subject himself to the ridicule of pretending, that any natural connexion subsists between the sun or the seasons, and the period within which human virtue can bear the temptations of power. Happily for mankind, liberty is not, in this respect, confined to any single point of time; but lies within extremes, which afford sufficient latitude for all the variations that may be required by the various situations and circumstances of civil society.

The election of magistrates might be, if it were found expedient, as in some instances it actually has been, daily, weekly, or monthly, as well as annual; and if circumstances may require a deviation from the rule on one side, why not also on the other side? Turning our attention to the periods established among ourselves, for the election of the most numerous branches of the state legislatures, we find them by no means coinciding any more in this instance, than in the elections of other civil magistrates. In Connecticut and Rhode-Island, the periods are half-yearly. In the other states, South Carolina excepted, they are annual. In South-Carolina, they are biennial; as is proposed in the federal government. Here is a difference, as four to one, between the longest and the shortest periods; and yet it would be not easy to show, that Connecticut or Rhode-Island is better governed, or enjoys a greater share of rational liberty, than South-Carolina; or that either the one or the other of these states are distinguished in these respects, and by these causes, from those whose elections are different from both.

In searching for the grounds of this doctrine, I can discover but one, and that is wholly inapplicable to our case. The important distinction, so well understood in America, between a constitution established by the people, and unalterable by the government; and a law established by the government, and alterable by the government, seems to have been little understood, and less observed in any other country. Wherever the supreme power of legislation has resided, has been supposed to reside also, a full power to change the form of the government. Even in Great Britain, where the principles of political and civil liberty have been most discussed, and where we hear most of the rights of the constitution, it is maintained, that the authority of the parliament is transcendent and uncontrolable, as well with regard to the constitution, as the ordinary objects of legislative provision. They have accordingly, in several instances, actually changed, by legislative acts, some of the most fundamental articles of the government. They have, in particular, on several occasions, changed the period of election; and on the last occasion, not only introduced septennial, in place of triennial elections; but, by the same act, continued themselves in place four years beyond the term for which they were elected by the people. An attention to these dangerous practices, has produced a very natural alarm in the votaries of free government, of which frequency of elections is the corner stone; and has led them to seek for some security to liberty, against the danger to which it is exposed. Where no constitution paramount to the government, either existed or could be obtained, no constitutional security, similar to that established in the United States, was to be attempted. Some other security, therefore, was to be sought for; and what better security would the case admit, than that of selecting and appealing to some simple and familiar portion of time, as a standard for measuring the danger of innovations, for fixing the national sentiment, and for uniting the patriotic exertions? The most simple and familiar portion of time, applicable to the subject, was that of a year; and hence the doctrine has been inculcated, by a laudable zeal to erect some barrier against the gradual innovations of an unlimited government, that the advance towards tyranny, was to be calculated by the distance of departure from the fixed point of annual elections. But what necessity can there be of applying this expedient to a government, limited as the federal government will be, by the authority of a paramount constitution? Or who will pretend, that the liberties of the people of America will not be more secure under biennial elections, unalterably fixed by such a constitution, than those of any other nation would be, where elections were annual, or even more frequent, but subject to alterations by the ordinary power of the government.

The second question stated is, whether biennial elections be necessary or useful? The propriety of answering this question in the affirmative, will appear from several very obvious considerations.

No man can be a competent legislator, who does not add to an upright intention and a sound judgment, a certain degree of knowledge of the subjects on which he is to legislate. A part of this knowledge may be acquired by means of information, which lie within the compass of men in private, as well as public stations. Another part, can only be attained, or at least thoroughly

37

attained, by actual experience in the station which requires the use of it. The period of service ought, therefore, in all such cases, to bear some proportion to the extent of practical knowledge, requisite to the due performance of the service. The period of legislative service, established in most of the states for the more numerous branch, is, as we have seen, one year. The question then may be put into this simple form: Does the period of two years bear no greater proportion to the knowledge requisite for federal legislation, than one year does to the knowledge requisite for state legislation? The very statement of the question, in this form, suggests the answer that ought to be given to it.

In a single state, the requisite knowledge relates to the existing laws, which are uniform throughout the state, and with which all the citizens are more or less conversant; and to the general affairs of the state, which lie within a small compass, are not very diversified, and occupy much of the attention and conversation of every class of people. The great theatre of the United States presents a very different scene. The laws are so far from being uniform, that they vary in every state; whilst the public affairs of the union are spread throughout a very extensive region, and are extremely diversified by the local affairs connected with them, and can with difficulty be correctly learnt in any other place, than in the central councils, to which a knowledge of them will be brought by the representatives of every part of the empire. Yet some knowledge of the affairs, and even of the laws of all the states, ought to be possessed by the members from each of the states. How can foreign trade be properly regulated by uniform laws, without some acquaintance with the commerce, the ports, the usages, and the regulations of the different states? How can the trade between the different states be duly regulated, without some knowledge of their relative situations in these, and other points? How can taxes be judiciously imposed, and effectually collected, if they be not accommodated to the different laws and local circumstances relating to these objects in the different states? How can uniform regulations for the militia be duly provided, without a similar knowledge of some internal circumstances, by which the states are distinguished from each other? These are the principal objects of federal legislation, and suggest most forcibly, the extensive information which the representatives ought to acquire. The other inferior objects, will require a proportional degree of information with regard to them.

It is true, that all these difficulties will, by degrees, be very much diminished. The most laborious task, will be the proper inauguration of the government, and the primeval formation of a federal code. Improvements on the first draught, will every year become both easier and fewer. Past transactions of the government, will be a ready and accurate source of information to new members. The affairs of the union, will become more and more objects of curiosity and conversation among the citizens at large. And the increased intercourse among those of different states, will contribute not a little to diffuse a mutual knowledge of their affairs, as this again will contribute to a general assimilation of their manners and laws. But, with all these abatements, the business of federal legislation must continue so far to exceed, both in novelty and difficulty, the legislative business of a single state, as to justify the longer period of service assigned to those who are to transact it.

A branch of knowledge, which belongs to the acquirements of a federal representative, and which has not been mentioned, is that of foreign affairs. In regulating our own commerce, he ought to be not only acquainted with the treaties between the United States and other nations, but also with the commercial policy and laws of other nations. He ought not to be altogether ignorant of the law of nations; for that, as far it is a proper object of municipal legislation, is submitted to the federal government. And although the house of representatives, is not immediately to participate in foreign negociations and arrangements, yet from the necessary connexion between the several branches of public affairs, those particular subjects will frequently deserve attention in the ordinary course of legislation, and will sometimes demand particular legislative sanction and co-operation. Some portion of this knowledge may, no doubt, be acquired in a man's closet; but some of it also can only be derived from the public sources of information; and all of it will be acquired to best effect, by a practical attention to the subject, during the period of actual service in the legislature.

There are other considerations, of less importance perhaps, but which are not unworthy of notice. The distance which many of the representatives will be obliged to travel, and the arrangements rendered necessary by that circumstance, might be much more serious objections with fit men for this service, if limited to a single year, than if extended to two years. No argument can be drawn on this subject, from the case of the delegates to the existing congress. They are elected annually, it is true; but their re-election is considered by the legislative assemblies almost as a matter of course. The election of the representatives by the people, would not be governed by the same principle.

A few of the members, as happens in all such assemblies, will possess superior talents; will, by frequent re-elections, become members of long standing; will be thoroughly masters of the public business, and perhaps not unwilling to avail themselves of those advantages. The greater the proportion of new members, and the less the information of the bulk of the members, the more apt will they be to fall into the snares that may be laid for them. This remark, is no less applicable to the relation, which will subsist between the house of representatives and the senate.

It is an inconvenience mingled with the advantages of our frequent elections, even in single states, where they are large, and hold but one legislative session in the year, that spurious elections cannot be investigated and annulled, in time for the decision to have its due effect. If a return can be obtained, no matter by what unlawful means, the irregular member, who takes his seat of course, is sure of holding it a sufficient time to answer his purposes. Hence a very pernicious encouragement, is given to the use of unlawful means, for obtaining irregular returns. Were elections for the federal legislature to be annual, this practice might become a very serious abuse, particularly in the more distant states. Each house is, as it necessarily must be, the judge of the elections, qualifications, and returns of its members, and whatever improvements may be suggested by experience, for simplifying and accelerating the process in disputed cases, so great a portion of a year would unavoidably elapse, before an illegitimate member could be dispossessed of his seat, that the prospect of such an event would be little check to unfair and illicit means of obtaining a seat.

All these considerations taken together, warrant us in affirming, that biennial elections will be as useful to the affairs of the public, as we have seen that they will be safe to the liberties of the people.

PUBLIUS.

THE FEDERALIST.

NUMBER LIV.

NEW YORK, FEBRUARY 12, 1788.

HAMILTON.

THE SAME SUBJECT CONTINUED, WITH A VIEW TO THE RATIO OF REPRESENTATION.

THE next view which I shall take of the house of representatives, relates to the apportionment of its members among the several states, which is to be determined by the same rule, with that of direct taxes.

It is not contended, that the number of people in each state, ought not to be the standard for regulating the proportion of those, who are to represent the people of each state. The establishment of the same rule for the apportionment of taxes, will probably be as little contested; though the rule itself in this case, is by no means founded on the same principle. In the former case, the rule is understood to refer to the personal rights of the people, with which it has a natural and universal connexion. In the latter, it has reference to the proportion of wealth, of which it is in no case a precise measure, and in ordinary cases, a very unfit one. But notwithstanding the imperfection of the rule as applied to the relative wealth and contributions of the states, it is evidently the least exceptionable among those that are practicable; and had too recently obtained the general sanction of America, not to have found a ready preference with the convention.

All this is admitted, it will perhaps be said: But does it follow from an admission of numbers for the measure of representation, or of slaves combined with free citizens, as a ratio of taxation, that slaves ought to be included in the numerical rule of representation? Slaves are considered as property, not as persons. They ought, therefore, to be comprehended in estimates of taxation which are founded on property, and to be excluded from representation, which is regulated by a census of persons. This is the objection, as I understand it, stated in its full force. I shall be equally candid in stating the reasoning, which may be offered on the opposite side.

We subscribe to the doctrine, might one of our southern brethren observe, that representation relates more immediately to persons, and taxation more immediately to property; and we join in the application of this distinction to the case of our slaves. But we must deny the fact, that slaves are considered merely as property, and in no respect whatever as persons. The true state of the case is, that they partake of both these qualities; being considered by our laws, in some respects, as persons, and in other respects, as property. In being compelled to labour not for himself, but for a master; in being vendible by one master to another master; and in being subject at all times to be restrained in his liberty, and chastised in his body, by the capricious will of his owner, the slave may appear to be degraded from the human rank, and classed with those irrational animals, which fall under the legal denomination of property. In being protected, on the other hand, in his life and in his limbs, against the violence of all others, even the master of his labour and his liberty; and in being punishable himself for all violence committed against others; the slave is no less evidently regarded by the law as a member of the society; not as a part of the irrational creation; as a moral person, not as a mere article of property. The federal constitution, therefore, decides with great propriety on the case of our slaves, when it views them in the mixt character of persons and of property. This is in fact their true character. It is the character bestowed on them by the laws under which they live; and it will not be disputed that these are the proper criterion; because it is only under the pretext, that the laws have transformed the negroes into subjects of property, that a place is denied to them in the computation of numbers; and it is admitted that if the laws were to restore the rights which have been taken away, the negroes could no longer be refused an equal share of representation, with the other inhabitants.

This question may be placed in another light. It is agreed on all sides, that numbers are the best scale of wealth and taxation, as they are the only proper scale of representation. Would the convention have been impartial or consistent, if they had rejected the slaves from the list of inhabitants, when the shares of representation were to be calculated; and inserted them on the lists when the tariff of contributions was to be adjusted? Could it be reasonably expected, that the southern states would concur in a system, which considered their slaves in some degree as men, when burdens were to be imposed, but refused to consider them in the same light, when advantages were to be conferred? Might not some surprise also be expressed, that those who reproach the southern states with the barbarous policy of considering as property, a part of their human brethren, should themselves contend, that the government to which all the states are to be parties, ought to consider this unfortunate race more completely in the unnatural light of property, than the very laws of which they complain?

It may perhaps be replied, that slaves are not included in the estimate of representatives in any of the states possessing them. They neither vote themselves, nor increase the votes of their masters. Upon what principle then, ought they to be taken into the federal estimate of representation? In rejecting them altogether, the constitution would, in this respect, have followed the very laws which have been appealed to, as the proper guide.

This objection is repelled by a single observation. It is a fundamental principle of the proposed constitution, that as the aggregate number of representatives allotted to the several states, is to be determined by a federal rule, founded on the aggregate number of inhabitants; so, the right of choosing this allotted number in each state, is to be exercised by such part of the inhabitants, as the state itself may designate. The qualifications on which the right of suffrage depend, are not perhaps the same in any two states. In some of the states, the difference is very material. In every state, a certain proportion of inhabitants, are deprived of this right by the constitution of the state, who will be included in the census by which the federal constitution apportions the representatives. In this point of view, the southern states might retort the complaint, by insisting, that the principle laid down by the convention, required that no regard should be had to the policy of particular states towards their own inhabitants; and consequently, that the slaves, as well as inhabitants, should have been admitted into the census according to their full number, in like manner with other inhabitants, who by the policy of other states, are not admitted to all the rights of citizens. A rigorous adherence, however, to this principle, is waved by those who would be gainers by it. All that they ask is, that equal moderation be shown on the other side. Let the case of the slaves be considered, as it is in truth a peculiar one. Let the compromising expedient of the constitution be mutually adopted, which regards them as inhabitants, but as debased by servitude below the equal level of free inhabitants, which regards the *slave* as divested of two fifths of the *man*.

After all, may not another ground be taken on which this article of the constitution will admit of a still more ready defence? We have hitherto proceeded on the idea, that representation related to persons only, and not at all to property. But is it a just idea? Government is instituted no less for protection of the property, than of the persons of individuals. The one, as well as the other, therefore, may be considered as represented by those who are charged with the government. Upon this principle it is, that in several of the states, and particularly in the state of

New-York, one branch of the government is intended more especially to be the guardian of property and is accordingly elected by that part of the society which is most interested in this object of government. In the federal constitution, this policy does not prevail. The rights of property, are committed into the same hands, with the personal rights. Some attention ought, therefore, to be paid to property, in the choice of those hands.

For another reason, the votes allowed in the federal legislature to the people of each state, ought to bear some proportion to the comparative wealth of the states. States have not, like individuals, an influence over each other, arising from superior advantages of fortune. If the law allows an opulent citizen but a single vote in the choice of his representative, the respect and consequence which he derives from his fortunate situation, very frequently guide the votes of others to the objects of his choice; and through this imperceptible channel, the rights of property are conveyed into the public representation. A state possesses no such influence over other states. It is not probable, that the richest state in the confederacy, will over influence the choice of a single representative, in any other state. Nor will the representatives of the larger and richer states, possess any other advantage in the federal legislature, over the representatives of other states, than what may result from their superior number alone; as far, therefore, as their superior wealth and weight may justly entitle them to any advantage, it ought to be secured to them by a superior share of representation. The new constitution is, in this respect, materially different from the existing confederation, as well as from that of the United Netherlands, and other similar confederacies. In each of the latter, the efficacy of the federal resolutions, depends on the subsequent and voluntary resolutions of the states composing the union. Hence the states, though possessing an equal vote in the public councils, have an unequal influence, corresponding with the unequal importance of these subsequent and voluntary resolutions. Under the proposed constitution, the federal acts will take effect without the necessary intervention of the individual states. They will depend merely on the majority of votes in the federal legislature, and consequently each vote, whether proceeding from a larger or smaller state, or a state more or less wealthy or powerful, will have an equal weight and efficacy; in the same manner as the votes individually given in a state legislature, by the representatives of unequal counties or other districts, have each a precise equality of value and effect; or if there be any difference in the case, it proceeds from the difference in the personal character of the individual representative, rather than from any regard to the extent of the district from which he comes.

Such is the reasoning, which an advocate for the southern interests, might employ on this subject: And although it may appear to be a little strained in some points, yet on the whole, I must confess that it fully reconciles me to the scale of representation, which the convention have established.

In one respect, the establishment of a common measure for representation and taxation, will have a very salutary effect. As the accuracy of the census to be obtained by the congress, will necessarily depend, in a considerable degree, on the disposition, if not the co-operation of the states, it is of great importance that the states should feel as little bias as possible, to swell or to reduce the amount of their numbers. Were their share of representation alone to be governed by this rule, they would have an interest in exaggerating their inhabitants. Were the rule to decide their share of taxation alone, a contrary temptation would prevail. By extending the rule to both objects, the states will have opposite interests, which will control and balance each other; and produce the requisite impartiality.

PUBLIUS.

THE FEDERALIST.

NUMBER LV.

NEW YORK, FEBRUARY 15, 1788.

HAMILTON.

THE SAME SUBJECT CONTINUED, IN RELATION TO THE TOTAL
NUMBER OF THE BODY.

THE number of which the house of representatives is to consist, forms another, and a very interesting point of view, under which this branch of the federal legislature may be contemplated. Scarce any article indeed in the whole constitution, seems to be rendered more worthy or attention, by the weight of character, and the apparent force of argument, with which it has been assailed.

The charges exhibited against it are, first, that so small a number of representatives, will be an unsafe depository of the public interests; secondly, that they will not possess a proper knowledge of the local circumstances of their numerous constituents; thirdly, that they will be taken from that class of citizens which will sympathize least with the feelings of the mass of the people, and be most likely to aim at a permanent elevation of the few, on the depression of the many; fourthly, that defective as the number will be in the first instance, it will be more and more disproportionate, by the increase of the people, and the obstacles which will prevent a correspondent increase of the representatives.

In general it may be remarked on this subject, that no

political problem is less susceptible of a precise solution, than that which relates to the number most convenient for a representative legislature; nor is there any point on which the policy of the several states is more at variance; whether we compare their legislative assemblies directly with each other, or consider the proportions which they respectively bear to the number of their constituents. Passing over the difference between the smallest and largest states, as Delaware, whose most numerous branch consists of twenty-one representatives, and Massachusetts, where it amounts to between three and four hundred, a very considerable difference is observable, among states nearly equal in population. The number of representatives in Pennsylvania, is not more than one fifth of that, in the state last mentioned. New-York, whose population is to that of South-Carolina as six to five, has little more than one third of the number of representatives. As great a disparity prevails between the states of Georgia and Delaware, or Rhode-Island In Pennsylvania, the representatives do not bear a greater proportion to their constituents, than of one for every four or five thousand. In Rhode-Island, they bear a proportion of at least one for every thousand. And according to the constitution of Georgia, the proportion may be carried to one for every ten electors; and must unavoidably far exceed the proportion in any of the other states.

Another general remark to be made is, that the ratio between the representatives and the people, ought not to be the same, where the latter are very numerous, as where they are very few. Were the representatives in Virginia, to be regulated by the standard in Rhode-Island, they would, at this time, amount to between four and five hundred; and twenty or thirty years hence, to a thousand. On the other hand, the ratio of Pennsylvania, if applied to the state of Delaware, would reduce the representative assembly of the latter to seven or eight members. Nothing can be more fallacious, than to found our political calculations on arithmetical principles. Sixty or seventy men, may be more properly trusted with a given degree of power, than six or seven. But it does not follow, that six or seven hundred would be proportionally a better depository. And if we carry on the supposition to six or seven thousand, the whole reasoning ought to be reversed. The truth is, that in all cases, a certain number at least seems to be necessary, to secure the benefits of free consultation and discussion; and to guard against too easy a combination for improper purposes: As on the other hand, the number ought at most to be kept within a certain limit, in order to avoid the confusion and intemperance of a multitude. In all very numerous assemblies of whatever characters composed, passion never fails to wrest the scepter from reason. Had every Athenian citizen been a Socrates; every Athenian assembly would still have been a mob.

It is necessary also to recollect here, the observations which were applied to the case of biennial elections. For the same reason that the limited powers of the congress, and the control of the state legislatures, justify less frequent elections, than the public safety might otherwise require; the members of the congress need be less numerous, than if they possessed the whole power of legislation, and were under no other, than the ordinary restraints of other legislative bodies.

With these general ideas in our minds, let us weigh the objections which have been stated against the number of members proposed for the house of representatives. It is said, in the first place, that so small a number cannot be safely trusted with so much power.

The number of which this branch of the legislature is to consist, at the outset of the government, will be sixty-five. Within three years a census is to be taken, when the number may be augmented to one for every thirty thousand inhabitants; and within every successive period of ten years, the census is to be renewed, and augmentations may continue to be made under the above limitation. It will not be thought an extravagant conjecture, that the first census will, at the rate of one for every thirty thousand, raise the number of representatives to at least one hundred. Estimating the negroes in the proportion of three-fifths, it can scarcely be doubted, that the population of the United States will by that time, if it does not already, amount to three millions. At the expiration of twenty-five years, according to the computed rate of increase, the number of representatives will amount to two hundred; and of fifty years, to four hundred. This is a number, which I presume will put an end to all fears, arising from the smallness of the body. I take for granted here, what I shall, in answering the fourth objection, hereafter show, that the number of representatives will be augmented, from time to time, in the manner provided by the constitution. On a contrary supposition, I should admit the objection to have very great weight indeed.

The true question to be decided then is, whether the smallness of the number, as a temporary regulation, be dangerous to the public liberty? Whether sixty-five members for a few years, and a hundred, or two hundred, for a few more, be a safe depository for a limited and well guarded power of legislating for the United States? I must own that I could not give a negative answer to this question, without first obliterating every impression which I have received, with regard to the present genius of the people of America, the spirit which actuates the state legislatures, and the principles which are incorporated with the political character of every class of citizens. I am unable to conceive, that the people of America, in their present temper, or under any circumstances which can speedily happen, will choose, and every second year repeat the choice, of sixty-five or an hundred men, who would be disposed to form and pursue a scheme of tyranny or treachery. I am unable to conceive, that the state legislatures, which must feel so many motives to watch, and which possess so many means of counteracting the federal legislature, would fail either to detect or to defeat, a conspiracy of the latter, against the liberties of their common constituents. I am equally unable to conceive that there are at this time, or can be in any short time in the United

States, any sixty-five or an hundred men, capable of recommending themselves to the choice of the people at large, who would either desire or dare, within the short space of two years, to betray the solemn trust committed to them. What change of circumstances, time, and a fuller population of our country, may produce, requires a prophetic spirit to declare, which makes no part of my pretensions. But judging from the circumstances now before us, and from the probable state of them within a moderate period of time, I must pronounce, that the liberties of America cannot be unsafe, in the number of hands proposed by the federal constitution.

From what quarter can the danger proceed? Are we afraid of foreign gold? If foreign gold could so easily corrupt our federal rulers, and enable them to ensnare and betray their constituents, how has it happened that we are at this time a free and independent nation? The congress which conducted us through the revolution, were a less numerous body than their successors will be; they were not chosen by, nor responsible to, their fellow citizens at large: though appointed from year to year, and recallable at pleasure, they were generally continued for three years; and prior to the ratification of the federal articles, for a still longer term; they held their consultations always under the veil of secrecy; they had the sole transaction of our affairs with foreign nations; through the whole course of the war, they had the fate of their country more in their hands, than it is to be hoped will ever be the case with our future representatives; and from the greatness of the prize at stake, and the eagerness of the party which lost it, it may well be supposed, that the use of other means than force would not have been scrupled: Yet we know by happy experience, that the public trust was not betrayed; nor has the purity of our public councils in this particular ever suffered, even from the whispers of calumny.

Is the danger apprehended from the other branches of the federal government? But where are the means to be found by the president or the senate, or both? Their emoluments of office, it is to be presumed, will not, and without a previous corruption of the house of representatives cannot, more than suffice for very different purposes: Their private fortunes, as they must all be American citizens, cannot possibly be sources of danger. The only means then which they can possess, will be in the dispensation of appointments. Is it here that suspicion rests her charge? Sometimes we are told, that this fund of corruption is to be exhausted by the president, in subduing the virtue of the senate. Now, the fidelity of the other house is to be the victim. The improbability of such a mercenary and perfidious combination of the several members of government, standing on as different foundations as republican principles will well admit, and at the same time accountable to the society over which they are placed, ought alone to quiet this apprehension. But fortunately, the constitution has provided a still further safeguard. The members of the congress, are rendered ineligible to any civil offices, that may be created, or of which the emoluments may be increased, during the term of their election. No offices therefore can be dealt out to the existing members, but such as may become vacant by ordinary casualties; and to suppose that these would be sufficient to purchase the guardians of the people, selected by the people themselves, is to renounce every rule by which events ought to be calculated, and to substitute an indiscriminate and unbounded jealousy, with which all reasoning must be vain. The sincere friends of liberty, who give themselves up to the extravagancies of this passion, are not aware of the injury they do their own cause. As there is a degree of depravity in mankind, which requires a certain degree of circumspection and distrust: So there are other qualities in human nature, which justify a certain portion of esteem and confidence. Republican government, presupposes the existence of these qualities in a higher degree, than any other form. Were the pictures which have been drawn by the political jealousy of some among us faithful likenesses of the human character, the inference would be, that there is not sufficient virtue among men for self-government; and that nothing less than the chains of despotism, can restrain them from destroying and devouring one another.

Publius

THE FEDERALIST.

NUMBER LVI.

NEW YORK, FEBRUARY 19, 1788.

HAMILTON.

THE SAME SUBJECT CONTINUED, IN RELATION TO THE SAME POINT.

THE *second* charge against the house of representatives is, that it will be too small to possess a due knowledge of the interests of its constituents.

As this objection evidently proceeds from a comparison of the proposed number of representatives, with the great extent of the United States, the number of their inhabitants, and the diversity of their interests, without taking into view, at the same time, the circumstances which will distinguish the congress from other legislative bodies, the best answer that can be given to it, will be a brief explanation of these peculiarities.

It is a sound and important principle, that the representative ought to be acquainted with the interests and circumstances of his constituents. But this principle can extend no farther, than to those circumstances and interests, to which the authority and care of the representative relate. An ignorance of a variety of minute and particular objects, which do not lie within the compass of legislation, is consistent with every attribute necessary to a due performance of the legislative trust. In determining the extent of information required in the exercise of a particular authority, recourse then must be had to the objects within the purview of that authority.

What are to be the objects of federal legislation? Those which are of most importance, and which seem most to require local knowledge, are commerce, taxation, and the militia.

A proper regulation of commerce requires much information, as has been elsewhere remarked; but as far as this information relates to the laws, and local situation of each individual state, a very few representatives would be sufficient vehicles of it to the federal councils.

Taxation will consist, in great measure, of duties which will be involved in the regulation of commerce. So far the preceding remark is applicable to this object. As far as it may consist of internal collections, a more diffusive knowledge of the circumstances of the state may be necessary. But will not this also be possessed in sufficient degree by a very few intelligent men, diffusively elected within the state. Divide the largest state into ten or twelve districts, and it will be found that there will be no peculiar local interest in either, which will not be within the knowledge of the representative of the district. Besides this source of information, the laws of the state, framed by representatives from every part of it, will be almost of themselves a sufficient guide. In every state there have been made, and must continue to be made, regulations on this subject, which will, in many cases, leave little more to be done by the federal legislature, than to review the different laws, and reduce them into one general act. A skilful individual in his closet, with all the local codes before him, might compile a law on some subjects of taxation for the whole union, without any aid from oral information; and it may be expected, that whenever internal taxes may be necessary, and particularly in cases requiring uniformity throughout the states, the more simple objects will be preferred. To be fully sensible of the facility which will be given to this branch of federal legislation, by the assistance of the state codes, we need only suppose for a moment, that this or any other state were divided into a number of parts, each having and exercising within itself a power of local legislation. Is it not evident that a degree of local information and preparatory labour, would be found in the several volumes of their proceedings, which would very much shorten the labours of the general legislature, and render a much smaller number of members sufficient for it? The federal councils will derive great advantage from another circumstance. The representatives of each state will not only bring with them a considerable knowledge of its laws, and a local knowledge of their respective districts; but will probably in all cases have been members, and may even at the very time be members of the state legislature, where all the local information and interests of the state are assembled, and from whence they may easily be conveyed by a very few hands into the legislature of the United States.

With regard to the regulation of the militia, there are scarcely any circumstances in reference to which local knowledge can be said to be necessary. The general face of the country, whether mountainous or level, most fit for the operations of infantry or cavalry, is almost the only consideration of this nature that can occur. The art of war teaches general principles of organization, movement; and discipline, which apply universally.

The attentive reader will discern, that the reasoning here used, to prove the sufficiency of a moderate number of representatives, does not, in any respect, contradict what was urged on another occasion, with regard to the extensive information which the representatives ought to possess, and the time that might be necessary for acquiring it. This information, so far as it may relate to local objects, is rendered necessary and difficult, not by a difference of was and local circumstances within a single state, but of those among different states. Taking each state by itself, its laws are the same, and its interests but little diversified. A few men, therefore, will possess all the knowledge requisite for a proper representation of them. Were the interests and affairs of each individual state, perfectly simple and uniform, a knowledge of them in one part, would involve a knowledge of them in every other, and the whole state might be competently represented by a single member taken from any part of it. On a comparison of the different states together, we find a great dissimilarity in their laws, and in many other circumstances connected with the objects of federal legislation, with all of which the federal representatives ought to have some acquaintance. Whilst a few representatives, therefore, from each state, may bring with them a due knowledge of their own state, every representative will have much information to acquire concerning all the other states. The changes of time, as was formerly remarked, on the comparative situation of the different states, will have an assimilating tendency. The effect of time on the internal affairs of the states, taken singly, will be just the contrary. At present, some of the states are little more than a society of husbandmen. Few of them have made much progress in those branches of industry, which give a variety and complexity to the affairs of a nation. These, however, will in all of them be the fruits of a more advanced population; and will require, on the part of each state, a fuller representation. The foresight of the convention, has accordingly taken care, that the progress of population, may be accompanied with a proper increase of the representative branch of the government.

The experience of Great Britain, which presents to mankind so many political lessons, both of the monitory and exemplary kind, and which has been frequently consulted in the course of these inquiries, corroborates the result of the reflections which we have just made. The number of inhabitants in the two kingdoms of England and Scotland, cannot be stated at less than eight millions. The representatives of these eight millions in the house of commons, amount to five hundred and fifty-eight. Of this number, one ninth are elected by three hundred and sixty-four persons, and one half, by five thousand seven hundred and twenty-three persons.* It cannot be supposed that the half thus elected, and who do not even reside among the people at large, can add any thing either to the security of the people against the government, or to the knowledge of their circumstances and

---

* Burgh's Political Disquisitions.

interests in the legislative councils. On the contrary, it is notorious, that they are more frequently the representatives and instruments of the executive magistrate, than the guardians and advocates of the popular rights. They might, therefore, with great propriety, be considered as something more than a mere deduction from the real representatives of the nation. We will, however, consider them in this light alone, and will not extend the deduction to a considerable number of others, who do not reside among their constituents, are very faintly connected with them, and have very little particular knowledge of their affairs. With all these concessions, two hundred and seventy-nine persons only, will be the depository of the safety, interest, and happiness, of eight millions; that is to say, there will be one representative only, to maintain the rights, and explain the situation, of *twenty-eight thousand six hundred and seventy* constituents, in an assembly exposed to the whole force of executive influence, and extending its authority to every object of legislation within a nation, whose affairs are in the highest degree diversified and complicated. Yet it is very certain, not only that a valuable portion of freedom has been preserved under all these circumstances, but that the defects in the British code are chargeable in a very small proportion, on the ignorance of the legislature concerning the circumstances of the people. Allowing to this case the weight which is due to it; and comparing it with that of the house of representatives as above explained, it seems to give the fullest assurance, that a representative for every *thirty thousand inhabitants*, will render the latter both a safe and competent guardian of the interests which will be confided to it.

PUBLIUS.

THE FEDERALIST.

NUMBER LVII.

NEW YORK, FEBRUARY 19, 1788.

HAMILTON.

THE SAME SUBJECT CONTINUED, IN RELATION TO THE SUPPOSED TENDENCY OF THE PLAN OF THE CONVENTION TO ELEVATE THE FEW ABOVE THE MANY.

THE *third* charge against the house of representatives is, that it will be taken from that class of citizens which will have least sympathy with the mass of the people; and be most likely to aim at an ambitious sacrifice of the many, to the aggrandizement of the few.

Of all the objections which have been framed against the federal constitution, this is perhaps the most extraordinary. Whilst the objection itself is levelled against a pretended oligarchy, the principle of it strikes at the very root of republican government.

The aim of every political constitution is, or ought to be, first, to obtain for rulers men who possess most wisdom to discern, and most virtue to pursue, the common good of the society; and in the next place, to take the most effectual precautions for keeping them virtuous, whilst they continue to hold their public trust. The elective mode of obtaining rulers, is the characteristic policy of republican government. The means relied on in this form of government for preventing their degeneracy, are numerous and various. The most effectual one, is such a limitation of the term of appointments, as will maintain a proper responsibility to the people.

Let me now ask, what there is in the constitution of the house of representatives, that violates the principles of republican government; or favours the elevation of the few, on the ruins of the many? Let me ask whether every circumstance is not, on the contrary, strictly conformable to these principles; and scrupulously impartial to the rights and pretensions of every class and description of citizens?

Who are to be the electors of the federal representatives? Not the rich, more than the poor; not the learned, more than the ignorant; not the haughty heirs of distinguished names, more than the humble sons of obscure and unpropitious fortune. The electors are to be the great body of the people of the United States. They are to be the same, who exercise the right in every state of electing the correspondent branch of the legislature of the state.

Who are to be the objects of popular choice? Every citizen whose merit may recommend him to the esteem and confidence of his country. No qualification of wealth, of birth, of religious faith, or of civil profession, is permitted to fetter the judgment, or disappoint the inclination of the people.

If we consider the situation of the men on whom the free suffrages of their fellow citizens may confer the representative trust, we shall find it involving every security which can be devised or desired for their fidelity to their constituents.

In the first place, as they will have been distinguished by the preference of their fellow citizens, we are to presume, that in general, they will be somewhat distinguished also, by those qualities which entitle them to it, and which promise a sincere and scrupulous regard to the nature of their engagements.

In the second place, they will enter into the public service under circumstances, which cannot fail to produce a temporary affection at least to their constituents. There is in every breast a sensibility to marks of honour, of favour, of esteem, and of confidence, which, apart from all considerations of interest, is some pledge for grateful and benevolent returns. Ingratitude is a common topic of declamation against human nature; and it must be confessed, that instances of it are but too frequent and flagrant, both in public and in private life. But the universal and extreme indignation which it inspires, is itself a proof of the energy and prevalence of the contrary sentiment.

In the third place, those ties which bind the representative to his constituents, are strengthened by motives of a more selfish nature. His pride and vanity attach him to a form of government which favours his pretensions, and gives him a share in its honours and distinctions. Whatever hopes or projects might be entertained by a few aspiring characters, it must generally happen, that a great proportion of the men deriving their advancement from their influence with the people, would have more to hope from a preservation of their favour, than from innovations in the government subversive of the authority of the people.

All these securities, however, would be found very insufficient without the restraint of frequent elections. Hence, in the fourth place, the house of representatives is so constituted, as to support in the members an habitual recollection of their dependence on the people. Before the sentiments impressed on their minds by the mode of their elevation, can be effaced by the exercise of power, they will be compelled to anticipate the moment when their power is to cease, when their exercise of it is to be reviewed, and when they must descend to the level from which they were raised; there for ever to remain, unless a faithful discharge of their trust shall have established their title to a renewal of it.

I will add, as a fifth circumstance in the situation of the house of representatives, restraining them from oppressive measures: that they can make no law which will not have its full operation on themselves and their friends, as well as on the great mass of the society. This has always been deemed one of the strongest bonds by which human policy can connect the rulers and the people together. It creates between them that communion of interest, and sympathy of sentiments, of which few governments have furnished examples; but without which every government degenerates into tyranny. If it be asked, what is to restrain the house of representatives from making legal discriminations in favour of themselves, and a particular class of the society? I answer, the genius of the whole system; the nature of just and constitutional laws; and, above all, the vigilant and manly spirit which actuates the people of America; a spirit which nourishes freedom, and in return is nourished by it.

If this spirit shall ever be so far debased, as to tolerate a law not obligatory on the legislature, as well as on the people, the people will be prepared to tolerate any thing but liberty.

Such will be the relation between the house of representatives and their constituents. Duty, gratitude, interest, ambition itself, are the cords by which they will be bound to fidelity and sympathy with the great mass of the people. It is possible that these may all be insufficient, to control the caprice and wickedness of men. But are they not all that government will admit, and that human prudence can devise? Are they not the genuine, and the characteristic means, by which republican government provides for the liberty and happiness of the people? Are they not the identical means on which every state government in the union relies for the attainment of these important ends? What then are we to understand by the objection which this paper has combatted? What are we to say to the men who profess the most flaming zeal for republican government, yet boldly impeach the fundamental principle of it; who pretend to be champions for the right and the capacity of the people to choose their own rulers, yet maintain that they will prefer those only who will immediately and infallibly betray the trust committed to them?

Were the objection to be read by one, who had not seen the mode prescribed by the constitution for the choice of representatives, he could suppose nothing less, than that some unreasonable qualification of property was annexed to the right of suffrage; or that the right of eligibility was limited to persons of particular families or fortunes; or at least, that the mode prescribed by the state constitutions was, in some respect or other, very grossly departed from. We have seen how far such a supposition would err, as to the two first points. Nor would it, in fact, be less erroneous as to the last. The only difference discoverable between the two cases is, that each representative of the United States will be elected by five or six thousand citizens; whilst, in the individual states, the election of a representative is left to about as many hundred. Will it be pretended, that this difference is sufficient to justify an attachment to the state governments, and an abhorrence to the federal government? If this be the point on which the objection turns, it deserves to be examined.

Is it supported by *reason*? This cannot be said, without maintaining, that five or six thousand citizens are less capable of choosing a fit representative, or more liable to be corrupted by an unfit one, than five or six hundred. Reason, on the contrary, assures us that, as in so great a number, a fit representative would be most likely to be found; so the choice would be less likely to be diverted from him, by the intrigues of the ambitious, or the bribes of the rich.

Is the *consequence* from this doctrine admissible? If we say that five or six hundred citizens are as many as can jointly exercise their right of suffrage, must we not deprive the people of the immediate choice of their public servants in every instance, where the administration of the government does not require as many of them as will amount to one for that number of citizens.

Is the doctrine warranted by *facts*? It was shown in the last paper, that the real representation in the British house of commons, very little exceeds the proportion of one for every thirty thousand inhabitants. Besides a variety of powerful causes, not existing here, and which favour in that country, the pretensions of rank and wealth, no person is eligible as a representative of a county, unless he possesses real estate of the clear value of six hundred pounds sterling per year; nor of a city or borough, unless he possesses a like estate of half that annual value. To this qualification, on the part of the county representatives, is added another on the part of the county electors, which restrains the right of suffrage to persons having a freehold estate of the annual value of more than twenty pounds sterling, according to the present rate of money. Notwithstanding these unfavourable circumstances, and notwithstanding some very unequal laws in the British code, it cannot be said, that the representatives of the nation have elevated the few, on the ruins of the many.

But we need not resort to foreign experience on this subject. Our own is explicit and decisive. The districts in New-Hampshire, in which the senators are chosen immediately by the people, are nearly as large as will be necessary for her representatives in the congress. Those of Massachusetts are larger than will be necessary for that purpose. And those of New-York still more so. In the last state, the members of assembly; for the cities and counties of New-York and Albany, are elected by very nearly as many voters as will be entitled to a representative in the congress, calculating on the number of sixty-five representatives only. It makes no difference that, in these senatorial districts and counties, a number of representatives are voted for by each elector at the same time. If the same electors, at the same time, are capable of choosing four or five representatives, they cannot be incapable of choosing one. Pennsylvania is an additional example. Some of her counties, which elect her state representatives, are almost as large as her districts will be by which her federal representatives will be elected. The city of Philadelphia is supposed to contain between fifty and sixty thousand souls. It will, therefore, form nearly two districts for the choice of federal representatives. It forms, however, but one county, in which every elector votes for each of its representatives in the state legislature. And what may appear to be still more directly to our purpose, the whole city actually elects a *single member* for the executive council. This is the case in all the other counties of the state.

Are not these facts the most satisfactory proofs of the fallacy, which has been employed against the branch of the federal government under consideration? Has it appeared on trial, that the senators of New-Hampshire, Massachusetts, and New-York; or the executive council of Pennsylvania; or the members of the assembly in the two last states, have betrayed any peculiar disposition to sacrifice the many to the few; or are in any respect less worthy of their places, than the representatives and magistrates appointed in other states, by very small divisions of the people?

But there are cases of a stronger complexion, than any which I have yet quoted. One branch of the legislature of Connecticut is so constituted, that each member of it is elected by the whole state. So is the governor of that state, of Massachusetts, and of this state, and the president of New-Hampshire. I leave every man to decide, whether the result of any one of these experiments, can be said to countenance a suspicion, that a diffusive mode of choosing representatives of the people, tends to elevate traitors, and to undermine the public liberty.

PUBLIUS.

THE FEDERALIST.

NUMBER LVIII.

NEW YORK, FEBRUARY 22, 1788.

HAMILTON.

THE SAME SUBJECT CONTINUED, IN RELATION TO THE FUTURE AUGMENTATION OF THE MEMBERS.

THE remaining charge against the house of representatives, which I am to examine, is grounded on a supposition that the number of members will not be augmented from time to time, as the progress of population may demand.

It has been admitted that this objection, if well supported, would have great weight. The following observations will show, that, like most other objections against the constitution, it can only proceed from a partial view of the subject; or from a jealousy which discolours and disfigures every object which it beholds.

1. Those who urge the objection, seem not to have recollected, that the federal constitution will not suffer by a comparison with the state constitutions, in the security provided for a gradual augmentation of the number of representatives. The number which is to prevail in the first instance, is declared to be temporary. Its duration is limited to the short term of three years.

Within every successive term of ten years, a census of inhabitants is to be repeated. The unequivocal objects of these regulations are, first, to re-adjust, from time to time, the apportionment of representatives to the number of inhabitants; under the single exception, that each state shall have one representative at least: Secondly, to augment the number of representatives at the same periods; under the sole limitation, that the whole number shall not exceed one for every thirty thousand inhabitants. If we review the constitutions of the several states, we shall find that some of them contain no determinate regulations on this subject; that others correspond pretty much on this point with the federal constitution; and that the most effectual security in any of them, is resolvable into a mere directory provision.

2. As far as experience has taken place on this subject, a gradual increase of representatives under the state constitutions, has at least kept pace with that of the constituents; and it appears that the former have been as ready to concur in such measures, as the latter have been to call for them.

3. There is a peculiarity in the federal constitution, which insures a watchful attention in a majority both of the people and of their representatives, to a constitutional augmentation of the latter. The peculiarity lies in this, that one branch of the legislature is a representation of citizens; the other of the states: In the former, consequently, the larger states will have most weight; in the latter, the advantage will be in favour of the smaller states. From this circumstance it may with certainty be inferred, that the larger states will be strenuous advocates for increasing the number and weight of that part of the legislature, in which their influence predominates. And it so happens, that four only of the largest, will have a majority of the whole votes in the house of representatives. Should the representatives or people, therefore, of the smaller states, oppose at any time a reasonable addition of members, a coalition of a very few states will be sufficient to over-rule the opposition; a coalition, which, notwithstanding the rivalship and local prejudices which might prevent it on ordinary occasions, would not fail to take place, when not merely prompted by common interest, but justified by equity and the principles of the constitution.

It may be alleged, perhaps, that the senate would be prompted by like motives to an adverse coalition; and as their concurrence would be indispensable, the just and constitutional views of the other branch might be defeated. This is the difficulty which has probably created the most serious apprehensions in the jealous friends of a numerous representation. Fortunately it is among the difficulties which, existing only in appearance, vanish on a close and accurate inspection. The following reflections will, if I mistake not, be admitted to be conclusive and satisfactory on this point.

Notwithstanding the equal authority which will subsist between the two houses on all legislative subjects, except the originating of money bills, it cannot be doubted, that the house composed of the greater number, when supported by the more powerful states, and speaking the known and determined sense of a majority of the people, will have no small advantage in a question depending on the comparative firmness of the two houses.

This advantage must be increased by the consciousness felt by the same side, of being supported in its demands, by right, by reason, and by the constitution; and the consciousness on the opposite side, of contending against the force of all these solemn considerations.

It is farther to be considered, that in the gradation between the smallest and largest states, there are several, which, though most likely in general to arrange themselves among the former, are too little removed in extent and population from the latter, to second an opposition to their just and legitimate pretensions. Hence it is by no means certain, that a majority of votes, even in the senate, would be unfriendly to proper augmentations in the number of representatives.

It will not be looking too far to add, that the senators from all the new states may be gained over to the just views of the house of representatives, by an expedient too obvious to be overlooked. As these states will, for a great length of time advance in population with peculiar rapidity, they will be interested in frequent re-apportionments of the representatives to the number of inhabitants. The large states, therefore, who will prevail in the house of representatives, will have nothing to do, but to make re-apportionments and augmentations mutually conditions of each other; and the senators from all the most growing states will be bound to contend for the latter, by the interest which their states will feel in the former.

These considerations seem to afford ample security on this subject; and ought alone to satisfy all the doubts and fears which have been indulged with regard to it. Admitting, however, that they should all be insufficient to subdue the unjust policy of the smaller states, or their predominant influence in the councils of the senate; a constitutional and infallible resource still remains with the larger states, by which they will be able at all times to accomplish their just purposes. The house of representatives can not only refuse, but they alone can propose the supplies requisite for the support of government. They, in a word, hold the purse; that powerful instrument by which we behold in the history of the British constitution an infant and humble representation of the people, gradually enlarging the sphere of its activity and importance, and finally reducing, as far as it seems to have wished, all the overgrown prerogatives of the other branches of the government. This power over the purse, may in fact be regarded as the most complete and effectual weapon, with which any constitution can arm the immediate representatives of the people, for obtaining a redress of every grievance, and for carrying into effect every just and salutary measure.

But will not the house of representatives be as much interested as the senate, in maintaining the government in its proper functions, and will they not therefore be unwilling to stake its existence or its reputation on the pliancy of the senate? Or if such a trial of firmness between the two branches were hazarded, would not the one be as likely first to yield as the other? These questions will create no difficulty with those who reflect, that in all cases, the smaller the number, and the more permanent and conspicuous the station of men in power, the stronger must be the interest which they will individually feel in whatever concerns the government. Those who represent the dignity of their country in the eyes of other nations, will be particularly sensible to every prospect of public danger, or of a dishonorable stagnation in public affairs. To those causes we are to ascribe the continual triumph of the British house of commons over the other branches of the government, whenever the engine of a money bill has been employed. An absolute inflexibility on the side of the latter, although it could not have failed to involve every department of the state in the general confusion, has neither been apprehended nor experienced. The utmost degree of firmness that can be displayed by the federal senate or president, will not be more than equal to a resistance, in which they will be supported by constitutional and patriotic principles.

In this review of the constitution of the house of representatives, I have passed over the circumstance of economy, which, in the present state of affairs, might have had some effect in lessening the temporary number of representatives; and a disregard of which would probably have been as rich a theme of declamation against the constitution, as has been furnished by the smallness of the number proposed. I omit also any remarks on the difficulty which might be found, under present circumstances, in engaging in the federal service a large number of such characters as the people will probably elect. One observation, however, I must be permitted to add on this subject, as claiming, in my judgment, a very serious attention. It is, that in all legislative assemblies, the greater the number composing them may be, the fewer will be the men who will in fact direct their proceedings. In the first place, the more numerous any assembly may be, of whatever characters composed, the greater is known to be the ascendancy of passion over reason. In the next place, the larger the number, the greater will be the proportion of members of limited information and of weak capacities. Now it is precisely on characters of this description, that the eloquence and address of the few are known to act with all their force. In the ancient republics, where the whole body of the people assembled in person, a single orator, or an artful statesman, was generally seen to rule with as complete a sway, as if a sceptre had been placed in his single hands. On the same principle, the more multitudinous a representative assembly may be rendered, the more it will partake of the infirmities incident to collective meetings of the people. Ignorance will be the dupe of cunning; and passion the slave of sophistry and declamation. The people can never err more than in supposing, that by multiplying their representatives beyond a certain limit, they strengthen the barrier against the government of a few. Experience will for ever admonish them, that, on the contrary, *after securing a sufficient number for the purposes of safety, of local information, and of diffusive sympathy with the whole society*, they will counteract their own views, by every addition to their representatives. The countenance of the government may become more democratic; but the soul that animates it, will be more oligarchic. The machine will be enlarged, but the fewer, and often the more secret, will be the springs by which its motions are directed.

As connected with the objection against the number of representatives, may properly be here noticed, that which has been suggested against the number made competent for legislative business. It has been said that more than a majority ought to have been required for a quorum, and in particular cases, if not in all, more than a majority of a quorum for a decision.

That some advantages might have resulted from such a precaution, cannot be denied. It might have been an additional shield to some particular interests, and another obstacle generally to hasty and partial measures. But these considerations are outweighed by the inconveniences in the opposite scale. In all cases where justice, or the general good; might require new laws to be passed, or active measures to be pursued, the fundamental principle of free government would be reversed. It would be no longer the majority that would rule; the power would be transferred to the minority. Were the defensive privilege limited to particular cases, an interested minority might take advantage of it to skreen themselves from equitable sacrifices to the general weal, or in particular emergencies to extort unreasonable indulgences. Lastly, it would facilitate and foster the baneful practice of secessions; a practice which has shown itself, even in states where a majority only is required; a practice subversive of all the principles of order and regular government; a practice which leads more directly to public convulsions, and the ruin of popular governments, than any other which has yet been displayed among us.

PUBLIUS.

THE FEDERALIST.

NUMBER LIX.

NEW YORK, FEBRUARY 22, 1788.

HAMILTON.

CONCERNING THE REGULATION OF ELECTIONS.

THE natural order of the subject leads us to consider, in this place, that provision of the constitution which authorizes the national legislature to regulate, in the last resort, the election of its own members.

It is in these words: "The *times*, *places*, and *manner* of holding elections for senators and representatives, shall be prescribed in each state by the legislature thereof; but the congress may, at any time, by law, make or alter *such regulations*, except as to *places* of choosing senators."* This provision has not only been declaimed against by those who condemn the constitution in the gross; but it has been censured by those who have objected with less latitude, and greater moderation; and, in one instance, it has been thought exceptionable by a gentleman who has declared himself the advocate of every other part of the system.

I am greatly mistaken, notwithstanding, if there be any article in the whole plan more completely defensible than this. Its propriety rests upon the evidence of this plain proposition, that *every government ought to contain in itself the means of its own preservation*. Every just reasoner will, at first sight, approve an

* 1st Clause, 4th Section of the 1st Article.

adherence to this rule in the work of the convention; and will disapprove every deviation from it, which may not appear to have been dictated by the necessity of incorporating into the work some particular ingredient, with which a rigid conformity to the rule was incompatible. Even in this case, though he may acquiesce in the necessity, yet he will not cease to regard a departure from so fundamental a principle, as a portion of imperfection in the system which may prove the seed of future weakness, and perhaps anarchy.

It will not be alleged, that an election law could have been framed and inserted in the constitution, which would have been applicable to every probable change in the situation of the country; and it will, therefore, not be denied, that a discretionary power over elections ought to exist somewhere. It will, I presume, be as readily conceded, that there were only three ways in which this power could have been reasonably organized; that it must either have been lodged wholly in the national legislature, or wholly in the state legislatures, or primarily in the latter, and ultimately in the former. The last mode has with reason been preferred by the convention. They have submitted the regulation of elections for the federal government, in the first instance, to the local administrations; which, in ordinary cases, and when no improper views prevail, may be both more convenient and more satisfactory; but they have reserved to the national authority a right to interpose, whenever extraordinary circumstances might render that interposition necessary to its safety.

Nothing can be more evident, than that an exclusive power of regulating elections for the national government, in the hands of the state legislatures, would leave the existence of the union entirely at their mercy. They could at any moment annihilate it, by neglecting to provide for the choice of persons to administer its affairs. It is to little purpose to say, that a neglect or omission of this kind would not be likely to take place. The constitutional possibility of the thing, without an equivalent for the risk, is an unanswerable objection. Nor has any satisfactory reason been yet assigned for incurring that risk. The extravagant sur-mises of a distempered jealousy, can never be dignified with that character. If we are in a humour to presume abuses of power, it is as fair to presume them on the part of the state governments, as on the part of the general government. And as it is more consonant to the rules of a just theory, to intrust the union with the care of its own existence, than to transfer that care to any other hands; if abuses of power are to be hazarded on the one side or on the other, it is more rational to hazard them where the power would naturally be placed, than where it would unnaturally be placed.

Suppose an article had been introduced into the constitution, empowering the United States to regulate the elections for the particular states, would any man have hesitated to condemn it, both as an unwarrantable transposition of power, and as a pre-meditated engine for the destruction of the state governments! The violation of principle, in this case, would have required no comment; and, to an unbiassed observer, it will not be less apparent in the project of subjecting the existence of the national government, in a similar respect, to the pleasure of the state governments. An impartial view of the matter cannot fail to result in a conviction that each, as far as possible, ought to depend on itself for its own preservation.

As an objection to this position, it may be remarked, that the constitution of the national senate, would involve in its full extent the danger which it is suggested might flow from an exclusive power in the state legislatures to regulate the federal elections. It may be alleged, that by declining the appointment of senators, they might at any time give a fatal blow to the union; and from this it may be inferred, that as its existence would be thus rendered dependent upon them in so essential a point, there can be no objection to intrusting them with it, in the particular case under consideration. The interest of each state, it may be added, to maintain its representation in the national councils, would be a complete security against an abuse of the trust.

This argument, though specious, will not, upon examination, be found solid. It is certainly true, that the state legislatures, by forbearing the appointment of senators, may destroy the national government. But it will not follow, that because they have the power to do this in one instance, they ought to have it in every other. There are cases in which the pernicious tendency of such a power may be far more decisive, without any motive to recommend their admission into the system, equally cogent with that which must have regulated the conduct of the convention, in respect to the formation of the senate. So far as that mode of formation may expose the union to the possibility of injury from the state legislatures, it is an evil; but it is an evil, which could not have been avoided without excluding the states, in their political capacities, wholly from a place in the organization of the national government. If this had been done, it would doubtless have been interpreted into an entire dereliction of the federal principle; and would certainly have deprived the state governments of that absolute safe-guard, which they will enjoy under this provision. But however wise it may have been, to have submitted in this instance to an inconvenience, for the attainment of a necessary advantage or a greater good, no inference can be drawn from thence to favour an accumulation of the evil, where no necessity urges, nor any greater good invites.

It may also be easily discerned, that the national government would run a much greater risk, from a power in the state legislatures over the elections of its house of representatives, than from their power of appointing the members of its senate. The senators are to be chosen for the period of six years; there is to be a rotation, by which the seats of a third part of them are to be vacated, and replenished every two years; and no state is to be entitled to more than two senators: A quorum of the body, is to consist of sixteen members. The joint result of these circumstances would be, that a temporary combination of a few states, to intermit the appointment of senators, could neither annual the existence, nor impair the activity, of the body? And it is not from a general and permanent combination of the states, that we can have any thing to fear. The first might proceed from sinister designs in the leading members of a few of the state legislatures; the last would suppose a fixed and rooted disaffection in the great body of the people; which will either never exist at all, or will, in all probability, proceed from an experience of the inaptitude of the general government to the advancement of their happiness; in which event, no good citizen could desire its continuance.

But with regard to the federal house of representatives, there is intended to be a general election of members once in two years. If the state legislatures were to be invested with an exclusive power of regulating these elections, every period of making them would be a delicate crisis in the national situation; which might issue in a dissolution of the union, if the leaders of a few of the most important states should have entered into a previous conspiracy to prevent an election.

I shall not deny that there is a degree of weight in the observation, that the interest of each state to be represented in the federal councils, will be a security against the abuse of a power over its elections in the hands of the state legislatures. But the security will not be considered as complete, by those who attend to the force of an obvious distinction between the interests of the people in the public felicity, and the interest of their local rulers in the power and consequence of their offices. The people of America may be warmly attached to the government of the union, at times when the particular rulers of particular states, stimulated by the natural rivalship of power, and by the hopes of personal aggrandizement, and supported by a strong faction in each of those states, may be in a very opposite temper. This diversity of sentiment between a majority of the people, and the individuals who have the greatest credit in their councils, is exemplified in some of the states at the present moment, on the present question. The scheme of separate confederacies, which will always multiply the chances of ambition, will be a never failing bait to all such influential characters in the state administrations, as are capable of preferring their own emolument and advancement to the public weal. With so effectual a weapon in their hands as the exclusive power of regulating elections for the national government, a combination of a few such men, in a few of the most considerable states, where the temptation will always be the strongest, might accomplish the destruction of the union; by seizing the opportunity of some casual dissatisfaction among the people, and which perhaps they may themselves have excited, to discontinue the choice of members for the federal house of representatives. It ought never to be forgotten, that a firm union of this country, under an efficient government, will probably be an increasing object of jealousy to more than one nation of Europe; and that enterprises to subvert it will sometimes originate in the intrigues of foreign powers, and will seldom fail to be patronised and abetted by some of them. Its preservation therefore ought in no case, that can be avoided, to be committed to the guardianship of any but those, whose situation will uniformly beget an immediate interest in the faithful and vigilant performance of the trust.

PUBLIUS.

THE FEDERALIST.

NUMBER LX.

NEW YORK, FEBRUARY 26, 1788.

HAMILTON.

THE SAME SUBJECT CONTINUED.

We have seen, that an incontrolable power over the elections for the federal government could not, without hazard, be committed to the state legislatures. Let us now see what are the dangers on the other side; that is, from confiding the ultimate right of regulating its own elections to the union itself. It is not pretended, that this right would ever be used for the exclusion of any state from its share in the representation. The interest of all would, in this respect at least, be the security of all. But it is alleged, that it might be employed in such a manner as to promote the election of some favourite class of men in exclusion of others; by confining the places of election to particular districts, and rendering it impracticable for the citizens at large to partake in the choice. Of all chimerical suppositions, this seems to be the most chimerical. On the one hand, no rational calculation of probabilities would lead us to imagine, that the disposition, which a conduct so violent and extraordinary would imply, could ever find its way into the national councils; and on the other hand, it may be concluded with certainty, that if so improper a spirit should ever gain admittance into them, it would display itself in a form altogether different and far more decisive.

The improbability of the attempt, may be satisfactorily inferred from this single reflection, that it could never be made without causing an immediate revolt of the great body of the people, headed and directed by the state governments. It is not difficult to conceive, that this characteristic right of freedom may, in certain turbulent and factious seasons, be violated in respect to a particular class of citizens by a victorious majority; but that so fundamental a privilege, in a country situated and enlightened as this is, should be invaded to the prejudice of the great mass of the people, by the deliberate policy of the government, without occasioning a popular revolution, is altogether inconceivable and incredible.

In addition to this general reflection, there are considerations of a more precise nature, which forbid all apprehension on the subject. The dissimilarity in the ingredients, which will compose the national government, and still more in the manner in which they will be brought into action in its various branches, must form a powerful obstacle to a concert of views, in any partial scheme of elections. There is sufficient diversity in the state of property, in the genius, manners, and habits of the people of the different parts of the union, to occasion a material diversity of disposition in their representatives towards the different ranks and conditions in society. And though an intimate intercourse under the same government, will promote a gradual assimilation of temper and sentiment, yet there are causes as well physical as moral, which may, in a greater or less degree, permanently nourish different propensities and inclinations in this particular. But the circumstance which will be likely to have the greatest influence in the matter, will be the dissimilar modes of constituting the several component parts of the government. The house of representatives being to be elected immediately by the people; the senate by the state legislatures; the president by electors chosen for that purpose by the people; there would be little probability of a common interest to cement these different branches in a predilection for any particular class of electors.

As to the senate, it is impossible that any regulation of "time and manner," which is all that is proposed to be submitted to the national government in respect to that body, can affect the spirit which will direct the choice of its members. The collective sense of the state legislatures, can never be influenced by extraneous circumstances of that sort: A consideration which alone ought to satisfy us that the discrimination apprehended would never be attempted. For what inducement could the senate have to concur in a preference in which itself would not be included? Or to what purpose would it be established in reference to one branch of the legislature, if it could not be extended to the other? The composition of the one would in this case counteract that of the other. And we can never suppose that it would embrace the appointments to the senate, unless we can at the same time suppose the voluntary co-operation of the state legislatures. If we make the latter supposition, it then becomes immaterial where the power in question is placed; whether in their hands, or in those of the union.

But what is to be the object of this capricious partiality in the national councils? Is it to be exercised in a discrimination between the different departments of industry, or between the different kinds of property, or between the different degrees of property? Will it lean in favour of the landed interest, or the monied interest, or the mercantile interest, or the manufacturing interest? Or, to speak in the fashionable language of the adversaries of the constitution, will it court the elevation of the "wealthy and the well-born," to the exclusion and debasement of all the rest of the society?

If this partiality is to be exerted in favour of those, who are concerned in any particular description of industry or property, I presume it will readily be admitted, that the competition for it, will lie between landed men and merchants. And I scruple not to affirm, that it is infinitely less likely that either of them should gain an ascendant in the national councils, than that the one or the other of them should predominate in all the local councils. The inference will be, that a conduct tending to give an undue preference to either, is much less to be dreaded from the former than from the latter.

The several states are in various degrees addicted to agriculture and commerce. In most, if not all of them, the first is predominant. In a few of them, however, the latter nearly divides its empire; and in most of them has a considerable share of influence. In proportion as either prevails, it will be conveyed into the national representation; and for the very reason, that this will be an emanation from a greater variety of interests, and in much more various proportions, than are to be found in any single state, it will be much less apt to espouse either of them, with a decided partiality, than the representation of any single state.

In a country consisting chiefly of the cultivators of land, where the rules of an equal representation obtain, the landed interest must, upon the whole, preponderate in the government. As long as this interest prevails in most of the state legislatures, so long it must maintain a correspondent superiority in the national senate, which will generally be a faithful copy of the majorities of those assemblies. It cannot therefore be presumed, that a sacrifice of the landed to the mercantile class, will ever be a favourite object of this branch of the federal legislature. In applying thus particularly to the senate a general observation suggested by the situation of the country, I am governed by the consideration, that the credulous votaries of state power cannot, upon their own principles, suspect that the state legislatures would be warped from their duty by any external influence. But as in reality the same situation must have the same effect, in the primitive composition at least of the federal house of representatives; an improper biass towards the mercantile class, is as little to be expected from this quarter or from the other.

In order perhaps to give countenance to the objection at any rate, it may be asked, is there not danger of an opposite biass in the national government, which may produce an endeavour to secure a monoply of the federal administration to the landed

class? As there is little likelihood that the supposition of such a
biass will have any terrors for those who would be immediately
injured by it, a laboured answer to this question will be dispensed with. It will be sufficient to remark, first, that for the
reasons elsewhere assigned, it is less likely that any decided
partiality should prevail in the councils of the union, than in
those of any of its members. Secondly, that there would be no
temptation to violate the constitution in favor of the landed
class, because that class would, in the natural course of things,
enjoy as great a preponderancy as itself could desire. And
thirdly, that men accustomed to investigate the sources of public prosperity, upon a large scale, must be too well convinced of
the utility of commerce, to be inclined to inflict upon it so deep
a wound, as would be occasioned by the entire exclusion of those
who would best understand its interests, from a share in the
management of them. The importance of commerce in the view
of revenue alone, must effectually guard it against the enmity of
a body, which would be continually importuned in its favor, by
the urgent calls of public necessity.

I the rather consult brevity in discussing the probability of a
preference founded upon a discrimination between the different
kinds of industry and property, because, as far as I understand
the meaning of the objectors, they contemplate a discrimination
of another kind. They appear to have in view, as the objects of
the preference with which they endeavour to alarm us, those
whom they designate by the description of the "wealthy and the
well-born." These, it seems, are to be exalted to an odious pre-
eminence over the rest of their fellow citizens. At one time,
however, their elevation is to be a necessary consequence of the
smallness of the representative body; at another time, it is to be
effected by depriving the people at large of the opportunity of
exercising their right of suffrage in the choice of that body.

But upon what principle is the discrimination of the places of
election to be made, in order to answer the purpose of the meditated preference? Are the wealthy and the well-born, as they
are called, confined to particular spots in the several states?

Have they, by some miraculous instinct or foresight, set apart in each of them, a common place of residence? Are they only to be met with in the towns and the cities? Or are they, on the contrary, scattered over the face of the country, as avarice or chance may have happened to cast their own lot, or that of their predecessors? If the latter is the case, (as every intelligent man knows it to be*) is it not evident that the policy of confining the places of elections to particular districts, would be as subversive of its own aim, as it would be exceptionable on every other account? The truth is, that there is no method of securing to the rich the preference apprehended, but by prescribing qualifications of property either for those who may elect, or be elected. But this forms no part of the power to be conferred upon the national government. Its authority would be expressly restricted to the regulation of the *times*, the *places*, and the *manner* of elections. The qualifications of the persons who may choose or be chosen, as has been remarked upon another occasion, are defined and fixed in the constitution; and are unalterable by the legislature.

Let it however be admitted, for argument sake, that the expedient suggested might be successful; and let it at the same time be equally taken for granted, that all the scruples which a sense of duty, or an apprehension of the danger of the experiment might inspire, were overcome in the breasts of the national rulers; still, I imagine, it will hardly be pretended, that they could ever hope to carry such an enterprise into execution, without the aid of a military force sufficient to subdue the resistance of the great body of the people. The improbability of the existence of a force equal to that object, has been discussed and demonstrated in different parts of these papers; but that the futility of the objection under consideration may appear in the strongest light, it shall be conceded for a moment, that such a force might exist; and the national government shall be supposed to be in the actual possession of it. What will be the con-

---

* Particularly in the southern states and in this state.

clusion? With a disposition to invade the essential rights of the community, and with the means of gratifying that disposition, is it presumable that the persons who were actuated by it would amuse themselves in the ridiculous task of fabricating election laws for securing a preference to a favourite class of men? Would they not be likely to prefer a conduct better adapted to their own immediate aggrandizement? Would they not rather boldly resolve to perpetuate themselves in office by one decisive act of usurpation, than to trust to precarious expedients, which, in spite of all the precautions that might accompany them, might terminate in the dismission, disgrace, and ruin of their authors? Would they not fear that citizens not less tenacious than conscious of their rights, would flock from the remotest extremes of their respective states to the places of election, to overthrow their tyrants, and to substitute men who would be disposed to avenge the violated majesty of the people?

PUBLIUS.

THE FEDERALIST.

NUMBER LXI.

NEW YORK, FEBRUARY 26, 1788.

HAMILTON.

THE SAME SUBJECT CONTINUED, AND CONCLUDED.

THE more candid opposers of the provision, contained in the plan of the convention, respecting elections, when pressed in argument, will sometimes concede the propriety of it; with this qualification, however, that it ought to have been accompanied with a declaration, that all elections should be held in the counties where the electors reside. This, say they, was a necessary precaution against an abuse of the power. A declaration of this nature, would certainly have been harmless: So far as it would have had the effect of quieting apprehensions, it might not have been undesirable. But it would, in fact, have afforded little or no additional security against the danger apprehended; and the want of it will never be considered, by an impartial and judicious examiner, as a serious, still less as an insuperable, objection to the plan. The different views taken of the subject in the two preceding papers, must be sufficient to satisfy all dispassionate and discerning men, that if the public liberty should ever be the victim of the ambition of the national rulers, the power under examination, at least, will be guiltless of the sacrifice.

If those who are inclined to consult their jealousy only, would exercise it in a careful inspection of the several state constitutions, they would find little less room for disquietude and alarm, from the latitude which most of them allow in respect to elections, than from that which is proposed to be allowed to the national government in the same respect. A review of their situation, in this particular, would tend greatly to remove any ill impressions which may remain in regard to this matter. But, as that review would lead into long and tedious details, I shall content myself with the single example of the state in which I write. The constitution of New-York makes no other provision for *locality* of elections, than that the members of the assembly shall be elected in the *counties*; those of the senate, in the great districts into which the state is, or may be divided: these at present are four in number, and comprehend each from two to six counties. It may readily be perceived, that it would not be more difficult for the legislature of New-York to defeat the suffrages of the citizens of New-York, by confining elections to particular places, than for the legislature of the United States to defeat the suffrages of the citizens of the union, by the like expedient. Suppose, for instance, the city of Albany was to be appointed the sole place of election for the county and district of which it is a part, would not the inhabitants of that city speedily become the only electors of the members both of the senate and assembly for that county and district? Can we imagine, that the electors who reside in the remote subdivisions of the counties of Albany, Saratoga, Cambridge, &c. or in any part of the county of Montgomery, would take the trouble to come to the city of Albany, to give their votes for members of the assembly or senate, sooner than they would repair to the city of New-York, to participate in the choice of the members of the federal house of representatives? The alarming indifference discoverable in the exercise of so invaluable a privilege under the existing laws, which afford every facility to it, furnishes a ready answer to this question. And, abstracted from any experience on the subject, we can be at no loss to determine, that when the place of election is at an *inconvenient distance* from the elector, the effect upon his conduct will be the same, whether that distance be twenty miles, or twenty thousand miles. Hence it must appear, that objections to the particular modification of the federal power of regulating elections, will, in substance, apply with equal force to the modification of the like power in the constitution of this state; and for this reason it will be impossible to acquit the one, and to condemn the other. A similar comparison would lead to the same conclusion, in respect to the constitutions of most of the other states.

If it should be said, that defects in the state constitutions furnish no apology for those which are to be found in the plan proposed; I answer, that, as the former have never been thought chargeable with inattention to the security of liberty, where the imputations thrown on the latter can be shown to be applicable to them also, the presumption is, that they are rather the cavilling refinements of a predetermined opposition, than the well founded inferences of a candid research after truth. To those who are disposed to consider, as innocent omissions in the state constitutions, what they regard as unpardonable blemishes in the plan of the convention, nothing can be said; or, at most, they can only be asked to assign some substantial reason why the representatives of the people, in a single state, should be more impregnable to the lust of power, or other sinister motives, than the representatives of the people of the United States? If they cannot do this, they ought, at least, to prove to us, that it is easier to subvert the liberties of three millions of people, with the advantage of local governments to head their opposition, than of two hundred thousand people who are destitute of that advantage. And in relation to the point immediately under consideration, they ought to convince us that it is less probable that a predominant faction, in a single state, should, in order to maintain its superiority, incline to a preference of a particular class of electors, than that a similar spirit should take possession of the representatives of thirteen states, spread over a vast region, and in several respects distinguishable from each other by a diversity of local circumstances, prejudices, and interests.

Hitherto my observations have only aimed at a vindication of
the provision in question, on the ground of theoretic propriety,
on that of the danger of placing the power elsewhere, and on
that of the safety of placing it in the manner proposed. But
there remains to be mentioned a positive advantage, which will
accrue from this disposition, and which could not as well have
been obtained from any other: I allude to the circumstance of
uniformity, in the time of elections for the federal house of representatives. It is more than possible, that this uniformity may
be found by experience to be of great importance to the public
welfare; both as a security against the perpetuation of the same
spirit in the body, and as a cure for the diseases of faction. If
each state may choose its own time of election, it is possible
there may be at least as many different periods as there are
months in the year. The times of election in the several states,
as they are now established for local purposes, vary between
extremes as wide as March and November. The consequence of
this diversity would be, that there could never happen a total
dissolution or renovation of the body at one time. If an improper
spirit of any kind should happen to prevail in it, that spirit
would be apt to infuse itself into the new members, as they
come forward in succession. The mass would be likely to remain
nearly the same; assimilating constantly to itself its gradual
accretions. There is a contagion in example, which few men have
sufficient force of mind to resist. I am inclined to think, that treble the duration in office, with the condition of a total dissolution
of the body at the same time, might be less formidable to liberty, than one third of that duration subject to gradual and successive alterations.

Uniformity, in the time of elections, seems not less requisite
for executing the idea of a regular rotation in the senate; and for
conveniently assembling the legislature at a stated period in
each year.

It may be asked, why then could not a time have been fixed
in the constitution? As the most zealous adversaries of the plan
of the convention in this state, are in general not less zealous

admirers of the constitution of the state, the question may be retorted, and it may be asked, why was not a time for the like purpose fixed in the constitution of this state? No better answer can be given, than that it was a matter which might safely be intrusted to legislative discretion; and that, if a time had been appointed, it might, upon experiment, have been found less convenient than some other time. The same answer may be given to the question put on the other side. And it may be added, that the supposed danger of a gradual change being merely speculative, it would have been hardly advisable upon that speculation to establish, as a fundamental point, what would deprive several states of the convenience of having the elections for their own governments, and for the national government, at the same epoch.

PUBLIUS.

THE FEDERALIST.

NUMBER LXII.

NEW YORK, FEBRUARY 29, 1788.

HAMILTON.

CONCERNING THE CONSTITUTION OF THE SENATE, WITH REGARD TO THE QUALIFICATIONS OF THE MEMBERS; THE MANNER OF APPOINTING THEM; THE EQUALITY OF REPRESENTATION; THE NUMBER OF THE SENATORS, AND THE DURATION OF THEIR APPOINTMENTS.

HAVING examined the constitution of the house of representatives, and answered such of the objections against it as seemed to merit notice, I enter next on the examination of the senate.

The heads under which this member of the government may be considered, are—I. The qualifications of senators—II. The appointment of them by the state legislatures—III. The equality of representation in the senate—IV. The number of senators, and the term for which they are to be elected—V. The powers vested in the senate.

I. The qualifications proposed for senators, as distinguished from those of representatives, consist in a more advanced age, and a longer period of citizenship. A senator must be thirty years of age at least; as a representative must be twenty-five. And the former must have been a citizen nine years; as seven years are required for the latter. The propriety of these distinctions, is explained by the nature of the senatorial trust; which, requiring greater extent of information and stability of character, requires at the same time, that the senator should have reached a period of life most likely to supply these advantages; and which, participating immediately in transactions with foreign nations, ought to be exercised by none, who are not thoroughly weaned from the prepossessions and habits, incident to foreign birth and education. The term of nine years appears to be a prudent mediocrity between a total exclusion of adopted citizens, whose merit and talents may claim a share in the public confidence; and an indiscriminate and hasty admission of them, which might create a channel for foreign influence on the national councils.

II. It is equally unnecessary to dilate on the appointment of senators by the state legislatures. Among the various modes which might have been devised for constituting this branch of the government, that which has been proposed by the convention is probably the most congenial with the public opinion. It is recommended by the double advantage of favouring a select appointment, and of giving to the state governments such as agency in the formation of the federal government, as must secure the authority of the former, and may form a convenient link between the two systems.

III. The equality of representation in the senate is another point, which, being evidently the result of compromise between the opposite pretensions of the large and the small states, does not call for much discussion. If indeed it be right, that among a people thoroughly incorporated into one nation, every district ought to have a *proportional* share in the government: and that among independent and sovereign states bound together by a simple league, the parties, however unequal in size, ought to have an *equal* share in the common councils, it does not appear to be without some reason, that in a compound republic, partaking both of the national and federal character, the government ought to be founded on a mixture of the principles of proportional and equal representation. But it is superfluous to try, by the standard of theory, a part of the constitution which is allowed on all hands to be the result, not of theory, but "of a spirit of amity, and that mutual deference and concession which

the peculiarity of our political situation rendered indispensable."
A common government, with powers equal to its objects, is
called for by the voice, and still more loudly by the political situation, of America. A government founded on principles more
consonant to the wishes of the larger states, is not likely to be
obtained from the smaller states. The only option then for the
former, lies between the proposed government, and a government still more objectionable. Under this alternative, the advice
of prudence must be, to embrace the lesser evil; and, instead of
indulging a fruitless anticipation of the possible mischiefs which
may ensue, to contemplate rather the advantageous consequences which may qualify the sacrifice.

In this spirit it may be remarked, that the equal vote allowed
to each state, is at once a constitutional recognition of the portion of sovereignty remaining in the individual states, and an
instrument for preserving that residuary sovereignty. So far the
equality ought to be no less acceptable to the large than to the
small states; since they are not less solicitous to guard by every
possible expedient against an improper consolidation of the
states into one simple republic.

Another advantage accruing from this ingredient in the constitution of the senate is, the additional impediment it must
prove against improper acts of legislation. No law or resolution
can now be passed without the concurrence, first, of a majority
of the people, and then, of a majority of the states. It must be
acknowledged that this complicated check on legislation may, in
some instances, be injurious as well as beneficial; and that the
peculiar defence which it involves in favour of the smaller
states, would be more rational, if any interests common to them,
and distinct from those of the other states, would otherwise be
exposed to peculiar danger. But as the larger states will always
be able, by their power over the supplies, to defeat unreasonable exertions of this prerogative of the lesser states; and as the
facility and excess of law-making seem to be the diseases to
which our governments are most liable, it is not impossible, that

this part of the constitution may be more convenient in practice, than it appears to many in contemplation.

IV. The number of senators, and the duration of their appointment, come next to be considered. In order to form an accurate judgment on both these points, it will be proper to inquire into the purposes which are to be answered by the senate; and, in order to ascertain these, it will be necessary to review the inconveniences which a republic must suffer from the want of such an institution.

First. It is a misfortune incident to republican government, though in a less degree than to other governments, that those who administer it, may forget their obligations to their constituents, and prove unfaithful to their important trust. In this point of view, a senate, as a second branch of the legislative assembly, distinct from, and dividing the power with, a first, must be in all cases a salutary check on the government. It doubles the security to the people, by requiring the concurrence of two distinct bodies in schemes of usurpation or perfidy, where the ambition or corruption of one would otherwise be sufficient. This is a precaution founded on such clear principles, and now so well understood in the United States, that it would be more than superfluous to enlarge on it. I will barely remark, that, as the improbability of sinister combinations will be in proportion to the dissimilarity in the genius of the two bodies, it must be politic to distinguish them from each other by every circumstance which will consist with a due harmony in all proper measures, and with the genuine principles of republican government.

Second. The necessity of a senate is not less indicated by the propensity of all single and numerous assemblies, to yield to the impulse of sudden and violent passions, and to be seduced by factious leaders into intemperate and pernicious resolutions. Examples on this subject might be cited without number; and from proceedings within the United States, as well as from the history of other nations. But a position that will not be contradicted, need not be proved. All that need be remarked, is, that a body which is to correct this infirmity, ought itself to be free from it, and consequently ought to be less numerous. It ought moreover to possess great firmness, and consequently ought to hold its authority by a tenure of considerable durations.

Third. Another defect to be supplied by a senate, lies in a want of due acquaintance with the objects and principles of legislation. It is not possible that an assembly of men, called, for the most part, from pursuits of a private nature, continued in appointment for a short time, and led by no permanent motive to devote the intervals of public occupation to a study of the laws, the affairs, and the comprehensive interests of their country, should, if left wholly to themselves, escape a variety of important errors in the exercise of their legislative trust. It may be affirmed, on the best grounds, that no small share of the present embarrassments of America is to be charged on the blunders of our governments; and that these have proceeded from the heads, rather than the hearts of most of the authors of them. What indeed are all the repealing, explaining, and amending laws, which fill and disgrace our voluminous codes, but so many monuments of deficient wisdom; so many impeachments exhibited by each succeeding, against each preceding, session; so many admonitions to the people, of the value of those aids, which may be expected from a well constituted senate?

A good government implies two things; first, fidelity to the object of government, which is the happiness of the people; secondly, a knowledge of the means by which that object can be best attained. Some governments are deficient in both these qualities: Most governments are deficient in the first. I scruple not to assert, that, in the American governments, too little attention has been paid to the last. The federal constitution avoids this error: and what merits particular notice, it provides for the last in a mode which increases the security for the first.

Fourth. The mutability in the public councils, arising from a rapid succession of new members, however qualified they may be, points out, in the strongest manner, the necessity of some stable institution in the government. Every new election in the states, is found to change one half of the representatives. From this change of men must proceed a change of opinions; and from a change of opinions, a change of measures. But a continual change even of good measures is inconsistent with every rule of prudence, and every prospect of success. The remark is verified in private life, and becomes more just as well as more important, in national transactions.

To trace the mischievous effects of a mutable government, would fill a volume. I will hint a few only, each of which will be perceived to be a source of innumerable others.

In the first place, it forfeits the respect and confidence of other nations, and all the advantages connected with national character. An individual who is observed to be inconstant to his plans, or perhaps to carry on his affairs without any plan at all, is marked at once by all prudent people, as a speedy victim to his own unsteadiness and folly. His more friendly neighbours may pity him, but all will decline to connect their fortunes with his; and not a few will seize the opportunity of making their fortunes out of his. One nation is to another, what one individual is to another; with this melancholy distinction perhaps, that the former, with fewer of the benevolent emotions than the latter, are under fewer restraints also from taking undue advantage of the indiscretions of each other. Every nation, consequently, whose affairs betray a want of wisdom and stability, may calculate on every loss which can be sustained from the more systematic policy of its wiser neighbours. But the best instruction on this subject is unhappily conveyed to America by the example of her own situation. She finds that she is held in no respect by her friends; that she is the derision of her enemies; and that she is a prey to every nation which has an interest in speculating on her fluctuating councils and embarrassed affairs.

The internal effects of a mutable policy are still more calamitous. It poisons the blessings of liberty itself. It will be of little avail to the people, that the laws are made by men of their own choice, if the laws be so voluminous that they cannot be read, or so incoherent that they cannot be understood: if they be repealed or revised before they are promulged or undergo such incessant changes, that no man who knows what the law is to-day, can guess what it will be to-morrow. Law is defined to be a rule of action; but how can that be a rule, which is little known and less fixed?

Another effect of public instability, is the unreasonable advantage it gives to the sagacious, the enterprising, and the monied few, over the industrious and uninformed mass of the people. Every new regulation concerning commerce or revenue, or in any manner affecting the value of the different species of property, presents a new harvest to those who watch the change, and can trace its consequences; a harvest, reared not by themselves, but by the toils and cares of the great body of their fellow citizens. This is a state of things in which it may be said, with some truth, that laws are made for the *few*, not for the *many*.

In another point of view, great injury results from an unstable government. The want of confidence in the public councils, damps every useful undertaking; the success and profit of which may depend on a continuance of existing arrangements. What prudent merchant will hazard his fortunes in any new branch of commerce, when he knows not but that his plans may be rendered unlawful before they can be executed? What farmer or manufacturer, will lay himself out for the encouragement given to any particular cultivation or establishment, when he can have no assurance, that his preparatory labours and advances will not render him a victim to an inconstant government? In a word, no great improvement or laudable enterprise can go forward, which requires the auspices of a steady system of national policy.

But the most deplorable effect of all, is that diminution of attachment and reverence, which steals into the hearts of the people, towards a political system which betrays so many marks of infirmity, and disappoints so many of their flattering hopes. No government, any more than an individual, will long be respected, without being truly respectable; nor be truly respectable, without possessing a certain portion of order and stability.

PUBLIUS.

THE FEDERALIST.

NUMBER LXIII.

NEW YORK, MARCH 7, 1788.

HAMILTON.

A FURTHER VIEW OF THE CONSTITUTION OF THE SENATE, IN REGARD TO THE DURATION OF THE APPOINTMENT OF ITS MEMBERS.

A FIFTH desideratum, illustrating the utility of a senate, is the want of a due sense of national character. Without a select and stable member of the government, the esteem of foreign powers will not only be forfeited by an unenlightened and variable policy, proceeding from the causes already mentioned; but the national councils will not possess that sensibility to the opinion of the world, which is perhaps not less necessary in order to merit, than it is to obtain, its respect and confidence.

An attention to the judgment of other nations, is important to every government, for two reasons: The one is, that, independently of the merits of any particular plan or measure, it is desirable on various accounts, that it should appear to other nations as the offspring of a wise and honourable policy: The second is, that in doubtful cases, particularly where the national councils may be warped by some strong passion, or momentary interest, the presumed or known opinion of the impartial world, may be the best guide that can be followed. What has not America lost with foreign nations by her want of character? And how many errors and follies would she not have avoided, if the justice and propriety of her measures had, in every instance, been previously tried by the light in which they would probably appear to the unbiassed part of mankind.

Yet however requisite a sense of national character may be, it is evident that it can never be sufficiently possessed by a numerous and changeable body. It can only be found in a number so small, that a sensible degree of the praise and blame of public measures, may be the portion of each individual; or in an assembly so durably invested with public trust, that the pride and consequence of its members may be sensibly incorporated with the reputation and prosperity of the community. The half-yearly representatives of Rhode-Island, would probably have been little affected in their deliberations on the iniquitous measures of that state, by arguments drawn from the light in which such measures would be viewed by foreign nations, or even by the sister states; whilst it can scarcely be doubted, that if the concurrence of a select and stable body had been necessary, a regard to national character alone, would have prevented the calamities under which that misguided people is now labouring.

I add, as a *sixth* defect, the want in some important cases of a due responsibility in the government to the people, arising from that frequency of elections, which in other cases produces this responsibility. The remark will, perhaps, appear not only new, but paradoxical. It must nevertheless be acknowledged, when explained, to be as undeniable as it is important.

Responsibility, in order to be reasonable, must be limited to objects within the power of the responsible party; and in order to be effectual, must relate to operations of that power, of which a ready and proper judgment can be formed by the constituents. The objects of government may be divided into two general classes; the one depending on measures, which have singly an immediate and sensible operation; the other depending on a succession of well chosen and well connected measures, which have a gradual and perhaps unobserved operation. The importance of the latter description to the collective and permanent welfare of every country, needs no explanation. And yet it is evident, that an assembly elected for so short a term as to be unable to provide more than one or two links in a chain of measures, on which the general welfare may essentially depend, ought not to be answerable for the final result, any more than a steward or tenant, engaged for one year, could be justly made to answer for plans or improvements, which could not be accomplished in less than half a dozen years. Nor is it possible for the people to estimate the *share* of influence, which their annual assemblies may respectively have on events resulting from the mixed transactions of several years. It is sufficiently difficult, at any rate, to preserve a personal responsibility in the members of a *numerous* body, for such acts of the body as have an immediate, detached, and palpable operation on its constituents.

The proper remedy for this defect, must be an additional body in the legislative department, which, having sufficient permanency to provide for such objects as require a continued attention, and a train of measures, may be justly and effectually answerable for the attainment of those objects.

Thus far I have considered the circumstances, which point out the necessity of a well constructed senate, only as they relate to the representatives of the people. To a people as little blinded by prejudice, or corrupted by flattery, as those whom I address, I shall not scruple to add, that such an institution may be sometimes necessary, as a defence to the people against their own temporary errors and delusions. As the cool and deliberate sense of the community ought, in all governments, and actually will, in all free governments, ultimately prevail over the views of its rulers; so there are particular moments in public affairs, when the people, stimulated by some irregular passion, or some illicit advantage, or misled by the artful misrepresentations of interested men, may call for measures which they themselves will afterwards be the most ready to lament and condemn. In these critical moments, how salutary will be the interference of some temperate and respectable body of citizens, in order to check the misguided career, and to suspend the blow meditated by the people against themselves, until reason, justice, and truth, can regain their authority over the public mind? What bitter anguish would not the people of Athens have often avoided, if their government had contained so provident a safeguard, against the tyranny of their own passions? Popular liberty, might then have escaped the indelible reproach, of decreeing to the same citizens, the hemlock on one day, and statues on the next.

It may be suggested, that a people spread over an extensive region, cannot, like the crowded inhabitants of a small district, be subject to the infection of violent passions; or to the danger of combining in the pursuit of unjust measures. I am far from denying, that this is a distinction of peculiar importance. I have, on the contrary, endeavoured in a former paper to show, that it is one of the principal recommendations of a confederated republic. At the same time, this advantage ought not to be considered, as superseding the use of auxiliary precautions. It may even be remarked, that the same extended situation, which will exempt the people of America from some of the dangers incident to lesser republics, will expose them to the inconveniency of remaining for a longer time, under the influence of those misrepresentations which the combined industry of interested men may succeed in distributing among them.

It adds no small weight to all these considerations, to recollect, that history informs us of no long-lived republic, which had not a senate. Sparta, Rome, and Carthage, are, in fact, the only states to whom that character can be applied. In each of the two first, there was a senate for life. The constitution of the senate in the last, is less known. Circumstantial evidence makes it probable, that it was not different in this particular from the two others. It is at least certain, that it had some quality or other, which rendered it an anchor against popular fluctuations; and that a smaller council, drawn out of the senate, was appointed not only for life, but filled up vacancies itself. These examples, though as unfit for the imitation, as they are repugnant to the genius, of America, are, notwithstanding, when compared with the fugitive and turbulent existence of other ancient republics, very instructive proofs of the necessity of some institution, that will blend stability with liberty. I am not unaware of the circumstances which distinguish the American, from other popular governments, as well ancient as modern; and which render extreme circumspection necessary, in reasoning from the one case to the other. But after allowing due weight to this consideration, it may still be maintained, that there are many points of similitude, which render these examples not unworthy of our attention. Many of the defects, as we have seen, which can only be supplied by a senatorial institution, are common to a numerous assembly frequently elected by the people, and to the people themselves. There are others peculiar to the former, which require the control of such an institution. The people can never wilfully betray their own interests: but they may possibly be betrayed by their representatives, and the danger will be evidently greater, where the whole legislative trust is lodged in the hands of one body of men, than where the concurrence of separate and dissimilar bodies is required in every public act.

The difference most relied on, between the American, and other republics, consists in the principle of representation, which is the pivot on which the former move, and which is supposed to have been unknown to the latter, or at least to the ancient part of them. The use which has been made of this difference, in reasonings contained in former papers, will have shown that I am disposed neither to deny its existence, nor to undervalue its importance. I feel the less restraint therefore in observing, that the position concerning the ignorance of the ancient governments on the subject of representation, is by no means precisely true, in the latitude commonly given to it. Without entering into a disquisition which would here be misplaced, I will refer to a few known facts in support of what I advance.

In the most pure democracies of Greece, many of the executive functions were performed, not by the people themselves, but by officers elected by the people, and *representing* them in their *executive* capacity.

Prior to the reform of Solon, Athens was governed by nine archons, annually *elected by the people at large.* The degree of power delegated to them, seems to be left in great obscurity. Subsequent to that period we find an assembly, first of four, and afterwards of six hundred members, annually *elected by the people*; and *partially* representing them in their *legislative* capacity, since they were not only associated with the people in the function of making laws, but had the exclusive right of originating legislative propositions to the people. The senate of Carthage, also, whatever might be its power, or the duration of its appointment, appears to have been elective by the suffrages of the people. Similar instances might be traced in most, if not all the popular governments of antiquity.

Lastly, in Sparta we meet with the Ephori, and in Rome with the Tribunes; two bodies, small indeed in number, but annually *elected by the whole body of the people*, and considered as the *representatives* of the people, almost in their *plenipotentiary* capacity. The Cosmi of Crete were also annually *elected by the people*; and have been considered by some authors as an institution analagous to those of Sparta and Rome, with this difference only, that in the election of that representative body, the right of suffrage was communicated to a part only of the people.

From these facts, to which many others might be added, it is clear, that the principle of representation was neither unknown to the ancients, nor wholly overlooked in their political constitutions. The true distinction between these, and the American governments, lies *in the total exclusion of the people in their collective capacity* from any share in the *latter*, and not in the *total exclusion of the representatives of the people* from the administration of the *former*. The distinction, however, thus qualified, must be admitted to leave a most advantageous superiority, in favour of the United States. But to insure to this advantage its full effect, we must be careful not to separate it from the other advantage, of an extensive territory. For it cannot be believed that any form of representative government, could have succeeded within the narrow limits occupied by the democracies of Greece.

In answer to all these arguments, suggested by reason, illustrated by examples, and enforced by our own experience, the jealous adversary of the constitution will probably content himself with repeating, that a senate appointed not immediately by the people, and for the term of six years, must gradually acquire a dangerous pre-eminence in the government, and finally transform it into a tyrannical aristocracy.

To this general answer, the general reply ought to be sufficient; that liberty may be endangered by the abuses of liberty, as well as by the abuses of power; that there are numerous instances of the former, as well as of the latter; and that the former, rather than the latter, is apparently most to be apprehended by the United States. But a more particular reply may be given.

Before such a revolution can be effected, the senate, it is to be observed, must in the first place, corrupt itself; must next corrupt the state legislatures; must then corrupt the house of representatives; and must finally corrupt the people at large. It is evident, that the senate must be first corrupted, before it can attempt an establishment of tyranny. Without corrupting the legislatures, it cannot prosecute the attempt, because the periodical change of members would otherwise regenerate the whole body. Without exerting the means of corruption with equal success on the house of representatives, the opposition of that co-equal branch of the government, would inevitably defeat the attempt; and without corrupting the people themselves, a succession of new representatives would speedily restore all things to their pristine order. Is there any man who can seriously persuade himself, that the proposed senate can, by any possible means within the compass of human address, arrive at the object of a lawless ambition, through all these obstructions?

If reason condemns the suspicion, the same sentence is pronounced by experience. The constitution of Maryland, furnishes the most apposite example. The senate of that state is elected, as the federal senate will be, indirectly by the people; and for a term less by one year only, than the federal senate. It is distinguished, also, by the remarkable prerogative of filling up its own vacancies within the term of its appointment; and, at the same time, is not under the control of any such rotation as is provided for the federal senate. There are some other lesser distinctions, which would expose the former to colourable objections, that do not lie against the latter. If the federal senate, therefore, really contained the danger which has been so loudly proclaimed, some symptoms at least of a like danger, ought by this time to have been betrayed by the senate of Maryland; but no such symptoms have appeared. On the contrary, the jealousies at first entertained by men of the same description with those who view with terror the correspondent part of the federal constitution, have been gradually extinguished by the progress of the experiment; and the Maryland constitution is daily deriving from the salutary operation of this part of it, a reputation in which it will probably not be rivalled by that of any state in the union.

But if any thing could silence the jealousies on this subject, it ought to be the British example. The senate there, instead of being elected for a term of six years, and of being unconfined to particular families or fortunes, is an hereditary assembly of opulent nobles. The house of representatives, instead of being elected for two years, and by the whole body of the people, is elected for seven years: and in a very great proportion, by a very small proportion of the people. Here, unquestionably, ought to be seen in full display, the aristocratic usurpations and tyranny, which are at some future period to be exemplified in the United States. Unfortunately, however, for the anti-federal argument, the British history informs us, that this hereditary assembly has not even been able to defend itself against the continual encroachments of the house of representatives; and that it no sooner lost the support of the monarch, than it was actually crushed by the weight of the popular branch.

As far as antiquity can instruct us on this subject, its examples support the reasoning which we have employed. In Sparta the Ephori, the annual representatives of the people, were found an overmatch for the senate for life; continually gained on its authority, and finally drew all power into their own hands. The tribunes of Rome, who were the representatives of the people, prevailed, it is well known, in almost every contest with the senate for life, and in the end gained the most complete triumph over it. This fact is the more remarkable, as unanimity was required in every act of the tribunes, even after their number was augmented to ten. It proves the irresistible force possessed by that branch of a free government, which has the people on its side. To these examples might be added that of Carthage, whose senate, according to the testimony of Polybius, instead of drawing all power into its vortex, had, at the commencement of the second punic war, lost almost the whole of its original portion.

Besides the conclusive evidence resulting from this assemblage of facts, that the federal senate will never be able to transform itself, by gradual usurpations, into an independent and aristocratic body; we are warranted in believing, that if such a revolution should ever happen from causes which the foresight of man cannot guard against, the house of representatives with the people on their side, will at all times be able to bring back the constitution to its primitive form and principles. Against the force of the immediate representatives of the people, nothing will be able to maintain even the constitutional authority of the senate, but such a display of enlightened policy, and attachment to the public good, as will divide with that branch of the legislature, the affections and support of the entire body of the people themselves.

PUBLIUS.

THE FEDERALIST.

NUMBER LXIV.

NEW YORK, MARCH 7, 1788.

JAY.

A FURTHER VIEW OF THE CONSTITUTION OF THE SENATE, IN REGARD TO THE POWER OF MAKING TREATIES.

It is a just, and not a new observation, that enemies to particular persons, and opponents to particular measures, seldom confine their censures to such things only in either, as are worthy of blame. Unless on this principle, it is difficult to explain the motives of their conduct, who condemn the proposed constitution in the aggregate, and treat with severity some of the most unexceptionable articles in it.

The 2d section gives power to the president, *"by and with the advice and consent of the senate, to make treaties*, PROVIDED TWO THIRDS OF THE SENATORS PRESENT CONCUR."

The power of making treaties is an important one, especially as it relates to war, peace, and commerce; and it should not be delegated but in such a mode, and with such precautions, as will afford the highest security, that it will be exercised by men the best qualified for the purpose, and in a manner most conducive to the public good. The convention appear to have been attentive to both these points—they have directed the president to be chosen by select bodies of electors, to be deputed by the people for that express purpose; and they have committed the appointment of senators to the state legislatures. This mode has, in such cases, vastly the advantage of elections by the people in their collective capacity, where the activity of party zeal, taking advantage of the supineness, the ignorance, the hopes, and fears of the unwary and interested, often place men in office, by the votes of a small proportion of the electors.

As the select assemblies for choosing the president, as well as the state legislatures who appoint the senators, will, in general, be composed of the most enlightened and respectable citizens, there is reason to presume, that their attention and their votes will be directed to those men only who have become the most distinguished by their abilities and virtue, and in whom the people perceive just grounds for confidence. The constitution manifests very particular attention to this object. By excluding men under thirty-five from the first office, and those under thirty from the second, it confines the elections to men of whom the people have had time to form a judgment, and with respect to whom they will not be liable to be deceived by those brilliant appearances of genius and patriotism, which, like transient meteors, sometimes mislead as well as dazzle. If the observation be well founded, that wise kings will always be served by able ministers, it is fair to argue that, as an assembly of select electors possess, in a greater degree than kings, the means of extensive and accurate information relative to men and characters, so will their appointments bear at least equal marks of discretion and discernment. The inference which naturally results from these considerations is this, that the president and senators so chosen, will always be of the number of those who best understand our national interests, whether considered in relation to the several states or to foreign nations, who are best able to promote those interests, and whose reputation for integrity inspires and merits confidence. With such men the power of making treaties may be safely lodged.

Although the absolute necessity of system, in the conduct of any business, is universally known and acknowledged, yet the high importance of it in national affairs, has not yet become sufficiently impressed on the public mind. They who wish to com-

mit the power under consideration to a popular assembly, composed of members constantly coming and going in quick succession, seem not to recollect that such a body must necessarily be
inadequate to the attainment of those great objects, which
require to be steadily contemplated in all their relations and circumstances, and which can only be approached and achieved by
measures, which not only talents, but also exact information,
and often much time, are necessary to concert and to execute. It
was wise, therefore, in the convention to provide, not only that
the power of making treaties should be committed to able and
honest men, but also that they should continue in place a sufficient time to become perfectly acquainted with our national concerns, and to form and introduce a system for the management
of them. The duration prescribed, is such as will give them an
opportunity of greatly extending their political information, and
of rendering their accumulating experience more and more beneficial to their country. Nor has the convention discovered less
prudence in providing for the frequent elections of senators in
such a way, as to obviate the inconvenience of periodically transferring those great affairs entirely to new men—for, by leaving
a considerable residue of the old ones in place, uniformity and
order, as well as a constant succession of official information,
will be preserved.

There are few who will not admit, that the affairs of trade
and navigation should be regulated by a system cautiously
formed and steadily pursued; and that both our treaties and our
laws should correspond with, and be made to promote it. It is of
much consequence that this correspondence and conformity be
carefully maintained, and they who assent to the truth of this
position, will see and confess that it is well provided for, by
making the concurrence of the senate necessary, both to treaties
and to laws.

It seldom happens in the negociation of treaties, of whatever
nature, but that perfect *secrecy* and immediate *dispatch* are
sometimes requisite. There are cases where the most useful
intelligence may be obtained, if the persons possessing it can be

relieved from apprehensions of discovery. Those apprehensions will operate on those persons, whether they are actuated by mercenary or friendly motives; and there doubtless are many of both descriptions, who would rely on the secrecy of the president, but who would not confide in that of the senate, and still less in that of a large popular assembly. The convention have done well, therefore, in so disposing of the power of making treaties, that although the president must, in forming them, act by the advice and consent of the senate, yet he will be able to manage the business of intelligence in such a manner as prudence may suggest.

They who have turned their attention to the affairs of men, must have perceived that there are tides in them; tides, very irregular in their duration, strength, and direction, and seldom found to run twice exactly in the same manner or measure. To discern and to profit by these tides in national affairs, is the business of those who preside over them; and they who have had much experience on this head inform us, that there frequently are occasions when days, nay, even when hours, are precious. The loss of a battle, the death of a prince, the removal of a minister, or other circumstances intervening to change the present posture and aspect of affairs, may turn the most favourable tide into a course opposite to our wishes. As in the field, so in the cabinet, there are moments to be seized as they pass, and they who preside in either, should be left in capacity to approve them. So often and so essentially have we heretofore suffered, from the want of secrecy and dispatch, that the constitution would have been inexcusably defective, if no attention had been paid to those objects. The matters which in negociations usually require the most secrecy, and the most dispatch, are those preparatory and auxiliary measures, which are no otherways important in a national view, than as they tend to facilitate the attainment of the main objects. For these the president will find no difficulty to provide; and should any circumstance occur, which requires the advice and consent of the senate, he may at any time convene them. Thus we see, that the constitution provides that our negociations for treaties shall have every advantage which can be derived from talents, information, integrity, and deliberate investigation, on the one hand; and from secrecy and dispatch, on the other.

But to this plan, as to most others that have ever appeared, objections are contrived and urged.

Some are displeased with it, not on account of any errors or defects in it, but because, as the treaties, when made, are to have the force of laws, they should be made only by men invested with legislative authority. These gentlemen seem not to consider that the judgments of our courts, and the commissions constitutionally given by our governor, are as valid and as binding on all persons whom they concern, as the laws passed by our-legislature. All constitutional acts of power, whether in the executive or in the judicial department, have as much legal validity and obligation as if they proceeded from the legislature, and therefore, whatever name be given to the power of making treaties, or however obligatory they may be when made, certain it is, that the people may, with much propriety, commit the power to a distinct body from the legislature, the executive, or the judicial. It surely does not follow, that because they have given the power of making laws to the legislature, that therefore they should likewise give them power to do every other act of sovereignty, by which the citizens are to be bound and affected.

Others, though content that treaties should be made in the mode proposed, are averse to their being the *supreme* law of the land. They insist, and profess to believe, that treaties, like acts of assembly, should be repealable at pleasure. This idea seems to be new and peculiar to this country, but new errors, as well as new truths, often appear. These gentlemen would do well to reflect, that a treaty is only another name for a bargain; and that it would be impossible to find a nation who would make any bargain with us, which should be binding on them *absolutely*, but on us only so long and so far as we may think proper to be bound by it. They who make laws, may without doubt, amend or repeal them, and it will not be disputed that they who make treaties, may alter or cancel them; but still let us not forget, that treaties are made not by one only of the contracting parties, but by both; and consequently, that as the consent of both was essential to their formation at first, so must it ever afterwards be to alter or cancel them The proposed constitution, therefore, has not in the least extended the obligation of treaties. They are just as binding, and just as far beyond the lawful reach of legislative acts now, as they will be at any future period, or under any form of government.

However useful jealousy may be in republics, yet when, like bile in the natural, it abounds too much in the body politic; the eyes of both become very liable to be deceived, by the delusive appearances which that malady casts on surrounding objects. From this cause, probably, proceed the fears and apprehensions of some, that the president and senate may make treaties without an equal eye to the interests of all the states. Others suspect, that the two-thirds will oppress the remaining third, and ask, whether those gentlemen are made sufficiently responsible for their conduct; whether, if they act corruptly, they can be punished? and if they make disadvantageous treaties, how are we to get rid of those treaties?

As all the states are equally represented in the senate, and by men the most able and the most willing to promote the interest of their constituents, they will all have an equal degree of influence in that body, especially while they continue to be careful in appointing proper persons, and to insist on their punctual attendance. In proportion as the United States assume a national form, and a national character, so will the good of the whole be more and more an object of attention; and the government must be a weak one indeed, if it should forget, that the good of the whole can only be promoted, by advancing the good of each of the parts or members which compose the whole. It will not be in the power of the president and senate to make any treaties, by which they, and their families and estates, will not be equally bound and affected with the rest of the community; and having no private interest distinct from that of the nation, they will be under no temptations to neglect the latter.

As to corruption, the case is not supposable. He must either have been very unfortunate in his intercourse with the world, or possess a heart very susceptible of such impressions, who can think it probable, that the president and two-thirds of the senate, will ever be capable of such unworthy conduct. The idea is too gross, and too invidious to be entertained. But if such a case should ever happen, the treaty so obtained from us would, like all other fraudulent contracts, be null and void by the law of nations.

With respect to their responsibility, it is difficult to conceive how it could be increased. Every consideration that can influence the human mind, such as honour, oaths, reputation, conscience, the love of country, family affections and attachments, afford security for their fidelity. In short, as the constitution has taken the utmost care that they shall be men of talents and integrity, we have reason to be persuaded, that the treaties they make will be as advantageous as, all circumstances considered, could be made; and so far as the fear of punishment and disgrace can operate, that motive to good behaviour is amply afforded by the article on the subject of impeachments.

PUBLIUS.

THE FEDERALIST.

NUMBER LXV.

NEW YORK, MARCH 7, 1788.

HAMILTON.

A FURTHER VIEW OF THE CONSTITUTION OF THE SENATE, IN
RELATION TO ITS CAPACITY, AS A COURT FOR THE TRIAL OF
IMPEACHMENTS.

THE remaining powers which the plan of the convention allots
to the senate, in a distinct capacity, are comprised in their participation with the executive in the appointment to offices, and
in their judicial character as a court for the trial of impeachments. As in the business of appointments, the executive will be
the principal agent, the provisions relating to it, will most properly be discussed in the examination of that department. We will
therefore conclude this head, with a view of the judicial character of the senate.

A well constituted court for the trial of impeachments, is an
object not more to be desired, than difficult to be obtained in a
government wholly elective. The subjects of its jurisdiction are
those offences which proceed from the misconduct of public men,
or in other words, from the abuse or violation of some public
trust. They are of a nature which may with peculiar propriety
be denominated POLITICAL, as they relate chiefly to injuries done
immediately to the society itself. The prosecution of them, for
this reason, will seldom fail to agitate the passions of the whole
community, and to divide it into parties, more or less friendly,

or inimical, to the accused. In many cases, it will connect itself with the pre-existing factions, and will enlist all their animosities, partialities, influence, and interest on one side, or on the other; and in such cases there will always be the greatest danger, that the decision will be regulated more by the comparative strength of parties, than by the real demonstrations of innocence or guilt.

The delicacy and magnitude of a trust, which so deeply concerns the political reputation and existence of every man engaged in the administration of public affairs, speak for themselves. The difficulty of placing it rightly in a government resting entirely on the basis of periodical elections, will as readily be perceived, when it is considered that the most conspicuous characters in it will, from that circumstance, be too often the leaders, or the tools of the most cunning or the most numerous faction; and on this account, can hardly be expected to possess the requisite neutrality towards those whose conduct may be the subject of scrutiny.

The convention, it appears, thought the senate the most fit depository of this important trust. Those who can best discern the intrinsic difficulty of the thing, will be least hasty in condemning that opinion; and will be most inclined to allow due weight to the arguments, which may be supposed to have produced it.

What, it may be asked, is the true spirit of the institution itself? Is it not designed as a method of NATIONAL INQUEST into the conduct of public men? If this be the design of it, who can so properly be the inquisitors for the nation, as the representatives of the nation themselves? It is not disputed that the power of originating the inquiry, or in other words, of preferring the impeachment, ought to be lodged in the hands of one branch of the legislative body; will not the reasons which indicate the propriety of this arrangement, strongly plead for an admission of the other branch of that body to a share of the inquiry? The model, from which the idea of this institution has been borrowed, pointed out that course to the convention. In

Great Britain, it is the province of the house of commons to prefer the impeachment; and of the house of lords to decide upon it. Several of the state constitutions have followed the example. As well the latter, as the former, seem to have regarded the practice of impeachments, as a bridle in the hands of the legislative body, upon the executive servants of the government. Is not this the true light in which it ought to be regarded?

Where else, than in the senate, could have been found a tribunal sufficiently dignified, or sufficiently independent? What other body would be likely to feel *confidence enough in its own situation,* to preserve unawed and uninfluenced, the necessary impartiality between an *individual* accused, and the *representatives of the people, his accusers*?

Could the supreme court have been relied upon as answering this description? It is much to be doubted whether the members of that tribunal would, at all times, be endowed, with so eminent a portion of fortitude, as would be called for in the execution of so difficult a task; and it is still more to be doubted, whether they would possess the degree of credit and authority, which might, on certain occasions, be indispensable towards reconciling the people to a decision that should happen to clash with an accusation, brought by their immediate representatives. A deficiency in the first, would be fatal to the accused; in the last, dangerous to the public tranquillity. The hazard in both these respects could only be avoided, if at all, by rendering that tribunal more numerous than would consist with a reasonable attention to economy. The necessity of a numerous court for the trial of impeachments, is equally dictated by the nature of the proceeding. This can never be tied down by such strict rules, either in the delineation of the offence by the prosecutors, or in the construction of it by the judges, as in common cases serve to limit the discretion of courts in favour of personal security. There will be no jury to stand between the judges, who are to pronounce the sentence of the law, and the party who is to receive or suffer it. The awful discretion, which a court of impeachments must necessarily have, to doom to honour or to infamy the most confidential and the most distinguished characters of the community, forbids the commitment of the trust to a small number of persons.

These considerations seem alone sufficient to authorize a conclusion, that the supreme court would have been an improper substitute for the senate, as a court of impeachments. There remains a further consideration, which will not a little strengthen this conclusion. It is this: the punishment, which may be the consequence of conviction upon impeachment, is not to terminate the chastisement of the offender. After having been sentenced to a perpetual ostracism from the esteem and confidence, and honours and emoluments of his country, he will still be liable to prosecution and punishment in the ordinary course of law. Would it be proper that the persons, who had disposed of his fame, and his most valuable rights as a citizen in one trial, should in another trial, for the same offence, be also the disposers of his life and his fortune? Would there not be the greatest reason to apprehend, that error, in the first sentence, would be the parent of error in the second sentence? That the strong biass of one decision, would be apt to overrule the influence of any new lights, which might be brought to vary the complexion of another decision? Those who know any thing of human nature, will not hesitate to answer these questions in the affirmative; and will be at no loss to perceive, that by making the same persons judges in both cases, those who might happen to be the objects of prosecution would, in a great measure, be deprived of the double security intended them by a double trial. The loss of life and estate, would often be virtually included in a sentence, which, in its terms, imported nothing more than dismission from a present, and disqualification for a future office. It may be said, that the intervention of a jury, in the second instance, would obviate the danger. But juries are frequently influenced by the opinions of judges. They are sometimes induced to find special verdicts, which refer the main question to the decision of the court. Who would be willing to stake his life and his estate upon the verdict of a jury, acting under the auspices of judges, who had predetermined his guilt?

Would it have been an improvement of the plan, to have united the supreme court with the senate, in the formation of the court of impeachments? This union would certainly have been attended with several advantages; but would they not have been overbalanced by the signal disadvantage already stated, arising from the agency of the same judges in the double prosecution to which the offender would be liable? To a certain extent, the benefits of that union will be obtained from making the chief justice of the supreme court, the president of the court of impeachments, as is proposed to be done in the plan of the convention; while the inconveniences of an entire incorporation of the former into the latter, will be substantially avoided. This was perhaps the prudent mean. I forbear to remark upon the additional pretext for clamour against the judiciary, which so considerable an augmentation of its authority would have afforded.

Would it have been desirable to have composed the court for the trial of impeachments of persons wholly distinct from the other departments of the government? There are weighty arguments, as well against, as in favour of such a plan. To some minds, it will not appear a trivial objection, that it would tend to increase the complexity of the political machine, and to add a new spring to the government, the utility of which would at best be questionable. But an objection, which will not be thought by any unworthy of attention, is this: a court formed upon such a plan, would either be attended with heavy expense, or might in practice be subject to a variety of casualties and inconveniences. It must either consist of permanent officers, stationary at the seat of government, and of course entitled to fixed and regular stipends, or of certain officers of the state governments, to be called upon whenever an impeachment was actually depending. It will not be easy to imagine any third mode materially different, which could rationally be proposed. As the court, for reasons already given, ought to be numerous; the first scheme will be reprobated by every man, who can compare the extent of the public wants, with the means of supplying them; the second will be espoused with caution by those, who will seriously consider the difficulty of collecting men dispersed over the whole union; the injury to the innocent, from the procrastinated determination of the charges which might be brought against them; the advantage to the guilty, from the opportunities which delay would afford for intrigue and corruption, and in some cases the detriment to the state, from the prolonged inaction of men, whose firm and faithful execution of their duty, might have exposed them to the persecution of an intemperate or designing majority in the house of representatives. Though this latter supposition may seem harsh, and might not be likely often to be verified; yet it ought not to be forgotten, that the demon of faction will, at certain seasons, extend his sceptre over all numerous bodies of men.

But though one or the other of the substitutes which have been examined, or some other that might be devised, should, in this respect, be thought preferable to the plan, reported by the convention, it will not follow that the constitution ought for this reason to be rejected. If mankind were to resolve to agree in no institution of government, until every part of it had been adjusted to the most exact standard of perfection, society would soon become a general scene of anarchy, and the world a desert. Where is the standard of perfection to be found? Who will undertake to unite the discordant opinions of a whole community, in the same judgment of it; and to prevail upon one conceited projector to renounce his *infallible* criterion, for the *fallible* criterion of his more *conceited neighbour?* To answer the purpose of the adversaries of the constitution, they ought to prove not merely, that particular provisions in it are not the best, which might have been imagined; but that the plan upon the whole, is bad and pernicious.

PUBLIUS.

THE FEDERALIST.

NUMBER LXVI.

NEW YORK, MARCH 11, 1788.

HAMILTON.

THE SAME SUBJECT CONTINUED.

A REVIEW of the principal objections that have appeared against the proposed court for the trial of impeachments, will not improbably eradicate the remains of any unfavourable impressions which may still exist, in regard to this matter.

The *first* of these objections is, that the provision in question confounds legislative and judiciary authorities in the same body, in violation of that important and well-established maxim, which requires a separation between the different departments of power. The true meaning of this maxim has been discussed and ascertained in another place, and has been shown to be entirely compatible with a partial intermixture of those departments for special purposes, preserving them, in the main, distinct and unconnected. This partial intermixture is even, in some cases, not only proper, but necessary to the mutual defence of the several members of the government, against each other. An absolute or qualified negative in the executive upon the acts of the legislative body, is admitted by the ablest adepts in political science, to be an indispensable barrier against the encroachments of the latter upon the former. And it may, perhaps, with not less reason, be contended, that the powers relating to impeachments are, as before intimated, an essential check in the hands of that body, upon the encroachments of the executive. The division of them between the two branches of the legislature; assigning to one the right of accusing, to the other the right of judging; avoids the inconvenience of making the same persons both accusers and judges: and guards against the danger of persecution, from the prevalency of a factious spirit in either of those branches. As the concurrence of two-thirds of the senate will be requisite to a condemnation, the security to innocence, from this additional circumstance, will be as complete as itself can desire.

It is curious to observe with what vehemence this part of the plan is assailed, on the principle here taken notice of, by men who profess to admire, without exception, the constitution of this state; while that very constitution makes the senate, together with the chancellor and judges of the supreme court, not only a court of impeachments, but the highest judiciary in the state in all causes, civil and criminal. The proportion, in point of numbers, of the chancellor and judges to the senators, is so inconsiderable, that the judiciary authority of New-York, in the last resort may, with truth, be said to reside in its senate. If the plan of the convention be, in this respect, chargeable with a departure from the celebrated maxim which has been so often mentioned, and seems to be so little understood, how much more culpable must be the constitution of New-York?*

A *second* objection to the senate, as a court of impeachments, is, that it contributes to an undue accumulation of power in that body, tending to give to the government a countenance too aristocratic. The senate, it is observed, is to have concurrent authority with the executive in the formation of treaties, and in the appointment to offices: If, say the objectors, to these prerogatives is added that of determining in all cases of impeachment, it will give a decided predominancy to senatorial

---

* In that of New-Jersey, also, the final judiciary authority is in a branch of the legislature. In New-Hampshire, Massachusetts, Pennsylvania, and South-Carolina, one branch of the legislature is the court for the trial of impeachments.

influence. To an objection so little precise in itself, it is not easy to find a very precise answer. Where is the measure or criterion to which we can appeal, for estimating what will give the senate too much, too little, or barely the proper degree of influence? Will it not be more safe, as well as more simple, to dismiss such vague and uncertain calculations, to examine each power by itself, and to decide on general principles, where it may be deposited with most advantage, and least inconvenience?

If we take this course, it will lead to a more intelligible, if not to a more certain result. The disposition of the power of making treaties, which has obtained in the plan of the convention, will then, if I mistake not, appear to be fully justified by the considerations stated in a former number, and by others which will occur under the next head of our inquiries. The expediency of the junction of the senate with the executive, in the power of appointing to offices, will, I trust, be placed in a light not less satisfactory, in the disquisitions under the same head. And I flatter myself the observations in my last paper, must have gone no inconsiderable way towards proving, that it was not easy, if practicable, to find a more fit receptacle for the power of determining impeachments, than that which has been chosen. If this be truly the case, the hypothetical danger of the too great weight of the senate, ought to be discarded from our reasonings.

But this hypothesis, such as it is, has already been refuted in the remarks applied to the duration of office prescribed for the senators. It was by them shown, as well on the credit of historical examples, as from the reason of the thing, that the most *popular* branch of every government, partaking of the republican genius, by being generally the favourite of the people, will be as generally a full match, if not an overmatch, for every other member of the government.

But, independent of this most active and operative principle; to secure the equilibrium of the national house of representatives, the plan of the convention has provided in its favour, sev-

eral important counterpoises to the additional authorities to be
conferred upon the senate. The exclusive privilege of originating
money bills, will belong to the house of representatives. The
same house will possess the sole right of instituting impeachments: Is not this a complete counterbalance to that of determining them?—The same house will be the umpire in all elections of the president, which do not unite the suffrages of a
majority of the whole number of electors; a case which it cannot
be doubted will sometimes, if not frequently, happen. The constant possibility of the thing, must be a fruitful source of influence to that body. The more it is contemplated, the more important will appear this ultimate, though contingent power, of
deciding the competitions of the most illustrious citizens of the
union, for the first office in it. It would not perhaps be rash to
predict, that as a mean of influence, it will be found to outweigh
all the peculiar attributes of the senate.

A third objection to the senate as a court of impeachments, is
drawn from the agency they are to have in the appointments to
office. It is imagined that they would be too indulgent judges of
the conduct of men, in whose official creation they had partici-
pated. The principle of this objection would condemn a practice,
which is to be seen in all the state governments, if not in all the
governments with which we are acquainted: I mean that of rendering those, who hold offices during pleasure, dependent on the
pleasure of those who appoint them. With equal plausibility
might it be alleged in this case, that the favouritism of the latter, would always be an asylum for the misbehaviour of the former. But that practice, in contradiction to this principle, proceeds upon the presumption, that the responsibility of those who
appoint, for the fitness and competency of the persons, on whom
they bestow their choice, and the interest they have in the
respectable and prosperous administration of affairs, will inspire
a sufficient disposition, to dismiss from a share in it, all such
who, by their conduct, may have proved themselves unworthy of
the confidence reposed in them. Though facts may not always
correspond with this presumption, yet if it be in the main just,

it must destroy the supposition, that the senate, who will merely sanction the choice of the executive, should feel a bias, towards the objects of that choice, strong enough to blind them to the evidences of guilt so extraordinary, as to have induced the representatives of the nation to become its accusers.

If any further argument were necessary to evince the improbability of such a bias, it might be found in the nature of the agency of the senate, in the business of appointments.

It will be the office of the president to *nominate*, and with the advice and consent of the senate to *appoint*. There will of course be no exertion of *choice*, on the part of the senate. They may defeat one choice of the executive, and oblige him to make another; but they cannot themselves *choose*—they can only ratify or reject the choice he may have made. They might even entertain a preference to some other person, at the very moment they were assenting to the one proposed; because there might be no positive ground of opposition to him; and they could not be sure, if they withheld their assent, that the subsequent nomination would fall upon their own favourite, or upon any other person in their estimation more meritorious than the one rejected. Thus it could hardly happen, that the majority of the senate would feel any other complacency towards the object of an appointment, than such as the appearances of merit might inspire, and proofs of the want of it destroy.

A fourth objection to the senate, in the capacity of a court of impeachments, is derived from their union with the executive in the power of making treaties. This, it has been said, would constitute the senators their own judges, in every case of a corrupt or perfidious execution of that trust. After having combined with the executive in betraying the interests of the nation in a ruinous treaty, what prospect, it is asked, would there be of their being made to suffer the punishment they would deserve, when they were themselves to decide upon the accusation brought against them for the treachery of which they had been guilty?

This objection has been circulated with more earnestness and with a greater show of reason, than any other which has appeared against this part of the plan; and yet I am deceived if it does not rest upon an erroneous foundation.

The security essentially intended by the constitution against corruption and treachery in the formation of treaties, is to be sought for in the numbers and characters of those who are to make them. The JOINT AGENCY of the chief magistrate of the union, and of two-thirds of the members of a body selected by the collective wisdom of the legislatures of the several states, is designed to be the pledge for the fidelity of the national councils in this particular. The convention might with propriety have meditated the punishment of the executive, for a deviation from the instructions of the senate, or a want of integrity in the conduct of the negociations committed to him: They might also have had in view the punishment of a few leading individuals in the senate, who should have prostituted their influence in that body, as the mercenary instruments of foreign corruption: But they could not with more or with equal propriety have contemplated the impeachment and punishment of two-thirds of the senate, consenting to an improper treaty, than of a majority of that or of the other branch of the national legislature, consenting to a pernicious or unconstitutional law: a principle which I believe has never been admitted into any government. How, in fact, could a majority of the house of representatives impeach themselves? Not better, it is evident, than two-thirds of the senate might try themselves. And yet what reason is there, that a majority of the house of representatives, sacrificing the interests of the society, by an unjust and tyrannical act of legislation, should escape with impunity, more than two-thirds of the senate, sacrificing the same interests in an injurious treaty with a foreign power? The truth is, that in all such cases, it is essential to the freedom, and to the necessary independence of the deliberations of the body, that the members of it should be exempt from punishment for acts done in a collective capacity; and the security to the society must depend on the care which is taken to confide the trust to proper hands, to make it their interest to execute it with fidelity, and to make it as difficult as possible for them to combine in any interest opposite to that of the public good.

So far as might concern the misbehaviour of the executive in perverting the instructions, or contravening the views of the senate, we need not be apprehensive of the want of a disposition in that body to punish the abuse of their confidence, or to vindicate their own authority. We may thus far count upon their pride, if not upon their virtue. And so far even as might concern the corruption of leading members, by whose arts and influence the majority may have been inveigled into measures odious to the community; if the proofs of that corruption should be satisfactory, the usual propensity of human nature will warrant us in concluding, that there would be commonly no defect of inclination in the body, to divert the public resentment from themselves, by a ready sacrifice of the authors of their mismanagement and disgrace.

PUBLIUS.

THE FEDERALIST.

NUMBER LXVII.

NEW YORK, MARCH 11, 1788.

HAMILTON.

CONCERNING THE CONSTITUTION OF THE PRESIDENT: A GROSS AT-
TEMPT TO MISREPRESENT THIS PART OF THE PLAN DETECTED.

THE constitution of the executive department of the proposed government, next claims our attention.

There is hardly any part of the system, the arrangement of which could have been attended with greater difficulty; and there is perhaps none, which has been inveighed against with less candour, or criticised with less judgment.

Here the writers against the constitution, seem to have taken pains to signalize their talent of misrepresentation. Calculating upon the aversion of the people to monarchy, they have endeavoured to enlist all their jealousies and apprehensions in opposition to the intended president of the United States; not merely as the embryo, but as the full grown progeny of that detested parent. To establish the pretended affinity, they have not scrupled to draw resources even from the regions of fiction. The authorities of a magistrate, in a few instances greater, in some instances less, than those of a governor of New-York, have been magnified into more than royal prerogatives. He has been decorated with attributes, superior in dignity and splendour to those of a king of Great Britain. He has been shown to us with a diadem sparkling on his brow, and the imperial

purple flowing in his train. He has been seated on a throne sur-
rounded with minions and mistresses; giving audience to the
envoys of foreign potentates, in all the supercilious pomp of
majesty. The images of Asiatic despotism and voluptuousness,
have not been wanting to crown the exaggerated scene. We
have been taught to tremble at the terrific visages of murder-
ing janisaries; and to blush at the unveiled mysteries of a future
seraglio.

Attempts extravagant as these to disfigure, or rather to meta-
morphose the object, render it necessary to take an accurate view
of its real nature and form; in order to ascertain its true aspect
and genuine appearance, to unmask the disingenuity, and to
expose the fallacy of the counterfeit resemblances which have
been so insidiously, as well as industriously, propagated.

In the execution of this task, there is no man who would not
find it an arduous effort either to behold with moderation, or
to treat with seriousness, the devices not less weak than
wicked, which have been contrived to pervert the public opinion in relation to the subject. They so far exceed the usual,
though unjustifiable, licences of party-artifice, that even in a
disposition the most candid and tolerant, they must force the
sentiments which favour an indulgent construction of the conduct of political adversaries to give place to a voluntary and
unreserved indignation. It is impossible not to bestow the imputation of deliberate imposture and deception upon the gross
pretence of a similitude between a king of Great Britain, and
a magistrate of the character marked out for that of the president of the United States. It is still more impossible to withhold that imputation, from the rash and barefaced expedients
which have been employed to give success to the attempted
imposition.

In one instance, which I cite as a sample of the general spirit,
the temerity has proceeded so far as to ascribe to the president
of the United States a power, which by the instrument reported,
is *expressly* allotted to the executives of the individual states. I
mean the power of filling casual vacancies in the senate.

This bold experiment upon the discernment of his country-men, has been hazarded by the writer who (whatever may be his real merit) has had no inconsiderable share in the applauses of his party;* and who, upon this false and unfounded sugges-tion, has built a series of observations equally false and unfounded. Let him now be confronted with the evidence of the fact; and let him, if he be able, justify or extenuate the shame-ful outrage he has offered to the dictates of truth, and to the rules of fair dealing.

The second clause of the second section of the second article, empowers the president of the United States "to nominate, and by and with the advice and consent of the senate to appoint ambassadors, other public ministers and consuls, judges of the supreme court, and all other *officers* of the United States, whose appointments are *not* in the constitution *otherwise provided for*, and *which shall be established by law.*" Immediately after this clause follows another in these words: "The president shall have power to fill up all *vacancies* that may happen *during the recess of the senate*, by granting commissions which shall *expire at the end of their next session.*" It is from this last provision, that the pretended power of the president to fill vacancies in the senate has been deduced. A slight attention to the connexion of the clauses, and to the obvious meaning of the terms, will satisfy us, that the deduction is not even colourable.

The first of these two clauses, it is clear, only provides a mode for appointing such officers, "whose appointments are *not other-wise provided for* in the constitution, and which *shall be estab-lished by law;*" of course it cannot extend to the appointment of senators; whose appointments are *otherwise provided for* in the constitution,† and who are *established by the constitution*, and will not require a future establishment by law. This position will hardly be contested.

The last of these two clauses, it is equally clear, cannot be understood to comprehend the power of filling vacancies in the

* See Cato, No. 5. † Article 1. Sec. 3. Clause 1.

senate, for the following reasons: *First.* The relation in which that clause stands to the other, which declares the general mode of appointing officers of the United States, denotes it to be nothing more than a supplement to the other; for the purpose of establishing an auxiliary method of appointment, in cases to which the general method was inadequate. The ordinary power of appointment is confided to the president and senate *jointly*, and can therefore only be exercised during the session of the senate: but, as it would have been improper to oblige this body to be continually in session for the appointment of officers; and as vacancies might happen *in their recess*, which it might be necessary for the public service to fill without delay, the succeeding clause is evidently intended to authorise the president, *singly*, to make temporary appointments "during the recess of the senate, by granting commissions which should expire at the end of their next session." *Second.* If this clause is to be considered as supplementary to the one which precedes, the *vacancies* of which it speaks must be construed to relate to the "officers" described in the preceding one; and this, we have seen, excludes from its description the members of the senate. *Third.* The time within which the power is to operate, "during the recess of the senate," and the duration of the appointments, "to the end of the next session" of that body, conspire to elucidate the sense of the provision, which, if it had been intended to comprehend senators, would naturally have referred the temporary power of filling vacancies to the recess of the state legislatures, who are to make the permanent appointments, and not to the recess of the national senate, who are to have no concern in those appointments; and would have extended the duration in office of the temporary senators to the next session of the legislature of the state, in whose representation the vacancies had happened, instead of making it to expire at the end of the ensuing session of the national senate. The circumstances of the body authorized to make the permanent appointments, would, of course, have governed the modification of a power which related to the temporary appointments; and, as the national senate is the body, whose situation is alone contemplated in the clause upon which the suggestion under examination has been founded, the vacancies to which it alludes can only be deemed to respect those officers, in whose appointment that body has a concurrent agency with the president. But, *lastly*, the first and second clauses of the third section of the first article, obviate all possibility of doubt. The former provides, that "the senate of the United States shall be composed of two senators from each state, chosen *by the legislature thereof* for six years;" and the latter directs, that "if vacancies in that body should happen by resignation or otherwise, *during the recess of the legislature of* ANY STATE, the executive THEREOF may make temporary appointments until the *next meeting of the legislature*, which shall then fill such vacancies." Here is an express power given, in clear and unambiguous terms, to the state executives, to fill the casual vacancies in the senate, by temporary appointments; which not only invalidates the supposition, that the clause before considered, could have been intended to confer that power upon the president of the United States; but proves, that this supposition, destitute as it is even of the merit of plausibility, must have originated in an intention to deceive the people, too palpable to be obscured by sophistry, too atrocious to be palliated by hypocrisy.

I have taken the pains to select this instance of misrepresentation, and to place it in a clear and strong light, as an unequivocal proof of the unwarrantable arts, which are practised, to prevent a fair and impartial judgment of the real merits of the plan submitted to the consideration of the people. Nor have I scrupled in so flagrant a case, to indulge a severity of animadversion, little congenial with the general spirit of these papers. I hesitate not to submit it to the decision of any candid and honest adversary of the proposed government, whether language can furnish epithets of too much asperity, for so shameless and so prostitute an attempt to impose on the citizens of America.

PUBLIUS.

THE FEDERALIST.

NUMBER LXVIII.

NEW YORK, MARCH 14, 1788.

HAMILTON.

THE VIEW OF THE CONSTITUTION OF THE PRESIDENT CONTINUED, IN RELATION TO THE MODE OF APPOINTMENT.

THE mode of appointment of the chief magistrate of the United States, is almost the only part of the system, of any consequence, which has escaped without severe censure, or which has received the slightest mark of approbation from its opponents. The most plausible of these, who has appeared is print, has even deigned to admit, that the election of the president is pretty well guarded.* I venture somewhat further, and hesitate not to affirm, that if the manner of it be not perfect, it is at least excellent. It unites in an eminent degree all the advantages, the union of which was to be wished for.

It was desirable, that the sense of the people should operate in the choice of the person to whom so important a trust was to be confided. This end will be answered by committing the right of making it, not to any pre-established body, but to men, chosen by the people for the special purpose, and at the particular conjuncture.

It was equally desirable, that the immediate election should be made by men most capable of analizing the qualities adapted to the station, and acting under circumstances favourable to

* Vide Federal Farmer.

deliberation, and to a judicious combination of all the reasons and inducements that were proper to govern their choice. A small number of persons, selected by their fellow citizens from the general mass, will be most likely to possess the information and discernment requisite to so complicated an investigation.

It was also peculiarly desirable, to afford as little opportunity as possible to tumult and disorder. This evil was not least to be dreaded in the election of a magistrate, who was to have so important an agency in the administration of the government. But the precautions which have been so happily concerted in the system under consideration, promise an effectual security against this mischief. The choice of *several*, to form an intermediate body of electors, will be much less apt to convulse the community, with any extraordinary or violent movements, than the choice of *one*, who was himself to be the final object of the public wishes. And as the electors, chosen in each state, are to assemble and vote in the state, in which they are chosen, this detached and divided situation will expose them much less to heats and ferments, that might be communicated from them to the people, than if they were all to be convened at one time, in one place.

Nothing was more to be desired, than that every practicable obstacle should be opposed to cabal, intrigue, and corruption. These most deadly adversaries of republican government, might naturally have been expected to make their approaches from more than one quarter, but chiefly from the desire in foreign powers to gain an improper ascendant in our councils. How could they better gratify this, than by raising a creature of their own to the chief magistracy of the union? But the convention have guarded against all danger of this sort, with the most provident and judicious attention. They have not made the appointment of the president to depend on pre-existing bodies of men, who might be tampered with beforehand to prostitute their votes; but they have referred it in the first instance to an immediate act of the people of America, to be exerted in the choice of persons for the temporary and sole purpose of making the appointment. And they have excluded from eligibility to this trust, all those who from situation might be suspected of too great devotion to the president in office. No senator, representative, or other person holding a place of trust or profit under the United States, can be of the number of the electors. Thus, without corrupting the body of the people, the immediate agents in the election will at least enter upon the task, free from any sinister bias. Their transient existence, and their detached situation, already noticed, afford a satisfactory prospect of their continuing so, to the conclusion of it. The business of corruption, when it is to embrace so considerable a number of men, requires time, as well as means. Nor would it be found easy suddenly to embark them, dispersed, as they would be over thirteen states, in any combinations founded upon motives which, though they could not properly be denominated corrupt, might yet be of a nature to mislead them from their duty.

Another, and no less important, desideratum was, that the executive should be independent for his continuance in office, on all, but the people themselves. He might otherwise be tempted to sacrifice his duty to his complaisance for those whose favour was necessary to the duration of his official cousequence. This advantage will also be secured, by making his re-election to depend on a special body of representatives, deputed by the society for the single purpose of making the important choice.

All these advantages will be happily combined in the plan devised by the convention, which is, that each state shall choose a number of persons as electors, equal to the number of senators and representatives of such state in the national government, who shall assemble within the state, and vote for some fit person as president. Their votes, thus given, are to be transmitted to the seat of the national government; and the person who may happen to have a majority of the whole number of votes, will be the president. But as a majority of the votes might not always happen to centre in one man, and as it might be unsafe to permit less than a majority to be conclusive, it is provided, that, in such a contingency, the house of representatives shall select out of the candidates, who shall have the five highest numbers of votes, the man who, in their opinion, may be best qualified for the office.

This process of election affords a moral certainty, that the office of president will seldom fall to the lot of any man who is not in an eminent degree endowed with the requisite qualifications. Talents for low intrigue, and the little arts of popularity, may alone suffice to elevate a man to the first honours of a single state; but it will require other talents, and a different kind of merit, to establish him in the esteem and confidence of the whole union, or of so considerable a portion of it, as would be necessary to make him a successful candidate for the distinguished office of president of the United States. It will not be too strong to say, that there will be a constant probability of seeing the station filled by characters pre-eminent for ability and virtue. And this will be thought no inconsiderable recommendation of the constitution, by those who are able to estimate the share which the executive in every government must necessarily have in its good or ill administration. Though we cannot acquiesce in the political heresy of the poet, who says:

"For forms of government, let fools contest—
That which is best administered, is best,"

—yet we may safely pronounce, that the true test of a good government is, its aptitude and tendency to produce a good administration.

The vice-president is to be chosen in the same manner with the president; with this difference, that the senate is to do, in respect to the former, what is to be done by the house of representatives, in respect to the latter.

The appointment of an extraordinary person, as vice-president, has been objected to as superfluous, if not mischievous. It has been alleged, that it would have been preferable to have authorized the senate to elect out of their own body an officer, answering to that description. But two considerations seem to justify the ideas of the convention in this respect. One is, that to secure at all times the possibility of a definitive resolution of the body, it is necessary that the president should have only a casting vote. And to take the senator of any state from his seat as senator, to place him in that of president of the senate, would be to exchange, in regard to the state from which he came, a constant for a contingent vote. The other consideration is, that, as the vice-president may occasionally become a substitute for the president, in the supreme executive magistracy, all the reasons which recommend the mode of election prescribed for the one, apply with great, if not with equal, force to the manner of appointing the other. It is remarkable, that, in this, as in most other instances, the objection which is made, would lie against the constitution of this state. We have a lieutenant-governor, chosen by the people at large, who presides in the senate, and is the constitutional substitute for the governor in casualties similar to those, which would authorize the vice-president to exercise the authorities, and discharge the duties of the president.

PUBLIUS.

THE FEDERALIST.

NUMBER LXIX.

NEW YORK, MARCH 14, 1788.

HAMILTON.

THE SAME VIEW CONTINUED, WITH A COMPARISON BETWEEN THE PRESIDENT AND THE KING OF GREAT BRITAIN, ON THE ONE HAND, AND THE GOVERNOR OF NEW-YORK, ON THE OTHER.

I PROCEED now to trace the real characters of the proposed executive, as they are marked out in the plan of the convention. This will serve to place in a strong light the unfairness of the representations which have been made in regard to it.

The first thing which strikes our attention is, that the executive authority, with few exceptions, is to be vested in a single magistrate. This will scarcely, however, be considered as a point upon which any comparison can be grounded; for if, in this particular, there be a resemblance to the king of Great Britain, there is not less a resemblance to the Grand Seignor, to the Khan of Tartary, to the man of the seven mountains, or to the governor of New-York.

That magistrate is to be elected for *four* years; and is to be re-eligible as often as the people of the United States shall think him worthy of their confidence. In these circumstances, there is a total dissimilitude between *him* and a king of Great Britain; who is an *hereditary* monarch, possessing the crown as a patrimony descendible to his heirs for ever: but there is a close analogy between *him* and a governor of New-York, who is elected for *three* years, and is re-eligible without limitation or intermission. If we consider how much less time would be requisite for establishing a dangerous influence in a single state, than for establishing a like influence throughout the United States, we must conclude, that a duration of *four* years for the chief magistrate of the union, is a degree of permanency far less to be dreaded in that office, than a duration of *three* years for a correspondent office in a single state.

The president of the United States would be liable to be impeached, tried, and, upon conviction of treason, bribery, or other high crimes or misdemeanors, removed from office; and would afterwards be liable to prosecution and punishment in the ordinary course of law. The person of the king of Great Britain, is sacred and inviolable: There is no constitutional tribunal to which he is amenable; no punishment to which he can be subjected, without involving the crisis of a national revolution. In this delicate and important circumstance of personal responsibility, the president of confederated America would stand upon no better ground than a governor of New-York, and upon worse ground than the governors of Virginia and Delaware.

The president of the United States is to have power to return a bill, which shall have passed the two branches of the legislature, for re-consideration; and the bill, so returned, is not to become a law, unless, upon that re-consideration, it be approved by two-thirds of both houses. The king of Great Britain, on his part, has an absolute negative upon the acts of the two houses of parliament. The disuse of that power for a considerable time past, does not affect the reality of its existence; and is to be ascribed wholly to the crown's having found the means of substituting influence to authority, or the art of gaining a majority in one or the other of the two houses, to the necessity of exerting a prerogative which could seldom be exerted without hazarding some degree of national agitation. The qualified negative of the president, differs widely from this absolute negative of the British sovereign; and tallies exactly with the revisionary authority of the council of revision of this state, of which the governor is a constituent part. In this respect, the power of the president would exceed that of the governor of New-York; because the former would possess singly, what the latter shares with the chancellor and judges: But it would be precisely the same with that of the governor of Massachusetts, whose constitution, as to this article, seems to have been the original from which the convention have copied.

The president is to be the "commander in chief of the army and navy of the United States, and of the militia of the several states, when called into the actual service of the United States. He is to have power to grant reprieves and pardons for offences against the United States, *except in cases of impeachment*; to recommend to the consideration of congress such measures as he shall judge necessary and expedient; to convene, on extraordinary occasions, both houses of the legislature, or either of them, and in case of disagreement between them *with respect to the time of adjournment*, to adjourn them to such time as he shall think proper; to take care that the laws be faithfully executed; and to commission all officers of the United States." In most of these particulars, the power of the president will resemble equally that of the king of Great Britain, and of the governor of New-York. The most material points of difference are these:—*First*. The president will have only the occasional command of such part of the militia of the nation, as by legislative provision may be called into the actual service of the union. The king of Great Britain and the governor of New-York, have at all times the entire command of all the militia within their several jurisdictions. In this article, therefore, the power of the president, would be inferior to that of either the monarch, or the governor. *Second*. The president is to be commander in chief of the army and navy of the United States. In this respect his authority would be nominally the same with that of the king of Great Britain, but in substance much inferior to it. It would amount to nothing more than the supreme command and direction of the military and naval forces, as first general and admiral of the confederacy; while that of the British king extends to the *declaring* of war, and to the *raising* and *regulating* of fleets and armies; all which, by the constitution under consideration, would appertain to the legislature.* The governor of New-York, on the other hand, is by the constitution of the state vested only with the command of its militia and navy. But the constitutions of several of the states, expressly declare their governors to be commanders in chief, as well of the army as navy; and it may well be a question, whether those of New-Hampshire and Massachusetts, in particular, do not, in this instance, confer larger powers upon their respective governors, than could be claimed by a president of the United States. *Third.* The power of the president, in respect to pardons, would extend to all cases, *except those of impeachment.* The governor of New-York may pardon in all cases, even in those of impeachment, except for treason and murder. Is not the power of the governor in this article, on a calculation of political consequences, greater than that of the president? All conspiracies and plots against the government, which have not been matured into actual treason, may be screened from punishment of every kind, by the interposition of the prerogative of pardoning. If a governor of New-York, therefore, should be at the head of any such conspiracy, until the design had been ripened into actual hostility, he could insure his accomplices and adherents an entire impunity. A president of the union, on the other hand, though he may even pardon treason, when prosecuted in the ordinary course of law,

---

* A writer in a Pennsylvania paper, under the signature of TAMONY, has asserted, that the king of Great Britain owes his prerogatives, as commander in chief, to an annual mutiny bill. The truth is, on the contrary, that his prerogative, in this respect, is immemorial, and was only disputed, "contrary to all reason and precedent," as Blackstone, vol. 1. page 262. expresses it, by the long parliament of Charles First; but by the statute the 13th of Charles Second, chap. 6. it was declared to be in the king alone, for that the sole supreme government and command of the militia within his majesty's realms and dominions, and of all forces by sea and land, and of all forts and places of strength, EVER WAS AND IS the undoubted right of his majesty and his royal predecessors kings and queens of England, and that both or either house of parliament cannot nor ought to pretend to the same.

could shelter no offender, in any degree, from the effects of impeachment and conviction. Would not the prospect of a total indemnity for all the preliminary steps, be a greater temptation to undertake, and persevere in an enterprise against the public liberty, than the mere prospect of an exemption from death and confiscation, if the final execution of the design, upon an actual appeal to arms, should miscarry? Would this last expectation have any influence at all, when the probability was computed, that the person who was to afford that exemption might himself be involved in the consequences of the measure; and might be incapacitated by his agency in it, from affording the desired impunity? The better to judge of this matter, it will be necessary to recollect that, by the proposed constitution, the offence of treason is limited "to levying war upon the United States, and adhering to their enemies, giving them aid and comfort;" and that by the laws of New-York, it is confined within similar bounds. *Fourth.* The president can only adjourn the national legislature, in a single case of disagreement about the time of adjournment. The British monarch may prorogue, or even dissolve the parliament. The governor of New-York may also prorogue the legislature of this state for a limited time; a prerogative which, in certain situations, may be employed to very important purposes.

The president is to have power, with the advice and consent of the senate, to make treaties, provided two-thirds of the senators present concur. The king of Great Britain is the sole and absolute representative of the nation, in all foreign transactions. He can of his own accord make treaties of peace, commerce, alliance, and of every other description. It has been insinuated, that his authority in this respect is not conclusive, and that his conventions with foreign powers are subject to the revision, and stand in need of the ratification of parliament. But I believe this doctrine was never heard of, till it was broached upon the present occasion. Every jurist* of that kingdom, and every

* Vide Blackstone's Commentaries, vol. 1. page 257.

other man acquainted with its constitution, knows, as an established fact, that the prerogative of making treaties exists in the crown in its utmost plenitude; and that the compacts entered into by the royal authority, have the most complete legal validity and perfection, independent of any other sanction. The parliament, it is true, is sometimes seen employing itself in altering the existing laws to conform them to the stipulations in a new treaty; and this may have possibly given birth to the imagination, that its co-operation was necessary to the obligatory efficacy of the treaty. But this parliamentary interposition, proceeds from a different cause; from the necessity of adjusting a most artificial and intricate system of revenue and commercial laws, to the changes made in them by the operation of the treaty; and of adapting new provisions and precautions, to the new state of things, to keep the machine from running into disorder. In this respect, therefore, there is no comparison between the intended power of the president, and the actual power of the British sovereign. The one can perform alone, what the other can only do with the concurrence of a branch of the legislature. It must be admitted, that, is this instance, the power of the federal executive would exceed that of any state executive. But this arises naturally from the exclusive possession by the union, of that part of the sovereign power which relates to treaties. If the confederacy were to be dissolved, it would become a question, whether the executives of the several states were not solely invested with that delicate and important prerogative.

The president is also to be authorized to receive ambassadors, and other public ministers. This, though it has been a rich theme of declamation, is more a matter of dignity than of authority. It is a circumstance which will be without consequence in the administration of the government; and it was far more convenient that it should be arranged in this manner, than that there should be a necessity of convening the legislature, or one of its branches, upon every arrival of a foreign minister; though it were merely to take the place of a departed predecessor.

The president is to nominate, and *with the advice and consent of the senate*, to appoint ambassadors and other public ministers, judges of the supreme court, and in general all officers of the United States established by law, and whose appointments are not otherwise provided for by the constitution. The king of Great Britain, is emphatically and truly stiled, the fountain of honour. He not only appoints to all offices, but can create offices. He can confer titles of nobility at pleasure; and has the disposal of an immense number of church preferments. There is evidently a great inferiority in the power of the president in this particular, to that of the British king; nor is it equal to that of the governor of New-York, if we are to interpret the meaning of the constitution of the state by the practice which has obtained under it. The power of appointment is with us lodged in a council, composed of the governor and four members of the senate, chosen by the assembly. The governor *claims*, and has frequently *exercised* the right of nomination, and is *entitled* to a casting vote in the appointment. If he really has the right of nominating, his authority is in this respect equal to that of the president, and exceeds it in the article of the casting vote. In the national government, if the senate should be divided, no appointment could be made: In the government of New-York, if the council should be divided, the governor can turn the scale and confirm his own nomination.* If we compare the publicity which must necessarily attend the mode of appointment by the president and an entire branch of the national legislature, with the privacy in the mode of appointment by the governor of New-York, closetted in a secret apartment with at most four, and frequently with only two persons; and if we at the same time consider how much more easy it must be to influence the small number of which a council of appointment consists, than

* Candor however demands an acknowledgement, that I do not think the claim of the governor to a right of nomination well founded. Yet it is always justifiable to reason from the practice of a government, till its propriety has been constitutionally questioned. And independent of this claim, when we take into view the other considerations, and pursue them through all their consequences, we shall be inclined to draw much the same conclusion.

the considerable number of which the national senate would consist, we cannot hesitate to pronounce, that the power of the
chief magistrate of this state, in the disposition of offices must,
in practice, be greatly superior to that of the chief magistrate of
the union.

Hence it appears, that, except as to the concurrent authority
of the president in the article of treaties, it would be difficult to
determine whether that magistrate would, in the aggregate,
possess more or less power than the governor of New-York.
And it appears yet more unequivocally, that there is no pretence
for the parallel which has been attempted between him and the
king of Great Britain. But to render the contrast, in this respect,
still more striking, it may be of use to throw the principal circumstances of dissimilitude into a closer groupe.

The president of the United States, would be an officer
elected by the people for *four* years. The king of Great Britain,
is a perpetual and *hereditary* prince. The one would be amenable
to personal punishment and disgrace: The person of the other is
sacred and inviolable. The one would have a *qualified* negative
upon the acts of the legislative body: The other has an *absolute*
negative. The one would have a right to command the military
and naval forces of the nation: The other, in addition to this
right, possesses that of *declaring* war, and of *raising* and *regulating* fleets and armies by his own authority. The one would
have a concurrent power with a branch of the legislature in the
formation of treaties: The other is the *sole possessor* of the
power of making treaties. The one would have a like concurrent
authority in appointing to offices: The other is the sole author of
all appointments. The one can confer no privileges whatever:
The other can make denizens of aliens, noblemen of commoners;
can erect corporations with all the rights incident to corporate
bodies. The one can prescribe no rules concerning the commerce
or currency of the nation: The other is in several respects the
arbiter of commerce, and in this capacity can establish markets
and fairs, can regulate weights and measures, can lay embargoes
for a limited time, can coin money, can authorize or prohibit the

circulation of foreign coin. The one has no particle of spiritual jurisdiction: The other is the supreme head and governor of the national church!—What answer shall we give to those who would persuade us, that things so unlike resemble each other?— The same that ought to be given to those who tell us, that a government, the whole power of which would be in the hands of the elective and periodical servants of the people, is an aristocracy, a monarchy, and a despotism.

PUBLIUS.

THE FEDERALIST.

NUMBER LXX.

NEW YORK, MARCH 18, 1788.

HAMILTON.

THE SAME VIEW CONTINUED, IN RELATION TO THE UNITY OF THE EXECUTIVE, AND WITH AN EXAMINATION OF THE PROJECT OF AN EXECUTIVE COUNCIL.

THERE is an idea, which is not without its advocates, that a vigorous executive is inconsistent with the genius of republican government. The enlightened well-wishers to this species of government must at least hope, that the supposition is destitute of foundation; since they can never admit its truth, without, at the same time, admitting the condemnation of their own principles. Energy in the executive, is a leading character in the definition of good government. It is essential to the protection of the community against foreign attacks: It is not less essential to the steady administration of the laws, to the protection of property against those irregular and high-handed combinations, which sometimes interrupt the ordinary course of justice, to the security of liberty against the enterprises and assaults of ambition, of faction, and of anarchy. Every man, the least conversant in Roman story, knows how often that republic was obliged to take refuge in the absolute power of a single man, under the formidable title of dictator, as well against the intrigues of ambitious individuals, who aspired to the tyranny, and the seditions of whole classes of the community, whose conduct threatened the existence of all government, as against the invasions of external enemies, who menaced the conquest and destruction of Rome.

There can be no need, however, to multiply arguments or examples on this head. A feeble executive, implies a feeble execution of the government. A feeble execution, is but another phrase for a bad execution: and a government ill executed, whatever it may be in theory, must be, in practice, a bad government.

Taking it for granted, therefore, that all men of sense will agree in the necessity of an energetic executive, it will only remain to inquire, what are the ingredients which constitute this energy? How far can they be combined with those other ingredients, which constitute safety in the republican sense? And how far does this combination characterize the plan which has been reported by the convention?

The ingredients which constitute energy in the executive are, unity; duration; an adequate provision for its support; competent powers.

The ingredients which constitute safety in the republican sense are, a due dependence on the people; a due responsibility.

Those politicians and statesmen, who have been the most celebrated for the soundness of their principles, and for the justness of their views, have declared in favour of a single executive, and a numerous legislature. They have, with great propriety, considered energy as the most necessary qualification of the former, and have regarded this as most applicable to power in a single hand; while they have, with equal propriety, considered the latter as best adapted to deliberation and wisdom, and best calculated to conciliate the confidence of the people, and to secure their privileges and interests.

That unity is conducive to energy, will not be disputed. Decision, activity, secrecy, and dispatch, will generally characterize the proceedings of one man, in a much more eminent degree than the proceedings of any greater number; and in proportion as the number is increased, these qualities will be diminished.

This unity may be destroyed in two ways; either by vesting the power in two or more magistrates, of equal dignity and authority; or by vesting it ostensibly in one man, subject, in whole or in part, to the control and co-operation of others, in the capacity of counsellors to him. Of the first, the two consuls of Rome may serve as an example; of the last, we shall find examples in the constitutions of several of the states. New-York and New-Jersey, if I recollect right, are the only states, which have intrusted the executive authority wholly to single men.* Both these methods of destroying the unity of an the executive have their partizans; but the votaries of an executive council are the most numerous. They are both liable, if not to equal, to similar objections, and may in most lights be examined in conjunction.

The experience of other nations will afford little instruction on this head. As far, however, as it teaches any thing, it teaches us not to be enamoured of plurality in the executive. We have seen that the Achæans, on an experiment of two prætors, were induced to abolish one. The Roman history records many instances of mischiefs to the republic from the dissentions between the consuls, and between the military tribunes, who were at times substituted to the consuls. But it gives us no specimens of any peculiar advantages derived to the state, from the plurality of those magistrates. That the dissentions between them were not more frequent or more fatal, is matter of astonishment; until we advert to the singular position in which the republic was almost continually placed, and to the prudent policy pointed out by the circumstances of the state, and pursued by the consuls, of making a division of the government between them. The patricians, engaged in a perpetual struggle with the plebeians, for the preservation of their ancient authorities and

---

* New-York has no council except for the single purpose of appointing to offices; New-Jersey has a council, whom the governor may consult. But I think, from the terms of the constitution, their resolutions do not bind him.

dignities; the consuls, who were generally chosen out of the former body, were commonly united by the personal interest they had in the defence of the privileges of their order. In addition to this motive of union, after the arms of the republic had considerably expanded the bounds of its empire, it became an established custom with the consuls to divide the administration between themselves by lot; one of them remaining at Rome to govern the city and its environs; the other taking the command in the more distant provinces. This expedient must, no doubt, have had great influence in preventing those collisions and rivalships which might otherwise have embroiled the republic.

But quitting the dim light of historical research, and attaching ourselves purely to the dictates of reason and good sense, we shall discover much greater cause to reject, than to approve, the idea of plurality in the executive, under any modification whatever.

Wherever two or more persons are engaged in any common enterprise or pursuit, there is always danger of difference of opinion. If it be a public trust or office, in which they are cloathed with equal dignity and authority, there is peculiar danger of personal emulation and even animosity. From either, and especially from all these causes, the most bitter dissentions are apt to spring. Whenever these happen, they lessen the respectability, weaken the authority, and distract the plans and operations of those whom they divide. If they should unfortunately assail the supreme executive magistracy of a country, consisting of a plurality of persons, they might impede or frustrate the most important measures of the government, in the most critical emergencies of the state. And what is still worse, they might split the community into violent and irreconcilable factions, adhering differently to the different individuals who composed the magistracy.

Men often oppose a thing, merely because they have had no agency in planning it, or because it may have been planned by those whom they dislike. But if they have been consulted, and have happened to disapprove, opposition then becomes, in their estimation, an indispensable duty of self-love. They seem to think themselves bound in honour, and by all the motives of personal infallibility, to defeat the success of what has been resolved upon, contrary to their sentiments. Men of upright and benevolent tempers, have too many opportunities of remarking with horror, to what desperate lengths this disposition is sometimes carried, and how often the great interests of society are sacrificed to the vanity, to the conceit, and to the obstinacy of individuals, who have credit enough to make their passions and their caprices interesting to mankind. Perhaps the question now before the public, may, in its consequences, afford melancholy proofs of the effects of this despicable frailty, or rather detestable vice in the human character.

Upon the principles of a free government, inconveniences from the source just mentioned, must necessarily be submitted to in the formation of the legislature; but it is unnecessary, and therefore unwise, to introduce them into the constitution of the executive. It is here, too, that they may be most pernicious. In the legislature, promptitude of decision is oftener an evil than a benefit. The differences of opinion, and the jarrings of parties in that department of the government, though they may sometimes obstruct salutary plans, yet often promote deliberation and circumspection; and serve to check excesses in the majority. When a resolution too is once taken, the opposition must be at an end. That resolution is a law, and resistance to it punishable. But no favourable circumstances palliate, or atone for the disadvantages of dissention in the executive department. Here they are pure and unmixed. There is no point at which they cease to operate. They serve to embarrass and weaken the execution of the plan or measure to which they relate, from the first step to the final conclusion of it. They constantly counteract those qualities in the executive, which are the most necessary ingredients in its composition—vigour and expedition; and this without any counter-balancing good. In the conduct of war, in which the energy of the executive is the bulwark of the national security, every thing would be to be apprehended from its plurality.

It must be confessed, that these observations apply with principal weight to the first case supposed, that is, to a plurality of magistrates of equal dignity and authority; a scheme, the advocates for which are not likely to form a numerous sect: But they apply, though not with equal, yet with considerable weight, to the project of a council, whose concurrence is made constitutionally necessary to the operations of the ostensible executive. An artful cabal in that council, would be able to distract and to enervate the whole system of administration. If no such cabal should exist, the mere diversity of views and opinions, would alone be sufficient to tincture the exercise of the executive authority with a spirit of habitual feebleness and dilatoriness.

But one of the weightiest objections to a plurality in the executive, and which lies as much against the last as the first plan, is, that it tends to conceal faults, and destroy responsibility. Responsibility is of two kinds, to censure and to punishment. The first is the most important of the two; especially in an elective office. Men in public trust, will much oftener act in such a manner as to render them unworthy of being any longer trusted, than in such a manner as to make them obnoxious to legal punishment. But the multiplication of the executive adds to the difficulty of detection in either case. It often becomes impossible, amidst mutual accusations, to determine on whom the blame or the punishment of a pernicious measure, or series of pernicious measures, ought really to fall. It is shifted from one to another with so much dexterity, and under such plausible appearances, that the public opinion is left in suspense about the real author. The circumstances which may have led to any national miscarriage or misfortune, are sometimes so complicated, that where there are a number of actors who may have had different degrees and kinds of agency, though we may clearly see upon the whole that there has been mismanagement, yet it may be impracticable to pronounce, to whose account the evil which may have been incurred is truly chargeable.

"I was overruled by my council. The council were so divided in their opinions, that it was impossible to obtain any better resolution on the point." These and similar pretexts are constantly at hand, whether true or false. And who is there that will either take the trouble, or incur the odium, of a strict scrutiny into the secret springs of the transaction? Should there be found a citizen zealous enough to undertake the unpromising task, if there happen to be a collusion between the parties concerned, how easy is it to cloath the circumstances with so much ambiguity, as to render it uncertain what was the precise conduct of any of those parties?

In the single instance in which the governor of this state is coupled with a council, that is, in the appointment to offices, we have seen the mischiefs of it in the view now under consideration. Scandalous appointments to important offices have been made. Some cases indeed have been so flagrant, that ALL PARTIES have agreed in the impropriety of the thing. When inquiry has been made, the blame has been laid by the governor on the members of the council; who on their part have charged it upon his nomination: while the people remain altogether at a loss to determine by whose influence their interests have been committed to hands so manifestly improper. In tenderness to individuals, I forbear to descend to particulars.

It is evident from these considerations, that the plurality of the executive, tends to deprive the people of the two greatest securities they can have for the faithful exercise of any delegated power. *First*. The restraints of public opinion, which lose their efficacy as well on account of the division of the censure attendant on bad measures among a number, as on account of the uncertainty on whom it ought to fall; and *secondly*, the opportunity of discovering with facility and clearness the misconduct of the persons they trust, in order either to their removal from office, or to their actual punishment, in cases which admit of it.

In England, the king is a perpetual magistrate; and it is a maxim which has obtained for the sake of the public peace, that he is unaccountable for his administration, and his person sacred. Nothing, therefore, can be wiser in that kingdom, than to annex to the king a constitutional council, who may be responsible to the nation for the advice they give. Without this, there would be no responsibility whatever in the executive department, an idea inadmissible in a free government. But even there, the king is not bound by the resolutions of his council, though they are answerable for the advice they give. He is the absolute master of his own conduct in the exercise of his office; and may observe or disregard the counsel given to him at his sole discretion.

But in a republic, where every magistrate ought to be personally responsible for his behaviour in office, the reason which in the British constitution dictates the propriety of a council, not only ceases to apply, but turns against the institution. In the monarchy of Great Britain, it furnishes a substitute for the prohibited responsibility of the chief magistrate; which serves in some degree as a hostage to the national justice for his good behaviour. In the American republic it would serve to destroy, or would greatly diminish the intended and necessary responsibility of the chief magistrate himself.

The idea of a council to the executive, which has so generally obtained in the state constitutions, has been derived from that maxim of republican jealousy which considers power as safer in the hands of a number of men than of a single man. If the maxim should be admitted to be applicable to the case, I should contend, that the advantage on that side would not counterbalance the numerous disadvantages on the opposite side. But I do not think the rule at all applicable to the executive power. I clearly concur in opinion in this particular with a writer whom the celebrated Junius pronounces to be "deep, solid, and ingenious," that "the executive power is more easily confined when it is ONE:"* That it is far more safe there should be a single object for the jealousy and watchfulness of the people; in a word, that all multiplication of the executive, is rather dangerous than friendly to liberty.

A little consideration will satisfy us, that the species of security sought for in the multiplication of the executive, is unattainable. Numbers must be so great as to render combination difficult; or they are rather a source of danger than of security. The united credit and influence of several individuals, must be more formidable to liberty, than the credit and influence of either of them separately. When power, therefore, is placed in the hands of so small a number of men, as to admit of their interests and views being easily combined in a common enterprise, by an artful leader, it becomes more liable to abuse, and more dangerous when abused, than if it be lodged in the hands of one man; who, from the very circumstance of his being alone, will be more narrowly watched and more readily suspected, and who cannot unite so great a mass of influence as when he is associated with others. The decemvirs of Rome, whose name denotes their number,† were more to be dreaded in their usurpation than any ONE of them would have been. No person would think of proposing an executive much more numerous than that body; from six, to a dozen, have been suggested for the number of the council. The extreme of these numbers, is not too great for an easy combination; and from such a combination America would have more to fear, than from the ambition of any single individual. A council to a magistrate, who is himself responsible for what he does, are generally nothing better than a clog upon his good intentions; are often the instruments and accomplices of his bad, and are almost always a cloak to his faults.

I forbear to dwell upon the subject of expense; though it be evident that if the council should be numerous enough to answer the principal end, aimed at by the institution, the salaries of the members, who must be drawn from their homes to reside at the

* De Lolme.   † Ten.

seat of government, would form an item in the catalogue of public expenditures, too serious to be incurred for an object of equivocal utility.

I will only add, that prior to the appearance of the constitution, I rarely met with an intelligent man from any of the states, who did not admit as the result of experience, that the unity of the executive of this state was one of the best of the distinguishing features of our constitution.

PUBLIUS.

THE FEDERALIST.

NUMBER LXXI.

NEW YORK, MARCH 21, 1788.

HAMILTON.

THE SAME VIEW CONTINUED, IN REGARD TO THE DURATION OF THE OFFICE.

DURATION in office, has been mentioned as the second requisite to the energy of the executive authority. This has relation to two objects: To the personal firmness of the chief magistrate, in the employment of his constitutional powers; and to the stability of the system of administration, which may have been adopted under his auspices. With regard to the first, it must be evident, that the longer the duration in office, the greater will be the probability of obtaining so important an advantage. It is a general principle of human nature, that a man will be interested in whatever he possesses, in proportion to the firmness or precariousness of the tenure by which he holds it; will be less attached to what he holds by a momentary or uncertain title, than to what he enjoys by a title durable or certain; and, of course, will be willing to risk more for the sake of the one, than of the other. This remark is not less applicable to a political privilege, or honour, or trust, than to any article of ordinary property. The inference from it is, that a man acting in the capacity of chief magistrate, under a consciousness that, in a very short time, he *must* lay down his office, will be apt to feel himself too little interested in it, to hazard any material censure or perplexity, from the independent exertion of his powers, or from encountering the ill-humours, however transient, which may happen to prevail, either in a considerable part of the society itself, or even in a predominant faction in the legislative body. If the case should only be, that he *might* lay it down, unless continued by a new choice; and if he should be desirous of being continued, his wishes, conspiring with his fears, would tend still more powerfully to corrupt his integrity, or debase his fortitude. In either case, feebleness and irresolution must be the characteristics of the station.

There are some, who would be inclined to regard the servile pliancy of the executive, to a prevailing current, either in the community, or in the legislature, as its best recommendation. But such men entertain very crude notions, as well of the purposes for which government was instituted, as of the true means by which the public happiness may be promoted. The republican principle demands, that the deliberate sense of the community should govern the conduct of those to whom they intrust the management of their affairs; but it does not require an unqualified complaisance to every sudden breeze of passion, or to every transient impulse which the people may receive from the arts of men, who flatter their prejudices to betray their interests. It is a just observation, that the people commonly *intend* the PUBLIC GOOD. This often applies to their very errors. But their good sense would despise the adulator who should pretend, that they always *reason right* about the *means* of promoting it. They know, from experience, that they sometimes err; and the wonder is, that they so seldom err as they do, beset, as they continually are, by the wiles of parasites and sycophants; by the snares of the ambitious, the avaricious, the desperate; by the artifices of men who possess their confidence more than they deserve it; and of those who seek to possess, rather than to deserve it. When occasions present themselves, in which the interests of the people are at variance with their inclinations, it is the duty of the persons whom they have appointed, to be the guardians of those interests; to withstand the temporary delusion, in order to give them time and opportunity for more cool and sedate reflection. Instances might be cited, in which a conduct of this kind has saved the people from very fatal consequences of their own mistakes, and has procured lasting monuments of their gratitude to the men who had courage and magnanimity enough to serve them at the peril of their displeasure.

But however inclined we might be, to insist upon an unbounded complaisance in the executive to the inclinations of the people, we can, with no propriety, contend for a like complaisance to the humours of the legislature. The latter may sometimes stand in opposition to the former; and at other times the people may be entirely neutral. In either supposition, it is certainly desirable, that the executive should be in a situation to dare to act his own opinion with vigour and decision.

The same rule which teaches the propriety of a partition between the various branches of power, teaches, likewise, that this partition ought to be so contrived as to render the one independent of the other. To what purpose separate the executive or the judiciary from the legislative, if both the executive and the judiciary are so constituted as to be at the absolute devotion of the legislative? Such a separation must be merely nominal, and incapable of producing the ends for which it was established. It is one thing to be subordinate to the laws, another to be dependent on the legislative body. The first comports with, the last violates, the fundamental principles of good government; and whatever may be the forms of the constitution, unites all power in the same hands. The tendency of the legislative authority to absorb every other, has been fully displayed and illustrated by examples in some preceding numbers. In governments purely republican, this tendency is almost irresistible. The representatives of the people, in a popular assembly, seem sometimes to fancy, that they are the people themselves, and betray strong symptoms of impatience and disgust at the least sign of opposition from any other quarter, as if the exercise of its rights, by either the executive or judiciary, were a breach of their privilege, and an outrage to their dignity. They often appear disposed to exert an imperious control over the other departments; and, as they commonly have the people on their side, they always act with such momentum, as to make it very difficult for the other members of the government to maintain the balance of the constitution.

It may perhaps be asked, how the shortness of the duration in office can affect the independence of the executive on the legislature, unless the one were possessed of the power of appointing or displacing the other? One answer to this inquiry may be drawn from the principle already mentioned, that is, from the slender interest a man is apt to take in a short-lived advantage, and the little inducement it affords him to expose himself, on account of it, to any considerable inconvenience or hazard. Another answer, perhaps more obvious, though not more conclusive, will result from the circumstance of the influence of the legislative body over the people; which might be employed to prevent the re-election of a man who, by an upright resistance to any sinister project of that body, should have made himself obnoxious to its resentment.

It may be asked also, whether a duration of four years would answer the end proposed? and if it would not, whether a less period, which would at least be recommended by greater security against ambitious designs, would not, for that reason, be preferable to a longer period, which was, at the same time, too short for the purpose of inspiring the desired firmness and independence of the magistrate?

It cannot be affirmed, that a duration of four years, or any other limited duration, would completely answer the end proposed; but it would contribute towards it in a degree which would have a material influence upon the spirit and character of the government. Between the commencement and termination of such a period, there would always be a considerable

interval, in which the prospect of an annihilation would be sufficiently remote, not to have an improper effect upon the conduct of a man endued with a tolerable portion of fortitude; and
in which he might reasonably promise himself, that there would
be time enough before it arrived, to make the community sensible of the propriety of the measures he might incline to pursue. Though it be probable that, as he approached the moment
when the public were, by a new election, to signify their sense
of his conduct, his confidence, and with it his firmness, would
decline; yet both the one and the other would derive support
from the opportunities which his previous continuance in the
station had afforded him, of establishing himself in the esteem
and good will of his constituents. He might then, with prudence,
hazard the incurring of reproach, in proportion to the proofs he
had given of his wisdom and integrity, and to the title he had
acquired to the respect and attachment of his fellow citizens.
As, on the one hand, a duration of four years will contribute to
the firmness of the executive in a sufficient degree to render
it a very valuable ingredient in the composition; so, on the
other, it is not long enough to justify any alarm for the public
liberty. If a British house of commons, from the most feeble
beginnings, *from the mere power of assenting or disagreeing to
the imposition of a new tax*, have, by rapid strides, reduced the
prerogatives of the crown, and the privileges of the nobility,
within the limits they conceived to be compatible with the principles of a free government; while they raised themselves to
the rank and consequence of a coequal branch of the legislature; if they have been able, in one instance, to abolish both
the royalty and the aristocracy, and to overturn all the ancient
establishments, as well in the church as state; if they have been
able, on a recent occasion, to make the monarch tremble at the
prospect of an innovation* attempted by them; what would be

---

* This was the case with respect to Mr. Fox's India bill, which was carried in the house of commons, and rejected in the house of lords, to the
entire satisfaction, as it is said, of the people.

to be feared from an elective magistrate of four years duration, with the confined authorities of a president of the United States? What but that he might be unequal to the task which the constitution assigns him? I shall only add, that if his duration be such as to leave a doubt of his firmness, that doubt is inconsistent with a jealousy of his encroachments.

PUBLIUS.

THE FEDERALIST.

NUMBER LXXII.

NEW YORK, MARCH 21, 1788.

HAMILTON.

THE SAME VIEW CONTINUED, IN REGARD TO THE RE-ELIGIBILITY
OF THE PRESIDENT.

THE ADMINISTRATION of government, in its largest sense, comprehends all the operations of the body politic, whether legislative, executive, or judiciary; but in its most usual, and perhaps
in its most precise signification, it is limited to executive details,
and falls peculiarly within the province of the executive department. The actual conduct of foreign negociations, the preparatory plans of finance, the application and disbursement of the
public monies, in conformity to the general appropriations of the
legislature, the arrangement of the army and navy, the direction
of the operations of war; these, and other matters of a like
nature, constitute what seems to be most properly understood
by the administration of government. The persons, therefore, to
whose immediate management these different matters are committed, ought to be considered as the assistants or deputies of
the chief magistrate; and, on this account, they ought to derive
their offices from his appointment, at least from his nomination,
and to be subject to his superintendence. This view of the thing
will at once suggest to us the intimate connexion between the

duration of the executive magistrate in office, and the stability of the system of administration. To undo what has been done by a predecessor, is very often considered by a successor, as the best proof he can give of his own capacity and desert; and, in addition to this propensity, where the alteration has been the result of public choice, the person substituted is warranted in supposing, that the dismission of his predecessor has proceeded from a dislike to his measures, and that the less he resembles him, the more he will recommend himself to the favour of his constituents. These considerations, and the influence of personal confidences and attachments, would be likely to induce every new president to promote a change of men to fill the subordinate stations; and these causes together, could not fail to occasion a disgraceful and ruinous mutability in the administration of the government.

With a positive duration of considerable extent, I connect the circumstance of re-eligibility. The first is necessary, to give the officer himself the inclination, and the resolution to act his part well, and to the community time and leisure to observe the tendency of his measures, and thence to form an experimental estimate of their merits. The last is necessary to enable the people, when they see reason to approve of his conduct, to continue him in the station, in order to prolong the utility of his talents and virtues, and to secure to the government, the advantage of permanency in a wise system of administration.

Nothing appears more plausible at first sight, nor more ill founded upon close inspection, than a scheme which, in relation to the present point, has had some respectable advocates—I mean that of continuing the chief magistrate in office for a certain time, and then excluding him from it, either for a limited period or for ever after. This exclusion, whether temporary or perpetual, would have nearly the same effects; and these effects would be for the most part rather pernicious than salutary.

One ill effect of the exclusion would be, a diminution of the inducements to good behaviour. There are few men who would not feel much less zeal in the discharge of a duty, when they were conscious that the advantage of the station, with which it was connected, must be relinquished at a determinate period, than when they were permitted to entertain a hope of *obtaining* by *meriting* a continuance of them. This position will not be disputed, so long as it is admitted, that the desire of reward is one of the strongest incentives of human conduct; or that the best security for the fidelity of mankind, is to make interest coincide with duty. Even the love of fame, the ruling passion of the noblest minds, which would prompt a man to plan and undertake extensive and arduous enterprises for the public benefit, requiring considerable time to mature and perfect them, if he could flatter himself with the prospect of being allowed to finish what he had begun, would, on the contrary, deter him from the undertaking, when he foresaw that he must quit the scene before he could accomplish the work, and must commit that, together with his own reputation, to hands which might be unequal or unfriendly to the task. The most to be expected from the generality of men, in such a situation, is the negative merit of not doing harm, instead of the positive merit of doing good.

Another ill effect of the exclusion, would be the temptation to sordid views, to peculation, and in some instances, to usurpation. An avaricious man, who might happen to fill the office, looking forward to a time when he must at all events yield up the advantages he enjoyed, would feel a propensity, not easy to be resisted by such a man, to make the best use of his opportunities, while they lasted; and might not scruple to have recourse to the most corrupt expedients to make the harvest as abundant as it was transitory; though the same person probably, with a different prospect before him, might content himself with the regular emoluments of his station, and might even be unwilling to risk the consequences of an abuse of his opportunities. His avarice might be a guard upon his avarice. Add to this, that the same man might be vain or ambitious as well as avaricious. And if he could expect to prolong his honours by his good conduct, he might hesitate to sacrifice his appetite for them, to his appetite for gain. But with the prospect before him of approaching an inevitable annihilation, his avarice would be likely to get the victory over his caution, his vanity, or his ambition.

An ambitious man too, finding himself seated on the summit of his country's honours, looking forward to the time at which he must descend from the exalted eminence for ever, and reflecting that no exertion of merit on his part could save him from the unwelcome reverse, would be much more violently tempted to embrace a favourable conjuncture for attempting the prolongation of his power, at every personal hazard, than if he had the probability of answering the same end by doing his duty.

Would it promote the peace of the community, or the stability of the government, to have half a dozen men who had had credit enough to raise themselves to the seat of the supreme magistracy, wandering among the people like discontented ghosts, and sighing for a place, which they were destined never more to possess?

A third ill effect of the exclusion would be, the depriving the community of the advantage of the experience gained by the chief magistrate in the exercise of his office. That experience is the parent of wisdom, is an adage, the truth of which is recognized by the wisest as well as the simplest of mankind. What more desirable or more essential than this quality in the governors of nations? Where more desirable or more essential, than in the first magistrate of a nation? Can it be wise to put this desirable and essential quality under the ban of the constitution; and to declare that the moment it is acquired, its possessor shall be compelled to abandon the station in which it was acquired, and to which it is adapted? This, nevertheless, is the precise import of all those regulations which exclude men from serving their country, by the choice of their fellow citizens, after they have, by a course of service, fitted themselves for doing it with a greater degree of utility.

A fourth ill effect of the exclusion would be, the banishing men from stations in which, in certain emergencies of the state, their presence might be of the greatest moment to the public interest or safety. There is no nation which has not, at one period or another, experienced an absolute necessity of the services of particular men, in particular situations, perhaps it would not be too strong to say, to the preservation of its political existence. How unwise, therefore, must be every such self-denying ordinance, as serves to prohibit a nation from making use of its own citizens, in the manner best suited to its exigencies and circumstances! Without supposing the personal essentiality of the man, it is evident that a change of the chief magistrate, at the breaking out of a war, or any similar crisis, for another even of equal merit, would at all times be detrimental to the community; inasmuch as it would substitute inexperience to experience, and would tend to unhinge and set afloat the already settled train of the administration.

A fifth ill effect of the exclusion would be, that it would operate as a constitutional interdiction of stability in the administration. By inducing the necessity of a change of men, in the first office in the nation, it would necessarily lead to a mutability of measures. It is not generally to be expected, that men will vary; and measures remain uniform. The contrary is the usual course of things. And we need not be apprehensive that there will be too much stability, while there is even the option of changing; nor need we desire to prohibit the people from continuing their confidence where they think it may be safely placed, and where, by constancy on their part, they may obviate the fatal inconveniences of fluctuating councils and a variable policy.

These are some of the disadvantages, which would flow from the principle of exclusion. They apply most forcibly to the scheme of a perpetual exclusion; but when we consider, that even a partial one would always render the re-admission of the person a remote and precarious object, the observations which have been made will apply nearly as fully to one case as to the other.

What are the advantages promised to counterbalance the evils? They are represented to be: 1st. Greater independence in the magistrate: 2d. Greater security to the people. Unless the exclusion be perpetual, there will be no pretence to infer the first advantage. But even in that case, may he have no object beyond his present station to which he may sacrifice his independence? May he have no connexions, no friends, for whom he may sacrifice it? May he not be less willing, by a firm conduct, to make personal enemies, when he acts under the impression, that a time is fast approaching, on the arrival of which he not only MAY, but MUST be exposed to their resentments, upon an equal, perhaps upon an inferior footing? It is not an easy point to determine, whether his independence would be most promoted or impaired by such an arrangement.

As to the second supposed advantage, there is still greater reason to entertain doubts concerning it, especially if the exclusion were to be perpetual. In this case, as already intimated, a man of irregular ambition, of whom alone there could be reason in any case to entertain apprehensions, would, with infinite reluctance, yield to the necessity of taking his leave for ever of a post, in which his passion for power and preeminence had acquired the force of habit. And if he had been fortunate or adroit enough to conciliate the good will of the people, he might induce them to consider as a very odious and unjustifiable restraint upon themselves, a provision which was calculated to debar them of the right of giving a fresh proof of their attachment to a favourite. There may be conceived circumstances in which this disgust of the people, seconding the thwarted ambition of such a favourite, might occasion greater danger to liberty, than could ever reasonably be dreaded from the possibility of a perpetuation in office, by the voluntary suffrages of the community, exercising a constitutional privilege.

There is an excess of refinement in the idea of disabling the people to continue in office men who had entitled themselves, in their opinion, to approbation and confidence; the advantages of which are at best speculative and equivocal, and are overbalanced by disadvantages far more certain and decisive.

PUBLIUS.

THE FEDERALIST.

NUMBER LXXIII.

NEW YORK, MARCH 21, 1788.

HAMILTON.

THE SAME VIEW CONTINUED, IN RELATION TO THE PROVISION
CONCERNING SUPPORT, AND THE POWER OF THE NEGATIVE.

THE third ingredient towards constituting the vigour of the executive authority, is an adequate provision for its support. It is evident that, without proper attention to this article, the separation of the executive from the legislative department, would be merely nominal and nugatory. The legislature, with a discretionary power over the salary and emoluments of the chief magistrate, could render him as obsequious to their will, as they might think proper to make him. They might, in most cases, either reduce him by famine, or tempt him by largesses, to surrender at discretion his judgment to their inclinations. These expressions, taken in all the latitude of the terms, would no doubt convey more than is intended. There are men who could neither be distressed, nor won, into a sacrifice of their duty; but this stern virtue is the growth of few soils: And in the main it will be found, that a power over a man's support, is a power over his will. If it were necessary to confirm so plain a truth by facts, examples would not be wanting, even in this country, of the intimidation or seduction of the executive by the terrors, or allurements, of the pecuniary arrangements of the legislative body.

It is not easy, therefore, to commend too highly the judicious attention which has been paid to this subject in the proposed constitution. It is there provided, that "The president of the United States shall at stated times receive for his service a compensation, *which shall neither be increased nor diminished, during the period for which he shall have been elected,* and he shall *not receive within that period any other emolument* from the United States, or any of them." It is impossible to imagine any provision which would have been more eligible than this. The legislature, on the appointment of a president, is once for all to declare what shall be the compensation for his services during the time for which he shall have been elected. This done, they will have no power to alter it either by increase or diminution, till a new period of service by a new election commences. They can neither weaken his fortitude by operating upon his necessities, nor corrupt his integrity by appealing to his avarice. Neither the union, nor any of its members, will be at liberty to give, nor will he be at liberty to receive, any other emolument, than that which may have been determined by the first act. He can of course have no pecuniary inducement to renounce or desert the independence intended for him by the constitution.

The last of the requisites to energy, which have been enumerated, is competent powers. Let us proceed to consider those which are proposed to be vested in the president of the United States.

The first thing that offers itself to our observation, is the qualified negative of the president upon the acts or resolutions of the two houses of the legislature; or, in other words, his power of returning all bills with objections, which will have the effect of preventing their becoming laws, unless they should afterwards be ratified by two-thirds of each of the component members of the legislative body.

The propensity of the legislative department to intrude upon the rights, and to absorb the powers, of the other departments, has been already more than once suggested; the insufficiency of a mere parchment delineation of the boundaries of each, has also been remarked upon; and the necessity of furnishing each with constitutional arms for its own defence, has been inferred and proved. From these clear and indubitable principles results the propriety of a negative, either absolute or qualified, in the executive, upon the acts of the legislative branches. Without the one or the other, the former would be absolutely unable to defend himself against the depredations of the latter. He might gradually be stripped of his authorities by successive resolutions, or annihilated by a single vote. And in the one mode or the other, the legislative and executive powers might speedily come to be blended in the same hands. If even no propensity had ever discovered itself in the legislative body, to invade the rights of the executive, the rules of just reasoning and theoretic propriety would of themselves teach us, that the one ought not to be left at the mercy of the other, but ought to possess a constitutional and effectual power of self-defence.

But the power in question has a further use. It not only serves as a shield to the executive, but it furnishes an additional security against the enaction of improper laws. It establishes a salutary check upon the legislative body, calculated to guard the community against the effects of faction, precipitancy, or of any impulse unfriendly to the public good, which may happen to influence a majority of that body.

The propriety of a negative has, upon some occasions, been combatted by an observation, that it was not to be presumed a single man would possess more virtue or wisdom than a number of men; and that, unless this presumption should be entertained, it would be improper to give the executive magistrate any species of control over the legislative body.

But this observation, when examined, will appear rather specious than solid. The propriety of the thing does not turn upon the supposition of superior wisdom or virtue in the executive; but upon the supposition, that the legislative will not be infallible; that the love of power may sometimes betray it into a disposition to encroach upon the rights of the other members of the government; that a spirit of faction may sometimes pervert its deliberations; that impressions of the moment may sometimes hurry it into measures which itself, on mature reflection, would condemn. The primary inducement to conferring the power in question upon the executive, is to enable him to defend himself; the secondary, is to increase the chances in favour of the community against the passing of bad laws, through haste, inadvertence, or design. The oftener a measure is brought under examination, the greater the diversity in the situations of those who are to examine it, the less must be the danger of those errors which flow from want of due deliberation, or of those missteps which proceed from the contagion of some common passion or interest. It is far less probable, that culpable views of any kind should infect all the parts of the government at the same moment, and in relation to the same object, than that they should by turns govern and mislead every one of them.

It may perhaps be said, that the power of preventing bad laws includes that of preventing good ones; and may be used to the one purpose as well as to the other. But this objection will have little weight with those who can properly estimate the mischiefs of that inconstancy and mutability in the laws, which form the greatest blemish in the character and genius of our governments. They will consider every institution calculated to restrain the excess of law-making, and to keep things in the same state in which they may happen to be at any given period, as much more likely to do good than harm; because it is favourable to greater stability in the system of legislation. The injury which may possibly be done by defeating a few good laws, will be amply compensated by the advantage of preventing a number of bad ones.

Nor is this all. The superior weight and influence of the legislative body in a free government, and the hazard to the executive in a trial of strength with that body, afford a satisfactory security, that the negative would generally be employed with great caution; and that, in its exercise, there would oftener be room for a charge of timidity than of rashness. A king of Great Britain, with all his train of sovereign attributes, and with all the influence he draws from a thousand sources, would, at this day, hesitate to put a negative upon the joint resolutions of the two houses of parliament. He would not fail to exert the utmost resources of that influence to strangle a measure disagreeable to him, in its progress to the throne, to avoid being reduced to the dilemma of permitting it to take effect, or of risking the displeasure of the nation, by an opposition to the sense of the legislative body. Nor is it probable, that he would ultimately venture to exert his prerogative, but in a case of manifest propriety, or extreme necessity. All well-informed men in that kingdom will accede to the justness of this remark. A very considerable period has elapsed since the negative of the crown has been exercised.

If a magistrate, so powerful, and so well fortified, as a British monarch, would have scruples about the exercise of the power under consideration, how much greater caution may be reasonably expected in a president of the United States, cloathed, for the short period of four years, with the executive authority of a government wholly and purely republican?

It is evident, that there would be greater danger of his not using his power when necessary, than of his using it too often, or too much. An argument, indeed, against its expediency, has been drawn from this very source. It has been represented, on this account, as a power odious in appearance, useless in practice. But it will not follow, that because it might rarely, it would never be exercised. In the case for which it is chiefly designed, that of an immediate attack upon the constitutional rights of the executive, or in a case in which the public good was evidently and palpably sacrificed, a man of tolerable firmness would avail himself of his constitutional means of defence, and would listen to the admonitions of duty and responsibility. In the former supposition, his fortitude would be stimulated by his immediate interest in the power of his office; in the latter, by the probability of the sanction of his constituents; who, though they would naturally incline to the legislative body in a doubtful case, would hardly suffer their partiality to delude them in a very plain one. I speak now with an eye to a magistrate possessing only a common share of firmness. There are men who, under any circumstances, will have the courage to do their duty at every hazard.

But the convention have pursued a mean in this business, which will both facilitate the exercise of the power vested in this respect in the executive magistrate, and make its efficacy to depend on the sense of a considerable part of the legislative body. Instead of an absolute, it is proposed to give the executive the qualified negative, already described. This is a power which would be much more readily exercised than the other. A man who might be afraid to defeat a law by his single VETO, might not scruple to return it for re-consideration; subject to being finally rejected, only in the event of more than one-third of each house, concurring in the sufficiency of his objections. He would be encouraged by the reflection, that if his opposition should prevail, it would embark in it a very respectable proportion of the legislative body, whose influence would be united with his in supporting the propriety of his conduct in the public opinion. A direct and categorical negative has something in the appearance of it more harsh, and more apt to irritate, than the mere suggestion of argumentative objections to be approved or disapproved, by those to whom they are addressed. In proportion as it would be less apt to offend, it would be more apt to be exercised; and for this very reason it may in practice be found more effectual. It is to be hoped that it will not often happen, that improper views will govern so large a proportion as two-thirds of both branches of the legislature at the same time; and this too in defiance of the counterpoising weight of the executive. It is at any rate far less probable, that this should be the case, than that such views should taint the resolutions and conduct of a bare majority. A power of this nature in the executive, will often have a silent and unperceived, though forcible, operation. When men, engaged in unjustifiable pursuits, are aware, that obstructions may come from a quarter which they cannot control, they will often be restrained by the bare apprehension of opposition, from doing what they would with eagerness rush into, if no such external impediments were to be feared.

This qualified negative, as has been elsewhere remarked, is in this state vested in a council, consisting of the governor, with the chancellor and judges of the supreme court, or any two of them. It has been freely employed upon a variety of occasions, and frequently with success. And its utility has become so apparent, the persons who, in compiling the constitution, were its violent opposers, have from experience become its declared admirers.*

I have in another place remarked, that the convention, in the formation of this part of their plan, had departed from the model of the constitution of this state, in favour of that of Massachusetts. Two strong reasons may be imagined for this preference. One, that the judges, who are to be the interpreters of the law, might receive an improper bias, from having given a previous opinion in their revisionary capacity. The other, that by being often associated with the executive, they might be induced to embark too far in the political views of that magistrate, and thus a dangerous combination might by degrees be cemented between the executive and judiciary departments. It is impossible to keep the judges too distinct from every other avocation than that of expounding the laws. It is peculiarly dangerous to place them in a situation to be either corrupted or influenced by the executive.

PUBLIUS.

* Mr. Abraham Yates, a warm opponent of the plan of the convention, is of this number.

THE FEDERALIST.

NUMBER LXXIV.

NEW YORK, MARCH 25, 1788.

HAMILTON.

THE SAME VIEW CONTINUED, IN RELATION TO THE COMMAND
OF THE NATIONAL FORCES, AND THE POWER OF PARDONING.

THE president of the United States, is to be commander "in chief of the army and navy of the United States, and of the militia of the several states *when called into the actual service* of the United States." The propriety of this provision is so evident, and it is, at the same time, so consonant to the precedents of the state constitutions in general, that little need be said to explain or enforce it. Even those of them which have, in other respects, coupled the chief magistrate with a council, have for the most part concentrated the military authority in him alone. Of all the cares or concerns of government, the direction of war most peculiarly demands those qualities which distinguish the exercise of power by a single hand. The direction of war, implies the direction of the common strength: and the power of directing and employing the common strength, forms an usual and essential part in the definition of the executive authority.

"The president may require the opinion, in writing, of the principal officer in each of the executive departments, upon any subject relating to the duties of their respective offices." This I consider as a mere redundancy in the plan; as the right for which it provides would result of itself from the office.

He is also authorized "to grant reprieves and pardons for offences against the United States, *except in cases of impeachment.*" Humanity and good policy conspire to dictate, that the benign prerogative of pardoning, should be as little as possible fettered or embarrassed. The criminal code of every country partakes so much of necessary severity, that without an easy access to exceptions in favour of unfortunate guilt, justice would wear a countenance too sanguinary and cruel. As the sense of responsibility is always strongest, in proportion as it is undivided, it may be inferred, that a single man would be most ready to attend to the force of those motives, which might plead for a mitigation of the rigour of the law, and least apt to yield to considerations, which were calculated to shelter a fit object of its vengeance. The reflection that the fate of a fellow creature depended on his *sole fiat*, would naturally inspire scrupulousness and caution: The dread of being accused of weakness or connivance, would beget equal circumspection, though of a different kind. On the other hand, as men generally derive confidence from their number, they might often encourage each other in an act of obduracy, and might be less sensible to the apprehension of censure for an injudicious or affected clemency. On these accounts, one man appears to be a more eligible dispenser of the mercy of the government than a body of men.

The expediency of vesting the power of pardoning in the president has, if I mistake not, been only contested in relation to the crime of treason. This, it has been urged, ought to have depended upon the assent of one, or both of the branches of the legislative body. I shall not deny that there are strong reasons to be assigned for requiring in this particular the concurrence of that body, or of a part of it. As treason is a crime levelled at the immediate being of the society, when the laws have once ascertained the guilt of the offender, there seems a fitness in referring the expediency of an act of mercy towards him to the judgment of the legislature. And this ought the rather to be the case, as the supposition of the connivance of the chief magistrate ought not to be entirely excluded. But there are also strong objections to such a plan. It is not to be doubted that a single man of prudence and good sense, is better fitted, in delicate conjunctures, to balance the motives which may plead for and against the remission of the punishment, than any numerous body whatever. It deserves particular attention, that treason will often be connected with seditions, which embrace a large proportion of the community; as lately happened in Massachusetts. In every such case, we might expect to see the representation of the people tainted with the same spirit which had given birth to the offence. And when parties were pretty equally poised, the secret sympathy of the friends and favourers of the condemned, availing itself of the good nature and weakness of others, might frequently bestow impunity where the terror of an example was necessary. On the other hand, when the sedition had proceeded from causes which had inflamed the resentments of the major party, they might often be found obstinate and inexorable, when policy demanded a conduct of forbearance and clemency. But the principal argument for reposing the power of pardoning in this case in the chief magistrate, is this: In seasons of insurrection or rebellion, there are often critical moments, when a well-timed offer of pardon to the insurgents or rebels may restore the tranquillity of the commonwealth; and which, if suffered to pass unimproved, it may never be possible afterwards to recall. The dilatory process of convening the legislature, or one of its branches, for the purpose of obtaining its sanction, would frequently be the occasion of letting slip the golden opportunity. The loss of a week, a day, an hour, may sometimes be fatal. If it should be observed that a discretionary power, with a view to such contingencies, might be occasionally conferred upon the president; it may be answered in the first place, that it is questionable whether, in a limited constitution, that power could be delegated by law;

and in the second place, that it would generally be impolitic before-hand to take any step which might hold out the prospect of impunity. A proceeding of this kind, out of the usual course, would be likely to be construed into an argument of timidity or of weakness, and would have a tendency to embolden guilt.

PUBLIUS.

46

THE FEDERALIST.

NUMBER LXXV.

NEW YORK, MARCH 28, 1788.

HAMILTON.

THE SAME VIEW CONTINUED, IN RELATION TO THE POWER OF MAKING TREATIES.

THE president is to have power, "by and with the advice and consent of the senate, to make treaties, provided two-thirds of the senators present concur."

Though this provision has been assailed on different grounds, with no small degree of vehemence, I scruple not to declare my firm persuasion, that it is one of the best digested and most unexceptionable parts of the plan. One ground of objection is, the trite topic of the intermixture of powers; some contending, that the president ought alone to possess the prerogative of making treaties; others, that it ought to have been exclusively deposited in the senate. Another source of objection, is derived from the small number of persons by whom a treaty may be made: Of those who espouse this objection, a part are of opinion, that the house of representatives ought to have been associated in the business, while another part seem to think that nothing more was necessary than to have substituted two-thirds of *all* the members of the senate, to two-thirds of the members *present*. As I flatter myself the observations made in a preceding number, upon this part of the plan, must have sufficed to place it, to a discerning eye, in a very favourable light.

I shall here content myself with offering only some supplementary remarks, principally with a view to the objections
which have been just stated.

With regard to the intermixture of powers, I shall rely upon
the explanations heretofore given, of the true sense of the rule
upon which that objection is founded; and shall take it for
granted, as an inference from them, that the union of the executive with the senate, in the article of treaties, is no infringement of that rule. I venture to add, that the particular nature of
the power of making treaties, indicates a peculiar propriety in
that union. Though several writers on the subject of government place that power in the class of executive authorities, yet
this is evidently an arbitrary disposition: For if we attend carefully to its operation, it will be found to partake more of the legislative than of the executive character, though it does not seem
strictly to fall within the definition of either. The essence of the
legislative authority is to enact laws, or, in other words, to prescribe rules for the regulation of the society; while the execution
of the laws, and the employment of the common strength, either
for this purpose, or for the common defence, seem to comprise
all the functions of the executive magistrate. The power of making treaties is, plainly neither the one nor the other. It relates
neither to the execution of the subsisting laws, nor to the enaction of new ones; and still less to an exertion of the common
strength. Its objects are, CONTRACTS with foreign nations, which
have the force of law, but derive it from the obligations of good
faith. They are not rules prescribed by the sovereign to the subject, but agreements between sovereign and sovereign. The
power in question seems, therefore, to form a distinct department, and to belong, properly, neither to the legislative nor to
the executive. The qualities elsewhere detailed, as indispensable
in the management of foreign negociations, point out the executive as the most fit agent in those transactions; while the vast
importance of the trust, and the operation of treaties as laws,
plead strongly for the participation of the whole, or a portion, of
the legislative body in the office of making them.

However proper or safe it may be in governments, where the executive magistrate is an hereditary monarch, to commit to him the entire power of making treaties, it would be utterly unsafe and improper to intrust that power to an elective magistrate of four years duration. It has been remarked, upon another occasion, and the remark is unquestionably just, that an hereditary monarch, though often the oppressor of his people, has personally too much at stake in the government, to be in any material danger of being corrupted by foreign powers: But that a man raised from the station of a private citizen to the rank of chief magistrate, possessed of but a moderate or slender fortune, and looking forward to a period not very remote, when he may probably be obliged to return to the station from which he was taken, might sometimes be under temptations to sacrifice duty to interest, which it would require superlative virtue to withstand. An avaricious man might be tempted to betray the interests of the state for the acquisition of wealth. An ambitious man might make his own aggrandizement, by the aid of a foreign power, the price of his treachery to his constituents. The history of human conduct does not warrant that exalted opinion of human virtue, which would make it wise in a nation to commit interests of so delicate and momentous a kind, as those which concern its intercourse with the rest of the world, to the sole disposal of a magistrate created and circumstanced as would be a president of the United States.

To have intrusted the power of making treaties to the senate alone, would have been to relinquish the benefits of the constitutional agency of the president in the conduct of foreign negociations. It is true, that the senate would, in that case, have the option of employing him in this capacity; but they would also have the option of letting it alone; and pique or cabal might induce the latter rather than the former. Besides this, the ministerial servant of the senate, could not be expected to enjoy the confidence and respect of foreign powers in the same extent with the constitutional representative of the nation; and, of course, would not be able to act with an equal degree of weight or efficacy. While the Union would, from this cause, lose a considerable advantage in the management of its external concerns, the people would lose the additional security which would result from the co-operation of the executive. Though it would be imprudent to confide in him solely so important a trust; yet it cannot be doubted, that his participation would materially add to the safety of the society. It must indeed be clear, to a demonstration, that the joint possession of the power in question, by the president and senate, would afford a greater prospect of security, than the separate possession of it by either of them. And whoever has maturely weighed the circumstances which must concur in the appointment of a president, will be satisfied, that the office will always bid fair to be filled by men of such characters, as to render their concurrence, in the formation of treaties, peculiarly desirable, as well on the score of wisdom, as on that of integrity.

The remarks made in a former number, will apply with conclusive force against the admission of the house of representatives to a share in the formation of treaties. The fluctuating, and taking its future increase into the account, the multitudinous composition of that body, forbid us to expect in it those qualities which are essential to the proper execution of such a trust. Accurate and comprehensive knowledge of foreign politics; a steady and systematic adherence to the same views; a nice and uniform sensibility to national character; decision, *secrecy*, and dispatch; are incompatible with the genius of a body so variable and so numerous. The very complication of the business, by introducing a necessity of the concurrence of so many different bodies, would of itself afford a solid objection. The greater frequency of the calls upon the house of representatives, and the greater length of time which it would often be necessary to keep them together when convened, to obtain their sanction in the progressive stages of a treaty, would be a source of so great inconvenience and expense, as alone ought to condemn the project.

The only objection which remains to be canvassed, is that which would substitute the proportion of two-thirds of all the members composing the senatorial body, to that of two-thirds of the members *present*. It has been shown, under the second head of our inquiries, that all provisions which require more than the majority of any body to its resolutions, have a direct tendency to embarrass the operations of the government, and an indirect one to subject the sense of the majority to that of the minority. This consideration seems sufficient to determine our opinion, that the convention have gone as far in the endeavour to secure the advantage of numbers in the formation of treaties, as could have been reconciled either with the activity of the public councils, or with a reasonable regard to the major sense of the community. If two-thirds of the whole number of members had been required, it would, in many cases, from the non-attendance of a part, amount in practice to a necessity of unanimity. And the history of every political establishment in which this principle has prevailed, is a history of impotence, perplexity, and disorder. Proofs of this position might be adduced from the examples of the Roman tribuneship, the Polish diet, and the states general of the Netherlands; did not an example at home, render foreign precedents unnecessary.

To require a fixed proportion of the whole body, would not, in all probability, contribute to the advantages of a numerous agency, better than merely to require a proportion of the attending members. The former, by increasing the difficulty of resolutions disagreeable to the minority, diminishes the motives to punctual attendance. The latter, by making the capacity of the body to depend on a *proportion* which may be varied by the absence or presence of a single member, has the contrary effect. And as, by promoting punctuality, it tends to keep the body complete, there is great likelihood, that its resolutions would generally be dictated by as great a number in this case, as in the other; while there would be much fewer occasions of delay. It ought not to be forgotten, that under the existing confederation, two members *may*, and usually *do*, represent a state; whence it happens that congress, who now are solely invested with *all the powers* of the union, rarely consists of a greater number of persons than would compose the intended senate. If we add to this, that as the members vote by states, and that where there is only a single member present from a state, his vote is lost, it will justify a supposition that the active voices in the senate, where the members are to vote individually, would rarely fall short in number of the active voices in the existing congress. When, in addition to these considerations, we take into view the co-operation of the president, we shall not hesitate to infer, that the people of America would have greater security against an improper use of the power of making treaties, under the new constitution, than they now enjoy under the confederation. And when we proceed still one step further, and look forward to the probable augmentation of the senate, by the erection of new states, we shall not only perceive ample ground of confidence in the sufficiency of the numbers, to whose agency that power will be intrusted; but we shall probably be led to conclude, that a body more numerous than the senate is likely to become, would be very little fit for the proper discharge of the trust.

PUBLIUS.

THE FEDERALIST.

NUMBER LXXVI.

NEW YORK, APRIL 1, 1788.

HAMILTON.

THE SAME VIEW CONTINUED, IN RELATION TO THE APPOINT-MENT OF THE OFFICERS OF THE GOVERNMENT.

THE president is "to *nominate*, and by and with the advice and consent of the senate, to appoint ambassadors, other public ministers and consuls, judges of the supreme court, and all other officers of the United States, whose appointments are not otherwise provided for in the constitution. But the congress may by law vest the appointment of such inferior officers as they think proper, in the president alone, or in the courts of law, or in the heads of departments. The president shall have power to fill up *all vacancies* which may happen *during the recess of the senate*, by granting commissions which shall *expire* at the end of their next session."

It has been observed in a former paper, that "the true test of a good government, is its aptitude and tendency to produce a good administration." If the justness of this observation be admitted, the mode of appointing the officers of the United States contained in the foregoing clauses, must, when examined, be allowed to be entitled to particular commendation. It is not easy to conceive a plan better calculated to promote a judicious choice of men for filling the offices of the union; and it will not need proof, that on this point must essentially depend the character of its administration.

It will be agreed on all hands, that the power of appointment, in ordinary cases, can be properly modified only in one of three ways. It ought either to be vested in a single man; or in a *select* assembly of a moderate number; or in a single man, with the concurrence of such an assembly. The exercise of it by the people at large, will be readily admitted to be impracticable; since, waving every other consideration, it would leave them little time to do any thing else. When, therefore, mention is made in the subsequent reasonings, of an assembly or body of men, what is said must be understood to relate to a select body or assembly, of the description already given. The people collectively, from their number and from their dispersed situation, cannot be regulated in their movements by that systematic spirit of cabal and intrigue, which will be urged as the chief objections to reposing the power in question in a body of men.

Those who have themselves reflected upon the subject, or who have attended to the observations made in other parts of these papers, in relation to the appointment of the president, will, I presume, agree to the position, that there would always be great probability of having the place supplied by a man of abilities, at least respectable. Premising this, I proceed to lay it down as a rule, that one man of discernment is better fitted to analize and estimate the peculiar qualities adapted to particular offices, than a body of men of equal, or perhaps even of superior discernment.

The sole and undivided responsibility of one man, will naturally beget a livelier sense of duty, and a more exact regard to reputation. He will, on this account, feel himself under stronger obligations, and more interested to investigate with care the qualities requisite to the stations to be filled, and to prefer with impartiality the persons who may have the fairest pretensions to them. He will have *fewer* personal attachments to gratify, than a body of men who may each be supposed to have an equal number, and will be so much the less liable to be misled by the sentiments of friendship and of affection. There is nothing so apt to agitate the passions of mankind as personal considerations, whether they relate to ourselves or to others, who are to be the objects of our choice or preference. Hence, in every exercise of the power of appointing to offices by an assembly of men, we must expect to see a full display of all the private and party likings and dislikes, partialities and antipathies, attachments and animosities, which are felt by those who compose the assembly. The choice which may at any time happen to be made under such circumstances, will of course be the result either of a victory gained by one party over the other, or of a compromise between the parties. In either case, the intrinsic merit of the candidate will be too often out of sight. In the first, the qualifications best adapted to uniting the suffrages of the party, will be more considered than those which fit the person for the station. In the last, the coalition will commonly turn upon some interested equivalent, "Give us the man we wish for this office, and you shall have the one you wish for that." This will be the usual condition of the bargain. And it will rarely happen that the advancement of the public service, will be the primary object either of party victories, or of party negociations.

The truth of the principles here advanced, seems to have been felt by the most intelligent of those who have found fault with the provision made, in this respect, by the convention. They contend, that the president ought solely to have been authorized to make the appointments under the federal government. But it is easy to show, that every advantage to be expected from such an arrangement would, in substance, be derived from the power of *nomination*, which is proposed to be conferred upon him; while several disadvantages which might attend the absolute power of appointment in the hands of that officer would be avoided. In the act of nomination, his judgment alone would be exercised; and as it would be his sole duty to point out the man, who with the approbation of the senate should fill an office, his responsibility would be as complete as if he were to make the final appointment. There can, in this view, be no difference between nominating and appointing. The same motives which would influence a proper discharge of his duty in one case, would exist in the other. And as no man could be appointed but upon his previous nomination, every man who might be appointed would be, in fact, his choice.

But his nomination may be overruled: This it certainly may; yet it can only be to make place for another nomination by himself. The person ultimately appointed, must be the object of his preference, though perhaps not in the first degree. It is also not probable, that his nomination would often be overruled. The senate could not be tempted, by the preference they might feel to another, to reject the one proposed; because they could not assure themselves, that the person they might wish would be brought forward by a second or by any subsequent nomination. They could not even be certain, that a future nomination would present a candidate in any degree more acceptable to them: And as their dissent might cast a kind of stigma upon the individual rejected; and might have the appearance of a reflection upon the judgment of the chief magistrate; it is not likely that their sanction would often be refused, where there were not special and strong reasons for the refusal.

To what purpose then require the co-operation of the senate? I answer, that the necessity of their concurrence would have a powerful, though in general a silent, operation. It would be an excellent check upon a spirit of favouritism in the president, and would tend greatly to prevent the appointment of unfit characters from state prejudice, from family connexion, from personal attachment, or from a view to popularity. In addition to this, it would be an efficacious source of stability in the administration.

It will readily be comprehended, that a man who had himself the sole disposition of offices, would be governed much more by his private inclinations and interests, than when he was bound to submit the propriety of his choice to the discussion and determination of a different and independent body; and that body an entire branch of the legislature. The possibility of rejection, would be a strong motive to care in proposing. The danger to his own reputation, and, in the case of an elective magistrate, to his political existence, from betraying a spirit of favouritism, or an unbecoming pursuit of popularity, to the observation of a body whose opinion would have great weight in forming that of the public, could not fail to operate as a barrier to the one and to the other. He would be both ashamed and afraid to bring forward, for the most distinguished or lucrative stations, candidates who had no other merit than that of coming from the same state to which he particularly belonged, or of being, in some way or other, personally allied to him, or of possessing the necessary insignificance and pliancy to render them the obsequious instruments of his pleasure.

To this reasoning it has been objected, that the president, by the influence of the power of nomination, may secure the complaisance of the senate to his views. The supposition of universal venality in human nature, is little less an error in political reasoning, than that of universal rectitude. The institution of delegated power implies, that there is a portion of virtue and honour among mankind, which may be a reasonable foundation of confidence; and experience justifies the theory. It has been found to exist in the most corrupt periods of the most corrupt governments. The venality of the British house of commons has been long a topic of accusation against that body, in the country to which they belong, as well as in this; and it cannot be doubted, that the charge is, to a considerable extent, well founded. But it is as little to be doubted, that there is always a large proportion of the body, which consists of independent and public spirited men, who have an influential weight in the councils of the nation. Hence it is, (the present reign not excepted) that the sense of that body is often seen to control the inclinations of the monarch, both with regard to men and to measures. Though it might therefore be allowable to suppose, that the executive might occasionally influence some individuals in the senate, yet the supposition, that he could in general purchase the integrity of the whole body, would be forced and improbable. A man disposed to view human nature as it is, without either flattering its virtues, or exaggerating its vices, will see sufficient ground of confidence in the probity of the senate, to rest satisfied, not only that it will be impracticable to the executive to corrupt or seduce a majority of its members, but that the necessity of its co-operation, in the business of appointments, will be a considerable and salutary restraint upon the conduct of that magistrate. Nor is the integrity of the senate the only reliance. The constitution has provided some important guards against the danger of executive influence upon the legislative body: It declares, "that no senator or representative shall, during the time *for which he was elected*, be appointed to any civil office under the United States, which shall have been created, or the emoluments whereof shall have been increased during such time; and no person holding any office under the United States, shall be a member of either house during his continuance in office."

PUBLIUS.

THE FEDERALIST.

NUMBER LXXVII

NEW YORK, APRIL 4, 1788

HAMILTON.

THE VIEW OF THE CONSTITUTION OF THE PRESIDENT CON-
CLUDED, WITH A FURTHER CONSIDERATION OF THE POWER OF
APPOINTMENT, AND A CONCISE EXAMINATION OF HIS REMAIN-
ING POWERS.

IT has been mentioned as one of the advantages to be
expected from the co-operation of the senate, in the business
of appointments, that it would contribute to the stability of the
administration. The consent of that body would be necessary to
displace as well as to appoint.* A change of the chief magistrate, therefore, would not occasion so violent or so general a
revolution in the officers of the government as might be
expected, if he were the sole disposer of offices. Where a man,
in any station, had given satisfactory evidence of his fitness for
it, a new president would be restrained from attempting
a change in favour of a person more agreeable to him, by
the apprehension that the discountenance of the senate might
frustrate the attempt, and bring some degree of discredit upon
himself. Those who can best estimate the value of a steady
administration, will be most disposed to prize a provision,
which connects the official existence of public men with the

---

* This construction has since been rejected by the legislature; and it is
now settled in practice, that the power of displacing belongs exclusively to
the president.

approbation or disapprobation of that body, which, from the greater permanency of its own composition, will, in all probability, be less subject to inconstancy than any other member of the government.

To this union of the senate with the president, in the article of appointments, it has in some cases been objected, that it would serve to give the president an undue influence over the senate; and in others, that it would have an opposite tendency; a strong proof that neither suggestion is true.

To state the first in its proper form, is to refute it. It amounts to this—the president would have an improper *influence over* the senate; because the senate would have the power of *restraining* him. This is an absurdity in terms. It cannot admit of a doubt, that the entire power of appointment would enable him much more effectually to establish a dangerous empire over that body, than a mere power of nomination subject to their control.

Let us take a view of the converse of the proposition, "The senate would influence the executive." As I have had occasion to remark in several other instances, the indistinctness of the objection forbids a precise answer. In what manner is this influence to be exerted? In relation to what objects? The power of influencing a person, in the sense in which it is here used, must imply a power of conferring a benefit upon him. How could the senate confer a benefit upon the president by the manner of employing their right of negative upon his nominations? If it be said they might sometimes gratify him by an acquiescence in a favourite choice, when public motives might dictate a different conduct; I answer, that the instances in which the president could be personally interested in the result, would be too few to admit of his being materially affected by the compliances of the senate. Besides this, it is evident, that the POWER which can *originate* the disposition of honours and emoluments, is more likely to attract than to be attracted by the POWER which can merely obstruct their course. If by influencing the president be meant *restraining* him, this is precisely what must have been intended. And it has been shown that the restraint would be salutary, at the same time that it would not be such as to destroy a single advantage to be looked for from the uncontroled agency of that magistrate. The right of nomination would produce all the good, without the ill.

Upon a comparison of the plan for the appointment of the officers of the proposed government, with that which is established by the constitution of this state, a decided preference must be given to the former. In that plan, the power of nomination is unequivocally vested in the executive. And as there would be a necessity for submitting each nomination to the judgment of an entire branch of the legislature, the circumstances attending an appointment, from the mode of conducting it, would naturally become matters of notoriety; and the public could be at no loss to determine what part had been performed by the different actors. The blame of a bad nomination would fall upon the president singly and absolutely. The consure of rejecting a good one, would lie entirely at the door of the senate; aggravated by the consideration of their having counteracted the good intentions of the executive. If an ill appointment should be made, the executive for nominating, and the senate for approving, would participate, though in different degrees, in the opprobrium and disgrace.

The reverse of all this, characterizes the manner of appointment in this state. The council of appointment consists of from three to five persons, of whom the governor is always one. This small body, shut up in a private apartment, impenetrable to the public eye, proceed to the execution of the trust committed to them. It is known, that the governor claims the right of nomination, upon the strength of some ambiguous expressions in the constitution; but it is not known to what extent, or in what manner he exercises it; nor upon what occasions he is contradicted or opposed. The censure of a bad appointment, on account of the uncertainty of its author, and for want of a determinate object, has neither poignancy nor duration. And while an unbounded field for cabal and intrigue lies open, all idea of responsibility is lost. The most that the public can know, is, that the governor claims the right of nomination: That *two*, out of the considerable number of *four* men, can often be managed without much difficulty: That if some of the members of a particular council should happen to be of an uncomplying character, it is frequently not impossible to get rid of their opposition, by regulating the times of meeting in such a manner as to render their attendance inconvenient: And that, from whatever cause it may proceed, a great number of very improper appointments are from time to time made. Whether a governor of this state avails himself of the ascendant he must necessarily have, in this delicate and important part of the administration, to prefer to offices men who are best qualified for them; or whether he prostitutes that advantage to the advancement of persons, whose chief merit is their implicit devotion to his will, and to the support of a despicable and dangerous system of personal influence, are questions which, unfortunately for the community, can only be the subjects of speculation and conjecture.

Every mere council of appointment, however constituted, will be a conclave, in which cabal and intrigue will have their full scope. Their number, without an unwarrantable increase of expense, cannot be large enough to preclude a facility of combination. And as each member will have his friends and connexions to provide for, the desire of mutual gratification will beget a scandalous bartering of votes and bargaining for places. The private attachments of one man might easily be satisfied; but to satisfy the private attachments of a dozen, or of twenty men, would occasion a monopoly of all the principal employments of the government, in a few families, and would lead more directly to an aristocracy or an oligarchy, than any measure that could be contrived. If to avoid an accumulation of offices, there was to be a frequent change in the persons who were to compose the council, this would involve the mischiefs of a mutable administration in their full extent. Such a council would also be more liable to executive influence than the senate, because they would be fewer in number, and would act less immediately under the public inspection. Such a council, in fine, as a substitute for the plan of the convention, would be productive of an increase of expense, a multiplication of the evils which spring from favouritism and intrigue in the distribution of public honours, a decrease of stability in the administration of the government, and a diminution of the security against an undue influence of the executive. And yet such a council has been warmly contended for, as an essential amendment in the proposed constitution.

I could not with propriety conclude my observations on the subject of appointments, without taking notice of a scheme, for which there has appeared some, though but few advocates; I mean that of uniting the house of representatives in the power of making them. I shall, however, do little more than mention it, as I cannot imagine that it is likely to gain the countenance of any considerable part of the community. A body so fluctuating, and at the same time so numerous, can never be deemed proper for the exercise of that power. Its unfitness will appear manifest to all, when it is recollected that in half a century it may consist of three or four hundred persons. All the advantages of the stability, both of the executive and of the senate, would be defeated by this union; and infinite delays and embarrassments would be occasioned. The example of most of the states in their local constitutions, encourages us to reprobate the idea.

The only remaining powers of the executive, are comprehended in giving information to congress of the state of the union; in recommending to their consideration such measures as he shall judge expedient; in convening them, or either branch, upon extraordinary occasions; in adjourning them when they cannot themselves agree upon the time of adjournment; in receiving ambassadors and other public ministers; in faithfully executing the laws; and in commissioning all the officers of the United States.

Except some cavils about the power of convening *either* house of the legislature, and that of receiving ambassadors, no objection has been made to this class of authorities; nor could they possibly admit of any. It required indeed an insatiable avidity for censure, to invent exceptions to the parts which have been assailed. In regard to the power of convening either house of the legislature, I shall barely remark, that in respect to the senate at least, we can readily discover a good reason for it. As this body has a concurrent power with the executive in the article of treaties, it might often be necessary to call it together with a view to this object, when it would be unnecessary and improper to convene the house of representatives. As to the reception of ambassadors, what I have said in a former paper will furnish a sufficient answer.

We have now completed a survey of the structure and powers of the executive department, which I have endeavoured to show, combines, as far as republican principles will admit, all the requisites to energy. The remaining inquiry is—Does it also combine the requisites to safety in the republican sense—a due dependence on the people—a due responsibility? The answer to this question has been anticipated in the investigation of its other characteristics, and is satisfactorily deducible from these circumstances, the election of the president once in four years by persons immediately chosen by the people for that purpose; his liability, at all times, to impeachment, trial, dismission from office, incapacity to serve in any other, and to the forfeiture of life and estate by subsequent prosecution in the common course of law. But these precautions, great as they are, are not the only ones which the plan of the convention has provided in favour of the public security. In the only instances in which the abuse of the executive authority was materially to be feared, the chief magistrate of the United States would, by that plan, be subjected to the control of a branch of the legislative body. What more can an enlightened and reasonable people desire?

PUBLIUS.

THE FEDERALIST.

NUMBER LXXVIII.

NEW YORK, JUNE 17, 20, 1788.

HAMILTON.

A VIEW OF THE CONSTITUTION OF THE JUDICIAL DEPARTMENT, IN RELATION TO THE TENURE OF GOOD BEHAVIOUR.

WE proceed now to an examination of the judiciary department of the proposed government.

In unfolding the defects of the existing confederation, the utility and necessity of a federal judicature have been clearly pointed out. It is the less necessary to recapitulate the considerations there urged; as the propriety of the institution in the abstract is not disputed: The only questions which have been raised being relative to the manner of constituting it, and to its extent. To these points, therefore, our observations shall be confined.

The manner of constituting it seems to embrace these several objects: 1st. The mode of appointing the judges: 2d. The tenure by which they are to hold their places: 3d. The partition of the judiciary authority between different courts, and their relations to each other.

First. As to the mode of appointing the judges: This is the same with that of appointing the officers of the union in general, and has been so fully discussed in the two last numbers, that nothing can be said here which would not be useless repetition.

Second. As to the tenure by which the judges are to hold their places: This chiefly concerns their duration in office; the provisions for their support; the precautions for their responsibility.

According to the plan of the convention, all the judges who may be appointed by the United States are to hold their offices *during good behaviour*; which is conformable to the most approved of the state constitutions—among the rest, to that of this state. Its propriety having been drawn into question by the adversaries of that plan, is no light symptom of the rage for objection, which disorders their imaginations and judgments. The standard of good behaviour for the continuance in office of the judicial magistracy, is certainly one of the most valuable of the modern improvements in the practice of government. In a monarchy, it is an excellent barrier to the despotism of the prince: in a republic, it is a no less excellent barrier to the encroachments and oppressions of the representative body. And it is the best expedient which can be devised in any government, to secure a steady, upright, and impartial administration of the laws.

Whoever attentively considers the different departments of power must perceive, that, in a government in which they are separated from each other, the judiciary, from the nature of its functions, will always be the least dangerous to the political rights of the constitution; because it will be least in a capacity to annoy or injure them. The executive not only dispenses the honours, but holds the sword of the community: The legislature not only commands the purse, but prescribes the rules by which the duties and rights of every citizen are to be regulated: The judicary, on the contrary, has no influence over either the sword or the purse; no direction either of the strength or of the wealth of the society; and can take no active resolution whatever. It may truly be said to have neither FORCE nor WILL, but merely judgment; and must ultimately depend upon the aid of the executive arm for the efficacious exercise even of this faculty.

This simple view of the matter suggests several important consequences: it proves incontestibly, that the judiciary is, beyond comparison, the weakest of the three departments of power,* that it can never attack with success either of the other two; and that all possible care is requisite to enable it to defend itself against their attacks. It equally proves, that, though individual oppression may now and then proceed from the courts of justice, the general liberty of the people can never be endangered from that quarter: I mean so long as the judiciary remains truly distinct from both the legislature and executive. For I agree, that "there is no liberty, if the power of judging be not separated from the legislative and executive powers."† It proves, in the last place, that as liberty can have nothing to fear from the judiciary alone, but would have every thing to fear from its union with either of the other departments; that, as all the effects of such an union must ensue from a dependence of the former on the latter, notwithstanding a nominal and apparent separation; that as, from the natural feebleness of the judiciary, it is in continual jeopardy of being overpowered, awed or influenced by its co-ordinate branches; that, as nothing can contribute so much to its firmness and independence as PERMANENCY IN OFFICE, this quality may there fore be justly regarded as an indispensable ingredient in its constitution; and, in a great measure, as the CITADEL of the public justice and the public security.

The complete independence of the courts of justice is peculiarly essential in a limited constitution. By a limited constitution, I understand one which contains certain specified exceptions to the legislative authority; such, for instance, as that it shall pass no bills of attainder, no *ex post facto* laws, and the like. Limitations of this kind can be preserved in practice no other way than through the medium of the courts of justice; whose duty it must be to declare all acts contrary to the man-

---

* Montesquieu, speaking of them, says, "of the three powers above mentioned, the JUDICIARY is next to nothing." Spirit of Laws, vol. 1, page 186.

† Idem. page 181.

ifest tenor of the constitution void. Without this, all the reservations of particular rights or privileges would amount to nothing.

Some perplexity respecting the right of the courts to pronounce legislative acts void, because contrary to the constitution, has arisen from an imagination that the doctrine would imply a superiority of the judiciary to the legislative power. It is urged that the authority which can declare the acts of another void, must necessarily be superior to the one whose acts may be declared void. As this doctrine is of great importance in all the American constitutions, a brief discussion of the grounds on which it rests cannot be unacceptable.

There is no position which depends on clearer principles, than that every act of a delegated authority, contrary to the tenor of the commission under which it is exercised, is void. No legislative act, therefore, contrary to the constitution, can be valid. To deny this, would be to affirm, that the deputy is greater than his principal; that the servant is above his master; that the representatives of the people are superior to the people themselves; that men, acting by virtue of powers, may do not only what their powers do not authorize, but what they forbid.

If it be said that the legislative body are themselves the constitutional judges of their own powers, and that the construction they put upon them is conclusive upon the other departments, it may be answered, that this cannot be the natural presumption, where it is not to be collected from any particular provisions in the constitution. It is not otherwise to be supposed, that the constitution could intend to enable the representatives of the people to substitute their *will* to that of their constituents. It is far more rational to suppose, that the courts were designed to be an intermediate body between the people and the legislature, in order, among other things, to keep the latter within the limits assigned to their authority. The interpretation of the laws is the proper and peculiar province of the courts. A constitution is, in fact, and must be, regarded by the judges as a fundamental law. It must therefore belong to them to ascertain its meaning, as well as the meaning of any particular act proceeding from the legislative body. If there should happen to be an irreconcilable variance between the two, that which has the superior obligation and validity ought, of course, to be preferred; in other words, the constitution ought to be preferred to the statute, the intention of the people to the intention of their agents.

Nor does the conclusion by any means suppose a superiority of the judicial to the legislative power. It only supposes that the power of the people is superior to both; and that where the will of the legislature declared in its statutes, stands in opposition to that of the people declared in the constitution, the judges ought to be governed by the latter, rather than the former. They ought to regulate their decisions by the fundamental laws, rather than by those which are not fundamental.

This exercise of judicial discretion, in determining between two contradictory laws, is exemplified in a familiar instance. It not uncommonly happens, that there are two statutes existing at one time, clashing in whole or in part with each other, and neither of them containing any repealing clause or expression. In such a case, it is the province of the courts to liquidate and fix their meaning and operation: So far as they can, by any fair construction be reconciled to each other, reason and law conspire to dictate that this should be done: Where this is impracticable, it becomes a matter of necessity to give effect to one, in exclusion of the other. The rule which has obtained in the courts for determining their relative validity is, that the last in order of time shall be preferred to the first. But this is a mere rule of construction, not derived from any positive law, but from the nature and reason of the thing. It is a rule not enjoined upon the courts by legislative provision, but adopted by themselves, as consonant to truth and propriety, for the direction of their conduct as interpreters of the law. They thought it reasonable, that between the interfering acts of an *equal* authority, that which was the last indication of its will, should have the preference.

But in regard to the interfering acts of a superior and subordinate authority, of an original and derivative power, the nature and reason of the thing indicate the converse of that rule as proper to be followed. They teach us, that the prior act of a superior, ought to be preferred to the subsequent act of an inferior and subordinate authority; and that, accordingly, whenever a particular statute contravenes the constitution, it will be the duty of the judicial tribunals to adhere to the latter, and disregard the former.

It can be of no weight to say, that the courts, on the pretence of a repugnancy, may substitute their own pleasure to the constitutional intentions of the legislature. This might as well happen in the case of two contradictory statutes; or it might as well happen in every adjudication upon any single statute. The courts must declare the sense of the law; and if they should be disposed to exercise WILL instead of JUDGMENT, the consequence would equally be the substitution of their pleasure to that of the legislative body. The observation, if it proved any thing, would prove that there ought to be no judges distinct from that body.

If then the courts of justice are to be considered as the bulwarks of a limited constitution, against legislative encroachments, this consideration will afford a strong argument for the permanent tenure of judicial offices, since nothing will contribute so much as this to that independent spirit in the judges, which must be essential to the faithful performance of so arduous a duty.

This independence of the judges is equally requisite to guard the constitution and the rights of individuals, from the effects of those ill humours which the arts of designing men, or the influence of particular conjunctures, sometimes disseminate among the people themselves, and which, though they speedily give place to better information, and more deliberate reflection, have a tendency, in the mean time, to occasion dangerous innovations in the government, and serious oppressions of the minor party in the community. Though I trust the friends of the proposed constitution will never concur with its enemies,* in questioning that fundamental principle of republican government, which admits the right of the people to alter or abolish the established constitution whenever they find it inconsistent with their happiness; yet it is not to be inferred from this principle, that the representatives of the people, whenever a momentary inclination happens to lay hold of a majority of their constituents incompatible with the provisions in the existing constitution, would, on that account, be justifiable in a violation of those provisions; or that the courts would be under a greater obligation to connive at infractions in this shape, than when they had proceeded wholly from the cabals of the representative body. Until the people have, by some solemn and authoritative act, annulled or changed the established form, it is binding upon themselves collectively, as well as individually; and no presumption, or even knowledge of their sentiments, can warrant their representatives in a departure from it, prior to such an act. But it is easy to see, that it would require an uncommon portion of fortitude in the judges to do their duty as faithful guardians of the constitution, where legislative invasions of it had been instigated by the major voice of the community.

But it is not with a view to infractions of the constitution only, that the independence of the judges may be an essential safe-guard against the effects of occasional ill humours in the society. These sometimes extend no farther than to the injury of the private rights of particular classes of citizens, by unjust and partial laws. Here also the firmness of the judicial magistracy is of vast importance in mitigating the severity, and confining the operation of such laws. It not only serves to moderate the immediate mischiefs of those which may have been passed, but it operates as a check upon the legislative body in passing them; who, perceiving that obstacles to the success of an iniquitous intention are to be expected from the scruples of the courts, are in a manner compelled by the very motives of the injustice they

* VideProtest of the minority of the convention of Pennsylvania, Martin's speech, &c.

meditate, to qualify their attempts. This is a circumstance calculated to have more influence upon the character of our governments, than but few may imagine. The benefits of the integrity and moderation of the judiciary have already been felt in more states than one; and though they may have displeased those whose sinister expectations they may have disappointed, they must have commanded the esteem and applause of all the virtuous and disinterested. Considerate men, of every description, ought to prize whatever will tend to beget or fortify that temper in the courts; as no man can be sure that he may not be to-morrow the victim of a spirit of injustice, by which he may be a gainer to-day. And every man must now feel, that the inevitable tendency of such a spirit is to sap the foundations of public and private confidence, and to introduce in its stead universal distrust and distress.

That inflexible and uniform adherence to the rights of the constitution, and of individuals, which we perceive to be indispensable in the courts of justice, can certainly not be expected from judges who hold their offices by a temporary commission. Periodical appointments, however regulated, or by whomsoever made, would, in some way or other, be fatal to their necessary independence. If the power of making them was committed either to the executive or legislature, there would be danger of an improper complaisance to the branch which possessed it: if to both, there would be an unwillingness to hazard the displeasure of either; if to the people, or to persons chosen by them for the special purpose, there would be too great a disposition to consult popularity, to justify a reliance that nothing would be consulted but the constitution and the laws.

There is yet a further and a weighty reason for the permanency of judicial offices; which is deducible from the nature of the qualifications they require. It has been frequently remarked, with great propriety, that a voluminous code of laws is one of the inconveniences necessarily connected with the advantages of a free government. To avoid an arbitrary discretion in the courts, it is indispensable that they should be bound down by strict rules and precedents, which serve to define and point out their duty in every particular case that comes before them; and it will readily be conceived, from the variety of controversies which grow out of the folly and wickedness of mankind, that the records of those precedents must unavoidably swell to a very considerable bulk, and must demand long and laborious study to acquire a competent knowledge of them. Hence it is, that there can be but few men in the society, who will have sufficient skill in the laws to qualify them for the stations of judges. And making the proper deductions for the ordinary depravity of human nature, the number must be still smaller, of those who unite the requisite integrity with the requisite knowledge. These considerations apprize us, that the government can have no great option between fit characters; and that a temporary duration in office, which would naturally discourage such characters from quitting a lucrative line of practice to accept a seat on the bench, would have a tendency to throw the administration of justice into hands less able, and less well qualified, to conduct it with utility and dignity. In the present circumstances of this country, and in those in which it is likely to be for a long time to come, the disadvantages on this score would be greater than they may at first sight appear; but it must be confessed, that they are far inferior to those which present themselves under the other aspects of the subject.

Upon the whole, there can be no room to doubt, that the convention acted wisely in copying from the models of those constitutions with have established *good behaviour* as the tenure of judicial offices, in point of duration; and that, so far from being blameable on this account, their plan would have been inexcusably defective, if it had wanted this important feature of good government. The experience of Great Britain affords an illustrious comment on the excellence of the institution.

PUBLIUS.

THE FEDERALIST.

NUMBER LXXIX.

NEW YORK, JUNE 24, 1788.

HAMILTON.

A FURTHER VIEW OF THE JUDICIAL DEPARTMENT, IN RELATION TO THE PROVISIONS FOR THE SUPPORT AND RESPONSIBILITY OF THE JUDGES.

NEXT to permanency in office, nothing can contribute more to the independence of the judges, than a fixed provision for their support. The remark made in relation to the president, is equally applicable here. In the general course of human nature, *a power over a man's subsistence amounts to a power over his will.* And we can never hope to see realized in practice the complete separation of the judicial from the legislative power, in any system, which leaves the former dependent for pecuniary resource on the occasional grants of the latter. The enlightened friends to good government, in every state, have seen cause to lament the want of precise and explicit precautions in the state constitutions on this head. Some of these indeed have declared that *permanent** salaries should be established for the judges; but the experiment has in some instances shown, that such expressions are not sufficiently definite to preclude legislative evasions. Something still more positive and unequivocal has been evinced to be requisite. The plan of the convention accordingly has provided, that the judges of the United States "shall

* Vide Constitution of Massachusetts, Chap. 2. Sect. 1. Art. 13.

at *stated times* receive for their services a compensation, which shall not be *diminished* during their continuance in office."

This, all circumstances considered, is the most eligible provision that could have been devised. It will readily be understood, that the fluctuations in the value of money, and in the state of society, rendered a fixed rate of compensation in the constitution inadmissible. What might be extravagant to-day, might in half a century become penurious and inadequate. It was therefore necessary to leave it to the discretion of the legislature to vary its provisions in conformity to the variations in circumstances; yet under such restrictions as to put it out of the power of that body to change the condition of the individual for the worse. A man may then be sure of the ground upon which he stands, and can never be deterred from his duty by the apprehension of being placed in a less eligible situation. The clause which has been quoted combines both advantages. The salaries of judicial offices may from time to time be altered, as occasion shall require, yet so as never to lessen the allowance with which any particular judge comes into office, in respect to him. It will be observed that a difference has been made by the convention between the compensation of the president and of the judges. That of the former can neither be increased nor diminished. That of the latter can only not be diminished. This probably arose from the difference in the duration of the respective offices. As the president is to be elected for no more than four years, it can rarely happen that an adequate salary, fixed at the commencement of that period, will not continue to be such to its end. But with regard to the judges, who if they behave properly, will be secured in their places for life, it may well happen, especially in the early stages of the government that a stipend, which would be very sufficient at their first appointment, would become too small in the progress of their service.

This provision for the support of the judges bears every mark of prudence and efficacy; and it may be safely affirmed that, together with the permanent tenure of their offices, it affords a better prospect of their independence than is discoverable in the constitutions of any of the states, in regard to their own judges.

The precautions for their responsibility, are comprised in the article respecting impeachments. They are liable to be impeached for mal-conduct by the house of representatives, and tried by the senate, and if convicted, may be dismissed from office and disqualified for holding any other. This is the only provision on the point, which is consistent with the necessary independence of the judicial character, and is the only one which we find in our own constitution in respect to our own judges.

The want of a provision for removing the judges on account of inability, has been a subject of complaint. But all considerate men will be sensible that such a provision would either not be practised upon, or would be more liable to abuse, than calculated to answer any good purpose. The mensuration of the faculties of the mind has, I believe, no place in the catalogue of known arts. An attempt to fix the boundary between the regions of ability and inability, would much oftener give scope to personal and party attachments and enmities, than advance the interests of justice, or the public good. The result, except in the case of insanity, must for the most part be arbitrary; and insanity, without any formal or express provision, may be safely pronounced to be a virtual disqualification.

The constitution of New-York, to avoid investigations that must forever be vague and dangerous, has taken a particular age as the criterion of inability. No man can be a judge beyond sixty. I believe there are few at present who do not disapprove of this provision. There is no station, in relation to which, it is less proper than to that of a judge. The deliberating and comparing faculties generally preserve their strength much beyond that period, in men who survive it; and when, in addition to this circumstance, we consider how few there are who outlive the season of intellectual vigour, and how improbable it is that any considerable proportion of the bench, whether more or less numerous, should be in such a situation at the same time, we shall be ready to conclude that limitations of this sort have little to recommend them. In a republic, where fortunes are not affluent, and pensions not expedient, the dismission of men from stations in which they have served their country long and usefully, on which they depend for subsistence, and from which it will be too late to resort to any other occupation for a livelihood, ought to have some better apology to humanity, than is to be found in the imaginary danger of a superannuated bench.

PUBLIUS.

THE FEDERALIST.

NUMBER LXXX.

NEW YORK, JUNE 27 AND JULY 1, 1788.

HAMILTON.

A FURTHER VIEW OF THE JUDICIAL DEPARTMENT, IN RELATION
TO THE EXTENT OF ITS POWERS.

To judge with accuracy of the due extent of the federal judicature, it will be necessary to consider, in the first place, what
are its proper objects.

It seems scarcely to admit of controversy, that the judiciary
authority of the union ought to extend to these several descriptions of cases. 1st. To all those which arise out of the laws of the
United States, passed in pursuance of their just and constitutional powers of legislation; 2d. To all those which concern the
execution of the provisions expressly contained in the articles of
union; 3d. To all those in which the United States are a party;
4th. To all those which involve the PEACE of the CONFEDERACY,
whether they relate to the intercourse between the United
States and foreign nations, or to that between the States themselves; 5th. To all those which originate on the high seas, and
are of admiralty or maritime jurisdiction; and lastly, to all those
in which the state tribunals cannot be supposed to be impartial
and unbiassed.

The first point depends upon this obvious consideration, that
there ought always to be a constitutional method of giving efficacy to constitutional provisions. What, for instance, would avail

restrictions on the authority of the state legislatures, without some constitutional mode of enforcing the observance of them? The states, by the plan of the convention, are prohibited from doing a variety of things; some of which are incompatible with the interests of the union, others, with the principles of good government. The imposition of duties on imported articles, and the emission of paper money, are specimens of each kind. No man of sense will believe that such prohibitions would be scrupulously regarded, without some effectual power in the government to restrain or correct the infractions of them. This power must either be a direct negative on the state laws, or an authority in the federal courts, to over-rule such as might be in manifest contravention of the articles of union. There is no third course that I can imagine. The latter appears to have been thought by the convention preferable to the former, and I presume will be most agreeable to the states.

As to the second point, it is impossible, by any argument or comment, to make it clearer than it is in itself. If there are such things as political axioms, the propriety of the judicial power of a government being co-extensive with its legislative, may be ranked among the number. The mere necessity of uniformity in the interpretation of the national laws, decides the question. Thirteen independent courts of final jurisdiction over the same causes, arising upon the same laws, is a hydra in government, from which nothing but contradiction and confusion can proceed.

Still less need be said in regard to the third point. Controversies between the nation and its members or citizens, can only be properly referred to the national tribunals. Any other plan would be contrary to reason, to precedent, and to decorum.

The fourth point rests on this plain proposition, that the peace of the WHOLE, ought not to be left at the disposal of a PART. The union will undoubtedly be answerable to foreign powers for the conduct of its members. And the responsibility for an injury, ought ever to be accompanied with the faculty of preventing it.

As the denial or perversion of justice by the sentences of courts, is with reason classed among the just causes of war, it will follow, that the federal judiciary ought to have cognizance of all causes in which the citizens of other countries are concerned. This is not less essential to the preservation of the public faith, than to the security of the public tranquillity. A distinction may perhaps be imagined, between cases arising upon treaties and the laws of nations, and those which may stand merely on the footing of the municipal law. The former kind may be supposed proper for the federal jurisdiction, the latter for that of the states. But it is at least problematical, whether an unjust sentence against a foreigner, where the subject of controversy was wholly relative to the *lex loci*, would not, if unredressed, be an aggression upon his sovereign, as well as one which violated the stipulations of a treaty, or the general law of nations. And a still greater objection to the distinction would result from the immense difficulty, if not impossibility, of a practical discrimination between the cases of one complexion and those of the other. So great a proportion of the controversies in which foreigners are parties, involve national questions, that it is by far most safe, and most expedient, to refer all those in which they are concerned to the national tribunals.

The power of determining causes between two states, between one state and the citizens of another, and between the citizens of different states, is perhaps not less essential to the peace of the union, than that which has been just examined. History gives us a horrid picture of the dissentions and private wars which distracted and desolated Germany, prior to the institution of the IMPERIAL CHAMBER by Maximilian, towards the close of the fifteenth century: and informs us, at the same time, of the vast influence of that institution, in appeasing the disorders, and establishing the tranquillity of the empire. This was a court invested with authority to decide finally all differences among the members of the Germanic body.

A method of terminating territorial disputes between the

states, under the authority of the federal head, was not unattended to, even in the imperfect system by which they have been hitherto held together. But there are other sources, besides interfering claims of boundary, from which bickerings and animosities may spring up among the members of the union. To some of these we have been witnesses in the course of our past experience. It will readily be conjectured, that I allude to the fraudulent laws which have been passed in too many of the states. And though the proposed constitution establishes particular guards against the repetition of those instances, which have heretofore made their appearance, yet it is warrantable to apprehend, that the spirit which produced them, will assume new shapes that could not be foreseen, nor specifically provided against. Whatever practices may have a tendency to disturb the harmony of the states, are proper objects of federal superintendence and control.

It may be esteemed the basis of the union, that "the citizens of each state shall be entitled to all the privileges and immunities of citizens of the several states." And if it be a just principle, that every government *ought to possess the means of executing its own provisions, by its own authority*, it will follow, that in order to the inviolable maintenance of that equality of privileges and immunities, to which the citizens of the union will be entitled, the national judiciary ought to preside in all cases, in which one state or its citizens are opposed to another state or its citizens. To secure the full effect of so fundamental a provision against all evasion and subterfuge, it is necessary that its construction should be committed to that tribunal, which, having no local attachments, will be likely to be impartial, between the different states and their citizens, and which, owing its official existence to the union, will never be likely to feel any bias inauspicious to the principles on which it is founded.

The fifth point will demand little animadversion. The most bigotted idolizers of state authority, have not thus far shown a disposition to deny the national judiciary the cognizance of maritime causes. These so generally depend on the laws of nations, and so commonly affect the rights of foreigners, that they fall within the considerations which are relative to the public peace. The most important part of them are, by the present confederation, submitted to federal jurisdiction.

The reasonableness of the agency of the national courts, in cases in which the state tribunals cannot be supposed to be impartial, speaks for itself. No man ought certainly to be a judge in his own cause, or in any cause, in respect to which he has the least interest or bias. This principle has no inconsiderable weight in designating the federal courts, as the proper tribunals for the determination of controversies between different states and their citizens. And it ought to have the same operation, in regard to some cases, between the citizens of the same state. Claims to land under grants of different states, founded upon adverse pretensions of boundary, are of this description. The courts of neither of the granting states could be expected to be unbiassed. The laws may have even prejudged the question, and tied the courts down to decisions in favour of the grants of the state to which they belonged. And where this had not been done, it would be natural that the judges, as men, should feel a strong predilection to the claims of their own government.

Having thus laid down and discussed the principles which ought to regulate the constitution of the federal judiciary, we will proceed to test, by these principles, the particular powers of which, according to the plan of the convention, it is to be composed. It is to comprehend "all cases in law and equity arising under the constitution, the laws of the United States, and treaties made, or which shall be made, under their authority; to all cases affecting ambassadors, other public ministers and consuls; to all cases of admiralty and maritime jurisdiction; to controversies to which the United States shall be a party; to controversies between two or more states; between a state and citizens of another state; between citizens of different states; between citizens of the same state, claiming lands under grants

of different states; and between a state or the citizens thereof,
and foreign states, citizens and subjects." This constitutes the
entire mass of the judicial authority of the union. Let us now
review it in detail. It is then to extend,

First. To all cases in law and equity, *arising under the constitution* and *the laws of the United States.* This corresponds
with the two first classes of causes, which have been enumerated, as proper for the jurisdiction of the United States. It has
been asked, what is meant by "cases arising under the constitution," in contra-distinction from those "arising under the laws of
the United States?" The difference has been already explained.
All the restrictions upon the authority of the state legislatures
furnish examples. They are not, for instance, to emit paper
money; but the interdiction results from the constitution, and
will have no connexion with any law of the United States.
Should paper money, notwithstanding, be emitted, the controversies concerning it would be cases arising under the constitution, and not under the laws of the United States, in the
ordinary signification of the terms. This may serve as a sample
of the whole.

It has also been asked, what need of the word "equity?" What
equitable causes can grow out of the constitution and laws of the
United States? There is hardly a subject of litigation, between
individuals, which may not involve those ingredients of *fraud,
accident, trust,* or *hardship* which would render the matter an
object of equitable, rather than of legal jurisdiction, as the distinction is known and established in several of the states. It is
the peculiar province, for instance, of a court of equity to relieve
against what are called hard bargains: These are contracts, in
which, through there may have been no direct fraud or deceit,
sufficient to invalidate them in a court of law; yet there may
have been some undue and unconscionable advantage taken of
the necessities or misfortunes of one of the parties, which a
court of equity would not tolerate. In such cases, where foreigners were concerned on either side, it would be impossible for the
federal judicatories to do justice without an equitable, as well as

a legal jurisdiction. Agreements to convey lands claimed under the grants of different states, may afford another example of the necessity of an equitable jurisdiction in the federal courts. This reasoning may not be so palpable in those states where the formal and technical distinction between LAW and EQUITY is not maintained, as in this state, where it is exemplified by every day's practice.

The judiciary authority of the union is to extend—

Second. To treaties made, or which shall be made, under the authority of the United States, and to all cases affecting ambassadors, other public ministers and consuls. These belong to the fourth class of the enumerated cases, as they have an evident connexion with the preservation of the national peace.

Third. To cases of admiralty and maritime jurisdiction. These form, altogether, the fifth of the enumerated classes of causes, proper for the cognizance of the national courts.

Fourth. To controversies to which the United States shall be a party. These constitute the third of those classes.

Fifth. To controversies between two or more states; between a state and citizens of another state; between citizens of different states. These belong to the fourth of those classes, and partake, in some measure, of the nature of the last.

Sixth. To cases between the citizens of the same state, *claiming lands under grants of different states*. These fall within the last class, and *are the only instances in which the proposed constitution directly contemplates the cognizance of disputes between the citizens of the same state.*

Seventh. To cases between a state and the citizens thereof, and foreign states, citizens or subjects. These have been already explained to belong to the fourth of the enumerated classes; and have been shown to be, in a peculiar manner, the proper subjects of the national judicature.

From this review of the particular powers of the federal judiciary, as marked out in the constitution, it appears, that they are all conformable to the principles which ought to have governed the structure of that department, and which were necessary to the perfection of the system. If some partial inconveniences should appear to be connected with the incorporation of any of them into the plan, it ought to be recollected, that the national legislature will have ample authority to make such *exceptions*, and to prescribe such regulations, as will be calculated to obviate or remove these inconveniences. The possibility of particular mischiefs can never be viewed, by a well-informed mind, as a solid objection to a principle which is calculated to avoid general mischiefs, and to obtain general advantages.

PUBLIUS.

THE FEDERALIST.

NUMBER LXXXI.

NEW YORK, JULY 4, 8, 1788.

HAMILTON.

A FURTHER VIEW OF THE JUDICIAL DEPARTMENT, IN RELATION
TO THE DISTRIBUTION OF ITS AUTHORITY.

LET us now return to the partition of the judiciary authority
between different courts, and their relations to each other.

"The judicial power of the United States is to be vested in
one supreme court, and in such inferior courts as the congress
may from time to time ordain and establish."* That there ought
to be one court of supreme and final jurisdiction, is a proposition
which is not likely to be contested. The reasons for it have been
assigned in another place, and are too obvious to need repetition. The only question that seems to have been raised concerning it, is, whether it ought to be a distinct body, or a branch of
the legislature. The same contradiction is observable in regard
to this matter, which has been remarked in several other cases.
The very men who object to the senate as a court of impeachments, on the ground of an improper intermixture of powers,
are advocates, by implication at least, for the propriety of vesting the ultimate decision of all causes, in the whole, or in a part
of the legislative body.

The arguments, or rather suggestions, upon which this
charge is founded, are to this effect: "The authority of the

* Article 3. Sect. 1.

supreme court of the United States, which is to be a separate and independent body, will be superior to that of the legislature. The power of construing the laws according to the *spirit* of the constitution, will enable that court to mould them into whatever shape it may think proper; especially as its decisions will not be in any manner subject to the revision or correction of the legislative body. This is as unprecedented as it is dangerous. In Britain, the judicial power in the last resort, resides in the house of lords, which is a branch of the legislature; and this part of the British Government has been imitated in the state constitutions in general. The parliament of Great Britain, and the legislatures of the several states, can at any time rectify by law, the exceptionable decisions of their respective courts. But the errors and usurpations of the supreme court of the United States, will be uncontrolable and remediless." This, upon examination, will be found to be altogether made up of false reasoning upon misconceived fact.

In the first place, there is not a syllable in the plan, which *directly* empowers the national courts to construe the laws according to the spirit of the constitution, or which gives them any greater latitude in this respect, than may be claimed by the courts of every state. I admit, however, that the constitution ought to be the standard of construction for the laws, and that wherever there is an evident opposition, the laws ought to give place to the constitution. But this doctrine is not deducible from any circumstance peculiar to the plan of the convention; but from the general theory of a limited constitution; and as far as it is true, is equally applicable to most, if not to all the state governments. There can be no objection, therefore, on this account, to the federal judicature, which will not lie against the local judicatures in general, and which will not serve to condemn every constitution that attempts to set bounds to legislative discretion.

But perhaps the force of the objection may be thought to consist in the particular organization of the supreme court; in its being composed of a distinct body of magistrates, instead of being one of the branches of the legislature, as in the government of Great Britain and in that of this state. To insist upon this point, the authors of the objection must renounce the meaning they have laboured to annex to the celebrated maxim, requiring a separation of the departments of power. It shall, nevertheless, be conceded to them, agreeably to the interpretation given to that maxim in the course of these papers, that it is not violated by vesting the ultimate power of judging in a *part* of the legislative body. But though this be not an absolute violation of that excellent rule; yet it verges so nearly upon it, as on this account alone, to be less eligible than the mode preferred by the convention. From a body which had had even a partial agency in passing bad laws, we could rarely expect a disposition to temper and moderate them in the application. The same spirit which had operated in making them, would be too apt to influence their construction: Still less could it be expected, that men who had infringed the constitution, in the character of legislators, would be disposed to repair the breach in that of judges. Nor is this all: Every reason which recommends the tenure of good behaviour for judicial offices, militates against placing the judiciary power, in the last resort, in a body composed of men chosen for a limited period. There is an absurdity in referring the determination of causes, in the first instance, to judges of permanent standing; in the last, to those of a temporary and mutable constitution. And there is a still greater absurdity in subjecting the decisions of men selected for their knowledge of the laws, acquired by long and laborious study, to the revision and control of men who, for want of the same advantage, cannot but be deficient in that knowledge. The members of the legislature will rarely be chosen with a view to those qualifications which fit men for the stations of judges; and as, on this account, there will be great reason to apprehend all the ill consequences of defective information; so, on account of the natural propensity of such bodies to party divisions, there will be no less reason to fear, that the pestilential breath of faction may poison the fountains of justice. The habit of being continually marshalled on opposite sides, will be too apt to stifle the voice both of law and of equity.

These considerations teach us to applaud the wisdom of those states who have committed the judicial power, in the last resort, not to a part of the legislature, but to distinct and independent bodies of men. Contrary to the supposition of those who have represented the plan of the convention, in this respect, as novel and unprecedented, it is but a copy of the constitutions of New-Hampshire, Massachusetts, Pennsylvania, Delaware, Maryland, Virginia, North-Carolina, South-Carolina, and Georgia; and the preference which has been given to these models is highly to be commended.

It is not true, in the second place, that the parliament of Great Britain, or the legislatures of the particular states, can rectify the exceptionable decisions of their respective courts, in any other sense than might be done by a future legislature of the United States. The theory neither of the British nor the state constitutions, authorizes the revisal of a judicial sentence by a legislative act. Nor is there any thing in the proposed constitution, more than in either of them by which it is forbidden. In the former, as in the latter, the impropriety of the thing, on the general principles of law and reason, is the sole obstacle. A legislature, without exceeding its province, cannot reverse a determination once made, in a particular case; though it may prescribe a new rule for future cases. This is the principle, and it applies, in all its consequences, exactly in the same manner and extent, to the state governments, as to the national government now under consideration. Not the least difference can be pointed out in any view of the subject.

It may in the last place be observed, that the supposed danger of judiciary encroachments on the legislative authority, which has been upon many occasions reiterated, is, in reality, a phantom. Particular misconstructions and contraventions of the will of the legislature, may now and then happen; but they can never be so extensive as to amount to an inconvenience, or in any sensible degree to affect the order of the political system. This may be inferred with certainty from the general nature of the judicial power; from the objects to which it relates; from the manner in which it is exercised; from its comparative weakness; and from its total incapacity to support its usurpations by force. And the inference is greatly fortified by the consideration of the important constitutional check, which the power of instituting impeachments in one part of the legislative body, and of determining upon them in the other, would give to that body upon the members of the judicial department. This is alone a complete security. There never can be danger that the judges, by a series of deliberate usurpations on the authority of the legislature, would hazard the united resentment of the body intrusted with it, while this body was possessed of the means of punishing their presumption, by degrading them from their stations. While this ought to remove all apprehensions on the subject, it affords, at the same time, a cogent argument for constituting the senate a court for the trial of impeachments.

Having now examined, and I trust removed, the objections to the distinct and independent organization of the supreme court; I proceed to consider the propriety of the power of constituting inferior courts,* and the relations which will subsist between these and the former.

The power of constituting inferior courts, is evidently calculated to obviate the necessity of having recourse to the supreme court in every case of federal cognizance. It is intended to enable the national government to institute or *authorize* in each state or district of the United States, a tribunal competent to the determination of matters of national jurisdiction within its limits.

---

* This power has been absurdly represented as intended to abolish all the county courts in the several states, which are commonly called inferior courts. But the expressions of the constitution are to constitute "tribunals INFERIOR TO THE SUPREME COURT," and the evident design of the provision is, to enable the institution of local courts, subordinate to the supreme, either in states or larger districts. It is ridiculaus to imagine, that county courts were in contemplation.

But why, it is asked, might not the same purpose have been accomplished by the instrumentality of the state courts? This admits of different answers. Though the fitness and competency of these courts should be allowed in the utmost latitude: yet the substance of the power in question, may still be regarded as a necessary part of the plan, if it were only to authorize the national legislature to commit to them the cognizance of causes arising out of the national constitution. To confer upon the existing courts of the several states the power of determining such causes, would perhaps be as much "to constitute tribunals," as to create new courts with the like power. But ought not a more direct and explicit provision to have been made in favour of the state courts? There are, in my opinion, substantial reasons against such a provision: The most discerning cannot foresee how far the prevalency of a local spirit may be found to disqualify the local tribunals for the jurisdiction of national causes; whilst every man may discover, that courts constituted like those of some of the states, would be improper channels of the judicial authority of the union. State judges, holding their offices during pleasure, or from year to year, will be too little independent to be relied upon for an inflexible execution of the national laws. And if there was a necessity for confiding to them the original cognizance of causes arising under those laws, there would be a correspondent necessity for leaving the door of appeal as wide as possible. In proportion to the grounds of confidence in, or distrust of the subordinate tribunals, ought to be the facility or difficulty of appeals. And well satisfied as I am of the propriety of the appellate jurisdiction, in the several classes of causes to which it is extended by the plan of the convention, I should consider every thing calculated to give, in practice, an *unrestrained course* to appeals, as a source of public and private inconvenience.

I am not sure but that it will be found highly expedient and useful, to divide the United States into four or five, or half a dozen districts; and to institute a federal court in each district, in lieu of one in every state. The judges of these courts may hold circuits for the trial of causes in the several parts of the respective districts. Justice through them may be administered with ease and dispatch; and appeals may be safely circumscribed within a narrow compass. This plan appears to me at present the most eligible of any that could be adopted, and in order to it, it is necessary that the power of constituting inferior courts should exist in the full extent in which it is seen in the proposed constitution.

These reasons seem sufficient to satisfy a candid mind, that the want of such a power would have been a great defect in the plan. Let us now examine in what manner the judicial authority is to be distributed between the supreme and the inferior courts of the union.

The supreme court is to be invested with original jurisdiction only "in cases affecting ambassadors, other public ministers and consuls, and those in which A STATE shall be a party." Public ministers of every class, are the immediate representatives of their sovereigns. All questions in which they are concerned, are so directly connected with the public peace, that as well for the preservation of this, as out of respect to the sovereignties they represent, it is both expedient and proper, that such questions should be submitted in the first instance to the highest judicatory of the nation. Though consuls have not in strictness a diplomatic character, yet as they are the public agents of the nations to which they belong, the same observation is in a great measure applicable to them. In cases in which a state might happen to be a party, it would ill suit its dignity to be turned over to an inferior tribunal.

Though it may rather be a digression from the immediate subject of this paper, I shall take occasion to mention here a supposition which has excited some alarm upon very mistaken grounds: It has been suggested that an assignment of the public securities of one state to the citizens of another, would enable them to prosecute that state in the federal courts for the amount of those securities. A suggestion, which the following considerations prove to be without foundation.

It is inherent in the nature of sovereignty, not to be amenable
to the suit of an individual *without its consent*. This is the general sense, and the general practice of mankind; and the exemption, as one of the attributes of sovereignty, is now enjoyed by
the government of every state in the union. Unless, therefore,
there is a surrender of this immunity in the plan of the convention, it will remain with the states, and the danger intimated
must be merely ideal. The circumstances which are necessary to
produce an alienation of state sovereignty, were discussed in
considering the article of taxation, and need not be repeated
here. A recurrence to the principles there established will satisfy us, that there is no colour to pretend that the state governments would, by the adoption of that plan, be divested of the
privilege of paying their own debts in their own way, free from
every constraint but that which flows from the obligations of
good faith. The contracts between a nation and individuals, are
only binding on the conscience of the sovereign, and have no
pretension to a compulsive force. They confer no right of action,
independent of the sovereign will. To what purpose would it be
to authorize suits against states for the debts they owe? How
could recoveries be enforced? It is evident that it could not be
done, without waging war against the contracting state: and to
ascribe to the federal courts, by mere implication, and in
destruction of a pre-existing right of the state governments, a
power which would involve such a consequence, would be altogether forced and unwarrantable.

Let us resume the train of our observations; we have seen
that the original jurisdiction of the supreme court would be confined to two classes of causes, and those of a nature rarely to
occur. In all other cases of federal cognizance, the original jurisdiction would appertain to the inferior tribunals, and the
supreme court would have nothing more than an appellate jurisdiction, "with such *exceptions*, and under such *regulations*, as
the congress shall make."

The propriety of this appellate jurisdiction has been scarcely
called in question in regard to matters of law; but the clamours

have been loud against it as applied to matters of fact. Some well-intentioned men in this state, deriving their notions from the language and forms which obtain in our courts, have been induced to consider it as an implied supersedure of the trial by jury, in favour of the civil law mode of trial, which prevails in our courts of admiralty, probates, and chancery. A technical sense has been affixed to the term "appellate," which in our law parlance, is commonly used in reference to appeals in the course of the civil law. But if I am not misinformed, the same meaning would not be given to it in any part of New-England. There an appeal from one jury to another, is familiar both in language and practice, and is even a matter of course, until there have been two verdicts on one side. The word "appellate," therefore, will not be understood in the same sense in New-England, as in New-York, which shows the impropriety of a technical interpretation derived from the jurisprudence of a particular state. The expression taken in the abstract, denotes nothing more than the power of one tribunal to review the proceedings of another, either as to the law or fact, or both. The mode of doing it may depend on ancient custom or legislative provision; in a new government it must depend on the latter, and may be with or without the aid of a jury, as may be judged advisable. If, therefore, the re-examination of a fact, once determined by a jury, should in any case be admitted under the proposed constitution, it may be so regulated as to be done by a second jury, either by remanding the cause to the court below for a second trial of the fact, or by directing an issue immediately out of the supreme court.

But it does not follow, that the re-examination of a fact once ascertained by a jury, will be permitted in the supreme court. Why may it not be said, with the strictest propriety, when a writ of error is brought from an inferior to a superior court of law in this state, that the latter has jurisdiction* of the fact, as well as the law? It is true it cannot institute a new inquiry con-

* This word is a compound of JUS and DICTIO, juris, dictio, or a speaking or pronouncing of the law.

cerning the fact, but it takes cognizance of it as it appears upon the record, and pronounces the law arising upon it. This is jurisdiction of both fact and law, nor is it even possible to separate them. Though the common law courts of this state ascertain disputed facts by a jury, yet they unquestionably have jurisdiction of both fact and law; and accordingly, when the former is agreed in the pleadings, they have no recourse to a jury, but proceed at once to judgment. I contend, therefore, on this ground, that the expressions, "appellate jurisdiction, both as to law and fact," do not necessarily imply a re-examination in the supreme court of facts decided by juries in the inferior courts.

The following train of ideas may well be imagined to have influenced the convention, in relation to this particular provision. The appellate jurisdiction of the supreme court, it may have been argued, will extend to causes determinable in different modes, some in the course of the COMMON LAW, others in the course of the CIVIL LAW. In the former, the revision of the law only will be, generally speaking, the proper province of the supreme court; in the latter, the re-examination of the fact is agreeable to usage, and in some cases, of which prize causes are an example, might be essential to the preservation of the public peace. It is therefore necessary, that the appellate jurisdiction should, in certain cases, extend in the broadest sense to matters of fact. It will not answer to make an express exception of cases which shall have been originally tried by a jury, because in the courts of some of the states, *all causes* are tried in this mode;* and such an exception would preclude the revision of matters of fact, as well where it might be proper, as where it might be improper. To avoid all inconveniences, it will be safest to declare generally, that the supreme court shall posses appellate jurisdiction, both as to law and *fact*, and that this jurisdiction shall be subject to such *exceptions* and regulations as the national legislature may prescribe. This will enable

* I hold, that the states will have concurrent jurisdiction with the subordinate federal judicatories, in many cases of federal cognizance, as will be explained in my next paper.

the government to modify it in such a manner as will best answer the ends of public justice and security.

This view of the matter, at any rate, puts it out of all doubt, that the supposed *abolition* of the trial by jury, by the operation of this provision, is fallacious and untrue. The legislature of the United States would certainly have full power to provide, that in appeals to the supreme court there should be no re-examination of facts, where they had been tried in the original causes by juries. This would certainly be an authorized exception; but if, for the reason already intimated, it should be thought too extensive, it might be qualified with a limitation to such causes only as are determinable at common law in that mode of trial.

The amount of the observations hitherto made on the authority of the judicial department is this: That it has been carefully restricted to those causes which are manifestly proper for the cognizance of the national judicature; that, in the partition of this authority, a very small portion of original jurisdiction has been reserved to the supreme court, and the rest consigned to the subordinate tribunals; that the supreme court will possess an appellate jurisdiction, both as to law and fact, in all the cases referred to them, but subject to any *exceptions* and *regulations* which may be thought advisable; that this appellate jurisdiction does, in no case, *abolish* the trial by jury; and that an ordinary degree of prudence and integrity in the national councils, will insure us solid advantages from the establishment of the proposed judiciary, without exposing us to any of the inconveniences which have been predicted from that source.

PUBLIUS.

THE FEDERALIST.

NUMBER LXXXII.

NEW YORK, JULY 11, 1783.

HAMILTON.

A FURTHER VIEW OF THE JUDICIAL DEPARTMENT, IN REFERENCE TO SOME MISCELLANEOUS QUESTIONS.

THE erection of a new government, whatever care or wisdom may distinguish the work, cannot fail to originate questions of intricacy and nicety; and these may, in a particular manner, be expected to flow from the establishment of a constitution founded upon the total or partial incorporation of a number of distinct sovereignties. Time only can mature and perfect so compound a system, liquidate the meaning of all the parts, and adjust them to each other in a harmonious and consistent WHOLE.

Such questions accordingly have arisen upon the plan proposed by the convention, and particularly concerning the judiciary department. The principal of these respect the situation of the state courts, in regard to those causes which are to be submitted to federal jurisdiction. Is this to be exclusive, or are those courts to possess a concurrent jurisdiction? If the latter, in what relation will they stand to the national tribunals? These are inquiries which we meet with in the mouths of men of sense, and which are certainly entitled to attention.

The principles established in a former paper* teach us, that the states will retain all *pre-existing* authorities, which may not be exclusively delegated to the federal head; and that this exclusive delegation can only exist in one of three cases; where an exclusive authority is, in express terms, granted to the union; or where a particular authority is granted to the union, and the exercise of a like authority is prohibited to the states; or, where an authority is granted to the union, with which a similar authority in the states would be utterly incompatible. Though these principles may not apply with the same force to the judiciary, as to the legislative power; yet I am inclined to think, that they are in the main, just with respect to the former, as well as the latter. And under this impression I shall lay it down as a rule, that the state courts will *retain* the jurisdiction they now have, unless it appears to be taken away in one of the enumerated modes.

The only thing in the proposed constitution, which wears the appearance of confining the causes of federal cognizance, to the federal courts, is contained in this passage: "The JUDICIAL POWER of the United States *shall be vested* in one supreme court, and in *such* inferior courts as the congress shall from time to time ordain and establish." This might either be construed to signify, that the supreme and subordinate courts of the union should alone have the power of deciding those causes, to which their authority is to extend; or simply to denote, that the organs of the national judiciary should be one supreme court, and as many subordinate courts, as congress should think proper to appoint; in other words, that the United States should exercise the judicial power with which they are to be invested, through one supreme tribunal, and a certain number of inferior ones, to be instituted by them. The first excludes, the last admits, the concurrent jurisdiction of the state tribunals: And as the first would amount to an alienation of state power by implication, the last appears to me the most defensible construction.

* No. XXXII.

But this doctrine of concurrent jurisdiction, is only clearly applicable to those descriptions of causes, of which the state courts have previous cognizance. It is not equally evident in relation to cases which may grow out of, and be *peculiar* to, the constitution to be established: For not to allow the state courts a right of jurisdiction in such cases, can hardly be considered as the abridgement of a pre-existing authority. I mean not therefore to contend, that the United States, in the course of legislation upon the objects intrusted to their direction, may not commit the decision of causes arising upon a particular regulation, to the federal courts solely, if such a measure should be deemed expedient; but I hold that the state courts will be divested of no part of their primitive jurisdiction, further than may relate to an appeal; and I am even of opinion, that in every case in which they were not expressly excluded by the future acts of the national legislature, they will of course take cognizance of the causes to which those acts may give birth. This I infer from the nature of judiciary power, and from the general genius of the system. The judiciary power of every government looks beyond its own local or municipal laws, and in civil cases, lays hold of all subjects of litigation between parties within its jurisdiction, though the causes of dispute are relative to the laws of the most distant part of the globe. Those of Japan, not less than of New-York, may furnish the objects of legal discussion to our courts. When in addition to this we consider the state governments and the national governments, as they truly are, in the light of kindred systems, and as parts of ONE WHOLE, the inference seems to be conclusive, that the state courts would have a concurrent jurisdiction in all cases arising under the laws of the union, where it was not expressly prohibited.

Here another question occurs; what relation would subsist between the national and state courts in these instances of concurrent jurisdiction? I answer, that an appeal would certainly lie from the latter, to the supreme court of the United States. The constitution in direct terms, gives an appellate jurisdiction to the supreme court in all the enumerated cases of federal cognizance, in which it is not to have an original one; without a single expression to confine its operation to the inferior federal courts. The objects of appeal, not the tribunals from which it is to be made, are alone contemplated. From this circumstance, and from the reason of the thing, it ought to be construed to extend to the state tribunals. Either this must be the case, or the local courts must be excluded from a concurrent jurisdiction in matters of national concern, else the judiciary authority of the union may be eluded at the pleasure of every plaintiff or prosecutor. Neither of these consequences ought, without evident necessity, to be involved; the latter would be entirely inadmissible, as it would defeat some of the most important and avowed purposes of the proposed government, and would essentially embarrass its measures. Nor do I perceive any foundation for such a supposition. Agreeably to the remark already made, the national and state systems are to be regarded as ONE WHOLE. The courts of the latter will of course be natural auxiliaries to the execution of the laws of the union, and an appeal from them will as naturally lie to that tribunal, which is destined to unite and assimilate the principles of national justice and the rules of national decision. The evident aim of the plan of the convention is, that all the causes of the specified classes shall, for weighty public reasons, receive their original or final determination in the courts of the union. To confine, therefore, the general expressions which give appellate jurisdiction to the supreme court, to appeals from the subordinate federal courts, instead of allowing their extension to the state courts, would be to abridge the latitude of the terms, in subversion of the intent, contrary to every sound rule of interpretation.

But could an appeal be made to lie from the state courts, to the subordinate federal judicatories? This is another of the questions which have been raised, and of greater difficulty than the former. The following considerations countenance the affirmative. The plan of the convention, in the first place, authorizes the national legislature "to constitute tribunals inferior to the supreme court."* It declares in the next place, that "the JUDI-

CIAL POWER of the United States *shall be vested* in one supreme court, and in such inferior courts as congress shall ordain and establish;" and it then proceeds to enumerate the cases, to which this judicial power shall extend. It afterwards divides the jurisdiction of the supreme court into original and appellate, but gives no definition of that of the subordinate courts. The only outlines described for them are, that they shall be "inferior to the supreme court," and that they shall not exceed the specified limits of the federal judiciary. Whether their authority shall be original or appellate, or both, is not declared. All this seems to be left to the discretion of the legislature. And this being the case, I perceive at present no impediment to the establishment of an appeal from the state courts, to the subordinate national tribunals; and many advantages attending the power of doing it may be imagined. It would diminish the motives to the multiplication of federal courts, and would admit of arrangements calculated to contract the appellate jurisdiction of the supreme court. The state tribunals, may then be left with a more entire charge of federal causes; and appeals in most cases in which they may be deemed proper, instead of being carried to the supreme court, may be made to lie from the state courts, to district courts of the union.

PUBLIUS.

* Section 8th, Article 1st.

THE FEDERALIST.

NUMBER LXXXIII.

NEW YORK, JULY 15, 18, 22, 25, 1788.

HAMILTON.

A FURTHER VIEW OF THE JUDICIAL DEPARTMENT, IN RELATION
TO THE TRIAL BY JURY.

THE objection to the plan of the convention, which has met
with most success in this state, is relative to *the want of a constitutional provision* for the trial by jury in civil cases. The
disingenuous form in which this objection is usually stated, has
been repeatedly adverted to and exposed; but continues to be
pursued in all the conversations and writings of the opponents
of the plan. The mere silence of the constitution in regard to
civil causes, is represented as an abolition of the trial by jury;
and the declamations to which it has afforded a pretext, are art-
fully calculated to induce a persuasion that this pretended abolition is complete and universal; extending not only to every
species of civil, but even to *criminal causes*. To argue with
respect to the latter, would be as vain and fruitless, as to
attempt to demonstrate any of those propositions which, by
their own internal evidence, force conviction when expressed in
language adapted to convey their meaning.

With regard to civil causes, subtleties almost too contemptible for refutation, have been employed to countenance
the surmise that a thing, which is only *not provided for*, is
entirely *abolished*. Every man of discernment must at once per-

ceive the wide difference between *silence* and *abolition*. But as the inventors of this fallacy have attempted to support it by certain *legal maxims* of interpretation, which they have perverted from their true meaning, it may not be wholly useless to explore the ground they have taken.

The maxims on which they rely are of this nature, "a specification of particulars, is an exclusion of generals;" or, "the expression of one thing, is the exclusion of another." Hence, say they, as the constitution has established the trial by jury in criminal cases, and is silent in respect to civil, this silence is an implied prohibition of trial by jury, in regard to the latter.

The rules of legal intepretation, are rules of *common sense*, adopted by the courts in the construction of the laws. The true test, therefore, of a just application of them, is its conformity to the source from which they are derived. This being the case, let me ask if it is consistent with common sense to suppose, that a provision obliging the legislative power to commit the trial of criminal causes to juries, is a privation of its right to authorize or permit that mode of trial in other cases? Is it natural to suppose, that a command to do one thing, is a prohibition to the doing of another, which there was a previous power to do, and which is not incompatible with the thing commanded to be done? If such a supposition would be unnatural and unreasonable, it cannot be rational to maintain, that an injunction of the trial by jury, in certain cases, is an interdiction of it in others.

A power to constitute courts, is a power to prescribe the mode of trial; and consequently, if nothing was said in the constitution on the subject of juries, the legislature, would be at liberty either to adopt that institution, or to let it alone. This discretion, in regard to criminal causes, is abridged by an express injunction; but it is left at large in relation to civil causes, for the very reason that there is a total silence on the subject. The specification of an obligation to try all criminal causes in a particular mode, excludes indeed the obligations of employing the same mode in civil causes, but does not abridge *the power* of the legislature to appoint that mode, if it should be thought proper. The pretence, therefore, that the national legislature would not be at liberty to submit all the civil causes of federal cognizance to the determination of juries, is a pretence destitute of all foundation.

From these observations, this conclusion results, that the trial by jury in civil cases would not be abolished, and that the use attempted to be made of the maxims which have been quoted, is contrary to reason, and therefore inadmissible. Even if these maxims had a precise technical sense, corresponding with the ideas of those who employ them upon the present occasion, which, however, is not the case, they would still be inapplicable to a constitution of government. In relation to such a subject, the natural and obvious sense of its provisions, apart from any technical rules, is the true criterion of construction.

Having now seen that the maxims relied upon will not bear the use made of them, let us endeavour to ascertain their proper application. This will be best done by examples. The plan of the convention declares, that the power of congress, or in other words of the *national legislature*, shall extend to certain enumerated cases. This specification of particulars evidently excludes all pretension to a general legislative authority; because an affirmative grant of special powers would be absurd as well as useless, if a general authority was intended.

In like manner, the authority of the federal judicatures, is declared by the constitution to comprehend certain cases particularly specified. The expression of those cases, marks the precise limits beyond which the federal courts cannot extend their jurisdiction; because the objects of their cognizance being enumerated, the specification would be nugatory, if it did not exclude all ideas of more extensive authority.

These examples are sufficient to elucidate the maxims which have been mentioned, and to designate the manner in which they should be used.

From what has been said, it must appear unquestionably

true, that trial by jury is in no case abolished by the proposed constitution; and it is equally true, that in those controversies between individuals in which the great body of the people are likely to be interested, that institution will remain precisely in the situation in which it is placed by the state constitutions. The foundation of this assertion is, that the national judiciary will have no cognizance of them, and of course they will remain determinable as heretofore by the state courts only, and in the manner which the state constitutions and laws prescribe. All land causes, except where claims under the grants of different states come into question, and all other controversies between the citizens of the same state, unless where they depend upon positive violations of the articles of union, by acts of the state legislatures, will belong exclusively to the jurisdiction of the state tribunals. Add to this, that admiralty causes, and almost all those which are of equity jurisdiction, are determinable under our own government without the intervention of a jury, and the inference from the whole will be, that this institution, as it exists with us at present, cannot possibly be affected, to any great extent, by the proposed alteration in our system of government.

The friends and adversaries of the plan of the convention, if they agree in nothing else, concur at least in the value they set upon the trial by jury: Or if there is any difference between them, it consists in this; the former regard it as a valuable safeguard to liberty, the latter represent it as the very palladium of free government. For my own part, the more the operation of the institution has fallen under my observation, the more reason I have discovered for holding it in high estimation; and it would be altogether superfluous to examine to what extent it deserves to be esteemed useful or essential in a representative republic, or how much more merit it may be entitled to, as a defence against the oppressions of an hereditary monarch, than as a barrier to the tyranny of popular magistrates in a popular government. Discussions of this kind would be more curious than beneficial, as all are satisfied of the utility of the institution, and of its friendly aspect to liberty. But I must acknowledge, that I cannot readily discern the inseparable connexion between the existence of liberty, and the trial by jury in civil cases. Arbitrary impeachments, arbitrary methods of prosecuting pretended offences, arbitrary punishments upon arbitrary convictions, have ever appeared to me the great engines of judicial despotism; and all these have relation to criminal proceedings. The trial by jury in criminal cases, aided by the *habeas corpus* act, seems therefore to be alone concerned in the question. And both of these are provided for, in the most ample manner, in the plan of the convention.

It has been observed, that trial by jury is a safeguard against an oppressive exercise of the power of taxation. This observation deserves to be canvassed.

It is evident that it can have no influence upon the legislature, in regard to the *amount* of the taxes to be laid, to the *objects* upon which they are to be imposed, or to the *rule* by which they are to be apportioned. If it can have any influence, therefore, it must be upon the mode of collection, and the conduct of the officers intrusted with the execution of the revenue laws.

As to the mode of collection in this state, under our own constitution, the trial by jury is in most cases out of use. The taxes are usually levied by the more summary proceeding of distress and sale, as in cases of rent. And it is acknowledged on all hands, that this is essential to the efficacy of the revenue laws. The dilatory course of a trial at law to recover the taxes imposed on individuals, would neither suit the exigencies of the public, nor promote the convenience of the citizens. It would often occasion an accumulation of costs, more burthensome than the original sum of the tax to be levied.

And as to the conduct of the officers of the revenue, the provision in favour of trial by jury in criminal cases, will afford the desired security. Wilful abuses of a public authority, to the oppression of the subject, and every species of official extortion, are offences against the government; for which, the persons who commit them, may be indicted and punished according to the circumstances of the case.

The excellence of the trial by jury in civil cases, appears to depend on circumstances foreign to the preservation of liberty. The strongest argument in its favour is, that it is a security against corruption. As there is always more time, and better opportunity, to tamper with a standing body of magistrates, than with a jury summoned for the occasion, there is room to suppose, that a corrupt influence would more easily find its way to the former than to the latter. The force of this consideration is, however, diminished by others. The sheriff, who is the summoner of ordinary juries, and the clerks of courts who have the nomination of special juries, are themselves standing officers, and acting individually, may be supposed more accessible to the touch of corruption than the judges, who are a collective body. It is not difficult to see, that it would be in the power of those officers to select jurors, who would serve the purpose of the party, as well as a corrupted bench. In the next place, it may fairly be supposed, that there would be less difficulty in gaining some of the jurors promiscuously taken from the public mass, than in gaining men who had been chosen by the government for their probity and good character. But making every deduction for these considerations, the trial by jury must still be a valuable check upon corruption. It greatly multiplies the impediments to its success. As matters now stand, it would be necessary to corrupt both court and jury; for where the jury have gone evidently wrong, the court will generally grant a new trial, and it would be in most cases of little use to practise upon the jury, unless the court could be likewise gained. Here then is a double security; and it will readily be perceived, that this complicated agency tends to preserve the purity of both institutions By increasing the obstacles to success, it discourages attempts to seduce the integrity of either. The temptations to prostitution, which the judges might have to surmount, must certainly be much fewer, while the co-operation of a jury is necessary, than they might be, if they had themselves the exclusive determination of all causes.

Notwithstanding, therefore, the doubts I have expressed, as to the essentiality of trial by jury in civil suits to liberty, I admit that it is in most cases, under proper regulations, an excellent method of determining questions of property; and that on this account alone, it would be entitled to a constitutional provision in its favour, if it were possible to fix with accuracy the limits within which it ought to be comprehended. This, however, is in its own nature an affair of much difficulty; and men not blinded by enthusiasm, must be sensible, that in a federal government, which is a composition of societies whose ideas and institutions in relation to the matter, materially vary from each other, the difficulty must be not a little augmented. For my own part, at every new view I take of the subject, I become more convinced of the reality of the obstacles, which we are authoritatively informed, prevented the insertion of a provision on this head in the plan of the convention.

The great difference between the limits of the jury trial in different states, is not generally understood. And as it must have considerable influence on the sentence we ought to pass upon the omission complained of, in regard to this point, an explanation of it is necessary. In this state, our judicial establishments resemble more nearly, than in any other, those of Great Britain. We have courts of common law, courts of probates (analogous in certain matters to the spiritual courts in England) a court of admiralty, and a court of chancery. In the courts of common law only, the trial by jury prevails, and this with some exceptions. In all the others, a single judge presides, and proceeds in general either according to the course of the canon or civil law, without the aid of a jury.* In New-Jersey there is a court of chancery which proceeds like ours, but neither courts of admi-

---

* It has been erroneously insinuated, with regard to the court of chancery, that this court generally tries disputed facts by a jury. The truth is, that references to a jury in that court rarely happen, and are in no case necessary but where the validity of a devise of land comes into question.

ralty, nor of probates, in the sense in which these last are established with us. In that state, the courts of common law have the cognizance of those causes, which with us are determinable in the courts of admiralty and of probates, and of course the jury trial is more extensive in New-Jersey, than in New-York. In Pennsylvania, this is perhaps still more the case, for there is no court of chancery in that state, and its common law courts have equity jurisdiction. It has a court of admiralty, but none of probates, at least on the plan of ours. Delaware has in these respects imitated Pennsylvania. Maryland approaches more nearly to New-York, as does also Virginia, except that the latter has a plurality of chancellors. North-Carolina bears most affinity to Pennsylvania; South-Carolina to Virginia. I believe however, that in some of those states which have distinct courts of admiralty, the causes depending in them are triable by juries. In Georgia there are none but common law courts, and an appeal of course lies from the verdict of one jury to another, which is called a special jury, and for which a particular mode of appointment is marked out. In Connecticut they have no distinct courts, either of chancery or of admiralty, and their courts of probates have no jurisdiction of causes. Their common law courts have admiralty, and, to a certain extent, equity jurisdiction. In cases of importance, their general assembly is the only court of chancery. In Connecticut, therefore, the trial by jury extends in *practice* further than in any other state yet mentioned. Rhode-Island is, I believe, in this particular, pretty much in the situation of Connecticut. Massachusetts and New-Hampshire, in regard to the blending of law, equity, and admiralty jurisdictions, are in a similar predicament. In the four eastern states, the trial by jury not only stands upon a broader foundation than in the other states, but it is attended with a peculiarity unknown, in its full extent, to any of them. There is an appeal *of course* from one jury to another, till there have been two verdicts out of three on one side.

From this sketch it appears, that there is a material diversity as well in the modification as in the extent of the institution of trial by jury in civil cases in the several states; and from this fact, these obvious reflections flow. First, that no general rule could have been fixed upon by the convention which would have corresponded with the circumstances of all the states; and secondly, that more, or at least as much might have been hazarded, by taking the system of any one state for a standard, as by omitting a provision altogether, and leaving the matter as has been done to legislative regulation.

The propositions which have been made for supplying the omission, have rather served to illustrate, than to obviate the difficulty of the thing. The minority of Pennsylvania have proposed this mode of expression for the purpose, "trial by jury shall be as heretofore;" and this I maintain would be inapplicable and indeterminate. The United States, in their collective capacity, are the OBJECT to which all general provisions in the constitution must be understood to refer. Now, it is evident, that though trial by jury, with various limitations, is known in each state individually, yet in the United States, *as such*, it is, strictly speaking, unknown; because the present federal government has no judiciary power whatever; and consequently there is no antecedent establishment, to which the term *heretofore* could properly relate. It would therefore be destitute of precise meaning, and inoperative from its uncertainty.

As on the one hand, the form of the provision would not fulfil the intent of its proposers; so on the other, if I apprehend that intent rightly, it would be in itself inexpedient. I presume it to be, that causes in the federal courts should be tried by jury, if in the state where the courts sat, that mode of trial would obtain in a similar case in the state courts—that is to say, admiralty causes should be trial in Connecticut by a jury, in New-York without one. The capricious operation of so dissimilar a method of trial in the same cases, under the same government, is of itself sufficient to indispose every well regulated judgment towards it. Whether the cause should be tried with or without a

jury, would depend, in a great number of cases, on the accidental situation of the court and parties.

But this is not, in my estimation, the greatest objection. I feel
a deep and deliberate conviction, that there are many cases in
which the trial by jury is an ineligible one. I think it so particularly, in suits which concern the public peace with foreign
nations; that is in most cases where the question turns wholly
on the laws of nations. Of this nature, among others, are all
prize causes. Juries cannot be supposed competent to investigations, that require a thorough knowledge of the laws and usages
of nations; and they will sometimes be under the influence of
impressions which will not suffer them to pay sufficient regard
to those considerations of public policy, which ought to guide
their inquiries. There would of course be always danger, that
the rights of other nations might be infringed by their decisions,
so as to afford occasions of reprisal and war. Though the true
province of juries be to determine matters of fact, yet in most
cases, legal consequences are complicated with fact in such a
manner, as to render a separation impracticable.

It will add great weight to this remark, in relation to prize
causes, to mention, that the method of determining them has
been thought worthy of particular regulation in various treaties
between different powers of Europe, and that, pursuant to such
treaties, they are determinable in Great Britain in the last
resort before the king himself in his privy council, where the
fact as well as the law, undergoes a re-examination. This alone
demonstrates the impolicy of inserting a fundamental provision
in the constitution which would make the state systems a standard for the national government in the article under consideration, and the danger of incumbering the government with
any constitutional provisions, the propriety of which is not
indisputable.

My convictions are equally strong, that great advantages
result from the separation of the equity from the law jurisdiction; and that the causes which belong to the former, would be
improperly committed to juries. The great and primary use of a

court of equity, is to give relief *in extraordinary cases*, which are *exceptions** to general rules. To unite the jurisdiction of such cases, with the ordinary jurisdiction, must have a tendency to unsettle the general rules, and to subject every case that arises to a *special* determination: While a separation between the jurisdictions, has the contrary effect of rendering one a sentinel over the other, and of keeping each within the expedient limits. Besides this, the circumstances that constitute cases proper for courts of equity, are in many instances so nice and intricate, that they are incompatible with the genius of trials by jury. They require often such long and critical investigation, as would be impracticable to men called occasionally from their occupations, and obliged to decide before they were permitted to return to them. The simplicity and expedition which form the distinguishing characters of this mode of trial require, that the matter to be decided should be reduced to some single and obvious point; while the litigations usual in chancery, frequently comprehend a long train of minute and independent particulars.

It is true, that the separation of the equity from the legal jurisdiction, is peculiar to the English system of jurisprudence; the model which has been followed in several of the states. But it is equally true, that the trial by jury has been unknown in every instance in which they have been united. And the separation is essential to the preservation of that institution in its pristine purity. The nature of a court of equity will readily permit the extension of its jurisdiction to matters of law, but it is not a little to be suspected, that the attempt to extend the jurisdiction of the courts of law to matters of equity, will not only be unproductive of the advantages which may be derived from courts of chancery, on the plan upon which they are established in this state, but will tend gradually to change the nature of the courts of law, and to undermine the trial by jury, by

* It is true that the principles by which that relief is governed are now reduced to a regular system; but it is not the less true that they are in the main applicable to SPECIAL circumstances, which form exceptions to general rules.

introducing questions too complicated for a decision in that mode.

These appear to be conclusive reasons against incorporating the systems of all the states, in the formation of the national judiciary; according to what may be conjectured to have been the intent of the Pennsylvania minority. Let us now examine how far the proposition of Massachusetts is calculated to remedy the supposed defect.

It is in this form: "In civil actions between citizens of different states, every issue of fact, arising in *actions at common law*, may be tried by a jury, if the parties, or either of them, request it."

This, at best, is a proposition confined to one description of causes; and the inference is fair either that the Massachusetts convention considered that as the only class of federal causes, in which the trial by jury would be proper; or that, if desirous of a more extensive provision, they found it impracticable to devise one which would properly answer the end. If the first, the omission of a regulation respecting so partial an object, can never be considered as a material imperfection in the system. If the last, it affords a strong corroboration of the extreme difficulty of the thing.

But this is not all: If we advert to the observations already made respecting the courts that subsist in the several states of the union, and the different powers exercised by them, it will appear, that there are no expressions more vague and indeterminate than those which have been employed to characterize *that* species of causes which it is intended shall be entitled to a trial by jury. In this state, the boundaries between actions at common law and actions of equitable jurisdiction, are ascertained in conformity to the rules which prevail in England upon that subject. In many of the other states, the boundaries are less precise. In some of them, every cause is to be tried in a court of common law, and upon that foundation every action may be considered as an action at common law, to be determined by a jury, if the parties, or either of them, choose it.

Hence the same irregularity and confusion would be introduced by a compliance with this proposition, that I have already noticed as resulting from the regulation proposed by the Pennsylvania minority. In one state a cause would receive its determination from a jury, if the parties, or either of them, requested it; but in another state, a cause exactly similar to the other, must be decided without the intervention of a jury, because the state tribunals varied as to common law jurisdiction.

It is obvious, therefore, that the Massachusetts proposition cannot operate as a general regulation, until some uniform plan, with respect to the limits of common law and equitable jurisdictions, shall be adopted by the different states. To devise a plan of that kind, is a task arduous in itself, and which it would require much time and reflection to mature. It would be extremely difficult, if not impossible, to suggest any general regulation that would be acceptable to all the states in the union, or that would perfectly quadrate with the several state institutions.

It may be asked, why could not a reference have been made to the constitution of this state, taking that, which is allowed by me to be a good one, as a standard for the United States? I answer, that it is not very probable the other states should entertain the same opinion of our institutions which we do ourselves. It is natural to suppose that they are more attached to their own, and that each would struggle for the preference. If the plan of taking one state as a model for the whole had been thought of in the convention, it is to be presumed that the adoption of it in that body, would have been rendered difficult by the predilection of each representation in favour of its own government; and it must be uncertain which of the states would have been taken as the model. It has been shown, that many of them would be improper ones. And I leave it to conjecture whether, under all circumstances, it is most likely that New-York, or some other state, would have been preferred. But admit that a judicious selection could have been effected in the convention, still there would have been great danger of jealousy and disgust in the other states, at the partiality which had been shown to the institutions of one. The enemies of the plan would have been furnished with a fine pretext, for raising a host of local prejudices against it, which perhaps might have hazarded, in no inconsiderable degree, its final establishment.

To avoid the embarrassments of a definition of the cases which the trial by jury ought to embrace, it is sometimes suggested by men of enthusiastic tempers, that a provision might have been inserted for establishing it in all cases whatsoever. For this, I believe no precedent is to be found in any member of the union; and the considerations which have been stated in discussing the proposition of the minority of Pennsylvania, must satisfy every sober mind, that the establishment of the trial by jury in *all* cases, would have been an unpardonable error in the plan.

In short, the more it is considered, the more arduous will appear the task of fashioning a provision in such a form, as not to express too little to answer the purpose, or too much to be advisable; or which might not have opened other sources of opposition, to the great and essential object, of introducing a firm national government.

I cannot but persuade myself on the other hand, that the different lights in which the subject has been placed in the course of these observations, will go far towards removing in candid minds, the apprehensions they may have entertained on the point. They have tended to show, that the security of liberty is materially concerned only in the trial by jury in criminal cases, which is provided for in the most ample manner in the plan of the convention; that even in far the greatest proportion of civil cases, those in which the great body of the community is interested, that mode of trial will remain in full force, as established in the state constitutions, untouched and unaffected by the plan of the convention: That it is in no case abolished* by that plan;

---

* Vide No. LXXXI. in which the supposition of its being abolished by the appellate jurisdiction in matters of fact being vested in the supreme court, is examined and refuted.

and that there are great, if not insurmountable difficulties in the way of making any precise and proper provision for it, in a constitution for the United States.

The best judges of the matter will be the least anxious for a constitutional establishment of the trial by jury in civil cases, and will be the most ready to admit, that the changes which are continually happening in the affairs of society, may render a different mode of determining questions of property, preferable in many cases, in which that mode of trial now prevails. For my own part, I acknowledge myself to be convinced that, even in this state, it might be advantageously extended to some cases to which it does not at present apply, and might as advantageously be abridged in others. It is conceded by all reasonable men, that it ought not to obtain in all cases. The examples of innovations which contract its ancient limits, as well in these states as in Great Britain, afford a strong presumption that its former extent has been found inconvenient; and give room to suppose that future experience may discover the propriety and utility of other exceptions. I suspect it to be impossible in the nature of the thing, to fix the salutary point at which the operation of the institution ought to stop; and this is with me a strong argument for leaving the matter to the discretion of the legislature.

This is now clearly understood to be the case in Great Britain, and it is equally so in the state of Connecticut; and yet it may be safely affirmed, that more numerous encroachments have been made upon the trial by jury in this state since the revolution, though provided for by a positive article of our constitution, than has happened in the same time either in Connecticut or Great Britain. It may be added, that these encroachments have generally originated with the men who endeavour to persuade the people they are the warmest defenders of popular liberty, but who have rarely suffered constitutional obstacles to arrest them in a favourite career. The truth is, that the general GENIUS of a government is all that can be substantially relied upon for permanent effects. Particular provisions, though not altogether useless, have far less virtue and efficacy than are commonly ascribed to them; and the want of them, will never be with men of sound discernment, a decisive objection to any plan which exhibits the leading characters of a good government.

It certainly sounds not a little harsh and extraordinary to affirm, that there is no security for liberty in a constitution which expressly establishes the trial by jury in criminal cases, because it does not do it in civil also; while it is a notorious fact that Connecticut, which has been always regarded as the most popular state in the union, can boast of no constitutional provision for either.

PUBLIUS.

THE FEDERALIST.

NUMBER LXXXIV.

NEW YORK, JULY 29 AND AUGUST 8, 12, 1788.

HAMILTON.

CONCERNING SEVERAL MISCELLANEOUS OBJECTIONS.

IN the course of the foregoing review of the constitution, I have endeavoured to answer most of the objections which have appeared against it. There remain, however, a few which either did not fall naturally under any particular head, or were forgotten in their proper places. These shall now be discussed: but as the subject has been drawn into great length, I shall so far consult brevity, as to comprise all my observations on these miscellaneous points in a single paper.

The most considerable of the remaining objections is, that the plan of the convention contains no bill of rights. Among other answers given to this, it has been upon different occasions remarked, that the constitutions of several of the states are in a similar predicament. I add, that New-York is of the number. And yet the persons who in this state oppose the new system, while they profess an unlimited admiration for our particular constitution, are among the most intemperate partizans of a bill of rights. To justify their zeal in this matter, they allege two things: one is, that though the constitution of New-York has no bill of rights prefixed to it, yet it contains, in the body of it, various provisions in favour of particular privileges and rights, which, in substance, amount to the same thing; the other is, that the constitution adopts, in their full extent, the common and statute law of Great Britain, by which many other rights, not expressed, are equally secured.

To the first I answer, that the constitution offered by the convention contains, as well as the constitution of this state, a number of such provisions.

Independent of those which relate to the structure of the government, we find the following: Article I. section 3. clause 7. "Judgment in cases of impeachment shall not extend further than to removal from office, and disqualification to hold and enjoy any office of honour, trust, or profit under the United States; but the party convicted shall, nevertheless, be liable and subject to indictment, trial, judgment, and punishment, according to law." Section 9. of the same article, clause 2. "The privilege of the writ of *habeas corpus* shall not be suspended, unless when in cases of rebellion or invasion the public safety may require it." Clause 3. "No bill of attainder or *ex post facto* law shall be passed." Clause 7. "No title of nobility shall be granted by the United States; and no person holding any office of profit or trust under them, shall, without the consent of the congress, accept of any present, emolument, office, or title, of any kind whatever, from any king, prince, or foreign state." Article III. section 2. clause 3. "The trial of all crimes, except in cases of impeachment, shall be by jury; and such trial shall be held in the state where the said crimes shall have been committed; but when not committed within any state, the trial shall be at such place or places as the congress may by law have directed" Section 3. of the same article, "Treason against the United States shall consist only in levying war against them, or in adhering to their enemies, giving them aid and comfort. No person shall be convicted of treason, unless on the testimony of two witnesses to the same overt act, or on confession in open court." And clause 3. of the same section, "The congress shall have power to declare the punishment of treason; but no attainder of treason shall work corruption of blood, or forfeiture, except during the life of the person attainted."

It may well be a question, whether these are not, upon the whole, of equal importance with any which are to be found in the constitution of this state. The establishment of the writ of *habeas corpus*, the prohibition of *ex post facto* laws, and of TITLES OF NOBILITY, *to which we have no corresponding provisions in our constitution*, are perhaps greater securities to liberty than any it contains. The creation of crimes after the commission of the fact, or, in other words, the subjecting of men to punishment for things which, when they were done, were breaches of no law; and the practice of arbitrary imprisonments have been, in all ages, the favourite and most formidable instruments of tyranny. The observations of the judicious Blackstone,* in reference to the latter, are well worthy of recital: "To bereave a man of life (says he) or by violence to confiscate his estate, without accusation or trial, would be so gross and notorious an act of despotism, as must at once convey the alarm of tyranny throughout the whole nation; but confinement of the person, by secretly hurrying him to jail, where his sufferings are unknown or forgotten, is a less public, a less striking, and therefore a *a more dangerous engine* of arbitrary government." And as a remedy for this fatal evil, he is every where peculiarly emphatical in his encomiums on the *habeas corpus* act, which in one place he calls "the BULWARK of the British constitution."†

Nothing need be said to illustrate the importance of the prohibition of titles of nobility. This may truly be denominated the corner stone of republican government; for so long as they are excluded, there can never be serious danger that the government will be any other than that of the people.

To the second, that is, to the pretended establishment of the common and statute law by the constitution, I answer, that they are expressly made subject "to such alterations and provisions as the legislature shall from time to time make concerning the same." They are therefore at any moment liable to

---

* Vide Blackstone's Commentaries, vol. 1, p. 136.
† Idem, vol. 4, page 438.

repeal by the ordinary legislative power, and of course have no constitutional sanction. The only use of the declaration was to recognize the ancient law, and to remove doubts which might have been occasioned by the revolution. This consequently can be considered as no part of a declaration of rights; which under our constitutions must be intended to limit the power of the government itself.

It has been several times truly remarked, that bills of rights are, in their origin, stipulations between kings and their subjects, abridgements of prerogative in favour of privilege, reservations of rights not surrendered to the prince. Such was MAGNA CHARTA, obtained by the Barons, sword in hand, from king John. Such were the subsequent confirmations of that charter by succeeding princes. Such was the *petition of right* assented to by Charles the First, in the beginning of his reign. Such also, was the declaration of right presented by the lords and commons to the prince of Orange in 1688, and afterwards thrown into the form of an act of parliament, called the bill of rights. It is evident, therefore, that according to their primitive signification, they have no application to constitutions professedly founded upon the power of the people, and executed by their immediate representatives and servants. Here, in strictness, the people surrender nothing; and as they retain every thing, they have no need of particular reservations. "WE THE PEOPLE of the United States, to secure the blessings of liberty to ourselves and our posterity, do *ordain* and *establish* this constitution for the United States of America:" This is a better recognition of popular rights, than volumes of those aphorisms, which make the principal figure in several of our state bills of rights, and which would sound much better in a treatise of ethics, than in a constitution of government.

But a minute detail of particular rights, is certainly far less applicable to a constitution like that under consideration, which is merely intended to regulate the general political interests of the nation, than to one which has the regulation of every species of personal and private concerns. If therefore the loud clamours against the plan of the convention, on this score, are well founded, no epithets of reprobation will be too strong for the constitution of this state. But the truth is, that both of them contain all which, in relation to their objects, is reasonably to be desired.

I go further, and affirm, that bills of rights, in the sense and to the extent they are contended for, are not only unnecessary in the proposed constitution, but would even be dangerous. They would contain various exceptions to powers not granted; and on this very account, would afford a colourable pretext to claim more than were granted. For why declare that things shall not be done, which there is no power to do? Why, for instance, should it be said, that the liberty of the press shall not be restrained, when no power is given by which restrictions may be imposed? I will not contend that such a provision would confer a regulating power; but it is evident that it would furnish, to men disposed to usurp, a plausible pretence for claiming that power. They might urge with a semblance of reason, that the constitution ought not to be charged with the absurdity of providing against the abuse of an authority, which was not given, and that the provision against restraining the liberty of the press afforded a clear implication, that a right to prescribe proper regulations concerning it, was intended to be vested in the national government. This may serve as a specimen of the numerous handles which would be given to the doctrine of constructive powers, by the indulgence of an injudicious zeal for bills of rights.

On the subject of the liberty of the press, as much has been said, I cannot forbear adding a remark or two: In the first place, I observe that there is not a syllable concerning it in the constitution of this state; in the next, I contend that whatever has been said about it in that of any other state, amounts to nothing. What signifies a declaration, that "the liberty of the press shall be inviolably preserved?" What is the liberty of the press? Who can give it any definition which would not leave the utmost latitude for evasion? I hold it to be impracticable;

and from this I infer, that its security, whatever fine declarations may be inserted in any constitution respecting it, must altogether depend on public opinion, and on the general spirit of the people and of the government.* And here, after all, as intimated upon another occasion, must we seek for the only solid basis of all our rights.

There remains but one other view of this matter to conclude the point. The truth is, after all the declamation we have heard, that the constitution is itself, in every rational sense, and to every useful purpose, A BILL OF RIGHTS. The several bills of rights, in Great Britain, form its constitution, and conversely the constitution of each state is its bill of rights. In like manner the proposed constitution, if adopted, will be the bill of rights of the union. Is it one object of a bill of rights to declare and specify the political privileges of the citizens in the structure and administration of the government? This is done in the most ample and precise manner in the plan of the convention; comprehending various precautions for the public security, which are not to be found in any of the state constitutions. Is another object of a bill of rights to define certain immunities

---

* To show that there is a power in the constitution, by which the liberty of the press may be affected, recourse has been had to the power of taxation. It is said, that duties may be laid upon publications so high as to amount to a prohibition. I know not by what logic it could be maintained, that the declarations in the state constitutions, in favour of the freedom of the press, would be a constitutional impediment to the imposition of duties upon publications by the state legislatures. It cannot certainly be pretended that any degree of duties, however low, would be an abridgement of the liberty of the press. We know that newspapers are taxed in Great Britain, and yet it is notorious that the press no where enjoys greater liberty than in that country. And if duties of any kind may be laid without a violation of that liberty, it is evident that the extent must depend on legislative discretion, regulated by public opinion; so that after all, general declarations respecting the liberty of the press, will give it no greater security than it will have without them. The same invasions of it may be effected under the state-constitutions which contain those declarations through the means of taxation, as under the proposed constitution, which has nothing of the kind. It would be quite as significant to declare, that government ought to be free, that taxes ought not to be excessive, &c. as that the liberty of the press ought not to be restrained.

and modes of proceeding, which are relative to personal and private concerns? This we have seen has also been attended to, in a variety of cases, in the same plan. Adverting therefore to the substantial meaning of a bill of rights, it is absurd to allege that it is not to be found in the work of the convention. It may be said that it does not go far enough, though it will not be easy to make this appear; but it can with no propriety be contended that there is no such thing. It certainly must be immaterial what mode is observed as to the order of declaring the rights of the citizens, if they are provided for in any part of the instrument which establishes the government. Whence it must be apparent that much of what has been said on this subject rests merely on verbal and nominal distinctions, entirely foreign to the substance of the thing.

Another objection, which, from the frequency of its repetition, may be presumed to be relied on, is of this nature: It is improper (say the objectors) to confer such large powers, as are proposed, upon the national government: because the seat of that government must of necessity be too remote from many of the states to admit of a proper knowledge on the part of the constituent, of the conduct of the representative body. This argument, if it proves any thing, proves that there ought to be no general government whatever. For the powers which it seems to be agreed on all hands, ought to be vested in the union, cannot be safely intrusted to a body which is not under every requisite control. But there are satisfactory reasons to show, that the objection is, in reality, not well founded. There is in most of the arguments which relate to distance, a palpable illusion of the imagination. What are the sources of information, by which the people in any distant county must regulate their judgment of the conduct of their representatives in the state legislature? Of personal observation they can have no benefit. This is confined to the citizens on the spot. They must therefore depend on the information of intelligent men, in whom they confide: and how must these men obtain their information? Evidently from the complexion of public measures, from the public prints, from correspondences with their representatives, and with other persons who reside at the place of their deliberations.

It is equally evident that the like sources of information would be open to the people, in relation to the conduct of their representatives in the general government; and the impediments to a prompt communication which distance may be supposed to create, will be overbalanced by the effects of the vigilance of the state governments. The executive and legislative bodies of each state will be so many sentinels over the persons employed in every department of the national administration; and as it will be in their power to adopt and pursue a regular and effectual system of intelligence, they can never be at a loss to know the behaviour of those who represent their constituents in the national councils, and can readily communicate the same knowledge to the people. Their disposition to apprize the community of whatever may prejudice its interests from another quarter, may be relied upon, if it were only from the rivalship of power. And we may conclude with the fullest assurance, that the people, through that channel, will be better informed of the conduct of their national representatives, than they can be by any means they now possess, of that of their state representatives.

It ought also to be remembered, that the citizens who inhabit the country at and near the seat of government will, in all questions that affect the general liberty and prosperity, have the same interest with those who are at a distance; and that they will stand ready to sound the alarm when necessary, and to point out the actors in any pernicious project. The public papers will be expeditious messengers of intelligence to the most remote inhabitants of the union.

Among the many curious objections which have appeared against the proposed constitution, the most extraordinary and the least colourable is derived from the want of some provision respecting the debts due *to* the United States. This has been represented as a tacit relinquishment of those debts, and as a wicked contrivance to screen public defaulters. The newspapers have teemed with the most inflammatory railings on this head; yet there is nothing clearer than that the suggestion is entirely void of foundation, the offspring of extreme ignorance or extreme dishonesty. In addition to the remarks I have made upon the subject in another place, I shall only observe, that as it is a plain dictate of common sense, so it is also an established doctrine of political law, that *"States neither lose any of their rights, nor are discharged from any of their obligations, by a change in the form of their civil government."**

The last objection of any consequence at present recollected, turns upon the article of expense. If it were even true, that the adoption of the proposed government would occasion a considerable increase of expense, it would be an objection that ought to have no weight against the plan. The great bulk of the citizens of America, are with reason convinced that union is the basis of their political happiness. Men of sense of all parties now, with few exceptions, agree that it cannot be preserved under the present system, nor without radical alterations; that new and extensive powers ought to be granted to the national head, and that these require a different organization of the federal government; a single body being an unsafe depository of such ample authorities. In conceding all this, the question of expense is given up; for it is impossible, with any degree of safety, to narrow the foundation upon which the system is to stand. The two branches of the legislature are, in the first instance, to consist of only sixty-five persons; the same number of which congress, under the existing confederation, may be composed. It is true that this number is intended to be increased; but this is to keep pace with the progress of the population and resources of the country. It is evident, that a less number would, even in the first instance, have been unsafe; and that a continuance of the present number would, in a more advanced stage of population, be a very inadequate representation of the people.

---

* Vide Rutherford's Institutes, vol. 2. book 11. chap. x. sect. xiv. and xv. —Vide also Grotius, book 11. chap. ix. sect. viii. and ix.

Whence is the dreaded augmentation of expense to spring? One source indicated, is the multiplication of offices under the new government. Let us examine this a little.

It is evident that the principal departments of the administration under the present government, are the same which will be required under the new. There are now a secretary at war, a secretary for foreign affairs, a secretary for domestic affairs, a board of treasury consisting of three persons, a treasurer, assistants, clerks, &c. These offices are indispensable under any system, and will suffice under the new, as well as the old. As to ambassadors and other ministers and agents in foreign countries, the proposed constitution can make no other difference, than to render their characters, where they reside, more respectable, and their services more useful. As to persons to be employed in the collection of the revenues, it is unquestionably true that these will form a very considerable addition to the number of federal officers; but it will not follow, that this will occasion an increase of public expense. It will be in most cases nothing more than an exchange of state for national officers. In the collection of all duties, for instance, the persons employed will be wholly of the latter description. The states individually, will stand in no need of any for this purpose. What difference can it make in point of expense, to pay officers of the customs appointed by the state, or by the United States?

Where then are we to seek for those additional articles of expense, which are to swell the account to the enormous size that has been represented? The chief item which occurs to me, respects the support of the judges of the United States. I do not add the president, because there is now a president of congress, whose expenses may not be far, if any thing, short of those which will be incurred on account of the president of the United States. The support of the judges will clearly be an extra expense, but to what extent will depend on the particular plan which may be adopted in regard to this matter. But upon no reasonable plan can it amount to a sum which will be an object of material consequence.

Let us now see what there is to counterbalance any extra expense that may attend the establishment of the proposed government. The first thing which presents itself is, that a great part of the business, that now keeps congress sitting through the year, will be transacted by the president. Even the management of foreign negotiations will naturally devolve upon him, according to general principles concerted with the senate, and subject to their final concurrence. Hence it is evident, that a portion of the year will suffice for the session of both the senate and the house of representatives: We may suppose about a fourth for the latter, and a third, or perhaps half, for the former. The extra business of treaties and appointments may give this extra occupation to the senate. From this circumstance we may infer, that until the house of representatives shall be increased greatly beyond its present number, there will be a considerable saving of expense from the difference between the constant session of the present, and the temporary session of the future congress.

But there is another circumstance, of great importance in the view of economy. The business of the United States has hitherto occupied the state legislatures, as well as congress. The latter has made requisitions which the former have had to provide for. It has thence happened, that the sessions of the state legislatures have been protracted greatly beyond what was necessary for the execution of the mere local business. More than half their time has been frequently employed in matters which related to the United States. Now the members who compose the legislatures of the several states amount to two thousand and upwards; which number has hitherto performed what, under the new system, will be done in the first instance by sixty-five persons, and probably at no future period by above a fourth or a fifth of that number. The congress under the proposed government will do all the business of the United States themselves, without the intervention of the state legislatures, who thenceforth will have only to attend to the affairs of their particular states, and will not have to sit in any proportion as long as they have heretofore done. This difference, in the time of the sessions of the state legislatures, will be clear gain, and will alone form an article of saving, which may be regarded as an equivalent for any additional objects of expense that may be occasioned by the adoption of the new system.

The result from these observations is, that the sources of additional expense from the establishment of the proposed constitution are much fewer than may have been imagined; that they are counterbalanced by considerable objects of saving; and that, while it is questionable on which side the scale will preponderate, it is certain that a government less expensive would be incompetent to the purposes of the union.

PUBLIUS.

THE FEDERALIST.

NUMBER LXXXV.

NEW YORK, AUGUST 15, 1788.

HAMILTON.

CONCLUSION.

ACCORDING to the formal division of the subject of these papers, announced in my first number, there would appear still to remain for discussion two points—"the analogy of the proposed government to your own state constitution," and "the additional security which its adoption will afford to republican government, to liberty, and to property." But these heads have been so fully anticipated, and so completely exhausted in the progress of the work, that it would now scarcely be possible to do any thing more than repeat, in a more dilated form, what has been already said; which the advanced stage of the question, and the time already spent upon it, conspire to forbid.

It is remarkable, that the resemblance of the plan of the convention to the act which organizes the government of this state holds, not less with regard to many of the supposed defects, than to the real excellencies of the former. Among the pretended defects, are the re-eligibility of the executive; the want of a council; the omission of a formal bill of rights; the omission of a provision respecting the liberty of the press: These, and several others, which have been noted in the course of our inquiries, are as much chargeable on the existing constitution of this state, as on the one proposed for the Union: and a man must have slender pretensions to consistency, who can rail at the latter for imperfections which he finds no difficulty in excusing in the former. Nor indeed can there be a better proof of the insincerity and affectation of some of the zealous adversaries of the plan of the convention, who profess to be devoted admirers of the government of this state, than the fury with which they have attacked that plan, for matters in regard to which our own constitution is equally, or perhaps more vulnerable.

The additional securities to republican government, to liberty, and to property, to be derived from the adoption of the plan, consist chiefly in the restraints which the preservation of the union will impose upon local factions and insurrections, and upon the ambition of powerful individuals in single states, who might acquire credit and influence enough, from leaders and favourites, to become the despots of the people; in the diminution of the opportunities to foreign intrigue, which the dissolution of the confederacy would invite and facilitate; in the prevention of extensive military establishments, which could not fail to grow out of wars between the states in a disunited situation; in the express guarantee of a republican form of government to each; in the absolute and universal exclusion of titles of nobility; and in the precautions against the repetition of those practices on the part of the state governments, which have undermined the foundations of property and credit; have planted mutual distrust in the breasts of all classes of citizens; and have occasioned an almost universal prostration of morals.

Thus have I, fellow citizens, executed the task I had assigned to myself; with what success your conduct must determine. I trust, at least, you will admit, that I have not failed in the assurance I gave you respecting the spirit with which my endeavours should be conducted. I have addressed myself purely to your judgments, and have studiously avoided those asperities which are too apt to disgrace political disputants of all parties, and which have been not a little provoked by the language and conduct of the opponents of the constitution. The charge of a conspiracy against the liberties of the people, which has been indiscriminately brought against the advocates of the plan, has something in it too wanton and too malignant not to excite the indignation of every man who feels in his own bosom a refutation of the calumny. The perpetual changes which have been rung upon the wealthy, the well-born, and the great, are such as to inspire the disgust of all sensible men. And the unwarrantable concealments and misrepresentations, which have been in various ways practised to keep the truth from the public eye, are of a nature to demand the reprobation of all honest men. It is possible that these circumstances may have occasionally betrayed me into intemperances of expression which I did not intend: It is certain that I have frequently felt a struggle between sensibility and moderation; and if the former has in some instances prevailed, it must be my excuse, that it has been neither often nor much.

Let us now pause, and ask ourselves whether, in the course of these papers, the proposed constitution has not been satisfactorily vindicated from the aspersions thrown upon it; and whether it has not been shown to be worthy of the public approbation, and necessary to the public safety and prosperity. Every man is bound to answer these questions to himself, according to the best of his conscience and understanding, and to act agreeably to the genuine and sober dictates of his judgment. This is a duty from which nothing can give him a dispensation. It is one that he is called upon, nay, constrained by all the obligations that form the bands of society, to discharge sincerely and honestly. No partial motive, no particular interest, no pride of opinion, no temporary passion or prejudice, will justify to himself, to his country, to his posterity, an improper election of the part he is to act. Let him beware of an obstinate adherence to party: Let him reflect, that the object upon which he is to decide is not a particular interest of the community, but the very existence of the nation: And let him remember, that a majority of America has already given its sanction to the plan which he is to approve or reject.

I shall not dissemble, that I feel an entire confidence in the arguments which recommend the proposed system to your adoption; and that I am unable to discern any real force in those by which it has been assailed. I am persuaded, that it is the best which our political situation, habits, and opinions will admit, and superior to any the revolution has produced.

Concessions on the part of the friends of the plan, that it has not a claim to absolute perfection, have afforded matter of no small triumph to its enemies. Why, say they, should we adopt an imperfect thing? Why not amend it, and make it perfect before it is irrevocably established? This may be plausible, but it is plausible only. In the first place I remark, that the extent of these concessions has been greatly exaggerated. They have been stated as amounting to an admission, that the plan is radically defective; and that, without material alterations, the rights and the interests of the community cannot be safely confided to it. This, as far as I have understood the meaning of those who make the concessions, is an entire perversion of their sense. No advocate of the measure can be found, who will not declare as his sentiment, that the system, though it may not be perfect in every part, is, upon the whole, a good one; is the best that the present views and circumstances of the country will permit; and is such an one as promises every species of security which a reasonable people can desire.

I answer in the next place, that I should esteem it the extreme of imprudence to prolong the precarious state of our national affairs, and to expose the union to the jeopardy of successive experiments, in the chimerical pursuit of a perfect plan. I never expect to see a perfect work from imperfect man. The result of the deliberations of all collective bodies, must necessarily be a compound as well of the errors and prejudices, as of the good sense and wisdom of the individuals of whom they are composed. The compacts which are to embrace thirteen distinct states, in a common bond of amity and union, must as necessarily be a compromise of as many dissimilar interests and inclinations. How can perfection spring from such materials?

The reasons assigned in an excellent little pamphlet lately published in this city,* unanswerably show the utter improbability of assembling a new convention, under circumstances in any degree so favourable to a happy issue, as those in which the late convention met, deliberated, and concluded. I will not repeat the arguments there used, as I presume the production itself has had an extensive circulation. It is certainly well worth the perusal of every friend to his country. There is however one point of light in which the subject of amendments still remains to be considered; and in which it has not yet been exhibited. I cannot resolve to conclude, without first taking a survey of it in this aspect.

It appears to me susceptible of complete demonstration, that it will be far more easy to obtain subsequent than previous amendments to the constitution. The moment an alteration is made in the present plan, it becomes, to the purpose of adoption, a new one, and must undergo a new decision of each state. To its complete establishment throughout the union, it will therefore require the concurrence of thirteen states. If, on the contrary, the constitution should once be ratified by all the states as it stands, alterations in it may at any time be effected by nine states. In this view alone the chances are as thirteen to nine† in favour of subsequent amendments, rather than of the original adoption of an entire system.

This is not all. Every constitution for the United States must inevitably consist of a great variety of particulars, in which thirteen independent states are to be accomodated in their interests or opinions of interest. We may of course expect to see, in any body of men charged with its original formation, very different

* Entitled "An Address to the people of the state of New-York."

† It may rather be said TEN, for though two-thirds may set on foot the measure, three-fourths must ratify.

combinations of the parts upon different ferent points. Many of those who form the majority on one question, may become the minority on a second, and an association dissimilar to either, may constitute the majority on a third. Hence the necessity of moulding and arranging all the particulars which are to compose the whole, in such a manner, as to satisfy all the parties to the compact; and hence also an immense multiplication of difficulties and casualties in obtaining the collective assent to a final act. The degree of that multiplication must evidently be in a ratio to the number of particulars and the number of parties.

But every amendment to the constitution, if once established, would be a single proposition, and might be brought forward singly. There would then be no necessity for management or compromise, in relation to any other point; no giving nor taking. The will of the requisite number, would at once bring the matter to a decisive issue. And consequently whenever nine,* or rather ten states, were united in the desire of a particular amendment, that amendment must infallibly prevail. There can, therefore, be no comparison between the facility of effecting an amendment, and that of establishing in the first instance a complete constitution.

In opposition to the probability of subsequent amendments it has been urged, that the persons delegated to the administration of the national government, will always be disinclined to yield up any portion of the authority of which they were once possessed. For my own part, I acknowledge a thorough conviction that any amendments which may, upon mature consideration, be thought useful, will be applicable to the organization of the government, not to the mass of its powers; and on this account alone, I think there is no weight in the observation just stated. I also think there is little force in it on another account. The intrinsic difficulty of governing THIRTEEN STATES, independent of calculations upon an ordinary degree of public spirit and integrity, will, in my opinion, constantly *impose* on the national

* See note in the preceding page.

rulers, the *necessity* of a spirit of accommodation to the reasonable expectations of their constituents. But there is yet a further consideration, which proves beyond the possibility of doubt, that the observation is futile. It is this, that the national rulers, whenever nine states concur, will have no option upon the subject. By the fifth article of the plan the congress will be *obliged*, "on the application of the legislatures of two-thirds of the states, (which at present amount to nine) to call a convention for proposing amendments, which *shall be valid* to all intents and purposes, as part of the constitution, when ratified by the legislatures of three-fourths of the states, or by conventions in three-fourths thereof." The words of this article are peremptory. The congress "*shall* call a convention." Nothing in this particular is left to discretion. Of consequence all the declamation about the disinclination to a change, vanishes in air. Nor, however difficult it may be supposed to unite two-thirds, or three-fourths of the state legislatures, in amendments which may affect local interests, can there be any room to apprehend any such difficulty in a union on points which are merely relative to the general liberty or security of the people. We may safely rely on the disposition of the state legislatures to erect barriers against the encroachments of the national authority.

If the foregoing argument be a fallacy, certain it is that I am myself deceived by it; for it is, in my conception, one of those rare instances in which a political truth can be brought to the test of mathematical demonstration. Those who see the matter in the same light, however zealous they may be for amendments, must agree in the propriety of a previous adoption, as the most direct road to their object.

The zeal for attempts to amend, prior to the establishment of the constitution, must abate in every man, who is ready to accede to the truth of the following observations of a writer, equally solid and ingenious: "To balance a large state or society (says he) whether monarchical or republican, on general laws, is a work of so great difficulty, that no human genius, however comprehensive, is able by the mere dint of reason and reflection, to effect it. The judgments of many must unite in the work: EXPERIENCE must guide their labour: TIME must bring it to perfection: And the FEELING of inconveniences must correct the mistakes which they *inevitably* fall into, in their first trials and experiments."* These judicious reflections contain a lesson of moderation to all the sincere lovers of the union, and ought to put them upon their guard against hazarding anarchy, civil war, a perpetual alienation of the states from each other, and perhaps the military despotism of a victorious demagogue, in the pursuit of what they are not likely to obtain, but from TIME and EXPERIENCE. It may be in me a defect of political fortitude, but I acknowledge that I cannot entertain an equal tranquillity with those who affect to treat the dangers of a longer continuance in our present situation as imaginary. A NATION without a NATIONAL GOVERNMENT, is an awful spectacle. The establishment of a constitution, in time of profound peace, by the voluntary consent of a whole people, is a PRODIGY, to the completion of which I look forward with trembling anxiety. In so arduous an enterprise, I can reconcile it to no rules of prudence to let go the hold we now have, upon seven out of the thirteen states; and after having passed over so considerable a part of the ground, to re-commence the course. I dread the more the consequences of new attempts, because I KNOW that POWERFUL INDIVIDUALS, in this and in other states, are enemies to a general national government in every possible shape.

PUBLIUS.

* Hume's Essays, vol. 1, page 128.—The rise of arts and sciences.

COLLATED TEXTS.

The TEXT in the copies as *revised* and *corrected* by Hamilton and Madison collated with a reprint, purporting to be from the Essays as printed when first issued, in the Gazettes. The first quoted passages are from the *revised copies*, being *substitutes* for the quoted passages in the *Reprint*.

No. I. Page 49. For; After *full* experience—after an *unequivocal* experience. For; *existing* Federal Government—*subsisting* Federal Government. For; to decide by their conduct and example—by their conduct and example to decide. For; *period, aera.* For; this idea by *adding*, willadd. For; will heighten, to heighten. Page 50. For; *uninfluenced by considerations foreign* to the public good—*unperplexed* and *unbiassed* by *considerations not connected with* the public good. For; but this *is more ardently to be wished for*—but this is *a thing* more ardently to be wished. For; *extraneous—foreign.* For; I am aware—I am *well* aware. For; "into interested or ambitious views, merely because their situations might subject them to suspicion," sentence transposed. For; *which has already shown itself,* or *that* may—*which has made its appearance,* or *may.* For; would always furnish—would furnish. For; *however well persuaded of being in the right*—to those, *who are ever so much persuaded of their being in the right, in any controversy.* Page 51. For; are *actuated*—are *influenced.* For; And yet *just as these sentiments must appear to candid men*—And yet *however just these sentiments will be allowed to be.* For; fond of power— fond of *despotic* power. Page 52. For; appearances—appearance. For; *it has been my aim,* Fellow Citizens, to put you—*I have had an eye, my* Fellow Citizens, *to putting* you. Page 53. For; claim *to attention*—claim *to your* attention, For; *its* open avowal—*an open avowal of it.* For; of the Constitution—of the *new* Constitution. For; *It may therefore be essential to examine particularly—It will. therefore be of use to begin by examining the.* For; *This shall accordingly be done*—This shall accordingly constitute the subject of my next address.

No. II. Page 54. For; When the people of America reflect that the question now submitted to their determination, is one of the most important that has engaged, or can well engage their attention, the propriety of their taking a very comprehensive, as well as a very serious view of it, must be evident—When the people of America reflect that they are now called upon to decide a question, which in its consequences must prove one of the most important that ever engaged their attention, the propriety of their taking a very comprehensive, as well as a very serious view of it, will be evident. For; *than that, or* that. Page 56. For; many of *them*—many of their *citizens.* For; tried the *souls* of men—tried the *minds* and *hearts* of men. Page 57. For; *passion—passions.* For; *But as has been already remarked*—But *this (as was remarked in the foregoing number of this paper.)* For; *from* the undue—*or* the undue. For; the great majority reasoned—the great majority of *the people* reasoned. For; such *measures only—only* such measures—omitted—after, great and weighty reasons—which I shall endeavor to develop and explain in some ensuing papers.

No. III. Page 60. For; *any* erroneous—*an* erroneous. For; as against dangers arising from domestic causes—as from dangers of the *like kind* arising from domestic causes. Page 61. For; or *may* happen—or *will* happen. For; has the additional circumstance, has in addition, the circumstance omitted after, "distinct confederacies"—for this opinion various reasons may be assigned. For; *When* once—*Because* when once. For; town or *county*—town or *country.* Page 62. For; *to the other* nations—to other nations. For; to *ourselves*—to *us.* For; Under the national—Because, under the national. For; *The* prospect—*Because* the prospect. For tempta*tions*—tempta*tion.* For; *If even—Because even if.* Page 63. For; such violences—*Because* such violences. For; *occasioned—caused.* For; *produced—occasioned.* For; irritation*s*—irritation. For; in *a* capacity to act *with circumspection—in* capacity to *act advisedly.*

No. IV. Page 65. For; proposed Confederacies—proposed *little* Confederacies. Page 66. For; not *sanctioned*—not *sanctified.* For; *most* prevalent—*more* prevalent. For; see *these* flourish *in our hands*—see *it* flourish. Page 67. For; *like* considerations—*such* like considerations. Page 68. For; will, in a manner—will, as it were. For; and if we are wise, the time may come—and the time may come, if we are wise. Page 69. For; which of the *associates*—which of *them*. For; combining—and combining. For; *than* to provoke—*than* provoke.

No. V. Page 73. For; not very *far* distant—not *very* distant. For; reasons—reason. Page 74. For; in which we should be formidable only to each other—formidable only to each other. For; those *persons*—those *Gentlemen*. For; and *which* would—*and would*. For; would have to regulate its commerce with foreigners—would have its commerce with foreigners to regulate. Page 75 For; character—characters.

No. VI. Page 76. For; this *work*—this *Paper*. Sentence beginning: "If these States should either be wholly disunited," transposed. Page 79. For; *We may ask*—*Is it not*, we may ask. For: acquisi*tion*—acquisi*tions*. For; and that they are of course liable—*and are* of course liable. Page 80. For; and *even* to—and *to*. For; *that* haughty—*this* haughty. For; Yet few nations have been more—Few nations, nevertheless, have been more. Omitted on Page 81, and sometimes even the more culpable desire of sharing in the commerce of other nations, without their consent. The last war but two between Britain and Spain sprang from the attempts of the English merchants, to prosecute an illicit trade with the Spanish main. These unjustifiable practices on their part, produced severities on the part of the Spaniards, towards the subjects of Great Britain which were not more justifiable; because they exceeded the bounds of a just retaliation, and were chargeable with inhumanity and cruelty. Many of the English who were taken on the Spanish coasts, were sent to dig in the mines of Potosi; and by the usual progress of a spirit of resentment, the innocent were after a while confounded with the guilty in indiscriminate punishment. The complaints of the merchants kindled a violent flame throughout the nation, which soon after broke out in the House of Commons, and was communicated from that body to the Ministry. Letters of reprisal were granted and a war ensued; which in its consequences overthrew all the alliances that but twenty years before had been formed with sanguine expectations of the most beneficial fruits. For; and *the* evils—*and evils*. Page 82. For; CONFEDERATE—CONFEDERATIVE.

No. VII. Page 83. For; the States could have—could the States have. For; difference—differences. Page 84. For; *by* the treaty of peace—*in* the treaty of peace. For; the *States which have made cessions*—the States which made the *cession*. Page 85. For; the lands—the land. For; another—and the other. Page 88. For; would be exposed—would be *hazarded*. For; *in the* experiment—*upon* experiment. For; Their refusal would afford to the complaining States a pretext for withholding—Their refusal would be too plausible a pretext to the complaining States to withhold. Note in reprint omitted to Page 89.

No. VIII. Page 92. For; establishment—establishments. For; *thence*—*therefore*. In note; *rational* precaution—*natural* precaution. For; *This inference*, from the very *form* of the proposition is *at best* problematical and uncertain—Their existence, however, from the *very terms* of the proposition is, at *most* problematical and uncertain. Page 92 For; they would be *obliged*—they would be *necessitated*. Page 93. For; be likely—be the *more* likely. For; *deduced from speculative*—*drawn from supposed or speculative*. For; by way of objection—by way of objection *to this*. Page 93. For; *which by its situation* is seldom exposed to invasions—*seldom exposed by its situation to internal invasions*. Page 94. For; Forbids competition with the natural strength—renders the natural strength of the community an overmatch for it. For; *though it may*—may. For; will be utterly incompetent to the purpose of enforcing—*but it will be unable to enforce*. Next sentence transposed. For; *his* services—*their* services. Omitted; There has been, for a long time past little room for the operation of the other causes, which have been enumerated as the consequences of internal war. *Note* omitted. Page 95. *Note* omitted. For; *If Britain had*,—If on *the contrary*, Britain had. For; at this day *be*—*be* at this day. For; *the* kingdom—*that* kingdom. For; *nor* futile—*or* futile. For; *on its vast* importance—*on the* importance of this interesting idea. Page 96. For; that *now* flit—*that flit*. For; would *then* quickly—would quickly. For; *prospects*—*forms*.

No. IX. Page 97. For; kept perpetually vibrating—kept in a state of perpetual vibration. Page 98. For; *error*—*errors*. For; friends *of* liberty—friends *to* liberty. Page 99. For; *receive* his ideas—*take* his ideas. Note to page 100. *Publius* omitted. Page 101. For; to *produce*—to *make*. Page 103. For; *writer*—*civilian*.

No. X. Page 105. For; a less folly—less folly. Page 107. For; of government—of the government. Page 109. For; *from* the mischiefs of faction—*for* the mischiefs of faction. Page 111. For: Does *this* advantage—Does *the* advantage.

No. XI. Page 113. For; look forward with painful solicitude—look forward to what this country is capable of becoming with painful solicitude. Page 114. For; this would answer *then* the—for, answer *the*. For; the wings *on*—the wings *by* which. For; we may in a variety of ways counteract—we may counteract a policy so unfriendly to our prosperity in a variety of ways. For; importance *to any manufacturing nation* of the markets of—importance of the markets of. For; to remain in this disposition—to remain so, to any manfacturing nation. Page 115. For: to *Great* Britain—*Britain*. Page 116. For; *a* flourishing—*and* a flourishing. Page 117. For; the *Lakes*—the *Western* Lakes. Page 118. For; and the conduciveness of that species of commerce to the prosperity of a navy, are points too manifest to require a particular elucidation—does not require a particular elucidation, no more than the conduciveness of that species of commerce to the prosperity of a navy. Page 119. For; newspaper discussion—*a* newspaper discussion.

No. XII. Page 121. For; *A prosperous commerce*—the *prosperity of commerce*. For; *all* the channels—the channels. For; to the *entire* satisfaction—*to the* satisfaction. Page 123. For; *illy* brook—*ill* brook. For; be the *best*—be best. Page 124. For; be driven—be *necessitated*. For; dealers in *contraband*—contraband *trade*. Page 124. For; this *proves*—this *shows*. For; and *shows*—and *places*. Page 125. For; to *expose*—to *hazard*. For; stationed *and employed*, might—stationed *at the entrances of our ports*. For; *an adjoining* State—a *neighboring* State. For; in Britain the proportion is still greater—in Britain they exceed this proportion.* *Note* omitted. If my memory be right they amount to twenty per cent. Page 126. For; *according to the* ratio—*Upon a* ratio. For; may, at a low computation be estimated at—may be estimated at. For; health of society—health of *the* society. For; *as this very article—as these spirits.* For; *revenue—revenues.* For; as before remarked—*as has been* before remarked. For; populous—popular. For; in some mode—in some mode or other. Page 127. For; of citizens—of *the* citizens.

No. XIII. Page 128. If the States be united—*are* united. For; another *conjecture*—another *supposition.*

No. XIV. Page 131. For; *errour—error.* Page 132. For; *must be* confined—*will be* confined. Page 135. For; *errour—error.* For; *scenes—scene.*

No. XV. Page 139. For; which is *neither* controverted, *nor* doubted—which is *not* either controverted *or* doubted. For; *in the* opinion—in *this sentiment* at least. For; of the reality *of many* of those defects—of the reality of those defects. For; *people—nation.* Page 141. For; the *very elements*—the *first principles.* For; of *whom—of* which. Page 142. For; *a* Government—Government. Page 143. For; still adhere—still *will* adhere. For; their observance—*the* observance. Page 144. For; *which* disposes—*that* disposes. Page 145. For; of *man*—of *human nature.*

No. XVI. Page 148. For; between *different* parts—*between parts.* For; to the *general*—to the *common.* Page 149. For; to the majority that happened to prevail in the national council for the exercise of factious views, of partiality, and of oppression—for the exercise of factions views, of partiality, and of oppression, in the majority that happened to prevail in the national council. Page 150. For; attributed—*which is* attributed. For; the *other*—the other *half.*

No. XVII. Page 153. For; be urged—be *likewise* urged. Page 154. For; to exercise *them*—exercise *those powers.* Page 155. For; to impress upon—to *impressing* upon. Page 157. For; *depositories—Deposits.*

No. XVIII. Page. 158. For; from the best transmitted accounts—from the best accounts *transmitted.* Page 159. For; the *weakest*—the *weaker.* Page 160. For; had in fact become—had become, in fact. For: who secretly—who *had* secretly. Page 161. For; that the monuments which remain of this curious political fabric are so imperfect—that such imperfect monuments remain of this curious political fabric. Page 163. For; *Cleomenes—Cleomens.*

No. XIX. Page 167. For; revenues—revenue. For; farther—*further.* Page 170. For; sprang—sprung. Page 171. For; *as* the head—*at* the head.

No. XX. Page 173. For; *an* hereditary—*a* hereditary. For; *his* independent—*this* independent. For; *audience—audiences.* Page 176. For; *in some measure*—in some *degree.* For; *operation—tendency* of these vices. Page 177. For; in *the* place—in place.

No. XXI. Page 178. For; which depict—which *have* depicted. For; the *existing* Confederation—the *subsisting* Confederation. For; no power—no powers. For; constitutional *means*—constitutional *mode.* Page 179. For; The want of such a right involves no doubt a striking absurdity—There is, doubtless, a striking absurdity in supposing that a right of this kind does not exist. For; supposing that deficiency—of embracing that supposition. For; considerations of utility—consideration of utility. Page 180. For; *directed* against—*levelled* against. Page 181. For; *produce* and *constitute national* wealth—produce *constitutional* wealth. For; the *contracted territory* of that republic—*that contracted district.* For; *those kingdoms*—the *three last mentioned countries.* For; no man acquainted—no man who is acquainted. Page 182. For; which *distributed*—which distributes. Page 183. For; *are* considered—*have been* considered. For; *an* Herculean—*a* Herculean. For; *the thing—things.*

No. XXII. Page 184. For; of the existing federal system enumerated in the last number—*already enumerated* in the existing Federal system. Page 184. For; conceding on their part privileges of importance—by which they conceded privileges of any importance to them. Page 187. For; ever will be able—will ever be able. For; Considering how peculiarly the safety and welfare of the smaller states depend on Union—The smaller States, considering how peculiarly their safety and welfare depend on Union. Page 188. For; VETO—VOTE. Page 189. For; *fortunate—happy.* Page 189. For; that which it is necessary to do—the doing what may be necessary. Page 190. For; *that the* interest—*the* interest. For; and *his* intrigues—*and* intrigues. For; corrupt a *smaller*—corrupt a smaller *number.* For; minds *actuated* by—minds *animated* and *guided* by. Page 191. For; *disclosed—delineated.* For; the *rival* parties—*the* parties. For; one *tribunal*—one *court.* Page 192. For; *an* uniform—*a* uniform. For; *decision—jurisdiction.* For; *should* happen—*was to* happen. For; from the deference with which men in office naturally look up to that authority to which they owe their official existence—nothing is more natural to men in office than to look with peculiar deference towards that authority. For; of which *these are* composed—of which *it is* composed. For; a *considerable* part—a *great* part. For; who are either free from erroneous prepossessions or can divest themselves of them—who can divest themselves of the prepossessions of preconceived opinions. Page 193. For; of Union—of *the* Union.

No. XXIII. Page 196. For; *and* the correspondent—*or* the correspondent. For; open *to* discussion—open *for* discussion. Page 197. For; THOSE *which may be* committed—*the objects* committed. Page 198. For; *achieved—accomplished.* For; *in respect to*—*as* to all. Page 199. For; *intrusted* with—*trusted* with. For; *would have given a better impression of their candour* if they had confined themselves to showing—*ought to have* confined themselves to showing. For; National concerns—National interests. Page 200. For; *is* susceptible of—*can be* susceptible of. For; If we embrace as *the standard of our political creed* the tenets of those—If we embrace the tenets of those who oppose the adoption of the proposed Constitution, as the standard of our political creed.

No. XXIV. Page 201. For; *which is* that proper—*which, if I understand it right, is this,* that proper. Page 202. For; against *military establishments*—against the *keeping up of troops.* Note, Page 203. For; other States, and their Constitutions—other States, *except the foregoing,* and their Constitutions. For; *pronouncing these clamours to be the—regarding these clamors as* the. Page 204. For; *obscured—entangled.* For; establishments would be improper—establishments *in time of peace.* would be improper. Page 205. For; only be *to guard* against—*only be against.* For; The militia, *in times of profound peace,* would not long—The militia would not long, etc., *in times of profound peace.*

No. XXV. Page 207. For; provided by the—provided *for*, by the. Page 208. For; If *from* the resources—*If the* resources. For; least likely *to be so*—least likely *to be jealous*. Page 209. For; There are other *views*—There are other *lights*. Page 210. For; The utility of a provision of this kind can only be *vindicated* on the *hypothesis of a* probability, at least—The *supposed* utility of a provision of this kind can only be *founded on the supposed probability or* at least. For; would at all times *be*—would *be* at all times. Page 212. For; how unequal *are* parchment provisions—how unequal parchment provisions *are*.

No. XXVI. Page 213. For; hardly *to have been* expected—hardly *to be* expected. For; they *wisely judged*—*wisely judging*. Page 214. For; nation from *which*—nation from *whom*. Page 216. For; *Without the consent of* the *Legislature* (in *italics*) instead of *capitals*. For; *monitory—cautionary*. For; *the actual*—the *necessities*. Page 218 For; transmitted through—transmitted *along* through. For; *parted with*—parted with *out of their own hands*. For; From the votes—from the acts. Page 219. For; *principle—principles*.

No. XXVII. Page 220. For; and *their* obedience to—and *obedience to*. Page 221. For; the principal of which are—the principal of which *reasons* are. For; *who* are select—*which* are select. For; more *comprehensive* information—more *extensive* information. For; public *deliberations*—public *councils*. For; *will occur* to fortify that probability—to fortify that probability will occur. For; a more *critical* eye—a more *critic* eye. Page 222. For; equal to—a match for. For; I will in the first place—I will, *in this* place. For; will have *but a transient* influence—*will generally have but little* influence. Page 223. For; than *the* species—than that species. For; will perceive, that if its powers are administered with a common share of prudence there is good ground—will perceive, that is there good ground to calculate upon a regular and peaceable execution of the laws of the Union, if its powers are administered with a common share of prudence.

No. XXVIII. Page 225. For; *under the necessity* of—be *necessitated* to. For; will sometimes *exist*—will sometimes *arise*. Page 226. For; *suppressing—repressing*. Page 227. For; or as many unconnected governments as there are states—or even if there should be an entire separation of the states. For; and after all *the* only—and after all, only. For: an infinitely—infinitely. Page 229. For: foreign *enemy*—foreign *power*.

No. XXIX. Page 230. According to Reprint, No. 35. Page 231. For; to *this* plan—to *the plan of the Convention*. For; in the same body ought, as far as possible to take away the inducement and the pretext—in the body to whose care the protection of the State is committed, ought, etc. For; for requiring the aid of the POSSE COMITATUS—for calling out the POSSE COMITATUS. Page 232. For; *extraordinary* manner—*this* manner. For; Federal Legislature on the subject—Federal Legislature *from this State* on the subject. For; *nor a week nor even a month—or even a week*. Page 233 For; short of a million of pounds—short of the whole expense of the civil establishments of all the States. For; moderate *size*—moderate *extent*. Page 235. For; *irritated at being required to undertake*—irritated *by being called upon to undertake*. For; and *make* them—and to make them. Page 236. For; *violences—violence*. *(Last paragraph in Reprint omitted in Page 236.)*

No. XXX. Page 237. For; supply *of revenue*—supply *of it*. Page 239. For; *abundantly—amply*. Page 240. For; *an* invincible—*invincible*. Page 241. For; *import duties—impost* duties. Page 242. For; *creating by its own authority new funds from new objects—creating new funds upon new objects of taxation, by its own authority*. For; to see the *halcyon scenes of the poetic or fabulous age realized in America—to see realized in America*, etc.

No. XXXI. Page 243. For; *are such direct*—are *yet* such direct. Page 246. For; to *escape from the apparitions which itself has raised—to extricate itself from the perplexities into which it has so rashly adventured*. Page 247. For; nature *and* extent—nature *or* extent.

No. XXXII. Page 249. For; consequences to the State Governments which seem to be apprehended—consequences which seem to be apprehended to the State Governments. Page 251. For; *is deducible—is to be deduced*. Page 252. For; why was it not left—*why not leave it*. For; that a further—that *thus* a further. For; State system—State systems. Page 253. For; is not *only* a—is *not a*.

No. XXXIII. Page 254. For; The residue of the argument against the provisions of the Constitution in respect to taxation is ingrafted upon the following clauses. (This paragraph omitted in Reprint.) For; first Article authorizes—the first Article of the plan under consideration authorizes. For; *sources—source*. Page 255. For; a test of the true nature—a test by which to judge of the true nature. Page 256. For; if there *be*—if there *is*. Page 257. For; *the* Constitution—its Constitution. Page 258. For; *abrogating—for* abrogating. For; of *a* power—of power. Page 258. For; of state—of *the* State.

No. XXXIV. Page 259. For; to develope—to advert. Page 260. For; TRIBUTIA—TRIBUTA. Page 260. For; *pinacle*—utmost *height*. Page 261. For; If we must be obliged to exceed this point—If, on the contrary, we ought to exceed this point. Page 262. For; would *already*—would *so soon*. For; *would be* to calculate—*is to* calculate. For; which *relate*—which *are relative*. For; *Judiciary—Judicial*. Page 263. For; But let us *take a view*—But let us *advert*. For; expenditure—expenditures. For; a *million of dollars—two hundred thousand pounds*. For; If it cannot be denied to be a just principle, that in framing a constitution of government for a nation, we ought—In framing a Government for posterity as well as ourselves, we ought. Page 264. For; ourattention—If this principle be a just one, our attention. For; one million of dollars—two hundred thousand pounds. Page 264. For; *twentieth of its—twentieth part*.

No. XXXV. Page 266. For; that this can never be the case—that they can never be carried to too great a length. For; *serve to beget—would beget*. Page 267. For; *most* natural—*more* natural. Page 268. For; and from a greater disproportion between her population and territory is less likely than some other states speedily to become in any considerable degree—and is not likely speedily to be, to any great extent. Page 268. For; *might beget—would beget*. Page 269. For; habits *of* life—habits *in* life. Page 270. For; *thousands* of acres—*millions* of acres Page 271. For; *among* between. For; *community—society*.

No. XXXVI. Page 275. For; *law—laws*. Page 277. For; *should be judged beforehand upon mature consideration, or should be discovered on experiment—should be discovered.* For; may forbear—may *then* forbear. Page 277. For; the first is, that the actual exercise of the power, may be found both convenient and necessary—the first is, that the exercise of that power, if convenient, will be preferable, because it will be more effectual. Page 279. For; if by the authority of the Federal government then it will not remain to be done—if *to be done* by the authority of the Federal government, it will not be to be done.

No XXXVII. Page 284. For; this foundation—this *first* foundation. For; dangers—danger. Page 285. For; energy *of* Government—energy *in* Government. Page 286. For; the statue law— *and* the statute law. Page 287. For; *conceived—considered.* Page 289. For; degra*ding*—degraded.

No. XXXVIII. Page 296. For; *scarcely—scarce.*

No. XXXIX. Page 303. For; *explicit* provision—*constitutional* provision. Page 306. For; *is by the adversaries of the plan of the Convention,* supposed to consist in this—*is supposed to consist in this.* For; But, the operation of the Government on the people in their individual capacities, in its ordinary and most essential proceedings, will, on the whole, in the sense of its opponents, designate it in this relation, a National Government—So far the National countenance of the Government on this side, seems to be disfigured by a few Federal features. But this blemish is perhaps unavoidable in any plan, and the operation of the Government on the People, in their individual capacities, in its ordinary and most essential proceedings, may, on the whole, designate it, in this relation, a *National* Government. Page 308. For; therefore, even when tested by the rules laid down by its antagonists, is in strictness—*therefore is, in strictness.*

No. XL. Page 314. For; confirmation *of all the States*—confirmation of the *Legislatures* of all the States. For; to be confirmed—to be confirmed by the *People.*

No. XLI. Page 319. For; field *of* rhetoric—field *for* rhetoric. Page 320. For; *war—War.* For; means and danger—and *the* danger. Page 321. For; *mistress—the* mistress. Page 324. For; *If* they have—*and* if they have. Page 325. For; may *be* almost—*may almost be.* For; *objects— object.*

No. XLII. Page 331. For; no farther—no *further.*

No. XLIII. Page 347. For; founded *on acts*—founded on *ordinary* acts.

No. XLIV. Page 352. For; *neat* produce—*net* produce. Page 352. Omitted in Reprint after, the Government of the United States, *or in any department or officer thereof.* For; yet on a fair investigation of it *as has been elsewhere shown,* no part can appear—yet on a fair investigation *of it,* no part can appear. Page 356. For; distinct*ions—distinction.*

No. XLV. Page 362. For; would not *bear* a comparison—would not *be* a comparison.

No. XLVI. Page 365. For; *instituted* with different powers—*constituted* with different powers. Page 367. For; *and* faculty—and *the* faculty. For; members of *the* Congress—members of Congress.

No. XLVII. Page 380. For; prerogative of pardoning—prerogative of *pardon.* ditto—below.

No. XLVIII. Page 384. Omitted after, multiplied without end. *I might find a witness in every citizen who has shared in, or been attentive to, the course of public administrations.*

No. XLIX. Page 392. For; parties preëxisting—preëxisting parties.

No. L. Page 400. For; which place *it* in—which place *that system* in. Page 402. For; powerful factions be gradually—powerful factions *or parties* be gradually. For; within a *practicable* sphere—within a practical sphere.

No. LI. Page 404. For; *Subject* to these—*Under* these. Page 405. For; *being but imperfectly*— being *at most but very.* Page 406. For; with *some* other—with *the* other. Page 407. For; proof— proofs.

No. LIII. Page 409. For; the *case*—the *instance.* Page 412. For; other *points*—other respects. Page 413—For; *some* internal—*many* internal. Page 414. For; particular *subjects*—particular *branches.* Page 415. For; *liberties—liberty.*

No. LIV. Page 416. For; *among—to.* Page 417. For; will of *his* owner—will of *another.* Page 418. For; *disputed—denied.*

No. LVI. Page 430. For; *be sufficient*—be *very* sufficient. For; *into—in.* Page 431. For; With regard to the regulation of the militia, there are scarcely any circumstances in reference to which local knowledge can be said to be necessary. The general face of the country, whether mountainous or level, most fit for the operations of infantry or cavalry, is almost the only consideration of this nature that can occur. The art of war teaches general principles of organization, movement, ???aud discipline, which apply universally—The observations made on the subject of taxation, apply with greater force to the case of the militia. For, however different the rules of discipline may be in different States, they are the same throughout each particular State; and depend on circumstances which can differ but little in different parts of the same State. Page 432. For; *tendency—effect.*

No. LVII. Page 435. For; sons of *obscure* and unpropitious fortune—sons of obscurity and unpropitious fortune. Page 436. For; *their* favor—*the* favor. Page 437. For; *men—man.* Page 438. For; hundred—*hundreds.* Page 438. For; unless he *possesses*—unless he *possess.*

No. LVIII. Page 441. For; which it *beholds*—which *is beheld.* Page 443. For; the greater number—the greater number *of members.*

No. LIX. Page 449. For; *regard* a departure—regard and *regret* a departure. For; *have been applicable*—have been *always* applicable. For; *organized—modified* and *disposed.* Page 451. For; without any motive to recommend their admission into the system, equally cogent with that which must have regulated the conduct of the convention, in respect to the formation of the Senate—without any motive equally cogent with that which must have regulated the conduct of the Convention in respect to the formation of the Senate, to recommend their admission into the system.

No. LX. Page 454. For; incontrollable—uncontrollable. For; what *are* the *dangers*—what *would be the danger.* For; and on the other *hand*—and on the *other.* Page 455. For; *assimilation of temper and sentiment*—*in some of these respects.* For; victorious majority—victorious and overbearing. Page 457. For; *the first—agriculture.* For; *the latter—commerce.* For; But *as* in reality—For; *in* reality. But *or—as.* For; *which may produce an endeavor—dispose to eudeavor.* Page 459. For; *and the cities*—or cities. For *another occasion—other occasions.*

No. LXI. Page 461. For; The more candid opposers of the provision, contained in the plan of the Convention *respecting Elections* when pressed in argument will sometimes concede the propriety of *it;* with this qualification, however, that it ought to have been accompanied with a declaration, that all elections should be *held* in the counties where the electors *reside*—The more candid opposers of the provision *respecting elections,* contained in the plan of the Convention, when pressed in argument, will sometimes concede the propriety of *that provision;* with this qualification, however, that it ought to have been accompanied with a declaration, that all elections should be *had* in the counties where the electors *resided.* Page 462. For; that which is proposed—*the latitude* which is proposed. For; *counties—county.* Page 464. For; which will *accrue*—which will *result.*

No. LXII. Page 466. For; *under—into.* Page 467. For; *merit—merits.* Page 469. For; *the* Senate—*a* Senate. Page 470. For; *in the* American Governments—in American Governments.

No. LXIII. Page 475. For; *The* remark—*This* remark. Page 476. For; *plans—places.* For; difficult *at any rate* to preserve—difficult to preserve. Page 478. For; *their* Representatives—the Representatives of the people. Page 479. For; *them*—the *People.* Page 480. For; *the Legislatures*—the *State* Legislatures. Page 482. For; *This* fact—*The* fact.

No. LXIV. Page 484. For; *the Elections*—the *Electors.* Page 486. For; *The* matters—*Those* matters. For; *the main objects*—the *objects of the negotiation.* Page 487. For; *law—laws.* Page 488. For; *that the two thirds*—that two-thirds. Page 489. For; But if such a case should ever happen—But in such a case, if it should ever happen.

No. LXV. Page 495. For; should in this respect be thought preferable to the plan—should be thought preferable to the plan in this respect.

No. LXVI. Page 496. For; with *not* less reason—with *no* less reason. Page 497. For; that of *determining*—that of *deciding.* Page 498. For; for *estimating*—for *determining.* For; *danger—dread.* For; *of* office—in office. Page 499. For; *they have*—they *will* have. For; *may have* proved—*shall* have proved. Page 500. For; *argument—arguments.* For; the choice *he may have made*—the choice *of the President.* Page 501. For; *a greater* show—with greater show.

No. LXVII. Page 503. For; the arrangement of which could have been attended with greater difficulty—which could have been attended with grater difficulty in the arrangement of it than this. Page 504. For; attempts extravagant—attempts *so* extravagant. For; in order to ascertain—in order *as well* to ascertain. Page 506. For; is *confided*—is confined. Page 507. For; *the plan*—the *Constitution.* For; to *indulge a severity*—to *allow myself in a severity.*

No. LXVIII. Page 509. For; *so complicated an investigation,* such *complicated investigations.* Omitted—*as the President of the United States.* For; *on preexisting*—on *any* preëxisting. Page 510. For; *already noticed*—already taken notice of. For; that *each State*—the *People* of each State. Page 511. For; *This* process—*The* process. For; *of* a—*in* a.

No. LXIX. Page 514. For; *is not to become a law unless*—is to *become a law if.* Page 516 (in note.) For; prerogatives—prerogative.

No. LXX. Page 523. For; are, unity, duration, an adequate provision for its support; competent powers—are, first, unity; secondly duration; thirdly, an adequate provision for its support; fourthly, competent powers. Page 524. For; *from the plurality—from the circumstance of the plurality.* Page 525. For; *embroiled the Republic*—embroiled the *peace* of the Republic. For; *into violent*—into the *most* violent. Page 527. For; *men—man.* For; *as to render them*—as to *render him.* Page 528. For; *a collusion—collusion.* For; *so manifestly improper*—so *unqualified.*

No. LXXI. Page 532. For; the *Chief* Magistrate—the *Executive* Magistrate. For; title *durable* or *certain—durable* or *certain* title. Page 535. For; already *mentioned*—already *remarked.* For; *circumstance—consideration.* Page 536. For; *an* annihilation—*annihilation.* For; He might, then, *with prudence, hazard—hazard with safety*—For; it is not *long enough—not enough.*

No. LXXII. Page 538. For; *the thing*—the *subject.* Page 539. For; to undo—to reverse and undo. For; to give the officer—to give *to* the officer. Page 540. For; make interest—make *their* interest. For; *advantages—emoluments.* For; *use of his opportunities while they lasted*—use of *the opportunity he enjoyed while it lasted.* For; *emoluments—perquisites.* Page 541. For; *finding himself—when he found himself.* For; *looking—when he looked.* For; *reflecting—reflected.* (*Omitted—such a man, in such a situation.*) Page 542. For; By inducing the necessity of—By *necessitating* a change. For; partial *one*—partial *exclusion.* Page 543. For; *the evils—these disadvantages.* For; *especially* if—*If.*

LXXIII. Page 546. For; *is* competent—are competent. For; *which will* have—*to have* the effect. Page 547. For; *has been already* more than once *suggested*—has been already *suggested and repeated.* For; *or* wisdom—*and* wisdom. Page 548. For; the secondary—the secondary *one.* Page 549. For; and that in its exercise there would oftener be room for a*charge* of timidity than of rashness—and there would oftener be room for a charge of timidity than of rashness in the exercise of it. For; it might rarely, it would never be exercised—it might be rarely exercised, it would never be exercised. page 550. For; *plain one*—plain *case.* For; *absolute—absolute negative.* For; *in defiance—in spite.* Page 551. For; *were its violent opposers*—were *violent opposers of it.* For; One, that the,—One *is* that the. For; *capacity—capacities.* For; the other—the other *is.*

No. LXXIV. Page 552. For; *so evident*—so *evident in itself.* Page 553. For; *number—numbers.* For; *the apprehension of censure*—the *apprehension of suspicion or censure.* Page 554. For; *poised—matched.* For; *the condemned*—the *condemned person.* For; its sanction—its sanction to *the measure.*

No. LXXV. Page 556. For; *prerogative—power.* Page 557. For; *heretofore given—already given in other places.* For; *either—either of them.* Page 558. For; *duty to interest*—his duty to *his* interest. Page 559. For; same *extent*—same *degree.* For; *number, will apply—number, which has been alluded to in another part of this paper.* Page 560. For; The former, by increasing the difficulty of resolutions disagreeable to the minority—the former by making a determinate number, at all times requisite to a resolution. Page 561. For; than the Senate is likely—*than the Senate would be likely*.

No. LXXVI. Page 563. For; *can be properly* modified *only—ought to be modified in one* of three ways. For; *since* waiving—*as* waiving. Page 564. Omitted; A single well-directed man, by a single understanding, cannot be distracted and warped by that diversity of views, feelings, and interests, which frequently distract and warp the resolutions of a collective body. Page 565. For; *upon—on*. For; *But his* nomination may be overruled: This it certainly may; yet it can only be—But might not his nomination be overruled? I grant it might, yet this could only be to make place for another nomination by himself. For; *to prevent—to preventing*. Page 566. For; than that of universal rectitude—than the supposition of universal rectitude.

No. LXXVII. Page 569. For; *been objected—been suggested*. Page 569. For; Besides this it is evident that the Power—The Power. Page 570. For; all the good without the ill—all the good of that of appointment, and would in a great measure avoid its evils. Page 573. For; been *assailed—been excepted* to. For; *the election—from* the election. For; his liability at all times to impeachment—and from his being at all times, liable to impeachment. For; What more can an enlightened and reasonable people desire—What more could be desired by an enlightened and reasonable people.

No. LXXVIII. Page 575. For; all the Judges—all Judges. For; among the rest—and among the rest. For; arm for—arm *even* for. Page 576. For; It proves—*And* it proves.

For; *that* as nothing—*and* that as nothing. Page 577. For; the *right*—the *rights*. For; the *grounds*—the *ground*. For; It must therefore belong—It therefore belongs to them. Page 578. For; in other—*or* in other. For: Nor does *the*—Nor does *this*. Page 580. For; of *an* iniquitous— of iniquitous. Page 581. For; *may imagine*—may be aware of. Page 582. for; of Judicial—of their Judicial.

No. LXXX Page 587. For; *due*—proper. Page 589. For; the sentences of Courts. is with reason—the sentences of Courts, as well as in any other manner, is with reason. For; the *controversies*—the *cases*. Page 590. For; are other sources—are *many* other sources. For; *of* the States—*between* the States. Page 592. For; *examples*—examples *of it*. For; *under* the Constitution—upon the Constitution. Page 594. For; to a -principle—to a *general* principle.

No. LXXXI. Page 595. For; is to be vested—is (by the plan of the Convention) to be vested. For; are advocates—*advocate*. For; of the Supreme Court—of the proposed Supreme Court. Page 596. For; the plan which—the plan under consideration which. Page 597. For; too apt *to influence their construction*—too apt *in interpreting them*. Page 598. For; *these* models—*those* models. For; In the former as in the latter—In the former, *as well* as in the latter. Page 600. For; *these* Courts—*those* Courts. For; To confer upon the existing Courts of the several States, the power of determining such causes—To confer the power of determining such causes upon the existing Courts of the several States. Page 600. For; confiding to them—confiding the original cognisance of causes arising under those laws to them. For; Courts may hold circuits—with the aid of the State Judges, may hold circuits. Page 603. For; *a* particular—*any* particular.

No. LXXXII. Page 606. For; Time only can—'Tis time only that can. Page 607. For; the *most defensible* construction—the most *natural* and the most defensible construction. Page 609. For; *which* give appellate—*giving* appellate.

No. LXXXIII. Page 611. For; in this State, is relative—in this State, and perhaps in several of the other States, is that relative to. For; would be—would *however* be. Page 612. Omitted; trial by jury in all such cases. For; but it is left at large in relation to civil causes, for the very reason that there is a total silence on the subject—but it is *of course* left at large in relation to civil causes, there being a total silence on this *head*. Page 613. For; to *appoint*—to *exercise*. For; is contrary to reason and therefore inadmissible—is contrary to reason *and common* sense, and therefore inadmissible. For; their proper *application*—their proper use and true meaning. For; the *authority* of the Federal Judicatures—the *Judicial* authority of. Page 613. Omitted; paragraph commencing, *But that there may be no possibility*. Page 614. For; From what has been said—From these observations. Omitted; after State Constitutions; and will be in no degree altered or influenced by the adoption of the plan under consideration. Page 615. For; *the desired security—the security* aimed at. Page 617. For; civil *suits*—civil *cases*. For: to fix *with accuracy* the limits—*to fix the limits*. For; *the* difficulty—*that* difficulty. Page 619. For; *inapplicable and indeterminate—senseless and nugatory*. For; *strictly speaking* unknown—*altogether* unknown. For; there is *no antecedent establishment*—there is no proper antecedent or previous establishment. Page 620. For; *in suits*—in *cases*. Page 621. For; while a separation between the jurisdictions—while a separation of the one from the other. For; *critical—deliberate and critical*. For; *the model—which is* the model. Page 623. For; the State tribunals—the State Judicatories. For; Massachusetts, proposition can not—Massachusetts, proposition, upon this subject, can not. For; that they *are more* attached—that they are *hitherto* more attached. Page 624. For; in full force—in its full force.

No. LXXXIV. Page 627. For; I have endeavored to answer—I have taken notice of, and endeavored to answer. For; There *remain however*—There *however* remain. Page 627. For; And yet *the persons who* in this State *oppose—And yet the opposers of* the new system, in this State. Page 628. For; the Constitution *offered* by—*proposed* by. Page 629. For; to liberty than any it contains—to liberty and republicanism than any it contains. Page 630. For; must be intended to *limit* the power—must be intended as limitations of the power. Page 630. For; *This* is—*Here* is. For; than to one—than to a Constitution. Page 631. For; that a *right* to prescribe—that a *power* to prescribe. Page 632. In like manner, the proposed Constitution—And the proposed Constitution, if adopted. Page 633. For; *provided for*—found in. For: Another objection which from the frequency of its repetition—Another objection, which has been made, and which, from the frequency of its repetition. For; may be presumed to be relied on—it is to be presumed is relied on. Page 633. For; *in any distant county*—in *Montgomery* county. Page 635. For; *is* given up— *must* be given up. Page 636. Omitted after United States. There is no good reason to suppose that either the number or the salaries of the latter will be greater than those of the former.

Page 637. For; *It has thence* happened *Hence it has* happened. For; the mere local business—
the mere local business *of the States*.

No. LXXXV. Page 639. For; and so *completely* exhausted—and exhausted. Page 640. For;
the Convention—the Convention *among us*. For; Government of this State—Government under
which they live. For; upon local—*on* local. For; *upon* the ambition—on the ambition. Page 641.
For; *are such—have been* such. For; *are* of a nature—*have been* of a nature. Page 642. For
assailed—opposed. For; This may be plausible, but it is plausible *only*—This may be *plausible
enough*, but it is *only* plausible. Page 643. For; It is certainly *well worth—well worthy*. For;
complete—absolute. For; Constitution should.—*Constitution proposed should*. Page 644. For;
prveail—take place. For; *force—weight*. Page 645. For; *left to discretion*—left to *the discretion
of that body*. For; be a fallacy—*is* a fallacy. For; their *own* object. Page 646. For; is an awful
spectacle—is, in my view, an awful spectacle. For; In so arduous an enterprise, I can reconcile
it—I can reconcile it to no rules of prudence.

PHILO PUBLIUS.

NUMBER I.

NEW YORK, OCTOBER 27, 1787.

DUER.

IN the first number of the Federalist, which appeared in the Independent Journal of Saturday, the interest of certain Officers, under the State establishments, to oppose an increase of Federal authority, is mentioned as a principal source of the opposition to be expected to the new Constitution. The same idea has appeared in other publications, but has not hitherto been sufficiently explained. To ascertain its justness and extent, would, no doubt, be satisfactory to the public; and might serve to obviate misapprehensions.

A very natural enquiry presents itself on the subject:—

How happens it, that the interest of the Officers of a state should be different from that of its Citizens? I shall attempt an answer to this question.

The powers requisite to constitute Sovereignty, must be delegated by every people for their own protection and security. The people of each State have already delegated these powers; which are now lodged; partly in the PARTICULAR GOVERNMENT, and partly in the GENERAL GOVERNMENT. It is not necessary that they should grant greater or new ones. The only question with them is, in what manner the powers already granted shall be distributed; into what receptacles; and in what proportions. If they are represented in both, it will be immaterial to them so far as concerns their individual authority, independence or liberty, whether the principal share be deposited in the whole body, or in the distinct members. The re-partition, or division, is a mere question of expediency; for by whatever scale it be made, their personal rights will remain the same. If it be their interest to be united, it will be their interest to bestow as large a portion upon the Union as may be required to render it solid and effectual; and if experience has shown, that the portion heretofore conferred is inadequate to the object, it will be their interest to take away a part of that which has been left in the State reservoirs, to add it to the common stock.

But such a transfer of power, from the individual members to the Union, however it may promote the advantages of the citizens at large, may subtract not a little from the importance, and, what is with most men less easily submitted to, from the emolument of those, who hold a certain description of offices under the State establishments. These have one interest as Citizens, and another as OFFICERS. In the latter capacity, they are interested in the POWER and PROFIT of their offices, and will naturally be unwilling to put either in jeopardy. That men love power is no new discovery; that they are commonly attached to good salaries does not need elaborate proof; that they should be afraid of what threatens them with a loss of either, is but a plain inference from plain facts. A diminution of State authority is of course, a diminution of the POWER of those who are invested with the administration of that authority; and, in all probability, will in many instances produce an eventual decrease of salary. In some cases it may annihilate the offices themselves. But, while these persons may have to repine at the loss of official importance or pecuniary emolument, the private citizen may feel himself exalted to a more elevated rank. He may pride himself in the character of a citizen of America, as more dignified than that of a citizen of any single State. He may greet himself with the appellation of an American as more honourable than that of a New Yorker, a Pennsylvanian, or a Virginian.

From the preceding remarks, the distinction alluded to, between the private citizen and the citizen in office will, I presume, be sufficiently apparent. But it will be proper to observe, that its influence does not reach near so far as might at first sight be imagined. The offices that would be affected by the proposed change, though of considerable importance are not numerous. Most of the departments of the State Governments will remain untouched, to flow in their accustomed channels. This observation was necessary to prevent invidious suspicions from lighting where they would not be applicable.

PHILO PUBLIUS.

NUMBER II.

NEW YORK, NOVEMBER 15, 1787.

DUER.

THE government of Athens was a democracy. The people, as is usual in all democratical governments, were constantly alarmed at the spectre of ARISTOCRACY; and it was common in that republic as it is in the republics of America to pay court to them by encouraging their jealousies, and gratifying their prejudices. Pericles, to ingratiate himself with the citizens of Athens, whose favour was necessary to his ambition, was a principal agent in mutilating the privileges and the power of the court of AREOPAGUS; an institution acknowledged by all historians to have been a main pillar of the State. The pretence was that it promoted the POWER of the ARISTOCRACY.

The same man undermined the constitution of his country to ACQUIRE popularity—squandered the treasures of his country to PURCHASE popularity—and to avoid being accountable to his country precipitated it into a war which ended in its destruction. Pericles was, nevertheless a man endowed with many amiable and shining qualities, and, except in a few instances, was always the favorite of the people.

PHILO PUBLIUS.

NUMBER III.

NOVEMBER 28, 1787.

DUER.

PUBLIUS has shown us in a clear light the utility, it might be said, the necessity of Union to the formation and support of a navy. There is one point of view however on which he has left the subject untouched—the tendency of this circumstance to the preservation of liberty.

Will force be necessary to repell foreign attacks, or to guard the national rights against the ambition of particular members? A navy will be a much safer as well as a more effectual engine for either purpose. If we have a respectable fleet there will be the less call on any account for an army. This idea is too plain to need enlargement. Thus the salutary guardianship of the Union appears on all sides to be the palladium of American liberty.

INDEX TO THE FEDERALIST.*

* The editor takes pleasure in acknowledging that he is indebted to the kindness of P. H. Kendall, Esq., a leading member of the Washington Bar, and formerly a District Attorney of the United States, for permission to use this index prepared by him for a former edition of this work. It is very slightly modified. Feb., 1864.